Instant Notes

Vegetable Science Subjective Type

NIPA® GENX ELECTRONIC RESOURCES & SOLUTIONS P. LTD.
New Delhi-110 034

About the Authors

Nagendra Rai Began professional career as Junior Scientist in May 1993 and went up the ladder through Senior Scientist (Horticulture) at ICAR, Research Complex for NEH Region, Meghalaya and Principal Scientist and Head, Division of Vegetable Improvement at Indian Institute of Vegetable Research, Varanasi.Taught several graduate/ post-graduate level courses in horticulture (Vegetable Crops) and guided research of many students which led to award of M.Sc. and Ph.D. degrees in various disciplines of vegetable science. Developed more than 25 varieties/ lines/ hybrids of vegetable crops like tomato, brinjal , cowpea, French bean, Indian bean and turmeric. Also generated production technologies in Vegetable Crops for various part of the country like Udham Singh Nagar of Uttrakhand, Raipur of Chhattisgarh and Umiam of Meghalaya.Fellows of National Academy of Agricultural Sciences, International Society for Noni Sciences, Society for Horticultural Research and Development, Uttar Pradesh Academy of Agricultural Sciences and Indian Society of Vegetable Science. Recipient of Kirti Singh life Time Achievement Award, Harbhajan Singh Memorial Award, Research Paper Reviewer Award, Year of the Scientist Award ,Distinguished Scientist Award, Young Scientist Associate Award and Crop Research Award. Publications 275 comprising research papers, books, book chapters, popular articles, technical bulletins/ manuals/ souvenirs and extension folders related to vegetable crops. Editor of Current Horticulture, Progressive Agriculture- An International Journal & Legume Research and Joint -Editor of Vegetable Science. Leadership in both fund mobilization and human resource development.

B.S. Asati possesses a meritorious academic record. He has an illustrious university career in agriculture, with an array of medals, prizes and scholarships. He has completed M.Sc. (Ag) Horticulture from Indira Gandhi Agricultural University, Raipur obtaining first position in the department of Horticulture. He served for four years as Research Associate in ICAR Research Complex for NEH Region, Umiam (Meghalaya). Presently, he is Associate Professor, Rani Avanti Bai Lodhi College of Agriculture and Research Station, Chhuikhadan - Indira Gandhi Krishi Vishwavidyalaya, Raipur, Chattisgarh. He has number of research papers, popular articles, book chapters and technical bulletin to his credit. He has also a life membership of various journals and magazines.

Krishna Kumar Rai has completed his M.Sc. in Biotechnology from, Amity University, Noida. He has served 5 years as Senior Research Fellow (SRF) in DBT/ICAR funded projects at Indian Institute of Vegetable Research, Varanasi, where he has worked on deciphering biochemical and molecular mechanisms linked to biotic and abiotic stress tolerance in tomato and Indian bean plants. He has published quality research papers and book chapters in the field of plant physiology, biochemistry and molecular biology. He has completed his Ph.D. degree from Institute of Sciences, Department of Botany, Banaras Hindu University, Varanasi.

Instant Notes

Vegetable Science SubjectiveTypes

(ARS, NET, SET, SRF, JRF and PhD Entrance Examinations)

Nagendra Rai
Principal Scientist and Head
Division of Vegetable Improvement
ICAR- Indian Institute of Vegetable Research
Jakhini (Shahanshahpur)
Varanasi, Uttar Pradesh

Bhagwat Saran Asati
Associate Professor
Rani Avanti Bai Lodhi College of Agriculture and Research Station, Chhuikhadan
Indira Gandhi Krishi Vishwavidlaya
Raipur, Chhattisgarh

Krishna Kumar Rai
Research Associate
Institute of Sciences, Department of Botany
Banaras Hindu University, Varanasi, Uttar Pradesh

NIPA® GENX ELECTRONIC RESOURCES & SOLUTIONS P. LTD.
New Delhi-110 034

NIPA® GENX ELECTRONIC RESOURCES & SOLUTIONS P. LTD.

101,103, Vikas Surya Plaza, CU Block
L.S.C. Market, Pitam Pura, New Delhi-110 034
Ph : +91 11 27341616, 27341717, 27341718
E-mail: newindiapublishingagency@gmail.com
Web: www.nipabooks.com

For customer assistance, please contact
Phone: + 91-11-27 34 17 17
Fax: + 91-11-27 34 16 16

ISBN: 978-93-95763-16-5

Composed and Designed by NIPA®

Preface

The significance of vegetables in human nutrition is widely acknowledged, as they serve as a dependable source of essential nutrients for the human body. They are an indispensable component of a balanced diet, and are rich in carotene, vitamin C, calcium, iron, and other minerals. Despite providing only a small amount of energy and protein, vegetables are crucial due to their ability to provide the necessary vitamins, minerals, and amino acids required by the body. They also contain health-promoting non-nutritive bioactive phytochemicals, which are considered "***protective supplementary food***." Consuming sufficient quantities of vegetables can enhance taste, palatability, and appetite. They are essential for maintaining good health and can protect against certain degenerative diseases.

Apart from their nutritional value, vegetables are an important component of Indian agriculture due to their short duration, high yield, nutritional richness, economic viability, and potential to generate on-farm and off-farm employment. Our country's diverse agro-climatic conditions, with distinct seasons, enable the cultivation of a wide variety of vegetables.

The book "**VEGETABLE SCIENCE: SUBJECTIVE**" is a much-needed resource for Indian students pursuing graduate and post-graduate degrees in Olericulture. Designed to cover courses offered by various universities and institutes, as well as syllabi for competitive examinations such as ARS, NET, SRF, JRF, SET, and PhD entrance examinations, this book is presented in a subjective mode, comprising three sections and both textual and tabular formats.

The **SECTION-I** of the book deals with information's related to Advances in Vegetable Science which includes vegetable science education research and extension, vegetable scenario, nutrition and medicinal values, vertical expansion, high-tech production, nutrient management, production in changing climatic scenario, plant health managements and post-harvest and value addition.

The **SECTION-II** covers vegetable breeding, biotechnology including molecular breeding, nanotechnology, seed technology and intellectual property right.

In **SECTION-III** authors have given information's related to vegetable production aspects which cover varieties/hybrids, agro-techniques and plant protection including physiological disorders.

The authors express their sincere gratitude to their family members for their unwavering support and cooperation throughout the writing of this book. Additionally, the authors invite readers, particularly members of the teaching community and students, to offer any constructive feedback that may enhance the quality of this publication.

Nagendra Rai
Bhagwat Saran Asati
Krishna Kumar Rai

Contents

SECTION-I

1

Education, Research and Extension in Vegetable Science

1. Education

1.1. Some Landmarks of Agricultural Education Including Vegetable Science

Year	Landmarks
1952	Indian Council of Agricultural Education (ICAE) set up (worked up to 1964 under ICAR).
1958	First 'Deemed University' status bestowed on Indian Agricultural Research Institute (IARI).
1959	Chief of Agricultural Education and ex-officio Secretary to ICAE appointed.
1960	Emergence of SAUs, starting with Pantnagar, based on the recommendations of Joint Indo-American Teams.
1965	Standing Committee on Agricultural Education replaced the Education Panel.
1965	ICAR reorganization with four Divisions including Agricultural Education
1966	ICAR developed Model Act for Agricultural Universities in India.
1973	Department of Agricultural Research and Education (DARE) to provide greater autonomy to ICAR, and Regional Committees to take care of regional needs, and creation of Agricultural Research Services (ARS) and Agricultural Scientists Recruitment Board (ASRB).
1974	Norms and Accreditation Committee (NAC) replaced Standing Committee on Agricultural Education.
1988	G.V.K. Rao Committee recommendations to revamp the functioning of ICAR including its role in Agricultural Education.
1995	Agricultural Human Resource Development (AHRD) project, with World Bank Support, launched (ended in 2001).
1996	Accreditation Board established replacing NAC.
2007	IV Deans Committee revised UG course curricula and syllabi, and norms,standards and academic regulation.
2009	National Core Group revised PG (Master's and PhD) course curricula and syllabi and the common academic regulations.

1.2. Agriculture Universities/Organizations Under National Agricultural Research System Having Education in Vegetable Science

Name of Universities /Organisations	Particulars
Acharya N. G. Ranga Agricultural University Hyderabad, Telanagana	The University was formally inaugurated on March 20, 1965 by Late Shri Lal Bahadur Shastri, the then Hon'ble Prime Minister of India. The University was renamed as Acharya N.G. Ranga Agricultural University on November 7th 1996 in honour and memory of an outstanding Parliamentarian Acharya N.G. Ranga, who rendered remarkable selfless service for the cause of farmers and is regarded as an outstanding educationist, kisan leader and freedom fighter. In this university, there is separate department of Vegetable Science and both post graduate and Ph. D. degree in Vegetable Science are being awarded by this university
Agriculture University Jodhpur, Rajasthan	Agriculture University, Jodhpur (AUJ) was established on 14th September, 2013 by Government of Rajasthan under Agriculture University, Jodhpur Act 21 of 2013. The districts under jurisdiction of the university cover 3 agro-ecological zones of the state. These are Arid Western Plain Zone Ia (Jodhpur and Barmer districts), Transitional plain of Luni Basin Zone IIb (Jalore, Pali, and Sirohi districts) and part of Transitional Plain of Inland Drainage Zone IIa (Nagaur district). The different units of teaching, research and extension in agriculture including vegetable science are systematically run by the headquarter situated at Mandor, Jodhpur.
Agriculture University Kota, Rajasthan	The Agriculture University, Kota (AUK)was established on 14th Kota, Rajasthan September, 2013 after bifurcation of the Maharana Pratap University of Agriculture & Technology (MPUAT), Udaipur and Swami Keshwanand Rajasthan Agricultural University (SKRAU), Bikaner through promulgation of Act No. 22 of 2013.The Agriculture University has its headquarter at Borkhera Farm, Kota & is located on Kota-Baran National highway-76. Development and education of modern practices in the field of Agriculture, Horticulture & Forestry for sustainable livelihood of the rural masses is the main thrust of the service area of AUK.
Anand Agriculture University, Anand Gujarat	The Anand Agricultural University (AAU) was established in 2004 at Anand by the Act No. (Guj 5 of 2004) dated April 29, 2004, caved out of the erstwhile Gujarat Agricultural University (GAU). The AAU was set up to provide support to the farming community in three facets namely education, research and extension activities in Agriculture, Horticulture Engineering, Processing and Home Science.
Assam Agricultural University, Jorhat, Assam	Assam Agricultural University (AAU) was established in 1969 at Jorhat in the state of Assam, India. The jurisdiction of the University extends to the entire State of Assam with regard to teaching, research and extension education in the field of agriculture and allied sciences. The University has a number of campuses with its headquarters at, Jorhat. In this university, there is separate department of Horticulture

where both post graduate and Ph.D educations in Vegetable Science are going on.

Bidhan Chandra Krishi Viswavidyalaya, Mohanpur, West Bengal

The Bidhan Chandra Krishi Viswavidyalaya(BCKV), came into being in West Bengal in 1974.The huge sylvine campus having its teaching, administrative, extension and research units now at Mohanpur, Nadia, West Bengal, has got the district mandates for offering agricultural education both at UG and PG levels, conducting agricultural research as well as organizing extension programmes. The faculties of the university are Agriculture, Horticulture and Agricultural Engineering.

Bihar Agricultural University, Bhagalpur Bihar

The Bihar Agricultural University (BAU), Bhagalpur, Bihar was established in 2010. The headquarter of this university is located at present Bihar Agricultural College, Sabour Campus, the oldest and premier Agricultural College of the State, engaged in imparting education in agriculture and horticulture including Vegetable Science.

Birsa Agriculture University, Ranchi Jharkhand

The Birsa Agricultural University (BAU), Ranchi Jharkhand was established on 26th June 1981 after its formal inauguration by the Prime Minister of India, Late Smt. Indira Gandhi. The primary objective of this university is education, research and extension in the field of Agriculture, Animal husbandry, Forestry, Horticulture including Vegetable Science for economic upliftment of tribal and other backward class of plateau region of Jharkhand (earlier it was in Bihar).

Chaudhary Charan Singh Haryana Agricultural University, Hisar Haryana

Chaudhary Charan Singh Haryana Agricultural University (CCSHAU) popu larly known as HAU, was established in 1970, located at Hisar in Haryana. The HAU was initially a campus of Punjab Agricultural University, Ludhiana. After the formation of Haryana in 1966, it became an autonomous institution on February 2, 1970 through a Presidential Ordinance, later ratified as Haryana and Punjab Agricultural Universities Act, 1970, passed by the Lok Sabha on March 29, 1970. A. L. Fletcher, the first Vice-Chancellor of the university, was instrumental in its initial growth. This was first university where department of vegetable science was seprated very early and both postgraduate and Ph.D. degree are awarding seprately in Vegetable Science.

Central Agricultural University Imphal Manipur

The Central Agricultural University (CAU) was established by an act of Parliament, the Central Agricultural University Act 1992 (No.40 of 1992). The Act came into effect on 26 January 1993 with the issue of necessary notification by the Department of Agricultural Research and Education (DARE), Government of India. The university became functional with the joining of the first Vice-chancellor on 13th September 1993.The jurisdiction of the university extends to six North-Eastern Hill States viz; Arunachal Pradesh, Manipur, Meghalaya, Mizoram, Sikkim and Tripura. Under this university, there are separate colleges of horticulture established at Arunchal Pradesh, Sikkim and Mizoram. The college offers undergraduate and postgraduate teaching, research and extension activities in the field of horticulture including Vegetable Science.

Chaudhary Sarwan Kumar Himachal Pradesh Krishi Vishvavidyalaya Himachal Pradesh	The Himachal Pradesh Krishi Vishvavidyalaya (renamed as Chaudhary Sarwan Kumar Himachal Pradesh Krishi Vishvavidyalaya in June, 2001 was established on 1st November, 1978. In this university, there is a separate department of Vegetable Science.
Chandra Shekhar Azad University of Agriculture & Technology, Kanpur, Uttar Pradesh	Chandra Shekhar Azad University of Agriculture & Technology, Kanpur was recognized as premier institution of agricultural research and education in India since dates back to 1893 when a small school was started to impart training to revenue officers which rose step by step to the full-fledged Government Agriculture College in1906 in U.P. After that it became the Institute of Agricultural Sciences (1969) and finally to the C.S. Azad University of Agriculture & Technology in 1975. Education, research and extension on Vegetable Science in this university are going on by the separate department of Vegetable Science.
Dr. Balasaheb Sawant Konkan Krishi Vidyapeeth, Dapoli Maharashtra	The Government of Maharashtra established the Konkan Krishi Vidyapeeth on the 18th May 1972 which was renamed as Dr. Balasaheb Sawant Konkan Krishi Vidyapeeth (BSKKV), Dapoli on 12th February 2001 to impart education, research and dissemi nation of technologies in Agriculture, Horticulture including Vegetable Science. This university has separate department of Vegetable Science.
Dr. Panjabrao Deshmukh Krishi Vidyapeeth Akola, Maharashtra	Dr. Panjabrao Deshmukh Krishi Vidyapeeth (PDKV), Akola was established on 20th October, 1969 with its head-quarter at Akola. This Agricultural University was named after the illustrious son of Vidarbha Dr. Panjabrao Deshmukh, who was the Minister for Agriculture, Govt. of India. The university is entrusted with the responsibility of education, research and extension in Agriculture, horticulture including Vegetable Science along with breeder and foundation seed programmes on cereals, pulses, vegetables etc.
Dr. Yashwant Singh Parmar University of Horticulture and Forestry Solan, Himachal Pradesh	Himachal Agricultural College, Solan was established in 1962 and affiliated to the Punjab University. It became one of the campus of Agriculture Complex of Himachal Pradesh University on its formation in 1970. Consequent upon the establishment of Himachal Pradesh Krishi Vishvavidyalaya in 1978, this campus built its Horticulture Complex and finally established on 1st December, 1985 as Dr. Yashwant Singh Parmar University of Horticulture and Forestry, (YSPUH&F) Solan with objective to promote education, research and extension education in the fields of Horticulture, Forestry and allied disciplines including fulfaged separate department of Vegetable Crops.
Dr.Y.S.R Horticultural University, Venkataramannagudem Hyderabad, Telangana	Dr.Y.S.R Horticultural University, Venkataramannagudem (YSRHUV) started functioning independently from 10-05-2008 at its headquarters at Venkataramannagudem. This university com prised of three new colleges of Horticulture, one each at Venkataramannagudem in West Godavari District, Mojerla in Mahaboobnagar District and Anantharajupet in Kadapa District.The UG and PG educational programmes in horticultural crops including Vegetable Crops being offered at Rajendranagar, Hyderabad under Acharya NG Ranga Agricultural University.

Govind Ballabh Pant University of Agriculture and Technology, Udham Singh Nagar, Uttrakhand

Govind Ballabh Pant University of Agriculture and Technology, (GBPUA&T) Udham Singh Nagar, Uttrakhand earlier known as Govind Ballabh Pant University of Agriculture and Technology, Pantnagar, Nainital, Uttar Pradesh was established in 1960,the first agricultural university of India.In this university, education, research and technology dissemination on Vegetable Crops is going on by fulfaged separate department of Vegetable Science.

Indian Agricultural Research Institute (IARI), Pusa, New Delhi

The Indian Agricultural Research Institute (IARI), popularly known as Pusa Institute, began in 1905 at Pusa (Bihar) with the generous grant of 30,000 pounds from an American philanthropist, Mr. Henry Phipps. The institute was then known as Agricultural Research Institute (ARI) which functioned with five departments, namely Agriculture, Cattle Breeding, Chemistry, Economic Botany and Mycology. Bacteriology unit was added in 1907. The name of ARI was changed to Imperial Institute of Agricultural Research (IIAR) in 1911 and, in 1919, it was renamed as Imperial Agricultural Research Institute. Following a devastating earth quake on 15th January 1934, the institute was shifted to Delhi on 29th July 1936. Post independence, the institute has been renamed as Indian Agricultural Research Institute (IARI). In this institute, education, research and technology dissemination on Vegetable Crops is going on by fulfaged separate division of Vegetable Science.

Institute of Agricultural Sciences, Banaras Hindu University, Varanasi, Uttar Pradesh

The Institute of Agricultural Sciences (IAS) formaly established in August 1980 had its inception as Institute of Agricultural Research, Banaras Hindu University in 1931 upon the recommendation of the Royal Commission on Agriculture, of which, the illustrious founder of this university the late Mahamana Pt. Madan Mohan Malaviya Ji was a member. In 1945, undergraduate teaching started and the Institute of Agricultural Research was renamed as College of Agriculture and brought under the Faculty of Technology. In 1968, the College of Agriculture became an independent Faculty of Agriculture. Subsequently 6 departments viz. Plant Physiology, Agronomy, Genetics & Plant Breeding, Soil Science & Agricultural Chemistry, Plant Pathology and Agricultural Economics were created in 1969. Department of Horticulture and Entomology & Agricultural Zoology were added in 1971, and Extension Education, Animal Husbandry & Dairying and Farm Engineering were created in 1981. In August 1980, the Faculty of Agriculture rose its status to the Institute of Agricultual Sciences. In this institute, there is combined department of horticulture in which education and research on Vegetable Crops are going on.

Indira Gandhi Krishi Vishwavidyalaya, Raipur, Chattisgarh

Indira Gandhi Krishi Vishwavidyalaya(IGKV), Raipur, Chattisgarh was established on 20th January 1987 after bifurcating from Jawaharlal Nehru Krishi Vishwavidyalaya, Jabalpur. From that time to this date, the University has been expanded several folds. In the British regime one Agricultural Research Station was established in 1903 known as "Labhandi Farm" at Raipur. This Labhandi Farm had grown slowly and today it has become the campus of Indira Gandhi Krishi Viswavidyalaya, Raipur. In this university, there is a separate department of Vegetable Science in which the UG, PG and Ph.D. educational programmes on Vegetable Crops are being offered.

Jawahar Lal Nehru Krishi Vishwavidlaya, Jabalpur Madhya Pradesh	The university was established in 1964 in name of Pt. Jawaharlal Nehru based on the recommendations of Radhakrishnan commission (1949) on the concept of establishment of Agricultural University. At present, Jawahar Lal Nehru Krishi Vishwavidlaya (JNKV) encompasses five colleges of Agriculture; one Agricultural Engineering; 4 Zonal Agricultural Research Stations (ZARS); 2 Regional Research Stations and 20 Krishi Vigyan Kendras (KVK). In this university, there is separate department of Vegetable Science which provides education, research, extension on Vegetable Crops.
Junagarh Agricultural University, Gujarat	The Gujarat Agricultural University was separated into four different Agricultural Universities in the State by Gujarat Agricultural University Act-2004. Junagarh Agricultural University is one of them, which came in to existence from 1st May, 2004. Junagarh Agricultural University offers education in Agriculture and allied sciences i.e., Agriculture, Agricultural Engineering, Fisheries, Veterinary Science & Animal Husbandary and Agri-Business Management. In this university, there is separate department of Vegetable Science which provides education, research and extension on Vegetable Crops.
Kerala Agriculture University, Kerala	The Kerala Agricultural University (KAU) was established on 24th February 1971 by virtue of the Act 33 of 1971 and started functioning on 1st February 1972. The Kerala Agricultural University is the 15th in the series of the SAUs. During 2011, Kerala Agricultural University was trifurcated into Kerala Veterinary and Animal Sciences University (KVASU), Kerala University of Fisheries and Ocean Studies (KUFOS) and Kerala Agricultural University (KAU).In this university, there is separate department of Vegetable Science which provides education, research and extension on Vegetable Crops.
Maharana Pratap University of Agriculture and Technology, Udaipur, Rajasthan	Maharana Pratap University of Agriculture and Technology, (MPUAT) Udaipur, the second Agricultural University of Rajasthan, (initially named as Agricultural University, Udaipur) came into existence on 1st November, 1999 by bifurcation of the Rajasthan Agricultural University, Bikaner through promulgation of Government of Rajasthan Ordinance No. 6 of 1999, which became an Act in May, 2000.The University started functioning in full swing with effect from December 1, 1999. In this university, there is separate department of Vegetable Science which provides education, research and extension on Vegetable Crops.
Mahatma Phule Krishi Vidyapeeth (MPKV) Rahuri, Maharashtra	The Mahatma Phule Krishi Vidyapeeth (MPKV), Rahuri is the premier Agricultural University in Maharashtra that renders services to the farmers through education, research and extension education. In pursuance of the Maharashtra Agricultural University (Krishi Vidyapeeth) Act 1967, initially, the Maharashtra Agricultural University (Krishi Vidyapeeth) was established for the entire Maharashtra State and started functioning in March, 1968 with its office at Mumbai. The office was shifted to College of Agriculture, Pune in 1969. Later on in 1972, four agricultural universities were established in Maharashtra. Mahatma Phule Krishi Vidyapeeth, Rahuri is one of them established in 1969 for the western

Maharashtra having jurisdiction spread over 10 districts viz. Jalgaon, Nandurbar, Dhule, Nashik, Ahmednagar, Pune, Solapur, Satara, Sangli and Kolhapur. The University is named after the great social reformer "Mahatma Jyotiba Phule". In this university, there is separate department of Vegetable Science which provides education, research and extension on Vegetable Crops.

Banda Univeristy of Agriculture and Technology, Banda Uttar Pradesh

The University was notified vide Government Order No. 301/79-V-1-10-1 (Ka) 27-2009 Lucknow and established on 2nd March 2010 under Uttar Pradesh Agriculture University Act (Sanshodhan) 1958 Gazette-Adhiniyam 2010. Initially, it was named as "Manyawar Shri Kanshiram Ji University of Agriculture and Technology, Banda", which was changed as "Banda University of Agriculture and Technology, (BUA&T) Banda" vide Uttar Pradesh Agriculture University Act (Sanshodhan) Adhiniyam,2014.State Government of Uttar Pradesh has assigned the University with the responsibilities of (a) human resource generation and development, (b) generation and perfection of technologies, and (c) their dissemination to the farmers, orchardists and dairy farmers in the Chitrakoot Dham and Jhansi divisions. In this University, there is seperate college of Horticulture in which education, research and extension on Vegetable Science are going on.

Nagaland University Lumami, Zunheboto, Nagaland

Nagaland University, the 13th Central University and the only Central University in Nagaland (CUN) was established based on the Act of Parliament of India and received the assent of the President of India on 20th November 1989 as the Nagaland University Act 1989 (no. 35 of 1989) and came into force as notified in the Gazette of India Extraordinary Part-II Section-1 in October 1989 published by the Ministry of Law and Justice (Legislative Department), New Delhi. The University came into being on September 6, 1994 having jurisdiction over the entire state of Nagaland. At present the University has four campuses, viz. (i) Headquarters at Lumami in Zunheboto district (ii) Kohima Campus at Meriema in Kohima district (iii) Medziphema Campus (School of Agricultural Sciences and Rural Development) at Medziphema in Dimapur district and (iv) a temporary campus at Dimapur with two Schools (School of Engineering & Technology and School of Management Studies).There are 37 departments offering undergraduate and postgraduate and Ph.D. programmes in different disciplines of Arts, Commerce, Sciences, Agricultural Sciences, Engineering & Technology and Management streams. In this university, education, research and extension on Vegetable Crops, are in under college of Agriculture.

Narendra Dev University of Agriculture & Technology, Faizabad, Uttar Pradesh

On January 15, 1974 the foundation stone of Narendra Dev University of Agriculture & Technology was laid at Mashodha near Faizabad city. On 21, 1975 the Govenment of UP decided that the main campus of the university would be established at Kumarganj, Faizabad instead of Mashodha. Shri A.D. Pandey, IAS (retired) was appointed the first Vice-Chancellor of the university on 10th October, 1975.The university started functioning in a borrowed building of Gram Swalabi Vidyalaya Acharya Nagar, Naka, Faizabad. Dr.Kirti Singh took over the first Dean of the Agriculture Faculty, on February,12, 1977 got approved creation of 20 departments in the college of agriculture. The Mahamaya College of Agriculture Engineering and Technology(MCAET) a constituent college of ND university of Agriculture and Technology (NDUA&T), Kumarganj, Faizabad was established in 2002 at Ambedkarnagar. In this university, there is separate College of Horticulture which provides education, research and extension on Vegetable Crops.

Navsari Agriculture University, Gujarat

The Navsari Agriculture University (NAU), Gujarat gained the status of a separate agricultural university with effect from May 1, 2004.The University has four fully developed faculties of Agriculture, Horticulture, Forestry and Veterinary, two Zonal Research Stations (Navsari and Bharuch), three main crop-based research stations (cotton, sorghum and mango), three regional research stations (Waghai, Vyara and Gandevi) and six verification/ testing centers.

Orissa University of Agriculture & Technology, Odhisa

In 1956, Dr. J.H. Longwell from the University of Misouri visited Orissa and had discussion with the State Government which resulted in a contract between the Government of India and the University of Missouri to provide assistance to the Agriculture and Veterinary Colleges of the State. In 1960, a decision was taken to establish an Agricultural University in Orissa in the pattern of the Land Grant Colleges of USA and Dr. Ide P. Trotter joined the Utkal Krishi Mahavidyalaya on 1st April, 1960, as a consultant in Educational Administration. In this university, there is separate department of Vegetable Science which provides education, research and extension on Vegetable Crops.

Professor Jayashankar Telangana State Agriculture University, Hyderabad, Telangana

Professor Jayashankar Telangana Agricultural University (PJTSAU) was established as per the Telangana Govt's G.O. Ms No.7, Agricultural and Cooperation (Agri III) Department, Govt. of Telangana dated 31-07-2014 adapting the ANGRAU Act 1963 as "The ANGRAU Act of 1963 (Telangana Adaptation) order, 2014". After bifurcation, the PJTSAU has five constituent colleges with three of those devoted to faculty of Agriculture, one to faculty of Agricultural Engineering and Technology and one to faculty of Home Science. In this university, education, research and extension on Vegetable Crops is going on under faculty of Agriculture.

Punjab Agricultural University, Ludhiana Punjab

The Punjab Agricultural University was established in 1962 to serve the state of erstwhile Punjab. On trifurcation of Punjab in November 1966, Haryana Agricultural University was carved out of PAU by an Act of Parliament in February 1970. Later, in July 1970, Himachal Pradesh Krishi Vishvavidalya was established.

The Punjab Agricultural University now has four constituent colleges, viz. College of Agriculture, College of Agricultural Engineering, College of Home Science and College of Basic Sciences & Humanities. In this university, there is separate department of Vegetable Science which provides education, research and extension on Vegetable Crops.

Dr. Rajendra Prasad Central Agricultural University, Samastipur, Bihar	Dr. Rajendra Prasad Central Agricultural University (RPCAU), Samastipur, Bihar was established in1970 itself at Pusa and has become an important landmark in agricultural research & education in the eastern region of the country. The status of Rajendra Agricultural University changed from the State Agricultural University (SAU) to Central Agricultural University (CAU) on May 28, 2016 which was enacted as Dr. Rajendra Prasad Central Agricultural University Act, 2016 with effect from October 07, 2016.The Rajendra Prasad Central Agricultural University now at Pusa has various faculties and constituent colleges namely, Tirhut College of Agriculture (Dholi) Muzaffarpur, Bihar veterinary college, Patna, Sanjay Gandhi Institute of Dairy Technology, Patna, College of Fisheries, Dholi (Muzaffarpur), College of Home Science, College of Agricultural Engineering, College of Basic Sciences & Humanities and a postgraduate Faculty at Pusa. In this university, there is separate college of Horticulture at Motihari where education, research and extension on Vegetable Crops are going on.
Rajmata Vijayaraje Scindia Krishi Vishwavidyalaya, Gwalior, Madhya Pradesh	The Rajmata Vijayaraje Scindia Krishi Vishwavidyalaya (RVSKV), Gwalior was established by Government of Madhya Pradesh Vide Ordinance No. 4 of 2008 notified in the Extraordinary Gazette No. 507 dated 19th August 2008 as second Agricultural University by bifurcating the JNKVV, Jabalpur. As per RVSKVV act (No. 4, year 2009). In this university, education, research and extension on vegetable crops are going on a combined department of horticulture.
Rani Lakshmi Bai Central Agricultural University Jhansi, Uttar Pradesh	The Union Agriculture Minister dated 28.10.2010 addressed to the Chief Minister, Government of Uttar Pradesh indicated that the Government of India have decided to set up a Central Agricultural University for Bundelkhand region. The CAU headquarters is presently in ICAR campuses of Indian Grassland & Fodder Research Institute (IGFRI) and National Research Centre for Agroforestry (NRCAF) with colleges in both Uttar Pradesh and Madhya Pradesh portions of the Bundelkhand region. In this University, there is seperate College of Horticulture in which education, research and extension on Vegetable Crops are going on.
Sam Higginbottom Institute of Agriculture, Technology & Sciences, Allahabad, Uttar Pradesh	The Agricultural Institute was established under the leadership of Dr. Sam Higginbottom, in 1910, as an ecumenical Institution of the Christian Churches and Church organizations in India. Dr. Sam Higginbottom came to India in 1903 and joined the North India Mission of the Presbyterian Church from 1903 to 1909. In this institute education, research and extension on Vegetable Crops are going in combined department of horticulture.
Sardar Vallabh Bhai Patel University of Agriculture and Technology, Merrut, Uttar Pradesh	Sardar Vallabh Bhai Patel University of Agriculture and Technology (SVBPUA&T) established as a full-fledged University has unique honour of being called "First Agriculture University of the third millennium and the 21st century". The University was established on 2nd October 2000 under Uttar Pradesh Agriculture University Act (revised) 1958 gazette and notified vide 3204A/X12-8-2000. It was inaugurated on 28th March 2002 by the Honorable Chief Minister of Uttar Pradesh. It who recognized and funded by U.P. Govt. & ICAR, Govt. of India. It is included in the list of recognized

	Universities maintained by the University Grants Commission (UGC), Govt. of India. In this university, education, research and extension on Vegetable Crops are going in seperate College of Horticulture.
Sardar Krushinagar Datiwada Agriculture University, Gujarat	Sardar Krushinagar Dantiwada Agricultural University (SKDAU) was founded as one of the State Agricultural Universities in 2004 when the GAU was split into four campuses. In this University, faculty of Agricuture provides education, research and extension on Vegetable Crops.
Sher- e Kashimir University of Agricultural Sciences & Technology of Jammu, Jammu	Sher-e-Kashmir University of Agricultural Sciences and Technology of Jammu (SKUAST-Jammu) came into existence on 20th September 1999 following the amendment in Sher-e-Kashmir University of Agricultural Sciences and Technology Act, 1982, through the State Legislature. In this university, there is separate department of Vegetable Science which provides education, research and extension on Vegetable Crops.
Sher- e Kashimir University of Agricultural Sciences & Technology of Kashmir, Srinagar	Sher-e-Kashmir University of Agricultural Sciences and Technology (SKUAST) was an Agricultural University in the Indian state of Jammu and Kashmir. It was established in the year 1982 through an Act passed by the State Legislature.Initially, the university had jurisdiction over the entire State of Jammu & Kashmir with its headquarters at Shalimar, Srinagar. With the SKUAST Act in force, the agricultural education, research and extension training units were transferred to SKUAST from various departments viz; Agriculture, Animal Husbandry, Sheep Husbandry and Sericulture of Jammu & Kashmir State. In this university, there is separate department of Vegetable Science which provides education, research and extension on Vegetable Crops.
Sri Karan Narendra Agriculture University, Jobner- Jaipur, Rajasthan	The Sri Karan Narendra Agriculture University (SKNAU), Jobner-Jaipur was established in 2013 by Govt of Rajasthan under Agri culture University, Jobner Act, 2013 (Bill No 39) with a view to impart teaching at the University or college level, conduct research and extension and education programmes in the field of agriculture.The territorial jurisdiction and responsibility of this University extend to the districts of Jaipur, Sikar, Alwar, Dausa, Tonk, Ajmer, Bhartpur and Dholpur.
Swami Keshwanand Rajasthan Agricultural University, Bikaner, (SKRAU), Rajasthan	The Rajastan Agriculture University was established and renamed as Swami Keshwanand Rajasthan Agricultural University, Bikaner (SKRAU) vide Gazette Notification No. F. 4 (2) vidhi/ 2/ 2009 dated June 09, 2009.
Tamil Nadu Agricultural University, Coimbatore, Tamil Nadu	The Tamil Nadu Agricultural University (TNAU) had its genesis from establishment of an Agricultural School at Saidapet, Chennai, Tamil Nadu, India as early as 1868 which was later relocated at Coimbatore during 1906. In this university, there is full fledged department of Vegetable Science in which the UG and PG educational programmes in Vegetable Crops are being offered.
University of Agricultural and Horticultural Sciences, Shimoga (UAHS), Karnataka	The University of Agricultural and Horticultural Sciences (UAHS), Shimoga is the first integrated university in the state of Karnataka, which has both agricultural and horticultural sciences under its juridiction. It was established under the Karnataka Act no. 38 of

2012, The University of Agricultural and Horticultural Sciences, Shimoga, came into independent existence on 1st April 2013.

University of Agricultural Sciences, Bangalore, Karnataka

The University of Agricutural Sciences (UAS) was inaugurated by Dr Zakir Hussain, the Vice President of India on the 21st August, 1964. On October 1, 1965, the Colleges of Agriculture at Hebbal, and Dharwad, Veterinary College at Hebbal, 35 research stations located all over Karnataka and 45 ICAR schemes which were with the State Department of Agriculture, Horticulture, Animal Husbandry and Fisheries were transferred to the newly established University of Agricultural Sciences, Bangalore. Later, Marine Product Processing Training Centre (MPPTC) at Mangalore and the Krishi Vignana Kendra, Hanumanamatti, Dharwad district were transferred to the University. The University established Fisheries College at Mangalore in 1969 to offer Bachelor of Fisheries Science training and the Agricultural Engineering Institute at Raichur to offer three-year diploma in Agricultural Engineering. In 1974, Home Science College was started to impart education in rural home science at Dharwad campus, besides establishing a College of Basic Sciences and Humanities and College of Post Graduate Studies at Hebbal.

University of Agricultural Sciences, Dharwad, Karnataka

The University of Agricultural Sciences, Dharwad was established on October 1, 1986. The University has 5 Colleges, 30 Research Stations, 6 Extension Education Units, 5 Krishi Vigyan Kendras and ATIC. The University has its jurisdiction over 7 districts namely Bagalkot, Belgaum, Bijapur, Dharwad, Gadag, Haveri, and Uttar Kannada in northern Karnataka. In this University good research works have been done for upliftment of Vegetable Science.

University ofAgricultural Sciences, Raichur Karnataka

The initiation for new Agricultural University at Raichur began through a letter by Government of Karnataka (No. AHD: 165: UAS:99 dated 17-12-1999) directing University of Agricultural Sciences, Dharwad to submit a feasibility report on the proposal. An expert committee was constituted (No.AO/Est-V/LC/4778-B/99-00; dated 5-1-2000) which not only realized the need for new Agricultural University but also recommended the proposal. The cabinet approved the proposal for establishment of Agricultural University at Raichur, with an allocation of rupees five crore during 2008-09 academic year on 26-9-2008.During 2008-09 and 2009-10, PG program began in other departments, thus making a total of 13 departments offering Post Graduate program at the campus level. The Raichur campus has registered significant growth in last decade reaching newer heights in education, research and extension.

University of Horticultural Sciences (UHS) at Bagalkot, Karnataka

The University of Horticultural Sciences (UHS) at Bagalkot, Karnataka was established by Ordinance No 2 of 2008 dated: 22-11-2008. Thus, the exclusive University of Horticultural Sciences came in to being with effect from 22-11-2008 at Bagalkot.

Uttar Banga Krishi Viswavidyalaya, West Bengal

The "Uttar Banga Krishi Viswavidyalaya" was established by West Bengal Act XX of 2000 and started functioning from 1st February, 2001. The head quarter is situated at Pundibari, a rural block in the district of Cooch Behar. A new Technology faculty has come into existence with due accreditation by All India Council of Technical

	Education (AICTE) from 2005-2006 academic session for offering 4 years B. Tech degree in Agricultural Engineering with annual intake of 15 students.
VCSG, Uttarakhand University of Horticulture & Forestry, Bharsar	The VCSG, Uttarakhand University of Horticulture & Forestry, Bharsar was established by an Act of State Legislative Assembly [The Uttarakhand Krishi Evam Prodyogik Vishwavidhyalaya (Amendment) Act, 2011 {Uttarakhand Act No.13 of 2011}] dated 28th April, 2011 with Head Quarter at Bharsar,Pauri Garhwal. The Notification No. 732/XIII-II/2011-12(02)/2011, dated 26th September, 2011 has also been issued in this regard by the State Government. With the establishment of UUHF, various campuses, Colleges, Research Centres and KVKs viz., Veer Chandra Singh Garhwali College of Horticulture, Bharsar; Krishi Vigyan Kendra, Distt. Pauri Garhwal; College of Forestry & Hill Agriculture, Ranichauri; Krishi Vigyan Kendra, Distt. Tehri Garhwal; Research Centers at Kanatal and Gaja (Tehri Garhwal) of Govind Ballabh Pant University of Agriculture & Technology have been merged with UUHF.
Vasantrao Naik Marathwada Krishi Vidyapeeth Parbhani Maharashtra	The Maharashtra Agriculture University (MAU) was established on May 18, 1972 and renamed as Vasantrao Naik Marathwada Krishi Vidyapeeth Parbhani(Maharashtra). It is entrusted with the responsibilities to pro- vide education in agriculture and allied fields, undertake research and facilitate technology transfer in Marathwada region of Maharashtra.
Viswa- Bharati Central University, West, Bengal	Founded by the first non-European Nobel Laureate Rabindranath Tagore (popularly known as Tagore) in 1921, Visva-Bharati was declared to be a Central University and an institution of national importance by an Act of Parliament in 1951. The President of India is the Paridarsaka (Visitor) of the University, the Governor of West Bengal is the Pradhana (Rector), and the Prime Minister of India acts as the Acharya (Chancellor). The President of India appoints the Upacharya (Vice-chancellor) of the University. In May 1951, Visva-Bharati was declared to be a Central University and "An Institution of National Importance" by an Act of Parliament. It was granted the status of a unitary, teaching and residential university. The status and function of all the major institutions have been redefined in successive Amendment.

1.2.1. Horticultural Universities in India

- Dr. Y.S. Parmar University of Horticulture & Forestry, Nauni, Solan, Himachal Pradesh.
- Dr. YSR Horticultural University, Venkataramannagudem, Tadepalligudem, Andhra Pradesh.
- University of Horticultural Sciences, Bagalkot, Karnataka.
- VCSG Uttarakhand University of Horticulture and Forestry, Bharsar, District - Pauri Garhwal, Uttarakhand.

- Mahatama Gandhi University of Horticulture and Forestry Sankra Patah Durg, Chhattisgarh
- Sri Konda Laxman Telangana State Horticultural University, Rajendra Nagar Campus, Hyderabad
- Maharana Partap Horticultural University, Karnal, Haryana.
- University of Agricultural & Horticultural Sciences, Shivamogga, Karnataka

1.2.2. Horticulture Colleges in India

University	Constitute College
Indira Gandhi Krishi Vishwavidyalaya, Raipur, Chhattisgarh	• KLS College of Horticulture & Research Station, Rajnandgaon • College of Horticulture, Jagdalpur
Dr. YSR Horticultural University, Venkataramannagudem, Andhra Pradesh	• College of Horticulture, Anantharajupeta, Sankra Railway Kodur Mandal, YSR Kadapa District, • College of Horticulture, Venkataramannagudem, West Godavari, District. Dhantari • College of Horticulture, Parvathipuram, Ullibhadra Post, Garugubilli Mandal, Vijayanagaram District, Jashpur • College of Horticulture, Chinalatarapi Village, Gudlur Mandal, Prakasam District, Bemeta
Sri Konda Laxman Telangana State Horticultural University, Rajendra Nagar Campus, Hyderabad	• College of Horticulture, Mojerla, Mahaboobnagar District • College of Horticulture, Rajendranagar, Hyderabad District.
VCSG Uttarakhand University of Horticulture and Forestry, Bharsar, District -Pauri Garhwal ,Uttarakhand	• VCSG College of Horticulture, Bharsar, District -Pauri Garhwal
University of Horticultural Sciences, Bagalkot, Karnataka	• KRC College of Horticulture, Arabhavi (Belgaum) • College of Horticulture, Bagalkot • College of Horticulture, Bidar • College of Horticulture, Kolar • College of Horticulture, Sirsi • College of Horticulture, Koppal (Munirabad) • College of Horticulture, Bengaluru • College of Horticulture, Mysore • College of Horticulture Engineering and Food Technology (CHEFT), Devihosur
Dr. Y S. Parmar University of Horticulture & Forestry, Nauni, Solan, HP	• College of Horticulture, Nauni, Solan College of Horticulture and Forestry, Neri, District Hamirpur
Central Agricultural University, Imphal, Manipur	• College of Horticulture & Forestry - Pasighat, Arunachal Pradesh • College of Horticulture & Forestry, Sikkim • College of Horticulture & Forestry, Mizoram

University	College
Rani Lakshmi Bai Central Agricultural University, Jhansi, UP	• College of Horticulture & Jhansi,
Assam Agricultural University, Jorhat	• College of Horticulture, Lokhowpur, District Nalbari.
Bihar Agricultural University Sabour, Bhagalpur, Bihar	• College of Horticulture, Noorsarai, Nalanda.
Sardarkrushinagar Dantiwada Agricultural University, Sardarkrushinagar, Gujarat	• Horticulture College, Jagudan.
Anand Agricultural University, Anand, Gujarat	• College of Horticulture, Anand.
Navsari Agricultural University, Navsari, Gujarat	ASPEE College of Horticulture and Forestry, NAU, Navsari.
Maharana Partap Horticultural University, Karnal, Haryana	• College of Horticulture, Karnal.
University of Agricultural & Horticultural Sciences, Shivamogga, Karnataka	• Horticultural College, Mudigere. • Horticultural College, Hiriyur.
Kerala Agricultural University Vellanikkara, Thrissur, Kerala	• College of Horticulture, Vellanikkara.
Rajmata Viyayaraje Scindia Krishi Vishwavidyalaya, Gwalior, Madhya Pradesh	• College of Horticulture, Mandsaur.
Dr . Balasaheb Sawant Konkan Krishi Vidyapeeth, Dapoli, Dist. Ratnagiri, M.S.	• College of Horticulture, Mulde, Tal. Kudal, Dist. Sindhudurg. • College of Horticulture, Dapoli, Dist. Ratnagiri.
Vasantrao Naik Marathwada Krishi Vidyapeeth, Parbhani, (M.S.)	• College of Horticulture, Parbhani.
Dr. Panjabrao Deshmukh Krishi Vidyapeeth, Akola, (MS)	• College of Horticulture, Akola.
Orissa University of Agriculture and Technology, Bhubaneshwar, Odisha	• College of Horticulture, Chiplima.
Tamil Nadu Agricultural University, Coimbatore	• Horticultural College & Research Institute, Coimbatore. • Horticultural College and Research Institute for Women, Trichy - Dindigul. • Horticultural College & Research Institute, Periyakulam, Theni.
C.S.A. University of Agriculture & Technology, Kanpur, Uttar Pradesh	• College of Horticulture, Kanpur.
Narendra Dev University of Agriculture & Technology, Faizabad, Uttar Pradesh	• College of Horticulture and Forestry, Faizabad.
Banda University of Agriculture and Technology, Banda, Uttar Pradesh	• College of Horticulture, Banda.
SVBP University of Agriculture and Technology, Merrut, Uttar Pradesh	• College of Horticulture, Merrut

1.3. Course Structure on Vegetable Science

Code	Course Title	Credits
Undergraduate Programme		
FSC 101	Fundamentals of Horticulture	2+1
VSC 101	Botany of Horticultural Crops	1+1
FSC 102	Propagation of Horticultural Crops	2+1
VSC 102	Production Technology of Tropical Vegetable Crops	2+1
PBG 102	Principle of Genetics and Cytogenetics	2+1
VSC 201	Production Technology of Temperate Vegetable Crops	2+1
PSM 201	Production Technology of Spices and Plantation Crops	2+1
SST 212	Seed Production Technology of Horticultural Crops	1+1
FLG 307	Protected and Precision Horticulture	2+1
AEN 311	Pest Management in Horticultural Crops	2+1
PBG 301	Principle and Method of Plant Breeding	2+1
VSC 302	Breeding of Horticultural Crops	2+1
PAT 411	Diseases of Horticultural Crops and their Management	2+1
SAC 401	Nutrient Management and Fertilizer Technology	2+1
Master's and Doctoral Programme		
VSC 501*	Production Technology of Cool SeasonVegetable Crops	2+1
VSC 502*	Production Technology of Warm SeasonVegetable Crops	2+1
VSC 503*	Breeding 0f Vegetable Crops	2+1
VSC 504*	Growth and Development of Vegetable Crops	2+1
VSC 505	Seed Production Technology of Vegetable Crops	2+1
VSC 506	Systematic of Vegetable Crops	1+1
VSC 507	Production Technology of Underexploited Vegetable Crops	1+1
VSC 508	Organic Vegetable Production Technology	1+1
VSC 509	Fundamentals of Processing of Vegetables	1+1
VSC 591	Master's Seminar	1+0
VSC 599	Master's Research	20
VSC 601**	Advances in Vegetable Production	2+1
VSC 602**	Advances in Breeding of Vegetable Crops	2+1
VSC 603**	Protected Cultivation of Vegetable Crops	1+1
VSC 604**	Biotechnology of Vegetable Crops	2+1
VSC 605	Seed Certification, Processing and Storage of Vegetable Crops	1+1
VSC 606	Abiotic Stress Management in Vegetable Crops	2+1
VSC 691	Doctoral Seminar I	1+0
VSC 692	Doctoral Seminar II	1+0
VSC 699	Doctoral Research	45

* Compulsory for Master's programme; **Compulsory for Doctoral programme

Experimental Learning Programmes

- Commercial Horticulture.
- Protected Cultivation of high value horticulture crops.
- Processing of fruits and vegetables for value addition.
- Floriculture and landscape architecture.
- Bio-inputs: Bio-fertilizers and bio-pesticides.
- Mass multiplication of plant and Molecules through tissue culture.

- Mushroom culture.
- Bee Keeping

1.4. Fellowship

For recognition of talent and promotion of merit in general, and for encouraging talented students to undertake higher agricultural including Vegetable Science education in particular, the Indian Council of Agricultural Research (herein-after referred to as Council) awards a certain number of Junior and Senior Research Fellowships for post-graduate (PG) studies in different disciplines of agriculture including Vegetable Science and allied sciences. The number and subjects of study for award of Junior and Senior Research Fellowships are announced from time to time.

Nomenclature

Council's Junior Research Fellowships for PG studies will be called "ICAR-JRF (PGS)" and the Senior Research Fellowships for PG studies will be called "ICARSRF (PGS)". ICAR-JRF (PGS) will be awarded for post-graduate study (course and research work) leading to a Master's degree whereas ICAR-SRF (PGS) will be awarded for post-graduate study (course and research work) leading to a Ph.D. degree.

1.4.1. ICAR-Junior Research Fellowship for Post-Graduate Studies (ICAR-JRF (PGS)

Method of Award

ICAR-JRF (PGS) will be awarded on the basis of merit in the All India Competitive Entrance Examination for (i) ICAR-JRF (PGS) and (ii) concurrent admission to Master's degree program at State Agricultural Universities (SAUs), Deemed Universities viz. IARI (New Delhi) / IVRI (Izatnagar) / NDRI (Karnal) / CIFE (Mumbai) / AAU (Allahabad), Central Agricultural University (Imphal, Manipur), and Central Universities having faculty of agriculture viz. Banaras Hindu University (BHU), Aligarh Muslim University (AMU),Visva Bharti and Nagaland University, collectively hereinafter referred to as the Agricultural Universities (AUs).The ICAR-JRF (PGS) will not be available for admission in any university other than the AUs as mentioned above.

Eligibility

Only those candidates having passed their Bachelor's Degree or appearing at the Final Examination of the Bachelor's Degree in the concerned field, under 10+2+5, 10+2+4 or 10+2+3 (only for basic science subjects) are eligible to apply for admission. (For admission, the eligibility requirement lay down by the respective AUs including remedial courses and tenure will be treated as final). Candidates must have obtained 60% marks or Overall Grade Point Average (OGPA) of 6.60/10.00 or 3.25/5.00 or 2.6/4.00 for General, OBC and Under Privileged States (UPS) categories whereas for SC/ST/Physically Handicapped (PH) categories, the candidates must have obtained 55% marks or an OGPA of 5.5/10.00 or 2.75/5.00 or 2.20/4.00. The equivalence of OGPA to percent 1 marks, where needed, will be certified by the Registrar of the concerned University.

Condidates who have passend out from private Universities which are not accredited by ICAR are not eligible for the exminations. Whereas, students who have studied from private universities accredited by ICAR are eligible to take up the ICAR take up the ICAR JRF examination.

Age Limit

Applicants must be at least 20 years of age as on July 01, of the year of admission. There is no relaxation allowed in the case of a minimum age limit for any categery.

Duration

Duration of ICAR-JRF (PGS) will be two years and in no case it will be extended beyond the period of two years.

Rates

Rs. 8640/- per mnth with contimngency grant of Rs. 6,000/- per annum.

1.4.2. Senior Research Fellowship

Method of Award

ICAR-SRF (PGS) will be awarded on the basis of merit obtained in the All India Competitive Examination conducted by the Council and the candidates for award of ICAR-SRF (PGS) would have to secure admission only in the Agricultural Universities (AUs).

Eligibility Criteria

Candidates having completed their Master's degree program with a minimum of 55% marks or an OGPA of 5.5/10.00 or 2.75/5.00 or 2.20/4.00 or an equivalent OGPA from any recognized University in India and abroad would be eligible. For SC/ST and Physically Handicapped (PH) candidates, the minimum percent of marks will be relaxed by 5 per cent or an equivalent OGPA. The equivalence of OGPA to percent marks, where needed, will be certified by the Registrar of the concerned University. Candidates appearing in the final semester would also be eligible provided they complete their postgraduate degree in all respects by the date of examination and produce the complete degree certificate from the Registrar to this effect. Fellowship would be granted only when the candidate gets eventually admitted and pursues Ph.D. degree in an Agricultural University(AU) other than the Agricultural University(AU) from where the candidate has completed M.Sc./M.V.Sc./ M.E./M.Tech. degree. The condidate must have completed their postgraduate degree in all respects and should have all the degree-completition requirements at the time of counseling/ admission in the university failing which they will not be considered for admission and the award of the fellowship.

Age

The upper age limit would be 30 years as on the date of the examination. For SC/ST & PH categories the upper age limit will be relaxed by 5 years. For OBC the upper age limit will be relaxed by 3 years. For in-service candidates of 2 Agricultural Universities (AU), the upper age limit would be 45 years as on the date examination whereas; the academic performance requirement would remain as stated above.

Reservation

Reservation of various categories such as SC/ST/OBC and PH etc., will be given as per Government of India rules/instructions issued from time to time. The responsibility of verification of the genuineness of SC/ST/OBC and PH certificates will be of the concerned Agricultural University (AU) where the candidate has obtained admission.

Duration

Duration of ICAR-SRF (PGS) will be three years and in no case, it will be extended beyond the period of three years.

Rates

For ICAR Senior Research Fellowships for pursuing Ph. D. degree it is Rs. 12000/- pm for 1st and 2nd year and Rs. 14000/- pm for 3rd year + Contingency grant of Rs. 10000/ - per year. Institute Fellowship at ICAR Deemed to be universities

(a) For purswing master is degree: Rs 7560/- per month (Fixed)

(b) For pursing Ph.D degree: Rs 10, 500/- per month (Fixed)

Other Conditions for Award of ICAR-JRF (PGS) and ICAR-SRF (PGS).

- The fellowships will be admissible to persons of Indian nationality as defined in the constitution of India or persons domiciled in India.
- A fellow will be under the administrative control of the Head of the Agricultural Universities (AUs) where he/she joins. The Head of the Agricultural Universities (AUs) will ensure that all the rules and regulations of Council governing the award of fellowship are strictly adhered to. The fellow will work under a recognized guide on the faculty of Agricultural Universities (AUs).
- The fellowship will take effect from the date the fellow joins the course or the start of academic session for which fellowship has been offered whichever is later.
- The students must take admission for the relevant degree program within a period of one year from the date of issuance of award letter, failing which fellowship shall stand withdrawn automatically.
- Fellows will not be paid their fellowship during the period of strike or during the period the fellow remains on conduct probation or the day fellow does not attend the class or student seminar in the department/division.
- A fellow will not be allowed to avail of any other fellowship/scholarship during the tenure of fellowship of the Council. In case a candidate is already receiving any other fellowship or scholarship, it will be surrendered by him before accepting the fellowship of the Council.
- Funds will normally be paid to the Head of the Institute/AU in advance for the first year after the issue of sanction for fellowship. The payment of fellowship for subsequent years will be made on receipt of (a) a demand for funds from the Head of the Institute/AU and (b) a certificate in the prescribed form from the Guide of the candidate, duly approved by the Head of the Institute/AU that the progress of the candidate is satisfactory with respect to the time schedule and maintenance of required OGPA as per eligibility of the fellowship at the end of each year of the study. No renewal application would be entertained by the Council if the required OGPA has not been maintained.

Termination of Fellowship

Under following conditions, the fellowship is terminated

- The fellowship will be terminated without notice.
- On the date the fellow ceases to be on the rolls of the Agricultural University.
- On the date the sanction of the fellowship expires.
- If the fellow leaves the institution where the fellowship was offered.
- If a fellow is dropped by the institute due to poor performance.
- If at any time in the opinion of the Agricultural University (AU) a fellow is found to be negligent in his studies, does not devote full time for studies and research, progress report is unsatisfactory or is guilty of unbecoming conduct.
- If a fellow does not complete or leaves his studies before the expiry of sanctioned tenure of the fellowship the guide should immediately report such cases and no fellowship should be paid thereafter.

Note

- All the candidates awarded ICAR-JRF (PGS)/ ICAR-SRF (PGS) will have to execute a surety bond of appropriate amount as per the instructions of the Council from time to time, at the time of registration in the respective University to ensure completion of the program undertaken with fellowship support.
- A fellow shall not leave the course before its completion without prior approval of the Council and ensuring that the required obligations under surety bond are fulfilled. If any fellow leaves without permission he shall not be paid any fellowship amount due to him from the date of leaving. No fellowship amount will be paid if fellow leaves within six months of joining the course.
- Fellow will submit a soft copy of the thesis on Compact Disk (CD) to the Council within three months of the completion of his studies. The result of submission of thesis will be intimated to the Council in due course by the Head of the Agricultural Universities.
- The receipt of financial assistance from the Council should be suitably acknowledged by the fellow in the thesis / research papers
- ICAR will have the intellectual property rights/proprietary right on research outputs of the ICAR-JRF (PGS) and ICAR-SRF (PGS) made during the period of working in the ICAR as per the provisions of "ICAR guidelines for Intellectual Property Management and Technology Transfer/ Commercialization" mutatis mutandis. However, in case the candidate has done some research work, his/her name can accordingly be acknowledged/ included appropriately in the research paper(s) as solely decided by the Guide. No right in this regard can be claimed.

Leave

ICAR-JRF (PGS)/ICAR-SRF (PGS) will be governed by the extant rules of the concerned AU as applicable to the other students

1.5. Awards and Honor Exclusively in Vegetable Science

Dr. Harbhajan Singh Memorial Award

Dr. Harbhajan Singh memorial award had been constituted in the year 1990. This award is in the memory of Dr. Haribhajan Singh, the founder President of the Indian Society of Vegetable Science for giving to honor to the outstanding scientists in the field of vegetable research and published their papers in the journal every year.

Dwarika Nath Memorial Award

To encourage the young scientists below the age of 35 years in the field of Vegetable science, Executive council of the society has decided to give Gold Medal for best Ph. D. work. The Award was sponsored by Dr. Prem Nath in memory of his father late Shri Dwarika Nath in 1998.

Dr. Bishwajeet Choudhary Memorial Award

This award was constituted in 2014 in memory of late Dr. Bishwajeet Choudhary for outstanding contribution in Vegetable Science.

Dr. Kirti Singh Life Time Achievement Award

This award was also constituted in 2014 for life time research achievement in Vegetable crops.

Fellows of the Society

It has been great tradition of the Society to elect the Fellows of the Society, who have contributed significantly on Vegetable Science.

1.6. Government Initiatives for Promotion of Education in Agriculture including Vegetable Science

Following initiatives have been taken to enhance quality of education in agriculture including Vegetable Science. These are;

- ICAR gives the financial support to **RAWE** programme and in this programme, student of graduate final year is attached and placed in the rural area for effective work experience of rural agriculture for one semester. They participate in most of the rural agricultural activities and understand the rural life and understand the socioeconomic condition of the farmers. This programme gives clear understanding of the village life which helps to the students in marketing future programme of the village development.
- Another initiative to enhance the quality of agricultural graduate taken by ICAR was **Experiential Learning Programme (ELP)** during Xth plan.The major components of this scheme were to establish instructional farm for cultivation of vegetables, model plants for food processing and value addition, modules of plant tissue culture, high-tech vegetable production, mass production of bio-agents and bio-pesticides, and vegetable processing etc. In this case, students are involved in all the operational activities which generate confidence, competitiveness and competence. The experience gained in experiential learning by the students is of great help when they serve in private sector.

- Besides this, ICAR has also taken initiative the programme "**Attracting and Retaining Youth in Agriculture (ARYA)** including vegetable science which objectives are;

1. To attract and empower the youth in rural areas to take up various Agriculture, allied and service sector enterprises for sustainable income and gainful employment in selected district.
2. To enable the farm youth to establish net work groups to take up resource and capital-intensive activities like processing, value addition and marketing.
3. To demonstrate functional linkages with different institutions and stake holders for convenience of opportunities available under various scheme/ programme for sustainable development of youth.

- The **Student READY** programme of ICAR is a new step which signifies as a Finishing School for the undergraduate students. The term READY refers to Rural and Entrepreneurship Awareness Development Yojana. Student READY is skill development initiative to strengthen students with skills, so as to enable them to tackle global challenges and to improve both their employability as well as ability to setup a venture. There are five components in this programmes

1. Experiential Learning/Hands on Training
2. Skill Development Training
3. Rural Agriculture Work Experience
4. In Plant Training/ Industrial attachment
5. Students Projects

The education division of ICAR, New Delhi has developed **e- KrishiShiksha** under learning and capacity building programme of NAIP for several UG level interactive & multimedia **e- Courseware** contents with following objectives;

1. Establishment of an independent web based integrated e-learning portal of Agricultural education including Vegetable Science.
2. A useful tool for the agricultural education e- courses data management related to all disciplines of Agricultural Sciences including Vegetable Science.
3. An effective tool and solution for refinement, updating, maintenance and sustenance of the e- learning courseware developed under learning and capacity building programme of NAIP.
4. For remote area institutions/ faculty/ students/, e- learning courseware has been made available as down loadable component from the same portal. This will eliminate the process of physical supply of e- course on CDS/DVDs by post / courier services.
5. The reporting through this system will help in quantitatively measuring utility of the system and impact assessment.

1.7. ICAR Awards (up to October, 2022)

• ICAR Challenge Award

To find a solution for any immediate or long-standing problem, or limitation in agriculture, which is coming in the way of agricultural development and/ or enhancing productivity in any major agricultural, horticultural or animal/fish product, ICAR has instituted a Challenge Award. The award carries a cash prize of 10.00 lakh, a citation, in addition to a share in the income generated by ICAR from the commercialization of the technology/ product/ process developed by the scientist while solving any of the given challenges as per ICAR rules and norms.

• Sardar Patel Outstanding ICAR Institution Award

In order to recognize outstanding performance by the ICAR institutes, DUs of ICAR, CAU and State Agricultural Universities, three Awards of 10.00 lakh each, a citation and a plaque will be given to two ICAR Institutes/NRC/Project Directorates National Bureaus (a Large and a small institute each) and one State Agricultural University/ DUs/CAU.

• Chaudhary Devi Lal Outstanding All India Coordinated Research Project

In order to recognize outstanding performance of the AICRP and its cooperating centers and to provide incentive for outstanding performance in terms of linkages and research output and its impact, one annual award of 3.00 lakh (2.00 lakh for the main coordinating unit and 1.00 lakh for the best coordinating centre) in cash, a citation and a plaque is to be given to the selected AICRP. All India Coordinated Research Projects, which have been in operation for at least 10 years can apply for the award. Forwarding authority may give a clear-cut recommendation regarding the most significant achievements made in the AICRP and the best coordinating centre.

• Jawaharlal Nehru Award for Outstanding Doctoral Thesis Research in Agricultural and Allied Sciences

In order to promote high quality doctoral thesis research in priority/frontier areas of agriculture and allied sciences, ICAR has constituted this award of 50,000/-in cash plus a citation and silver medal (gold polished) for the outstanding original research work in agriculture and allied sciences. This award is meant exclusively for the doctoral thesis related to agricultural sciences from Indian Universities. The Ph.D. degree/provisional degree for this award must have been awarded during the year preceding the year of the award. A thesis will be considered only once for this award. Applicant must have evidence of publication of his/ her work in the form of published/ accepted form of at least one good research paper in a reputed journal having NAAS rating of 7.6 from the research work done for the Ph.D. thesis. The forwarding authority may give clear cut recommendation highlighting the merit of the research work.

• Panjabrao Deshmukh Outstanding Woman Scientist Award

All women scientists engaged in research in agricultural and allied subjects /extension in a recognized institution are eligible for this award. The award consists of 1.00 lakh in cash and citation along with provision of equal amount of 1.00 lakh for motivating woman scientists and female students across the country including travel within a year of receiving the award. The awards are exclusively meant for individual women scientists.

The forwarding authority may give clear cut recommendation highlighting the most significant achievements made by the scientists.

• Vasantrao Naik Award for Outstanding Research Application in Dry Land Farming Systems

In order to promote outstanding research and application in priority aspects of dry land farming systems & water conservation, an annual award of 1.00 lakh is awarded to an outstanding scientist engaged in research/ technology application work in dry land farming in India are eligible for the award. The award is also open to small inter disciplinary team of the scientists comprising up to six scientists/ team of scientists. The forwarding authority may give clear cut recommendation highlighting the most significant achievements made by the scientists/ team of scientists.

• Jagjivan Ram Abhinav Kisan Puruskar /Jagjivan Ram Innovative Farmer Award (National/Zonal)

In order to recognize the outstanding contributions of innovative farmers for initiatives in development adoption, modification and dissemination of improved technology and practices for increased income with sustainability, following national and zonal awards are announced:

(i) **National:** One annual national award of 1.00 lakh each in any of the areas of agriculture and allied sciences + equal amount of travel grant across the country to promote his achievement are to be given to farmers at national level.

Agricultural Production Commissioners / Secretaries / Directors of Agril. / Hort. /A.H. / Fisheries / Sericulture, Vice-Chancellors of Agricultural Universities / Directors of ICAR Institute will identify and nominate the farmers in their areas of jurisdiction and forward the authentic information to the Council.

(ii) **Zonal:** Eleven annual awards of 0.50 lakh each + equal amount of travel grant to promote his/ her achievement and motivate farmers in his/ her perspective zone. All the KVKs in the country are divided zone wise. There are eight zones in the country and each zone is headed by Zonal Project Director. The geographical area of each zone is given in the guidelines of award.

Agricultural Production Commissioners / Secretaries / Directors of Agriculture / Horticulture / Animal Husbandry / Fisheries / Sericulture, Vice-Chancellors of Agricultural universities/ Directors/ Joint Directors of ICAR Institutes and Directors of ATARIs /NGOs, shall identify and nominate the farmers in their respective areas of jurisdiction and forward the authenticated nomination form to the Council. Nominating authority may put on record a clear-cut recommendation highlighting the contributions made by the nominee and giving full justification for the nomination.

• N.G. Ranga Farmer Award for Diversified Agriculture

In order to recognize outstanding contribution of innovative farmers for diversified agriculture, one annual award of 1.00 lakh in any of the areas of Diversified Agriculture is given by ICAR.Agricultural Production Commissioners / Secretaries/ Directors of Agriculture/ Horticulture/ Animal Husbandry / Fisheries/ Sericulture Vice-Chancellors of Agriculture University/ Directors of ICAR Instt. / Zonal Directors of KVKs / NGOs, other organizations connected with plant and animal sciences will identify and nominate the farmers in their area of jurisdiction and forward the nomination after proper authentication to the Council. All farmers selected for National/ Zonal Award and meeting the criteria of this award are also eligible. Nominating authority may put on record a clear-cut recommendation highlighting the contributions made by the nominee and giving full justification for the nomination.

• Pandit Deen Dayal Upadhyay Antyodaya Krishi Puruskar (National & Zonal)
In order to recognize the contributions of marginal, small and landless farmers for developing sustainable integrated models of farming, the ICAR has instituted Pandit Deen Dayal Upadhyay Antyodaya Krishi Puruskar (National & Zonal) annually. For National level there is one award comprising of 1,00,000/- (Rupee one lakh only) and Award Certificate to be given annually. At zonal level there are total eleven awards: one for each zone of ATARIs comprising of 50,000/- (Rupees Fifty Thousand only). Nominating authority may put on record a clear-cut recommendation highlighting the contributions made by the nominee and giving full justification for the nomination.

• Haldhar Organic Farmer Award
In order to recognize outstanding contribution of organic farmers ICAR has instituted an award titled Haldhar Organic Farmer Award . The award consists of 1,00,000/- (Rupees one lakh only). The award is annual in nature. Any farmer involved in organic farming/ activities in the area of field crop/ horticultural crops/ medicinal crops/ milk products etc., with an experience of 10 years is eligible. Applications must be submitted in the recommended format and should be duly authenticated and forwarded by the competent forwarding authority.

• Chaudhary Charan Singh Award for Excellence in Journalism in Agricultural Research and Development
Six annual awards carrying cash award of 1,00,000/- (One lakh only) and a certificate are to be given to journalists for Print Media [Hindi Journalism/ English Journalism/ Journalism in Regional languages (Four awards)] and Electronic media (Two awards). The contribution made by the journalists would be judged on the basis of the articles/ success stories published in Hindi/English/ Regional languages Newspapers / Magazines /Journals / electronic media in India during the preceding three years. The applications shall be submitted in the proper format only and shall be submitted through proper channel and authenticated by their competent supervising authority.

• Fakhruddin Ali Ahmed Award for Outstanding Research in Tribal Farming Systems
The award is primarily meant for any person or team (With two or three associates, if any) engaged in applied research and its applications in tribal areas of the country aimed at improving the biological resources and livelihoods or in original work directly applicable to tribal farming system. Two awards each with the value of 1.00 lakh in cash and citation + provision of equal amount for study on related subject in geographical area of work for a year. The forwarding authority may give clear cut recommendation regarding the most significant contributions made by the concerned scientist/ team of scientists.

• Bharat Ratna Dr C. Subramaniam Award for Outstanding Teachers

In order to provide recognition to outstanding teachers and to promote quality teaching in the field of Agriculture, four outstanding teacher awards are given annually. Each award consists of 1.00 lakh in cash + travel grant of 1.00 lakh (Rupee one lakh only) to promote innovation in teaching. The applications through proper channel in respect of the eligible teachers are invited from SAUs, CAUs and DUs. The forwarding authority may give clear cut recommendation highlighting the most significant contributions made by the concerned teacher.

• Pandit Deen Dayal Upadhyay Krishi Vigyan Protshahan Puraskar (National & Zonal)

These awards promote healthy competition among Krishi Vigyan Kendras (KVKs) at Zonal and National Level for application of science and technology in agriculture. All KVKs are eligible to submit the application for these awards in the prescribed format duly forwarded and authenticated by the competent forwarding authority. For competition at national level, there is one award having prize money of 25.0 lakhs (20.00 lakhs for infrastructural development + 1.0 lakhs for sharing among staff + 4.0 lakh for training of KVK staff). At zonal level there are a total of eleven awards: one for each zone of KVKs. Each award consists of 2.25 lakh (1.50 lakh for purchase of office/farm equipments + 0.75 lakh for training of KVK staff). The Directors/ Joint Directors of ICAR institutes/ Vice-chancellors/ Directors of Extension of Agricultural Universities/ Directors of ATARIs may forward the applications in their respective areas of operations. The forwarding authority may give a 1-2 page note on the specific and most significant contributions made by the concerned KVK.

• Dr Rajendra Prasad Puruskar for Technical Books in Hindi in Agricultural and Allied Sciences

These awards recognize to authors of original Hindi Technical books in agriculture and allied sciences & incentivize Indian writers to write original standard works in agricultural and allied sciences in Hindi. The award is meant for individuals as well as teams of authors. An individual award consists of 1.00 lakh in cash and a citation. There are four awards, one each in the Crop / Horticultural Sciences; Natural Resource Management / Agricultural Engineering, Animal / Fisheries Sciences and Social Sciences. All original Hindi technical books in the designated subject areas of agriculture and allied sciences written by Indian authors, including editors of multi-author books in which the editor also has himself contributed substantially, are eligible. The author/editor must have had a substantial and active involvement in the relevant field of agriculture and allied sciences. The publication must be free from any infringement of copy rights. The publication must have been written and published during preceding year of the award. The forwarding authority may give clear cut recommendation on the originality and technical quality of the publication.

• Lal Bahadur Shastri Outstanding Young Scientist Award

In order to recognize the talented young scientists who have shown extraordinary originality and dedication in their research programmes, four individual awards are to be given annually. An individual award of 1.00 lakh in cash and a citation and a challenge project for three years with budgetary provision of 10.00 lakh per year + 5.00 lakhfor foreign training (upto 3 months), if deemed necessary by the ICAR. The challenge project and foreign training will be administered/monitored by Division of Agricultural Education of ICAR. All young scientists who have possessed a doctoral degree and are below forty years of age (on 31st December 2016) and hold a regular teaching, research, extension education job in the ICAR-SAU system of institutions and engaged in research in agricultural and allied sciences for at least five years continuously are eligible for consideration. The forwarding authority may give clear cut recommendation regarding the most significant contributions made by the concerned scientist.

- **Rafi Ahmed Kidwai Award for Outstanding Research in Agricultural Sciences**

In order to recognize outstanding research in agricultural and allied sciences & provide incentives for excellence in agricultural research, this award is to be given to agricultural scientists for outstanding contribution in specified areas. A total of four awards are provided under the award. Each award carries a cash prize of 5.00 lakh in addition to the citation. All Indian scientists engaged in agricultural research and overseas Indian scientists working in the areas relevant to Indian agriculture are eligible for these awards. The forwarding authority may give clear cut recommendation regarding the most significant contributions made by the concerned scientist.

- **Swami Sahajanand Saraswati Outstanding Extension Scientist Award**

The award is exclusively meant for individual extension scientist/teacher for excellence in agricultural extension methodology and education work. Two individual awards have been provided. An individual award would consist of 1.00 lakh in cash and a citation. Two awards have been assigned across the disciplines in agriculture & allied sciences. Applications must be submitted in the recommended format and should be duly authenticated and forwarded by the competent forwarding authority.

- **NASI-ICAR Award For Innovation and Research on Farm Implements**

In order to reduce drudgery of farm women by development of farm implements and to encourage researchers and innovators to develop farm implements for farm women, ICAR and NASI have instituted the NASI-ICAR Award For Innovation and Research on Farm Implements. The award consists of 1.00 lakh in cash, citation and certificate. The award is annual in nature. All Scientists/Engineers/ Innovators engaged in research in agricultural farm implements are eligible. Applications must be submitted in the recommended format and should be duly authenticated and forwarded by the competent forwarding authority.

- **ICAR Award for Outstanding Interdisciplinary Team Research in Agricultural and Allied Sciences**

In order to recognize, encourage and promote the understanding that practical and useful research would normally have to be interdisciplinary in approach, the ICAR has constituted the ICAR Award for Outstanding Interdisciplinary Team Research in Agricultural and Allied Sciences. The award is biennial in nature. All agricultural scientists engaged in interdisciplinary team research in India in the specified subject areas are eligible. The team must have scientist-level representation from a minimum of three well-recognized disciplines and may also have technical officers (T6 and above). They must have been working on an integrated research project dealing with an inherently interdisciplinary problem in a system based, problem solving mode. The final phase of the research work including its field validation must have been completed during the five years preceding the year of the award. Each member of the team must have remained its active member continuously for at least three years preceding the year of the award. Documentary evidence should be provided that the project has been running/ has run continuously for at least five years at that time of submission of the application. The award is not limited to NARS i.e. Agricultural Scientists outside NARS are also eligible if they meet the eligibility criteria as mentioned above. There would be maximum 4 awards, and each award would be of 5,00,000/- (Rupees five lakhs only). Not more than one award will be given in any discipline.

• **Cash Award Scheme for Administrative/Technical/Supporting category employees** of ICAR Research Institutes/NRCs/Bureaus/ZCUs has been instituted by the ICAR in order to recognize the excellence in performance. Three annual awards of 51,000/- (Rupees Fifty One Thousand only) are to be given to the awardees, selected among applications received from the regular employees of ICAR. The forwarding authority may provide a detailed note on the most significant activities made by the employee in his/ her service career.

New Awards Initiated (October, 2022 onwards) only there new National Awards with high stature and it will be instituted for Farmers Research and Technology. The awards will be given to ICAR Institutes, Deemed Universities, Central Agricultural Universities which may be converted into ranking.

1.8. Foreign Vegetable/Horticulture Science Institutes

Name of Institutes	Address	Discipline
Agricultural Cooperative for Vegetables	Haidestrasse 22, Vienna -1110, Austria	Marketing of vegetables.
Alata Horticultural Research Institute	Turkish Ministry of Agriculture and Rural Affairs, P.O. Box 27 Erdemli, Mersin-33740, Turkey	Breeding, biotechnology, protected culture and crop protection of fruits, vegetables & ornamentals.
All-Russian Research Institute of Breeding and Seed Production of Vegetables	Russian Academy of Agricultural Science, Moscow region, P.O. Lesnoy Gorodok, Odintsovo-143080, Russia	Breeding and culture (seed production) of veg etables.
All-Russian Research Institute of Irrigated Vegetables and Melons	Russian Academy of Agricultural Science, Astrakhan region, Lubitcha str.16, Kamyziak-416306, Russia	Culture, soil and water management (irrigation) of vegetales & melons.
All-Russian Research Institute of Vegetable Crops	Russian Academy of Agricultural Science, Moscow region, Ramenskoe district, Vereya village, 500, 140153, Russia	Culture of vegetables.
ARC-Roodeplaat Vegetable and Ornamental Plant Institute	Agricultural Research Council, Private Bag X293, Pretoria-0001, South Africa	Breeding, biotechnology, culture and crop protec tion of potato, vegetables, indigenous vegetables, ornamentals (indigenous flowers) & medicinal plants.
Asian Vegetable Research and Development Center (World Vegetable Center)	PO Box 42, Shanhua, 741, Taiwan	Breeding, culture (production), soil management, crop protection (IPM), training and outreach of vegetables (alliums, tomato, chili, sweet peppers, leafy vegetables, mungbean, soybean).
Ataturk Central Horticultural Research Institute	Turkish Ministry of Agriculture and Rural Affairs, Suleyman Bey Mah. Yalý Cad. P.O. Box 15, Yalova -77102, Turkey	Breeding, biotechnology, propagation, physiology, protected culture, crop protection, post-harvest (processing), economics and training of fruit, grape, vegetables & ornamentals.
Athalassa Experimental Station	Agricultural Research Institute, Agricultural Research Institute, Nicosia -1516, Cyprus	Culture of vegetables, subtropical fruits (olives, pistachio, date palm) and flowers (i.e. roses and greenery in soilless cultivation).

Contd.

Name of Institutes	Address	Discipline
Austrian Horticultural Museum	Lärbergstrasse 211, Im Kurpark, Vienna- 1100, Austria	Education of horticultural museum.
Austrian Horticultural Society	Parkring 12, Vienna -1010, Austria	Interest promotion of horticultural crops.
Beijing Union Medical	Chinese Academy of Medical Science, Medicinal Plant Research Institute, Xibeiwang, Haidian District, Beijing -100094, China	Culture (resources utilization and production) of medicinal plants.
Beijing Vegetable Research Center	Beijing Academy of Agricultural and Forestry Sciences, Banjingcun, Haidian District, Beijing-100089, China	Genetics, breeding, biotechnology, culture, (post harvest) physiology, nutrition and seed testing of vegetables & flowers
Biological Engineering applied to Horticulture	National Institute of Horticulture (INH), Rue Le Nôtre 2, Angers - 49045, France	Genetics, germplasm preservation, molecular and cellular biology, genetic engineering, developmental physiology of vegetables & ornamental plants.
Centre for Agro-industrial Research and Development	Universidad de Bogota Jorge Tadeo Lozano, Apartado Aereo 140196,Ch¡a-Cundinamarca, Colombia	Agronomy, culture, soil management (irrigation, fertilisation), crop protection and rural extension of fruit, vegetables & flowers.
Centre for Arboriculture and Horticulture, Les Fougères	Swiss Federal Research Station for Plant Production (Changins), Conthey, CH-1964, Switzerland	Culture (production) of fruit (berries), vegetables and medicinal plants.
Centre for Temperate Fruit Crops and Medicinal, Aromatic and Wild Plants	Bjelo Polje, - 84000, Yugoslavia	Breeding, cultivar selection, culture and pomology of fruit, medicinal plants, aromatic plants and wild plants.
Chiredzi Research Station	Dept of Research and Specialist Services, Horticultural Research Institute, P.O. Box 97, Chiredzi, Zimbabwe	Agronomy, culture, cultivar selection, physiology, plant protection of fruit (mainly tropical and sub tropical), vegetables, root and tuber crops.
Crops Research Institute	Council for Scientific and Industrial Research, P.O. Box 3785, Kumasi, Ghana	Breeding, genetics, propagation, culture, physiology, nutrition, crop protection (IPM) and post-harvest management of fruit (citrus, mango, plantain, banana, pineapple), cashew, & vegetables (tomato, pepper, okra, eggplant, leafy vegetables, onion).

Contd.

Name of Institutes	Address	Discipline
Department of Medicinal and Aromatic Plants	University of Horticulture and Food Industry, Villanyi ut 29, Budapest-1118, Hungary	Crop science, breeding, culture, (post-harvest) and physiology of horticultural crops (medicinal plants).
Department of Vegetable Crops	University of Applied Sciences of Weihenstephan, State Experiment Station of Horticulture, Freising-Weihenstephan - 85350, Germany	Crop science, culture, computer-controlled climate, irrigation and fertilization of vegetable crops.
Department of Vegetable Growing	Horticultural College and Research Institutes, Vienna Vienna -1131, Austria	Crop science and culture of vegetables.
Department of Vegetable Growing	University of Horticulture and Food Industry, Ménesiu. 44, Budapest- 1118, Hungary	Crop science, breeding and culture of vegetables & mushrooms.
Department of Vegetable Growing	University of Horticulture and Food Industry, Ecskemét -6000, Hungary,	Crop science and culture of vegetables.
Department of Vegetable Varieties Testing	Horticultural College and Research Institutes, Vienna-1131, Austria	Cultivar testing of vegetables.
Erzincan Horticultural Research Institute	Turkish Ministry of Agriculture and Rural Affairs, P.O. Box 18, Erzincan - 24070, Turkey	Breeding, propagation, culture and training of fruits & vegetables.
Fengshan Tropical Horticultural Experiment Station	Taiwan Agricultural Research Institute, Horticultural Lane 4, Wenshan Road, Fengshan, 830, Taiwan	Crop science, biotechnology, breeding, physiology and culture of fruit & vegetables.
Horticultural Crop Research and Development Institute	Department of Agriculture (DOA), P.O. Box 11, Gannoruwa, Kandy, Peradeniya -KY20400, Sri Lanka	Breeding, agronomy, culture, soil chemistry, crop protection, economics and extension of fruit, vegetables, root & tuber crops.
Horticultural Crops Research Institute	Xinjiang Academy of Agricultural Sciences, Nanchang Road 38, Urumchi-830000, China	Breeding, culture, micro-propagation and post harvest physiology of fruit (apricot, pear, pomegranate, almond), grape, vegetables, sweet melon, water melon & flowers.
Horticultural Crops Research Institute	Zhejiang Academy of Agricultural Sciences,	Culture and post harvest (storage, processing) fruit,

Contd.

Name of Institutes	Address	Discipline
	Shiqiao Road 198, Hangzhou - 310021, China	vegetables, edible fungi, flowers.
Horticultural Guild of Austria	Wiedner Hauptstrasse 63, Vienna-1045, Austria	Interest promotion of horticultural crops.
Horticultural Research	Agricultural Research Corporation (ARC), Rahad, P.O. Box 235, Sudan	Agronomy, breeding, entomology, and agricultural engineering of horticultural crops.
Horticulture Australia Limited	Level 1, 50 Carrington Street, Sydney, 2000	Research, development and marketing of horticultural crops.
Horticulture Research Centre	Department of Research and Specialist Services, Horticultural Research Institute, P.O. Box 810, Marondera, Zimbabwe	Agronomy, breeding and selection, plant propaga tion, physiology, plant protection and post-har vest of flowers, deciduous fruits & vegetables.
Horticulture Research Institute	Pakistan Agricultural Research Council, National Agricultural Research Centre, Park Road Chak Shehzad, Islamabad-1031, Pakistan	Cultivar evaluation, seedling production, physiol ogy, nutrition, crop protection, ecology, vinification, post-harvest, marketing and economy of fruit, grape-vine, vegetables & ornamental plants.
Horticulture Research Institute	Liaoning Academy of Agricultural Sciences, Dongling Road 84, Shenyang -110161, China	Breeding, biotechnology and culture of fruit, grape-vine & vegetables.
Horticulture Research Institute	Anhui Academy of Agricultural Sciences, Nongkeyuan Road, 40 Silihe, Hefei -230031, China	Genetics, breeding, biotechnology, culture, plant physiology, landscaping, gardening of fruit and vegetables.
Horticulture Research Institute	Qinghai Academy of Agricultural Sciences, Ningzhang Road 83, Xining -810016, China	Breeding and culture of fruit, vegetables & flow ers.
Horticulture Research International	Willington Road Kirton, Boston -PE20 1NN, United Kingdom	Agronomy, culture, crop physiology, entomology and plant physiology of field vegetables, bulbs & cut flowers.
Horticulture Research International	Wellesbourne, Warwick -CV35 9EF, United Kingdom	Genetics, breeding, agronomy, culture, biometrics, biochemistry, biotechnology, plant physiology, nutrition and phytopathology (entomology, pathology) of vegetables, mushrooms, protected ornamentals & protected edible crops.

Contd.

Name of Institutes	Address	Discipline
Horticulture Research International - Stockbridge House	Cawood, Selby-YO8 0TZ, United Kingdom	Agronomy, culture, plant physiology, nutrition, phytopathology (entomology, plant pathology), crop protection of protected crops and field vegetables.
Hudieba Research Station	Agricultural Research Corporation, El Dammer, P.O. Box 31, Sudan	Breeding, agronomy, crop protection (entomology, virology, mycology, weed control) of horticultural crops and legumes.
Institute of Breeding on Vegetables, and Medicinal and Spice Plants	Centre for Breeding Research on Cultivated Plants, Quedlinburg-06484, Germany	Breeding of vegetables, medicinal plants and spice plants.
Institute of Horticultural and Agricultural Engineering	University of Hannover, Herrenhäuser Straße, Hannover-30419, Germany	Greenhouse technology and expert systems for horticultural crops.
Institute of Horticultural Economics, Section Market and Policy Analysis	University of Hannover, Herrenhäuser Straße 2, Hannover-30419, Germany	Economics, marketing and communication of horticultural commodities.
Institute of Horticultural Economics, Section Production and Resources Economics	University of Hannover,Herrenhäuser Straße 2, Hannover-30419, Germany	Economics and marketing of horticultural commodities.
Institute of Post Harvest Technology of Horticultural Products	Mendel University of Agriculture and Forestry, Valtická 337, Lednice na Morave -691 44, Czech Republic	Post harvest physiology and technology of fruit, vine grapes, vegetables & cut flowers.
Institute of Vegetable and Floriculture	Mendel University of Agriculture and Forestry, Valtická337, Lednice na Morave -691 44, Czech Republic	Agrotechnologies, cultivar testing, (seed) physiology, plant nutrition, breeding and nutritional value of vegetables, flowers, medicinal & aromatic plants.
Institute of Vegetable and Fruit Science	University of Hannover, Herrenhäuser Straße 2, Hannover-30419, Germany	Crop science, culture and modeling plant growth of vegetables.
Institute of Vegetables and Flowers	Chinese Academy of Agricultural Sciences, Baishiqiao Road 30, Beijing-100081, China	Breeding, genetics, culture, crop protection and post harvest physiology of vegetables & flowers.
Institute of Viticulture, Vegetable Crops and Floriculture	National Agricultural Research Foundation (NAGREF), Mesa Katsampas, Heraklion - 71110,	Culture, plant physiology (hormones), irrigation, nutrition, fertilization and waste water management

Contd.

Name of Institutes	Address	Discipline
	Greece	of grape-vine, vegetables & flowers.
International Potato Center (CIP)	La Molina, outside of Lima, Peru's	Scientific research and related activities on potato, sweet potato, other root and tuber crops, and on the improved management of natural resources in the Andes and other mountain areas.
Inter-professional Technical Centre for fruit and Vegetables	Rue Bergère 22, Paris, 75009, France	Marketing and advertising of fruit and vegetables.
IRA Kebili station	Secetrtary of State of Scientific Research and Technology, Route de Douz, Jannoura, Kébili -4200, Tunisia	Fulture, soil management and crop protection of fruit trees & vegetables.
Jilin Vegetable and Flower Research Institute	Jilin Provincial Agricultural Bureau, Zhiyou Dalu 154, Changchun-130031, China	Breeding and culture of vegetables & flowers.
Lisavenko Research Institute of Horticulture for Siberia	Russian Academy of Agricultural Science, Zmeinogorsky tract 49, Barnaul-656045, Russia	Breeding, propagation, cultivar evaluation, seed production, water management, crop protection and mechanisation of fruit, berries, vegetables & ornamental plants.
Lithuanian Institute of Horticulture	Kauno28, Kaunas distr., Babtai- 4335, Lithuania	Breeding, biotechnology, physiology, culture, crop protection and processing of fruit & vegetables.
Lowlands Agricultural Experiment Station, Keravat	National Agricultural Research Institute, East New Britain, Kokopo, Papua New Guinea	Cultivar evaluation, culture, phytopathology (en tomology) and crop protection of sweet potato, banana, aibika (*Abelmoschus manihot*), vanilla & cashew nut.
Mediterranean Agricultural Institute - CIHEAM	Apartado 202, Zaragoza-50080, Spain	Plant resources conservation and utilization of horticultural crops.
National Agricultural Research Institute	NARI Main Highlands Program - Aiyura, P.O. Box 384 Eastern Highlands Province, Kainantu, Papua New Guinea	Germplasm collection and evaluation, cultivar and rootstock evaluation, culture, physiology (drought tolerance) of sweet potato, citrus and apple.

Contd.

Name of Institutes	Address	Discipline
National Agricultural Research Institute	Ministry of Agriculture, IRESA, Rue Hédi Karray, Ariana -2049, Tunisia	Breeding, biotechnology, propagation, culture, crop protection, soil and water management of fruit, vegetables & ornamentals.
National Agricultural Research Institute	Co-operative Republic of Guyana, East Coast Demerara, Mon Repos	Genetic resources management, propagation, seed production, soil management, crop protection, post-harvest technology and extension of horticultural crops: fruit (pineapple, citrus, West-Indian cherry, mango), vegetables (tomato, ochro, boulanger, pepper); root and tuber crops (sweet potato, eddo, yam) & food crops (plantation, legumes).
National Horticulture Research Centre	Kenya Agricultural Research Institute (KARI), PO Box 220, Kenya	Breeding, physiology, agronomy, culture, crop protection, post-harvest of fruit, vegetables & flowers.
National Potato Research Centre - Tigoni	Kenya Agricultural Research Institute (KARI), PO Box 338, Limuru, Kenya	Breeding, agronomy, culture, crop protection and post harvest (food science) of potato & flowers.
Potato Research Centre	Agricultural Research Institute 'Serbia', Albanske Spomenice 21, Guca -32230, Yugoslavia	Breeding, selection, culture, physiology, phyto pathology (virology) and crop protection of potato.
Pure State Horticultural Research Station	Latvia, Pure 26, Pure, Tukums- 3124	Breeding, tissue culture, cultivar evaluation, cul ture and crop protection of fruit & vegetables.
Research and Extension Division	Ministry of Agriculture and Forestry, P.O Box 14, Nuku'alofa, Tonga	Culture (crop production) and crop protection of root crops, vegetables, tree crops, coffee, spices, coconuts, vanilla & kava.
Research Institute for the Dry Regions of Médenine	Secretary of State of Scientific Research and Technology, El Fjé, Médenine-4119, Tunisia	Genetic resources, physiology, culture and water management of fruit trees & vegetables.
Research Institute of Organic	Research Institute of Organic Agriculture (FiBL),	Cultivar testing, quality of biological production,

Contd.

Name of Institutes	Address	Discipline
Agriculture	Ackerstrasse, Frick-CH-5070, Switzerland	seedling production, physiology, soil management, pest and disease management, marketing and economy of fruit, grape-vine, vegetables & ornamentals.
Research Institute of Vegetable Crops	Ministry of Agriculture and Food Economy, Konstytucji 3 Maja 1/3, Skierniewice -96-100, Poland	Breeding, tissue culture, biotechnology, culture, physiology, nutrition, soil science, crop protection and post-harvest (storage, processing) of vegetables.
Research Station for Floriculture and Glasshouse Vegetables	Linnaeuslaan 2a, Aalsmeer -1431 JV, Netherlands	Culture (production), crop protection (biological control, IPM), soil and water management (fertilizers, amendments) of flowers & vegetables.
School of Higher Horticulture Studies	Ministry of Agriculture, IRESA, Chott Mériem - 4042, Tunisia	Breeding, biotechnology, culture, crop protection and education of fruit, vegetables & flowers.
Sigatoka Research Station	Research Division of MAFF, P.O.Box 24, Sigatoka, Fiji Islands	Culture, cultivar evaluation, propagation, crop protection and package of management practice of vegetables & tropical fruit.
South-Urals Research Institute of Horticultural Crops and Potato	Russian Academy of Agricultural Science, Gidrostroy str. 16 P.O.Shershny, Tchelyabinsk-454902, Russia	Breeding, biotechnology, biochemistry, propaga tion, culture (seed production, cultural techniques) and mechanisation of fruit, berry crops & potato.
Station for Applied Research on Arable Farming and Field Production of Vegetables	Edelhertweg 1, P.O. Box 430, Lelystad -8200 AK, Netherlands	Crop cultivation of arable crops and vegetables.
Swiss Federal Research Station for Fruit-Growing, Viticulture and Horticulture	P.O. Box 185, Wädenswil -H-8820, Switzerland	Breeding, cultivar and rootstock testing, culture, physiology, crop protection and post harvest of fruit (pome, stone, soft) & vegetables, grape-vine.
Teaching and Experimental Station for Horticulture Hessen	Oberzwehrenerstraße, 103, Kassel -34132, Germany	Organic growing, landscape gardening and teach ing of horticultural crops (vegetables, garden plants).

Contd.

Name of Institutes	Address	Discipline
The Maritsa Vegetable Crops Research Institute	National Center for Agrarian Sciences of Bulgaria, Plovdiv -4003, Bulgaria	Genetics, breeding, biotechnology, biochemistry, cultivar testing, culture, seed production, physiology, nutrition, chemical analyses), crop protection, mechanization, economics and extension of vegetables.
Vegetable Crops Centre	Agricultural Research Institute'Serbia', Karadordeva 71, Smederevska Palanka -1420, Yugoslavia	Genetics, breeding, culture and crop protection of vegetables.
Vegetable Crops Research Institute	University of Horticulture and Food Industry, Budapest, Mészöly Gy. u.6 ,Kecskemét - 6004, Hungary	Breeding, culture (seed production, cleaning and selling) and marketing of vegetables.
Vegetable Research Institute	Shanxi Academy of Agricultural Sciences, Nongke Beilu 61, Taiyuan -030031, China	Breeding and culture of vegetables.
Vegetable Research Institute	Tianjin Academy of Agricultural Science, Tianjin high way, Tianjin -300381,China	Breeding, biotechnology, culture, physiology, stor age and processing of vegetables (Chinese cabbage, cauliflower, snap bean, fruit vegetables, water melon and sweet melons, cabbage, potato).
Vegetable Research Institute	Shandong Academy of Agricultural Sciences, Gongye Beilu 202, Jinan -250100, China	Breeding, biotechnology and culture of vegetables.
Zyghi Experimental Station	Agricultural research Institute, Zyghi, Larnaca, Cyprus	Culture of vegetables, olive, date palm, strawberry, citrus & flowers (i.e. roses, greenery and cut flowers).

1.9. Some Indian Authored Books Related to Vegetable/Horticulture Sciences

Name of books	Authors	Publication Agency
Advances in Arid Horticulture: Present Status Vol. I	P.L. Saroj, B.B. Vashishtha and D.G. Dhandar	International Book Distributing Co., Lucknow
Advances in Horticulture and Forestry Volume7, 8	Edited by S.P. Singh	Scientific Publishers, Jodhpur
Advances in Horticulture: Strategies, Production, Plant Protection and Value Addition	Edited by V.K. Sharma	Deep and Deep, New Delhi
Advances in Horticulture: Vegetable Crops (Vol 5& 6)	Ed. K. L. Chadha and G. Kalloo	Malhotra Publishing House, New Delhi
Advances in Vegetable Diseases	S. Gangopadhyay	Associated Publishing Co., New Delhi
Advances in Vegetable Production	N. Rai and D. S. Yadav	Researchco Book Centre, New Delhi
Advances in Potato Science	R. K. Maiti and V. P. Singh	The Gaurav Society of Agricultural Research Information Centre Hisar, India
Basic Concepts of Vegetable Science	Neeraj Partap Singh	International Book Distributing Co. Lucknow
Biotechnology in Horticultural and Plantation Crops	K.L. Chadha, P.N. Ravindran and Leela Sahijram	Malhotra Publishing House, New Delhi
Biotechnology of Horticultural Crops	Edited by V.A. Parthasarathy, T.K. Bose, P.C. Deka and P. Das	Naya Prokash, Kolkata
Breeding of Horticultural Crops: Principles and Practices	N. Kumar	New India Publishing, New Delhi
Breeding Procedures for Cross Pollinated Vegetable Crops	Vishnu Swarup	ICAR, New Delhi
Commercial Production of Horticultural Crops	H.N. Samaddar	Naya Udyog, Kolkata
Comprehensive Micropropagation of Horticultural Crops	Ramesh Chandra and Maneesh Mishra	International Book Distributing Co., Lucknow
Cultivation of Spice Crops	A.A. Farooqi, B.S. Sreeramu and Srinivasappa	Universities Press, Hyderabad
Dictionary of Horticulture	Dinesh Arora	Biotech Books, New Delhi
Diseases of Vegetables Crops	V. K. Gupta	Kalyani Publishers, New Delhi
Diseases of Vegetables Crops	R. S. Singh	Oxford and IBH Publishing Co. Pvt. Ltd, New Delhi

Contd.

Name of books	Authors	Publication Agency
Elements of Horticulture	D.K. Singh and S.K. Singh	AgrotechPublshingAcademy, Udaipur
Emerging Scenario in Vegetable Research and Development	Edited by G. Kalloo and Kirti Singh	Research Periodicals and Book Publishing House, New Delhi
Exploitation of Hybrid Vigour in Vegetables	Harbhajan Singh, Vishnu Swarup and Brijendra Singh	ICAR, New Delhi
Flowers and Vegetables of India	Romesh Kumar Sud and Sudhir Kumar	Scientific Publication, Jodhpur
Fruit and Vegetable Preservation	R.C. Bhutani	Biotech Books, New Delhi
Genetics and Breeding of Vegetables	K. V. Peter	ICAR, New Delhi
Gobivargeya Sabjiyon	Ramphal	ICAR, New Delhi
Hand Book of Horticulture	Ed. K. L. Chadha	ICAR, New Delhi
Handbook of Aromatic Plants	Supriya Kumar Bhattacharjee	Pointer Pub., Jaipur
Heterosis Breeding in Vegetable Crops	N. Rai and Mathura Rai	New India Publishing Agencey, New Delhi
Hi-Tech Horticulture	D.K. Singh	AgrotechPublshingAcademy, Udaipur
Horticulture for Sustainable Income and Environmental Protection	Edited by V.B. Singh, K. Akali Sema, Pauline	Concept, New Delhi
Horticulture Technology: Vision 2000 and Beyond	Edited by V.K. Sharma and K.C. Azad	Deep & Deep, NewDelhi
Innovative Pest and Disease Management in Horticultural and Plantation Crops	Edited by S. Narasimhan, G. Suresh and S. Daniel Wesley	SPIC Science Foundation, Chennai
Kheervargeya Sabjiyon	Nampal Singh and Pramod Joshi	ICAR, New Delhi
Laboratory Manual of Analytical Techniques in Horticulture	R.S. Saini, K.D. Sharma, O.P. Dhankhar and R.A. Kaushik	Agrobios, Jodhpur
Major Spices of India-Crop Management and Post Harvest Technology	J. S. Pruthi	ICAR, New Delhi
Minor Spices and Condiments Crop Management and Post-Harvest Technology	J. S. Pruthi	ICAR, New Delhi
Nutrition of Vegetable Crops	S. K. Mitra	Naya Prokash, Kolkata
Vegetable Science (Objective Type)	N. Rai, B.S. Asati and K.K. Rai	NIPA, New Delhi

Contd.

Name of books	Authors	Publication Agency
Pest and Soil Management of Horticultural Crops	S.K. Singh and D.K. Singh	Agrotech Pub., Udaipur
Pest Management in Horticulture Crops: Principles and Practices	Edited by L.R. Verma, A.K. Verma and D.C. Gautam	Asiatech Pub., New Delhi
Pest management in Vegetables, Vol I & II	K. P.Srivastava	Research Periodical and Book, New Delhi
Plant Growth Regulators in Agriculture and Horticulture: Their Role and Commercial Uses	Amarjit S. Basra.	International Book, Lucknow
Preservation of Fruits and Vegetables	Girdhari Lal, G.S. Siddappaa and G. L. Tandon	ICAR, New Delhi
Principles and Methods of Vegetable Cultivation	P. P. Sharma and R.C. Pandey	Ashiyan Publishers, New Delhi
Principles of Vegetable Production	S. P. Singh	Agro Tech Publishing, Udaipur
Producing Seed of Binnial Vegetables in Temperate Region	T.S. Verma, S. C. Sharma and P.V. Sane	ICAR, New Delhi
Production Technology of Vegetable crops	K. G. Shanmugavelu	Oxford and IBH Publishing Co. Pvt. Ltd, New Delhi
Propagation of Tropical and Subtropical Horticultural Crops, Vol. I	Edited by T.K. Bose, S.K. Mitra, M.K. Sadhu, P. Das, D. Sanyal and V.A. Parthasarathy.	Naya Udyog, Kolkata
Sabji Ottpadan ke Siddhant Avam Vidhiya	P.C. Sharma	Asian Publishers, Muzzafarpur
Sabji Vigyan	Prem Nath, Vishambarsharan Brahmchari and Dharmpal Singh	ICAR, New Delhi
Scientific Horticulture: Volume 2, 3,4, 5,6, 7, 8	Edited by S.P. Singh.	Scientific, Jodhpur
Techniques of Developing Hybrids in Vegetable Crops	J. C. Kumar	Agro Botanical Publication, Bikaner
Technology for Vegetable Production and Improvement	Hazra and M.G. Som	Naya Prokash, Calcutta
Terminology of Horticulture	N. P. Singh	International Book Distributing Co., Lucknow
The Potato	R. P. Pandey	Kalyani Publishers, New Delhi
The Potato Production and Utilization	SM Paul Khurana	Mehta Publishers, New Delhi
Tomato	G. Kalloo	Allied Publishers Pvt. Ltd, New Delhi
Genetic Improvement of Vegetable Crops	G. Kalloo and O. P. Burgh	
Genetic Improvement of Tomato	G. Kalloo	

Contd.

Name of books	Authors	Publication Agency
Treatise on Indian Medicinal Plants Vol. 1, 2, 3, 4	Edited by Asima Chatterjee	Naya Prokash, Calcutta
Tropical Horticulture, Vol. 1	Edited by T.K. Bose, S.K. Mitra, A.A. Farooqi and M.K. Sadhu.	Naya Prokash, Calcutta
Tropical Horticulture, Volume 2	Edited by T.K. Bose, J. Kabir, P. Das and P.P. Joy	Naya Prokash, Calcutta
Varieties of Horticultural Crops	U. Thapa, A.B. Sharangi and A.K. Pal	Agrotech, Udaipur
Vegetable Breeding	G. Kalloo	Panima Educational Book Agency, New Delhi
Vegetable Breeding Principles and Practices	Hari Har Ram	Kalyani Publisher, New Delhi
Vegetable Breeding, Production and Seed Production	Prem Singh Arya	Kalyani Publishers, Ludhiana
Vegetable Crops of India	K. S. Yawalkar	Agri-Horticultural Publishing House, Nagpur
Vegetable crops of India	P. C. Das	Kalyani Publishers, Ludhiana
Vegetable crops Vol. I, II and III	Ed. T. K. Bose, J. Kabir, T. K. Maity, V. A. Parthasarathy and M. G. Som	Naya Prokash, Calcutta
Vegetable Crops: Production Technology	M.S. Fageria	Kalyani Publishers, Ludhiana
Vegetable Growing	S.C. Dey	Agrobios, Jodhpur
Vegetable Growing in India	S. L. Katyal	Oxford and IBH Publishing Co. Pvt. Ltd, New Delhi
Vegetable Growing in India	Sasanka Barooach	Kalyani Publishers, Ludhiana
Vegetable Production in India	D.V. S. Chauhan	Ram Prasad and Sons, Agra
Vegetable Seed Production Principles	Prem Singh Arya	Kalyani Publisher, New Delhi
Vegetables	B. Choudhary	National Book Trust of India, New Delhi
Text Book of Vegetables Tuber crops and Spices	S. Thamburaj and Narendra Singh	Directroate of Information and Publications of Agriculture, Indian Council of Agriculture Research New Delhi.
Vegetable Science	N, Rai and B.S. Awasti	NIPA GENX Electronic Resources Pvt.Ltd, New Delhi-110088.

1.10. Some Foreign Authored Books Related to Vegetable/Horticulture Sciences

Name of books	Authors	Publication Agency
A Colour Atlas of Cucurbit Diseases	D. Blancard, H. Lecoq and M. Pitrat	CPL Press Tall Gables, The Sydings Speen, Newbury, Berks RG14 1RZ, UK
A Colour Atlas of Tomato Diseases	D. Blancard	CPL Press Tall Gables, The Sydings Speen, Newbury, Berks RG14 1RZ, UK
Advances in Potato Pest Biology and Management Mary L. Powelson and Richard K. Jansson	Edited by Geoffrey W. Zehnder,	CPL Press Tall Gables, The Sydings Speen, Newbury, Berks RG14 1RZ, UK
Compendium of Tomato Diseases	Edited by JB Jones, John Paul Jones, RE Stall and TA Zitter	CPL Press Tall Gables, The Sydings Speen, Newbury, Berks RG14 1RZ, UK
Cruciferous Vegetables, Isothiocyanates and Indoles IARC Handbooks of Cancer Prevention Volume 9	Harri Vainio, Franca Bianchini	OxfordUniversity Press Bookshop, 116 High Street OxfordOX1 4BZ. UK
Diseases of Fruits and Vegetables - Diagnosis and Management	Edited by S Naqvi	Springer Publishing Agency
Diseases of Vegetable Crops	Edited by Alfred Steferud	Biotech Books, New Delhi
Diseases of Vegetable Crops	John Charles Walker	Greenworld, Lucknow
Diseases of Vegetables Crops	John Charles Walker	McGraw Hill Book Company, New York
Fruit and vegetable biotechnology	Edited by Victoriano Valpuesta	CPL Press Tall Gables, The Sydings Speen, Newbury, Berks RG14 1RZ, UK
Fruit and Vegetable Biotechnology	Edited by Victoriano Valpuesta	CPL Press Tall Gables, The Sydings Speen, Newbury, Berks RG14 1RZ, UK
Fruit and Vegetable Diseases	Edited by Mukherji, K.G	Springer Publishing Agency
Fruit and Vegetable Processing	Wim Jonger	CPL Scientific Publishing Services Limited, The Sydings Speen, Newbury, Berks RG14 1RZ, UK
Fruit and Vegetable Processing	Mircea Enachescu Dauthy	International Book Distributing Co., Lucknow

Contd.

Name of books	Authors	Publication Agency
Fruit and Vegetable Processing - Improving Quality	Edited by W Jongen	CPL Press Tall Gables, The Sydings Speen, Newbury, Berks RG14 1RZ, UK
Fruit and Vegetables IARC Handbooks of Cancer Prevention Volume 8	Harri Vainio, Franca Bianchini	OxfordUniversity Press Bookshop, 116 High Street OxfordOX1 4BZ. UK
Handbook of Horticulture	G.H. Preston	Reprint Pub., Dehradun
Handbook of Vegetable Pests	John L. Capinera	Academic Press, London
Handbook of Vegetable Preservation and Processing	Edited by Y. H. Hui, Sue Ghazala, Dee M. Graham, K. D. Murrell, Wai-Kit Nip	Marcel Dekker
Onions and other Vegetable Alliums	J. L. Brewster	CAB International, Cambridge, UK
Pests and Diseases of Vegetable Crops	B.A. Gerasimov, and E.A. Osnitskaya	State Publishing House for Agricultural Literature, Moscow.
Phytochemistry of Fruits and Vegetables	F. A. Tomás-Barberán, R. J. Robins	OxfordUniversity Press Bookshop, 116 High Street OxfordOX1 4BZ. UK
Postharvest Oxidative Stress in Horticultural Crops	Edited by D. Mark Hodges	Lucknow, International Book
Postharvest Physiology and Pathology of Vegetables	Edited by J A Bartz and J K Brecht	Marcel Dekker
Producing Vegetable Crops	John M Swiader	International Book Distributing Co.Lucknow
The New Vegetable Grower's handbook	Arthur J. Simons	Penguin Books Ltd. Middlesex.
Vegetable Crops	Homer C. Thomson	McGraw Hill Book Company, New York
Vegetable Production	John H. MacGillivray	McGraw hill Book Company, Newyork
Vegetable Production and Marketing	Paul Work	John Wiley and Sons, New York

1.11. Some Indian Journals Related to Vegetable/Horticulture Science

Name of Journals	Subscription	Publishing Agency
Indian Journal of Horticuture	Quartely, (English)	The Horticultureal Society of India, Indian Agricultural Research Insititurte, New Delhi-110012.
Journal of Applied Horticulture	Half yearly (English)	Society for the Advancement of Horticulture, A-859, Indiranagar, Lucknow-226016
Orissa Journal of Horticulture	Half yearly (English)	Journal of Orissa Horticultural Society, Department of Horticulture, OUAT, Bhubaneswar-751003 (Orissa)
Plant Horti-Tech	Bimonthly (English)	Institute of Plantation and Horticulture Management, Bangalore, India
Potato Journal	Quartely, (English)	Indian Potato Association, Central Potato Research Institute, Shimla-171001 (IIP)
Progressive Horticulutre	Quartely, (English)	Horticultural Experiments and Training Centre, CHAUBATTIA-263651, Ranikhet, Almora (Uttaranchal) India
The Horticultural Journal	Thrice issues per year (English)	Society of the Advancment of Horticulture, Faculty of Horticulture, BCKV, Mohanpur, WB
Vegetable Science	Half yearly (English)	Indian Institute of Vegetable Research (IIVR), P.O. Jakhani (Shanshahpur), Varanasi 221305 (Uttar Pradesh)
The Horticulture Journal	Half yearly	Bidhan Chandra KrishiVishawavidlaya, Mohanpur-741252, Nadia, West Bengal
Current Horticulture	Half yearly	Society for Horticultural Research and Development (SHRD), Gaziabad, UP

1.12. Some Foreign Journals Related to Vegetable/Horticulture Sciences

Name of Journals	Subscription	Publishing Agency
Acta Horticulturae	Irregular, (English)	ISHS Secretariat, PO Box 500, 3001 Leuven 1, Belgium
Biological Agriculture & Horticulture	Quaterly (English)	AB Academic Publishers, P.O. Box 42Bicester, OX6 7NW , U.K
Hort Science	Monthly (English)	American Society for Horticultural Sciences (ASHS), 113 South West Street, Suite 200, Alexandria, VA22314-2851.
Hort Technology	Quarterly (English)	American Society for Horticultural Science, 113 South West Street, Suite 200, Alexandria, VA22314-2851
Horticultura Brasileira	Quarterly (English)	Sociedade de Olericultura do Brasil
Horticultural Science Abstracts	Monthly (English)	CAB International Wallingford, Oxfordshire, OX10 8DE, UK
HORTUS	Quarterly (English)	Smith Settle, Otley, West Yorkshire
Journal of American Society for Horticultural Sciences	Bimonthly, (English)	American Society for Horticultural Sciences (ASHS), 113 South West Street, Suite 200, Alexandria, VA22314.
Journal of Environmental Horticulture (JEH)	Quartely, (English)	Horticultural Research Institute, 1000 Vermont Avenue, N.W., Suite 300 Washington, D.C.20005.
Journal of Therapeutic Horticulture	Three issues/year (English)	American Horticultural Therapy Association (AHTA), 3570 East 12th Ave., Suite 206 - Denver, CO 80206
Journal of Vegetable Science	Quartely, (English)	The LaneResearchCenter, Lane, Oklahoma
New Zealand Journal of Crop and Horticultural Science	Quartely, (English)	The Royal Society of New Zealand
Nigerian Journal of Horticultural Science	Quartely, (English)	Dept. of Agronomy, University of Ibadan, Ibadan, Nigeria
Scientia Horticultural	Quartely, (English)	Elsevier, P.O. Box 1270, 1000 BG Amsterdam, The Netherlands.
The Horticulturist	Half yearly (English)	The Journal of the Institute of HorticultureInstitute of Horticulture, 14/15 Belgrave Square, LondonSW1X 8PS.
The Journal of Horticultural Science & Biotechnology	Bimonthly (English)	Department of Biological Sciences, University of WarwickCoventry, CV4 7AL, UK

1.13. Some Scientists that Contributed Significantly in the Field of Vegetable Science

Name of Scientists	Specilazation
Late Dr. B. Choudhury	Vegetable breeder, specialized in cucurbits and tomato
Dr. K. S. Nandpuri	Vegetable breeder, specialsied in cucurbits
Dr. S.S. Saini	Vegetable breeder, specialization in cucurbits
Late MR Thakur	Vegetable breeder, specialization in chilli
Late Dr. B. R. Sharma	Vegetable breeder specialization in okra
Dr. Prem Nath	Vegetable breeder
Late Dr. VishnuSwarup	Vegeta ble breeder, specialized in cole crops
Dr. V. S. Sheshadri	Vegetable breeder, specialized in cucurbits
Late Dr. Harbhajan Singh	Vegetable breeder, specialised in Okra
Late Dr. Kirti Singh	Vegetable breeder cum vegetable agronomist
Dr. G. Kalloo	Vegetable breeder, specialized in solanaceous vegetables
Dr. M. G. Som	Vegetable breeder, specialized in legume vegetables
Dr. O. P. Dutta	Vegetable breeder, specialized in okra, French bean and cucurbits
Dr. S.K. Pandey	Potato breeder
Late Dr. K.V. Peter	Vegetable breeder specialized in chilli
Late Dr. Brahma Singh	Vegetable agronomy, specialized in protected cultivation
Late Dr. C. R. Muthukrishanan	Vegetable breeder specialized in chilli
Dr. Pushkar Nath	Potato breeder
Dr, L. C. Sikka	Potato breeder
Dr. J. L. Mangal	Vegetable agromomy, specialized in soil salanity
Dr. K. S. Randhwa	Vegetable agronomy
Dr. S. S. Purewal	Vegetable agronomy
Dr. J. C. Anand	Vegetable post harvest management
Dr, S. K. Roy	Vegetable post harvest management
Dr. S. J. Singh	Vegetable virologist, specialized on tomato
Dr. Jambhale Nerkar	Okra breeder
Dr. Harihar Ram	Vegetable breeder, specialized in brinjal, French bean and cucurbits
Dr. Nohar Prasad Singh	Vegetable breeder specialized in pea
Dr. M.L. Chadha	Vegetable crops
Dr. T.A. More	Vegetable breeder, specialized in cucurbits
Dr. S.K. Tikkoo	Vegetable breeder specialized in tomato
Dr. K.E. Lavande	Specialized in onion and garlic breeding
Dr. N.C. Gautam	Vegetable breeder, specialized in legume breeding
Dr. Balraj Singh	Vegetable agronomy, specialized in protected cultivation
Dr. P.S. Sirohi	Specialzed in cucurbits breeding
Dr. Najeer Ahmad	Specialized in temperate vgetable crops
Dr. B. Singh	Vegetable breeder specialized in okra breeding
Dr. Major Singh	Specialized in vegetable biotechnology
Dr. Pratim Kalia	Vegetable breeder, specialized in cole crops and root crops
Dr. A.T. Sadashiva	Vegetable breeder, specialized in tomato
Dr. Madhavi Ready	Specilization chilli breeding
Dr. T.K. Behara	Cucurbits specialized in bitter gourd and cucumber
Dr N. Rai	Vegetable breeder, specialized in tomato and legume vegetables
Dr. Hira Lal	Cowpea breeder
Dr Sudhakar Pandey	Specilization on cucurbits breeding
Dr. Vijay Mahajan	Vegetable breeder specialized in onion
Dr. A.J. Gupta	Vegetable breeder specialized in onion
Dr. D.R. Bhardwaj	Specialization in cucurbits breeding
Dr. A.D. Munsi	Specialization in brinjal

1.14. Gaps in Agriculture Education including Vegetable Science

Lack of focus on leadership development

- Students not challenged with real world problems
- Lack of focus on MDGs (Millennium/Development Goals).

Poor employability of the graduates

- Lack of practical knowledge and skills
- Education more theoretical
- Not industry oriented.

Poor quality of education

- Obsolete and inadequate facilities.
- Negligible on-farm training's.
- Poor adoption of modem tools ICT in education.

Curriculum

- Not reviewed regularly.
- Regional problems not included.
- Not in pace with global technology development.

Students more of Job Seekers than Job Creators

- Lack required skill and confidence.
- Lack entrepreneurship and experiential learning.
- Disconnect between research and extension .
- Poor collaborations with premier institutes- nationally or globally

1.15. Critical Requirements of a World Class Learning Institution

- **Leadership:** Translating vision into actions.
- **Mindset:** Open environment where we are willing to listen.
- **Meritocracy:** Create and respect meritocracy.
- **Academic Ambience:** Quality teacher and teaching: laboratories and modern facilities; incubation and high-tech learning centres; clean green and airy surroundings; sports & cultural centres etc.
- **Humility:** Success should always be accompanied by humility.

1.16. Qualities of a Good Teacher

- Most powerful element in education -shape future generations.
- Knowledgeable and creative,
- Learner-centred.

- Collaborate, co-create, plan lesson, and monitor.
- Help students learn something new at the end of every lecture.
- Should put effort in "connecting" with students.
- Inspire and build confidence in students.
- Should have passion for subject and teaching.
- Should give the student an opportunity to discuss and air their thoughts.
- Identify the difficulties of the deficient students and make them learn the subject.
- 6 E's and S (Engage, Explore, Explain, Elaborate, Evaluate, Extend, and Standards) to add new knowledge to students.
- Mediocre teacher tells, Good teacher explains, Superior teacher demonstrates while Great teacher inspires and engages students in learning from each other as much as possible.

1.17. Ideal Student

- Proud of national identity.
- Proud of cultural heritage.
- Have high values.
- Conscious and strong.
- Equator and creative.
- Believes in moderation and tolerance.
- Have necessary skills and knowledge for future carrier.

1.18. Teaching methods

(A) Traditional Teaching Methods

- One way communication.
- The student is the receiver of the information which is delivered u. the "chalk and talk" method.
- Students are passive receptors and get distracted easily.
- The teacher delivers the lecture content and the students listen io the lecture.
- More emphasis given on the theory with out any practical and real life time situations.
- Learning from memorization but not understanding.
- Marks rather than result oriented.

Methods

A. Teacher Controlled Teaching (*Tell me and will forget, show me 1 will remember, involve me and I will understand*)

(Monologue, autocratic teaching: Lecture methods, demonstration methods, lecture demonstration method, team teaching, individualized teaching)

(B). Innovative Teaching Methods (I hear and I forget; I see and I believe; l do and I understand).

1. Interactive teaching: It is important to provide interactive act' that involve all students in small groups

(Democratic dialogue teaching: Question answer method, interactive methods, group discussion method, tutorial method, s-einhar method, panel method, symposium).

2. Learner controlled teaching *(Self study-fair teaching)*

Self study-fair teaching: Programmed instruction, library, methods, laboratery methods, Internet & computer assisted instruction £ assignments.

3. Group controlled teaching (*Action oriented democratic teaching*)

Role play method, project method, simulation method, field trip, methods field work survey method/' workshop method, problem solving method, problem based learning method, narrative method, story telling method, model building method and , buzz session method.

4. Other common teaching methods

The Internet, Computer managed instruction, Computer assisted insutruction. Computer technology and learning, Computer teaching strategies, Self learning modules

What is Leclture ?: A lecture is an oral present inforation or teach students about particular subject.

- L-Lively
- E-Edncativc
- C-Creative
- T-Thought provoking
- U-Understanding
- R-Relevant
- E-Enjoyable

Lecture Delivery: It depend upon;

- Speaker-audience distance
- Body movements and stand
- Facial expression.
- Gesture
- Voice
- Strength
- Enunciation
- Pronunciation.
- Rate of speech
- Variety
- Pauses
- Humour

1.19. Academic Ambience: These are

- Create modern teaching, laboratory and residential infrastructure.
- Develop high-tech, experiential learning, incubation and 24 x 7 library facilities.
- Foster an environment and atmosphere for best learning of students.
- Create and maintain a good classroom environment for learning with proper layout and arrangement of furniture, computers, audiovisuals, equipments, etc.
- Create a friendly environment to feel a sense of community and caring among the students.
- Create positive classroom climate and culture and interact with the students on disciplinary measures, mannerisms, support, encouragement, cooperation, and focus on individual students for conducive learning.
- Develop clean, green, airy surroundings, open air canteens, sports and cultural centres
- Develop learning by doing through Experiential Learning Programs to enhance skills of students and entrepreneurship
- Introduce modern tools and teaching aids like smart class rooms/ e-resources.
- Strengthen links with industry and farm community and involve external donars for funding.
- Placement cells and counselling in each faculty for student placement/competitive examination.
- Ensure adequate staff for teaching and appoint efficient teachers and avoid inbreeding
- Foster greater interaction of teacher/scientists in India with those in the developed countries.
- Reform recruitment and examination procedure to attract talented faculty
- Provide incentives to best performing staff/ scientists'

As a Leader in Education: It depend upon

- **Our Understanding:** The knowledge and skill of our workforce is the major determinant of ourfuture development and sustainability.
- **Our Focus** : Enquiry based learning.
- **Our Mission:** Reform education to build excellence in teaching and larening to produce next generation leaders to tackle the challenges in Agriculture.
- **Our Approach:** Replicate and improve upon our experiences at University level.

1.20. Vegetable Science: Educational Strides Recommendations

- Upgradation of facilities and course curriculum, and active linkage with foreign institutes having "Center of Excellence to make pace with global development
- Agriculture Technology School (ATS) should be promoted for skill development
- Industry oriented course curriculum for agriculture students and orientation programme for the faculty to meat the needs

- Creation of modern hi-tech/intelligent infrastructures to promote precision cultivation for national / export need
- Industry oriented education/hands on training to facilitate entrepreneurship.

1.21. New National Agriculture Education Policy 2020 for Agriculture including Vegetable Science Courses

- GIS
- Precision farming
- Conservation Agriculture
- Secondary Agriculture
- Hi-tech cultivation
- Speciality Agriculture
- Renewable Energy
- Artificial Intelligence
- Mechatronics
- Plastic in Agriculture
- Dryland Horticulture
- Introductory Nanotechnology
- Agro-meterology & climate change
- Waste Disposal and Pollution Abatement
- Food Plant Regulations and Licensing
- Food Quality
- Safety Standard and Certification
- Food Plant Sanitation and Environmental Control
- Emerging Food Processing Technologies

2. Research

2.1. Organizational Structure in Horticulture including Vegetable Science Deputy Director General (Horticulture)

Assistant Director General (Horticulture) I	10 Research Institutes
	6 Directorates
Assistant Director General (Horticulture) II	7 National Research Centres
	13 All India Coordinated Research Project
	6 Network Project / Outreach Programmes

2.2. ICAR Organizations for Horticulture including Vegetable Science

- Indian Institute of Horticulture Research, Banglore
- Central Tropical Research Insitiute, Lucknow
- Central Dryland Horticulture Research Institute, Bikaner
- Central Temperate Horticulture Institute, Srinagar
- Central Agriculture Research Institute, Portblair
- National Research Centre Trichanaplli, Tamil Nadu
- National Research Centre on Citrus, Nagpur
- National Research Centre on Grapes, Pune
- National Research Centre on Litchi, Muzzafarpur
- National Research Centre on Pomegranate, Maharashtra
- Indian Institute of Vegetable Research, Varanasi
- Central Potato Research Institute, Solan
- National Research and Training Centre on Mushroom, Solan
- Directorate of Onion and Garlic Research, Nasik, Maharashtra
- Central Plantation Crop Research Institute, Kerala
- Central Tuber Crop Research Institute, Thiruvananthapuram, Kerala
- Indian Institute of Species Research, Calicut
- National Research Centre on Cashewnut, Karnataka
- National Research Centre on Medicinal andAromatic Plants, Anand, Gujarat
- National Research Centre on Oilpalm, Pedawegi, Andhra Pradesh
- National Research Centre on Spices, Ajmer, Rajasthan

2.3 All India Coordinated Research Projects

• Central Dry Land Horticulture Institute, Bikaner	• Vegetables, India Institute of Vegetable Research, Varanasi	• Beetle, Vine, National Research Centre on Medicinal and Aromatic Plants, Anand, Gujarat
• Floriculture and Land Scapping Division, IARI, PUSA, New Delhi	• National Mushroom Research and Training Centre, Solan	• National Research Centre on Cashewnut, Karnataka
• Post Harvest Management Technology, Fruit and Horticulture Division, IARI, New Delhi	• Central Potato Research Institute, Solan	• Palm, Central Plantation Crops Research Institute, Kasaragod, Kerala
• Subtropical Fruits Central Tropical Research Institute, Lucknow	• Vegetable Seeds, India Institute of Vegetable Research, Varanasi	• National Research Centre on Spices, Calicut, Kerala
• Subtropical Fruits, Indian Instutute of Horticulture Research, Bangalore		• Central Tuber Crop Research Institute, Thiruvananthapuram, Kerala

2.4. Plan-wise Initiation of AICRP (Vegetable Crop) Centres in India

Regular Centre	Initiated in plan/year
ICAR-Indian Agricultural Research Institute, New Delhi	IV Plan (1971)
ICAR-IARI Regional Vegetable Reseearch Station, Katrain, Kullu	IV Plant (1971)
ICAR-Indian Agricultural Research Institute, New Delhi	IV Plan (1971)
ICAR-IARI Regional Vegetable Research Station, Katrain, Kullu, Himachal Pradesh	IV Plant (1971)
ICAR-Indian Institute of Horticultural Research, Bangalore, Karnataka	IV Plan (1971)
Punjab Agriculture University, Ludhiana, Punjab	IV Plan (1971)
Dr. Rajendra Prasad Central Agricultural University, Pusa Bihar	IV Plan (1971)
Mahatma Phule Krishi Vidyapeeth, Rahuri, Maharashtra	IV Plan (1971)
Chandra Shekhar Azad University of Agriculture & Technology, Kanpur, UP	IV Plan (1971)
Assam Agricultural University, Jorhat, Assam	IV Plan (1971)
Odisha University of Agricuture & Technology, Bhubaneshwar, Odisha	IV Plan (1971)
Jawaharlal Nehru Krishi Vishwa Vidyalaya, Jabalpur, Madhya Pradesh	IV Plan (1971)
Sher-e-Kashmir University of Agricultural Science, Srinagar, J&K	IV Plan (1971)
Andhra Pradesh Agricultural University, RS, Lam, Guntur, A.P.	IV Plan (1971)
Rajasthan Agricultural University, Durgapura, Rajasthan	IV Plan (1971)
Bidhan Chandra Krishi Vishwavidyalaya, Kalyani, West Bengal	V Plan (1974)
Marathwada Krishi Vishwavidyalaya, Ambajogi, Maharashtra	V Plan (1974)
Haryana Agricultural University, Hisar, Harayana	V Plan (1974)
Narendra Dev University of Agriculture & Technology, Faizabad, UP	VI Plan (1980)
Kerala Agricultural University, Vellanikkara, Kerala	VI Plan (1980)
Dr. Y.S. Parmar University of Horticulture & Forestry, Solan, H.P.	VII Plan (1985)
Andhra Pradesh Agricultural University, Hyderabad, AP	VII Plan (1985)
Gujarat Agricultural University, Junagarh, Gujarat	VII Plan (1985)
ICAR-Indian Institute of Vegetable Research, Varanasi, UP, Head Quarter	VII Plan (1992)
University of Agricultural Science, Dharwad, Karnataka	VIII Plan (1992)
Indira Gandhi Krishi Vishwavidyalaya, Raipur, CG	VIII Plan (1992)
IARI (Reg. Station), Karnal (After the Merger of AICRP-VC with NSP	XI Plan (2008)
CAU, Pasighat, Arunachal Pradesh	XI Plan (2008)
Rajendra Agricultural University, Smastipur, Bihar	XI Plan (2008)

Central Institute of arid Horticulture, Bikaner	XII Plan (2012)
ICAR Research Complex for NEH Region, Barapani	XII Plan (2012)
ICAR Reserch Complex for Eastern Region, Ranchi	XII Plan (2012)
ICAR Vivekanand Parvatiya Krishi Anusandhan Sansthan, Almora	XII Plan (2012)
ICAR Research Complex for Goa	XII Plan (2012)
ICAR Central Island Agricultural Research Institute, Portblair	XII Plan (2012)
School of Agricultural Sciences and Rural Development (SASRD), Medzipheme, Nagaland	XII Plan (2012)

Voluntary Centres

SAU based Voluntary Centres	Initiated in plan/year	Other Voluntary Centres
PDKV, Akola	ICAR-CITH, Srinagar	NHRDF, Nasik
SHIATS (AAI), Allahabad	ICAR-NBPGR, New Delhi	NHRDF, Karnal
AAU, Anand	ICAR Research Complex, Lembuchera, Tripura	
BSKKV, Dapoli	ICAR-CHES, Bhubaneshwar	
SKUAS&T, Jammu	ICAR-IASRI, New Delhi	
NAU, Navsari	ICAR_IIVR, Sargatia, Kushinagar	
CSK HPKV, Palampur	CITH, Mukteshwar	
PAJNCARI, Karaikal		
YYGH&F, Ranichauri		
GKVK, Bengaluru		
HC&RI, TNAU, Perriyankulum		
BUAT, Banda		
MGCGV, Chitrakoot		
UBKV, Cooch Behar		
UAS, Raichur		

Seed Companies

- Ankur Seeds Pvt. Ltd., 27, New Cotton Market Layout, Nagpur-440018 (Maharashtra).
- Century Seeds Pvt. Ltd., LusaTower, BA, 22-24, Mangolpuri Industrial Area, Phase-II, -110034 (New Delhi).
- Indo-American Hybrid Seeds, 214, Palika Bhawan, Street. XIII, RK Puram, -110066 (New Delhi).
- Maharashtra Hybrid Seeds Company Limited, PB No 27, Jalna-341203.
- Nirmal Seeds Limited Bhadgaon Road, Pachora-424201, Jalgaon.
- Nath Seeds Ltd., Nath Seeds House, Nath Research, PB No 318, Aurangabad-431005 (Maharashtra).
- Nimbkar Seeds, PB No 23, Phaltan.

- Sheetal Hybrid Seeds Co. Ltd., PB No 72, A-2, Mama Chowk, Jalna-431203 (Maharashtra Seeds).
- Novartis India Limited, Seed Sector, Wagholi, Gate No. 2347, Pune, Nagar Road, Taluk, Haveli.
- Namdhari Seeds Pvt. Ltd., Bidadi, Bangalore-562106, Karnataka.·Proagro PGS India Ltd., GM, A-305, Ansal Chamber No. 1,3, Bhikaji Cama Place, New Delhi.
- SPIC PHI Seeds Ltd., Main Building, 4th Floor, 97, Mount Road, Guiady, Chennai-600032.
- Sultan & Sons Pvt. Ltd., K-26, Connaught Circus Opp. Plaza Cinema, New Delhi-110001
- Nagarjun Agriculture Research and Development Institute, C-15, Vikrampuri, Secundrabad-500009.
- Ajeet Seeds Ltd., IInd Floor, Topadia Terrace, Adalat Road, Aurangabad-431001 (Maharashtra).
- Bayer (India) Ltd., Business Group-Agrochemicals 1-2 Community Centre, Aram Bagh, Opposite Panchkuian Road, -110055(New Delhi).
- Sunagro Seeds Ltd., 207, Aradhana Bhawan, Azadpur, -110033 (Delhi).
- JK Agri. Genetics, 20, Paigh Colony, Behind Anand Theatre, S.P. Road, Secundrabad-500003.
- Indofil Chemical Company, Nerlon House, Dr. Annie Besant Road, Mumbai-400025.
- Zeneca Agrochemical Ltd. 28, Dhandaythpani Nagar, 2nd Street, Katturpura, Chennai.
- Advanta India Pvt. Ltd. Koppa Road Begur, Bangalore - 560068 (Karnataka)
- Annoya Seeds Pvt. Ltd. 832, 25th Main Sector - 1 HSR Layout, Bangalore - 560 102, Karnataka
- Basant Agro Tech Ltd. Opp. Panchayat Samiti Tajna Peth, Akola - 444 001 (M.S.)
- Beejo Sheetal Research Pvt.Ltd. Beej Sheetal Corner, Mantha Road, Jalna - 421 203 (M.S.)
- Clause India Pvt. Ltd. 6-1-20/2 Walker Town, Bhoiguda, Sikanderabad - 500025 (AP)
- East West Ltd., C-12, Gautam Garden, Colony Shivapur Bypass Road, Varanasi - 221 003 (U.P.)
- Kaveri Seeds Company Ltd., 513B, 5th Floor Minerva Complex, S.D. Road, Secunderabad - 5000 03 (A.P.)
- Krishidhan Seed Pvt. Ltd. Sci. Capital, 9th Floor, Opposite ICC Complex, Sena Pati Bapat Road, Shivaji Nagar, Pune - 411 005 (M.S.)
- National Seeds Corporation Ltd. Beej Bhawan Pusa Complex, New Delhi - 110012.
- Nuziveedee Seeds Ltd. 403, Nilgiri Appartment, Barakhaba Road, Connaught Place, New Delhi - 110001.
- Proagro GGS India Ltd. GM, A-305, Ansal Chamber No 1, 3, Bhikaji Cama Place, New Delhi - 110066
- Syngenta India Ltd. Seed Sector, Waogholi, Gate, No. 2347, Pune - Nagar Road, Taluk, Haveli, Pune - 412 207
- VNR Seeds Pvt. Ltd. Ratnagiri, Opposite, R.K. College GE. Road, Raipur - 492 001 (C.G)

2.5. Organizations of AICRP on Tuber Crops

Name of the coordinated unit	Year of start	Crops deal with
(A) ICAR Institute		
• ICAR Research Complex for NEH Region, Umroi Road, Umiam-793103 (Meghalaya)	1975	Sweet Potato, Colocasia
• Central Agricultural Research Institute, Port Blair-744101 (Andamon & Nicobar)	2000	Cassava, Sweet Potato, Colocasia and Yams
(B) State Agricultural Universities		
• Rajendra Agricultural University, Dholi, Muzaffarpur-843121(Bihar)	1968	Sweet Potato, Colocasia, Dioscorea, Amorphophalus and Pachyrrhizus
• Tamil Nadu Agricultural University, Coimbatore-641003(Tamil Nadu)	1968	Cassava, Sweet Potato, Colocasia, Amorphophallus and Dioscorea
• Acharya NG Ranga Agricultural University, Rajendranagar, Hyderabad-500030 (Andhra Pradesh)	1969	Cassava, Sweet Potato, Colocasia, Amorphophallus and Dioscorea
• Assam Agricultural University, Jorhat-785013 (Assam)	1971	Cassava, Sweet Potato, Colocasia, Amorphophallus and Dioscorea
• Dr. Balasaheb Sawant Kankan Krishi Vidyapeeth, Dapoli, (Maharashtra)	1975	Cassava, Sweet Potato, Colocasia and Dioscorea
• Bidhan Chandra Krishi Viswavidyalaya, Nadia, Kalyani-741235(West Bengal)	1976	Cassava, Sweet Potato, Colocasia, Pachyrrhizus, Amorphophallus and Dioscorea
• Birsa Agricultural University, Kanke, Ranchi-834006 (Bihar)	1987	Sweet Potato, Colocasia and Pachyrrhizus
• Indira Gandhi Agricultural University, Kumharwand, Jagdalpur (Baster)-494005 (Chhattisgarh)	1987	Cassava, Sweet Potato, Colocasia and Dioscorea
• NarendraDevUniversity of Agriculture and Technology, Faizabad-224229 (Uttar Pradesh)	1987	Sweet Potato and Colocasia
• Gujarat Agricultural University, Navasari-396450, (Gujarat)	1994	Cassava, Sweet Potato, Colocasia and Dioscorea

2.6. Organizations of AICRP on Spices

State	Centres	Year of start	Crop
Andhra Pradesh	Chintapalli Jogital Guntur	198119861975	Pepper Ginger and turmeric Coriander and fenugreek
Gujarat	Jagudan	1975	Cumin, Coriander, fennel and fenugreek
Himachal Pradesh	Solan	1971	Ginger and turmeric
Karnataka	SirsiMudigere	19811971	PepperSmall cardamom
Kerala	Panniyur Pampadumparai	19711971	PepperSmall cardamom
Rajasthan	Jobner	1975	Cumin, coriander, fennel and fenugreek
Tamil Nadu	CoimbatoreYercaud	19851981	Coriander and fenugreekTree spices, pepper
Sikkim	Gangtok	1986	Large cardamom
Haryana	Hissar	1993	Seed spices
Bihar	Dholi	1993	Seed spices
Chhattisgarh	Raigarh	1995	Ginger, turmeric, coriander and fenugreek

2.7. Emerging Issues in Vegetable Production

- Climate change
- Organic farming
- Precision farming
- Production of heavy metal free vegetables
- Quality assurance
- Human resource development

2.8. Future Research in Vegetable Science

- Climate-proof vegetables.
- Root stock breeding and molecular genetics of root stock and scion interaction.
- Photosynthesis efficient varieties and hybrids.
- Thermo and photo-insensitive vegetables.
- Metabolomes profiling and development of nutrient-rich vegetables.
- Breeding for plant architecture and ideotype.
- Genetically edited vegetables.
- Multi-purpose vegetables including vegetables for biofuel.
- Genetically engineered vegetables for edible vaccines.
- Enhancing carbon sequestration/carbon capture through conservation practices in vegetable farming.
- Energy, water, nutrient efficient and off season vegetable production technology.
- Vegetable based cropping systems.
- Organic farming for safe nutrition and environment.

- Nano-technology for enhancing fertilizer use efficiency and smart delivery of nutrients.
- Integrated use of crop growth models and geo-informatics for climate change studies and development of climate change mitigation strategies.
- Remote sensing for assessment of crop stress.
- Terrace farming/roof farming.
- Physiology, biochemistry and processing of vegetables.
- Processing industry hubs and storage facility for enhancing the export of processing and reducing the post-harvest losses.
- Landscape epidemiology of plant diseases.
- Virus-vector-symbiont interaction.
- Applications of meta-genomics, robotics, nanotechnology in pest diagnosis and management.
- Connecting work to world in area of pest alert and diagnostics.
- Crop loss modeling and digital pest maps.
- Ecological engineering.
- Chemical ecology.
- Bio-threat detection and surveillance.
- Plant microbe interactions and rhizosphere engineering.
- Mechanization in vegetable production.

2.9. Doubling Farmers' Income Through Intervention of Vegetables in Farming system

- Crop intensification and diversification.
- Mechanization for small and medium farmers.
- Enhancing area under micro-irrigation.
- Fertigation and mulching.
- Government intervention for enhancing of infrastructure for protected cultivation.
- Government intervention for creation of fresh vegetables collection centers near villages.
- Sorting, grading, packing and cold chain infrastructure.
- Development of processing units.
- Use of honey bees.
- Development of adequate infrastructure for hybrid seed production.
- Seed to seedlings for enhanced production.
- Popularization and utilization of under-utilized and /or lesser known vegetables
- Waste to wealth.
- Seed production hubs and seed export zones for vegetables.
- E-farming and smart farmer concept.
- VegAppS.

2.10 Agro-climate zones of AICRP (Vegetable Crops)

Agro-climate zone	States
Humid Weswtern Himalaya Region	Jammu & Kashmir (J&K) Himachal Pradesh and Uttarakhand
Humid Bengal-Assam basin	West Bengal and Assam
Humid Eastern Himalaya and Bay Islands	Sikkim, Meghalaya, Manipur, Nagaland, Mizoram, Tripura, Arunachal Pradesh and Andaman & Nicobar Islands
Sub Humid Sutlej Ganga Alluvial Plain	Punjab, U.P. Bihar and Jharkhand
Sub Humid to Humid Eastern and South Eastern Uplands	Chattisgarh, Odisha, Telangana and Andhra Pradesh
Arid Western Plain	Rajasthan, Gujrat, Haryana and Delhi
Semi-Arid Lava Plateux and Central High Lands	Madhya Pradesh, Maharashtra and Goa
Humid to semi-Arid Western Ghats and Karnataka	Karnataka, Tamil Nadu, Kerala, Pondicherry

3. Extension

3.1. Technology Transfer/Extension Approach

- Demonstration
- Farmers' Trainings
- In-service Trainings
- Farmers-Scientist Interaction
- Meetings
- Exposure visits
- Field days
- Kisan Melas
- Exhibitions Radio/TV talk
- Decision making
- Group approach
- Para Extension workers
- Linkages
- Information Technology Support prices & Marketing
- Seed production and distribution of planting materials

3.2. Growth of KVKs

- First KVK established during 1974 at Pondicherry
- 19 KVKs established by the end of 5th Plan
- 36 KVKs established by the end of 6th Plan

- 56 KVKs established by the end of 7* Plan
- 261 KVKs established by the end of 8th Plan
- 327 KVKs established by the end of 9th Plan
- 551 KVKs established by the end of 10* Plan
- 569 KVKs by the end of 11 plan 7-6 KVKs have been established till date

3.3 Theme of KVKs

- Need based in approach
- Skill based in vocational training
- Comprehensive in activities
- Farm based support
- Inbuilt Research-Extension linkages
- Participatory management
- Multi-disciplinary team of scientists
- Mechanism for feed-back and feed-forward

3.4 Activities of KVK

- On farm testing to identify the location specificity of technologies in various farming systems.
- Frontline demonstrations to establish production potentials newly released technologies on farmers' fields and provide feed back.
- Training of farmers to update their knowledge and skills.
- Training of extension personnel to orient them in the frontier areas of technology development.
- Work as resources and knowledge centre of agricultural technology for supporting initiatives, of public, private and voluntary sector for improving the agricultural economy of the district.

3.5 Government Initiatives for Development of Horticulture Including Vegetables in India

National Horticulture Mission (NHM)	The scheme was started in the year 2005-06. The Scheme operates in all States and Union Territories, except North Eastern States including Sikkim, Himachal Pradesh, Jammu & Kashmir and Uttarakhand, for which a separate Technology Mission for Integrated Development of Horticulture exists, to promote holistic growth of the horticulture sector covering fruits, vegetables, root & tuber crops, mushroom, spices, flowers, aromatic plants, cashew and cocoa. Similarly, programme for development of coconut is being implemented by Coconut Development Board (CDB). NHM is a Centrally Sponsored Scheme in which Government of India contributes 85% and 15% is met by the State Governments.

Objectives: These are

- Promotion of holistic growth of the horticulture sector through area based regionally differentiated strategies, enhance horticulture production and to assure nutritional security and income support to farm households and others.
- Establishing convergence and synergy among multiple on-going and planned programmes for horticulture development
- Promotion, development and dissemination of technologies to generate employment for skilled and unskilled persons, especially unemployed youth.

Technology Mission for Integrated Development of Horticulture in North Eastern States, Sikkim, Jammu & Kashmir, Himachal Pradesh and Uttarakhand

This Centrally Sponsored Scheme was launched during the 9th Five- Year Plan period. The implementation of the scheme was later extended to the States of Jammu and Kashmir, Himachal Pradesh and Uttarakhand during 2003-04 in the 10thPlan. This is a hundred percent centrally sponsored scheme and operational in eleven States: Arunachal Pradesh, Assam, Manipur, Meghalaya, Mizoram, Nagaland, Sikkim, Tripura, Jammu & Kashmir, Himachal Pradesh and Uttarakhand. The Small Farmers' Agri-Business Conortium (SFAC) is involved in coordinating the scheme.

Objectives: These are

- Establishing convergence and synergy among numerous on going governmental programmes in the field of horticulture development to achieve horizontal and vertical integration.
- Ensuring adequate, appropriate, timely and concurrent attention to all the links in the production, post-harvest management and consumption chain.
- Maximize economic, ecological and social benefits from the existing investments and infrastructure created for horticulture development.
- Promotion of ecologically sustainable intensification, economically desirable diversification and skilled employment to generate value addition.
- Promoting development and dissemination of ecotechnologies based on the blending of traditional wisdom and technology with frontier knowledge such as bio-information and space technology
- Provide the missing links in on going horticulture development projects.

Micro-irrigation

The Centrally Sponsored Scheme on micro irrigation was launched in January 2006 under the 10thPlan for implementing drip and sprinkler irrigation in an area of 6.2 lakh hectares. The scheme envisages achieving greater water use efficiency resulting in enhanced productivity and better quality of produce. Under this scheme, drip and sprinkler irrigation is being promoted on a large scale. Assistance is provided to all categories of farmers at the rate of 50 per cent for drip/ sprinkler system implementation and at the rate of 75 per cent for training and demonstration in each district of the State for both horticulture crops as well as non-horticulture

	crops. Further, training and demonstration being done by the Precision Farming Development Centres (PFDCs) at 17 locations through the National Committee for Plasticulture Applications in Horticulture.
National Horticulture Board (NHB)	National Horticulture Board (NHB) was set up by the Government of India in 1984 as an autonomous society under the Societies Registration Act 1860. Board has its Head Quarter in Gurgaon (Haryana). The Managing Director is the Principal Executive of NHB who implements various schemes under overall supervision and guidance of the Board of Directors of NHB as well as the Department of Agriculture & Co-operation, Ministry of Agriculture, Government of India. **Objectives:** These are • Development of hi-tech commercial horticulture in identified belts. • Development of modern post-harvest management infrastructure as integral part of area expansion projects or as common facility for cluster of projects. • Development of integrated, energy efficient cold chain infrastructure for fresh horticulture produce. • Popularization of identified new technologies / tools / techniques for commercialization / adoption, after carrying out technology need assessment. • Assistance in securing availability of quality planting material by promoting setting up of scion and root stock banks / mother plant nurseries, carrying out accreditation/ rating of horticulture nurseries and need based imports of planting material. • Promotion and market development of fresh horticulture produce. • Promotion of field trials of newly developed/ imported planting materials and other farm inputs, production technology, PHM protocols, INM and IPM protocols, and applied R&D programmes for commercialization of proven technology. • Promotion of applied Research & Development for standardizing PHM protocols, prescribing critical storage conditions for fresh horticulture produce, bench marking of technical standards for cold chain infrastructure etc. • Transfer of technology to producers/farmers and service providers such as gardeners, farm level skilled workers, operators in cold storages, work force carrying out post harvest management including processing of fresh horticulture produce, and to the master trainers. • Promotion of consumption of horticulture produce and products. • Setting up Common Facility Centers in Horticulture Parks and Agri-Export Zones.

Contd.

- Strengthen market intelligence system by developing, collecting and disseminating horticulture database.
- Carrying out studies and surveys to identify constraints and develop short and long-term strategies for systematic development of horticulture and providing technical services including advisory and consultancy services.

Central Institute of Horticulture in Nagaland

Recognizing the potential for development of horticulture in Northeast region, and in order to provide adequate institutional support to tap this potential, Government of India set-up the "Central Institute of Horticulture" at Medziphema, Nagaland under the Central Sector Scheme in the year 2006 and on 27th March. The institute provides technical support on different aspects of horticulture for the holistic development in the North-East Region.

Objectives: These are

- The Institute has been set up with the objective of providing adequate institutional support for development of horticulture especially in North Eastern States.
- Institute imparts training to trainers, extension officers, farmers, entrepreneurs, processors and exporters with an objective of capacity building.
- Demonstration of improved technologies such as use of improved varieties/hybrids, adoption of INM/IPM practices, hi-tech farming, precision farming, protected cultivation, post-harvest technologies etc.
- Follow on extension support in the field of horticulture.
- Promotion of organic cultivation of horticultural crops.
- Establishing convergence and synergy among programmes in the field of horticultural research and development, and Monitoring of centrally sponsored schemes in the area of horticulture.

National Committee on Plasticulture Applications in Horticulture (NCPAH), New Delhi

NCPAH is responsible for coordinating and monitoring activities related to precision farming and hi-tech horticulture through the Precision Farming Development Centres (PFDCs).

Objectives: These are

- To coordinate in promotion of horticulture / agriculture development through use of plastics in agriculture (Plasticulture) with special reference to harnessing available natural resources such as water and sunlight in improving the productivity and quality of the produce.
- To recommend suitable policy measures for promotion of Plasticulture in the country.

Agricultural and Processed Food Products Export Development Authority (APEDA), New Delhi

The Agricultural and Processed Food Products Export Development Authority (APEDA) was established by the Government of India under the Agricultural and Processed Food Products Export Development Authority Act passed by the Parliament in December, 1985. The Act came into effect from 13th February, 1986 by a notification issued in

Contd.

the Gazette of India: Extraordinary: Part-II [Sec. 3(ii): 13.2.1986). The Authority replaced the Processed Food Export Promotion Council (PFEPC).

Objectives: These are

- Development of industries relating to the scheduled products for export by way of providing financial assistance or otherwise for undertaking surveys and feasibility studies, participation in enquiry capital through joint ventures and other reliefs and subsidy schemes.
- Registration of persons as exporters of the scheduled products on payment of such fees as may be prescribed.
- Fixing of standards and specifications for the scheduled products for the purpose of exports.
- Carrying out inspection of meat and meat products in slaughter houses, processing plants, storage premises, conveyances or other places where such products are kept or handled for the purpose of ensuring the quality of such products.
- Improving of packaging of the scheduled products.
- Improving of marketing of the scheduled products outside India.
- Promotion of export oriented production and development of the scheduled products.
- Collection of statistics from the owners of factories or establishments engaged in the production, processing, packaging, marketing or export of the scheduled products or from such other persons as may be prescribed on any matter relating to the scheduled products and publication of the statistics so collected or of any portions thereof or extracts therefrom.
- Training in various aspects of the industries connected with the scheduled products.
- Such other matters as may be prescribed.APEDA is mandated with the responsibility of export promotion and development of the following scheduled products:
- Fruits, Vegetables and their Products.
- Meat and Meat Products.
- Poultry and Poultry Products.
- Dairy Products.
- Confectionery, Biscuits and Bakery Products.
- Honey, Jaggery and Sugar Products.
- Cocoa and its products, chocolates of all kinds.
- Alcoholic and Non-Alcoholic Beverages.
- Cereal and Cereal Products.
- Groundnuts, Peanuts and Walnuts.
- Pickles, Papads and Chutneys.
- Guar Gum.
- Floriculture and Floriculture Products
- Herbal and Medicinal Plants In addition to this, APEDA has been entrusted with the responsibility to monitor import of

sugar.

Directorate of Marketing & Inspection (DMI), New Delhi

The Directorate of Marketing and Inspection (DMI) is an attached Office of the Ministry of Agriculture. It was set up in the year 1935 to implement the agricultural marketing policies and programmes of the Central Government. Since its very inception, the Directorate continues to be responsible for bringing about an integrated development of marketing of agricultural and allied produce in the country with a view to safeguard the interests of producer-sellers as well as the consumers. It maintains a close liaison between the Central and the State Governments in the implementation of agricultural marketing policies in the country.

*Objectives:*These are

- Promotion of Standardisation and Grading of Agricultural and allied produce under the Agricultural Produce (Grading & Marking) Act, 1937 as amended in 1986.
- Market Research, Surveys and Planning.
- Agricultural Marketing Reforms.
- Agricultural Marketing Information Network.
- Promotion of Cold Storage.
- Construction of Rural godowns.
- Development of Marketing Infrastructure, Grading & Standardization.
- Training in Agricultural Marketing.
- Marketing Extension.

Ministry of Food Processing Industries (MFPI), New Delhi

The Ministry of Food Processing Industries is concerned with formulation and implementation of the policies & plans for the food processing industries within the overall national priorities and objectives. A strong and dynamic food processing sector plays a vital role in reduction in the wastage of perishable agricultural produce, enhancing shelf life of food products, ensuring value addition to agricultural produce, diversification &commercialization of agriculture, generation of employment, enhancing income of farmers and creating surplus for the export of agro & processed foods. In the era of economic liberalization, all segments including private, public and co-operative sectors have defined roles to play and the Ministry promotes their active participation.

Objectives: These are

- Better utilization and value addition of agricultural produce for enhancement of income of farmers.
- Minimizing wastage at all stages in the food processing chain by the development of infrastructure for storage, transportation and processing of agro-food produce.
- Induction of modern technology into the food processing industries from both domestic and external sources.
- Encourage R&D in food processing for product and process development and improved packaging.
- Provide policy support, and support for creation of Infrastructure, capacity expansion/ Upgradation and other

	supportive measures form the growth of this sectors. • Promote export of processed food products.
National Medicinal Plants Board (NMPB), New Delhi	The National Medicinal Plants Board (NMPB) set-up in November 2000 by the Government of India has the primary mandate of coordinating all matters relating to medicinal plants and support policies and programmes for growth of trade, export, conservation and cultivation. The Board is located in the Department of Ayurveda, Yoga & Naturopathy, Unani, Siddha & Homeopathy (AYUSH) of the Ministry of Health & Family Welfare.
National Horticulture Research & Development Foundation (NHRDF), Nasik	The National Horticultural Research and Development Foundation (NHRDF) was established by National Agricultural Co-operative Marketing Federation of India Ltd. (NAFED) and its Associate Shippers of onion on 3 November, 1977 under Societies Registration Act, 1860 at New Delhi. During 1989, the Head Office of NHRDF was shifted to Nasik but the Registered Office is at New Delhi. The aim of establishment of NHRDF was to guide the farmers, exporters and others concerned for improving the productivity and quality of horticultural crops in order to make available sufficient quantity for domestic requirement and also to boost up export of onion and other such export oriented horticultural crops in the country. Onion was the first crop on which the NHRDF has started its Research and Development programmes to meet the above-mentioned aim and subsequently garlic, okra, chilli, French bean crops etc. have been added. The NHRDF initially started as a small center at New Delhi in 1978 and now it has 5 Regional Research Stations, Laboratories on different aspects and 20 Extension Centers spread all over the major onion and garlic growing pockets of the country. It has also established one Krishi Vigyan Kendra at Ujwa in New Delhi to cater the needs of farmers of Delhi State.

3.6 Some Remarkable Information Technology Center(ITC) Initiative in India for Diffusing Agro-information Including Vegetable Science

Projects	Location	Content	Benefits
TNAU agri-tech portal	Managed by Tamil Nadu University	Crop management	All agricultural stakeholder
E choupal	Initiative of ITC Limited, a conglomerate in India	Link directly with rural farmers via the internet for procurement of agricultural and aquaculture pproducts like soybeans, wheat, coffee and prawns	farmers, producers, buissnessman
Agrisnet	Managed by Department of Agricullture, Government of Tamil Nadu, Telengana	Identify the reason for gap in yield of individual farms and address them	Farmer, producer, buissnessman
E Sagu		eSagu is as web-based personalized agro-advisory system which uses Information Technology to solve the unscientific agricultural practiccs	It exploit the advances in Information Technology to build accost effective agricultural information dissemination system to disseminate expert agriculture knowledge to farming community
E Krishi Manch	ICAR Public interface	Direct scientist farmer interface	All agricultural stakeholders
PUSA Krishi online	ICAR Public interface	Direct scientist farmer interface	All agricultural stakeholders
Krishikosh Mobile Applications (ICAR-IARI)	ICAR Public interface	Direct scientist farmer interface	All agricultural stakeholders

2

Vegetable Scenario

2. Vegetable Scenario

2.1. Major Vegetable Crops

Crop	Botanical name	Chromosome number(2n)	Family	Origin	Distribution
Vegetatively Propagated					
Potato	*Solanum tuberosum*	48	Solanaceae	South America in the central Andean region	India, China, Russian Federal, Poland, USA, Ukraine, Germany, Netherland and UK
Sweet potato	*Ipomea batatas*	90	Convovulaceae	Tropics of America	India, America, Malaya, Archipelago, The Pacific Island, Oceania, South and Latin America, Temperate Zone of Japan, China, Korea and North America
Tapioca	*Manihot esculenta*	36 (72)	Euphorbeaceae	Brazil or Paraguay	India, South America, Mexico, Central America, The Caribean Island, Malaysia, Indonesia, Maynmar, The Philippines, Sri Lanka, Thialand and Vietanam.
Yam	*Dioscorea alata*	40	Dioscoreaceae	South East Asia	Africa, China, Japan and Oceania
Arvi (Colocasia)	*Colocasia esculenta*	28	Araceae	South central Asia perhaps India or Malaysia	India, Asia, Oceania, Central Africa, Wet Indies and Central America
Sexually Propagated					
Fruit Vegetables					
Eggplant	*Solanum melongena*	24	Solanaceae	Indo- Verma Region	India, China , Turkey, Japan, Egypt, Italy, Indonesia, Iraq, Syaria, Spain and Philippines
Chilli	*Capsicum frutescens*	24	Solanaceae	South America	India, USA, China, Turkey, Italy,

Contd.

Crop	Botanical name	Chromosome number(2n)	Family	Origin	Distribution
					Egypt, Spain, Iran and Greece
Capsicum	*Capsicum annum*	24	Solanaceae	Spain	India, USA, China, Turkey, Italy, Egypt, Spain, Iran and Greece
Tomato	*Lycopersicon esculentum (Solanum lycopersicon*- new name)	24	Solanaceae	Peru- Ecuador – Bolivia area of the Andes	India, USA, China, Turkey, Italy, Egypt, Spain, Iran and Greece
Okra	*Abelmoschus esculentus*	72, 120, 130, 132	Malvaceae	Tropical or sub tropical Aferica	India, USA, China, Turkey, Italy, Egypt, Spain, Iran and Greece
Legumes					
Pea	*Pisum sativum*	14	Fabaceae	Ethopia	India, Syria, Turkey, Jordan, Egypt
Broad bean	*Vicia faba*	12(24)	Fabaceae	North Africa or the South Caspain Sea	India China, Ethopia, Egypt, West Germany, Italy, Morocco, and France
Cluster bean	*Cyamopsis tetragonoloba*	14	Fabaceae	Either from India or Africa	India, Pakistan
Cowpea	*Vigna unguiculata*	22	Fabaceae	India	India, Nigeria, West Africa and Central
French bean	*Phaseolus vulgaris*	22	Fabaceae	South Mexico or Central America	India, Myanmar, Brazil, United States, Tanzania, China, Mexico, Indonesia
Indian bean	*Dolichos lablab*	22 (24)	Fabaceae	India	India, Kenya, Eastern Africa
Bulb Crops					
Garlic	*Allium sativum*	16	Amaryllidaceae	Central Asia	India, Egypt, USA, Korea Repbulic and Korea
Onion	*Allium cepa*	16	Amaryllidaceae	Central Asia	India, China, USA, France, Japan, Korea Republic, Brazil, Spain and Pakistan

Contd.

Crop	Botanical name	Chromosome number(2n)	Family	Origin	Distribution
Cole Crops					
Broccoli(Sprouting)	*Brassica oleracea* (Italica Group)	18	Brassicaceae	Italy	India, United State of America and North Europe
Brussels sprouts	*Brassica oleracea* (Gemmifera Group)	18	Brassicaceae	Europe	India and European Countries
Cauliflower	*Brassica oleracea* (Botrytis Group)	18	Brassicaceae	Mediterranean Region	India, China, France, Italy, UK, USA, Spain, Poland, Germany and Pakistan
Cabbage	*Brassica oleracea* (Capitata Group)	18	Brassicaceae	Mediterranean Region	India, China, Russian Federation, Japan, Korea, Repbulic, Poland, USA, Indonesia and Ukaraine
Knol-khol	*Brassica oleracea* (Gongylodes Group)	18	Brassicaceae	Mediterranean Region	India, USA, China, Turkey, Italy, Egypt, Spain, Iran and Greece
Cucurbits					
Ash gourd	*Benincasa hispida*	24	Cucurbitaceae	Malayasia	India, Burma and Ceylon
Bitter gourd	*Momordica charantia*	22	Cucurbitaceae	Indo- Verma Region	India, USA, China, Turkey, Italy, Egypt, Spain, Iran and Greece
Bottle gourd	*Lagenaria siceraria*	22 (44)	Cucurbitaceae	Costal Areas of Malabar (North India)	India, Ethopia, Africa, Central America
Cucumber	*Cucmis sativus*	14	Cucurbitaceae	India	India, Myanmar, Pakistan, Whote South-East Asia, Tropical Africa
Ivy gourd	*Coccinia grandis*	24	Cucurbitaceae	India	India, Malaysia, South east Asian countries
Muskmelon	*Cucumis melo*	24	Cucurbitaceae	China	India, China and Southern USSR
Pointed gourd	*Trichosanthes dioica*	22	Cucurbitaceae	India	India, Botswana,
Pumpkin	*Cucurbita moschata*	40	Cucurbitaceae	North and South America	India, China, Russia, Ukraine, United States
Ridge gourd	*Luffa acutangula*	26	Cucurbitaceae	India	India, Chine, Philipines, Mayanmar, Egypt

Contd.

Crop	Botanical name	Chromosome number(2n)	Family	Origin	Distribution
Smooth gourd	*Luffa cylindrica*	26	Cucurbitaceae	India	India, China, Philipines, Mayanmar
Snake gourd	*Trichosanthes anguina*	22	Cucurbitaceae	China	India, China, Japan and Australia
Water melon	*Cittruus lanatus*	22	Cucurbitaceae	Tropical Aferica	India, Russia, China, Turkey, Iran
Leafy Vegetables					
Amaranth	*Amaranthus tricolor*	32	Amaranthaceae	South East Asia	India, Central and South America, South East Asia
Basella	*Basella alba*	24	Basellaceae	Asia more particularly in India	India, China, Malaysia, Philippines, Ghana, Netherlands, Brazil, Russia, Indonesia
Celery (Salad)	*Apium graveolens* var. *dulce*	22	Apiaceae	Sweden to Algeria	India, Southern France, China and Egypt
Coriander (Salad)	*Coriandrum sativum*	22,24	Apiaceae	Mediterranean Region	India Morocco, erstwhile USSR, Russia, Bulgaria, Argentina, China, Japan, Italy, Hungary, Poland, Mexico and USA
Fenugreek	*Trigonella foenumgraecum*	16	Fabaceae	South Eastern Europe and West Asia	India, USA, China, Turkey, Italy, Egypt, Spain, Iran and Greece.
Lettuce	*Lactuca sativa*	18	Asteraceae	Mediterranean Region	India, USA, Southern eastern Australia, Japan, China, Isreal, Northern Mexico, Chile, Argentina, Brazil and Peru.
Root Crops					
Beet root	*Beta vulgaris*	18	Chenopodiaceae	Europe	India, Europe, North America, Middle East of Asia
Caroot	*Daucus carota*	18	Apiaceae	Afghanistan	India, Denmark, Isreal and Canada
Radish	*Raphanus sativus*	18	Brassicaceae	China	India, Europe, Asia
Turnip	*Brassica rapa* (Rapifera group)	20	Brassicaceae	Mediterranean Region	India, England, Scotland, Lreland, Eastern Canada

Contd.

Crop	Botanical name	Chromosome number(2n)	Family	Origin	Distribution
Spices					
Black Pepper	*Piper nigrum*	24-132	Piperaceae	West coast (Malabar)	India, Srilanka, Indonesia, Malayasia, Brazil and Thialand
Small Cardamom	*Elettaria cardamomum*	48	Zingiberaceae	South India and Srilanka	India, Tanzania, Srilanka, Esalydor, Vietnam, Loas, Combodia and New Guinea.
Large Cardamom	*Amomum subulatum*	52	Zingiberaceae	Unknown	India, China, Indonesia, Thialand, Laos and Bhutan.
Cinnamon	*Cinnamomum zeylanicum*	24	Lauraceae	Srilanka and Malabar coast of India	India, SriLanka, Malabar, Island, Seychelles, Myanmar South America and Malayan Peninsula.
Clove	*Syzygium aromaticum*	22	Myrateceae	MoluccaIsland of Indonesia	India, Malaysia and Haiti
Cumin	*Cuminum cyminum*	14	Apiaceae	Egypt and Syria	Turkey, Iran, Egypt, Pakistan and Syria
Fennel	*Foeniculum vulgare*	22	Apiaceae	Europe and Mediterranean Region	Egypt, China, Romaniaand Russia
Ginger	*Gingerber officinalis*	22, 24	Zingiberaceae	India or China	India, USA, China, Turkey, Italy, Egypt, Spain, Iran and Greece
Turmeric	*Curcuma domestica*	3n=63 or 4n= 84	Zingiberaceae	South east and Northern Eastern Region of India and Java	China, Pakistan, Haiti, Jamica, Peru, Bangaladesh, ElSavador and Tiwan.

2.2. Underutilized Solanaceae Vegetables

Common name	Botanical name	Chromosome number (2n)
African eggplant	*Solanum macrocarpon* L.	36
Local garden egg	*Solanum incanum* L.	24
Black nighshade	*Solanum nigrum* L.	24
Jilo	*Solanum gilo*	24
Naranjillo	*Solanum quitoense* L.	24
Pepino	*Solanum muricatum* Ait.	24
Sun berry	*Solanum intrusum*	2x to 14 x (x=7)
Tit began	*Solanum torvum* Swartz.	24
Tomatillo	*Physalis ixocarpa* Brot.	24
Tree tomato	*Cyphomandra betacea*	24
Wild cape goseberry	*Physalis minima* L.	48

2.3. Underutilized Cucurbitaceous Vegetables

Common name	Botanical name	Chromosome number (2n)
Sweet gourd	*Momordica cochinchinensis* Spreng	28
Spine gourd	*Momordica dioica* Roxb.	28
Balsam pear	*Momordica balsamina* L.	22
Fig leaf gourd	*Cucurbita ficifolia* Bouche	40
Buffalo gourd	*Cucurbita foetidissima* Kunth	40
Snap Melon	*Cucumis melo* Var. momordica	48
Chow-chow	*Sechium edule* (Jack.) Sw	28
Ash gourd	*Benincasa hispida* (Thunberg ex Murray) Cogn	24
Ivy gourd	*Coccinia grandis* (L.) Voigt	24
Snake gourd	*Trichosanthes cucumerina* L.	22
Bitter apple	*Citrullus colocynthis* (L.) Schard.	22
Melothria	*Solena amplexicaulis* (Lamk) Gandhi Syn	32
Sweet bitter gourd	*Cyclanthera pedata* (L.) Schrader	32
Pointed gourd	*Trichosanthes dioica* Roxb.	24

2.4. Underutilized Leafy Vegetables

Botanical name	Family
Acalypha indica L	Euphorbiaceae
Aerva lanata (L.) Juss.	Amaranthaceae
Aeschynomene aspera L.	Caselpiniaceae
Alternathera sessilis R. Br.	Amaranthaceae
Althaea officinalis L.	Malvaceae
Amaranthus caudatus L.	Amaranthaceae

Contd.

Amaranthus cruentus L.	Amaranthaceae
Amaranthus spinosus L.	Amaranthaceae
Amaranthus virdis L.	Amaranthaceae
Antidesma diandrum (Roxb.) Roth	Euphorbiaceae
Argyreia nervosa (Burm.f.) Boj	Convulvulaceae
Atriplex hortensis L.	Chenopodiaceae
Basella spp.	Basellaceae
Begonia spp.	Begoniaceae
Boerhaavia diffusa L.	Nyctanginaceae
Brassica juncea var. cuneifolia Roxb.	Brassicaceae
Brynopsis laciniosa (L.)	Cucurbitaceae
Cardiospermum halicacabum L.	Sapindaceae
Casearia esculenta Roxb.	Flacourtiaceae
Cassia tora L.	Caesalpiniaceae
Cayraia trifolia (L.) Don	Vitaceae
Celosia argentea L.	Amaranthaceae
Ceropegia bulbosa L.	Asclepiadaceae
Chenopdium album L.	Chenopodiaceae
Chlorophytum tuberosum Baker	Liliaceae
Cissus discolour Bl.	Vitaceae
Cissus repens Bl.	Vitaceae
Cleome viscosa Bl.	Cleomaceae
Clerodendrum indicum (L.) Kuntze	Verbenaceae
Clerodendrum serratum (L.) Moon	Verbenaceae
Commelina benghalensis L.	Commelinaceae
Commelina obliqua Ham.	Commelinaceae
Convolvulus spp.	Convulvulaceae
Cynotis tuberosa Roem. & Schult	Commelinaceae
Desmodium microphyllum	Papilionaceae
Digera muricata	Amaranthaceae
Embelia sonchifolia	Myrsinaceae
Enydra fluctuans	Asteraceae
Gymnema sylvestris R. Br	Asclepiadaceae
Hibiscus sabdariffa L.	Malvaceae
Hibiscus surattensis L.	Malvaceae
Holostemma annularis (Roxb.) Schum	Asclepiadaceae
Hydrocotyle sibthorpioides	Apiaceae
Hydrolea zeylanica	Hydrophyllacaceae
Hygrophilia salcifolia Nees	Acanthaceae
Ipomea aquatica Forsk.	Convulvulaceae
Lasia spinosa (L.) Thw	Araceae
Launea nudicaulis Hook.	Asteraceae
Leucas lantana Benth	Labiatae
Lysimachia candida Lindl	Primulaceae
Leucas lantana Benth	Labiatae
Malva parviflora L.	Malvaceae
Marsilea minuta L.	Marsileaceae
Medicago hispida Gaertn	Papilionaceae
Melochia corchorifolia	Sterculiaceae

Contd.

Merremia emarginata Hall.f.	Convulvulaceae
Meyna laxiflora Robyns	Rubiaceae
Molluga cerviana Scringe	Aizoaceae
Nothosaerva brachiate Wt.	Amaranthaceae
Neptunia oleracea Lour	Mimosaceae
Nymphoides cristatum O. Kuntze	Gentianaceae
Ottelia alismoides Pers	Hydrocharitaceae
Oxalis acetosella L.	Oxalidaceae
Oxalis corymbosa DC.	Oxalidaceae
Perilla frutesscens (L.) Britt	Labiatae
Phytolacca acinosa Roxb.	Phytolaccaceae
Pisonia alba Spanoghe	Nyctaginaceae
Plumbago zeylanica L.	Plimbaginaceae
Polygonum plebium R. Br.	Polygonaceae
Portulaca spp.	Portulacaceae
Pouzolzia viminea Wedd.	Utricaceae
Premna latifolia Roxb.	Verbenaceae
Rivia hypocerateriformis (Lamk)	Convulvulaceae
Rumex vesicarius L	Polygonaceae
Salsola foetida Del. Ex Spreng	Chenopodiaceae
Sauropus androgynus (L.)	Euphorbiaceae
Sesbania grandiflora (L.)	Papilionaceae
Sonchus oleraceus L.	Asteraceae
Sphenoclea zeylonica Gaerthner	Campanulaceae
Stellaria media (L.) Vill	Caryophyllaceae
Suaedea maritima (L.)	Chenopodiaceae
Talinum triangulare (Jacq.)	Portulacaceae
Tetragonia expansa Murr.	Aizoaceae
Trianthema portulacastrum L.	Aizoaceae
Tribullus terrestris L.	Zygophyllaceae
Typha angustata Bory and Chaub	Typhaceae
Vallaris solanacea (Roth) O. Kuntze	Apocynaceae
Vallisneria spp.	Hydrocharitaceae
Vernonia cinerea L.	Asteraceae
Wrightia tomentosa Roxb.	Apocynaceae

2.5. Underutilized Tuber Crops

Sub-groups	Common name	Botanical name
A. Yams	Yams	*Dioscorea spp.*
B. Tuber crops	Cassava	*Manihot esculenta* Crantz
	Sweet potato	*Ipomea batatas* L.
	Arrow root	*Maranta arundinacea* L.
	Chinese potato	*Solenostemon rotundifolius* (poiret)
	Winged bean	*Psophocarpus tetragonolobus* L.
	Yam bean	*Pachyrrhizus erosus* L.

Contd.

C. Aroids	Elephant foot yam	*Amorphophallus paenoiifolius* (dennst.)
	Giant taro	*Alocasia indica* (Roxb.)
	Tania	*Xanthosoma sagittifolium* L.
	Taro	*Colocasia esculenta* L.

2.6. Underutilized Yams

Cultivated largely	Underutilized yams
Greater yam (*Dioscorea alata* L.)	Potao yam (*Dioscorea bulbifera* L.)
Lesser yam (*Dioscorea esculenta* L.)	Yellow yam ((*Dioscorea cayenesis* L.)
White yam (*Dioscorea rotundata* Poir.)	Bitter yam (*Dioscorea dumentorum* Kunth.)
	Chinese yam (*Dioscorea opposita* Thumb.)
	Buck yam (*Dioscorea pentaphylla* L.)
	Cush-Cush yam (*Dioscorea trifida* L.)
	Dioscorea japonica L.
	Dioscorea nummularia L.
	Dioscorea belophylla Voight.
	Dioscorea anguina Roxb.

2.7. Underutilized Vegetables for Alkali Soils

Common name	Botanical name	Family
Agathi	*Sesbania grandiflora*	Papilionaceae
Amaranth	*Amaranthus spp.*	Amaranthaceae
Drumstick	*Moringa oleifera*	Moringaceae
Winged bean	*Psophocarpus tetragonolobus*	papilionaceae

2.8. Underutilized Vegetables for Flood Prone Conditions

Underutilized vegetables	Family	Parts used
Achyranthes spp.	Amaranthaceae	Leaves
Alternanthera philoxeroides	Amaranthaceae	Leaves
Aponogeton echinatum	Aponogetonaceae	Leaves
Aponogeton crispum	Aponogetonaceae	Leaves
Aponogeton natans	Aponogetonaceae	Leaves
Colocasia spp.	Araceae	Corms
Enydra fluctuans	Asteraceae	Leaves
Euryale ferox	Nymphaeaceae	Rhizome, young
Ipomea aquatica	Convolvulaceae	Leaves
Musa spp.	Musaceae	Inflorescence
Nelumbo nucifera	Nymphaeaceae	Rhizome
Nymphaea nouchali	Nymphaeaceae	Petioles and pedicels
Nymphoides cristatum	Menyanthaceae	Stem, fruit and leaves
Ottelia alismoides	Hydrocharitaceae	Stem, leaves
Sonneratia caseolaris	Sonneratiaceae	Unripe fruits
Trapa bispinosa	Trapaceae	Immature kernel
Typha angustata	Typhaceae	Rhizome

2.9. Underutilized Vegetables for Famine and Scarcity

Common name	Botanical name	Family
A. Leafy vegetables		
Chandlai	*Amaranthus gracilis*	Amaranthaceae
Lal Chaulai	*A. hybridus*	Amaranthaceae
Unda Kanta	*Achyranthes aspera*	Amaranthaceae
Khokte	*Acalypha indica*	Euphorbiaceae
Jangli Kulfa	*Portulaca oleracea*	Portulacaceae
Balukasag	*Giseka pharnaceodies*	Aizoaceae
Murga Kalgi	*Celosia argentea*	Amaranthaceae
Morang	*Digera muricata*	Amaranthaceae
Luni or Lunki	*Portulaca quadrifida*	Portulacaceae
Bagre	*Cleome viscosa*	
Bakna	*Commelina benghalensis*	Commenlinaceae
Kasira	*Commelina forskalii*	Commenlinaceae
Kesudo	*Cassia ociidentalis*	Caesalpiniceae
Goma	*Leucas aspera*	Labiatae
Halkhura	*Leucas cephalotes*	Labiatae
Bapchi	*Ocimum americanum*	Labiatae
Tulsi	*Ocimum balsicum*	Labiatae
Thor	*Euphorbia canducifolia*	Euphorbiaceae
Arg	*Securingea leucopyrus*	Euphorbiaceae
Balhua	*Chenopodium album*	Chinopodiaceae
Golia	*Chenopodium murale*	Chinopodiaceae
Peelwan	*Cocculus pendulus*	Menispermaceae
Kauphuti	*Cardiospermum halicacabum*	Sapindaceae
Sata	*Boerhaavia diffusa*	Nyctaginaceae
Mota sata	*Boerhaavia spp.*	Nyctaginaceae
B. Fruit Vegetables		
Kair	*Capparis decidua*	Capparidaceae
Gular	*Ficus glomerata*	Moraceae
Lasora	*Cordia myxa*	Boraginaceae
Drumstick	*Moringa oleifera*	Moringaseae
Kachari	*Cucumis callusus*	Cucurbitaceae
Mateera	*Citrullus spp*	Cucurbitaceae
Bankarela	*Momodica spp*	Cucurbitaceae
C. Underutilized Legumes		
Bekario	*Indigofera spp*	Papilionaceae
Arak Moth	*Vigna trilobata*	Papilionaceae
Khejri	*Prosopis cineraria*	Mimosaceae
D. Root, Tubers and Others		
Dhak	*Butea monosperma*	Papilonaceae
Semul	*Bombax ceiba*	Bombacaceae
Khandula	*Ceropegia tuberosa*	Asclepiadaceae
Motha	*Cyperus spp*	Cyperaceae
Satavar	*Asperagous racimosus*	Liliaceae
Canna	*Canna edulis*	Cannaceae

Contd.

E. Flowers and Buds		
Lasora	*Cardia myxa*	Boraginaceae
Drumstick	*Moringa oleifera*	Moringaceae
Phog	*Calligonum polygonoides*	Polygonaceae
Khejri	*Prosopis cineraria*	Mimosaceae

2.10. Underutilized Vegetables of Ladakh Area

Common/local name of vegetable	Botanical name
Buck wheat/dyat	*Fagopyrum esculentum*
Dittander/Shangsho	*Lepidium latifoloium*
Khala	*Lactuca dolichophylla*
Mountain sorrel/lamachu	*Oxyria digyna*
Sagani	*Chenopodium botrys*
Shoma	*Rumex patientia ssp. tibeticus*
Zacchout	*Urtica hyperborea*

2.11. Underutilized Leafy Vegetables for NEH Region

Botanical name	Family
Acronychia pedunculate (L.) Syn	Rutaceae
Alocasia macroorrhiza L.	Araceae
Ardisia crispa DC., Syn	Myrsinaceae
Ardisia polycephala Wall., Syn	Myrsinaceae
Casearia esculenta Roxb.	Flacourtiaceae
C. glomerate Roxb.	Flacourtiaceae
Cirsium lipski Petrak, Syn	Asteraceae
Cissus repens Lamk	Vitaceae
Calusena excavate Burm.f	Rutaceae
Calusena heptaphylla Wt & Arn	Rutaceae
Clerodendrum colebrookianum Walp	Verbenaceae
C. indicum (L.) Kuntze	Verbenaceae
Embelia subcoriacea (Clarke) Mez	Myrsinaceae
Enydra fuctuans Lour	Asteraceae
Fagara oxyphylla (Edgew.) Engl	Rutaceae

2.12. Underutilized Edible Leafy Vegetables for Ladakh Region

Botanical name	Family
Allium wallichii	Amaryllidaceae
Capparis spinosa	Capparidaceae
Capsella bursa PastorisMed.	Brassicaceae
Chenopodium botrys	Chenopodiaceae
Christolea crassifolia Camb.	Brassicaceae
Elsholtzia densa Benth.	Labiatae
Fagopyrum esculentum Moench	Polygonaceae
Lactucu dolichophylla Kitam	Asteraceae

Contd.

Lepidium latifolium L.	Brassicaeae
Mentha longifolia L.	Labiate
Orobanche cernua Loefl	Orbanchaceae
Oxyria digyna	Polygonceceae
Rhodiola imbricata	Crassulaceae
Rumex hastatus D. Don	Polygonaceae
Rumex patientia L. ssp. Tibeticus	Polygonaceae
Sonchus oleraceus	Asteraceae
Sedium ewersii L.	Crassulaceae
Taraxacum officinale Weber	Asteraceae

2.13. Fruit Plants Used for Vegetable Purposes

Common name	Botanical name	Family
Agathi	*Sesbania grandiflora* L.	Papilionaceae
Alpinia	*Alpinia galangal* L.	Zingiberaceae
Ardisia	*Ardisia Griffithii* C.B. Clarke	Mysinaceae
Asoka	*Saraca indica* L.	Casealpiniaceae
Bamboo	*Bambusa Bambos* L.	Poceae
Bitter cress	*Cardamine hirsute* L.	Brassicaceae
Broussonetia	*Broussonetia luzonica* Blanco	Moraceae
Buripalm	*Corypha utan* Lamk	Palmae
Butterbur	*Petasites japonicus* (Sieb. & Zuec.)	Asterceae
Clerodendrum	*Clerodendrum serratum* L.	Verbenaceae
Dioscorea	*Dioscorea pentaphylla* L.	Discoreaceae
Drumstick	*Moringa oleifera* Lamk.	Moringaceae
Elephant Apple	*Dillenia indica* L.	Dilleniaceae
Holostemma	*Holostemma annularis* (Roxb.)	Asclepiadaceae
Indian Sago Palm	*Caryota urens* L.	Palmae
Indigofera	*Indigofera pulchella* Roxb.	Papilionaceae
Kair	*Capparis aphylla* Roth	Capparidaceae
Karmal	*Dillenia Pentagyna* Roxb.	Dilleniaceae
Lisora	*Cordia dichotoma* Forst.	Boranginaceae
Monochoria	*Monochoria hastate* (L.)	Pontederiaceae
Mountain Ebony	*Bauhinia variegate* L.	Caesalpiniaceae
Mussaenda	*Mussaenda frondosa* L.	Rubiaceae
Orthanthera	*Orthathera viminea* Wt. & Arn.	Asclepiadaceae
Pala indigo plant	*Wrightia tinctoria* R. Br.	Apocynaceae
Periploca	*Periploca aphylla* Decne.	Asclepiadaceae
Pink Bahunia	*Bauhinia purpurea* L.	Caselpiniaceae
Plantain	*Musa sapientum* L.	Musaceae
Polygonum	*Polygonum rtuncinatum*	Polygonaceae
Pumpkin	*Curcurbita moschata* Poir.	Cucurbitaceae
Pygmy Water lily	*Nymphaea tetragona* Georg.	Nymphaceace
Sunhemp	*Crotolaria juncea* L.	Papilionaceae
Silk Cotton	*Bombax malabaricum* DC.	Bombacaceae
Vaccinium	*Vaccinium vacciniaceum* (Roxb.)	Vacciniaceae
White lotus	*Nymphaea nouchali* Burm. f.	Nymphaeaceae
Woodfordia	*Woodfordia fruticose* (L.) Krz.	Lythraceae

2.14. Production Share (%) of Various Horticulture Crops in India

Horticulture Crops	2012-13	2013-14	2014-15	2015-16	2016-17	2017-18
Fruits	30.2	32.1	30.8	31.5	30.9	31.2
Vegetable	60.3	58.7	60.3	59.1	59.3	59.2
Flowers and Aromatic Plants	1.0	1.1	1.1	1.1	1.1	1.2
Plantation Crop	6.3	5.9	5.5	5.8	6.0	5.8
Spices	2.1	2.1	2.2	2.4	2.7	2.6

Source: NHB Date Book 2016-2017

2.15. Leading Vegetable Producing Countries of the World

Country (tons)	Vegetable Production Combined 2021(tons)	Roots And TubersOnly Production 2021 (tons)	Vegetable Only Production 2021
China	74,90,13,077.00	14,90,00,000.00	60,00,13,077.00
India	20,02,80,472.00	6,22,92,000.00	13,79,88,472.00
Nigeria	13,77,94,510.00	12,20,00,000.00	1,57,94,510.00
United States	4,78,09,754.00	1,98,92,416.00	2,79,17,338.00
Indonesia	3,41,49,724.00	2,11,40,129.00	1,30,09,595.00
Thailand	3,33,98,955.00	3,06,18,052.00	27,80,903.00
Russia	3,18,39,496.00	1,82,95,535.00	1,35,43,961.00
Turkey	3,17,46,111.00	51,00,000.00	2,66,46,111.00
Brazil	3,16,00,910.00	2,30,29,138.00	85,71,772.00
Vietnam	2,93,44,953.00	1,21,20,743.00	1,72,24,210.00
Bangladesh	1,74,85,426.00	1,01,67,043.00	73,18,383.00
Mexico	1,70,85,027.00	23,37,974.00	1,47,47,053.00
Egypt	1,56,50,789.00	79,865.00	1,55,70,924.00
Germany	1,50,95,270.00	1,13,12,100.00	37,83,170.00
Tanzania	1,49,78,668.00	1,22,04,942.00	27,73,726.00
France	1,44,23,202.00	89,87,220.00	54,35,982.00
Japan	1,33,39,607.00	31,62,825.00	1,01,76,782.00
Pakistan	1,31,77,422.00	61,03,661.00	70,73,761.00
Italy	1,28,02,890.00	13,62,130.00	1,14,40,760.00
Iran	1,19,30,216.00	25,99,089.00	93,31,127.00
South Korea	1,06,72,712.00	9,03,805.00	97,68,907.00
Philippines	99,98,963.00	33,40,017.00	66,58,946.00
United Kingdom	78,81,855.00	53,06,720.00	25,75,135.00
Kenya	69,64,759.00	36,22,884.00	33,41,875.00
Ethiopia	66,49,364.00	49,97,295.00	16,52,069.00
Colombia	65,75,160.00	41,34,363.00	24,40,797.00
Myanmar	58,57,531.00	9,23,436.00	49,34,095.00
South Africa	53,75,308.00	26,76,893.00	26,98,415.00
DR Congo	9,62,716.00	3,70,916.00	5,91,800.00

Source: APEDA, 2022

2.16. Area and Production of Major Vegetable Crops in India

Vegetables	2013-14		2014-15		2015-16		216-17		2017-18	
	Area	Production	Area	Production	Area	Production	Area	Production	Area	Production
Beans	138	1370	218	2204	217	2135	198	2012	228	2277
Bitter gourd	79	807	76	770	90	983	95	1030	97	1137
Bottle gourd	103	1819	108	1826	144	2407	153	2529	157	2683
Brinjal	711	13558	673	12589	664	12552	733	12510	703	12801
Cabbage	400	9039	386	8585	388	8755	395	8807	399	9037
Capsicum	30	167	32	183	21	268	24	30	24	326
Carrot	62	1074	64	968	79	1254	86	1350	97	1648
Cauliflower	434	8573	411	7926	426	8199	454	1857	453	8668
8688Cucumber	43	678	43	678	64	1024	74	1142	82	1260
Chillies (Green)	140	1687	181	1998	238	2392	316	3624	309	3592
Muskmelon	37	761	42	863	47	936	29	748	30	774
Mushroom		17		51	5	76	182	441	198	487
Okra	533	6346	504	5709	485	5507	507	6003	509	6095
Onion	1204	19402	1173	18927	1225	20991	1306	22427	1285	23262
Pointed gourd	13	169	18	347	16	243	18	268	20	310
Peas	434	3869	476	4652	497	4814	530	5345	540	5422
Potato	1973	41555	2076	48009	2134	43770	2179	48605	2142	51310
Radish	173	2485	168	2307	193	2743	203	2898	209	3061
Pumpkin	20	416	49	1122	54	1197	74	1664	78	1714
Sweet Potato	106	1088	107	1228	130	1472	128	1460	131	1500
Tapioca	228	8139	208	4373	204	4554	179	4171	173	4950
Tomato	882	18736	767	16385	760	18399	797	20708	789	19759
Others	1574	19108	1654	25053	1513	22197	1558	21557	1580	22320
Total vegetables	9459	167429	9417	166566	9575	166608	10238	178172	10259	184394

Note: Area in 000' ha, production in 000' metric tonnes Source: Department of Agriculture, Cooperation & Farmers Welfare (Horticulture Statistics Division).

2.17: Global Status of Vegetable: Primary, Potatoes and Dry Onion

FAO, 2020)

Country	Area (Million ha)	Production (Million tonnes)	Productivity (MT/ha)	% Share of the countries in total global vegetables	
				Area	Production
China	28.64	696.01	24.30	35.68X	43.17
India	12.73	219.23	17.22	15.86	13.60
USA	1.27	55.73	43.88	1.58	3.46
Russia	1.87	35.30	18.88	2.33	2.19
Turkey	2.29	33.44	14.60	2.85	2.07
Egypt	0.92	24.52	26.65	1.15	1.52
Iran	0.57	19.15	33.60	0.71	1.19
Mexico	0.80	18.53	23.16	1.00	1.15
Nigeria	5.20	18.29	3.52	6.48	1.13
Vietnam	1.11	17.64	15.89	1.38	1.09
Spain	0.43	16.04	37.30	0.54	0.99
Indonesia	1.45	15.68	10.81	1.81	0.97
Others	22.98	442.51	19.26	28.63	27.47
Total (World)	**80.26**	**1612.07**	**20.09**		

Source: (FAOSTAT)

2.18: Vegetable Productivity Scenario (t/ha) (FAO, 2020)

Crops	India (Average)	World (Average)	Maximum productivity
Tomato	25.34	36.98	50.2 (Belgium)
Eggplants	17.36	30.17	50.0 (Netherland)
Chilli (green)	8.45	17.46	28.1 (Netherland)
Chilli (dry)	2.49	2.57	18.52 (Morocco)
Okra	12.28	4.17	12.4 (Guyana)
Peas (green)	10.13	7.85	13.00 (Cyprus)
Melons	22.54	26.65	61 ?29 (Cyprus)
Cucurbits	9.60	13.85	32.7(Guyana)
Cucumber	6.33	40.36	70.5 (Netherland)
Watermelons	25.34	33.28	119.78 (Botswana)
Cabbage	23.19	29.35	70.84 (Netherland)
Cauliflower	19.30	18.81	44.98 (Jordan)
Onion	18.65	21.37	79.62 (Republic of Korea)
Garlic	8.04	17.19	44.27 (Kuwait)
Beans	2.82	6.26	23.04 (Kazakhstan)

Source: (FAOSTAT)

2.19: Crop Wise Area, Production, and Productivity (2020-2021)

Crop	Area (000 ha)	Production (000MT)	Productivity (MT/ha)
Tomato	845.00	21181.00	25.07
Brinjal	749.00	12874.00	17.19
Okra	531.00	6466.00	12.18
Pea	567.00	5846.00	10.31
Cauliflower	473.00	9225.00	19.50
Cabbage	412.00	9560.00	23.20
Tapioca	183.00	6941.00	37.93
Radish	207.00	3263.00	15.76
Beans	261.00	2595.00	9.94
Sweet Potato	106.00	1121.00	10.58
Bottle gourd	193.00	3171.00	16.43
Bitter gourd	109.00	1330.00	12.20
Chilli (green)	411.00	4363.00	10.62
Carrot	108.00	1885.00	17.45
Cucumber	117.00	1652.00	14.12
Pumpkin	106.00	2205.00	20.80
Capsicum	37.00	563.00	15.22
Pointed gourd	62.00	725.00	11.69
Potato	2203.00	56173.00	25.50
Onion	1624.00	26641.00	16.40
Others Vegetables	1555.00	22665.00	14.58
All India	10859.00	200445.00	18.46

Source: (PIB, Govt, of India)

2.20: State-Wise Projected Demand of Vegetables in Subsequent Years (000mt)

States	Years	
	2025	2030
Andaman & Nicobar	66.62	71.77
Andhra Pradesh & Telangana	14845.29	15992.59
Arunachal Pradesh	242.43	261.16
Assam	5465.23	5887.61
Bihar	18201.15	19607.81
Chandigarh	184.93	199.22
Chhattisgarh	4478.23	4824.32
D & N Haveli	60.12	64.76
Daman & Din	42.59	45.88
Delhi	2937.52	3164.54
Goa	255.60	275.35
Gujrat	10587.69	11405.95
Haryana	4445.42	4788.98
Himanchal Pradesh	1202.22	1295.14
Jammu & Kashmir	2200.33	2370.38
Jharkhand	5465.23	5887.61
Karnataka	10718.68	11547.07

Kerala	5854.21	6306.65
Lakshadweep	11.30	12.17
M.P	12729.29	13713.06
Maharashtra	19703.53	21226.29
Manipur	477.23	514.12
Meghalaya	519.71	559.88
Mizoram	191.30	206.08
Nagaland	347.28	374.12
Odisha	7355.07	7923.50
Pondicherry	218.20	235.07
Punjab	4857.67	5233.09
Rajasthan	12032.04	12961.92
Sikkim	106.55	114.79
T.N	12648.88	13626.43
Tripura	643.68	693.43
Uttarakhand	1773.88	1910.97
U.P	34994.70	37699.23
West Bengal	16016.95	17254.81
India	212195.83	228595.18

2.21 Leading Vegetable Producing States (2016-17) in India

States	% Contribution
Uttar Pradesh	15
West Bengal	15
Madhya Pradesh	10
Bihar	8
Gujarat	8
Maharashtra	6
Odisha	5
Karnataka	5
Haryana	4
Chattisgarh	4
Others	22

Source: Data Book (2016-17).

2.22. Percentage Change in Area and Production of Vegetable Crops in India

Years	Area	Production
08-09 over 07-08	1.69	0.49
09-10 over 08-09	0.1	3.6
10-11 over 09-10	6.4	9.6
11-12 over 10-11	5.8	6.7
12-13 over 11-12	2.4	3.7
13-14 over 12-13	2.1	0.4
14-15 over 13-14	1.6	4.0
15-16 over 14-15	5.9	-0.2
16-17 over 15-16	1.8	3.5

2.23: Decadal growth rate of major cereals and vegetables

Decade	Paddy	Wheat	Vegetable
1960-70	2.65	8.14	4.57
1971-80	3.75	5.30	5.01
1981-90	3.99	4.99	3.13
1991-2000	1.47	4.53	4.14
2001-2010	2058	0.77	6.46\
2011-2020	1.61	1.54	8.95

Source: Agricultural Statistics at a Glance 2021, Govt. of India

2.24. Brinjal Growing Belts in India

State	Growing belts
Andhra Pradesh	East & West Godavari, Krishna, Guntur, Nellore, Kurnool, Anantapur, Srikakulam, Visakhapatnam.
Assam	All districts of Assam.
Bihar	Patna, Nalanda, Bhojpur, Buxar, Rohtas, Kaimur, Gaya, Jehanabad, Nawada, Aurangabad, Saran (Chhapra), Siwan, Gopalganj, East Champaran, West Champaran, Muzaffarpur, Sitamarhi, Vaishali, Bhagalpur, Banka, Munger, Khagaria, Darbhanga, Madhubani, Samastipur, Begusarai, Purnea, Araria, Katihar, Saharsa, Madhepura, Supaul.
Chhattisgarh	Raipur, Baloda Bazar, Balod, Bilaspur, Gariaband, Durg, Mahasamund, Janjgir-Champa, Jagdalpur, Kabirdham, Raigarh, Surguja, Surajpur, Kondagaon, Korba, Rajnandgaon, Dhamtari, Bemetera, Kanker, Mungeli, Jashpur, Balrampur, Koriya.
Gujarat	Ahmedabad, Gandhinagar, Dang, Narmada, Patan, Mehsana, Bhavnagar.
Haryana	Ambala, Yamunanagar, Karnal, Panipat, Sonipat, Rohtak, Gurgaon, Bhiwani, Hisar, Sirsa, Jind, Mewat.
Himachal Pradesh	Hamirpur, Una, Solan, Kangra, Bilaspur, Kulu.
Jharkhand	Ranchi (Bundu, Tamar, Mandar, Kanke), Ramgarh, Hazaribagh, Gumla, Dumka, Palamu
Karnataka	Kolar, Belgaum, Dharwar, Bijapur, Hassan, Mysore, Tumkur.
Kerala	Erattupetta (Melukavu, Thidanad, Poonjar Thekkekara, Thalappalam), Kanjirappally (Koottickal, Mundakkayam, Koruthde, Manimala, Erumely).
Maddhya Pradesh	Jabalpur, Narsinghpur, Damoh, Sagar, Hoshangabad, Chhattarpur, Satna, Vidisha, Raisen, Barwani, Ratlam, Bhopal, Harda, Ujjain, Dewas, Mandsaur, Rewa
Maharashtra	Nagpur, Satara, Solapur, Parbhani, Pune, Sangali, Bhandara, Amravati, Wardha, Chandrapur, Latur, Nashik, Dhule, Beed, Aurangabad.
Mizoram	Aizawl, Khawzawl, Lunglei, Tuidam.
Nagaland	Dimapur, Wokha.
Odisha	Puri (Astaranga, Nimapada, Satyabadi), Jaipur (Panikoili, Barabati, Nischintakoili), Cuttack (Banki, Athgarh, Tigria), Keonjhar (Dhenkikote, Jhumpura), Sambalpur (Padiabahal), Koraput (Narayanpatna, Bandhugaon).

Rajasthan	Alwar, Bundi, Dholpur, Ganganagar, Jaipur, Jhalawar, Jodhpur, Sawai Madhopur, Tonk, Ajmer, Baran, Hanumangarh, Kota.
Tamil Nadu	Dindigul, Coimbatore, Dharmapuri, Salem, Theni, Pudukottai, Vellore, Trippur.
Tripura	Major Part of Tripura.
Uttar Pradesh	Agra, Meerut, Mainpuri, Kanpur Nagar, Lucknow, Gonda, Raebareli, Hardoi, Banda, Chitrakoot, Mahoba, Firozabad, Bareilly, Etah, Allahabad.
Uttrakhand	Chamoli, Dehradun, Nainital, Udham Singh Nagar.
West Bengal	Nadia, Murshidabad, North & South 24 Parganas, Malda, Jalpaiguri, CoochBehar.

2.25. Cabbage Growing Belts in India

State	Growing belts
Andhra Pradesh	Kurnool, Rangareddy, Chittoor, Guntur.
Arunachal Pradesh	West Kameng, Twang, Lower Subansiri, Kurung Kumey, Upper Siang, Upper Dibang Valley.
Assam	All districts of Assam.
Bihar	Patna, Nalanda, Bhojpur, Rohtas, Gaya, Nawada, Aurangabad, Saran, Siwan, Gopalganj, East Champaran, West Champaran, Sitamarhi, Shoehar, Vaishali, Bhagalpur, Khagaria, Darbhanga, Madhubani, Samastipur, Begusarai, Purnea, Katihar, Saharsa, Madhepura.
Chhattisgarh	Gariaband, Baloda Bazar, Mahasamund, Dhamtari, Raipur, Durg, Balod, Bemetara, Jagdalpur, Kondagoan, Kanker, Bilaspur, Janjgir-Champa, Korba, Raigarh, Surguja, Surajpur, Koriya, Balrampur.
Gujarat	Ahmedabad, Anand, Gandhinagar, Dahod, Panchmahal, Patan, Banaskantha, Mehsana, Sabarkantha.
Haryana	Ambala, Sonipat, Rohtak, Faridabad, Narnaul, Gurgaon, Fatehabad, Sirsa, Jind, Palwal, Yamunanagar, Kurukshetra, Karnal.
Himachal Pradesh	Shimla (Theog, Mashobra), Kullu (Kullu, Bajaura, Banjar).
Jharkhand	Lohardaga, Ramgarh, Hazaribag, Gumla, Dumka, Palamu, Ranchi (Pithoria, Chutia, Mandar, Ratu).
Karnataka	Haveri, Hassan, Bellary, Dakshin Kannada, Chamarajanagar, Chikmagalur, Mandya, Raichur, Bengaluru Rural, Chikkaballapur, Ramanagara, Davanagere, Mysore, Bidar, Kolar, Belgaum, Dharwad.
Maddhya Pradesh	Jabalpur, Sagar, Tikamgarh, Reeva, Satna, Vidisha, Rajgarh, Indore, Dhar, Barwani, Ratlam, Shajapur, Dewas, Bhopal, Baitul, Chhindwara.
Maharashtra	Nasik, Pune, Satara, Chandrapur, Nagpur, Ahmednagar, Sangli.
Manipur	Ukhrul.
Meghalaya	All districts of Meghalaya.
Mizoram	Aizawl, Tuidam, Saiha, Kolashib, Serchhip, Khawzawl.
Nagaland	Kohima, Wokha, Mokochung, Zunheboto, Tuensang, Phek, Mon, Dimapur.
Odisha	Cuttack (Athgarh, Banki, Baranga), Puri (Nimapara, Astaranga), Sambalpur (Kuchinda), Dhenkanal (Kamakshyanagar, Shankarpur), Koraput (Patangi, Semiliguda, Lamtaput, Nandapur).
Punjab	Patiala (Sanaur, Nabha, Rajpura, Ghanaur), Fatehgarh Sahib (Khamano, Bassi Pathana).

Rajasthan	Ajmer, Alwar, Ganganagar, Jaipur, Tonk, Sikar, Jodhpur, Bundi, Bharatpur, Nagaur, Rajsamand.
Sikkim	North, East, West & South Districts.
Tamil Nadu	Krishnagiri, Theni, Nilgiris.
Tripura	West, South, Dhalai & North Districts.
Uttar Pradesh	Bulandshahar, Unnao, Mainpuri, Gorakhpur, Meerut, Etah, Agra, Mathura, Aligarh, Faizabad, Lucknow, Gonda, Firozabad, Pratapgarh.
Uttrakhand	Dehradun, Haridwar, Nainital, Tehri, Champawat.
West Bengal	Paschim Medinipur, South 24 Parganas, North 24 Parganas, Nadia, Murshidabad.

2.26. Cauliflower Growing Belts in India

State	Growing belts
Andhra Pradesh	Chittoor, Kurnool.
Arunachal Pradesh	West Kameng, Twang, Lower Subansiri, Kurung Kumey, Upper Siang, Upper Dibang Valley.
Assam	All districts of Assam.
Bihar	Patna, Nalanda, Bhojpur, Rohtas, Gaya, Nawada, Aurangabad, Saran, Siwan, Gopalganj,East Champaran,West Champaran,Muzaffarpur, Vaishali, Bhagalpur, Khagaria,Darbhanga, Madhubani, Samastipur, Begusarai, Purnea, Katihar, Saharsa, Madhepura.
Chhattisgarh	Baloda Bazar, Gariaband, Mahasamund, Dhamtari, Durg, Balod, Bemetara, Kabirdham, Jagdalpur, Kondagaon, Kanker, Raipur, Janjgir-Champa, Bilaspur, Korba, Raigarh, Surguja, Surajpur, Koriya, Balrampur, Narayanpur, Rajnandgaon.
Delhi	(Rural Area)
Gujarat	Ahmedabad, Anand, Gandhinagar, Dahod, Panchmahal, Patan, Banaskantha, Mehsana, Sabarkantha.
Haryana	Sonipat, Rohtak, Ambala, Kurukshetra, Karnal, Panipat, Faridabad, Gurgaon, Hisar, Fatehabad, Jind, Palwal, Yamunanagar.
Himachal Pradesh	Solan (Solan, Kandaghat, Kunihar, Dharmpur, Vaknaghat), Shimla (Theog, Mashobra).
Jharkhand	Lohardaga, Ramgarh, Hazaribag, Gumla, Dumka, Palamu, Ranchi (Pithoria, Chutia, Mandar, Ratu).
Karnataka	Chikkaballapur, Ramanagara, Kolar, Belgaum, Dharwad, Haveri, Hassan, Chamarajanagar, Chikmagalur, Mandya, Raichur, Bengaluru Rural, Davanagere, Mysore, Bidar.
Maddhya Pradesh	Baitul, Chhindwara, Jabalpur, Sagar, Tikamgarh, Reeva, Satna, Vidisha, Rajgarh, Indore, Dhar, Barwani, Ratlam, Shajapur, Dewas, Bhopal.
Maharashtra	Nashik, Satara, Pune, Nagpur, Ahmadnagar, Chandrapur, Buldhana, Parbhani, Beed.
Manipur	Tamenlong.
Meghalaya	All districts of Meghalaya.
Mizoram	Aizawl, Tuidam, Saiha, Kolashib, Serchhip, Khawzawl.
Nagaland	Kohima, Wokha, Mokochung, Zunheboto, Tuensang, Phek, Mon, Dimapur

Odisha	Jajpur (Chandikhol), Cuttack (Athgarh, Tigiria, Baranga), Puri (Kakatpur, Astaranga), Bolangir (Agalpur, Bongamunda, Titlagarh), Khordha (Balipatna, Balianta).
Punjab	Hoshiarpur (Hariana, Bhunga), Gurdaspur (Gurdaspur, Batala, Fatehgarh Churian, Dera Baba Nanak), Fatehgarh Sahib (Bassi Pathana, Sirhind).
Rajasthan	Ajmer, Alwar, Tonk, Sikar, Bundi, Bharatpur, Nagaur, Rajsamand, Ganganagar, Jaipur, Jodhpur.
Sikkim	North, East, West & South Districts.
Tripura	West, South, Dhalai & North Districts.
Uttar Pradesh	Agra, Muzaffarpur, Saharanpur, Bulandshahr, Moradabad, Maharajganj, Unnao, Gorakhpur, Kushinagar, Ghaziabad, Mainpuri, Badaun, Aligarh, Meerut, Lucknow, Bareilly.
Uttrakhand	Dehradun, Haridwar, Nainital, Pithoragarh, Udham Singh Nagar, Almora, Chamoli.
West Bengal	Paschim Medinipur, Bankura, Nadia, Murshidabad, North & South 24 Parganas.

2.27. Okra Growing Belts in India

State	Growing belts
Andhra Pradesh	Adilabad, Anantapur, Chittoor, East Godavari, Guntur, Karimnagar, Krishna, Kurnool, Mahbubnagar, Medak, Nalgonda, Nizamabad, Nellore, Prakasam, Rangareddy, Srikakulam, Visakhapatnam, Vizianagaram, Warangal, West Godavari.
Assam	Darrand, Nagaon, Sibsagar.
Bihar	Patna, Nalanda, Bhojpur, Buxar, Rohtas, Gaya, Nawada, Aurangabad, Saran, Siwan, Gopalganj, East Champaran, West Champaran, Muzaffarpur, Sitamarhi, Vaishali, Bhagalpur, Munger, Khagaria, Darbhanga, Madhubani, Samastipur, Begusarai, Purrnea, Katihar, Sahara, Madhepura.
Chhattisgarh	Raipur, Baloda Bazar, Gariaband, Mahasamund, Dhamtari, Durg, Balod, Bemetara, Rajnandgaon, Kabirdham, Jagdalpur, Kondagaon, Kanker, Janjgir- Champa, Bilaspur, Mungeli, Korba, Raigarh, Surguja, Surajpur, Koriya, Balrampur, Narayanpur.
Gujarat	Ahmedabad, Anand, Gandhinagar, Dang, Narmada, Navsari, Panchmahal,Bharuch, Sabarkantha, Surat, Tapi.
Haryana	Jind, Mewat Yamunanagar, Hisar, Karnal, Panipat, Ambala, Sonipat, Rohtak, Jhajjar, Faridabad, Narnaul, Gurgaon, Bhiwani, Fatehabad, Sirsa.
Karnataka	Haveri, Dharwad, Gulburga, Dakshin Kannada, Belguam, Shimoga.
Kerala	Erattupetta (Melukavu, Thidanad, Poonjar Thekkekara, Thalappalam), Kanjirappally Koottickal, Mundakayam, Koruthodu, Manimala, Erumeli), Vazhoor (Vellavoor).
Maddhya Pradesh	Jabalpur, Sagar, Hoshangabad, Vidisha, Barwani, Ratlam, Shajapur, Bhopal.
Maharashtra	Satara, Pune, Solapur, Jalgaon, Thane, Parbhani, Chandrapur, Dhule, Nasik, Sangli.
Mizoram	Aizawl, Khawzawl, Lunglei, Tuidam.
Nagaland	Kohima, Wokha, Mokochung, Zunheboto, Tuensang, Phek, Mon, Dimapur.

Odisha	Jajpur (Biribati, Rasulpur), Khordha (Balianta, Bolagarh), Cuttack (Narsinghpur, Badamba, Salepur), Puri (Pipil, Satyabadi).
Rajasthan	Ajmer, Alwar, Bundi, Dausa, Ganganagar, Jaipur, Pali, Sirohi.
Tamil Nadu	Dindigul, Coimbatore, Salem, Vellore, Kancheepuram, Dharmapuri.
Tripura	Major part of Tripura.
Uttar Pradesh	Agra, Meerut, Lucknow, Unnao, Mainpuri, Jalaun, Rae Bareli, Hardoi, Sitapur, Sultanpur, Kushinagar, Aligarh, Kanpur Nagar, Ghaziabad, Farrukhabad, Gonda, Bahraich, Varanasi, Fetehpur, Bulandshaher.
Uttrakhand	Dehradun, Udham Singh Nagar, Pithoragarh, Tehri, Nainital, Haridwar, Chamoli.
West Bengal	Nadia, Murshidabad, North & South 24 Parganas, Bardhaman.

2.28. Onion Growing Belts in India

State	Growing belts
Andhra Pradesh	Adilabad, Anantapur, Guntur, Kadapa, Kurnool, Rangareddy, Srikakulam.
Bihar	Patna, Nalanda, Bhojpur, Rohtas, Gaya, Aurangabad, East Champaran, West Champaran, Muzaffarpur, Sitamarhi, Vaishali, Bhagalpur, Munger, Sheikhpura, Darbhanga Madhubani, Samastipur, Begusarai, Purnea, Araria, Kishanganj, Katihar.
Chhattisgarh	Raipur, Baloda Bazar, Mahasamund, Dhamtari, Durg, Bemetara, Rajnandgaon, Kabirdham, Kanker, Janjgir-Champa, Bilaspur, Korba, Raigarh, Surguja, Surajpur, Koriya, Balrampur, Jashpur.
Gujarat	Dang, Dahod, Bhavnagar, Rajkot Amreli, Junagarh, Jamnagar, Sundarnagar.
Haryana	Sirsa, Jind, Yamunanagar, Kurukshetra, Panchkula, Ambala, Kaithal, Karnal, Panipat, Sonipat, Rohtak, Jhajjar, Biwani, Mewat.
Jharkhand	Palamu, Ramgarh.
Karnataka	Belgam, Dharwad, Gadag, Haveri, Bagalkot, Chitradurga, Bijapur, Chamarajanagar, Chikmaglur, Raichur, Bellary, Gulburga, Chikkaballapur, Davanagere, Koppal.
Madhya Pradesh	Shajapur, Jabalpur, Indore, Khandwa, Ujjain, Reeva, Bhopal, Dhar, Khargone, Mandsaur, Ratlam.
Maharashtra	Nasik, Ahmednagar, Pune, Satara, Solapur, Dhule, Jalgaon, Osmanabad, Beed, Aurangabad, Bhandara, Nandurbar, Latur.
Odisha	Bolangir (Bongamunda, Tureikela), Kalahandi (Bhawanipatna), Boudh (Harbhanga), Angul (Kishorenagar), Deogarh (Reamal), Nuapada (Khariar, Komna, Sinapalli).
Punjab	Sangrur (Sangrur, Malerkotla, Dhuri, Sunam), Patiala (Patiala, Rajpura, Ghanaur, Patran).
Rajasthan	Alwar, Ajmer, Chittorgarh, Jaipur, Jalore, Nagour, Jhunjhunu, Bharatpur, Bhilwara, Jhalawar.
Tamil Nadu	Perambalur, Trichy, Dindigul, Erode, Namakkal, Trippur, Tirunelveli.
Uttar Pradesh	Kannauj, Fatehpur, Sultanpur, Jaunpur, Mainpuri, Kanpur, Farrukhabad, Bahraich, Ballia, Azamgarh, Gonda, Sonabhadra, Ghazipur, Hardoi, Rae Bareli, Unnao, Barabanki, Kanpur Dehat, Pratapgarh, Jalaun, Allahabad, Badaun.

Uttarakhand	Almora, Chamoli, Dehradun, Pauri, Pithoragarh, Tehri, Udham Singh Nagar.
West Bengal	Hooghly, Murshidabad, Nadia, North 24 Parganas.

2.29. Pea Growing Belts in India

State	Growing belts
Andhra Pradesh	Chittoor, Rangareddy, Medak.
Assam	Darrang, Kamrup, Nagaon.
Bihar	Patna, Nalanda, Bhojpur, Gaya, Muzaffarpur, Vaishali, Samastipur, Katihar.
Chhattisgarh	Raipur, Baloda Bazar, Durg, Bemetara, Rajnandgaon, Janjgir-Champa, Bilaspur, Korba, Raigarh, Surguja, Surajpur, Koriya, Balrampur.
Haryana	Ambala, Yamunanagar, Kurukshetra, Kaithal, Karnal, Panipat, Sonipat, Gurgaon, Jind.
Himachal Pradesh	Lahul & Spiti (Keylong, Kazza), Kinnaur (Kalpa, Sangla Nichar Valley, Chango, Pooh), shimla (Rohroo, Theog, Shogi, Mashoba), Sirmour (Pacchad, Sangarh, Rajgarh).
Jharkhand	Ranchi (Ratu, Mandar), Ramgarh, Hazaribagh, Palamu.
Karnataka	Kolar, Bengaluru, Mysore, Tumkur, Hassan, Chikkaballapur.
Madhya Pradesh	Shajapur, Jabalpur, Ujjain, Dewas, Gwalior, Morena, Hoshangabad, Vidisha, Sagar.
Maharashtra	Pune, Parbhani, Thane, Jalna, Nandurbar, Chandrapur, Buldhana.
Manipur	Imphal, Valley.
Mizoram	Aizawl, Lunglei, Saiha.
Nagaland	Kohima, Wokha, Mokochung, Zunheboto, Tuensang, Phek, Mon, Dimapur
Odisha	Angul (Kishorenagar), Sambalpur (Sasan).
Punjab	Hoshiarpur (Hoshiarpur 1, Hoshiarpur 2, Chabbewal), Amritsar (Verka, Jandiala Guru, Majitha, Rayya), Patiala (Sanaur, Rajpura, Ghannaur, Patran), S.B.S. Nagar (Nawan Shahr, Bala, Chaur).
Rajasthan	Jaipur, Alwar, Jodhpur, Udaipur.
Uttar Pradesh	Lalitpur, Jalaun, Jhansi, Mohoba, Sultanpur, Hamirpur, Azamgarh, Basti, Allahabad, Pratapgarh, Etah, Mirzapur, Jaunpur, Kabir Nagar, Ambedkar Nagar, Sonbhadra, Faizabad, Barabanki, Raebareli, Sitapur, Siddharth Nagar, Gonda, Balia, Kanpur-Nagar, Kanpur-Dehat, Kanshi Ram Nagar.
Uttarakhand	Almora, Chamoli, Champawat, Dehradun, Nainital, Tehri, Udham Singh Nagar, Uttarkashi.
West Bengal	Nadia, Hoogly, 24 parganas.

2.30. Tomato Growing Belts in India

State	Growing belts
Andhra Pradesh	Adilabad, Anantapur, Chittoor, East Godavari, Karimnagar, Khammam, Mahbubnagar, Medak, Nalgonda, Nizamabad, Prakasam, Rangareddy, Vizianagaram, Warangal.
Arunachal Pradesh	West Kameng, Twang, Lower Subansiri, Kurung Kumey, Upper Siang, Upper Dibang Valley.

Assam	All districts of Assam.
Bihar	Patna, Nalanda, Bhojpur, Aurangabad, Saran, Siwan, Gopalganj, East Champaran, West Champaran, Muzaffarpur, Sitamarhi, Vaishali, Bhagalpur, Khagaria, Darbhanga, Madhubani, Samastipur, Begusarai, Katihar, Saharsa, Madhepura.
Chhattisgarh	Raipur, Baloda Bazar, Gariaband, Mahasamund, Durg, Balod, Dhamtari, Bemetara, Rajnandgaon, Janjgir-Champa, Kanker, Bilaspur, Mungeli, Korba, Raigarh, Jashpur, Surguja, Surajpur, Balrampur, Koriya, Kondagaon, Bijapur, Kabirdham, Dantewada, Sukma, Narayanpur.
Gujarat	Anand, Kheda, Gandhinagar, Dang, Dahod, Narmada, Panchmahal, Banaskantha, Vadodara, Valsad, Sabarkantha, Bhavnagar.
Haryana	Ambala, Yamunanagar, Kurukshetra, Karnal, Panipat, Sonipat, Rohtak, Jhajjar, Faridabad, Gurgaon, Mewat, Palwal, Bhiwani, Hisar, Fatehabad, Sirsa, Jind.
Himachal Pradesh	Solan (Solan, Kandaghat, Kunihar, Dharmpur, Vaknaghat), Sirmour (Pacchad, Sangarh, Rajgarh), Kullu (Kullu, Bajaura, Banjar).
Jharkhand	Ranchi (Bundu, Tamar, Mandar, Angara), Khunti (Karra, Arki, Murhu, Raniya), Chatra (Simariya, Itkhori), Ramgarh, Hazaribagh, Gumla, Dumka, Palamu, East Singhbhum, West Singhbhum, Lohardaga.
Karnataka	Kolar, Belgaum, Bagalkot, Chitradurga, Bijapur, Chamarajanagar, Chikmaglur, Mandya, Bellary, Koppal, Gulburga, Bengaluru Rural, Chikkaballapur, Ramanagara, Davanagere, Mysore, Tumkur.
Madhya Pradesh	Ratlam, Indore, Khargone, Dhar, Jhabua, Ujjain, Sagar, Raisen, Bhopal, Shajapur, Jabalpur, Chhindwara, Satna Vidish, Bhopal.
Maharashtra	Nasik, Ahmednagar, Pune, Beed, Satara, Solapur, Chandrapur, Latur, Parbhani, Nagpur.
Manipur	Imphal Valley.
Meghalaya	All districts of Meghalaya.
Mizoram	Aizawl, Khawzawl, Lunglei, Tuidam, Saih.
Nagaland	Dimapur, Mokokchung, Wokha.
Odisha	Keonjhar (Hatadihi, Anandapur), Sambalpur (Padiabahal), Bolangiri (Patnagarh, Belpara, Murihahal), Nuapada (Khariar), Cuttack (Tiglria, Kishornagar, Baranga), Koraput (Semiliguda, Patangi, Kotpada, Boriguma), Nawarangpur (Umarkote).
Punjab	Amritsar (Tarsika, Verka, Rayya, Jandiala Guru, Majitha), Patiala (Sanaur, Patiala, Rajpura, Ghanaur).
Rajasthan	Ajmer, Jaipur, Dholpur, Alwar, Tonk, Bharatpur, Dausa, Ganganagar, Jalore, Jhalawar, Kota, Sirohi, Karoli.
Sikkim	North, East, West & South Districts.
Tamil Nadu	Vellore, Salem, Dharmapuri, Coimbatore, Periyar, Trichy, Madurai, Dindigul, Erode, Krishnagiri.
Tripura	West, South, Dhalai & North Districts.
Uttar Pradesh	Etah, Mainpuri, Agra, Kanpur-Nagar, Jalaun, Meerut, Aligarh, Unnao, Barabanki, Faizabad, Firozabad, Lucknow, Sultanpur, Ghaziabad, Kanshi Ram Nagar, Kanpur Dehat, Kannauj.
Uttarakhand	Champawat, Dehradun, Haridwar, Nainital, Pauri, Pithoragarh, Tehri, Udham Singh Nagar, Uttarkashi.
West Bengal	Murshidabad, Nadia, North 24 Parganas, South 24 Parganas Jalpaiguri.

2.31. Export of Other Fresh Vegetables from India

Country	2012-13		2013-14		2014-15	
	Qty (MT)	Value (Lac)	Qty (MT)	Value (Lac)	Qty (MT)	Value (Lac)
Pakistan	2,84,094.22	43,796.33	3,88,474.97	83,706.63	3,34,641.17	71,095.53
Nepal	1,84,036.47	15,998.16	1,87,963.71	15,118.16	2,06,799.91	39,454.99
United Arab Emirates	1,08,547.91	25,777.57	1,01,938.36	28,306.84	79,503.65	30,784.68
United Kingdom	20,792.11	15,268.10	20,907.56	18,844.30	16,870.17	17,674.56
Saudi Arabia	25,827.41	9,354.25	31,533.56	13,676.02	22,015.19	11,606.35
Qatar	12,773.17	4,741.34	15,269.56	6,852.02	17,232.60	9,847.19
Sri Lanka	14,582.63	2,519.12	34,071.61	6,529.96	34,283.24	9,149.87
Kuwait	8,984.09	3,620.21	17,693.16	7,088.81	18,073.89	8,082.29
United States	6,734.99	3,207.02	6,435.28	4,693.91	5,484.35	5,031.16
Bangladesh	11,919.08	1,628.04	44,787.47	10,429.76	24,785.73	4,631.42

Source: APEDA Agrixchange Website

2.32. Export of Dried & Preserved Vegetables from India

Country	2012-13		2013-14		2014-15	
	Qty (MT)	Value (Lac)	Qty (MT)	Value (Lac)	Qty (MT)	Value (Lac)
Germany	8,102.93	10,008.64	5,853.92	11,459.43	9,096.08	14,341.45
United Kingdom	5,066.73	4,796.41	4,459.50	5,509.68	6,580.82	8,684.48
United States	6,562.72	6,609.55	3,889.07	5,425.54	6,248.15	8,132.47
Russia	5,150.89	4,306.49	4,506.53	5,933.35	3,917.62	4,896.27
Belgium	2,237.83	2,201.41	2,060.31	2,728.07	2,793.03	3,934.53
Brazil	2,620.87	2,416.51	2,241.74	2,885.68	2,561.73	3,250.51
South Africa	2,193.71	2,180.03	1,788.11	2,253.19	2,260.75	2,814.68
Netherland	1,627.29	1,542.89	1,326.53	1,670.52	2,211.69	2,678.56
Spain	2,207.24	1,926.88	1,817.87	2,095.92	2,383.31	2,670.55
France	684.07	2,668.62	403.98	5,034.64	728.82	2,451.50

Source: APEDA Agrixchange Website

2.33. India Export Statistics: Vegetable

	2022-23		2023-24	
Country	Qty (MT)	Value (Lacs)	Qty (MT)	Value (Lacs)
U Arab Emts	8,29,30,270.00	47,634.55	6,17,55,496.00	33,791.49
Nepal	36,56,87,135.00	44,198.11	18,51,99,519.00	21,184.38
U K	1,15,24,467.00	18,855.30	77,20,148.00	12,020.51
Qatar	2,36,73,857.00	17,272.93	1,22,61,027.00	8,323.14
Oman	4,43,07,331.00	12,782.87	3,48,01,383.00	10,318.64
Bangladesh	7,09,63,564.00	15,425.40	10,59,32,591.00	29,103.51
Saudi Arab	3,69,47,441.00	11,254.68	2,24,13,302.00	7,408.83
Malaysia	3,53,07,856.00	10,043.37	2,18,18,393.00	8,262.57
Maldives	1,62,37,506.00	8,913.66	95,85,882.00	4,619.97
Kuwait	1,72,08,629.00	8,661.28	1,33,86,063.00	7,653.97
Singapore	1,20,36,561.00	8,644.25	72,55,204.00	5,513.13
Indonesia	2,84,03,975.00	7,247.00	1,46,92,000.00	3,912.59
Bhutan	1,59,67,106.00	5,017.18	73,81,078.00	2,713.58
Sri Lanka Dsr	2,23,86,307.00	4,864.91	96,77,851.00	2,214.35
Canada	28,67,147.00	3,622.89	19,05,120.00	2,633.55
Baharain Is	57,87,357.00	3,388.24	34,73,939.00	2,308.79
Germany	21,85,751.00	1,871.76	14,23,684.00	1,624.73
U S A	8,09,982.00	1,384.76	4,47,533.00	769.53
France	8,38,206.00	1,106.93	6,65,304.00	1,098.63
Thailand	24,74,151.00	1,004.21	19,04,090.00	1,314.60
Hong Kong	21,60,268.00	926.57	18,34,876.00	756.37
Netherland	4,58,884.00	712.95	3,19,005.00	545.04
Ireland	3,78,473.00	501.29	3,66,397.00	543.07
Total	**82,72,88,051.00**	**2,35,335.09**	**54,69,81,554.00**	**1,75,714.62**

Source: DGCIS

2.34. Export of Fruits & Vegetables Seeds from India

Country	2012-13		2013-14		2014-15	
	Qty (MT)	Value (Lac)	Qty (MT)	Value (Lac)	Qty (MT)	Value (Lac
Pakistan	7,719.03	8,960.24	6,421.43	6,857.97	4,012.93	6,584.60
Bangladesh	4,266.75	3,487.65	4,681.93	4,068.10	5,329.58	5,559.77
United States	141.95	3,830.97	173.65	4,297.72	85.03	5,370.26
Netherland	326.33	3,352.28	105.54	3,546.13	82.16	3,666.26
Japan	189.31	1,643.81	187.99	2,073.57	194.86	2,178.98
Thailand	61.12	975.75	48.07	2,293.77	58.26	2,054.25
China P Rp	94.75	966.71	440.40	1,006.69	203.17	1,926.26
Singapore	17.66	404.80	59.12	1,473.55	56.35	1,590.53
Kenya	86.74	730.45	57.12	1,065.50	48.47	1,506.63
Korea Republic	287.65	849.24	263.91	802.15	110.29	1,047.19

Source: APEDA Agrixchange Website

2.35. Export Specifications of Important Vegetables

Crop	Specific requirements
Okra	Green, tender and 6-9 cm long.
Chillies	Green and 6-7 cm long.
Cluster bean	Green, tender and 7-10 cm long.
Bitter gourd	Green, 20-25 cm long having short neck.
Bottle gourd	Light green, straight cylindrical in shape and 25-30 cm long.
Gherkin	Green small sized having 160-300 fruits/kg in premium grade
Tomato	Round, medium size, red colour in Middle East, cherry tomatoes in European countries.
French bean	Straight 10-12 cm long, round green pods in bush beans, Flat beans having 12-13 cm length and pods are also in demand in European markets.
Big onion	4-6 cm, light to dark red colour, round shape, strong pungency in Gulf markets and South East Asian markets.3-4 cm, light red and round shape in Bagladesh.Yellow/brown colour, 7-8 cm, round or spindle shape in European and Japanese markets.
Small onion	Dark red 2-3 cm and round shape.
Multiplier onion	2.5-3.5 cm sized bulblets of bright red colour.
Garlic	White, round, 5 cm and above, bigger cloves of 10-12 mm and above with 10-15 in number. For Bangladesh and Sri Lanka 4-5 cm size bulbs are also acceptable.
Potato	White, oval, 4.5 to 6.0 cm size. Bangladesh demands red types and that Iran & Iraq demand potatoes with yellow flesh.

2.36. Export from India (2016-17) of Different Vegetables

Crops	Quantity (Thous and MT)	Valve (Lakh Rupees)
Onion	2415.75	3,10,650.09
Potato	384.24	64,056.48
Tomato	267.19	54,806.05
Cabbage	0.30	44.24
Chilli	43.49	21751.04
Garlic	1.27	2097.88

Source: NHB Data Book (2016-17)

2.37. Peak Harvesting Season of Major Vegetable Crops in India

Vegetable Crops	Peak Harvesting
Onion	Maharashtra – April Madhya Pradesh – March, April Seprate to October Gujarat – February Rajasthan – May and November Bihar – March -April

Contd.

Potato	Uttar Pradesh – December West Bengal – March Gujarat – January Madhya Pradesh – February to March
Tomato	Madhya Pradesh – January, February, October and December Andhra Pradesh – January to December Telangana – January ot December Gujarat – January, February, March adn December
Brinjal	West Bengal – Round Theyear Odisha – Janjuary, February, November, December Gujarat – January to April, October to December Madhya Pradesh – September, October Bihar – November, December
Cabbage	West Bengal – November to February Odisha – December to March Assam – November to February Bihar – January to February Gujarat – December to February
Chilli	Kharif – September to November Rabi – April - June
Garlic	March-April

3

Vegetable Nutrition and Medicinal Values

3.1. Nutritive Value of Various Vegetables per 100 g of Edible Portion

Name of the vegetable	Moisture content (%)	Carbohydrate (g)	Protein (g)	Fat	Vitamin (g)	Vitamin B (mg) A (I.U.)		Vitamin C (mg)
						Thiamine	Riboflavin	
1	2	3	4	5	6	7	8	9
Amaranthus	85.7	6.3	4.0	0.5	9,200	0.03	0.10	99
Ash gourd	96.5	1.9	0.4	0.1	0	0.06	0.01	1
Beetroot	87.7	8.8	1.7	0.1	0	0.04	0.09	88
Bitter gourd	92.4	4.2	1.6	0.2	210	0.07	0.09	88
Bottle gourd	96.1	2.5	0.2	0.1	0	0.03	0.01	6
Brinjal	92.7	4.0	1.4	0.3	124	0.04	0.11	12
Cabbage	91.9	4.6	1.8	0.1	2,000	0.06	0.03	124
Carrot	86.0	10.6	0.9	0.2	3,150	0.04	0.02	3
Cauliflower	90.8	4.0	2.6	0.4	51	0.04	0.10	56
Chilli (green)	85.7	3.0	2.9	0.6	292	0.19	0.39	111
Cluster bean	81.0	10.8	3.2	0.4	316	0.09	0.09	47
Coccinia	93.5	3.1	1.2	0.1	260	-	-	15
Cowpea	84.6	8.0	4.3	0.2	941	0.07	0.09	13
Cucumber	96.3	2.7	0.4	0.1	0	0.03	0.01	7
Dolichos bean	86.1	6.7	3.8	0.7	312	0.1	0.06	9
French bean	91.4	4.5	1.7	0.1	221	0.08	0.06	11
Garlic (dry)	62.0	29.80	6.3	0.1	0	0.06	0.03	13
Knol-khol	92.7	3.8	1.1	0.2	36	0.05	0.09	85
Lady's finger	89.6	6.4	1.9	0.2	88	0.07	0.10	13
Lettuce	93.4	2.5	2.1	0.3	1,650	0.09	0.13	10
Muskmelon	94.0	5.0	1.0	0	3,420	0.04	0.05	33
Onion	86.8	11.0	1.2	-	0	0.08	0.01	11

Contd.

Pea	72.0	15.8	7.2	0.1	139	0.25	0.01	9
Pointed gourd	92.0	2.2	2.0	0.3	255	0.05	0.06	29
Pumpkin	92.6	4.6	1.4	0.1	84	0.06	0.04	2
Radish (white)	94.4	3.4	0.7	0.1	5	0.06	0.02	15
Round melon	93.5	3.4	1.4	0.2	23	0.08	0.04	18
Snake gourd	94.6	3.3	0.5	0.3	160	0.04	0.06	0
Snap melon	95.7	3.0	0.3	0.1	265	-	-	10
Spinach	92.1	2.9	2.0	0.7	9,300	0.03	0.07	28
Spinach beet	90.7	-	2.3	-	25,000	0.13	0.28	40.9
Sponge gourd	94.3	4.4	0.8	0.2	330	-	-	8
Squash (summer)	94.0	2.4	1.0	0.1	80	0.05	0.03	19
Tomato (green)	93.1	3.6	1.9	0.1	320	0.07	0.01	31
Turnip	91.6	6.2	0.5	0.2	0	0.04	0.04	43
Watermelon	95.8	3.3	0.2	0.2	590	0.05	0.05	6

3.2. Mineral and Trace Element Rich Vegetables (mg/100g)

Underutilized vegetables	Minerals and trace elements								
	Fe	Ca	P	Mg	Na	K	Cu	S	Cl
Amaranth tender green	3.49	397	83	122	230	341	0.08	61	88
Bamboo tender shoot	0.1	20	65	32	91	-	0.19	-	76
Coriander leaves	1.42	184	71	31	58.3	256	0.14	49	43
Curry leaf	0.93	830	57	44	-	-	0.10	81	198
Drumstick leaves	0.85	440	70	42	-	259	0.07	137	423
Hibiscus cannabinus L.	2.28	172	40	66	-	-	0.08	60	19
Fenugreek leaves	1.93	395	51	33	76.1	31	0.01	167	165
Mint	15.6	200	62	60	-	-	0.18	84	34
Neem tender leaves	25.3	130	150	127	72.2	254	0.60	96	26
Purslane	14.8	111	45	120	67.2	716	0.19	63	73
Sonchal sag	19.5	300	60	-	-	680	0.39	-	-
Spinach	1.14	73	21	64	58.5	206	0.10	30	54
Tamarind leaves	0.30	101	140	26	-	-	0.02	63	94
Colocasia leaves	10	227	82	32	-	-	0.18	-	72
Yam (ordinary)	1.19	35	20	1.7	90	237	0.12	-	-
Yam (wild)	1.0	20	74	34	11	450	0.16	35	29
Drumstick (fruits)	0.18	30	110	28	-	259	0.01	137	423
Broad bean	1.4	50	64	33	43.5	39	0.17	53	43
Field bean	0.83	210	68	17	55.4	74	0.10	40	31
Jackfruit (tender)	1.7	30	40	-	35	328	-	-	-
Lotus (stem dry)	60.6	405	128	168	438	3007	1.22	258	444
Papaya green	0.9	28	40	-	23	216	-	-	-
Plantain flower	1.6	32	42	54	20.1	185	0.10	68	68
Plantain green	6.27	10	29	13	15	193	0.03	15	6
Snake gourd	1.53	26	20	28	25.4	34	0.14	35	21
Sword bean	2	60	40	-	29	1800	-	-	-
Round melon	0.9	25	24	14	35	24	0.12	-	44
Tomatillo	1.4	7	40	23	0.4	243	0.09	27	14
Tree tomato	1.0	12	46	34	1.7	539	0.17	37	10

3.3. Folic Acid Content in Some Underutilized Vegetables (μg/100g edible portion)

Underutilized vegetables	Folic acid	
	Free	Total
Amaranth	41.0	149.0
Cluster bean	50.0	144.0
Coccinia	18.0	55.0
Colocasia	16.0	94.0
Curry leaf	23.5	93.0
Mint	9.7	114.0
Plantain green	1.6	16.4
Snake gourd	7.5	15.5
Sorrel	40.0	125.0
Spinach	51.0	123.0
Yam	0.9	17.5

3.4. Antioxidants in Vegetables and Their Role in Human Health

Antioxidants	Role in plant system	Role in human health
Phenolics	Signaling molecules, pigments, flavor, defense	Antioxidative, anti-inflammatory, antimutagenic, anticarcinogenic, reduce cardiovascular diseases
Carotenoids	Pigmentation, attract pollinators	Anticancer, anti-cardiovascular, eye health, antioxidant,prostate cancer
Anthocyanin	Pigmentation	Antioxidant. anti-inflammatory (purple, red) and anti-carcinogenic activity, cardiovascular disease prevention, obesity control, and diabetes alleviation properties.
Glucosinolates	Plant defense	Anti-cancer compounds.
Omega-6-fatty acids (linoleic acid)	Plant defense and metabolic activities omega-6- fatty acids (ex. from	Balanced ratio of omega-3- fatty acids (ex. from fish) and vegetables) is essential for good health.
Vitamins	Plant growth and development, quality	Antioxidants, anti-therogenic, anti-carcinogenic, immuno modulator, prevents colon and breast cancers, cardiovascular diseases, cataract, arthritis, certain neurological disorders.
Organic acids	Precursor compounds, protective agents	Taste factor, human metabolism

3.5. Nutrient Rich Vegetables

Nutrients available	Vegetable crops
Protein	Pea, French bean, cowpea, cluster bean, amaranth and broad bean.
Carbohydrates	Potato, sweet potato, dry beans, yam and tapioca.
Vitamin-A	Carrot, palak, amaranth, pumpkin, methi and paprika
Vitamin-B	Garden pea and Indian bean
Vitamin-C	Tomato, sweet pepper, green chilli, cauliflower, knol-khol, bitter gourd, amaranth, methi, palak and cabbage.
Calcium	Methi, kale, beet leaf, amaranth, broccoli, onion, beet root, Indian bean, and cabbage.
Potassium	Sweet potato, potato, bitter gourd, raddish, dolichos, onion and green leafy vegetables.
Phosphorus	Garlic, garden pea, bitter gourd, broccoli, onion, leek, kale, amaranth.
Iron	bitter gourd, amaranth, methi, poi, beet leaf, leek and spinach.

3.6. Nutraceuticals in Vegetable Crops

Vegetables	Nutraceuticals	Health benefits
Allium vegetables (garlic, onions, chives and leeks)	Allyl sulfides, Aliin, Alicin, Quercetin	Protect against cancers and heart disease, boost the immune system.
Cruciferous vegetables (broccoli, cauliflower, cabbage, Brussels, sprout, kale, radish, turnip, kohlrabi and Chinese cabbage)	Indoles/glucosinolates, sulfaforaphane, Isothiocyanates/thiocyanates, Thiols	Protect against cancer, heart disease and stroke, Jaundice, liver infection and piles
Chilli	Capsaicin, Oleoresin	Anti-diarrhoel, Anti-rheumatic
Brinjal	Chlorogenic acid	Anti-carcinogenic, Anti-obesity and anti-diabetic properties
Umbelliferous vegetables (Carrot, celery, parsley, parsnips	Carotenoids, Phthalides, Polyacetylenes and Acid Oligosacchrides	Antioxidant and artery protecting
artichoke	Silymarin	Hepatoprotective, Anticarcinogenic
Beans	Flavonoids	Protect against cancer, lower cholestrol
Cucurbits (Cantaloupe and pumpkin)	Vitamin A, Momordicin and Charantin	Anticancerous, diabetes, blood purifier, hypertension, dysentry, anathematic
Green leafy vegetables	Vitamin E, C	Antioxidant, inhibition of platelet aggregation

3.7. Crop Specific Nutraceuticals and Their Health Effects

Vegetable	Active principle	Health effect
Okra	Mucilage	Blood sugar stabilizing, anti-ulcer, anti-cholestrol, bind to bile acid
Carrot	Acid oligosaccharides	Anti-cancer, artery-protecting, immuno-modulating infection fighting, decrease cholestrol
Radish	Raphanin	Anti-microbial, anti-viral, bronchitis, hyper-lipidemia
Beet	Betacyanin	Hepatic disorders
Chilli	Capsaicinoids	Antioxidant, anti-inflammatory
Tomato	Lycopene	Antioxidant, prevents cardio-vascular diseases
Potato	Glycoalkaloids, alpha-	Useful in dyspeptia. skin diseases, anti-chaconine cancer
Garlic	Aliin, allicin	Anti-parasitic, anti-cancer, antiviral, antibacterial
Onion	Quercetin	Anaemia, skin disorders, stomach cancer

3.8. Antinutrients in Plant Foods that Reduce Nutrient Bioavailability Impairing Health

Antinutrient	Effect	Dietary source
Phytic acid	Binds minerals K, Mg, Ca, Fe, Zn	Legumes and cereals
Trypsin inhibitor	Reduces the activity of the enzyme trypsin and other closely related enzymes that help digest protein	Legumes, cereals and potato
Hemaglutinin, eg. Lectin	Interfere with cells lining the gastrointestinal tract causing acute symptoms, can bind metals and some vitamins; can be toxic	Legumes
Polyphenolics, tanins	Form complexes with iron, zinc, copper that reduces mineral absorption	Beans, tea, coffee, sorghum
Cyanogens or glycoalkaloids	Inhibit acetylcholinestrase activity which impair nerve transmission, can damage cell membranes	Cassava, peas, beans
Oxalic acid	Binds calcium to prevent its absorption	Spinach leaf, amaranth, rhubarb, portulaca, colocasia, elephant foot yam
Solanine	Can be toxic, affect gastro intestinal and nervous system	Green parts of potato tubers
Saponins	May irritate the gastrointestinal tract and interfere with nutrient absorption	Soybeans, peas, sugar beets, pea nuts
Goitrogens	Suppress thyroids function	Brassica, alliums foods
Cadmium, mercury, lead	May have toxic effects, e.g.. High levels of Hg impair brain development	Contaminated leafy vegetables
Glycosides	Liberate toxic hydrocynic acid with enzymic action	Tapioca leaves

3.9. Pigments or Edible Colors

Colour	Pigments	Vegetables
Red	Lycopene, Betacyanins	Tomato, watermelon and carrot, beet root
Orange	Beta-carotene	Carrot, cantaloupe, pumpkin, sweet potato and cauliflower
Blue/purple/black	Anthocyanins	Eggplant, carrot, amaranth, dolichos, cabbage and broccoli
Yellow/Cream/Green	Lutein, Chlorophyll	Yellow corn, carrot, sweet pepper, broccoli, kale, spinach, cabbage and asparagus

3.10. Microgreen and Nutrition Security

- Microgreen and sprouts may fall into one vague category of tiny seedlings but they have subtle and important differences.
- Sprouts falls under the category of newly germinated seeds with visible immature cotyledons and roots and harvested before the development of true leaves.
- Sprouts are cultivated/grown in dark condition without soil and fertilizers feeded with clean water and air. They have relatively short growing periods ranging from 3-7 days.
- The nutrients are supplied by seed embryo and cotyledons. Sprouts are eaten as whole plant including stem and roots.
- Microgreens have fully developed cotyledons and a pair of very small partially developed true leaves. The growing period ranges from 7-14 days.
- At the time of harvest, the microgreens are cut above the roots and are eaten along with stem and leaves but not the roots.
- Sprouts and microgreen are incredibly easy and inexpensive to grow, taking minimum space and time.
- Sprouts and microgreen are considered as high energy foods that are alkaline, high in enzymes, predigested complete proteins, chelated minerals and rich in vitamins.
- The most common sprouts and microgreens suitable for consumption includes:

  Pulses: Legumes- alfalfa, clover, fenugreek, lentil, pea, chickpea, mung bean and soybean.

  Cereals: Oat, wheat, maize, rice, barley and rye.

  Pseudocereals: Quinoa, amaranth and buck wheat.

  Oil seeds: Sesame, sunflower, almond, hazelnut, hemp, linseed and peanut.

  Brassica: Broccoli, cabbage, watercress, mustard, radish, argula, turnip and tatsoi

  Umbellifer: Carrot, celery, funnel and parsley.

  Mucilaginous seeds: Arugala, basil, chia seed, cress, flax, yellow mustard

  Other: Spinach, lettuce and lemon grass
- Consumption of sprouts of cruciferous plants such as broccoli, cabbage, brussels sprout, cauliflower and radish are associated with the reduction of several cancer diseases.
- Japanese radish sprouts are reported to prevent breast cancer.
- Among the secondary products of plant metabolism, phenolic compounds have attracted more and more attention as potential agents for preventing and treating many oxidative stress treated disease such as cancer, cardiovascular diseases, diabetes, rheumatoid.
- Sprouting reduces the level of antinutrients present in sprouts and microgreens prevent several lifestyles generated non-communicable diseases.

Sprouts and Microgreen

Sprouts: Germinated seeds with emerging root.

- Microgreen: 2-3 inch in height; 7-21 days noryest stem cotyeedons and emergint true leaves.

3.11. Xenohormesis: Concept and Role of Vegetable Crops

- Xenohormesis explains how certain molecules such as plant polyphenols, which indicate stress in the plants, can have a longevity-conferring effect in consumers of plant (i.e. mammals).
- It was first used in the paper "Small molecules that regulate life span: evidence for xenohormesis." by Dr. David Sinclair and colleagues from Harvard Medical School.
- Polyphenols such as resveratrol and quercetin, which are produced by stressed plants, activate sirtuin enzymes and extend the life span of fungi and animals, ostensibly by mimicking the beneficial effects of caloric restriction.
- Xenohormesis is a biological principle that explains how environmentally stressed plants produce bioactive compounds that can confer stress resistance and survival benefits to animals that consume them.
- Xenohormetic plant compounds can yield benefits to the animal directly, or by activating the animal's own stress defense pathways. The xenohormetic benefit of the *Cecropia*–ant relationship, for example, comes mainly in the form of calories.
- Ascorbic acid, flavonoids, and alpha-tocopherol produced by lettuce and soy act primarily as antioxidants. Other hormetic compounds like podophyllum and paclitaxel have a low dose therapeutic effect, but are quite toxic at higher doses.
- A wide variety of phytochemicals present in our diet, including fruits, vegetables, and spices, have been shown to possess a broad range of health-beneficial properties.
- The cytoprotective and restorative effects of dietary phytochemicals are likely to result from the modulation of several distinct cellular signal transduction pathways. Many dietary phytochemicals that are synthesized as secondary metabolites function as toxins, that is, "phytoalexins," and hence protect plants against insects and other damaging organisms and stresses.
- For instance, the global spread of drug-resistant malaria has created a major demand for the anti-malarial artemisinin, a sesquiterpenoid compound that is synthesized in glandular trichomes of *Artemisia annua*.
- While the original concept of xenohormesis focused on micronutrients, the concept can also be extended at the macronutrient level.
- This xenohormetic process also provides a natural model for the action of the Hsp co-inducing hydroxylamines: like unsaturated plant lipids, these membrane-intercalating compounds are capable of simultaneously reducing the molecular order of specific membrane domains and correcting dysregulated expression of Hsps.

- The key alarm that initiates the response to caloric restriction is lack of available energy in the form of ATP deficit and/or oxidative stress.
- Continued focused research on plants' adaptive stress response will likely lead to the discovery of new health-promoting compounds with significant pharmaceutical promise. Close examination of bioactive products found in plants that survive and thrive in environmentally harsh conditions may reveal potent therapeutic substances.
- Another insight from an understanding of xenohormesis is that it may partially explain the conundrum currently surrounding many ethno-pharmaceutical studies that too often cannot stand up to standards of scientific reproducibility.
- The epidemic of the colony collapse syndrome, for example, has devastated honeybee populations. Is the honeybee no longer ingesting stress-derived and stress-protective bioactive nutrients from a variety of plant species, and therefore becoming more vulnerable itself to life's stresses.

3.12. Medicinal Values of Major Vegetable Crops

Vegetables	Medicinal values	Safety Profile
Tomato	Prostate cancer, colorectal cancer, blood pressure heart disease, diabetes	Although tomato allergy is rare individuals allergic to grass pollen are more likely to be allergic
Brinjal	Blood cholesterol control, heart attack control, cancer, memory loss control, weight loss, helps in digestion, helps quit smoking, flawless skin, glowing skin, soft and supple skin strong hair, hydrated scalp, hair growth and hair texture	Avoid eating brinjal if have acidity problem or excess bile humor. Avoid eating brinjal during pregnancy
Chilli	Detoxicants, anti-inflammatory properties, gastrointestinal disorders that produce diarrhea such as dysentery and other microbial disorders, chemo- preventive, cardiovascular, antioxidant properties, hypoglycemic, psoriasis, diabetic neuropathy, fibromyalgia, skin and aging, menopausal symptoms, pain killer, cancer, heart attack and lung diseases.	Chillies should not be used by person who has the problems of acidity, hyper-acidity, ulcer and stomach burning
Okra	Promotes a healthy pregnancy, okra fruits are rich in fiber and other nutrients which proves beneficial in normalizing blood sugar in the body, helping with diabetes, helps with kidney disease, supports colon health, asthma and promotes healthy skin.	In one study, it was shown that okra block the absorption of metformin. Metformin is a drug that is used to help manage blood sugar levels. If we are taking metformin currently, okra should not be taken in dict. The USDA notes that no copper, brass or iron cooking vessels should be employed in preparing okra because the metal will be absorbed and the pods covered or even rendered poisonous. The cooking should be done in agate, porcelain or earthenware.

Contd.

Vegetables	Medicinal values	Safety Profile
Broccoli	Cancer fighting power, anti-inflammatory, cardiovascular support, enhances detoxification, improving bone health, looking younger and improved digestion.	Broccoli is sometimes referred to as a "goitrogenic" food. According to the latest studies, foods themselves- broccoli included-are not "goitrogenic" in the sense of causing goiter whenever they are consumed, or even when they are consumed in excess.
Cabbage	Weight loss, brain food, it helps detoxify the body, cancer preventive, keep blood pressure, relieve headaches and an anti-inflammatory and blood sugar regulator.	Those with thyroid problems should avoid eating large amounts of cabbage. It interferes with the body's absorption of iodine, needed by the thyroid gland.
Cauliflower	Detox support, cancer prevention for women, cardiovascular support, digestive support, memory, boost brain health, anti-aging, bone heal, common cold and flu, crohn's disease, diabetes mellitus, peptic ulcer, pregnancy support and weight loss.	Cauliflower contains naturally occurring substances called purines. Purines are commonly found in plants, animals, and humans. In some individuals who are susceptible to purine-related problems, excessive intake of these substances can cause health problems. Since purines can be broken down to form uric acid, excess accumulation of purines in the body can lead to excess accumulation of uric acid. The health conditions called "gout" and the formation of kidney stones from uric acid are two examples of uric acid-related problems that can be related to excessive intake of purine-containing foods. Cauliflower is sometimes referred to as a "goitrogenic" food. According to the latest studies, foods themselves-cauliflower included-are not "goitrogenic" in the sense of causing goiter whenever they are consumed, or even when they are consumed in excess. It has non-digestible carbohydrates that can lead to smelly gas and bloating in digestive system.In rare cases, cauliflower can cause itching, hand and facial swelling, and even breathing

Contd.

Vegetables	Medicinal values	Safety Profile
		difficulties.
Chinese cabbage	Regulate blood pressure, fights anaemia and fatigue, acts as a preventative measure/helps fight cancer, keeps eyes healthy, great for weight loss, supports youthful and healthy skin, boosts the immune system, fights off bad bacteria.	The Chinese cabbage contains a compound called glucosinolates which prevents cancer if taken in small dose however becomes toxic if taken excessively. Over consumption of cBok Choy causes dizziness, nausea, and indigestion for people with weak digestive system.
Kale	Antioxidant, anti-inflammatory, cancer-preventive and cardiovascular support.	Because of its high vitamin K content, patients taking anti-coagulants such as warfarin are encouraged to avoid kale since it increases the vitamin K concentration in the blood, which is what the drugs are attempting to lower.
Knol-khol	Good for the circulatory system, fights cancer, promotes healthy digestion, boosts the immunity system, assists muscle and nerve functions, stabilizes blood pressure and weight loss.	Knol- khol may contain goitrogens, plant-based compounds found in cruciferous vegetable like cauliflower, broccoli, etc., may cause swelling of thyroid gland and should be avoided in individuals with thyroid dysfunction. However, knol-knols may be eaten freely in healthy person.
Bottle gourd	Weight loss, balancing liver function, prevents heart disease, for indigestion,urinary disorders, nervous diseases, bottle gourd juice for diabetics, premature graying of hair and reduces stress.	Some bottle gourds develop naturally occurring cucurbitacins in excess amounts under environmental adversities and may accumulate terpenoid toxin compounds such as cucurbitacin B,D,G,H, etc. Bottle gourd poisoning is a condition that occurs when a raw bitter (toxic) bottle gourd consumed either directly or in the form of juice. ICMR (Indian Council of Medical Research) recommends the following guidelines regarding bottle gourd consumption to the public:

Contd.

Vegetables	Medicinal values	Safety Profile
		· A small piece of bottle gourd should be tasted before extracting the whole fruit juice to ensure that it is not bitter. If found bitter; the whole fruit should be discarded. · Bitter bottle gourd juice should not be consumed at all. · Bottle gourd juice should not to be mixed with any other juice. · In case of discomfort after consumption (nausea, vomiting, diarrhea or any feeling of uneasiness), the person should be immediately taken to any nearby hospital.
Bitter gourd (Karela)	Blood disorders, cholera, diabetes mellitus, energy, eye problems, gout, hangover, immune booster, piles, psoriasis, respiratory disorders, toxemia, HIV/AIDS, cancer, asthma, karela juice is excellent for the skin, enhances digestion, weight loss and juice helps boost the immune system.	Bitter gourd may contain alkaloid substances like quinine and morodicine, resins and saponic glycosides, which may be cause intolerance in some people. Their bitterness and toxicity may be reduced somewhat by parboiling or soaking in salt water for upto 10 minutes. Toxicity symptoms may include excessive salivation, facial redness, dimness of vision, stomach pain, nausea, vomiting, diarrhea, muscular weakness
Cucumber	Cancer, skin problem, hair growth, diuretic, diabetics, weight loss, eye care, renal disorder, relieves bad breath, hangover cure and promotes joint health, relieves gout and arthritis pain.	Oftentimes, some cucumbers mat turn bitter akin to poisonous bottle gourds due to terpenoid toxin compounds such as cucurbitacin B,D,G,H, etc. A small slice of cucumber should be tasted before eating the whole fruit to ensure that it is not bitter. If found bitter; the whole fruit should be discarded. In case of discomfort after consumption (nausea, vomiting, diarrhea or any feeling of uneasiness), the person should be immediately taken to any nearby hospital.

Contd.

Vegetables	Medicinal values	Safety Profile
Pointed gourd (Parwal)	Improves digestion, treats constipation, aids in weight loss, blood purifier, reduces flu, fight with aging factors, controls blood sugar and cholesterol.	Over eating of parwal causes vomiting.
Watermelon	**Fruits:** Kidney disorders, prevents heat stroke, high blood pressure, prevents cancer, diabetes, heart care, macular degeneration and impotence. **Watermelon seeds:** Treatment of diabetes, treatment of prostate enlargement, antioxidant and analgesic properties, improve sexual health, treatment of gastric ulcer and diuretic action of watermelon seed.	People with serious hyperkalemia, or too much potassium in their blood, should probably not consume more than about one cup of watermelon a day, which has less than 140 mg of potassium.
Muskmelon	Age-related macular degeneration, asthma, blood pressure, cancer, digestion, hydration, inflammation, skin and hair, ulcers,relieves constipation, prevents kidney stones, helps during pregnancy, cures sleeping disorder, eases menstrual cramps and helps in quitting smoking.	Muskmelons have no known reported cases of allergic reactions, and may be safely eaten during pregnancy and in nursing mothers. However, being a member of cucurbita, some fruits may carry cucurbitacin toxin. It is therefore, unripe/bitter tasting melons should be avoided.
Luffas	Preventing eye disease (macular degeneration), preventing pain in the muscles, copper content in luffa provides a useful anti-inflammatory to soothe stiffness and pain associated with arthritis, may reduce the symptoms of anemia and prevent anemia, help the healing of wounds quickly, headaches associated with migraines, maintaining brain health, helps reduce type 2 diabetes, helpful in the swelling of the lymph glands, the leaves of the ridge gourd are useful in the treatment of dysentery conditions, the leaves or juice of the ridge gourd are used as dressing in the diseases such as inflammation of spleen, ringworms,	Pregnant and nursing women should consume but should be limited. While others can consume at will because luffa currently does not have serious side effects.

Contd.

Vegetables	Medicinal values	Safety Profile
	piles and even leprosy, oil is extracted from the seeds of ridge gourd which is used in the treatment of skin diseases and prevention of premature greying of hair.	
Snake gourd	Fevers, diabetes, heart disorders, jaundice, alopecia, as a purgative, great to cure dandruff, excellent to restrain in weight-loss and cures constipation.	The seeds of the snake gourd should not be taken in excess of prescribed dosage as their overdose may cause gastric discomfort, nausea, vomiting, abdominal pain, and diarrhea; due to their high content of oil. The fruits are contraindicated in cold with diarrhea. Snake gourd root should be used cautiously during pregnancy as high doses.
Radish	Jaundice, pile, urinary disorder, weight loss, cardiovascular condition, cancer, leucoderma, constipation, reespiratory disorders, bronchitis and asthma, blood pressure, diabetes, skin disorder, fever, kidney disorders, insect bites, dehydration, sore throat, and immune system,	Radish contains goitrogens. Goitrogens cause swelling of the thyroid gland and should be avoided in individuals with thyroid dysfunction. Eating large amounts of radish may irritate the digestive tract as well. Radishes may irritate anyone who has gallstones, so it may be best to avoid.
Carrot	Prevention of heart disease, blood pressure, immune booster, digestion, lung cancer, colorectal cancer, prostate cancer, macular degeneration, leukemia, improves eyesight, oral health, stroke and diabetes. Alternative medicinal uses: Anthelmintic (destroying or expelling worms), carminative (expelling flatulence), contraceptive, deobstruent, Diuretic (promoting the discharge of urine), emmenagogue (producing oils which stimulate the flow of menstrual blood), galactogogue (promoting the secretion of milk), ophthalmic (pertaining to the eye), stimulant, Oedema (water retention).	Carrot is rich in Vitamin A. Overconsumption of vitamin A can be toxic to humans, but is unlikely to be achieved through diet alone (most vitamin overconsumption occurs by supplementation). Over consumption of carotene may cause a slight orange tinge in skin color but is not harmful to health.

Contd.

Vegetables	Medicinal values	Safety Profile
Turnip	Cancer prevention, cardiovascular, bone health, lung health, aids in digestion, prevents atherosclerosis, treatment of common ailments, beneficial for weight loss and cures asthma.	Turnips and top greens are generally very safe to eat, including in pregnant women.However, the root and its top greens contain small amount oxalic acid (0.21 g per 100 g), a naturally-occurring substance found in some vegetables belonging to Brassica family, which may crystallize as oxalate stones in the kidneys and urinary tract in some people. It is therefore, those with known oxalate urinary tract stones may want to avoid them in the food. Adequate intake of water is advised to maintain normal urine output in these individuals to minimize the stone risk.
Beet root	Reduces birth defects, prevent certain cancers, good for liver health, prevents respiratory problems, prevents lung cancer, prevents cataracts, capillary fragility, aphrodisiac, boosts energy levels, macular degeneration and strokes.	Beetroots are usually well tolerated, except for individuals who are prone to kidney stones. Consumption of beet root may causes urine to become pink/red, which is harmless but often confused with blood in urine. Beet roots contain high levels of oxalates which can contribute to kidney stone formation. Oxalates also have antinutrient properties. This means that they may interfere with the absorption of micronutrients. The levels of oxalates are much higher in the leaves of the beetroot plant than in the root but the root is nevertheless considered high in oxalates.
French bean	Antioxidant properties, reduce blood cholesterol levels, preventing age related macular diseases, preventing neural tube defects in the offspring, control the heart rate and	People who are taking blood-thnners, such as cournadin or warfarin, they should to eat aboid, French bean. French bean contains lectin, more

Contd.

Vegetables	Medicinal values	Safety Profile
	blood pressure, French beans are a good source of molybdenum that helps in detoxification of sulfites from the blood, lower the risk of inflammatory diseases, like rheumatoid arthritis, helps in relieving fatigue, relaxing sore muscles, nerves and blood vessels, thereby relieving the symptoms of asthma and migraine headaches, regulates the blood sugar levels and prevents a sudden jump in blood sugar levels after meals. The folic acid present in French bean prevents the accumulation of an intermediary metabolite of protein metabolism, called homocysteine, which promotes the risk of atherosclerosis.	eating of French bean causes profcains in the digestive system. Cocking beans reduce the level of lectin.
Cowpea	Prevent cancer, prevents anemia, supports a healthy metabolism, helps in maintaining strong bones, encourages mental well-being, helps heal and repair muscle tissue, helps maintain bowel health, supports a healthy cardiovascular system , supports immune system, prevent cold sores, prevent depression and prevent diabetes.	Dried peas contain naturally-occurring substances called purines. Purines are commonly found in plants, animals, and humans.In some individuals who are susceptible to purine-related problems, excessive intake of these substances can cause health problems. Since purines can be broken down to form uric acid, excess accumulation of purines in the body can lead to excess accumulation of uric acid. The health conditions called "gout" and the formation of kidney stones from uric acid are two examples of uric acid-related problems that can be related to excessive intake of purine-containing foods. For this reason, individuals with kidney problems or gout may want to limit or avoid intake of purine-containing foods such as dried peas.

Contd.

Vegetables	Medicinal values	Safety Profile
Broad bean	Reduce blood cholesterol levels, broad beans are rich in phyto-nutrients such as isoflavone and plant-sterols. Isoflavone such as genistein and daidzein have been found to protect breast cancer, prevent Parkinson's disease and dopamine responsive dystonia disorders, prevent neural-tube defects in the newborn baby and helps counter pressing effects of sodium on heart and blood pressure.	Over consumption causes favism
Cluster bean	Heat associate illiness reduce chance of anemia, do not cause rapid fluctions in the blood sugar level, control blood pressure levels, avoid different bowel problems calms the brain and good for fetus in the womb.	If enough water is not consumed or high doses of guar gum are consumed it may block the throat or the intestine. Avoid if pregnant or breastfeeding, or if we suffer from GI obstruction. As it lowers blood sugar and blood pressure those taking medicines for this condition ought to keep this fact in mind. Also avoid it if we are about to undergo surgery as it affects blood sugar levels. Ethinyl estradiol, a form of estrogen, some anti diabetic drugs, pencillin, digoxin and some other medicines interact with guar gum. Guar Gum reduces absorption of carotenoids like beta carotene and lycopene.
Spinach	Anti-Inflammatory and anti-cancer, control atherosclerosis and high blood pressure, prevention of eye-related problems, helping bone up	Spinach has consistently been determined to have high oxalate content.Oxalates are naturally occurring organic acids found in a wide variety of foods, and in the case of certain medical conditions, they must be greatly restricted in a meal plan to prevent over-accumulation inside the body.

Contd.

Vegetables	Medicinal values	Safety Profile
Cassava	Healthy weight gain, increased circulation, birth defects, digestive health, metabolic activity, bone health, neurological health and blood pressure	· Cassava root contains natural toxic cyanogenic glycoside compounds linamarin and methyl-linamarin. Injury to tuber releases linamarase enzyme from the ruptured cells, which then converts linamarin to poisonous hydrocyanic acid (HCN). It is therefore, consumption of raw cassava root results in cyanide poisoning with symptoms of vomiting, nausea, dizziness, stomach pains, headache, and death. In general, cyanide content is substantially higher in its outer part and peel. While peeling lessens the cyanide content, sun drying, and soaking followed by boiling in salt-vinegar water results in evaporation of this compound and makes it safe for human consumption. Prolong consumption of monotonous cassava diet may result in chronic illness like tropical ataxic neuropathy (TAN) and diabetic mellitus, especially among rural and tribal inhabitants who are engaged in processing and consumption of exclusively cassava products.
Sweet potato	Diabetes, blood pressure, heart attack, cancer, digestion and regularity ,f ertility, immunity, inflammation, vision, skin and hair and stress.	Sweet potatoes contain oxalic acid, a naturally occurring substance found in some vegetables that may crystallize as oxalate stones in the urinary tract in some people. It is, therefore, individuals with known history of oxalate urinary tract stones may have to avoid eating sweet potato. Adequate intake of water is, therefore, advised to maintain normal urine output in these individuals to minimize stone risk.

Contd.

Vegetables	Medicinal values	Safety Profile
Elephant	Diabetes, blood pressure, heart attack, cancer, digestion	Sweet potatoes contain oxalic acid, a naturally occurring substance found in some vegetables that may crystallize as oxalate stones in the urinary tract in some people. It are, therefore, individuals with known history of oxalate urinary tract stones may have to avoid eating them. Adequate intake of water is, therefore, advised to maintain normal urine output in these individuals to minimize stone risk.
Potato	Anemia, arthritis, burns, rashes and other skin irritations, constipation and hemorrhoids,gastritis and gastric ulcers, reduces high blood pressure, joint and other types of pain, rheumatism, dark circles under the eyes and weight loss.	· Potatoes are among the foods on which pesticide residues are frequently found. Buy organic potatoes whenever possible. Do not eat either green potatoes or the sprouts that grow on potatoes because they contain the toxic alkaloid substance solanine may cause health symptoms like nausea, diarrhea, stomach cramps, headache, dizziness and shortness of breath.
Turmeric	Anti-inflammatory,curcumin present in turmeric is effective treatment for inflammatory bowel disease (IBD) such as Crohn's and ulcerative colitis,rheumatoid arthritis, cystic fibrosis,cancer prevention and reduce risk of childhood leukemia.	Irriate when it has taken in large amount. people who take blood thinning drugs, such as Warfarin, should avoid consuming large doses of turmeric. Pregnant women should avoid taking turmeric suppliments because of its blood-thinning effects.
Ginger	Treat nausea, reduce muscle pain and soreness, osteoarthritis, lower blood sugars and improve heart disease, help treat chronic indigestion, reduce menstrual pain, lower cholesterol levels, prevent cancer, protect against Alzheimer 's disease and help in fight infections.	Ginger stimulates many secretary glands in the body; it has "sialogogic" effect (increases salivary juice secretion in the mouth) on salivary glands; increase bile secretion and its release. Therefore, the root may be contraindicated in patients with history of gallstones.Ginger root is also known to potentiate the toxicity of anti-coagulant drug warfarin, resulting in

Contd.

Vegetables	Medicinal values	Safety Profile
		severe bleeding episodes.
Cardamom	Anti-carcinogenic properties, good for cardiovascular, control of cholesterol, anti-depressant, protection against gastrointestinal diseases, antimicrobial properties, anti-apasmodic properties,dental diseases, anti-asthmatic property, anti-inflammatory properties,detoxification, improved blood circulation,good for nausea and vomiting aphrodisiac properties,sore throat, hiccups, breath freshener,digestion, halitosis, diuretic, depression, oral health, cold and flu, cancer, blood pressure, blood clots andAnti-aging.	Cardamom pods should be used in small amounts. Too many spices in the food can cause gastrointestinal irritation.
Black pepper	Good for the stomach, weight loss, skinhealth, respiratory relief, antibacterial quality, antioxidant potential enhances bioavailabili, cognitive impairment and neurological health, peptic ulcers,asthma and whooping cough hernia, hoarseness and insect bites.	Consumption of dishes prepared with excessive amounts of black pepper can cause gastrointestinal irritation, and bleeding from the ulcer sites. Therefore, recipes prepared with pepper should be avoided in individuals with acid-peptic disease, stomach ulcers, ulcerative colitis, and diverticulitis conditions.
Clove	Better digestion, antibacterial properties,chemo-preventive properties, liver protection, diabetes control, bone preservation, anti-mutagenic properties, boosts the immune system, anti-inflammatory properties, cure for oral diseases and aphrodisiac properties.	Consumption of dishes prepared with large quantity of clove can cause gastrointestinal irritation, central nervous system disorders. Recipes prepared with this spice should be avoided in individuals with stomach ulcers, ulcerative colitis, and diverticulitis conditions. Eating cloves is also avoided during pregnancy.
Coriander	Skin inflammation, skin disorders, low cholesterol levels, diarrhea, preventing nausea, vomiting, and other stomach disorders, blood pressure, mouth ulcers, anemia, anti-allergic	There have been very few dangers associated with coriander, but as with almost any food, there is some danger of allergic reaction to it, and in some

Contd.

Vegetables	Medicinal values	Safety Profile
	properties, salmonella protection, bone health, digestion, smallpox, menstrual disorders, eye care, conjunctivitis, blood sugar and diabetsa and helps cure ulcers, inflammation, spasms, while acting as an expectorant and protecting the liver. It is anticarcinogenic, anticonvulsant, antihistaminic and hypnotic.	cases, it can be irritating to the skin. One of the more unusual side effects is that some patients complain of sunlight sensitivity, and that excessive coriander intake makes them more susceptible to sunburn, which could subsequently lead to skin cancer over the long term.

4

Vertical Expansion of Vegetable Production

4.1. Promotion of Kitchen Gardening

4.1.1. Essential Guide Lines for Kitchen Gardening

- The location should be in the backyard of the house. As far as practicable, kitchen garden plot should be located near to the well, water tap or other source of irrigation. It should never be located in the shady area of home, which is generally not suitable for most of the vegetables. There should be enough of sunlight for major part of day.
- It should be fenced with boundary wall or fruit crop or live fence all around.
- The layout should be such as to make the garden look attractive and allow access to all its parts. The land should be laid out in small paths and plots.
- The garden should preferably be rectangular in shape.
- About 200 m^2 area is sufficient for a five members family to supply about 1.5 kg vegetable per day.
- A separate plot on one side of the kitchen garden should be demarcated for perennial vegetables like drumstick, curry plant and tapioca. Quick growing fruit trees like banana, papaya, lemon etc. should be planted in the northern side of the garden and climbing type of vegetables like cucurbits, dolichos etc. can be grown on the other side.
- Several sowing of particular crop at short intervals should be done during the season to ensure regular supply of vegetables.
- Ridges which separate the bed may be utilized for growing root crops like radish, carrot, turnip etc.
- Early maturing crop should be planted together in continuous beds so that the area can be made available at once for putting late crop.
- Interspaced of the long duration crops like brinjal, tomato, chillies etc. may be utilized for quick growing crops like spinach, beet, lettuce, knoll-khol etc.
- One or two small compost pits should be dug in the corner of garden to dispose the plant residue, which will be utilized as compost materials.

4.1.2. Crops

The crops which are to be grown in the kitchen garden depend on the region, size of kitchen garden and choice of the family. Only those vegetable crops should be selected which are adopted and give satisfactory yield. Tomato, beans, cabbage, lettuce, palak, beet root, radish, carrot, mustard leaf, coriander, garlic, green onion etc. are desirable for small kitchen garden.

Cropping Sequence: It varies from place to place. However, in general, following cropping sequence may be follow:

- Cabbage (October - February) - Cowpea (March - June) - Mehti (July -September)
- Okra (September - December) - French bean (January - March) - Tomato (April - July)
- Carrot (November - January) - Chillies (February - June) - Cucumber (July - October).
- Potato (August - November) - Bitter gourd (December - April) - Amaranth (May - July).
- Pea (August - October) -Tomato (November - February) - Okra (April - July).
- Capsicum (June - October) - Onion (November - March) - Long melon (April - May)
- Carrot (August - October) - French bean (November - January) - Radish (February - March) - Cucumber (April - July).
- Capsicum (September-December)-Cluster bean (January-April)-Pumpkin (May-August).
- Beet root (September - November) - Cabbage (December - March) - Cluster bean (April - July).
- Potato (November - February) - Amaranth (March - May) - Cowpea (June - August) - Radish (September - October).
- Pea (October - December) - Tomato (January - April) - Bitter gourd (May - September).
- Spinach (October - December) - Okra (January - April) - Sweet potato (May - September)
- Methi (November - February) - Fench bean (March - June) - Onion (July -October).
- Palak (October - January) - Long melon (February - April) - Lima bean (May - September).
- Garlic (October - February) -Turnip (March-May) - Cauliflower (June-September).
- Turnip (November - February) - Lima bean (March - June) - Garlic (July -October).
- Knol Khol (October - January) - Carrot (February - April) - Amaranth (May-September).
- Cauliflower (August - November) - Potato (December - March) - sem (April - July).

- Okra (November - February) - Spinach (March - June) - Knol khol (July-October)
- Tomato (September - December) -Turnip (June - March) - Cabbage (April - August).
- Cabbage (September - December) - Brinjal (January - May) - Cucumber (June - August).
- Palak (November - January) - Capsicum (February - May)- Cowpea (June-September).
- Cauliflower (September - December) - Chilli (January - April) - Jack bean (May-August)

Crop Rotations for Bunds

- Knol khol (August- October) - Carrot (November - January) - Radish (February - March) - Fellow (April - July).
- Turnip (August - September) - Beet root (October - December) - Knol khol (January - March) - Radish (March - April) - Fallow (May - July).

Crop Rotations for Fence Side

- Bitter gourd (December - March) - Cucumber (April - June)- Sponge gourd (July - October).
- Pumpkin (November - February) - Ridges gourd (March - June) - Bitter gourd (July - October).
- Cucumber (December - March) - Bitter gourd (April - July) - Winged bean (August - December).

4.2. Promotion of Riverbed Cultivation

4.2.1. Concept

Diara land farming or riverbed cultivation is very old practice (possibly started during Mughal period with various cucurbits) of growing vegetables on the bank or basin of river after when flood level receded. Presently, in South Asian countries, cucurbitaceous vegetables are extensively being grown in riverbeds (called diara land). These diara lands are formed and subjected to alluvion and diluvion action of perennial Himalayan rivers and due to inundation caused by swollen rivers during South- West monsoon. Fresh silt and clay deposits received every year, during the monsoon months, especially in Himalayan Rivers, makes these lands suitable for growing vegetables crops, literally on sand. Even though upper layers of land seem unsuitable for growing crops, the subterranean moisture seeped from adjacent river streams, makes it possible to grow early crops. This system is unconnected with any other crop rotation and cucurbits are specially adapted to this system of growing due to their long tap root system. It can be treated as a kind of vegetables forcing where in the cucurbits are grown under sub-normal conditions, literally on sand, during winter months from November- February, especially in North and North- Western India. About 65% of total cucurbit cropped area of the country falls under riverbeds.

4.2.2. Tips for Cultivation

- Riverbed plots are chosen by farmers, with plots perpendicular to the river's flow. This allows every farmer equal access to different types of soil needed for the different crops. Short-rooted crops like cucumber and bitter gourd are planted close to the water; long rooted bottle gourds, pumpkins, and watermelon are planted further in the back. To prevent crop damage by thieves or wild animals, a fence is erected around the perimeter of the plots.A shelter is built in the vicinity to serve as protection from the sun during the day, and to function as a look-out during the night. Farmers choose either the pit or the ditch system when planting, depending on personal preferences and labor availability.
- Vegetable crops which could be sold in the local *haat* (Temporary market) and nearby markets. Cucurbit species are suitable crops to be grown on riverbed areas.
- The riverbed area selected consisted of silty soil (pure sand is not good) with water table of 0.60 m to 0.75 m below the land surface
- Some of the important river-bed cultivated crops and their cultivars are given below in Table

Musk melon	Arka Rajhans, Arka Jeet,Pusa Sharabati, Pusa Madhuras, Kashi Madhu
Water melon	Sugar Baby, Improved Shipper ,Asahi Yamato and Durgapura Meetha , Kalagolan
Pumpkin	Kashi Harit, Narendra Agrim
Long Melon	Arka Sheetal, Pusa Komal
Bittergoourd	Kalyanpur Baramasi
Parwal	Kashi Alankar, Kashi Suphal
Sponge gourd	Azard Sneha, Sujata,
Ridge gourd	Arka Sujeet, Swarn Manjari
Tomato	Kashi Aman, Kashi Chayan

- Pits or trenches or channels are prepared after the cessation of the south-west monsoon and recession of flood during October- November. The trenches are dug in North- West direction to manage the availability of moisture and higher temperature. The channel should be 50-60 cm wide and 45-90 cm deep depending on height of water table. Generally, 60cm to 90cm is the height of water table in riverbeds. Sometimes circular pits of about 35-45cm in diameter are prepared having a depth of 90cm. The pits/ trenches are filled manured with FYM or any other organic decomposed waste or oil cakes.Especially in North- Western India, where winter temperatures in December- January go down to 1-2^{0}C, the protection is provided by planting of grass stubbles (probably of *Saccharam sp.*). This protection has three fold uses: (i) it checks the sand drifting on the dug-up trenches and covering the hills sown with seeds, (ii) it provides partial through insufficient protection against chilly winds and (iii) this grass is available for spreading over the sand when the vines, especially when "Loo" or hot summer winds sweep these areas in May.

- Majority of farmers used to grow vegetable crops by direct sowing in the pits. Seed rate varies from crop to crop like 300-350 g/ha for cucumber, 450-500 g/ha for bottle gourd and sponge gourd, and 1.5 kg/ha for water melon and bitter gourd. Cucurbit seeds are soaked in water for 24 hrs, floated seeds are removed and remaining seeds are air dried. After that, seeds are wrapped in big sized green leaves, again wrapped by muslin clothes and it put into compost heap for 3-4 days for germination. After germination, two seeds are sown per pit. After sowing the seeds, mulching is done using locally available dry grasses. Sowing of seeds is done between November and December. However, early sown seeds showed better performance because of good emergence and early plant vigor before the extreme cold season. Some of the riverbed vegetable producer groups kept vegetable nursery under plastic tunnel sowing the seeds in soil and compost mixed poly pots. The plastic tunnel is managed by opening the plastic during the day time and closing it during the night time. Seedlings are transplanted in the pits starting from the second week of February.
- Earlier no practices of manures/ fertilizers were used for diara land cultivation but now day's farmers are slightly using. Since crop is taken only for one season, so organic manures and fertilizers are used. Well-decomposed FYM or compost, groundnut or caster cake is given in first application. River silt is generally used to enhance retentively of moisture in the feeding zone. These organic manures provide some kind of warmth to the germinating seeds or growing transplants. In some areas, single super phosphate, urea or any standard fertilizer mixture is also given as a basal application but it is not known whether all the nitrogen is fully available or some amount is leached away. Application of 30-60 g urea per pit at the time of thinning will be useful. After 30-40 days of sowing, top dressing of 40 g pit urea is usually done in two split doses. At the flowering stage, some farmers used two sprays of Miraculan (plant hormone) at 10 day intervals to enhance flowering and fruiting. If the plants showed the deficiency of micronutrients, 1.0-1.5 ml multiplex per liter of water is sprayed on standing crops. Crops are infested by red pumpkin beetles, aphids, fruit flies which are controlled by hand picking of insects and spraying of cattle urine (1:5 urine to water ratio) as pest repellant. Root rot, powdery mildew and downy mildew are major diseases which were controlled by spraying appropriate fungicides.
- Most of the cucurbits are having deep root system, which enable the plant to survive in diara land. Irrigation is given through pitcher or left as usual. Sprinkler or trickle irrigation system may be quite beneficial because most of the nutrients applied by the farmers are leached away because of sandy soil, unless water level is managed. Irrigations necessary for seedlings every 2 to 3 days if the soil does not contain enough moisture. However, if plants have ground water within 1 m depth, no further irrigation is necessary after this.
- Mulching is used to conserve soil moisture, support branch distribution, protect from wind damage, and minimize weed growth. No tillage is necessary.

- In north-west India, when winter temperature goes down to 1-2°C in December-January, young plants require protection in early stage against low temperature and frost. The protection is provided by thatch screen made of locally available materials like paddy straw, *Saccharum* grass or sugarcane leaves. In the month of February, grass is spread over the sand as a mulch and bedding. This helps to protect the young and tender plants/ fruits from heat of scorching sand during summer and also avoids drifting of vines during strong winds. Methods for using polyethylene cover as frost protection are yet to be developed. This will be economical and within the reach of ordinary growers.
- Cropping pattern usually practiced in riverbeds are bottle gourd, bitter gourd, cucumber and sponge gourd in North India, Ridge gourd in Rajasthan, M.P. and U.P. and pointed gourd in Bihar.
- In diara land areas major weeds are *Polygonum* sp., *Euphorbia hirta*, *Eclipta prostrata*, *Sida sp.*, and *Fimbristlylis dichotoma* etc. these weeds can be eradicated manually or by pulling, since soil is quite loosened due to excess sands. No weedicide should be used because it may mix with running water of river and may prove hazardous to human animal and fishes etc.
- In Cucurbits, harvesting should be done when fruits are quite tender and edible. Kartoli, Kakrol and pointed gourd start flowering after 50, 60 and 80 days of transplanting, respectively. Generally, after 8-10 nodes, every nodes bear's fruits 30-35, 28-35, 15-18 days after flowering. Edible mature fruits should be harvested at 2-3 days interval, otherwise, quality deterioration start and fruits hardened due to seed maturity continuous harvesting can be done end of June to end of October. Potential yield of various vegetables is given in Table 4.2.4. Early harvested crops had high market demand and fetched good prices as off-seasonal vegetables (4.2.5). In the vegetable market chain, there were local traders who collected vegetables from *haats* and delivered to different end markets within and outside the district. Where the production sites are bordering to India, large quantities of vegetables are exported to Indian markets. Vegetables are put in different sized locally made bamboo baskets for marketing.Bicycles and other means of transportation such as bullock drawn carts, public buses and jeeps are used for vegetable transportation to market places. Some innovative farmers growing vegetables in larger area used to carry vegetables to nearby markets instead of selling to local traders in *haats*. In this regards, there is prospect of operating collective marketing system by riverbed vegetable producer groups linking into value chain with wholesalers in the big end markets.

4.2.4. Crop Duration and Yield of Cucurbitaceous Vegetables in Diara Lands

Vegetables	Planting Time	Harvesting Time	Average Yield (q/ha)
Bottle gourd	November-December	March-July	200-350
Bitter gourd	Feburary-March	May-July	100-150
Pointed gourd	November-December	March-July	350-400
Ridge gourd	April-May	June-July	100-200
Sponge gourd	January-Feburory	April-May	100-200
Cucumber	January-Feburary	March-June	225-250

4.2.5. Important Considerations for Cucurbits Harvesting / Marketing

Crops	Harvesting	Test method	Stage of fruit	Remark
Cucumber	60-70 days after sowing	Anthesis duration	Tender green fruit	Optimum length 20-25 cm (depending upon variety/ consumers demand)
Bitter gourd	55-100 days after seed sowing (depending upon variety)	Anthesis duration	Tender green fruit	Optimum length 20-25 cm
Pointed gourd	80-90 days after transplanting	Anthesis duration	Green fruits having tender sceds	Optimum length 20-25 cm
Ivy gourd	Tender immature fruits	Anthesis duration	Green fruits having tender seeds	Optimum length 20-25 cm
Ash gourd	75-125 days after sowing	Anthesis duration	Full mature stage	White wax deposition on skin
Bottle gourd	60-100 days after sowing (12-15 days after fruit setting)	Pressing the skin and little pubescence persisting on the skin Nail test	Light green colour	Seed should be soft, if examined in transverse section
Luffa species	55-60 days after sowing, (6-7 days after anthesis)	Anthesis duration	Fruit should not turn fibrous and picking should be done earlier	Picking at 4-5 days interval

4.2.3. Constraints

There are some constraints to river bed vegetable farming to all farmers. These are;

- Farming on the riverbed is seasonal and only one crop can be grown by farmers in a year.
- Soil is poor and requires high level of plant nutrient sources for good crop production.
- There is the problem of stray animals and vegetable are also stolen because riverbed farms are general away from village or settlements.
- Strong wind storms with sand particles damage plants severely every year.
- Due to long spell of droughts in recent years, there is need for irrigation on riverbed farming which further increases the cost of production. Farmers manually collect water in buckets from river and irrigate the crops
- Rivers changes their courses every year and shifting of blocks for riverbed vegetable farming creates problems to farmers.
- Few farmers have dropped vegetable production on riverbed due to low profit margin
- Some times late mansoon and early mansoon heavily damage the crop.

4.2.6. Strategies

- Joint effort of government and non- government organization are needed for effective and sustainable scaling up of riverved vegetable farming intervention.

4.3. Promotion of Apartment Balcony Gardening

4.3.1. Concept

This is the perfect system for an apartment balcony garden because it gives someone the chance to raise at least a portion of their food, even without a yard or any landscaping at all. Since the system can be as elaborate or as small as we want, it usually works with most any sized balcony. Most balconies have plenty of air and sunlight which are the main two necessities from the environment to allow this system to thrive. There are many great benefits to having an apartment balcony garden, especially if its vegetables. The benefit is that everything grown there has been done so without the use of chemicals, so it's better for health .There are no pesticides, no carcinogens, and no preservatives. This means the food is actually healthier for eating. Another great benefit is that it will save some money.

4.3.2. Types

4.3.2.1. Square Foot Gardening

The idea behind square foot gardening is to plant a variety of plants in a small amount of space. We shall have to put a little bit of money into constructing the raised beds and filling them with soil, but once even if we don't do a square foot garden, a raised garden has its benefits. It prevents grass from growing in our garden space, we get easier access to our plants, and there is no wasted space.

4.3.2.2. Container Gardening

Another version of a raised garden is to grow vegetables in a container, or in wine crates. These are great because they are portable and we can move them around as needed. Container vegetable gardens are a great alternative for those that don't have access to a garden, backyard or even a balcony. Some good reasons to have this gardening.

- Mostly it's just lack of a spot of soil on our fair earth.
- Easy access to the kitchen.
- Handy or safer environments, especially for children.
- Better protected from unwanted attention of various pests.
- Easy for the less mobile and the handicapped.

4.3.3. Tips for Container Gardening

- Unlike ground gardening, there's no need to put a weed or seed blocking layer first in our pots; just a piece of something like a stone, clay, bark, sponge or whatever's handy, to go over the drainage hole or a thin layer of stones or clay bits and pieces to cover many holes if necessary.
- Have a plant pot saucer or use old dinner plates, lids etc to put under our containers. This ensures that some water can drain through the pot and be taken up slowly over hot weather.
- Don't have saucers that are too big, otherwise mosquitoes might breed in drainage water after a week. Also our vegetables are not like waterlilies, so they don't like perpetually sodden soil.
- Naturally if we are doing our container vegetable gardening on an outdoor patio or balcony and we don't mind water seeping out from the pots and staining the surrounds, then there's no need to put saucers underneath.
- Porous soil is a must in pots to allow for good drainage and air exchange. Just like garden soil, if it's too sandy it will not retain moisture and if too fine like clay it will compact.
- Drainage is vital, so get our set-up correct first. Ensure our containers have large enough drainage holes so they allow water to escape. If they clog up, the plants will 'drown' and suffer from lack of air to their roots and be susceptible to disease and rot.
- Avoid with rats as they climb up to balconies, shimming up walls or drainpipes even, and under cover of darkness they will dig up container plants, knock them over if small, eat any vestiges of un-rotted compost and nibble roots.
- To stop smells from compost, especially if our pots are inside or nearly, and to help control moisture and temperature, put 3-10 newspaper layers on top of soil before added mulch. This also deters birds from scratching up the soil. Check the soil for when to water, just in case it has dried out underneath the paper.
- If we have only a window-sill, a sunny table-top, a neaten tidy porch and don't want mess and muck, in which case buy our organic potting mix by the bag.

- In container gardening, roots are restricted, potted veggies need constant vigilance. Watch and correct signs of wilting in particular. It's so easy for pots, especially plastic pots to heat up and fry plant roots. Clay pots are prone to drying out their soil contents quickly so keep a watering system handy.
- Preferably set up an irrigation system of small, flexible pipes that drip into each pot when turn on a tap. Otherwise, use a hose or watering can and give our pots their main watering in the morning before the sun gets high and hot.
- Just like vegetables grown in the ground, stress by any means, such as lack of water even for a short time, lack of nutrients, cold snaps, blasts of wind and so on, will more often than not result in the vegetable plants producing small harvests, succumbing to disease, or in some varieties, bolting to seed.
- Roots go down and out a remarkably long way in most plants when grown unrestricted, so when contained by walls, roots have no means to go further and deeper in search of food and water. Due to extra watering, nutrients get washed away quicker in a container than in the ground also.
- As well as watering, regular feeding is a must. Use diluted liquid fertilizer every 1-3 weeks depending on what plants we are growing. Here some quick and easy recipes for making compost tea and other liquid fertilizers we can brew up at home in just days or a few weeks.
- It is also very important that a mulch is put on top of the container, especially when plants are small, pots are big, and there's lots of soil exposure. This will slow evaporation and keep the surface temperature of the soil cooler. Plants with smaller, fibrous roots like tomatoes can so easily dry and die in hot soil. Sharp gravel will act as a mulch and also deters diggers such as squirrels. Some of the rounded or coloured pea gravels are attractive and to a lesser degree will act as a pest barrier, but remember that it will be replanting or repotting vegetables often, so will need to remove these sorts of permanent mulches when necessary.

4.3.4. Inside Gardening

If there is no outdoor space and don't have any indoor space that gets sunlight, consider something like the 3-Tier *SunLite Garden* from Gardener's Supply Company. It is pricey but it may be an option if we are desperate for some indoor greens and can not get any sunlight.

4.3.5. Nano Gardening

It is a super cool concept for growing a vegetable garden right in the kitchen, without help from sun or rain. The concept takes tiered metal shelving, climate controlled panels, purposefully-directed lumens, and an attachment to a water source to make our indoor vegetable crop dreams a potential reality. Because light, water and nutrient supply is totally controllable, it's up to grower how quickly one want to grow. It is having arrangement for signaling against overwatering, over-sunning, or for nutrients needs. It even works to naturally purify the air in our home.

4.3.6. Key Hole Gardening

The raised beds, surrounded by stones, and built up of layers of organic material that serve the dual purpose of adding nutrients to the soil and retaining moisture make the keyhole garden extremely productive even in the cold, dry winter months. The keyhole garden is originally developed for use by the chronically ill. The original design is a relatively small, round garden with a low outer wall. A space is left in the middle of the keyhole garden to allow a person to sit or squat while they worked the garden around them. This proved an effective way to work the garden with minimal effort for people who are disabled or physically weak due to illness. Once built, the garden requires only limited maintenance and few additional inputs (such as fertilizer). In addition, the layer-based design helps the garden retain moisture, so it requires less water reduces the labour burden of collecting water for irrigation.

4.3.6.1. Advantages: These are

- Soil enrichment.
- Moisture retention in arid or semi-arid climate.
- Labour saving.
- Reducing dependence on external inputs.
- Year-round vegetable production.

4.3.6.2. Suitable Crops for Keyhole garden

- Root Crops: Carrots, beet root, radish, turnip and garlic.
- Leafy Crops: Spinach, swiss chard, lettuce, mustard, spinach and herbs.

4.3.7. Trench Gardening

Trench gardens use is the same principles and techniques of a keyhole garden, but instead of building a raised bed the layers are dug into the ground, leaving only a small mound of topsoil raised above ground level. Trench gardens have the same moisture-retaining and soil enrichment properties, but require fewer materials and allow for larger plants, such as tomato and eggplant. However, they require more space than a keyhole garden, and therefore may not be appropriate in urban areas or other areas where space is limited.

4.3.8. Pots/Boxes on Terraces Gardening

Lack of free ground space near the house compels the people, having interest in homestead gardening, to grow vegetables on terraces of the house. Vegetables grow well on terraces of house due to availability of ample sunlight. There is no competition among plants for moisture, nutrients, space and light, as only a limited number of plants are raised in a confined area of soil, and thus, they give very high yield.

Simple earthen pots having a diameter of 30-35cm are considered ideal for growing vegetables. The second choice may be of wooden boxes of size 75 x 45 x 50cm length, breadth and depth, respectively. The inner and outer surfaces of the pots or boxes should be properly painted with some water proof paints. The containers should have legs and holds for their convenient handling. If polythene bags are used, 5-6 holes are to be there on either side to drain out the excess water. Coconut fibre or earthen pot piece can be used to cover these holes to avoid the loss of soil from the bags. In case of earthen pots, there should be a drainage hole at the bottom, and this hole must be covered with a tile piece before filling it with potting mixture.

At the bottom of bags, pots, or boxes, first the sand is filled to a thickness of about 6cm, over this, a mixture of 1-part garden soil, 1-part sand and 1-part compost is filled up to a height of 4-5cm below upper brim of the container. Incorporation of organic manure in potting mixture increases the population of beneficial soil microorganisms. About 3-4 seeds of a particular species are generally sown per pot/bag to ensure germination. Upon germination, only the healthiest seedling is retained in a pot. After sowing seeds, the boxes or the pots are placed on the terraces. Some shade must be provided to the growing seedlings during hot summer to protect them from harmful effect of blazing sun.

4.3.9. Roof Gardening

On painted roofs, the rectangular cemented beds of convenient size may be constructed near boundary wall of the roof. The beds should be at least 45-60cm deep but not more than 75cm wide to allow easy intercultural operations. The entire roof should never be covered with beds otherwise that may create problem in cultural operations. The beds are filled with a mixture of garden soil, sand and compost.

4.3.10. Tips for Cultivation of Vegetable in Pots in Apartment Balcony Gardening

4.3.10.1. Tomato

- Tomato is the most productive vegetables we can grow in pots. Tomatoes need ample sun (5-6 hours minimum). The pot size depends on the type of tomato which are growing. In containers, growing dwarf varieties of determinate type should be preferred. We should also try cherry tomato for higher yield.
- Grow determinate varieties of tomato if there is short of space or growing tomatoes in containers. Determinate tomato does not grow too tall or wide (generally, 3-4 feet).
- If indeterminate tomatos are grown, requires sturdy support by caging or staking.
- Don't start the plants too early before the season, unless live in a warm climate otherwise; our tomato plants will be exposed to unexpected late frost and cold temperatures. The best planting time is when the temperature starts to stay above 10° C.
- Ideal pH for tomato is around 6 – 6.8 (Slightly acidic to neutral).
- Use tomato feed to fertilize our plants. Apply less dose than the instruction given on the packet but more often. Consider half of the recommended dose but twice.
- At the time of planting, place 2-3 crushed chicken egg shells in the bottom. This will provide a constant supply of minerals and calcium to the plant.
- Deficiency of calcium promotes blossom end rot in tomato. It is an essential element in the uptake of nutrients. Calcium also saves the plant from heat stress and affects the fruit quality.

- Sprinkle some bonemeal at the time of planting, especially if our soil lacks calcium. Bonemeal will also provide a slow and steady supply of phosphorus to the plant. It is an organic product that consists higher amount of phosphorus and calcium.
- Tomato must be planted deeply. Deep planting encourages healthy and strong root system. At the time of planting, cover bottom 2/3 part of our tomato seedling with potting soil.
- Space our tomato plants 40 cm apart (Determinate one). Ideally, we should leave the space of 60cm if possible. Tomato plants grown too close are prone to fungal diseases and are less productive.
- On a small balcony, we can even grow smaller varieties more closely. Consider cherry tomatoes. But remember, tomatoes growing too tightly require more attention: More fertilizer, water, and pruning.
- Pruning is not necessary unless plants are grown too close. Prune tangling branches that are blocking the air flow and penetration of sun. Also, remove suckers (emerging stems) up to 15-20 cm under each plant. This will improve the productivity of the plant.
- Support tomato by staking. If we are growing tomato on a balcony, consider tying them up to the railing.
- Don't grow tomato upside down. It is a fancy idea but not a practical one. However, we can grow tomato (Cherry tomato) in hanging baskets.
- Provide the sun, as much sun as possible. The more our tomato plant will soak the sunlight more they will fruit.
- Use soilless potting mix for the better result. We can buy it or make our own.
- When growing tomato in a container, regular watering is essential.Watering must be done in the morning. Almost every day in summer. In tropics, we may need to water twice a day.
- Avoid overhead watering. Wetting the foliage is a bad practice as wet leaves and stems are more prone to diseases.
- Mulch our tomato plants, it is important. For mulching, use organic matter, crushed egg shell, and coffee ground or tea.

4.3.10.2. French bean

- Most of the beans are climbers or bushier type and they grow upward. They are productive in pots and are easy to grow.
- French bean can grow them on a trellis near a wall and within weeks, we will get a green wall of beans running across the trellis.
- For growing beans we need a sunny place and a pot that is minimum 12 inches deep (the bigger the better) and a strong trellis like structure for support.
- Since French bean do not fix the nitrogen like other legume vegetables, hence requires more nitrogen, are good to grow underneath them.

4.3.10.3. Lettuce

- Lettuce grows up quickly and we will have the opportunity to harvest them multiple times throughout the growing season.
- As lettuce is a cool season crop, we'll have to decide what is the right time for its growth according to our climate, usually, seeds are started in spring. But if it live in a warm climate, grow lettuce in winter.
- For growing lettuce, choose a wide planter rather than deep (63 deep is enough). When planting, make sure to leave space of at least 4 inches between each plant.
- Remember, leaf lettuces can be grown more closely than head lettuces. Use well draining soil and do shallow and frequent watering to keep the soil slightly moist always.

4.3.10.4. Bell pepper

- Growing bell peppers require soil temperature above 15 °C for best growth. The optimum seed germination temperature is above 20 °C. It can tolerate temperature up to 35 °C) and down to 10° easily. The ideal growing temperature is between 21-32 °C.
- Planting bell pepper in containers requires a pot that is at least 25-30cm deep and wide and has sufficient drainage holes. We can grow up to 2-3 plants (smaller varieties) in such a pot. Avoid using the black color container if we are growing bell pepper in a tropical climate.
- Pepper love the sun.The most productive pepper plants are grown in warmth and heat. When we are growing bell peppers in pots, keep them in a position that receives at least 6 hours of sunlight daily. That place should be sheltered from strong wind.
- Good soil is the key to productive pepper plants. Buy best quality potting mix that is well drained, loose and fertile or make our own potting mix. Potting mix must be rich in organic matter. Add well-rotted manure or compost in the combination of peat moss/coco peat and vermiculite or perlite (Alternatively, sand). We can also add 5-10 g neem cake at the time of soil preparation, it will protect the young plant from soil-borne diseases and pests.
- Buy good quality seeds and fill small pots or seedling tray with the seed mix and plant two seeds in each pot, 2-3 cm deep.

- Start seeds 6-10 weeks before last spring frost date. Usually, in subtropical and tropical climate, we can start seeds anytime except in harsh summer.
- The seeds will germinate in 1 to 3 weeks depending on the weather conditions and seed quality. After they germinate thin out and only keep one plant per pot. When seedlings have two true-leaves they are ready to be transplanted into the desired containers.
- Growing bell peppers require regular watering to keep the soil slightly moist, soil should never dry out completely. In any case, avoid wetting the foliage, overhead watering may cause fungal infection. Water at the foot of the plant. Also, pepper plants suffer from overwatering so be careful that our plants don't sit in water.
- For our convenience and to reduce the evaporation of water, do mulching. Cover the base of the plant with organic matter such as leaves, pine barks, straws, paper or whatever that is readily available.
- Pepper plants are heavy feeders and we shall need to fertilize the plant in every 15 days or so. When fertilizing, remember too much nitrogen-rich fertilizer can promote foliage growth. Once in a month feed the plant with compost or manure tea. In the early stage, when the plant is young pinch growing tips regularly to make it bushier. Pruning is not necessary but can be carried out if required.
- If pepper plant is flowering too early dead head the flowers, it is important. This will direct the plant's energy into growing and becoming healthy. We can also stop the formation of new fruits if we want to speed up the maturation of pepper fruits that are already growing on the plant by pinching off emerging flowers.
- We may need to support the plants. For this, either use tomato cages or simply poke a stick near the main stem and tie the plant to it.
- Growing bell peppers in pots require care from virus and thrips as they are the enemy of pepper plants. In hot and dry weather, we shall also need to control spider mites.
- Bell peppers are ready for harvesting in 60-90 days after transplanting. We can harvest them green when they reach full size and remain firm. If left to ripen, the color will change into orange, yellow or red, depending upon varieties.

4.3.10.5. Radish

- Radishes are one of the quickest growing vegetables and suitable for container vegetable gardening.
- A planter that is just 15cm deep is enough but if we want to grow larger varieties use 20-25 cm deep pot.
- Allow 8-10cm of space between each plant.

4.3.10.6. Spinach

- For growing spinach in pots, choose a pot that is least 15-20cm deep.
- No need a very deep pot rather use a wide pot. It can either use so many small pots and grow one plant in each or select large window boxes, wooden boxes or crates.

- Sow seeds 1/2 inches deep directly in containers or a seed tray.
- Seedlings will germinate in 5-14 days depending on the variety and growing conditions.
- If seeds are sown in a seed tray wait until 2-3 true leaves appear on each plant and then transplant them into the original pots carefully.
- Provide each spinach plant a space of 8-10cm , if we want to pick large leaves, give more space to each plant,10-12cm.
- If we want to harvest leaves at very young age, then the spacing can be reduced to 5cm only. Divide the planter box into squares, and see how many plants will feel comfortable in it.
- If you are growing spinach in fall (autumn), keep the plant in a sunny spot (in mild climates) due to shorter days and less intensity of the sun.
- For spring and summer planting, keep our potted plants in a location where it receives some shade, especially in the afternoon.
- In subtropical or tropical climate, place the containers in a spot that receives plenty of shade.
- For growing spinach in containers, use quality potting mix rich in organic matter. The texture of soil must be crumbly and loamy. Avoid soil that clogs the drainage and remains waterlogged. Well-draining soil is most important factor for the optimum growth of spinach in containers. Soil pH must be neutral.
- When growing spinach in containers, avoid water stagnation because it will lead to the development of rot and various fungal diseases. Also, avoid wetting the foliage. Keep the soil moist but not soggy or wet. Taking care of good drainage in the pot is necessary.
- Spinach seeds germinate in temperatures as low as 4^0 C and in high temperatures too. The best soil temperature for growing spinach falls in the range of $10\text{-}27^0$ C. Many spinach cultivars can tolerate temperature down to -6^0C and up to 32^0 C easily. Once the temperature starts to so high, we may need to provide shade to plants.
- For growing healthy green spinach, you have to provide nitrogen. At the time of planting, mix time-based fertilizer, or can add a lot of compost or well-rotted manure, this will provide nutrients slowly. Feeding the plant with fish emulsion, compost or manure tea in the middle of the growth and so on is a nice organic way to promote the plants. If we have not done added time-based fertilizer, we can also feed the plant with balanced liquid fertilizer at regular intervals.
- Do mulching, even if we are growing spinach in pots. Mulching plants with organic matter will help in retaining moisture.
- Do not need to worry much about pests as we are growing spinach in containers, in a small space and we can easily control them. However, keeping an eye on leaf-eating insects like slugs and caterpillars and other common garden pests like aphids should be control in time.

- The spinach plant will be ready for harvest 37-50 days after germination depending on the growing conditions and cultivar.
- Harvesting can be done when the plant has formed at least 5-6 healthy leaves, and they are at least 3-4 inches long. Pick outer leaves first and leave the new inner leaves so that they continue to grow or cut the whole plant off at the base with a knife or scissor, the plant will resprout again.
- When the weather becomes humid and hot (in warm climates) the plant tends to form an erect stem, on which we can see some small yellow or green flowers developing. To coincide with the flowering and the subsequent production of flowers, the foliage of the plant thickens and changes in flavor (more bitter), which is called bolting, so it is convenient to harvest the plant before it starts flowering for better taste

4.3.10.7. Peas

- Peas prefer moderate conditions, they are a perfect crop for container gardening and don't require a large pot.
- They grow quickly without attention.
- We can even grow peas on a balcony.
- Choose a dwarf or bushier type varieties and do regular and frequent watering as peas prefer slightly moist soil.
- Keep the plants in a spot that receives full sun to part sun (Especially in warm climates).

4.3.10.8. Cucumber

- If we are growing cucumbers vertically in containers, prefer large containers that are about at least 12 inches deep and wide.
- A vining variety grows tall and send long roots, whereas bushier varieties are short.
- Choose a 5 to 6 feet tall trellis that is sturdy and doesn't topple. If growing climbing varieties use "A frame trellis" so that the plant crawls up and down from it easily.
- Sow seeds directly onto the desired spot or in small pots. Cover them with about 2 cm of soil. Once the seedlings germinate and have a few leaves, transplant the healthiest ones into a bigger pot or on the frost free ground in spring or summer when soil temperature is around 20^0 C. If there is tropical or subtropical climate, we can grow cucumber year round.
- Cucumber plant is a heavy feeder like tomatoes, prepare our soil well before planting by incorporating decomposed manure and compost.
- Cucumber loves a warm and sunny exposure that is less windy. It does not tolerate temperature 10^0 C. Optimum temperature to grow cucumbers falls in the range of 15 – 35^0 C.
- It prefers well drained, loose and deep soil, rich in organic matter and neutral in pH.

- Regular and deep watering is the key of productive harvest, when growing cucumber. It is due to the high water content of its fruits. While watering, avoid wetting the foliage as it may encourage fungal diseases.
- Mulch around the base of plant to improve moisture retaining ability of soil.
- At the time of planting, add all purpose slow release fertilizer in soil. Once the plant starts to flower, sides dress the plant with aged manure. Also apply balanced liquid fertilizer at that time according to manufacturer's instructions.
- Cucumber plants particularly suffer from anthracnose, powdery mildew and in pests look out for aphids.
- Cucumbers are ready for harvest in 60 to 90 days after seed sowing, depending on the variety. Pick cucumbers when they are developed enough, do not let the fruit to over ripe.

4.3.10.9. Brinjal

- Although eggplants are susceptible to many pests, still growing them is easy.
- They are heat-loving plants and need high temperatures both day and night, thus a suitable summer crop. But if we live in a warm climate we can grow it year round.
- Also, it is easier to maintain them in containers than in a large vegetable garden.
- It is necessary that we keep the pots in a full sun and feed heavily (like all other plants from tomato family– peppers, potatoes; eggplants are heavy feeders too).

4.3.10.10. Squash

- Squashes are easy to grow plants.
- Summer squashes (Zucchini) are more productive than winter squashes.
- We can harvest bountiful even in containers.
- It is one of the most suitable crops for rooftop, balcony or patio gardeners.

4.3.10.11 Suitable Varieties for pot-culture

Name of crop	Varieties
Tomato	VRT-02, Kashi Cherry Tomato-3, Kashi Cherry Tomato-14
Frenchbean	Kashi Rajhans, Kashi Sampann
Indianbean	Kashi Bouni Sem-9, Kashi Bounisen-18
Waterspinach	Kashi Manu
Chilli	Kashi Anmole
Brinjal	Kashi Sandesh
Carrot	
Winter Squash	
Palak	

4.4. Promotion of Peri- urban Vegetable Production

4.4.1. Genesis and Concept

India's agricultural policies have focused strongly on rural areas, aiming to achieve self-sufficiency in food production and to reduce rural poverty. Accordingly, urban food needs are expected, explicitly or implicitly, to be fulfilled by production in rural areas. With the emphasis on rural agriculture, the positive contribution that production closer to the cities can make has hardly been acknowledged. However, the role of urban and peri-urban agriculture as a major source of produce, a means of improving food security and enhancing the livelihoods of poor producers, is increasingly described in the literature. Much of the evidence to date has been gathered from African, Latin American, Caribbean and some Asian and Eastern European countries. The Indian subcontinent has been under represented, reflecting a neglect of this issue by the international and national research communities. Indeed, in India, government policies, scientific research communities and non-governmental organizations (NGOs) have shown little recognition of urban and peri-urban agriculture (UPA).

Peri-urban agriculture is defined as in the introduction can be subdivided in intra-urban and peri-urban agriculture. Intra-urban agriculture takes place within the inner city.

Peri-urban cultivation of vegetables is one of the solutions to convert urban poor to being employed while at the same time improving the built environment. There are hundreds of cities both in rich and poor countries that have set targets to make their cities green and sustainable cities. The cost of greening and cleaning can be borne by urban food production and urban agriculture. Different countries in the world like China, Australia, USA, South America, Europe and many Asian as well as African countries are doing it and constantly improving on this. In India, though the concept of peri-urban agriculture is beginning to become popular.

4.4.2. Advantages

- Cultivation of vegetables in peri-urban or urban areas is recognized for its potential role in increasing food security, employment and income generation, poverty alleviation, community resource development, waste management and environmental sustainability.
- Peri-urban areas offers opportunities for innovative science, living condition improvement and agricultural and ecosystem management requiring novel policies, and action to promote harmony both between society and nature and between groups of people.
- Most cities and towns have vacant and under-utilized land areas that are or can be used for peri-urban agriculture, including areas not suited for building (along streams, close to airports, etc.), public or private land not being used (land waiting for construction) that can have an interim use, community lands and household areas and peri-urban agriculture takes place in the urban periphery.
- A huge quantity of solid waste generated during handling and marketing of fresh vegetable produce in metro cities, which is creating health and

environmental hazards, can be used or recycled to produce vermicompost, etc., for use in organic vegetable production.

- Peri-urban vegetable cultivation can provide farmers the possibility to cultivate a small piece of land, and obtain an income to meet their essential and basic needs.
- In recent years, around big cities, green belts are being developed which can provide a very intensive and profitable network of small farms specialized in production of perishable vegetables for consumption by the urban consumers.

4.4.3. Distinguishing Characters of Peri-urban Cultivation of Vegetables

- It uses urban resources (land, labour, urban organic wastes and water).
- Produces for urban citizens is strongly influenced by the urban conditions (policies, competition for land, urban markets and prices).
- Impacts on the urban system (effects on urban food security and poverty, ecological and health impacts).
- Although some forms of peri-urban cultivation are based on temporal use of vacant lands thus an important component for sustainable city development.
- Longer-term peri-urban cultivation of vegetables seems to be sustainable; especially when it has potential for multi-functional land use is recognized and fully developed.
- This multi-functionality of peri-urban cultivation makes it a cheap producer of public goods.
- Sustainability of urban agriculture seems strongly related to its contribution to the development of a sustainable city – i.e. one that is inclusive, food-secure, productive, and environmentally healthy.

4.4.4. Major Challenges

- Increased urbon land values.
- Intensified competition for other land uses.
- Rapidly changing land rights.
- Labour availability.
- Irrigation with sewage contaminated with heavy metals.

4.4.5. Policy Needs

- Formulate land and water use policy in context to peri-urban cultivation.
- Encourage contact / cooperative farming producer companies with the concept of technology led development of peri-urban.
- Enforce laws for recycling and safe utilization of urban effluents and making available safe water and other inputs.
- Creating marketign hubs and strengthen market information system for periurban farmers.

4.5. Promotion of Hydroponics and Aeroponics

4.5.1. Definition

Hydroponics or soil-less culture is a system of growing plants, which helps reduce problems experienced in conventional crop cultivation. Hydroponics offers opportunities to provide optimal conditions for plant growth and therefore, higher yields of better quality produce can be obtained compared to open field condition. Hydroponics offers a means of control of soil-borne diseases and pests, which is especially desirable in the tropics where the life cycles of these organisms continues uninterrupted and so does the threat of infestation. Thus, the costly and time-consuming tasks of soil sterilization, soil amelioration, etc. can be avoided with hydroponics system of cultivation.

4.5.2. History

Soilless culture is considered as a modern-day practice, but growing plants in containers above ground has been tried at various times throughout the ages. Wall paintings found in the temple of Deir el Bahari appear to be the first documented case of container-grown plants (Naville, 1913).They transfer mature trees from native countries of origin to the king's palace and then grown as soilless culture, when local soils are not suitable for the particular plant. Many ancient civilizations have used soilless culture for their agricultural productions. Egyptian hieroglyphic records dating back several hundred years B.C. shows the growing of plants in water. Hydroponic gardens in history trace back to the hanging gardens of Babylon. The Aztec Indians had a system of growing crops on rafts in shallow lakes, near Mexico City. Developments did not start taking place in Europe until 1699, when Woodward found that he could grow plants in a solution of water to which soil had been added. Liebig, a German scientist, started using nutrient solutions to study the nutritional requirements of plants in the 1850's and was followed by Sachs in 1860 and Knop in 1861, who made studies of nutrient elements in water solutions. They were able to grow plants in nutrient solutions made up from mineral salts eliminating the need for soil." "Research continued and by 1925, practical applications of hydroponics were being made in the greenhouse industry. The next decade witnessed extensive development as researchers became aware of the potential of growing hydroponically The Aztecs used floating gardens for the cultivation of certain crops. The hanging garden of Babylon is also a fine example of soilless culture.

In 1929, Dr William F. Gericke of the University of California succeeded in growing tomato vines of 7.5 m height in nutrient solutions. He named this new production system "Hydroponics" a word derived from Greek to reflect the importance of '*Hydros*' (water) and '*Ponos*' (working). Thus, hydroponics broke the laboratory bounds and entered the world of practical horticulture. The term hydroponics originally meant nutrient solution culture. However, crop growing in inert solid media using nutrient solution is also included in hydroponics in broad sense. In 1930, Gericke produced the first commercial hydroponic unit in the USA. Later during World War II, the American forces in the Pacific grew vegetable crops hydroponically.

Since the inception of hydroponics, research to refine the methodology has continued. In the late 1960s researchers at the Glasshouse Crops Research Institute (GCRI), Little

Hampton, U.K. developed the nutrient film technique along with a number of subsequent refinements (Graves, 1983). This research gave rise to the hydroponic systems used today. Developments continued and the commercial use of hydroponics spread throughout the world, but it was the development of N.F.T. system by Dr. Alan Cooper in the 1970's, along with improved nutritional formulations, that made the hydroponic growing of a wide range of plants commercially viable. Since then many developed and developing countries all over the world are adopting this farming method with minor modifications, although basic principle remains the same.

In India, hydroponics was introduced in year 1946 by an English scientist, W. J. Shalto Duglas and he established a laboratory in Kalimpong area, West Bengal. He written a book on Hydroponics, named as Hydroponics the Bengal System. Later on during 1960s and 70s, commercial hydroponics farms were developed in Abu Dhabi, Arizona, Belgium, California, Denmark, German, Holland, Iran, Italy, Japan, Russian Federation and other countries. During 1980s, many automated and computerized hydroponics farms were established around the world. In recent decades, NASA has done extensive hydroponic research for their Controlled Ecological Life Support System or CELSS. Hydroponics intended to take place on Mars are using LED lighting to grow in different color spectrum with much less heat.

4.5.3. Advantages: These are

- Land is not a limiting factor, i.e. crops can be grown where no suitable soil exists or where the soil is contaminated with disease or it can be practiced even in upstairs, open spaces and in protected structures.
- Labours for tilling, cultivating, fumigating, watering and other traditional practices is largely eliminated. There is no need of making beds, weeding, watering, etc. It is easy to hire labour as hydroponics system is more attractive and easier than cultivation in soil.
- Maximum yields are possible, making the system economically viable in high-density and expensive land areas.
- Continuous cultivation and off-season production are possible.Many plants are found to give early and higher yields in hydroponics system.
- Possibility of growing a wide variety of vegetable and flower crops including anthuriums, marigolds, etc.
- Conservation of water and nutrients are a feature of all systems. This can lead to a reduction in pollution of land and streams.
- Soil-borne plant diseases are more readily eradicated in closed systems, which can be totally flooded with an eradicant, therefore, it is possible to grow plants and rooted cuttings for export purpose.
- Complete control of the environment is generally a feature of the system (i.e., root environments, timely nutrient feeding or irrigation), and in greenhouse-type operations, the light, temperature, humidity, and composition of the air can be manipulated.

- Water carrying high-soluble salts may be used if done with extreme care. If the soluble salts in the water supply are over 500 ppm, an open system of hydroponics may be used, if care is given to frequent leaching of the growing medium to reduce the salt accumulations.
- The hydroponics system can be adopted in house gardens, even in high-rise buildings. A hydroponic system is clean, light weight and mechanized.

4.5.4. Disadvantages: These are

- The initial capital expenditure per unit land area is high.
- High degree of management skills is necessary for solution preparation, maintenance of pH and EC, nutrient deficiency judgment and correction, ensuring aeration, maintenance of favorable condition inside protected structures, etc. trained personnel must direct the growing operation. Knowledge of how plants grow and the principles of nutrition are important.
- Energy inputs are necessary to run the system.
- Negligence may lead to introduction of soil-borne diseases and nematodes, which spread quickly to all beds on the same nutrient tank of a closed system.
- Considering the high cost, the soil-less culture is limited to high value crops cultivation.
- Most available plant varieties adapted to controlled growing conditions will require further research and development efforts.
- The grower has to observe the plants every day.

4.5.5. Precautions for Vegetable Productions in Hydroponics: These are

- If we have limited space and can not form a full-fledged vegetable garden, hydroponic gardening would be a rewarding experience for everybody. With the help of hydroponics growing systems, we can easily grow vegetables as desire without worrying about the outdoor setting or soil problems. It is important to provide plenty of lights for our hydroponic indoor garden to get a good result.
- In hydroponics, the plants roots are suspended in a solution of nutrient rich water solution to absorb essential nutrient from it. Plants grown in hydroponic systems filled with water leave fewer chances of problems caused by water.
- When we are planning to make our own hydroponic vegetable garden, choose from the assortment of types of containers available in the market for hydroponic growing.

- Use rock wool as a growing medium because it provides roots with a good balance of water and oxygen. It also helps the plants healthy growth in each stage.
- Right amount of hydroponic nutrients for our vegetable garden is very essential for plants vigorous growth. We have to understand the nutrient needs of our plants and accordingly provide well-mixed nutrient solution.
- Hydroponic vegetable gardens require plenty of lights for their growth. The type of lighting that we need to provide and ideal for our hydroponic system would depend on the plants that are to be grown.
- Try to maintain grow room temperature and humidity level, to create an ideal environment for vegetables to grow. Even if we live in place where environment is not suitable for growing plants, with hydroponics systems we can make growing possible.

4.5.6. List of Vegetable Crops that Can Be Grown on Commercial Level Using Soil-Less Culture

Type of crops	Name of the crops
Vegetables	*Lycopersicon esculentum* (Tomato), *Capsicum frutescens* (Chilli), *Solanum melongena* (Brinjal), *Phaseolus vulgaris* (Green bean), *Beta vulgaris* (Beet), *Psophocarpus tetragonolobus* (Winged bean), *Capsicum annum* (Bell pepper), *Brassica oleracea* var. capitata (Cabbage), *Brassica oleracea* var. botrytis (Cauliflower), *Cucumis sativus* (Cucumbers), *Cucumis melo* (Melons), *Raphanus sativus* (Radish), *Allium cepa* (Onion)
Leafy vegetables	*Lactuca sativa* (Lettuce), *Ipomoea aquatica* (Kang Kong)

Source: Hussan et al (2014).

4.5.7. Compatibility Chart for Some Soluble Fertilizers Used in Soil Less Culture

Soluble fertilizer	AN	AS	CAN	MAP	SOP	MOP
Ammonium nitrate (AN)	-	C	C	C	C	C
Ammonium sulphate (AS)	C	-	L	-	C	C
Calcium nitrate (CAN)	C	L	-	X	C	C
Mono ammonium phosphate (MAP)	C	C	X	-	C	C
Potassium sulphate (SOP)	C	C	L	C	-	C
Potassium chloride (MOP)	C	C	X	C	C	-
Gypsum (G)	X	X	X	X	C	C
Kieserite (KS)	C	C	C	X	C	C
Potassium nitrate (PN)	C	L	C	C	-	C

C: compatible, can be mixed in the solution L: Limited compatibility, mix at the time of use or some precautions must be taken; X: Incompatible, do not mix.

4.5.8. Elemental Concentrations for Several "Standard" Solutions Used in Soilless Culture

Element	Amount in mg/lit. (ppm)					
	Hoagland and Arnon	Cooper Modified	Steiner	Wilcox 1	Wilcox 2	Wilcox 3
Major nutrients						
Nitrogen (N)	210	200	171	132	162	175
Phosphorus (P)	31	60	48	58	58	65
Potassium (K)	234	300	304	200	284	400
Calcium (Ca)	200	170	180	136	136	197
Magnesium (Mg)	48	50	48	47	47	44
Micronutrients						
Boron (B)	0.5	1.5	0.3	1.5	1.5	0.5
Copper (Cu)	0.02	0.1	0.2	0.1	0.1	0.05
Iron (Fe)	5.0	12.0	3.0	4.0	4.0	2.0
Manganese (Mn)	0.5	2.0	1.0	0.5	0.5	0.5
Molybdenum (Mo)	0.01	0.2	0.1	0.1	0.1	0.02
Zinc (Zn)	0.05	0.1	0.4	0.3	0.3	0.05

4.5.9. Recommended Major Element Nutrient Solution Levels for Crops in Soilless

Vegetables	Major elements (mg/l, ppm)				
	N	P	K	Ca	Mg
Cucumber	230	40	315	175	42
Eggplant	175	39	235	150	28
Leafy	210	80	275	180	67
Lettuce	200	50	300	200	65
Melon	185	39	235	180	25
Pepper	175	39	235	150	28
Tomato	200	50	360	185	45

4.5.10. pH Values for Different Soilless Culture Crops

Plant	pH Range	Plant	pH Range
Beans	6.0-6.5	Onions	6.5-7.0
Broccoli	6.0-6.5	Peas	6.0-6.8
Cabbage	6.5-7.5	Pineapple	5.0-5.5
Carrots	5.8-6.4	Pumpkin	5.0-6.5
Cucumbers	5.8-6.0	Radish	6.0-7.0
Garlic	6.0-6.5	Strawberries	5.5-6.5
Lettuce	6.0-6.5	Tomatoes	5.5-6.5

Source: Hydroponic Food Production by Howard M. Resh Woodbridge Press, 1987

4.5.11. Irrigation Water Quality Classes

Factor	Unit	Water quality classes		
		Non-hazardous	Slight to Moderate	Severe
pH (Normal Range 6.5 - 8.4)				
Salinity ECw	dS/m	0.0 – 0.8	0.8 – 3.0	>3.0
Sodium	me/l	<3	<3.0	-
Chloride	me/l	<3	<3.0	-
Boron	me/l	<0.7	0.7-3.0	>3.0
Bicarbonates	me/l	<1.5	1.5-8.5	>8.5

4.5.12. Aeroponic

Concept and Use

The word aeroponic is derived from the Greek word *aero* means air and *ponos* means labour. Availability of disease free planting material is most important basic requirement for healthy seed potato production programme. Augmentation in subsequent generations for vegetatively propagated crop like potato is easily possible by aeroponic technology. Aeroponic is the method of growing plants in air mist enclosed and controlled chamber without the use of soil or any aggregated solid medium. In aeroponic system, plants are suspending its roots in air mist chamber and spraying nutrient solution intermittently at periodical interval for entire cropping period. The water soluble nutrients solution is re-circulated through desired pressure by motor pump fitted in nutrient tank and monitored regularly for pH, EC and solution which is changed at periodical interval. The tissue culture based microplant and microtuber techniques previously used for minituber production usually produces maximum of 6-10 minitubers per plant depending upon varieties. Aeroponic system offers production potential of three to four times more numbers of minitubers per plant than the conventional tissue culture technique. Aeroponic minituber based seed potato production is increasing in India due to more number of minituber per unit area and time as well desired temperature manipulation through controlled conditions round the year.

Aeroponic technology for potato seed production was first time standardized in India by Central Potato Research Institute, Shimla during 2009-10. Later on it became functional in the month of October, 2012 for first time at Shimla under hill conditions and series of experiments were started for successful disease-free aeroponic minituber production. Long day, short day and day neutral varieties of potato are being grown through this technique. There are several other added advantages of aeroponic system like avoid soil and tuber-borne diseases, easy inspection and desired size harvesting at periodical interval, limited space requirement with vertical growth.

Some advantages to using an aeroponic systems are they typically use little to no growing media. The roots get maximum oxygen, and the plants grow more rapidly as a result. Aeroponic systems also generally use less water than any other type of hydroponic system (especially true aeroponic systems). Also harvesting is usually easier, especially for root crops. However there are a few downsides to aeroponic systems as well. Besides being a bit more expensive to build. The mister/sprinkler heads can clog from build up of the dissolved mineral elements in the nutrient solution. So make sure to have extras on hand to swap out when they do clog while you clean them. Also because the plants roots are hanging in mid air by design in aeroponic systems, the plants roots are much more vulnerable to drying out if there is any interruption in the watering cycle. Therefore, even any temporary power outage (for any reason) could cause your plants to die much more quickly than any other type of hydroponic system. Also there's a reduced margin for error with the nutrient levels in aeroponic systems, especially the true high pressure systems.

The aeroponic system is probably the most high-tech type of hydroponic gardening. Like the N.F.T. system above the growing medium is primarily air. The roots hang in the air and are misted with nutrient solution. Because the roots are exposed to the air like the N.F.T. system, the roots will dry out rapidly if the misting cycles are interrupted.

4.5.13. Aquaponics

It involves production of fish and vegetables with same input resource of water and nutrients. This results in effective utilization of fish pond water and its nutrients for production of vegetables/plants simultaneously with added returns on input resources. Plants act as bio-filter for the recycled water to fish pond.

- Aquaponics combines aquaculture with hydroponics.,
- Fish produce ammonia (NH_4), which bacteria convert to nitrate (NH_3).
- The water is sent to plants, which absorb nutrients that they need
- The water returned to the fish,
- Asia: Farmers combined rice in paddies with fish to grow both.

4.5.14. Film Farming

- Film farming refers to an alternative method of organic farming that uses a hydromembrane composed of a water-soluble polymer (hydrophillic booster, SkyGel) and a hydrogel-based IMEC film as opposed to traditional soil.
- SkyGel acts as a reservoir and fertilizer for the plant, holding water up to 1,000 times its weight.
- The IMEC film and the SkyGel work together to reduce the plant's water intake by 90% while increasing crop yield and plant producti vity.
- IMEC- Interunixersity Micro Electronics Center Hydromembrane
- Film farming is the brainchild of Yuichi Mori (pictured), the chemical physicist who founded Mebiol in 1995.
- This unique method of farming was invented in 2009 by Dubai-based company Agricel, founded by Yalman A. Khan and Kunal G. Wadhwani.
- The Agricel network is primarily based in Japan but h has extended to China and Australia. Agricel's vision seeks to feed the future by promoting film farming and the use of hydrophillic boosters in an effort to limit the use of water and to fight world hunger.

- With the addition of a greenhouse, agriculture can be utilized anyw here in the world with film farming and hydrophillic technolcg.

4.5.15. Factors of Soilless Cultivation of Vegetables

- Contact Market-Without it great chance of failure.
- Suitable site for production.
- Suitable varieties/hybrids/planting material
- Good management by trained farmer.

4.5.16. International Status Soilless/Hydroponics

- The area under hydroponics/CEA began to expand significantly in Europe and Asia during 1950s and 1960s
- Large hydroponic systems were developed in the deserts of California, Arizona, Abu Dhabi, and Iran (1970) (Fontes, 1973; Jensen and Teran, 1971).
- In these desert locations, the advantages of the technology were augmented by the duration and interest of solar radiation, which maximized photosynthetic production.
- At present, the largest commercial hydroponics facility in the world is "Eurofresh" Farms in Wilcox, Arizona, Eurofresh has 318 acres (1.29 km2) under glass and represents about a third of the commercial hydroponic greenhouse area in the United States.
- Eurofresh does not consider its tomatoes organic, but they are pesticide-free. They are grown in rock wool with top irrigation.
- The future for hydroponics appears more positive today than any time over the last 50 years.

4.5.17. Global Trends

- According to recent estimates countries having substantial commercial hydroponics production area include
- Israel 30,000 acres,
- Holland 10,000 acres,
- England 4,200 acres and
- Australia and New Zealand around 8,000 acres
- China 250 acres

4.5.18. Basic requirements for a hydroponic system

- Light: is essential to carry on photosynthesis.
- Nutrient Strength: Nutrients must be solely designed for hydroponics.
- Growth Media: The growing medium, not soil, holds moisture and anchors roots. pH - pH is the level of acidity or alkalinity of the nutrient solution.

- Temperature: Requirements for plants are the same as out of a hydroponic system.
- Air: Plants require C02. Oxygen aeration for the roots is important for uptake Water Quality: Excessive salinity or high zinc content could be harmful.

4.5.19. Nutrients

There are approximately seventeen elements required for proper growth of hydroponic plants.

Macro-nutrients

1. Carbon - Formation of organic compounds,
2. Oxygen- Release of energy from sugar,
3. Hydrogen- Water formation,
4. Nitrogen- Chlorophyll, Amino Acids and Proteins synthesis,
5. Phosphorus- Vital for photosynthesis and growth,
6. Potassium- Enzyme activity,
7. Calcium- Cell growth, cell division and the components of cell wall,
8. Magnesium-Component of chloroph) 11. enzyme activation.
9. Sulfur- Formation of Amino Acids and Proteins.

B) Micro- nutrients

10. Iron- Used in Photosynthesis,
11. Boron - Vital for reproduction,
12. Chlorine Helps root growth,
13. Copper- Enzyme activation,
14. Manganese- Component of chlorophyll. Enzynre activation.
15. Zinc- Component of enzymes and auxins.
16. Molybdenum- Nitrogen fixation,
17. Cobalt- Nitrogen fixation.

Other elements like Sodium- Vital for water movement, Nickel-Nitrogen liberation, Silicon-Cell wall toughness, can also be used

Nutrient solution

- Most plants grow well with a basic nutrient solution. Many readymade choices are available.
- Care must be taken to avoid minor nutrient deficiencies.
- Several different herbs may be grown in a single nutrient solution.

Name nutrients	Quantity in (ppm)
Nitrogen	210
Phosphorous	70
Potassium	300
Calcium	180
Magnesium	67
Magnese	1.25
Iron	3.0
Cupper	0.26
Boron	0.5
Zinc	0.40
Molybednum	0.06

4.5.20. Vegetable Production Under Soil-Less Culture in India

Vegetables	Production (g/m2/day)
Carrot	56.5
Cucumber	226
Garlic	57
Ginger	57
Leek	57
Green Bean	113
Lettuce	226
Onion	56.5
Peapod	113
Potato	56.5
Salad greens	226
Tomato	113
Greens	113

4.5.21. Different Hydroponic Systems

- Capillary / wick systems
- Flood and drain system
- Drip system (recovery / non recovery)
- Nutrient film technique
- Aeroponic system
- Aquaponic System
- Microgreens

4.5.22. Soilless Culture Systems for Crop Production in Some Countries

Countries	NFT	DRFT	DFT	Aeroponic	Substrate culture
Thailand	√	√	√	√	√
Singapore	√	√	-	√	√
China	√	-	√	√	√
Korea	√	-	√	√	√
Japan	√	-	√	√	√
New Zealand	√	-	-	-	√
Australia	√	-	-	-	√

NFT = Nutrient film techniques, DRFT = Dynamic root floating techniques, DFT = Deep flow techniques.

Source: Wattanapreechanon *et al.*(2C12).

5

High-Tech Vegetable Production

5.1. Precision Farming

Precision farming is an emerging concept in modern agriculture. It is micro management system to arrive at improved agriculture and land management decisions that result from using information delivered by geospatial technologies. In other words it is "Digital Agriculture" involving very large scale farm level mapping, comprehensive data base creation on required resources generated through space based inputs and field observations and making a detailed plan of work for maximizing the yield and reducing the cost on inputs using the decision support system. ***Precision farming means to do the right thing, in the right place and in right time***. It is also called **site-specific management (SSM),** is the management of an agricultural crop at a spatial scale smaller than the individual field. In many fields, the crop's environment varies substantially from one part to another. Mineral nutrient levels, soil texture and chemistry, moisture content and pest patterns may all vary from location to location. By adjusting management practices and input levels according to what is appropriate for local conditions, the farmer can in principle save money, improve yields and reduce un-wanted environmental effects. At its most fundamental level, precision agriculture is information management. To effectively manage, a field on site-specific basis, the farmer must be able to measure variations in yield in order to determine whether intensive management is economically justified. The farmer must also be able to measure variations in factors that influence yield and identify the factors underlying yield variability in each specific field and season. Finally, it must exist to use this information to implement changes in management practices that increase profitability or reduce environmental impacts. The introduction of SSM practices into crop production was made possible by the confluence of a number of information-management technologies. These include yield monitoring, remote sensing, geographic information systems (GIS), global positioning systems (GPS) and variable rate application technology. Whether or not these practices are actually adopted will depend on development of the capability to interpret sit-specific data and act on that information to increase profitability.

5.1.1. Advantages: These are

- Improves crop yield.
- Provides information to make better management decisions.
- Reduces the chemical and fertilizer costs through more efficient application.
- Provides more accurate farm records.

- Increases profit margin.
- Reduces pollution.

5.1.2. Basic Principles: These includes

(a) *Characterization*: Measure extent, scales and dynamics of variation,

(b) *Interpretation*: Assess significance, identify major causes of uncertainty and formulate management targets,

(c) *Management:* Apply inputs at the appropriate scale and in a timely manner and

(d) *Monitoring:* Outcome in a continuous learning process of change. This may be accomplished in discrete steps (mapping approaches), as dynamic process executed in real-time (sensing approaches and modelling approaches) or as combination of both is also possible.

5.1.3. General Requirements: Following requirements

Crop Characteristics

Crop type, stage of the crop, crop health, special care, nutrient requirement, canopy etc;

Soil Characteristics

Physical and chemical properties, depth, texture, nutrient status, salinity and toxicity, soil temperature, productivity potential, etc.

Climate Characteristics

Temperature, wind direction and speed, humidity, rainfall, evaporation, evapo-transpiration etc.

Land Topography

Size and shape of field, slope of land, surface and sub surface drainage conditions.

Irrigation Facilities

Surface water and ground water availability, irrigation method, levels of irrigations, interval etc.

Precision Machinery

Tillage machinery, intercultural machinery, harvesting machinery.

Other Planning inputs

Electricity, road, secondary services, labour, market, etc.

Steps Used: The steps used in precision farming are;

- Assessing variation
- Managing variation and
- Evaluation

5.1.4. Methodologies Used

There are two methodologies for implementing precision farming. Each method has unique benefits and can even be used in a complementary or combined fashion.

Map Based

It includes grid sampling a field, performing laboratory analyses of the soil samples, generating a site-specific map of the properties and finally using this map to control a variable rate applicator. During both the sampling and application steps, a positioning system GPS/DGPS is used to identify the current location with higher accuracy in the field. This method is most popular due to lack of sufficient sensors for monitoring the soil conditions and also truth in a laboratory analyses and the reliability of the data. However, the cost of soil testing limits the number of samples that a farmer can afford to test. Thus, the usual practice is to grid sample a field every 2 to 2.5 acres. Site specific maps may also be used for grid wise site-specific input management. This methodology is most relevant for Indian agriculture at present.

Sensor Based

It utilizes real time sensors and feed back control to major the desired properties on-the-go, usually soil properties or crop characteristics and immediately use this signal to control the variable rate applicator. Sensors developed for on-the-go real time measurement of soil properties have the potential to provide benefits from increased density of measurements at a relatively low cost. A GPS receiver and a data logger are used to record the position of each soil sample or measurement, to generate a map which can be processed along with other layers of spatially variable information to control the variable rate applicator.

5.1.5. Constraints: These are

- Small land holding.
- Socio-economic status of Indian farmers.
- Lack of success stories or cost-benefit studied on precision farming.
- Lack of technical expertise, knowledge and technology.
- Heterogeneity of cropping systems and market imperfections.
- High cost.
- Provision of assured irrigation and other agricultural inputs.

5.2. Crop Modeling

The International Benchmark Sites Network for Agro-technology Transfer (IBSNAT) has published documentation for a set of crop model inputs and outputs. This system of files and data formats is used for the models integrated into the Decision Support System for Agro-technology Transfer (DSSAT), in which corn, wheat, soybean, and peanut crop models all used the same database software and strategy evaluation program. This system is useful for running and validating the models for conducting sensitivity analysis, and for evaluating the variability and risks of different management strategies for a range of locations specified by soil and weather data. The attempt to develop and use general files and formats provided a good start and demonstrated the utility of the endeavor. However, the introduction of other crops (such as rice), the introduction of other models of the same crops, and the introduction of other processes into the existing models revealed several deficiencies. Further, the large number of files presented difficulties to many users. Work has been initiated, therefore, to develop a more universal set of files.

5.2.1. Objectives

Crop models integrate the crop development growth and production as a function of weather and has many uses in agriculture. They serve as tools in land use planning, crop adaptation, crop monitoring and forecasting, crop management, pest and disease control and finally in prioritizing the research needs. An overview of crop models was studied and compiled by Rao (2011) describing the main purpose of developing the crop models, which are:

1. To understand crop weather interactions, processes involved and their limitations.
2. To assess the affect of environment, crop genotype and management of input resources on crop yields, and to quantify the yield gaps with existing knowledge.
3. To undertake strategic and policy decisions to increase the productivity of resource based efficient cropping systems.

5.2.2. Importance

Rao (2011) studied the importance of crop growth simulation models which are being used to solve practical problems during last four decades. The general utility of the crop growth simulation models are:

- Yield assessment of cereals, pulses an oilseed crops based on varying crop management decisions during the growing season as well as over different rainfall years for risk analysis.
- Potential productivity of crops for regional agricultural planning. Yield gaps and decision support systems.
- Genetic improvement of cereals, pulses and oilseeds for yield, pest resistance food value and input requirements.
- Quantifications of impact of global climate change on agricultural productivity.
- Management decisions on evaluating sowing date, row spacing, plant populations, scheduling irrigation, evaluation of yield variations in different rainfall years, impact of moisture and temperature stresses on yield.
- To simulate growth, development and yield levels.
- To define optimum management strategies regarding drainage, irrigation, soil, water, weather, fertilizer, pest control, planting dates, tillage, crop residue management.
- Evaluation of new crops for introducing at a location.

5.2.3. Types of Models

The models can be broadly categorized into

A. Empirical statistical models
B. Crop weather analysis models and
C. Crop growth simulation models

5.2.4. Crop Growth Simulation Models for Different Crop/Processes

Model Name	Crop	Processes involved	Reference
CERES-Sorghum	Sorghum	Growth and development, grain yield	Ritchie and Alagarswamy (1988)
RESCAP	Sorghum	Dry matter, water use, grain yield, radiation interception	Monteith *et al.* (1989)
RESCAP	Pearl Millet	Dry matter accumulation,	Monteith *et al.* (1989)
SIMAIZ	Maize	Growth, grain yield	Duncan (1975)
CERES-Maize	Maize	Growth and development, grain yield	Stapper and Arkin (1980)
COTTAM	Cotton	Growth, development, soil water budget, morphology	Jackson *et al.* (1988)
GOSSYM	Cotton	Growth, yield	Baker *et al.* (1983)
SUBSTOR	Potato	Growth, development, yield	Hodges *et al.* (1989)
IRRIMOD (1980)	Rice	Growth, development, yield	Angus and Zandstra
CERES-Rice	Rice	Growth, yield, phenology	Ritchie *et al.* (1986)
AUSCANE	Sugarcane	Growth, development, cane yield	Jones *et al.* (1989)
SOYGRO	Soybean	Vegetative, reproductive, grain yield, phenology	Wilkerson et al. (1985)
SOYMOD	Soybean	Growth, development, yield	Curry *et al.* (1975)
BEANGRO	Dry bean	Growth, development, phenology, grain yield	Hoogenboom et al. (1990)
PNUTGRO	Peanut	Growth, development, phenology, yield	Boote *et al.* (1989)
POTATO	Potato	Growth, yield	Loomis (1984)
SIMTAG	Wheat	Genotypes growth and development, grain yield	Stapper (1984)
CERES-Wheat	Wheat	Growth, development, grain yield	Ritchie *et al.* (1985)
EPIC	Any crop and cropping	Water use, nitrogen nutrition, Soil productivity, erosion, plant growth processes, yield	William *et al.* (1984)
SPAW	Any crop	Plant environment interaction, microclimate, dry matter, grain	Shawcroft *et al.* (1974)
ALMANAC	Crop-weed	Crop-weed competition competitions	Kiniry *et al.* (1992)
PLANTGRO	Any crop	Evapotranspiration and grain yield	Retta and Hanks (1980)

Source: Rao (2011).

5.2.5. Common Crop Growth Simulation Models

Various crop growth simulation models are used for the simulation of crop growth and development for various purposes. Some of the common models used for the purpose are:

S.No.	Crop Models	Reference
1.	APES	Donatelli *et al.* 2010
2.	APSIM	McCown *et al.* 1996
3.	CROPSYST	Stöckle et al., 2003
4.	DAISY	Hansen, 2000
5.	DSSAT	Jones *et al.*, 2003
6.	EPIC	Keating *et al.*, 2003
7.	FASSET	Berntsen *et al.* 2003
8.	HERMES	Kersebaum, 1995
9.	INFOCROP	Aggarwal *et al.*, 2006
10.	MONICA	Nendel *et al.*, 2011
11.	STICS	Brisson *et al.*, 2003
12.	WOFOST	Boogaard *et al.*, 1998

5.3. Vegetable Production Under Protected Structure

5.3.1. Status and Scope in India

In India, use of greenhouse technology started only during 1980's. In India, the technology is still in its nascent stage. The area under greenhouse cultivation in India, as reported by National Horticulture Mission, Government of India was about 2000 ha including 500 ha net house, shade nets net1500 ha greenhouse in the year 2005 which has grown up to 80,795.81 ha by the end of 2012.

Greenhouses are being built in the Ladakh region for extending the growing season of vegetables from 3 to 8 months. In the North-East, greenhouses are being constructed essentially as rain shelters to permit off-season vegetable production. In the Northern plains, seedlings of vegetables and flowers are being raised in the greenhouses either for capturing the early markets or to improve the quality of the seedlings. Propagation of difficult-to-root tree species has also been found to be very encouraging. Several commercial floriculture ventures are coming up in Maharashtra, Tamil Nadu and Karnataka states to meet the demands of both domestic and export markets. The commercial utilization of greenhouses started from 1988 onwards and now with the introduction of Government's liberalization policies and developmental initiatives, several corporate houses have entered to set up 100% export oriented units. In just four years, since implementation of the new policies in 1991, 103 projects with foreign investment of more than Rs.80 crores have been approved to be set up in the country at an estimated cost of more than Rs.1000 crores around Pune, Bangaluru, Hyderabad and Delhi.

Thus, the area under climatically controlled greenhouses of these projects was estimated to be around 300 ha. Out of which many have already commenced exports and have received very encouraging results in terms of the acceptance of the quality in major markets abroad and the profits obtained.

5.3.2. Basic Principles

A greenhouse is generally covered with a transparent material such as polythene or glass. Depending upon the cladding material and its transparency major fraction of sunlight is absorbed by vegetable crops and other objects. These objects in greenhouse in turn emit long wave thermal radiations for which cladding material has lower transparency. With the result, solar energy is trapped and raises the temperature inside the greenhouse. This is popularly known as greenhouse effect. This rise in temperature in greenhouse is responsible for growing vegetable in cold climates. During summer months, air temperature in greenhouse is to be brought down by providing cooling device. In commercial greenhouses besides temperature-controlled humidity, carbon dioxide, photoperiod, soil temperature, plant nutrients etc. facilitate round the year production of desired vegetable crops. Controlled climatic and soil conditions provide an opportunity to the vegetable crops to express their yield potentials.

5.3.3. Advantages: These are

- The yield may be 10-12 times higher than that of outdoor cultivation depending upon the type of greenhouse, type of crop, environmental control facilities.
- Vegetables can be raised successfully under adverse climatic conditions.
- Vegetables can be grown throughout the year in a particular area.
- Off season quality nursery can be raised which advances the harvesting period.
- Off-season production of vegetable flowers and fruit crops.
- Disease-free and genetically superior transplants can be produced continuously.
- Efficient utilization of chemicals, pesticides to control pest and diseases.
- Water requirement of crops very limited and easy to control.
- Maintenance of stock plants, cultivating grafted plant-lets and micro propagated plant-lets.
- Hardening of tissue cultured plants.
- Uniform production of quality produce free of blemishes.
- Most useful in monitoring and controlling the instability of various ecological system.
- Modern techniques of hydroponic (Soil less culture); aeroponics and nutrient film techniques are possible only under greenhouse cultivation.

5.3.4. Different Types: These are;

5.3.4.1. Naturally Ventilated Polyhouse

Naturally ventilated polyhouse increases temperature (2- 3°C) and CO_2 % and protect from cold energy to the crop during winter but there is no provision for lowering temperature and RH during day time in summer. Crop cycle is reduced 30-40 days. This structure avoids all type of abiotic stresses. The yield increase in this type is 25-30 percent

5.3.4.2. Fan–Pad or Hi-tech Polyhouse

Increased CO_2 % and temperature up to 3- 4°C more as compared to open during winter but this polyhouse can be increased and decreased up to 4-5 °C temperature and 5-10% RH and cut of 30-50% solar radiation in day time during summer according to crop. This structure avoids all type of abiotic stresses. The yield increase in this type is 40-50 percent.

5.3.4.3. Shade-net-house

Shade net covering reduces solar radiation (30-80%) and minimize temperature (1-2^{0}C), minimized evaporation rate 50%, saving 50% and increasing 15-20% RH during critical summer months (May-September). This structure is suitable for leafy vegetable production. The yield increase in this type is 20-25 percent.

5.3.4.4. Insect-Proof -net-house

Insect- Proof- Net-house minimized virus incidence (90-95%) through insect vector and decreased the use of insecticides/pesticides (80-85%), rain and hail injury , minimized solar radiation (10-15%) as compared to open field.The yield increase in this type is 25-30 percent.

5.3.4.5. Plastic Low-tunnel

Shade net covering reduces solar radiation 30-80% and minimize temperature 1-2^{0}C, minimized evaporation rate 50%, saving 50% and increasing 15-20% relative humidity during May-September. This structure is suitable for leafy vegetable production.The yield increase in this type is 20-25 percent.

5.3.4.6. Walk -in -tunnel

This is a short duration temporary structure suitable for early and off-season cucurbitaceous crops. This structure minimizes cold, frost, hail, rain and injury and increases 1-2^{O}C temperature and avoid all kind of abiotic stresses. Crop is advanced by 30 -40 days. The yield increase in this type is 15-20 percent.

5.3.4.7. Coloured Poly-mulching

Mulching technology saves 30- 40 % water, 25 % fertilizers and conserves up to 40-50 % moisture.Soil temperature is increased by 0.5-1.5^{O}C. It also minimizes weed incidences and save labour and time. The yield increase in this type is 20-30 percent.

5.3.5. Mode of protected cultivation: These are;

5.3.5.1. Low-cost greenhouse/polyhouse

The low cost polyhouse is a zero-energy chamber made of UV stabilized polyethylene sheet of 700 gauge supported on bamboos with sutli (ropes) and nails. It will be used for protecting the crop from high rainfall. Its size depends upon the purpose and availability of space. The structure depends on the sun for energy. The temperature within polyhouse increases by 6-10^{0}C more than outside.In UV stabilized plastic film covered pipe framed polyhouse, the day temperature is higher and night temperature is lower than the outside. The solar radiation entering the polyhouse is 30-40% lower than that reaching the soil surface outside.

5.3.5.2. Medium-cost greenhouse/polyhouse

With a slightly higher cost, a Quonset-shaped polyhouse (green house) can be framed with GI pipe (Class B) of 15 mm bore. This polyhouse will have a single layer covering of UV-stabilized polythene of 800 gauges. The exhaust fans are used for ventilation. These are thermostatically controlled. Cooling pad is used for humidifying the air entering the polyhouse. The polyhouse frame and glazing material have a life span of about 20 years and 2 years, respectively.

5.3.5.3. High cost green house/polyhouse

It is constructed on the structure (frame) made of iron/aluminum structure, designed domed shaped or cone shaped (as per choice). Temperature, humidity and the light are automatically controlled as per requirement of the users. Floor and a part of walls are made of concrete. It is highly durable, about 5-6 times costlier, required qualified operator, proper maintenance, care and precautions while operating. The low and medium-cost greenhouses have wide scope in production of domestic as well as export-oriented vegetables. NEH region recorded the highest rainfall in the world. The duration of rainy season is also wide (April-October). During this period, growing of vegetables such as cabbage, cauliflower, broccoli, tomato, brinjal and French bean in open conditions is very difficult. Severe attacks of pest and diseases occur due to heavy rains. So, growing of vegetable crops in low cost polyhouse during this period is very profitable. Control of disease and pest in polyhouse is also easy.

5.4. Other Plant Protection Structures: These are

5.4.1. Plastic Low Tunnels

Plastic low tunnels are miniature form of greenhouses to protect the plants from rains, winds, low temperature, frost and other vagaries of weather. The low tunnels are very simple structures requiring very limited skills to maintain are easy to constructs and offer multiple advantages. For construction of low tunnels, film of 100 micron would be sufficient. In cold conditions, they are used to conserve warmth, stimulate germination and early growth, protect plants from frost injury and improve the quality of the crops. The main purpose of growing vegetables in plastic low tunnels is to hasten growth for early markets.

5.4.2. Hot Bed and Cold Frame

Hot bed is made of wood, cement or brick stone and is prepared above ground with artificial heating. Used for growing vegetables in winter provide an early start of crops like – tomato, cucumber, okra, pepper, cabbage, muskmelon and watermelon etc. Cold frames are similar to hot beds except for absence of any form of artificial heat and having plastic on top for tapping solar energy or natural heat.

5.4.3. Net Houses

These simple framed structures are of two types, namely, shade nets and insect-proof nets.Shade nets are perforated plastic materials used to cut down the solar radiation so as to protect leaves from scorching. These nets are available in three colours i.e. black, green and white and are in different shading intensities ranging from 25 to 75 per cent. Leafy vegetables and ornamental greens are preferably grown under shade nets. Insect proof nylon nets with different intensities ranging from 25 to 60 meshes are effective means to control entry of most flying insects and save the crop from viral diseases.

5.4.4. Cloches

It is a protective enclosure, consisting of a structural frame and a transparent glazing material for one plant. It is used to provide protection to potted plants and young transplants in fruit orchard and forests.

5.4.5. Rain Shelter

Most suited protective structure in high rainfall states like – Assam and Kerala. Mostly even span low cost green house structures are used as rain shelter.

5.4.6. Floating Row Cover

It is a plastic film fabric used without any mechanical support in the form of hoops to protect crops from insect vectors, practiced for winter production of tender warm season crops to enhance early maturity, improve quality and extend the growing season.

5.4.7. Trench Cultivation

Trench cultivation, otherwise called as "underground greenhouse technology" is a simple and economically viable technology for growing vegetable during winter. Best utilization by farmers of Ladakh and Leh region of Himachal Pradesh and Jammu and Kashmir for extending vegetable production from three to eight months. Important vegetables are beet root, spinach, Chinese cabbage, celery, parsley, coriander etc.

5.5. Optimal Storage Conditions for Greenhouse-grown Vegetables

Vegetables	Temperature (p C)	Relative humidity (%)	Storage life (days)
Cucumber	10-13	95%	10-14
Pepper	08-13	90-95%	14-21
Tomato	10-13	90-95%	07-21

5.5.1. Percent Increase Yield in Different Type of Protected Structures

S.N.	Protected structure	% increase yield
1.	Naturally ventilated poly house	25-30
2.	Fan-pad or Hi-tech polyhouse	40-50
3.	Shade net house	20-25
4.	Insect proof net house	25-30
5.	Plastic low tunnel	20-25
6.	Walk in tunnel	15-20
7.	Coloured poly mulching	20-30

5.5.2. Major Barriers for Upscaling

- Lack of region-specific designs.
- No maintenance supports.
- Limited availability of suitable varieties.
- Lack of organized marketing chains.
- Huge shortage of skilled man-power.
- Nematodes and soil-borne fungus infestation.
- Scope of only limited vegetables.
- Limited availability of quality cladding materials.

5.5.3 Strategies for Promotion

- Suggest most suitable varieties and crop sequences.
- Promotion of low-pressure drip irrigation system.
- Selection of suitable designs of protected structures.
- Large scale use of different color plastic mulches and white colored drip and laterals for micro irrigation systems.
- Promotion of large-scale mechanization.
- Use of solar energy.
- Major ITIs in the country should include a diploma course on fabrication of protected structures, repair and their maintenance.
- Large scale training in the field of protected cultivation
- Government support to develop input hubs for protected cultivation in multi-locations in PPP mode.
- A special cluster club of protected cultivation growers may be established in blocks at state level.
- All the protected cultivation clusters must be mandatorily clubbed with rain water harvesting infrastructure facilities.
- Practical demonstration units at each state level may be established for low cost protected structures along with the production and pest management strategies.

5.6. Use of Mulching in Vegetable Production

Mulch is a general term for a protective ground cover that can include manure, wood chips, seaweed, leaves, straw, grasses, sands, stones (boulders), synthetic plastics, and other natural products. While the term mulching may be defined as *a practice of covering the surface of soil with these materials to reduce evaporation, and also to moderate wide fluctuations in diurnal soil temperatures, especially in the root zone environment.* It controls external evaporability and also reduces energy supply to the evaporating site by cutting off solar radiation falling on the ground. *Its main function is limited to controlling first stage of drying which helps in improved moisture status, reduced soil temperature*, besides checking seedling mortality and improving crop stand. Thus, mulches are effective means to conserve soil water and moderate surface soil temperature. It also suppresses weed-flora and reduces weed competition with crop for water and nutrients making them available in greater quantities for crop plants. Besides, the above, mulching helps in increasing downward movement of water. Its storage deep in the profiles escape evaporation due to reduction in thermal gradients and exchange of vapours. The effectiveness of mulches in conserving moisture has generally been found to be higher under more frequency of rainfall, drought conditions and also during early period of plant growth when canopy cover remains scanty.

5.6.1. Advantages: These are

- To improves fertility of soil.
- To protects soil from water and wind erosion.
- To preserves soil moisture.
- To accents landscape plantings.
- To provides a "finished" look to the garden.
- To helps in production of clean and quality products.
- To protects the plant and their produce from attack of insect-pest and diseases.
- To moderates the soil thermal regime throughout the cropping season.
- To prevents weed growth.
- Increasing overall crop production

5.6.2. Disadvantages: Mulches do have a few drawbacks, which are as follows;

- The cost of materials is major drawback to large-scale mulching.
- Some mulch is not readily available.
- In case of sawdust or straw mulch, nitrogen starvation sometimes occurs.
- Heavy mulching over a period of years may result in buildup of soil over the crown area of the plants.
- Continuously using the same type of mulch (pine bark, acidic in nature i.e., pH 3.5-4.5) may cause plant death by changing the soil's reaction. Conversely, hardwood bark mulch, although initially acidic, may cause the soil to become too basic or alkaline, causing acid-loving plants to quickly decline. Soil pH's above 6.5 usually create micronutrient deficiencies of iron and manganese for many common landscape plants. One can avoid this by periodically rotating the type of mulch used.
- Difficulty in application of top-dressed fertilizers.
- Some of the mulch materials (plastic mulches) are not degradable.
- In areas where the incidence of termites is very high, application of organic mulch needs frequent irrigation and spray of termiticides.
- Some of the organic mulches have allelopathic effects on crops.

5.6.3. Characteristics of Organic Mulch: These are:

- Undecomposed or partially decomposed mulch material should not have a nitrogenase activity after the application of mulch.
- Should not have any antagonistic effect on the crop.
- It should be free from the attack of insects/pests particularly termites and diseases.
- Determination of mulch depth and identification of plant for moisture and oxygen tolerance are the two important steps in organic mulching.

5.6.4. Selection of Organic Mulch: These are;

Material	Depth to apply	Comments
Composted leaves	2-3 inches	Breaks down rapidly. Add humus and food to soil.
Grass clippings	2 inches	Excellent mulch. Will break down rapidly in soil.
Ground corncobs	2-3 inches	Improves fertility in soil. Good for plants that require medium acid soil. Excellent for improving soil structure.
Hay	3-4 inches	Unattractive but repeated use builds up reserve of available nutrients which lasts for years. Reduces weeds and holds moisture well.
Peat	2 inches	Soak well before using as may scatter easily. Breaks down rapidly.
Pine needles	3 inches	Adds acid to soil. Will not mat down. Fairly durable.
Sawdust	2 inches	Use weathered sawdust if mixing with soil. Fresh sawdust may leach soil of nitrogen as it breaks down.
Peat moss	1-2 inches	Attractive, available but expensive for large areas. Should be kept moist at all times.
Peanut hulls	2-3 inches	Supplies plant nutrients and improve soil structure. Fairly durable. May contain nematodes.
Shredded tree leaves	2-3 inches	-
Whole tree leaves	6 inches	Excellent source of humus. Rots rapidly. High in plant nutrients.
Straw	6 inches	Same as grass clippings, but lower in nutrients although furnishes considerable potassium.
Bark	1-2 inches	Ground and packaged commercially. Especially attractive in this form.
News paper	¼ inches	News paper text pages printed with black ink should be used. Colour dyes may be harmful to soil micro-flora and fauna if composted and used, not recommended for windy areas.

5.6.5. Precautions While Laying Organic Mulch

- Weeds should be removed before spreading mulch.
- Soil should be periodically tested for pH.
- Slimy mould responsible for fungal attacks should not be allowed to develop.

5.6.6. Types of Mulches

There are of two basic type's viz., organic and non-organic mulches. The examples of only those mulch materials have been explained below which are mostly used in vegetable productions.

5.6.6.1. Organic Mulches

5.6.6.1.1. Compost/Manure/peat

These materials can be used for mulching and can be of quite an attractive appearance.

They need to be laid in a 2" – 3" thick layer. Manure should be well rotted before laying or damage can occur to plants. These materials will benefit the soil fertility. It is generally considered as the best mulching material for the home garden. It is usually free of weed seeds and is inexpensive. It may be highly satisfactory where available from commercial producers or homeowners. One can prepare compost from materials present in his yard. It is not necessary to purchase expensive materials for mulching.

5.6.6.1.2. Peat Moss

This mulch is attractive and easy to handle but somewhat expensive. Dry peat moss requires considerable time and water to become moist, so it should be applied only to a 3-inch or less depth and avoided in areas subject to drought. Its acidic pH makes it especially desirable for acid-loving plants.

5.7.6.1.3. Pine Bark and Pine Needles

A two to three inches layer of pine bark is good for weed control. Pine bark makes attractive, usually dark-colored mulch. It can be purchased in various particle sizes, from shredded to large-sized particles, called nuggets. Large pine bark nuggets float in water and may not stay in place during a heavy rain. They may also attract termites and other insects. Pine needles makes excellent mulch for acid-loving trees and shrubs.This mulch is very attractive and allows water to penetrate easily and supply nutrients as they decompose.

5.6.6.1.4. Sawdust

Aged partially rotted sawdust makes satisfactory mulch that lasts a long time. Since, it is prone to caking and has a high carbon to nitrogen ratio. It contains only half the nutrients of straw, is slow to break down and causes nitrogen robbery, so should not be incorporated into the soil unless and until it has broken down to a brown 'soil' and worms are found in it. Softwood sawdust takes longer than hardwoods to decompose. Even better, add nitrogen to sawdust, and then compost it before spreading it on our soil. Apply it two inches deep after adding nitrogen fertilizer to the soil to prevent nutrient deficiencies.

5.6.6.1.5. Grass-clippings

Grass clippings are very effective mulch and can be applied straight from the mower box. However, it must be applied as a 4" to 6" thickness and this can cause problems. If the layer is too thick, no air will penetrate to the bottom and they will become smelly and rotten and useless as a soil conditioner. These should be used only before grass seed has ripened. Add additional layers as clipping decompose. It is one of the most easily available mulches, underrated principally because of people's experience with smell rotting masses when clippings are continually dumped in one spot. Do not use clipping from lawn treated with herbicides. They provide their own nitrogen if incorporated fresh, but may cause nitrogen robbery after long drying. Grass clippings can be used satisfactorily in most areas of the garden.

Experiments have been done in Sweden for three years on mulching cauliflower with grass clippings. It was observed that grass mulching consistently resulted in increased yield and reduced damage by root maggots. The effect of grass mulching on root fly population was also studied for one year. The mulching did not reduce egg lying but did result in increased egg-predation. The effects were more pronounced when the mulching material completely covered the ground even close to the stems of the plants.

5.6.6.1.6. Straw

Straw has similar qualities to grass clippings provided that it should be put down in a thick layer (5-10 cm).

5.6.6.1.7. Newspaper

Apply sheets of newspaper and cover lightly with grass clippings or other mulch material to anchor. They are impractical on their own, as they are too prone to blow away and once wet are soon broken up or penetrated by weeds. Newspaper is mostly chlorine-free and there is no danger to lead from the ink any one. If other mulch materials are not available, cover edges of paper with soil.Applying on a windy day can be a problem. This is certainly readily available and economical but somewhat difficult to apply. A good use for newspaper is as an under mulch; that is, place two to three sheets under a thin layer of an attractive, more expensive mulch. They can be useful underneath loose mulches, as they stop the soil being mixed commercial papers are available. Though expensive, they are most effective at keeping saladings clean. Take care not to use waxed or colored paper as these may be contaminated with chemicals. The high carbon-to-nitrogen ratio necessitates the prior application of nitrogen fertilizer. Rolls of plain wallpaper can be as effective. Paper alone begins to tear and blow away within 2-3 weeks after field application due to rapid biodegradation and loss of strength when wet. One disadvantage of oil saturated paper mulches is the messiness associated with handling oily paper in the field.

5.6.6.2. Non-organic Mulches

5.6.6.2.1. Polyethylene Mulches

Non-organic mulches generally lack the soil improving properties particularly to improvement in soil particle aggregation, structure formation and regulation of soil reactions. Among the different inorganic mulches, the use of plastic mulches is most common owing to its properties of moderating the hydrothermal regimes of microclimate of crops, show positive effects on weed control, prevention of soil dryness and crusting, water saving by preventing evaporation from surface, prevention of soil erosion and reduction of nutrient loss by leaching.

Advantages: These are

- Increases soil temperature (black plastic: 4-5 °C, clear film: 8-10 °C) upto 2 inch depth of soil.
- Increases plant growth- higher CO_2 concentration due to chimney effect.
- Facilitate earlier harvesting- black plastic by 7-10 days & clear mulch by 14-21 days.
- Reduces evaporation, weed problems, fertilizer leaching.
- Eliminates root pruning.
- Facilitates cleaner vegetable cultivation.

- Mulches aids fumigation- necessary to control soil born diseases (*Fusarium* wilt).
- Helps in insect management.

Disadvantages

- Higher initial cost and encourages some pernicious forms (like sludge and snails), fungal and other diseases.
- Impermeable mulch also restricts soil aeration.
- Removal of non-degradable plastic mulches is essential.

5.6.6.2.2. Aluminum-coated Plastic and Foil

Use of aluminum-coated plastic and foil is limited primarily to vegetable plants where research findings have indicated a significant reduction in insect- pests, such as aphids, and viruses carried by insects.One layer of either one of these materials provides excellent weed control. These materials decompose very slowly, but they are very expensive and quite unattractive mulches.

5.6.7. Selection of Plastic Materials

The selection of mulches depends upon the ecological situations and primary and secondary aspects of mulching is summarized in tabular form as given below

Condition	Type of mulch preferred
Orchard and plantation	Thicker mulch
Soil solarization	Thin, transparent film
Weed control through solarization	Transparent film
Weed control in cropped land	Black film
Rainy season	Perforated mulch
Saline water use	Black film
Summer cropped land	White film
Insect repellent	Silver colour film
Yield	Appropriate colour mulch
Early germination	Thinner film

5.6.8. Effect of Straw Mulching on Yields of Crops and Soil Temperature

Crop	Mean yield increase (%)	Decrease in soil temperature (°C)
Tomato	107	4-10
Lady's finger	388	4-10
Green gram	178	1-7
Moth bean	90	1-7
Cluster bean	71	1-7

5.6.9. Effect of Plastic Mulching on Yield of Vegetable Crops

Crops/ Vegetables	Plastic sheet thickness (μ)	Yield increased (%)
Brinjal	25	10-27
Okra	25	48-55
Potato	50	49-50
Tomato	25	65-70
Snap bean	25	33-73.3
Cucumber	25	44-52
Cabbage/Cauliflower	50	10-71
Chilli	25	60
Carrot	50	10-50

5.7. Drip Irrigation and Fertigation

During 1990-2000, witnessed a quantum leap in expansion of micro irrigation technology both in developed and developing countries. The micro irrigated area grew slowly but steadily and it was 0.41 M ha in 1981 to about 3.0 Mha in 2000 of both sprinkler micro irrigation. The area under micro irrigation increased almost six folds during last 20 years- from 1.1 million ha in 1986 to about 6.1 million ha in 2006 (Reinders 2007).While drip method of irrigation is currently practiced over 35 countries, the United States of America alone accounts for over 35 percent of the world's total drip irrigated areas. In countries like Israel, Austria and Germany, all the irrigated areas are brought under micro-irrigation technology, due to its comparative advantages over surface irrigation. Whereas micro-irrigation accounts for over 21 percent of the USA's total irrigated area, it accounts just 1.6 percent of India's total irrigated area.

In India, there has been a tremendous growth in the area under drip irrigation during the last 20 years. However, an appreciable improvement in the adoption of drip irrigation technology has taken place only from the 1980s, mainly because of various promotional programmes introduced by the Central and State governments. Many crops are irrigated by the drip method in India with the tree crops occupying the maximum percentage of the total area under drip irrigation, followed by vine crops, vegetables, field crops, flowers and other crops.

5.7.1. Advantages: These are

- Increase irrigation and fertilizer efficiency.
- Hasten maturity and improve quality of produce.
- Increase yield of crop.
- Reduce water requirement considerably.
- Reduce the input cost like labour, fertilizer, weeding and other inter-cultural operations.
- Lower pest and disease incidence.
- Versatility in undulating and sandy land,
- Utility under poor water quality (EC of 3 mmhos/cm).

5.7.2. Comparative Advantages of Drip-irrigation Over Conventional Method

Variables	Drip-irrigation	Conventional method
Water saving	High: 40-70%	Less due to evaporation run-off, percolation etc.
Irrigation efficiency	90%	30-50%
Input cost	Less in labour, fertilizer, pesticides and tilling	Comparatively higher
Weed problem	Almost nil	High
Water quality	Even saline water can be used	Only normal water can be used
Disease and pest problem	Relatively less	High
Water logging, run-off	Nil	High
Water control	High and easy	Less
Efficiency of fertilizer use	Very high and regulated supply	Heavy loss due to leaching
Range of applicability	In wide range of soil	Not suitable for sandy and undulated type of soil
Yield	20-100% increase	Less compared to Drip-irrigation

5.7.3. Irrigation Scheduling in Vegetables

Vegetables	Preferred minimum soil moisture		Critical stages of moisture stress
	Soil moisture tension (bars)	ASM[*1]	
Asparagus	-0.70	40%	As ferns begin to grow their foliage.
Broccoli	-0.25	70%	As head begin to develop.
Cabbage	-0.34	60%	Head/curd formation and enlargement.
Carrot	-0.45	50%	Root enlargement.
Cauliflower	-0.34	60%	Head/curd formation and enlargement.
Cucumber	-0.45	50%	During flowering and throughout fruit development.
Eggplant	-0.45	50%	Flowering and fruit development.
French beans	-0.45	50%	Flowering and pod filling.
Turnip, Mustard, Kale	-0.25	70%	Sufficient soil moisture from sowing to harvesting.
Lettuce	-0.34	60%	Head and leaf development.
Okra	-0.70	40%	Flowering and pod development.
Onion	-0.25	70%	Bulb formation and enlargement.
Peas	-0.70	40%	Flowering and pod filling.
Chilli and Capsicum	-0.45	50%	Flowering and fruit set.
Potato	-0.35	70%	Tuberization and tuber enlargement.
Pumpkin	-0.70	40%	Flowering and fruit enlargement.
Radish	-0.25	70%	Root enlargement.
Sweet potato	-2.00	20%	Root development.
Tomato	-0.45	50%	Flowering and fruit enlargement.
Watermelon	-2.00	40%	Flowering and period of fruit enlargement.

[*1]= Available soil moisture at 23-30 cm depth

5.7.4. Fertigation

Applying plant nutrients by dissolving them in irrigation water (termed as fertigation) particularly with the micro-irrigation system is the most efficient and precise way of nutrient application close to the crop root zone. In vegetable production, nutrients and irrigation must be provided to reduce nutrient and moisture stress and to maximize production.Surface irrigation systems are inexpensive to install and easy to manage, but their water use efficiency is lower (33%) than that of drip irrigation (90% or more). Drip fertigation is generally used with polythene mulch in high valued crops such as tomato, capsicum, eggplant, cucurbits, etc. Since soluble nutrients move with the wetting front, precise management of irrigation quantity, and the rate and timing of N and K applications are essential for efficient vegetable production. For effective fertigation, water application and nutrient application must be precisely managed to prevent over watering and nutrient leaching. Over irrigation with fertigation can result in severe nutrient deficiencies and reduced crop yields. In fertigation, fertilizer application is made in small and frequent doses that fit within scheduled irrigation intervals matching the plant water use to avoid leaching. Fertilizer use efficiency upto 95 % can be achieved through drip fertigation. (5.7.4.1)

5.7.4.1. Fertilizer Use Efficiency in Different Methods of Applications

Nutrient	Fertilizer use efficiency (%)		
	Soil application	Drip	Drip and fertigation
N	30-50	65	95
P	20	30	45
K	50	60	80

5.7.4.2. Advantages of Fertigation: These are

- In drip fertigation, fertilizer application is synchronized with plant need which varies from plant to plant. In drip fertigation, the amount and form of nutrient supply is regulated as per the need of the critical stages of plant growth.
- Due to better water and fertilizer use efficiency and reduction in leaching, there are considerable water and fertilizer saving in fertigation.
- Optimisation of nutrient balance in soils by supplying the nutrients directly to the effective root zones as per the requirement.
- Reduction in labour and energy cost by making use of water distribution systems for nutrient application.
- Better yield and quality of products obtained.
- Timely application of small but precise amounts of fertilizers directly to the roots zone, this improves fertilizer use efficiency and reduces nutrient leaching below the root zone.
- Ensures a uniform flow of water and nutrients.
- Improves availability of nutrients and their uptake by crop.
- Less infestation of weeds and pests due limited area wetting.
- Soil and water erosion are prevented.

5.7.4.3. Effect of Fertigation on Fertilizer Savings and Yields

Vegetables	Saving in fertilizer (%)	Increase in yield(%)
Okra	40	18
Onion	40	16
Banana	20	11
Castor	60	32
Cotton	30	20
Potato	40	30
Tomato	40	33
Sugarcane	50	40

Source: (Rajput and Patel, 2002).

5.7.4.4. Commonly Used Fertilizers for Fertigation and Their Solubility in Water at 20°C

Fertilizers	N- P- K	Solubility (g/lit)
Urea	46-0-0	1100
Urea ammonium nitrate	32-0-0	Highly soluble
Ammonium nitrate	34-0-0	1500
Calcium nitrate	16-0-0	1290
Ammonium sulphate	21-0-0	744
Potassium nitrate	13-0-44	316
Potassium chloride	0-0-60	344
Potassium sulphate	0-0-50	110
Mono-ammonium phosphate	12-61-0	365
Mono-potassium phosphate	0-52-34	220
Phosphoric acid	0-52-0	Highly soluble
Urea phosphate	17-44-0	960
Water soluble fertilizers	19-19-19	Highly soluble
	20-20-20	
	15-30-15	
	14-7-28	
	13-0-46	

5.7.4.5. Commonly Used Stock Solution For Fertigation Scheduling*

Nutrients	N: P_2O_5: K_2O	N%	P%	K%	Quantity of fertilizer (kg/ 100 lit water)
NPK	1:1:1	3.3	3.3	3.3	Urea 7.2, PA 5.3, KCl 5.4
	1:1:1	4.4	4.6	4.9	Urea 9.6, MKP 8.8, KCl 3.0
	1:2:4	2.2	4.8	8.9	Urea 4.8, PA 7.7, KCl 14.6
	3:1:1	6.9	2.3	4.3	Urea 15.0, PA 3.7, KCl 7.0

Contd.

	3:1:3	6.4	2.1	6.4	Urea 13.9, PA 4.0, KCl 8.2
	1:2:1	2.5	5.0	2.5	Urea 5.4, PA 8.1, KCl 4.1
NK	1:0:1	4.6	0	4.6	Urea 10.0, KCl 7.5
	1:0:2	1.9	0	3.9	Ammonium sulphate 9.0, KCl 6.4
	2:0:1	5.8	0	2.9	Urea 12.6, KCl 4.8
PK	0:1:1	0	5.8	5.8	PA 9.4, KCl 9.5
	0:1:2	0	3.9	8.0	MPK 7.5, KCl 8.9

Abbrev., PA= Phosphoric acid, MKP= Monopotassium phosphate, KCl = potassium chloride
*Adopted from Technical Bulletin on Fertigation, NCPAH, Ministry of Agril., Govt. Of India, New Delhi

5.7.4.6. Drip Fertigation Schedule For Some Important Vegetable Crops

Crop	Crop development		Injection rate ($kg\ ha^{-1}\ day^{-1}$)		Total nutrients ($kg\ ha^{-1}$)[a]	
	Stage	Weeks	N	K	N	K
Cucumber(10 wks)	1	1	1.1	0.9	130	110
	2	2	1.7	1.4		
	3	6	2.2	1.8		
	4	1	1.7	1.4		
Eggplant(13 wks)	1	2	1.1	0.9		
	2	2	1.7	1.4	130	110
	3	6	2.2	1.8		
	4	3	1.1	1.4		
Capsicum(14 wks)	1	2	1.1	0.9	180	150
	2	3	1.7	1.4		
	3	7	2.2	1.8		
	4	1	1.7	1.4		
	5	1	1.1	0.9		
Tomato(14 wks)	1	2	1.1	0.9	180	150
	2	3	1.7	1.4		
	3	7	2.2	1.8		
	4	1	1.7	1.4		
	5	1	1.1	0.9		
Watermelon(13 wks)	1	4	1.1	0.9	130	110
	2	2	1.7	1.4		
	3	2	2.2	1.8		
	4	3	1.7	1.4		
	5	2	1.1	0.9		

[a]20% of N and K have been applied as starter. All required quantity of P applied as basal.
Source: Adopted from Hochmuth 1992

Contd.

5.7.4.7. Suggested N and K Fertigation Scheduling For Tomato and Capsicum (kg/ha)

N and K fertigation scheduling for tomato (kg/ha)						
Days after planting	Daily N	Weekly N	Seasonal N	Daily K_2O	Weekly K_2O	Seasonal K_2O
Pre-plant	57.0	114.0				
0-21	0.6	4.0	70	1.1	8.0	138
22-49	0.8	5.6	92	1.6	11.2	183
50-70	1.1	8.0	116	2.3	16.0	231
71-91	1.3	8.8	143	2.5	17.6	283
92-112	1.1	8.0	167	2.3	16.0	331
N and K fertigation scheduling for Capsicum (kg/ha)						
Pre-plant		57.0			114.0	
0-21	1.1	8.0	81	1.1	8.0	138
22-42	1.4	9.6	110	2.7	19.2	231
43-56	2.1	14.4	138	4.1	28.7	288
57-84	2.5	17.6	209	5.0	35.1	428
85-98	2.7	19.2	247	5.5	38.3	505

Source: Adopted from Rosen *et al*, (2004).

5.7.4.8. Acceptable Concentration of Different Nutrients

Nutrient	Acceptable limit of concentration (ppm)	Average acceptable concentration (ppm)
Nitrogen	150-1000	250
Phosphate	50-100	80
Potassium	100-400	300
Calcium	100-500	200
Magnesium	50-100	75
Sulphur	200-1000	400
Copper	0.1-0.5	0.5
Boron	0.5-5.0	1.0
Iron	2.0-10	5.0
Manganese	0.5-5.0	2.0
Molybdenum	0.01-0.05	0.02
Zinc	0.5-1.0	0.5
Sodium	20.0-100	50
Corbonates	20-100	60
Sulphate	200-300	250
Chloride	50-100	70

Source: Rajput and Patel (2002).

5.7.4.9. Sufficiency Concentration Range of Plant Leaf Petiole Fresh Sap NO_3-N and Potassium for Important Vegetable Crops

Vegetables	Growth stage	Petiole sap (mg l^{-1})		Whole leaf dry wt. (g kg^{-1})	
		N	K	N	K
Cucumber	First blossom	800-1000	-	40-50	20-30
	Fruit 8 cm long	600-800	-	25-50	20-30
	First harvest	400-600	-	25-35	15-25
Eggplant	First fruit (5 cm long)	1200-1600	4500-5000	45-55	45-60
	First harvest	1000-1200	4000-4500	45-50	35-50
	Mid harvest	800-1000	3500-4000	35-45	30-40
Muskmelon	First blossom	1000-1200	-	45-50	50-60
	First fruit (5 cm long)	800-1000	-	40-50	45-50
	First harvest	700-800	-	35-45	20-40
Capsicum	First flower bud	1400-1600	3200-3500	45-50	50-60
	First open flowers	1400-1600	3000-3200	40-45	45-50
	Fruit half grown	1200-1400	3000-3200	40-45	40-50
	First harvest	800-1000	2400-3000	35-40	35-45
	Second harvest	500-800	2000-2400	25-30	30-40
Tomato (field)	First buds	1000-1200	3500-4000	30-50	40-50
	First open flowers	600-800	3500-4000	35-40	35-40
	Fruit 2 cm dia.	400-600	3000-3500	35-40	35-40
	Fruit 5 cm dia.	400-600	3000-3500	30-40	30-40
	First harvest	300-400	2500-3000	25-35	25-35
	Second harvest	200-400	2000-2500	20-30	20-30
Tomato (greenhouse)	Transplant to 2nd cluster	1000-1200	4500-5000	40-60	40-50
	2nd cluster to 5th cluster	800-1000	4000-5000	40-50	35-40
	Harvest	700-900	3500-4000	35-40	25-35

Source: Hochmuth (1994).

5.7.4.10. Salt Index of Some Fertilizers Used in Fertigation

Fertilizer	Salt index
Ammonium sulfate (21 % N)	53.7
Ammonium nitrate (35 % N)	49.3
Muriate of potash (50 % K)	31.9
Urea (46 %)	26.7
Sulphate of potash (45 % K)	14.1
Anhydrous Ammonia (82 % N)	9.4
Di-ammonium Phosphate (21 % N, 27 % P)	7.5
Mono-Ammonium Phosphate (12 % N, 27 % P)	6.7
Super Phosphate (9 %)	6.4

5.7.4.11. The Compatibility of Commonly Used Fertilizers in Fertigation

	Urea	Ammo. nitrate	Ammo. sulphate	Calcium nitrate	Potassium nitrate	Potassium chloride	Potassium sulphate	Ammo. phosphate	Fe, Zn, Cu, Mn sulphate	Fe, Zn, Cu, Mn chelate	Mag. sulp-hate	Phos-phoric acid	Sulp-huric acid	Nitric acid
Urea	√													
Amm. Nitrate	√	√												
Ammo. Sulphate	√	√	√											
Calcium Nitrate	√	√	x	√										
Potassium Nitrate	√	√	√	√	√									
Potassium Chloride	√	√	√	√	√	√								
Potassium Sulphate	√	√	R	x	√	R	√							
Ammo. Phosphate	√	√	√	x	√	√	√	√						
Fe, Zn, Cu, Mn Sulphate	√	√	√	x	√	√	R	x	√					
Fe, Zn, Cu, Mn Chelate	√	√	√	R	√	√	√	R	√	√				
Mag. Sulphate	√	√	√	x	√	√	R	x	√	√	√			
Phosphoric Acid	√	√	√	x	√	√	√	√	√	R	√	√		
Sulphuric Acid	√	√	√	x	√	√	R	√	√	√	√	√	√	
Nitric Acid		√	√	√	√	√	√	√	√	x	√	√	√	√

“ = compatible x = incompatibleR = reduced compatibility

5.8. Mechanization for Vegetable Production

Farm mechanization often been criticized for displacement of employment opportunities in a labour abundant economy. However, changing scenario of Indian economy and labour flow dynamics, role of machines in farm sector has changed. This will not only affect the farm power availability scenario but compulsions of employing machines to complete farm operations well within time in absence of labour force will be added advantages to it. Potential of mechanization on improving productivity and profitability of farming sector can be well realized by careful analysis of the existing level of farm mechanization in the country, farm power availably and future perspective of improving the farm mechanization level.

5.8.1. Constraints for Using Mechanization in India

Major constraints in adoption of improved farm equipment are;

- Small land holding
- High initial cost of the equipment.
- Inadequate loan facilities.
- Low annual use of the equipment.
- Non-availability of spare parts at rural level.
- Inadequate repair and maintenance facilities in rural areas.

5.8.2. Inputs Utilization and Economics of Vegetable Crops Cultivation

Physical quantities of inputs used in the cultivation of brinjal, tomato, potato, garlic, cauliflower, onion and cabbage are given in Table 5.8.3. Highest human labour utilization (277-man days/ha) has been found in garlic cultivation followed by tomato (271-man days/ha), onion (200-man days/ha), cauliflower (168-man days /ha), cabbage (157-man days/ha), brinjal (138-man days/ha) and potato (77-man days/ha).

5.8.3. Willingness to Invest on Machinery and Implements by Vegetable Growers

Vegetable crops	Average Vegetable farm (ha)	Annual return from vegetable crops (Rs.)	Gross return of household (Rs.)	Willingness to invest on machinery/ Implements (Rs.)
Potato	3.01	2,17,443	4,41,245	32,000 – 84,000
Onion	0.55	26, 318	2,86,327	21,000-73,000
Garlic	1.78	5,02,601	7,57,654	54,000-1,35,000
Brinjal	0.48	26,558	1,43,245	9,000- 37,000
Tomato	0.76	66,575	3,03,565	13,000- 47,000
Cauliflower	1.8	1,53,820	3,47,700	21,000-52,000
Okra	0.48	38,700	1,54,400	10,000- 27,000
Cabbage	0.53	30,300	1,50,000	11,000-23,000

5.8.4. Inputs Used in Vegetable Crops Cultivation

Particulars	Brinjal	Tomato	Potato	Garlic	Cauli-flower	Onion	Cabbage	Okra
Human labour, man-days/ha	138.0	271.0	77.0	277.0	168.0	200.0	157.0	247.0
Tractor, h/ha	17.4	14.1	19.5	15.2	13.0	12.1	16.3	15.5
Electric motor, h/ha	177.5	503.0	70.8	77.0	122.0	56.4	146.0	247.0
Farmyard manure, t/ha	4.2	1.8	3.0	3.6	4.2	6.6	3.8	51.0
Seed, kg/ha	0.6	0.5	2197.0	554.0	0.6	8.4	0.7	14.4
Zaivik Khad, kg/ha	17.5	13.0	16.0	23.0	18.0	11.7	11.0	16.0
Fertilizers								
Nitrogen, kg/ha	62.5	64.0	80.0	76.4	60.0	73.3	50.0	48.0
Phosphorus, kg/ha	49.4	54.0	86.3	47.8	80.0	57.6	45.0	56.0
Potash, kg/ha	38.8	29.0	75.0	32.8	80.0	58.3	38.0	34.0
Agro-chemicals, kg/ha	2.1	3.3	1.9	2.7	4.2	1.1	2.4	5.8

Singh and Singh (2007).

5.8.5. Economics of Vegetable Crops Cultivation

Particulars	Brinjal	Tomato	Potato	Garlic	Cauliflower	Onion	Cabbage	Okra
Total cost, Rs./ha	33,000	41,274	39,475	58,503	33,509	14,772	32,238	34,737
Variable cost, Rs./ha	29,080(88.12)	38,509(93.30)	35,788(90.66)	54,437(93.05)	30,062(89.7)	11,690(79.40)	28,765(89.23)	30,971(89.15)
Fixed cost, Rs./ha	3920(11.88)	2765(6.70)	3687(9.34)	4066(6.95)	3447(10.3)	3032(20.60)	3473(10.77)	3766(10.85)
Yield, t/ha	12.5	14.7	16.8	7.8	19.6	15.9	20.4	12.3
Gross return, Rs./ha	55,350	87,598	72,240	282360	85456	47,851	57,120	80,565
Net return, Rs./ha	22,349	46,324	32, 765	223857	51947	33,079	24,882	45,828
B/C ratio	1.97	2.12	1.83	4.83	2.55	3.22	1.77	2.32

5.8.6. Seedbed Preparation Equipment's for Cultivation of Vegetable Crops

Sl.No.	Name of equipment	Size, mm (Approx.)	Working capacity, ha/h	Suitability
A. Animal operated				
1	M. B.Plough	150	0.024	For all regions
2	Disc arrow (4 to 8 disc)	600-1200	0.18-0.24	For light soils
3	Culitvator (3 tynes)	700-1000	0.08	For light soils
4	Bakhar	500	0.06	For heavy soils
5	Patela Harrow	1500-2000	0.2-0.25	For planking in all regions
B. Power tiller operated				
1.	Rotavator	500-600	0.07-0.09	For all regions
C. Tractor operated				
1.	M. B. Plough	2-3 x (350-360)	0.20-0.25	For all regions
2.	Disc Plough	2-3x (500-660)	0.25-0.30	For all regions
3.	Disc arrow (14-16 disc)	2000	0.40-0.50	For all region
4.	Cultivator (9-11 tyne)	2300	0.40-0.50	Light soils
5	Rotavator	1500-2100	0.25-0.30	All regions
6.	Sweep Cultivator	5 x (340-500)	0.30-0.35	Heavy soils
7.	Laser guided Land Leveler	2000	0.15-0.20	For all region to precisely level the field.

*M.B. Plough: Mould Board Plough.

5.8.7. Improved Sowing and Planting Equipment used for Cultivation of Vegetable Crops

Sl.No.	Name of equipment	Size, mm (Approx.)	Working capacity, ha/h	Suitability
A. Manually operated				
	Galric planter	1 x 600	0.075	For light soils
B. Animal Drawn Equipment				
1.	CIAE inclined plate planter	3 x 450	0.120	For medium size seeds
2.	Potato planter	2 x450	0.175	Light soil
B. Power tiller operated				
1.	Seed cum fertilizer drill	5 x 225-300	0.16-0.21	For all regions
C. Tractor operated				
1.	CIAE pneumatic planter	6 x 450	0.40-0.50	For all types of seed
2.	Potato planter	2 x 600	0.25	Suitable for all regions
3.	Vegetable transplanter	2000	0.15-0.20	For transplanting of vegetable seedlings

5.8.8. Improved Inter-culture and Spraying Equipments for Vegetable Cultivation

Sl.No.	Name of Implement	Size, mm (Approx.)	Working capacity, ha/h
A. Manually operated			
	Grubber	150-200	0.012
	Dry land peg weeder	150-200	0.025
	CIAE twin wheel hoe	150-200	0.025
	PAU wheel hoe	150-200	0.030
	Hand compression sprayer	16 litres	0.10
	Lever operated knapsack sprayer	13-16 litres	0.10
	Foot sprayer	-	0.150
	Duster	4-5 kg	0.20-0.25
	Controlled droplet sprayer	1 litres	0.20-0.25
B. Animal drawn equipment			
1.	Dora	300	0.10
2.	Three tyne sweep	600	0.20
3.	Bullock operated sprayer	2050	0.35
C. Power tiller operated			
1.	Three tyne cultivator	1000	0.20
D. Tractor operated			
1.	9-11 tyne tiller	2100	0.40
2.	5 tyne sweep	2250	0.45
3.	Tractor operated aero blast sprayer	2500	1.50
E. Self-propelled/power operated equipment			
1.	CIAE/TNAU weeder	500	0.120
2.	Knap sack sprayer cum duster	5 lit	0.22
3.	Mist blower	0.37 kW	0.15-0.20
4.	Power sprayer with Triplex pump	3.7-7.5 kW	0.40

5.8.9. Harvesting Equipment's for Vegetable Cultivation

Sl.No.	Name of Implement	Size, mm (Approx.)	Working capacity, ha/h
A. Manually operated			
	CIAE serrated sickle	-	0.008
B. Animal Drawn Equipment			
1.	CIAE groundnut cum potato digger	500	0.10
C. Tractor operated			
1.	Onion Harvester	2100	0.35-0.40
2.	Potato digger	2000	0.35-0.40

5.9. Resource Conservation Technologies

5.9.1. Concept

Cultivation is defined by the Oxford English dictionary as 'the tilling of land', 'the raising of a crop by tillage' or 'to loosen or break up soil'. Other terms used in this dictionary include 'improvement or increase in (soil) fertility'. All these definitions indicate that cultivation is synonymous with tillage or ploughing. The word 'sustainable' defined in the Oxford English dictionary as 'capable of being borne or endured, upheld, defended, maintainable'. Something that is sustained is 'kept up without intermission or flagging, maintained over a long period'. This is an important concept in today's agriculture, since the human race will not want to compromise the ability of its future offspring to produce their food needs by damaging the natural resources used to feed the population today.

Changes in the farmers' behaviour may be due to prices, weather, government policy and programmes, exports, international events, and other factors. In any case, price changes are a major source of risk that exists in agricultural production. New technology provides a constant source of information on new agricultural techniques, new seeds variety, new biological or chemicals agents for weed control, etc. Farmers must learn to continually rethink their decisions as environmental and economic condition change. Conservation agriculture is an alternative to traditional land use and management. It is a practical method to reduce soil erosion, restore organic matter and conserve soil moisture and soil fertility (Conservation agriculture web page). Therefore, *Conservation agriculture (CA) is defined as minimal soil disturbance (no-till) and permanent soil cover (mulch) combined with rotations (FAO CA, 1999), is a recent agricultural management system that is gaining popularity in many parts of the world.* The method is based on the following:

- Maintaining a permanent or semi-permanent organic soil cover to protect the soil physically from sun, rain and wind and to feed soil biota,
- No-Tillage (or Minimum Tillage): The idea is based on the elimination of mechanical tillage in order not to disturb soil micro-organisms and soil fauna activities.
- Crop Rotation: A varied crop rotation is also important to avoid disease and pest problems.

5.9.2. Irrigation Method and Efficiency

Methods of irrigation	Conveyance efficiency	Application efficiency	Overall efficiency
Surface	40-50 (Canal) 60-70 (well)	60-70	30-35
Sprinkler	100	70-80	50-60
Drip	100	90	80-90

Source: Raina, 2002.

5.9.3. Extent of Water Saving and Increase in Yield with Drip Irrigation System

Crops	Water saving (%)	Increase in yield (%)
Tomato	42	60
Watermelon	66	19
Cucumber	56	45
Chili	68	28
Cauliflower	68	70
Okra	37	33

Source: Singh & Singh, 2012, IIVR Technical bulletin No. 48

5.9.4. Effect of Irrigation and Mulching on Yield of Vegetables

Treatments	Tomato yield (t/ha)	Brinjal yield (t/ha)	Ridge gourd yield (t/ha)	Cucumber yield (t/ha)
Irrigation and Mulch				
Drip irrigation with mulch at IW:CPE=1	42.2	35.7	15.3	27.9
Drip irrigation without mulch at IW:CPE=1	32.7	26.7	12.4	22.5
Drip irrigation with mulch at IW:CPE=0.7	33.1	26.2	11.0	20.0
Drip irrigation without mulch at IW:CPE=0.7	26.4	24.1	9.2	16.2
Surface irrigation	31.1	26.1	11.9	21.0
C.D. at 5%	2.9	2.3	1.4	2.8

5.10. Contract Farming

5.10.1. Concept

Literarily contracts mean an agreement between two or more parties, especially one that is written and enforceable by law. Contracts are means by which people seek, identify and negotiate opportunities from exchange. In regards to agriculture, it is defined by various workers in many ways. Contract farming can be defined as an agreement between farmers and processing and/or marketing firms for the production and supply of agricultural products with conditions arranged in advance (Eaton and Shepherd, 2001). A contract is a legally binding or informal agreement concerning a bargain, which is essentially commercial in its nature and involves sale or hire of a commodity. Da Silva (2005) defines contract farming as an intermediate mode of coordination whereby the conditions of exchange are specifically set among transacting partners by some form of legally enforceable binding agreement. Specifications can include production technology, price discovery, risk sharing and other product and transaction attributes. Contractual agreements are shaped by a number of factors, which includes property rights relations, labour process and organizational form (Bellemare, 2009).

Contract farming has also been defined *as a system for the production and supply of agricultural and horticultural produce by farmers/primary producers under advance contracts, the essence of such arrangements being a commitment to provide an agricultural commodity of a type (quality/variety), at a specified time, price, and in specified quantity to a known buyer*. In fact, contract farming can be described as a halfway house between independent farm production and corporate/captive farming and can be a case of a step towards complete vertical integration or disintegration depending on the given context. Due to the efficiency (co-ordination and quality control in a vertical system) and equity (smallholder inclusion) benefits of this hybrid system, it has been promoted aggressively in the developing world by various agencies. It basically involves four things - pre-agreed price, quality, quantity or acreage (minimum/ maximum) and time. It is generally undertaken when there is market failure expressed in perishability of produce, quality of produce and technicalities of producing a new/ different product. On the other hand, "*Contract farming is the practice adopted by most retail chains in India which refers to just having registered farmers without any commitment to buy or sell or a pre-agreed price or quantity specified.*

5.10.2. Importance

Under the present circumstances contract farming is the only answer to bridge the gap between the farmers and consumers through quality and economic production as well as help to the different sectors of government, private and farmer farming himself due to the following reasons;

- To reduce the load on the central & state level procurement system.
- To increase private sector investment in agriculture.
- To bring about a market focus in terms of crop selection by Indian farmers.
- To generate a steady source of income at the individual farmer level.
- To promote processing & value addition.
- To generate gainful employment in rural communities, particularly for landless agricultural labour.
- To flatten as far as possible, any seasonality associated with such employment.
- To reduce migration from rural to urban areas.
- To promote rural self-reliance in general by pooling locally available resources & expertise to meet new challenges.

5.10.3. Steps Used

The managers must coordinate production activities and the delivery of products by farmers to the processing or marketing facilities. Stress is placed on the need to carry out all activities in a transparent and participatory fashion so that the farmers fully understand their obligations and those of management. For this to be achieved, the maintenance of harmonious relations between management and contracted farmers is essential.

5.10.4. Importance and Beneficial Effects of Conservation Tillage

Farm level	Community level	National level
Savings labour, power and time through reduced cultivation and weeding requirements	Reduced soil loss and improved water flow and recharge of water table	Reduced soil erosion and improved land quality
Reduced investment in farm implements due to prolonged life and reduced inventory	Improved water quality due to reduced sedimentation and movement of pollutants	Improved carbon balance through reduced carbon emission , lower fuel and energy consumption, and increased carbon sequestration
Reduced erosion and improved soil health	Increased awareness and protection of natural resources	Improved protection of biodiversity at microflora and fauna levels
More stable and higher yields	Reduced costs of maintenance of communal infrastructure, e. g. ruralroads, watershed protection measures	Improved hydrological cycles at river basin/ continental level
Reduced cost of production and improved farm income	Improved sustainability of production systems, food security and quality of life for rural communities	Recognition of role of farming communities inproviding environmental services for the society
Reduced drudgery and more available time for social needs		

5.10.5. Conservation Technologies Addressing Sustainable Farming Issues Compared to Conventional Techniques

Issues	Conventional agriculture	Conservation Farming
Nutrient deficiency	Corrected with inorganic fertilizers	Relies on integrated nutrient management through biological regeneration, plus targeted use of or ganic orinorganic fertilizers. Where appropriate, includes integration of livestock production for nutrient recycling.
Water deficiency	Corrected with irrigation	Emphasises on management of soil organic matter (use of cover crops and mulch) for efficient capture of rainfall,soil moisture conservation and targeted irrigation.
Erosion control	Corrected with physical barriers	Minimises erosion through reduced or no-till practices along with retention of cover crops/residue in arable agriculture and vegetation management in non-crop situations.
Soil structure deficiencies and compaction	Corrected with intensivet illage, which further decreases biological oxidation and soil carbon	Restores soil using cover crops, residue management,crop rotation, and minimum/zero tillage.
Pest management	Use of calendar or need based spraying of crop protection chemicals	Manages insect, weed, diseases and other pests using IPM approaches, which are economic, environmentally safe, and socially acceptable.
Environmental degradation	Corrective measures involve variations in intensive tillage and associated management practices, which provide limited protection against soil erosion and secondary damage through silting and contamination of surface and groundwater from leaching and run-off of applied chemicals.	Reduces soil erosion, water run-off from farms and emission of green houseg ases.
Loss of biodiversity and wildlife habitat	Caused by intensive soil cultivation, planting of similar biotypes over large areas, applied inputs during crop growth. Hig her productivity through intensification can slow spreadof agriculture to fragile and marginal areas.	Additional cover provided by crop mulch encourages micro-fauna and flora diversity and other wild lifes pecies. Sustainable increases in productivityfrom existing areas avoid spread of agriculture to marginal areas.

Source: UN. 2002. Report of the World Summit on Sustainable Development, Johannesburg, South Africa, 26 August - 5 September, 2002.United Nations, New York, USA

A number of specific organizational and administrative activities have to be carried out before production commences. The key issues that managers must address in advance are:

- Identifying suitable production areas.
- Selecting farmers.
- Forming working groups.
- Providing material inputs.
- Providing logistical support.
- Purchasing the product.

5.10.6. Models Used

Contract Farming(CF) is known by different variants like centralised model which is company farmer arrangement, outgrower scheme which is run by government/public sector/joint venture, nucleus-outgrower scheme involving both captive farming and CF by the contracting agency, multi-partite arrangement involving many types of agencies, intermediary model where middlemen are involved between the company and the farmer, and satellite farming referring to any of the above models. There are a few popular models of contract farming that are accepted globally and these are;

- Centralized model
- Nucleus Estate model
- Bi-partite CF model
- Multipartite model
- Informal model
- Intermediary model

5.10.7. Status and Experiences of Contract Farming in India

Some recently studies of the Contract Farming across crops, companies, and locations in Punjab confirms that the income through the contract farming is higher in compare to traditional farming. The studies in the states of Punjab and Haryana reveal that contract growers faced many problems like undue quality cut on produce by firms, delayed deliveries at the factory, delayed payments, low price and pest attack on the crop.

In CF, both companies and growers try to improve their own positions, as a negotiation, which change over time. Further, contract design is a complex matrix, there is always a problem of incomplete contracts due to bounded rationality of the contracting parties.

5.10.7.1. Punjab

The success storey of Green Revolution, once again may be repeated by the Punjab farmers, a ray of new hopes for the second Green Revolution through the contract farming. The success of operation flood is witness of cooperative farming. The case by case study shows that there is no doubt about its success. Punjab has witnessed a second Green Revolution through crop diversification from traditional crops like wheat and paddy to tomato and other vegetables with the help of contract farming practiced since 1989 by two processing firms, *viz.,* Hindustan Lever Limited (HLL) and Nijjer Agro Foods Ltd (NAL).

5.10.7.2. Karnataka Organisations Involved in Contract Farming of Fruits and Vegetables in Karnataka

Name of the organisations	Crop(s)	Service(s) rendered
IQF Foods Ltd., Bangalore	Fruits & vegetables	Exporters
Global green, Bangalore	Fruits, vegetables (gherkins)	Contract farming
Ken Agritech Pvt. Ltd., Hubli / Bangalore	Gherkins	Consultant & Facilitator for contract farming
SPA agro, Bangalore	Fruits & Vegetables	Facilitators for contract farming
Clean Foods Corporation Limited (Sun-Sip), Bangalore	Mango, tomato	Contracting farming for export & domestic
North Karnataka Onion Growers Co-operative Society, Hubli	Onion	Exporters
Indradhanu Farms, Belgum (Asoga)	Potato	Contract farming for Pepsi Foods Ltd.
NDDB	Fruits & vegetables	Procurement through multiple centres in Karnataka -comes into effect from 2002
APEDA, Bangalore	Fruits & vegetables	Facilitators for exports
State Land Use Board, Bangalore	-	Facilitators & drafting legislation for contract farming
KLE Socity's School of Agriculture, Belgaum	-	Facilitators for contract farming

5.10.7.3. Tamil Nadu

Appachi Cotton Company (ACC), the ginning and trading house from Pollachi (Coimbatore district of Tamil Nadu, India). It encouraged farmers in the Nachipalayam village in Kinathukadavu block of Coimbatore to sow cotton seeds in their fields..

5.10.7.4. Odisha

Odisha has also shown positive response to contract farming. Various MNCs are interested in investestment through contract farming. Organic cotton contract farming in Gujarat, Odisha and Madhya Pradesh in a big way.

5.10.7.5. Kerala

The small size of holdings is a key factor in unproductive harvests. About 2,400 small farmers of Thrissur in Kerala have demonstrated the virtues of cooperative farming. The Adat Farmers Cooperative Bank (AFCB) is supporting their experiment in cooperative organic paddy cultivation.

5.10.7.6. Andhra Pradesh

In Andhra Pradesh, about Rs 964 lakh has been invested to pilot contract farming on 200 acres of land in Kuppam, the then Chief Minister Chandra Babu Naidu's constituency. The place has become a laboratory of technological options at the cost of the farmers' interests.The Kuppam Pilot Project was primarily undertaken by the Government of Andhra Pradesh through its Rural Development Department to promote and demonstrate Corporate Agriculture as part of its new strategy for agricultural development in the State. The State cabinet approved the demonstration project with Israeli Technology offered by M/s.BHC (India) Pvt. Ltd. in September 1995.

5.10.7.7. Uttar Pradesh

In Meerut district, encouraged by success of Punjab, Rajasthan and Andhra Pradesh, Meerut farmers adopted the same pattern in conjugation with PepsiCo, specifically in potato production.

5.10.7.8. Maharashtra

Despite the hurdle of private agencies not buying back 100 per cent of the stock produced, thousands of farmers have still benefited from contract farming in cotton.Contract farming has, to a large extent, improved the productivity and quality of cotton bringing a better price for farmers of Deoli and Selu Talukas in Wardha district where it was taken up as an experiment for last two years. Looking at the 19% increase in yield and 37% increase in net profit of over 2,000 farmers in the district, two agencies involved in contract farming in cotton in Vidarbha.

5.10.8. Advantages and Disadvantages

By the above discussions, it is clearly beneficial for all the parties involved in contract *viz*; farmers, industries as well as government.

Farmer's benefits

The prime advantage of a contractual agreement for farmers is that the sponsor will normally undertake to purchase all produce grown, within specified quality and quantity parameters. Contracts can also provide farmers with access to a wide range of managerial, technical and extension services that otherwise may be unobtainable. Farmers can use the contract agreement as collateral to arrange credit with a commercial bank in order to fund inputs. Thus, the main potential advantages for farmers are:

- Provision of inputs and production services.
- Access to credit.
- Introduction of appropriate technology.
- Skill transfer.
- Guaranteed and fixed pricing structures.
- Access to reliable markets.

Problems Faced by the Farmers

For farmers, the potential problems associated with contract farming include;

- Increased risk.
- Unsuitable technology and crop incompatibility.
- Manipulation of quotas and quality specifications.
- Corruption.
- Domination by monopolies.
- Indebtedness and over reliance on advances.

Sponsor's Benefits

Companies and government agencies have a number of options to obtain raw materials for their processing and marketing activities.The benefits of contract farming are best examined in the light of the other alternatives, namely spot market purchases and large-scale estates. The main potential advantages for sponsors can be seen as:

- Political acceptability.
- Overcoming land constraints.
- Production reliability and shared risk.
- Quality consistency.
- Promotion of farm inputs.

Problems faced by sponsors

The main disadvantages faced by contract farming developers are;

- Land availability constraints.
- Social and cultural constraints.
- Farmer discontent.
- Extra-contractual marketing.
- Input diversion.

Government's benefit

- Use of waste land, by which land revenue may be generated.
- Taxes deposited by the processing industries.
- Decrease the pressure on government to purchase their produce.
- Relax by the farmers' subsidy.

5.11. Use of Vegetable Grafted Plants

5.11.1. Concept and History

Grafting is the process whereby the top of one plant (the scion) is attached via a graft union to the root system of another plant (the rootstock). The most common objective of grafting is to overcome some limitation of either the scion or the rootstock. For example, the root systems of many crops are susceptible to attack by a range of persistent soil-borne diseases (*Fusarium, Verticillium, Ralstonia*) or pests such as nematodes. If resistance to these pest problems can be identified in other cultivars or even in closely related species it may possible to make crosses that introduce this resistance into the pest sensitive crop. However, this crossing process may take years and there are no guarantees of success. A more rapid approach to accessing this pest resistance may be to simply use the pest resistant material as a rootstock. *A scion from a high quality, high yielding but disease/pest sensitive cultivars is then grafted onto the resistant rootstock – effectively capturing the strengths of both the high quality scion and the pest tolerant root stock in a single plant.*

Grafting traces back to antiquity with fruit and nut crops in ancient Chinese literature (1560 BC) discussed in the agricultural writing of Aristotle (384-322 BC) and

Theophrastus (371-287BC) .Pear grafting was discussed in "*Qi Min Yao Shu*" (*Si-xie Jia*, 386-543). Opo squash grafting was first described by *Sheng-zhi Fan* (100 BC). Later detailed by *Si-xie Jia* (286-543): sow 10 seeds in a circle, bundle growing vines and sealed them with soil, when stems fused, select only one vine to grow, resulting in large guards. Similar method described by Hong (1643-1715) in Korea.The real grafting of vegetables was done by a watermelon farmer in Japan (1927) to overcome Fusarium wilt disease. This technique quickly spread in Japan and then Korea from late 1920s to early 1930s. It then has been practiced for many years in east Asia to overcome issues associated with intensive cultivation on limited arable land.

Vegetable grafting was introduced to Europe and other countries in the late 20th century. Later, grafting was introduced to North America from Europe and it is now attracting growing interest, both from greenhouse growers and organic producers.

In India, grafting work has been started in Indian Institute of Horticulture Research (IIHR) Bangalore. At IIHR, the work was on identification of rootstocks for waterlogged conditions. For this purpose, IIHR has imported semi-automated grafting machine. The NBPGR regional station, Thrissur, Kerala have done work on cucurbit grafting by taking *Momordica cochinchinensis*, a dioecious plant.The female plants were grafted on to the male plants to increase its production. Graft success was 98%. CSKHPKV, Palampur initiated work on grafting and identified more than 22 rootstocks of brinjal, chilli, tomato and cucurbits for importing resistance to bacterial wilt and nematodes. Indian Institute of Vegetable Research (IIVR), Varanasi has also been taken lead in identification of brinjal root stock(IC-111056) for grafting of tomato as scion for cultivation of tomato under excess moisture condition under National Innovations of Climate Resilient Agriculture (NICRA) project. Some private players are also involved in grafting. One of them is 'VNR Seed Private Limited' in Chhattisgarh which is supplying grafted brinjal seedlings resistant to bacterial wilt to farmers. The other seed company is 'TAKII SEED INDIA PRIVATE LIMITED'.

5.11.2. Advantages: These are;

- Tolerance to soil-borne diseases.
- Tolerance to abiotic stresses.
- Effect on fruit quality.
- Plant vigour promotion.
- High yield.

5.11.3. Disadvantages: These are;

- Cost labour, if manually, cost, for a Robot if automatically, cost for root stock: not cheap.
- Grafting incompatibility.
- Fruit quality could be down: It depends on the combination of rootstock/scion varieties.

5.11.4. Suitable Rootstock for Grafting in Vegetable Crops

Scion	Root stock
Cucumber	*Cucurbita moschata ,Cucurbita ficifolia,Cucurbita maxima* and *Sicyos angulatus*
Melons (for open field)	Cucurbita sp., *C. moschata x C. maxima,Cucumis melo*
Bitter gourd	*Cucurbita moschata, Lagenaria siceraria* and *Luffa aegyptica*
Melons (for green house)	*Cucumis melo, Benincasa hispida, Cucurbita spp, C. moschata x C. Maxima*
Watermelon	*Citrus lanatus, Cucurbita maxima, C. moschata* and *Lagenaria siceraria*

5.11.5. Tips for Grafting

Following precautions should be taken while using grafting in vegetable crops

- The stem diameters of the rootstock and scion must be similar for successful grafting.
- Seeds for root stocks are sown 5 to 6 days before sowing seeds for scions.
- The growth rate of both scion and rootstock seedlings varies from season to season and variety to variety. Growers must adjust their sowing times according to their own specific conditions.
- Commercial potting mixes are recommended. Their quality, consistency, and freedom from plant pathogens allow for the development of uniform and healthy seedlings. If commercial mixes are not available, prepare a light weight, well-drained, pasteurized soil mix. One example is the AVRDC standard mix consisting of field soil, well-decomposed compost, rice husk, and river sand in a 2:3:1:1 ratio. If compost is not available, add 30 g of nitrogen (e.g., 65 g of urea (46% N) per 100 liters of soil mix for pepper seedlings, or 50 g of nitrogen for chili seedlings). If a field soil mix is used, cover seeds with fine compost to prevent crusting.
- Grow root stock seedlings in individual pots, 5 cm high x 6 cm in diameter. Sow two seeds per pot and thin to one seedling.
- Raise scion seedlings in individual pots or in open flats. If using open flats, space seeds at least 4 cm apart to prevent seedlings from becoming tall and spindly.
- Seedlings may be grafted after developing 2 to 3 true leaves. The stem diameter of scions and root stocks should be 1.6-1.8 mm at this point.
- This stage of development typically requires 35 to 40 days in case sweet peper.
- To maximize the efficiency of the technique, a perfect co-ordination of the vegetative cycles must be achieved before the conjunction of the two plants.
- Expose seedlings to full sun and some water stress before grafting to keep the plants short and increase tolerance to water stress.
- During grafting, timing of the operations needs to be strictly controlled. Make grafts early or late in the day to avoid water loss.

- Appropriate sanitation measures have to be adopted (use of pest free high quality seeds)
- Always match scions and rootstocks of equal stem diameter. Cut them at exactly the same angle. Graft in a location that is protected from direct sunlight and away from greenhouse heater discharge.
- Make sure the cut surfaces make good contact when the plants are clipped together so that they have the best chance of successfully connecting to each other.
- Use physical barriers against virus vectors and specific pesticides against insects and fungi.
- During the entire process, the environmental conditions (temperature, humidity, composition of the substrate, sun radiation, ventilation) should be to be optimized and controlled.

6

Production Management in Vegetable Crops

6.1. Organic Farming

6.1.1. Vegetable Crops Suitable for Organic Cultivation

Name of vegetables	Botanical name
Potato	*Solanum tuberosum* L.
Tomato	*Solanum lycopersium* L.
Brinjal	*Solanum melongena* L.
Water-melon (Matira)	*Citrullus lanatus*
Musk-melon	*Cucumis melo*
Cowpea	*Vigna ungiculata*
Peas	*Pisum sativum*
Cluster bean or guar	*Cyamopsis tetragonoloba*
Chilli	*Capsicum annum* L.
Garlic	*Allium cepa* L.
Radish	*Raphanus sativus* L.
Bottle gourd	*Lagenaria siceraria*
Coriander	*Coriandrum sativum*
Methi (Fenugreek)	*Trigonella foenue-graecum*

6.2. Nutrient Content of Organic Manures

Organic manures	% N	% P_2O_5	% K_2O
Cattle dung	0.40	0.20	0.17
Pig dung	0.55	0.50	0.40
Poultry manure	3.03	0.63	1.40
Farm yard manure	0.60	0.20	0.50
Rural compost	0.75	0.20	0.50
Urban compost	1.75	1.00	1.50
Vermicompost	3.00	1.00	1.50
Sesbania aculeata	3.97	0.37	4.80
Coir dust	0.20	0.18	0.96
Cow and bullocks urine	1.00	Trace	1.35
Sheep & goat droppings	3.00	1.00	2.00
Human faeces	1.35	0.75	0.50
Dry cow dung	1.23	0.50	0.73

6.3. Average Nutrient Content of Animal Based Concentrated Organic Manures

Concentrated organic manures	Nutrient content (%)		
Blood meal	N	P_2O_5	K_2O
Meat meal	10 - 12	1 - 2	1.0
Fish meal	10.5	2.5	0.5
Horn and Hoof meal	4 - 10	3 - 9	0.3 - 1.5
Raw bone meal	13	-	-
Steamed bone meal	3 - 4	20 - 25	-

6.4. Nutrient Composition in FYM

Total N	...	0.6 (%)	Zn	20.0 ppm
P_2O_5	...	0.3 (%)	Cu	4.0 ppm
K_2O	...	0.7 (%)	B	4.0 ppm
MgO	...	0.04 (%)	Mo	0.3 ppm
CaO	...	0.20 (%)	Fe	180.0 ppm
pH	...	8.0	Mn	45.0 ppm

6.5. C:N ratios in Various Organic Materials

Organic material	C:N ratio
Soil microorganisms	8:1
Soil organic matter	10:1
Sewage sludge	9:1
Alfalfa residues	16:1
Farm yard manure	20:1
Corn stover	60:1
Corn residues at physiological maturity stage	67:1
Rice straw at physiological maturity stage	69:1
Grain straw	80:1
Oak litter	200:1
Barley straw at physiological maturity stage	99:1
Pine litter	300:1
Crude oil	400:1
Conifer wood	625:1
Ryegrass at vegetative stage	30:1
Pea straw at physiological maturity stage	21:1
Cowpea (green pod stage)	13.9:1
Sunnhemp	20.2:1
Pigeon pea	25.9:1

6.6. Standard for Quality Compost

Parameter	Range
Moisture content	15-25 % W/ W
Total Organic Carbon	16-20% (Minimum)
Total Nitrogen	0.8% (Minimum)
C : N ratio	< 20 : 1
Phosphorus	0.5 – 0.8 % P_2O_5
Potassium	1-2% K_2O
pH	6.5 – 7.5

6.7. Nutritional Composition of Vermicompost and Conventional Compost

Nutrient element	Vermicompost	P-enriched vermicompost	Conventional compost
Ash (%)	52.0	52.5	38.5
Water-soluble carbon (%)	0.88	0.88	1.60
Total organic carbon (%)	26.5	26.5	28.0
Nitrogen (%)	1.9	1.95	1.0
C/N ratio	13.6	13.6	20.6
Phosphorus (P_2O_5) (%)	2.0	4.0	1.0
Potassium (K_2O) (%)	0.8	0.86	0.6
Zinc (ppm)	100	100	80
Copper (ppm)	48	46	40
Iron (ppm)	9458	9960	7756
Manganese (ppm)	500	540	260

6.8. Physical and Chemical Characteristics of Flyash

Properties	Values
Bulk Density (g /cm)	<1.0
pH	6.0 - 10.0
Electrical conductivity (dS/m)	0.15 - 0.45
Water Holding Capacity (%)	35-40
Porosity (%)	50-60
CaO (%)	0.2-8.0
K_2O (%)	0.04-0.9
MgO (%)	0.01-0.5
P (%)	0.004-0.8 0
K (%)	0.19-3.0
S (%)	0.1-1.50
Fe (%)	36-1333
Zn (ppm)	14-1000
Cu (ppm)	1-26
Mn (ppm)	100-3000
B (ppm)	46-618

6.9. Characteristics of Natural Plant Residue and Crops

Residue Nutrient Content	Rice straw	Maize straw	Lentil straw	Subabul leaves	Karanj leaves	Water hycinth
C%	47.70	52.8	48.0	48.6	46.0	42.7
N%	0.54	0.64	1.64	3.24	2.53	2.39
P%	0.11	0.14	0.12	0.24	1.10	0.12
K%	1.68	0.94	1.68	2.54	1.06	2.89
Ca%	0.80	0.80	4.0	4.4	4.0	2.40
Mg%	0.09	0.13	0.47	0.15	1.42	0.45
S%	0.09	0.13	0.47	0.15	1.42	0.45
Zn mg kg^{-1}	119	123	148	133	139	130
C/N ratio	88	85	29	15	18	18
C/P ratio	434	377	100	203	460	356

6.10. Nutrient Content of Green Leaf Manure Crops

Plant	Nutrient content (%) on air dry basis		
	N	P	K
Gliricidia	2.76	0.28	4.60
Pongania	3.31	0.44	2.39
Neem	2.83	0.28	0.35
Gulmohur	2.76	0.46	0.50
Peltophorum	2.63	0.37	0.50
Su-babul	3.50	0.26	1.78
Parthenium	2.68	0.68	1.45
Water hyacinth	3.01	0.90	0.15
Trianthema	2.64	0.43	1.30
Ipomoea	2.01	0.33	0.40
Calotrophis	2.06	0.54	0.31
Cassia	1.60	0.24	1.20
Sesbania aculeatea	*3.2*	*0.7*	*1.3*
Crotalaria juncea	2.6	0.6	2.0
Sesbania speciosa	2.7	0.5	2.2
Tephrosia purpurea	2.4	0.3	0.8
Phaseolus trilobus	2.1	0.5	-
Green leaf Manure			
Pongamia glabra	3.2	0.3	1.3
Glyricidia maculeata	2.9	0.5	2.8
Azadirachta indica	2.8	0.3	0.4
Calatropis gigantea	2.1	0.7	3.6

6.11. Quality and Recovery of NADEP Compost Produced from Vegetable Wastes

Vegetable residues	C:N ratio	Nutrient content (%)			Dry matter content (%)	Recovery of VC (%)
		N	P	K		
Brinjal	36.14	0.69	0.32	0.67	72.51	65.32
Cucurbits	32.52	0.61	0.24	0.54	74.31	64.27
Cowpea	25.42	1.11	0.46	0.72	76.12	66.40
Crucifers	34.21	0.71	0.31	0.74	68.23	61.12

6.12. Quality and Recovery of Vermicompost Produced from Vegetables Wastes

Vegetable residues	C:N ratio	Nutrient content (%)			Dry matter content (%)	Recovery of VC (%)
		N	P	K		
Waste of Solanaceae (brinjal, tomato) + Leguminosae (Garden pea, French bean, Indian bean) in 1:1 ratio	25.17	1.72	0.74	1.32	46.45	46.24
Waste of Cruciferae (Cabbage, cauliflower) + Leguminosae in 1:1 ratio	26.20	1.73	0.75	1.34	45.62	42.54
Waste of Cucurbitaceae (bottle gourd, pumpkin, spong gourd, bitter gourd) + Leguminosae in 1:1 ratio	27.32	1.62	0.69	1.31	45.12	45.86
Leguminosae + cow dung only	22.14	1.74	0.81	1.36	38.27	48.56
Cow dungs only	26.84	1.54	0.76	1.20	40.23	51.20

6.13. Liquid Manures

6.13.1. Panchagavya

Ingredients for making panchagavya

Fresh cow dung	5 kg
Cow's urine	3 liters
Cow's Milk	2 liters
Cow's Curd	2 kg
Cow's ghee	1/2 kg
Sugarcane juice or Jaggery	3 liters OR500 g with 3 litre water
Tender Coconut water	3 liters
Banana (ripe)	12 No.
Toddy Or grape juice Or yeast powder + Jaggery	2 liters 100 g – 100 g In 2 L of warm water

6.13.2 Jivamrut (Soil rejuvenator)

Ingredients for making Jivamrut

Fresh cow dung	10 kg
Cow's urine	10 liters
Sugarcane juice Or Jaggery	4 liters Or2 kg
Virgin Soil	1 kg
Pulse flour	2 kg
Water	200 liters
Container	Plastic/ earthen/ cement

6.13.3. Copper and Manganese Content in Jeevamruta

Days after preparation (DAP)	Content in ppm	
	Copper	Manganese
7	51.00	46.0
10	35.70	26.10
13	25.20	15.10
16	16.00	13.60

6.14. Ingredients Used for Making Beejamrut

Fresh cow dung	5 kg
Cow's urine	5 litres
Lime	50 g

6.15. Micro- nutrients Contents of Beejamruta and Jeevamruta

Micro-nutrients	Content in ppm	
	Beejamruta (Fresh)	Jeeva mruta (7 days old)
Zinc	18	12
Copper	36	51
Manganese	16	46
Iron	168	318

6.16. Ingredients Used for Making Amritpani

Fresh cow dung	10 kg
Cow ghee	250 g
Honey	500 g

6.17. Microbial Load in Different Organic Liquid Manures

Organisms	Colony count (cfu/ml)			
	Panchgavya	Jeevamruta	Beejamruta	Biodigester
Bacteria (X10^5)	26.1	20.4	15.4	12.9
Fungi (X10^3)	18.0	13.8	10.5	9.2
Actinomycetes	4.2	3.6	6.8	3.0
P-solublizer(X10^2)	5.7	4.0	2.7	1.0
Free living N_2 fixer(X 10^2)	2.7	5.0	3.1	2.1

6.18. Nutrient Status in Different Organic Liquid Manures

Parameters	Panchagavya	Jeevamruta	Beejamruta	Bio- digester
pH	6.82	7.07	8.20	7.29
Soluble salts	1.88dsm^2	3.40dsm^2	5.5dsm^{-2}	1.09dsm^{-1}
Total Nitrogen	1000ppm	770ppm	40.ppm	255ppm
Total hosphorus	174.4	166.0ppm	155.3ppm	79ppm
Total potassium	194.1ppm	126.0ppm	252.0ppm	79ppm
Total Zinc	0.38ppm	4.29ppm	2.96ppm	0.52ppm
Total copper	29.71ppm	1.58ppm	0.52ppm	1.24ppm
Total iron	29.71ppm	282ppm	15.35ppm	9.60ppm
Totalmanganese	1.84ppm	10.7ppm	3.32ppm	8.30ppm

6.19. Intercrop Combination Effective in Organic Vegetable Pest Management

Crop combination	Target pest
Cabbage + Carrot	Diamond back moth
Broccoli + Faba bean	Flea beetle
Okra + Cowpea	Yellow vein mosaic
Cabbage + French bean	Root fly
Cabbage + Tomato	Diamond back moth

6.20. Role of Micro Nutrients in Vegetable Production

6.20.1. Born

6.20.1.1. Importance

Warington first demonstrated the essentiality of boron in plants in 1923 in broad bean (*Vigna fava* L.). Boron markedly affects nitrogen uptake and the metabolism of nitrogen compounds. The protein contents of young leaves decrease and soluble nitrogen compounds, particularly nitrate accumulate under the condition of severe boron deficiency. The increased nitrate content may be the results of intensified nitrate uptake and/or decreased activity of nitrate reductase. Sen *et al.* (1993), have reported that the nitrate reductase activity in the leaves of rape plants increased with increasing nitrogen level in soil and the enhancement caused by nitrogen was more with boron than without boron added. Both with and without boron added, nitrate reductase activity was obviously higher with Ca $(NO_3)_2$ than with $(NH_4)_2SO_4$. With boron added, nitrate reductase activity in leaves increased from the basal to the top parts of the plant.

6.20.1.2. Status of Available Boron in Indian Soils

Name of the state	Soil group	Samples analysed	Available soil B(mg/ Kg)	% Soil deficient
Assam	Acid soil	320	0.05-0.72	43
Bihar	Calcareous soil	1201	0.06-8.00	48
Madhya Pradesh	Red & yellow	544	0.5	49
Meghalaya	Alfisols	20	0.10-0.50	50
Orissa	Red & Laterite	882	0.10-2.20	69
Punjab	Ustochrept	116	0.30-2.00	43
Uttar Pradesh	Saline-Alkali	45	0.20-4.10	23
West Bengal	Red & Laterite	2544	0.02-3.30	64
	Terai-Tista alluvial	633	0.05-0.76	84

6.20.1.3. Deficiency Symptoms

Boron deficiency occurs on vegetable crops with high boron requirements when grown on acidic soils where native boron has been leached, on acid organic soils, on alkaline soils with free lime and on sandy soils with a low organic matter contents. Hollow stems of cruciferous crops like cabbage, cauliflower and broccoli are found to result due to inadequate boron. Brown heart of turnip appears first in irregularly shaped water soaked areas. Black heart or canker of beat root occurs in internal and external necrotic areas in the root. In celery, cracked stem appears as cross splitting of vascular bundles in the fleshy petiole resulting from a decrease in collenchyma cell wall thickness and in the number of cellulose lamellae. In tomato, the disorders appears as open locules in the fruit, internal browning, stem resetting when the boron levels in fruit are about 6 ppm and when the leaf boron is about 15 ppm on a dry weight basis. Boron deficiency occurs in most of the vegetable crop if the level is less than 30 ppm on dry weight basis. "Brown heart", "Heart rot" or "Hollow centre" occurs in the roots of radish, turnip and beet root due to deficiency of boron. In Chinese cabbage, the deficiency symptoms appear on fifth to tenth leaves from the outside of the plant when the head begins to form. The inner parts of the midribs became cracked and corky. The vegetables show variations for their boron requirements. Beet chard, globe artichoke and asparagus are quite tolerant to high boron. Pea, lima bean, sweet potato, onion, carrot, pepper, potato, cabbage, radish, celery, lettuce and tomato are semi-tolerant to high boron. Jerusalem artichoke, cowpea and French bean are sensitive to high boron levels

6.20.1.4. Causes of Deficiency

Boron deficiency particularly prevalent in light-textured, highly leached acid soils, calcarious soils, high clay soils, soils with low organic matter. Adoption of high yielding cultivars, intensive cropping with increased use of high analysis B-free fertilizers, drought condition also favours deficiency of Boron.

6.20.2. Sources of Boron Fertilizer

Name	Chemical formula	Boron content (%)
Borax	$Na_2B407 .10H_2O$	11
Sodium tetraborate (FertilizerBorate-48, Agribol)	$Na_2B407.5H_2O$	14-15
Fertilizer Borate-68	Na_2B407	21
Boric acid	H_3BO_3	17
Solubor	$Na_2B_4O7.5H_2O$ + Na2 B10O16.$10H_2O$	20-21
Colemanite (Portabor)	$Ca_2B6O11.\ 5H_2O$	10-16
Boron frits Complex borosilicates		2-6

6.20.3. Molybdenum

6.20.3.1. Importance

Molybdenum (Mo) is one of the six 'minor' chemical elements required by green plants. The other five are iron, copper, zinc, manganese and boron. Arnon and Stout (1939) first demonstrated its essential role in the tomato plant. It is essential for the utilisation of nitrate and boron. It reduces nitrate to ammonium and helps in the formation of amino acid. Also it helps in the fixation of nitrogen. According to Spencer and Wood (1954) in tomato, there has been a marked increase in the level of nitrate two days after molybdenum treatment in deficient conditions. However, the concentration of nitrate, ammonia, amides, amino acid and protein has increased. At high levels of molybdenum in the soil, the nitrate reduction activity is high. Molybdenum helps in the absorption of iron and other cations. Molybdenum in acid soils tends to be unavailable to plants. This is why most molybdenum deficiencies occur on acid, rather than on neutral or alkaline soils. A few cases of molybdenum deficiency have been reported on soils with a pH above 6.0, but most occur where pH is 5.5 or less. (Note: On the pH scale 7.0 is neutral. Less than 7 indicates acidity, and above 7.0 alkalinity. A normal plant should have 3mg/kg dry weight of molybdenum.

Molybdenum deficiencies occur in vegetable crops when grown on very acidic soils, or, when molybdenum is unavailable, or on soils where molybdenum is fixed by secondary soil minerals, or, on very well drained alkaline soils. Molybdenum deficiency symptoms in vegetable crops are given in 6.20.3.2

6.20.3.2. Deficiency Symptoms

Crop	Symptoms
French bean	Leaves are pale green and mottled interveinally with rapidly developing brown scorched areas in interveinal tissues. Green bands remain close to midribs and veins even after death of affected tissue.
Beetroot	Red veins are more conspicuous against chlorotic background.

Cabbage	Older leaves become mottled, bleached, scorched and coupled with irregular margins and head formation is poor.
Cauliflower	'Whiptail' develops; leaves are twisted and elongated with laminae showing various degrees of narrowness and irregularity. Laminae are often corrugated irregularly, cupped, relatively thick, turgid and abnormally dark green or blue green. Flower curds are irregular with 'ricey' and leafy formation in slightly affected plants.
Tomato	Leaves become pale with diffused marginal and interveinal yellow mottling. Margins curl upward and leaflets appear rolled. A pale brown scorching being at the tip of the apical leaflet of the oldest leaf. In severe cases, the plants die.
Turnip	Leaves show cupping, whiptail, chlorosis, mottling and marginal burn.
Beetroot	Leaves die in crown, which may be covered with small, deformed leaves; older leaves wilt and become necrotic. Roots show heart rot and dry rot.
Cabbage	Leaves are distorted, brittle stiff, thick mottled along margins and wilted. Leaves making up head are unattached; petioles having swellings, which later become corky.
Carrot	Leaves show marginal yellowing followed by red extending inward. Roots have wide deep splits.
Onion	Leaves are of deep blue colour, later the youngest leaves become conspicuously mottled, yellow and green, with distorted shrunken areas.
Pea	Leaves develop yellow or white veins, followed by small changes in interveinal areas. Growing points die and blossom shed.
Chillies	Leaf veins show decomposition and granulation, older leaves turn yellow at tips.
Radish	Terminal growing tip dies and leaves are discoloured and distorted. Roots show internal darkening.

6.20.4. Manganese

6.20.4.1. Importance

Manganese (Mn) is the eleventh abundant element forming the Earth's crust. In terms of abundance, manganese-containing compounds are after iron (Fe) in the earth's crust. Total amount of manganese in soil is between 20 to 3000 ppm and 600 ppm on average. Divalent manganese is absorbed by clay minerals and organic material, and in terms of nutrition plant, divalent manganese ions ($Mn^{2}+$) is most important. In soil manganese occurs as exchangeable manganese, manganese oxide, organic manganese and component of Ferro-manganese silicate minerals, the manganese ion ($Mn^{2}+$) is similar in size to magnesium ($Mg^{2}+$) and ferrous iron ($Fe^{2}+$) and can substitute for these elements in silicate minerals and iron oxides. Manganese reactions in soils are quite complex. The amount of available manganese is influenced by soil pH, organic matter, moisture, and soil aeration.

6.20.4.2. Deficiency Symptoms in Vegetable Crops

Crop	Symptoms
Bean	Young leaves first exhibit chlorosis followed by necrosis. Later the leaves turn yellow and drop and plants die.
Beet root	Leaves are chlorotic between veins, with erect growth. Margin is curled towards upper surface. Red purple tinting appears.
Cabbage	Leaves are smaller and yellower than normal and marked by yellowing mottling between veins.
Pea	Stem may appear normal or leaves show a slight interveinal chlorosis, flat surfaces of seeds have a brown spot or cavity in the centre.
Tomato	Shoot growth varies from normal to severe stunting. Leaves near shoot tips are small, rolled forward and some hot chlorotic. Most of the variety show small dark brown spots along veins or distributed sporadically on younger leaves.

6.20.4.3. Sources of Manganese

Sources of manganese fertilizer	Chemical formula	Mn%
Manganese sulfate	$MnSO_4.3H2O$	26-28
Manganese oxide	MnO	41-68
Manganese carbonate	$MnCO_3$	31
Manganese kalat	Mn-EDTA	12
Manganese chloride	$MnCl_2$	17
Manganese dioxide	MnO_2	63

6.20.5. Zinc

6.20.5.1. Importance

The Zinc (Zn) plays very important role in plant metabolism by influencing the activities of hydrogenase and carbonic anhydrase, stabilization of ribosomal fractions and synthesis of cytochrome. Plant enzymes activated by Zn are involved in carbohydrate metabolism, maintenance of the integrity of cellular membranes, protein synthesis, and regulation of auxin synthesis and pollen formation. The regulation and maintenance of the gene expression required for the tolerance of environmental stresses in plants are Zn dependent. Its deficiency results in the development of abnormalities in plants which become visible as deficiency symptoms such as stunted growth, chlorosis and smaller leaves, spikelet sterility. Micronutrient Zn deficiency can also adversely affect the quality of harvested products; plants susceptibility to injury by high light or temperature intensity and to infection by fungal diseases can also increase. Zinc may be involved in the biosynthesis of the plant auxin indole-3 acetic acid (IAA). Skoog (1940) observed a marked decrease in auxin content of zinc deficient tomato plants and a significant increase in the IAA content when zinc was added to the deficient plants. It appears that deficiency symptom could be associated with the decrease in the plant auxin concentration. It is also reported that zinc reduces auxin content through its involvement in the synthesis of tryptophan, a precursor of auxin. Nason (1956), found that zinc deficient *Neurospora* showed low tryptophan synthatase activity. This enzyme catalyses the reaction of the serine with indole to form tryptophan. Zinc acts as an activator of several enzymes, alcoholic dehydrogenase, pyridine nucleotide deydrogenase and carbonic anhydrase. Carbonic anhydrase is the first zinc containing enzyme found in some marine plants and animals. It may also act as an activator for some phosphate-transferring enzyme, such as hexokinase or triose phosphate dehydranase. It has been found that zinc deficiency leads to accumulation of soluble nitrogen compounds such as amino acids and amides. It can thus, be assumed that zinc must play an important role in protein synthesis. Zinc deficient tomato plants may have greatly increased polyphenol oxidase and peroxidase activities, and these changes might contribute to the accumulation of tannins that is observed in Zn deficient tissues.

6.20.5.2. Deficiency

Deficiency of zinc occurs under varied soil conditions. Deficiency symptoms in vegetable crops are mostly species related. In general, zinc deficiency results in shortened internodes and chlorotic areas in older leaves or may appear in younger plants also. Shortened internodes may be due to non-availibility of indoleacetic acid, since zinc is essential for the synthesis of tryptophane, a precursor of Indole acetic acid. Normal healthy leaves contain 20 ppm zinc. When zinc is deficient, young leaves turn yellow, then white and brown. Tomato leaves become smaller, chlorosis appears and the whole plant is dwarfed with small leaves curling inward. Onion leaves turn yellow. In Bakers garlic whole plants turn yellow and develop a rosette form with poor growth. Zinc deficiency may be controlled by soil or foliar application of soluble or chealated zinc compounds. Spraying of zinc salt and zinc EDTA were effective in alleviating yellowing on Bakers garlic. Beans and lima beans are quite susceptible to zinc deficiency. Potatoes, tomatoes and onion are somewhat sensitive to zinc deficiency and peas, asparagus and carrot are insensitive to zinc deficiency. Many researchers reported the plants are able to dissolve in the soil solution under the conditions.

6.21. Foliar Sampling Techniques for Determining the Nutrient Status for Vegetable Crops

Crop	Symptoms
Asparagus	Fern needles-take tops 12 inches of ferns in September and after drying, strip needles from stem and discards the stem.
Beans (*Phaseolus sp.*)	Leaf blades-select upper most mature leaf blades without petioles when 10 per cent of the plants are in bloom 50 to 100 leaves should be taken for sampling.
Beans (Lima beans and soybeans)	Petioles-take petioles from second lateral leaf blades from top of the plant at 10 per cent bloom.
Beetroot	Leaf blades without petioles-take from intermediate rings.
Cabbage	Take midrib of wrapper leaf-take samples at time when cabbage is beginning to form head.

Contd.

Carrot	Leaves with petioles-take mature leaf and petioles (cut off carrot crown at time root begins to enlarge).
Cauliflower	Midribs of outside leaves-take samples at time of curd are beginning to form.
Celery	Petioles-take petioles of youngest fully elongated leaf at mid-growth period when the plant is 10-15" tall.
Lettuce	Leaf midrib-taken from wrapper leaf at heading time.
Peas	Leaf blades or leaf petioles-take leaf blade or a leaf petiole from third node down from the top of plant when it has reduced eight or nine stages.
Potato	Leaves with petioles-select fourth or fifth leaf and petiole from primary stalk at early bloom stage counting down from the growing tip.
Tomato	Leaf blades without petioles- select petioles of 4th leaf from growing tip at early bloom stage. Lucaus and Wittwer (1963) used the dried petioles of leaves subtending flower truss, while Kagayama *et al.* (1961) utilised the petioles of third to fifth mature leaves for analysis of the nitrate content of the tomato plants.

6.22. Foliar Application of Micro-nutrients

Name of nutrients	Chemical used for spray	Quantity (kg/ha)
Boron	Sodium borate (Borax)	4.5
Zinc	Zinc sulphate	0.50
Manganese	Manganese sulphate	6.8
Molybdenum	Sodium molybdate	0.2-0.3
Iron	Ferrous sulphate	0.50
Copper	Copper sulphate	0.50

6.23. Use of Plant Growth Regulators

6.23.1. Concept and History

Plant hormone: "A plant hormone is an organic compound synthesized in one part of a plant and translocated to another part where in every low concentrations it causes a physiological response". To distinguish it from animal hormone, it was termed as phytohormone.

Plant growth regulator: "Plant growth regulators are defined as organic compound other than the nutrients which in small amount promotes/inhibits or otherwise modify any physiological response in plants".

During the mid 1800s the famous German Plant Physiologist Julius Van Sachs suggested that plant form is attained through the action of specific 'organ-farming' substances, such as "leaf forming" substances, "root forming" substances and "flower forming" substances. Early efforts to isolate and identify such substances were unsuccessful and Sachs views were not strongly supported by other botanist at this time. The botanist groups were thinking that plant form resulted from the maintenance of specific levels of organic constituents, such as carbohydrates, soluble nitrogen, protein or other substances. Support for this view came from studies on the chemical composition of plants at different stages of development when grown under various levels of inorganic nutrition, light and temperature. During this period there was great interest in the isolation and identification of plant constituents. Such compounds as starch, sucrose, glucose, fructose, organic acid, amino acid, protein and nucleic acids were found in plants and methods were developed for their analysis. Later work indicates that the two points of view are not mutually exclusive. Instead of specific organ-forming substances, as suggested by Sachs, plant contain substances that trigger or initiate biochemical process, which is turn, ultimately lead to organ formation or to other aspects of growth. Several distinctly different groups of components are recognized as triggering substances (The triggering substances, referred to as phytohormones, initiate biochemical reactions and changes in chemical composition with the plants); auxins, gibberellins, cytokinins and phenolics. There are five classes of phytohormones namely auxins, gibberellins, cytokinins, abscisic acid and ethylene. The details about these hormones are described below.

6.23.2. Auxin: The term auxin (Greek *auxein*, to increase) was first used by Frits Went, who as a graduate student in Holland in 1926, discovered that some unidentified compound probably caused curvature of oat coleoptiles toward light. Auxin occurs in two forms **(i) Free auxin:** These are diffusible auxin, which move out of the tissue quite redily (e.g. auxin diffusing out of coleoptile tips into agar). They are readily extractable in various solvents like diethyl ether at 0° to 5 °C. **(ii) bound Auxins:** These auxins are released from plant tissues only after they are subjected to hydrolysis, autolysis or enzymolysis. Bound auxins include reserve or storage forms and detoxification forms. Detoxification products are not active *per se*. The chemical nature of auxins are an unsaturated ring, a carboxylic (-COOH) group, at least one carbon atom between the ring and carboxlic group, the molecule should posses a negative and positive charge and the distance between the charges should be 5.5A°. The physiological effects of auxin are cell elongations, secondary growth, rooting of cutting, apical dominance, parthanocarpy, fruit size, abscission, organogenesis, crowngall, as herbicides and fruit ripeness. The pathway of auxin particularly IAA synthesis involves the amino acid and tryptophan. Two mechanisms for synthesis are involved, both of which involve removal of the amino acid group and the terminal carboxyl group from the side chain of tryptophan. Several intermediates are recognized between tryptophan and IAA-indolepyruvic acid, tryptoamine and indoleacetaldehyde. Tryptophan itself is synthesised from phosphoenolypyruvate (PEP) and erythrose-4-phosphate. The pathway also provides intermediates in the synthesis of a wide range of phenolic compounds. Indole is an intermediate and IAA can be formed directly by a reaction between the amino acid serine and indole. The pathway from indole to tryptophan involves several intermediates. The enzymes necessary for the conversion of tryptophan to IAA are most active in young tissues, such as shoot meristems, growing leaves and fruits. In these the auxin contents are also highest, suggesting that IAA is synthesized there.

6.23.3 Gibberellins: Gibberellins were first discovered by Plant Physiologist in Japan in the 1930s from studies with diseased rice plants that grew excessively tall. As early as the 1890s, the Japanese called this the "bakanae" (foolish seedling) disease. It is caused by the fungus *Gibberella fujikuroi* (the asexual or imperfect stage is *Fusarium* *moniliformae*). As of 1990, 84 gibberellins have been discovered in various fungi and plants. Seeds of the cucurbit *Sechium edule* contain at least 20 gibberellins and seeds of the common bean (*Phaseolus vulgaris*) contain at least 16, but most species may contain fewer. Almost all gibberellins are chemically related to a large group of naturally occurring compounds terpenoids (sterol and carotenoids are occur in plant tissues). Kaurene is the precursor of gibberllins. Gibberellins are made of basic skeleton of ent-gibberellane (20 carbons) or ent-20 non- gibberellane (C-19). The presence or absence of the lacton configuration (internal ester) differentiates them from another in the ring A and the substituents, mainly –OH (hydroxyl) groups, about the whole ring structure. The physiological responses of gibberellins are fruit thinning agent, breaking dormancy, flowering, sex expression and fruit russetting. Both gibberellins and abscisic acid are synthesized from acetate. The intermediate, isopentenyl pyrophosphate, appears to be a branch point in the biosynthesis pathways. There are some evidences that ABA can be formed from degradation products of carotenoids that are also synthesized via isopentenyl pyrophosphate. The anabolic pathway from isopentenyl pyrophosphate to ABA may predominate in actively growing tissue whereas the catabolic pathway from carotenoides may occur during aging and senescence. Isopentenyl pyrophosphate is also an intermediate in the synthesis of cytokinins. The another pathway of gibberellins may be by diterpenes synthesized from acetate units of acetyl co-enzymes A by the mevalonic acid pathway- *Geranygeranyl pyrophosphate*, a 20-carbon compound, serves as the donor for all gibberellins carbon atoms. It is converted to copalypyrophosphate, which has two ring systems, and the later is then converted to *Kaurene*. Conversion of *kaurene* further along the pathway involves oxidations occurring in the endoplasmic reticulum, producing the intermediate compounds *kaurenol* (an alcohol), *kaurenal* (an aldehyde) and *kaurenoic acid*.

6.23.4. Cytokinin: It is also known as juvenile hormone. About 1913 Gottlieb Haberlandt discovered in Australia that unknown compound present in vascular tissues of various plants stimulated cell division that caused cork-cambium formation and wound healing in cut potato tubers. This discovery was apparently the first demonstration that plants contain compounds, now called cytokinins that stimulate cytokinesis. In the 1940s Johannes Van Overbreak found that the milkey endosperm from immature coconuts are also rich in compounds that promote cytokinensis. Zeatin, zeatin riboside, isopentyl allenine and dihydrozeatin are natural cytokinin, while kinetin and benzyladenine are synthetic. The cytokinin is effective in plant development, seed germination and early seedling development, cotyledon expansion, chlorophyll synthesis, cell division and organ differentiation, control of leaf senescence and root-shoot interaction. There is less known about the synthesis of cytokinin in plants than the synthesis other growth substances. Nucleotide synthesis in bacteria is rather well understood, but similar information for plant is lacking. The cytokinin, isopentenyladenine apparently is formed by the addition of isopentenyl to adenine.

6.23.5 Ethylene: In 1910, an annual report by H.H. Cousins to the Jamaican Agricultural Department mention that oranges should not be stored with bananas on ships because some emanation from the oranges caused the banana ripen prematurely. This report was apparently the first suggestion that fruit release a gas that stimulate ripening but it was not until 1934 that R. Gane proved that ethylene is synthesized by plants and is responsible for faster ripening.

The Russian physiologist Dimitry N. Neljubow first established that ethylene affects plant growth. In 1901 he identified ethylene is illuminating gas and showed that it causes a triple response on pea seedlings i.e., inhibited stem elongation, increased stem thickening and a horizontal growth habit. Ethylene is natural compound while ethrel or ethephon are synthetic. The physiological effects of ethylene are induction of female flowers, male sterility, stimulation of germination and growth inhibition. The synthesis of ethylene in plants has been of interest for years. Because of its simple structure, it might imagine that ethylene could be formed from metabolic intermediate in ethylene synthesis. The conversion of S. adenosyl methionine (SAM) to ACC is mediated by ACC.

6.23.6. Growth Retardant: These are synthetic organic compounds consisting of carbon and hydrogen, which counteract the effect of gibberellin biosynthesis. Several growth retardants are available. These include tetcyclasis (BAS 106), triazols such as Uniconazole (S-3307; x E-1019) paclobutrazol (PP_{333} or cultar), triapenthenol (RSW 0411) and BAS 111, pyrimidines e.g. flurprimidol (EL 500) and 4-pyridines such as inabenfide (CGR-811). There are other 'old time retardants also and these include AMO-1618, CCC, Phosphon-D, C-111, B-Nine and Maleic hydrazide.

6.23.7. Growth Inhibitors: These are both natural and synthetic organic compounds, which counteract the effect of auxin biosynthesis. The natural inhibitors are caffeic, ferullic, juglone, abscisic acid etc. Benzyle adenine is a synthetic growth inhibitor. In 1963 abscisic acid was first identified and chemically characterized in California by Federick T. Addicott and his coworkers, who were studying compounds responsible for abscission of cotton fruits. The physiological responses of growth inhibitors are stomatal closure and water relation, photosynthesis, root growth, elongation of coleoptile, bud and seed dormancy and abscission. There are two alternative metabolic routes of ABA biosynthesis. One pathway involves mevalonic acid, which is precursor of all terpenoids in plants. In this pathway, 15-carbon ABA is formed from mevalonic acid and 15-carbon ABA precursor farnesyl pyrophosphate. In the indirect pathway, ABA is formed from the cleavage of 40-carbon carotenoid. The indirect pathway involves a neutral growth inhibitor with physiological properties similar to ABA. Xanthoxin is converted to ABA when it is supplied to shoot. Xanthoxin is break down product of carotenoids such as violaxanthine. A major cause of inactivated of free ABA is oxidation with results in the formation of unstable intermediate 6' hydroxy methyl ABA, which is converted to phasic acid (PA) and dihydrophasic acid (DPA). Free ABA is also inactivated by conjunction, in which the hormone forms a covalent link with another molecules such as monosasaccharides. When water potential or turgor of the chloroplast falls, there is block is the conversion of FPP to genanyl-geranyl pyrophosphate and some production of farenol may occur. This could alter the nature of chloroplast membranes and as a consequence release existing ABA into the cytoplasm. Fresh biosynthesis of ABA in the chloroplast will follow because of the raised level of precursor FPP.

6.23.8. Names and Structure of Some Plant Growth Regulators Used in Vegetable Production

Abbreviation or Common Name	Chemical Name or Structure	Major uses
ABA	Abscisic acid	Defoliant
Chlormequat (CCC)	2-chloroethyl-trimethyl ammonium chloride	LP, SR
3-CPA	2-(3-chlorophenoxy) propionic acid	FT
4-CPA	4-chlorophenoxy-acetic acid	FT
2,4-D	(2,4-dichlorophenoxy)acetic acid	Herbs.
Daminozide (B9 , Alar)	Succinic acid-2, 2-demethyl hydrazine	GR
Ethephon	2-chloroethyl phosphonic acid	SR
GA_3	Gibberellic acid	GE
Kinetin	6-furfuryl aminopurine	DB
IAA	Indole-3-acetic acid	Enlarge.
IBA	Indole-3-butyric acid	Enlarge.
Maleic hydrazide	1,2-dihydro-3, 6-pyridazinedione	Herb. GR
Mepiquat chloride	N,N-dimethyl piperidinium chloride	GR
NAA	1-naphthaleneacetic acid	FT GR
NOXA BNOA	2-naphthalenyloxyacetic acid	GS
Paclobutrazol	(2RS, 3RS)-1-(4-chlorophenyl)-4, 4-dimethyl-2-(1,2,4-triazol-1-yl)-pentan-3-ol	GR
2,4,5-T	(2,4,5-trichlorophenoxy) acetic acid	Herb.
TIBA	2,3,5-triiodo-benzoic acid	GR
Uniconazol	(E)-(4-chlorophenyl)-4, 4-dimethyl-2-(1,2,4-triazol-1-yl)-1-penten-3-ol	GR Fung.

Abbreviations: DB = Dormancy Breaker; Enlarg.= Plant Cell Enlarger; FT = Fruit Thinner; Fung.= Fungicide; GR = Growth Retardant; GS = Growth Stimulant; Herb. = Herbicide; LP = Lodging Preventor; GE = Grape Enlarger; SR = Sugarcane Ripener.

6.24. Use of Plant Growth Promoting Rhizobacteria (PGPR)

6.24.1. Concept and Importance

There are some soil microorganisms plays an important role in improving soil fertility and crop productivity due to their capacity to fix atmospheric nitrogen, insoluble phosphate and decompose farm wastes resulting in the release of plant nutrient. The extents of benefit from these microorganisms depend their number and efficiency, which however, is governed by a large number of soil and environmental factors. When the number and activity of specific microorganism called microbial inoculant or biofertilizer is used to hasten biological activity to improve availability of plant nutrients. A number of products are now available that are generally referred to as soil and plant additives of non-traditional nature. These products include (i) microbial fertilizers and soil microoraganisms, (ii) microbial activators that contain special chemical formulations for increasing the numbers and activity of beneficial microorganisms in soil, (iii) soil conditions that claim to create favourable soil physical and chemical conditions which result in increased growth and yield of crops, and (iv) vermi-compost which helps in improving soil health and fertility.

Nitrogen fixing organisms can be provided to the farmers in the name of microbial inoculants otherwise termed as biofertilizers. The biofertilizers containing biological nitrogen fixing organisms are very effective in vegetable production. Biofertoilizers harper atmospheric nitrogen with the help specilized soil microorganisms. Such nitrogen fixing microorganisms are either free living in soil and symbiotic with plants and directly or indirectly contribute towards the nitrogen nutrition of the plant. There are following advantages in using biofertilizers in vegetable crops;

- They help in the establishment and growth of crop plants and trees.
- They enhance biomass production and grain yields by 10-20 per cent.
- They are useful in sustainable agriculture.
- They are suitable in organic farming.
- They play an important role in agroforestry/silvipastoral systems.

6.24.2. Types of Biofertilizers

6.24.2.1. Nitrogen Fixing

These include symbiotic (Rhizobium) as well as non-symbiotic (Azotobacter, Azospirillum) microorganisms which are capable of fixing atmospheric nitrogen into the soil. As an estimate, Rhizobia, Cyanobacteria and Azospirillium can fix atmospheric nitrogen in the range of 50-300, 15-25 and 10-30 kg/ha, respectively.

Rhizobium

The most widely used biofertilizer is Rhizobium, which colonizes the roots of specific legumes to form tumour like growths called root nodules. These nodules act as factories of ammonia production. Rhizobia have the ability to fix atmospheric nitrogen in symbiotic association with legumes and certain non-legumes like Parasponia, Rhizobia. A mature nodule consists of a central 'bacteroid zone' surrounded by several layers of cortical cells. The process of N-fixation is wholly dependent on the activity of the enzyme nitrogenase, which is located within the bacteriods. The volume and number of bacteriods have a direct positive relationship with the amount to nitrogen fixed. The Rhizobium legume association can fix upto 100-300 kg N/ha in one crop season and in certain situations can leave behind substantial nitrogen for the following crop. The range of nitrogen fixed per year by different legume vegetables is 80-85 kg for cowpea and 240-320 kg for faba bean.

Azotobacter

Azotobacter is one of most important non-symbiotic N-fixing microorganism and considered to be very important for fixation of nitrogen in non-leguminous plants. Based on morphological and physiological features the genus Azotobacter has been classified in 3 species i.e. *Azotobacter chroococcum*, *A. beijerinckii* and *A. vinelandii*. The first two species are deemed to be the most commonly occurring species in India. *Azotobacter chroococcum* appeared in acid soils while *A. beijerinckii* in neutral and alkali soils. The beneficial effects of Azotobacter biofertiliser on vegetables under both irrigated and rainfed field conditions has been substantiated and documented.

Azospirillum

Azospirillum lipoferum and *A. brasilense* are primary inhabitants of soil, the rhizosphere and intercellular spaces of root cortex of graminaceous plants. They perform the associative symbiotic relation with the graminaceous plants. The bacteria of Genus *Azospirillum* are N_2 fixing organisms isolated from the root and above ground parts of a variety of crop plants. They are Gram negative, *Vibrio* or *Spirillum* having abundant accumulation of polybetahydroxybutyrate (70 %) in cytoplasm. Five species of *Azospirillum* have been described to date *A. brasilense, A.lipoferum, A.amazonense, A.halopraeferens* and *A.irakense*. The organism proliferates under both anaerobic and aerobic conditions but it is preferentially micro-aerophilic in the presence or absence of combined nitrogen in the medium. Apart from nitrogen fixation, growth promoting substance production (IAA), disease resistance and drought tolerance are some of the additional benefits due to *Azospirillum* inoculation.

6.24.2.2 Phosphate Solubilizing (PS)

Several soil bacteria and fungi, notably species of *Pseudomonas, Bacillus, Penicillium, Aspergillusetc.* secrete organic acids and lower the pH in their vicinity to bring about dissolution of bound phosphates in soil. Increased yields of wheat and potato were demonstrated due to inoculation of peat based cultures of *Bacillus polymyxa* and *Pseudomonas striata.* Currently, phosphate solubilizers are manufactured by agricultural universities and some private enterprises and sold to farmers through governmental agencies. These appear to be no check on either the quality of the inoculants marketed in India or the establishment of the desired organisms in the rhizosphere.

The transfer of nutrients mainly phosphorus and also zinc and sulphur from the soil *milieu* to the cells of the root cortex is mediated by intracellular obligate fungal endosymbionts of the genera *Glomus, Gigaspora, Acaulospora, Sclerocysts* and *Endogone* which possess vesicles for storage of nutrients and arbuscles for funneling these nutrients into the root system.

6.24.2.3. Silicate Solubilizing(SS)

These microorganisms are capable of degrading silicates and aluminum silicates. During the metabolism of microbes several organic acids are produced and these have a dual role in silicate weathering. They supply H^+ ions to the medium and promote hydrolysis and the organic acids like citric, oxalic acid, Keto acids and hydroxy carbolic acids which from complexes with cations, promote their removal and retention in the medium in a dissolved state.

6.24.3. Spectrum of Resistance Shown by Plant Growth Promoting Rhizobacter (PGPR) Against Various Diseases of Vegetables

Bio-agent	Disease	Crop
B. sublitis	*Rhizoctonia solani*	Tomato
B. pumilus	*Colletotrichum orbiculare*	Cucumber
B. pumilus	*Fusarium oxysporum.*	Tomato
B. pumilusB. subtilis	*Colletotrichum orbiculare*	Cucumber
B. subtilis BS 107	*Erwinia carotovora* subsp. *atroseptica* and *Erwiniacarotovora* subsp. *carotovora*	Potato
B. subtilis strainLS213	Bacterial spot and lateblight of tomato Angularleaf spot of cucumber	Tomato and cucumber
B. subtilis, *B. cereus*,*P. putida.*	*Pythium* sp	Cucumber
P. putida	*Fusarium oxysporum* f.sp. *cucurbitacearum*	Cucumber
B. polymyxa and *P. fluorescens* PRS9,	*Fusarium oxysporum* f.sp. lycopersici	Tomato
Bacillus amyloliquefaciens strain 1 N 937a	Tomato mottle virus	Tomato
P.fluorescens Pf1	*Fusarium oxysporum* f.sp. *lycopersici*	Tomato
Pseudomonas fluorescens Pf1	*Pythium* sp	Tomato and hot pepper
B. pumilus SE34	*Phytophthora infestans*	Tomato
B. cereus X16	*Fusarium roseum* var.*sambucinum*	Potato
B. subtilis and *P. chlororaphis* (PA23)	Damping off	Tomato
B. subtilis BS 21; BS 22; BS 23	*Colletotrichum lindemuthianum*	Cowpea
P.putida	*Fusarium oxysporum* f.sp. *melonis*	Muskmelon
B. subtilis	*Rhizoctorua solani*	Tomato
Bacillus spp	*Xanthomonas campestris* pv. *campestris* Leila	Crucifers
B. subtilis RB 14–CS	*Rhizoctorua solani*	Tomato
B. subtilis RB 14–CS	*Rhizoctorua solani*	Tomato
B. subtilis UM AF6614; UM AF6619; UM AF6639; UM AF8561	*Podosphaera fusca*	Cucurbit
B. subtilis EU07	*Fusarium oxysporum* f.sp. radicis lycopersici	Tomato
Bacillus spp.	*Fusarium oxysporum* f.sp. *lycopersici* and *Sclerotiumrolfsii*	Tomato and cowpea
B. subtilis ZK8	*Rhizoctonia* rot	Tomato

6.24.4. PGPR Formulations on Disease Control and Productivity in Vegetables

PGPR	Crop	Formulation	Target pathogen	Disease control (% reduction over control)	Yield (% increase over control)
B. japonicum Tal 629	Radish	Bacterial cell	-	-	15(dry matter)
B. pumilus strain SE34 or *B. amyloliquefaciens* strain IN937a or *B. subtilus*strain IN937	Tomato	Bacterial cells	Cucumber mosaic virus disease	40-60	5-55
Mixture of *Serratia plymuthica* strain C-1, *Chromobacterium*sp. strain C-61 and *Lysobacterenzymogenes* strain C-3 + Chitin	Pepper	Bioformulation +chitin	*Phytophthora* blight	80-90	-
B. pumilus (T4) + *B.subtilis* (GBO3)	Cowpea	Talc based	Beancommon mosaic virus	62.1	-
Bacillus sp C2+*Streptomyces* sp. C32	Chilli	Bacterial suspension	-	-	69.9
Pseudomonas fluorescens	Tomato	Bacterial cells	*Ralstonia solanacearum*	57.9	>100

6.24.5. Some of Commercial Bio-pesticides used in Vegetables Crop

Available Biocontrol Agents in India

Tradeproduct	Bioagent	Manufacturer
Antagon Combi Antagon TV	*Trichoderma viride*	Green Teen Agro Products, Rajaji Road, Coimbatore
Trichogaurd	*Trichoderma viride*	Anu Biotech International Tigocon Road, Faridabad 121 002
Niprot	*Trichoderma viride*	Pest Control India Ltd., Biocontrol Research Laboratory, Post Box No. 3228, Bangalore - 560 032
Biomonas	*Pseudomonas fluorescence*	Biotech International, New Delhi
Tridhodex XP	*Trichoderma viride*, *Paceilomyces* sp.	Excel Industry Ltd. Bombay
Bioderma	*Trichoderma viride*	Biotech International, New Delhi

6.25. Weed Management

6.25.1. Major Weeds of Vegetable Crops

Scientific name	English name	Family
Rainy (*kharif*)/summer season		
Grasses		
Cynodondactylon Pers.	Bermuda grass	Poaceae
Brachiaria ramosa L.	Brown top millet	Poaceae
Digitaria sanguinalis (L.) Scop.	Crab grass	Poaceae
Dactylocteniumaegyptium L.	Crow foot grass	Poaceae
Dinebraretroflexa Vahl.	Viper grass	Poaceae
Chlorisbarbata Sw.	Peacock plume grass	Poaceae
Eleusine indica (L.) Gaertn.	Goose grass	Poaceae
Echinochoa colona Link.	Jungle rice	Poaceae
Eragrostis major		Poaceae
Sorghum halepense (L.) Pers.	Johnson grass	Poaceae
Setaria glauca Beauv.	Yellow fox tail	Poaceae
Setaria viridis L.	Green foxtail	Poaceae
Panicum repens L.	Tarpedo grass	Poaceae
Paspalum paspaloides	Hilo grass, Sour grass	Poaceae
Broad-leaved		
Commelina benghalensis L.	Tropical spider wort	Commelinaceae
Ageratum conyzoides L.	Bill goat weed	Compositae
Amaranthus viridis L.	Pigweed	Amaranthaceae
Amaranthus palmeri S. Wats.	Palmer amaranth	Amaranthaceae
Amaranthusretroflexus L.	Redroot pigweed	Amaranthaceae
Boerhaavia diffusa L.	Hog weed	Nyctaginaceae
Celosia argentea L.	White cock's comb	Amaranthaceae

Contd.

Cleome viscosa L.	Cleome	Capparridaceae
Digera arvensis Forsk.	False amaranth	Amaranthaceae
Portulaca oleracea L.	Common purslane	Portulacaceae
Euphorbia hirta L.	Pill pod spurge	Euphorbiaceae
Eclipta alba Hassk.	False daisy	Compositae
Corchorus acutangulus Lamk.	Jew's mallow	Tiliaceae
Trianthema portulacastrum L.	Horse purslane	Aizoaceae
Tridax procumbens L.	Coat buttons,tridax daisy	Compositae
Sedges		
Cyperus rotundus L.	Purple nut sedge	Cyperaceae
Winter (*Rabi*) season		
Grasses		
Phalaris minor Retz.	Littleseed canay grass	Poaceae
Avena ludoviciana Dur.	Wild oat	Poaceae
Polypogon monspeliensis L.	Foxtail grass	Poaceae
Cynodondactylon Pers.	Bermuda grass	Poaceae
Broad-leaved		
Asphodelus tenuifolius Cav.	Wild onion	Liliaceae
Anagallis arvensis L.	Scarlet pimpernel	Primulaceae
Chenopodium album L.	Lambs quarters	
Chenopodiaceae		
Convolvulus arvensis L.	Field bind weed	Convolvulaceae
Fumaria parviflora,	Bansoya	Fumariaceae
Melilotus indica/ M. alba	Yellow sweet clover/white sweet clover	
Leguminosae		
Rumex retroflexus L.	Golden dock	Polygonaceae
Spergula arvensis	Corn spurry	
Caryophyllaceae		
Vicia sativa	Common vetch	Leguminosae
Lathyrus aphaca L.	Wild pea	Leguminosae
Sedges		
Cyperus rotundus L.	Purple nut sedge	Cyperaceae
Parasitic		
Orobanche spp.	Broomrapes	*Orobanchaceae*

6.25.2. Critical Period of Crop-Weed Competition in Different Vegetable Crops

Name of the crop	Critical period
Cole crops	2-6 weeks after transplanting
Okra	2-4 weeks after sowing
Tomato and brinjal	2-6 weeks after transplanting
Onion	2-9 weeks after transplanting
Potato	3-6 weeks after planting
Chilli	4-6 weeks after transplanting
Cabbage	2-6 weeks after transplanting

Contd.

Radish, turnip, beet root	2-4 weeks after sowing
Carrot	2-8 weeks after sowing
Field peas	2-6 weeks after sowing
Frenchbean	2-6 weeks after sowing
Cowpea	2-4 weeks after sowing
Garlic	2-8 weeks after planting

6.25.3. Recommended Herbicides in Different Vegetable Crops

Vegetables	Herbicides	Dose (kg ai/ha)	Time of application
Chilli/Capsicum	Fluchloralin	0.50	PPI
	Oxadiazon	1.0-1.25	PE (seeded crop)
	Oxyfluorfen	0.10	PE
	Pendimethalin	0.75	PE
	Metolachlor	1.0	PE
Onion	Oxadiazon	0.50	PE (3 DAS)
	Alachlor	1.5-2.0	PE
	Butachlor	1.0	(2 DAT)
	Oxyfluorfen	0.12-0.37	PE
	Pendimethalin	0.75-1.0	PE
	Oxadiagryl	0.06-0.09	PE
	Metolachlor	0.75-1.0	
Okra	Fluchloralin	1.0-1.5	PPI
	Oxyfluorfen	0.10-0.20	PE
	Pendimethalin	1.0-1.5	PE
	Alachlor	2.0-2.5	PE
Tomato	Alachlor	1.0	PE
	Trifluralin	0.75	PPI
	Fluchloralin	1.0-1.25	PPI
	Metribuzin	0.75-1.0	PE
	Pendimethalin	1.0-1.5	PE
	Oxadiazon	1.0-1.5	PE
Brinjal	Alachlor	2.0	PE
	Pendimethalin	1.0-1.5	PE
	Oxadiazon	1.0	PE
	Fluchloralin	1.0-1.25	PPI
	Oxyfluorfen	0.125-0.250	PE
Cole crops	Alachlor	2.0-2.5	PE
	Trifluralin	0.75-1.5	PPI
	Oxyfluorfen	0.1-0.250	PE
	Pendimethalin	1.0-1.25	PE
Fenugreek	Pendimethalin	1.0	PE
	Fluchloralin	1.0	PPI
Root crops	Oxyfluorfen	0.2	PE
	Pendimethalin	1.0	PE
	Alachlor	1.0-1.5	PE
	Fluchloralin	1.0	PPI
Coriander	Pendimethalin	1.0	PE

Contd.

Beans	Fluchloralin	1.0-1.5	PPI
	Pendimethalin	1.0-1.5	PE
	Alachlor	2.0-2.5	PE
Potato	Pendimethalin	1.0-1.50	PE
	Paraquat	0.50	POE to weeds (before potato emergence)
	Oxyfluorfen	0.125-0.250	PE
	Alachlor	2.0-2.5	PE
	Metribuzin	0.50-0.75	PE
Peas	Alachlor	0.75-1.0	PE
	Fluchlorlin	1.0	PPI
	Pendimethalin	1.0-1.5	PE

DAS – Days after sowing, DAT - Days after transplanting; PE- Pre-emergence, PPI-Pre-plant soil incorporation, POE-Post-emergence

6.25.4. List of Herbicides Commonly Used in Vegetable Crops with their Common names and Company

Name of herbicide	Trade name	Company
Pendimethalin (30% EC)	Stomp, Prowl, Herbadox, Pentagon	BASF
Trifluralin (48% EC)	Treflan	Dow Agro Science
Flucholarin (45% EC)	Basalin	BASF
Alachlor (50% EC)	Lasso	Monsanto
Butachlor (50% EC)	Machete	Monsanto
Metolachor (72% EC)	Dual, Medal, Falcon	Syngenta
Oxyfluorfen (23.5% EC)	Goal, Koltar	Dow Agro Science
Metribuzin (75 % WG)	Sencor, Sencorex, Lexone	Bayer Crop Science, DuPont
Oxadiazon (25% EC)	Ronstar, Foresite	Bayer Crop Science
Oxadiargyl (80% WP)	Raft, Topstar	Bayer Crop Science
Paraquat (24% SL)	Gramaxone, Cyclone, Dextrone	Syngenta

7

Vegetable Production in Climate Change

7.1. Status

Vegetables are generally sensitive to environmental extremes, and thus high temperatures and limited soil moisture are the major causes of low yields as they greatly affect several physiological and biochemical processes like reduced photo-synthetic activity, altered metabolism and enzymatic activity, thermal injury to the tissues, reduced pollination and fruit set etc., which will be further magnified by climate change. The consequences of the climate change badly hit the vegetable production. Under changing climatic situations crop failures, shortage of yields, reduction in quality and increasing pest and disease problems are common and they render the vegetable cultivation unprofitable. This ultimately questions the availability of nutrient source in human diet. Due to climate change South Asian summer monsoon will be delayed and become less certain and that temperature increases will be most intense during the winter season. The failure of the monsoons results in water shortages, resulting in below-average crop yields.This is particularly true of major drought-prone regions such as southern and eastern Maharashtra, northern Karnataka, Andhra Pradesh, Orissa, Gujarat and Rajasthan. High temperatures and inadequate rainfall at the time of sowing and heavy rainfall at the time harvesting cause severe crop losses in Andhra Pradesh, Tamilnadu and Karnataka. According to Network Project on Climate Change (Impact, Adaptation and Vulnerability of Indian Agriculture to Climate Change), the maximum and minimum temperature (1960-2003) analysis for northwest region of India showed that the minimum temperature is increasing at annual, *kharif* and *rabi* season time scales. The rate of increase of minimum temperature during *rabi* is much higher than during *kharif*. The maximum temperature showed increasing in annual, *kharif* and *rabi* time scales but very sharp rise was observed from the year 2000 onwards and significant negative rainfall trends were observed in the Eastern parts of Madhya Pradesh, Chhattisgarh and parts of Bihar, Uttar Pradesh, parts of north west and north east India and also a small pocket in Tamil Nadu.

7.2. The Effect of Increase in Temperature on Vegetable Crops

- Potato productivity is expected to decline in all potato growing states of India. It is expected that 16% decline in tuber yield of potato by 2050 for West Bengal if any special strategies are not adapted. However, it is suggested that planting of potato crop at a new optimal date of mid November in order to minimize the yield losses up to 8%.Increase in temperature favours the potato cultivation by prolonging the crop growing season in high altitudes and temperate regions of the world like Europe, Russia and in India, Himalayan and other mountain regions and frost prone states like Haryana and Punjab. Whereas, it disfavours the potato production by shortening the growing period in subtropical plains such as West Bengal and Bihar during winter season. Potato requires long days and low temperatures for its flowering. It makes possible the hybridization or heterosis breeding of potato in high altitudes of Himachal Pradesh. Due to increase in temperature the potato breeding area is shifting towards the further more high altitudes. Potato is very strict to its temperature requirement for tuber formation. Optimum tuber formation takes place at 20°C. An increase in temperature of above 21°C cause sharp reduction in the potato tuber yield at 30°C complete inhibition of tuber formation occurs. In potato, high harvesting index (HI) of 0.8 is recorded at 15°C night temperatures of and zero at 28°C in Northern Indian (Punjab, Haryana, Uttar Pradesh, Bihar) and Northern hills. A moderate harvest index(HI) of 0.4-0.6 is recorded at 20°C night temperatures in Central Indian states like Gujarat, Chattisgarh, some parts of Maharashtra and West Bengal indicating temperature stress limiting the partitioning of photosynthates to the tubers. A low HI of 0.2 is recorded at more than 20°C night temperature in South India. Potato tubers with high starch content are favored by the processing industry. At low temperatures starch is converted into the sugar, which causes browning due to charring of sugar while chips making there by reduces their preference by the processing industry. This ultimately results in increased post-harvest losses more than the present level, which is figured as 40- 50%. This is most common problem in areas where night temperatures fell below optimum during winter season.

7.3. Predicted Impact of Climate Change on Tuber Yield Productivity in Major Potato Growing States of India Under Optimal Management Without Adaption

States	Change (%) from current productivity		States	Change (%) from current productivity	
	By 2020	By 2050		By 2020	By 2050
UttarPradesh	-1.61	9.08	MadhyaPradsh	-6.64	-20.63
West Bengal	-4.86	-16.11	Gujarat	-16.75	55.10
Bihar	-3.01	-11.50	Maharashtra	-8.82	35.29
Punjab & Haryana	+7.31	+3.66	Karnataka	-18.68	-45.73

Source: Kondinya *et al*; (2014).

- High temperature can affect tomato through their direct and indirect effects on the plants, soils, livestock and pests. An increase in atmospheric carbon dioxide level will have a fertilization effect on crops with C_3 photosynthetic pathway and thus will promote their growth and productivity. The increase in temperature, depending upon the current ambient temperature, can reduce crop duration, increase crop respiration rates, alter photosynthetic partitioning to economic products, affect the survival and distribution of pest populations, hasten nutrient mineralization in soils, decrease fertilizer-use efficiencies, and increase evapotranspiration rate. Indirectly, there may be considerable effects on land use due to snow melt, availability of irrigation water, frequency and intensity of inter- and intra-seasonal stress.

- In pepper, exposure to high temperature at post-pollination stage inhibits fruit set. High temperature affects red colour development in ripen chilli fruits and also causes flower drop, ovule abortion, poor fruit set and fruit drop. It is observed that high percentage (90%) seed germination of chilli at 20°C and complete inhibition at 10°C indicating that fall in minimum temperatures affect seed germination in chilli.
- Germination of cucumber and melon seeds is greatly suppressed at 42 and 45°C, respectively besides germination will not occur at 42°C in watermelon, summer squash, winter squash and pumpkin seeds. The temperature fluctuations delay the ripening of fruits and reduce the sweetness in melons. Low moisture content in the soil effects fruit quality and development in melons and gourds. Warm humid climate increase the vegetative growth and result in poor production of female flowers in cucurbitaceous vegetables like ash gourd, bottle gourd, pumpkin which causes low yield.
- In French bean, high temperatures will cause enhanced abscission of flower buds, flowers and young pods and reduce pod production, mature pod size and seeds per pod. Onsets of anthesis and pod development stages are most sensitive to high night temperature. Pods larger than 3 cm do not abscise but usually abort and shrivel under high night temperatures. Moisture stress in the months of April and May and intense rain during flowering and fruiting stage (Jun-July) reduces the productivity of French bean. Flower abscission and ovule abortion in French bean occurs at temperature above 35^0 C.
- In okra, high temperatures cause poor germination of seed during-spring 32^0 C summer season. Flower drop in okra is recorded at high temperatures above 42°C. High temperature causes bolting in cole crops, which is not desirable when they are grown for vegetable purposes.
- Climate change resulting in increased temperature could show impact on insect-pest populations in several complex ways. Although some climate change effects might tend to depress insect populations, the warmer temperature in temperate climate will result in more types and higher populations of insects. Climate change also influences the ecology and biology of insect-pests. Anticipated effect of climate change on some insect-pests of vegetables is presented in Table 7.4. Increased temperature, in some group of insects with short life cycles such as aphids and diamond back moth, increases fecundity, earlier completion of life cycle. Hence, these can produce more generations per year than their usual rate. Contrary to it, some insects may take several years to complete their life cycle. Temperature may change gender ratios of some pest species such as thrips potentially affecting reproduction rates. Some insect species which reside in soil for the whole or some stages of life cycle tend to suffer more than insects present above the soil surface, because soil provides an insulating medium that will tend to buffer temperature changes more than the air.

7.4. Anticipated Effect of Climate Change on Some Insect-pest of Vegetables (*Source*: Kondinya *et al*., 2014)

Pest	Present Position	Anticipated effect of climate change
Melon fly(*Bactrocera cucurbitae*)	South of Japanese archipelago	Invasion to Japanese archpelago
Sweet potato weevil (*Cylas fprmicarius)*	Tropical and subtropica refion of the world	Invasion to temperate zones due to increase in temperature
Aphids (*Aphis gossypi*; *Aulacorthum solani*	World wide distribution	Increase in number of generations per year resulted in more infestation due to lower developmental zero point, low thermal total requirement for one generation
Fruit and pod borer (*Helcoverpa armigera*: *Spodoptera litura*)	World wide distribution	Increase in number of generation per year resulted in more infestation
Colorado potato beetle (*Leptinotarsa decemileata*)	North America, South Europe, Asia and much of Pacific ocean	Expansion in its potential northern limit by 400 km causing more potential risk to 99% potato growing areas.
Diamond back moth	European origin, cosmopolitan in distribution	More frequent overwintering and increase in pest status drastically
Cabbage butterfly (*Pieris brassicae*)	Europe, North-West Africa and Asia, introduced to America and Australia	Increase in range, abundance and diversity. Decrease in diversity.
Cabbage root fly(*Delia radicum*)	Europe, North Africa, West Asia and North America	Populations become active a month earlier in UK with a mean temperature increase of 3°C

- Temperature and frost sensitivity effect the distribution of pathogen species as irrespective of their huge host range the soil borne pathogens such as *Sclerotium rolfsii* and *Macrophomina phaseolina* do not occur in temperate climates due to their high temperature optimum and frost sensitivity. Higher temperatures cause faster disease cycles in air borne pathogens and increase their survival due to reduction in frost. The earlier appearance and increase in number of insect vectors of viral diseases due to rise in temperature during winter, results in increasing viral diseases of crops like potato and sugar beet. In potatoes, diseases like late blight, early blight, black scurf, soft rot, and apical leaf curl and mosaics are more prevalent under Haryana (India) ecological conditions. During the last 10 years (2001-2010) late blight was observed most destructive disease with a mean intensity of 16.5 in the state. The incidence of black scurf was observed in an increasing order. Common scab decreased from 2.8% to 0.1%. Early blight incidence ranged from 1.6 to 25.5% and was noticed to be serious in late sown conditions because relatively high temperature (20-28°C) and high RH

(>80%) prevailed for longer duration. High severity of severe mosaic (11.0%) and leaf roll (10.8%) were coincided with high aphid population (98/10 compound leaves) in the month of February, where the ETL for aphid population in potato is 20/100 leaves. In West Bengal (India), the late blight disease intensity was found to be less than 20% in 1990-91 to 1999-2000, except in the 1994-95 seasons, but more frequent late blight epidemics have been reported throughout West Bengal in the last few years. The late blight epidemics were observed during the year 2006-07 and 2008-09. Onset of late blight is likely to be earlier in the growing season in the future decades as compared to the present decades (2011-2020).The future trend is that the disease severity is likely to reduce by 5-7% from 1981-2010 periods to 2031-40 periods in the intensive potato growing areas of West Bengal. Potato and tomato late blight fungus Phytophthora infestans infects and reproduces most successfully during periods of high moisture within the temperature range between 7.2°C and 26.8°C. Increased night time and winter temperatures are contributing to the greater prevalence of tomato diseases.Wet vegetation promotes the germination of spores and the proliferation of fungi. Based on analysis of plant/disease/climate relations, late blight onset on tomatoes 1-2 weeks earlier than normal which means 2-3 additional sprays to achieve sufficient control of late blight. Accordingly, 1-3 more sprays will be applied at the incoming decades of the 2025-2100. Reduction in frost due to increased average minimum temperatures implies the removal of a limiting factor for pathogens such as *Fusarium*.

- Climate change effects are likely to increase the incidence of *Brassica* crop disorders due to global warming in cases where negative affects result in stress, nutritional deficiencies or excesses. Therefore, growers should learn to positively identify the various physiological disorders that occur in their agro-ecological zones/areas and be able to manipulate the environment and to use locally available resources such as fertilization of *Brassica* crops with animal manure to mitigate nutritional deficiencies in order to control particular disorders. Evaluation of cultivars adaptable to the different agro-ecological zones coupled with sound horticultural practices, such as timely seedling transplanting, adequate fertilization and irrigation will go a long way towards alleviating the devastating effects of physiological disorders of Brassicas

7.5. Critical Stages of Drought Stress and its Impact on Vegetable Crops

Vegetable crops	Critical period for watering	Impact of water stress
Tomato	Early flowering, fruit set and enlargement	Flower shedding, lack of fertilization, reduced fruit size, fruit splitting, puffiness and development of calcium deficiency disorder i.e. blossom end rot(BER) , poor seed viability.
Brinjal	Flower and fruit development	Reduces yield with poor colour development in fruits, poor seed viability.

Contd.

Chilli and capsicum	Flowering and fruit set	Shedding of flowers and young fruits, reduction in dry matter production and nutrient uptake, poor seed viability.
Potato	Tuberization and tuber enlargement	Poor tuber growth and yield, splitting and internal brown spot.
Okra	Flowering and pod development	Considerable yield loss, development of fibers high infestation of mites poor seed viability.
Cauliflower, cabbage and broccoli	Head/ curd formation and enlargement	Tip burning and splitting of head in cabbage; browning and buttoning in cauliflower.
Carrot, radish and turnip	Root enlargement	Distorted , rough and poor growth of roots, strong and pungent odor in carrot, accumulation of harmful nitrates in roots
Onion	Bulb formation and enlargement	Splitting and doubling of bulb, poor storage life.
Cucumber	Flowering as well as through fruit development	Deformed and no- viable pollen grains, bitterness and deformity in fruits poor seed viability.
Melons	Flowering and evenly throughout fruit development	Poor fruit quality in muskmelon due to decrease in TSS, reucing sugar and ascorbic acid, increase nitrate content in watermelon fruit, poor seed viability.
Summer squash	Bud development and flowering	Deformed and no- viable pollen grains , misshapen fruits.
Leafy vegetables	Throughout growth and development of plants	Toughness of leaves, poor foliage growth, accumulation of nitrate.
Asparagus	Spear production and fern (foliage) developement	Reduce spear quality through reduced spear size and increased fiber content, leading to toughness, lower grade spears.
Lettuce	Consistently throughout development	Toughness of leaves, poor plant growth, tip burning.
Vegetable pea	Flowering and pod filling	Reduction in root nodulation and plant growth, poor pod filling, poor seed viability.
Lima bean	Pollination and pod development	Leaf colour takes on a slight grayish cast, blossom drop, poor seed viability.
Snap bean	Flowering and pod enlargement	Blossom drop with inadequate moisture levels and pods fail to fill poor seed viability.
Sweet corn	Silking , tasseling and ear development	Crop may tassel and shed pollen before silks on ears are ready for pollination, lack og pollination may result in missing rows of kernels reduced yields, or even eliminate ear production, poor seed viability.
Sweet potato	Root enlargement	Reduced root enlargement with poor yield, growth crack.

Source: Modified from Bahadur *et al.* (2011).

7.6. Response of Physiological Traits to Drought Conditions

Plant traits	Effects relevant for yield	Modulation under stress
Stomatal conductance/ leaf temperature	More/less rapid water consumption. Leaf temperature reflects the evaporationand hence is a function of stomatal conductance.	Stomatal tolerance increases under stress.
Photosynthetic capacity	Modulation of concentration of Calvincycle enzymes and elements of the lightreactions.	Reduction under stress.
Timing of phenological phases	Early/late flowering. Maturity and growth duration, synchrony of silk emergence and anthesis, reduced grain number.	Wheat and barley advanced flowering, rice delayed, maize ynchrony.
Anthesis-silkinginterval (ASI)	ASI is negatively associated with in maize	Drought stress at flowering causes a delay in silk emergence relative to yield in drought conditions anthesis.
Starch availability duringovary/ embryo development	A reduced starch availability leads to abortion, reduced grain number.	Inhibition of photosynthetic activity reduces starch availability.
Partitioning and stem reserve utilization	Lower/higher remobilization of reserves from stems for grain-filling, effecting kernel weight.	Compensation of reduced current leaf photosynthesis by increased remobilization.
Stay green	Delayed senescence	-
Single plant leaf area	Plant size and related productivity.	Reduced under stress (wilting, senescence, abscission)
Rooting depth	Higher/lower tapping of soil water resources	Reduced total mass but increased root/shoot ratio, growth into wet soil layers, re-growth on stress release
Cuticular tolerance and surface roughness	Higher or lower water loss, modification of boundary layer and reflectance.	-
Photosynthetic pathway	C_3/C_4/CAM, higher water use efficiency and greaterheat tolerance of C_4 and CAM	-
Osmotic adjustment	Accumulation of solutes: ions, sugars, poly-sugars, amino acids, glycinebetaine.	Slow response to water potential.
Membrane composition	Increased membrane stability and changes in aquaporine function	Regulation in response to water potential changes.
Antioxidative defense	Protection against active oxygen species.	Acclimation of defence systems.
Accumulation ofstress-related proteins	Involved in the protection of cellular structure and protein activities.	Accumulated under stress.

Contd.

Source: Kumar *et al.* (2012).

7.7. General Limit of Vegetable Crop Tolerance

	Irrigation water content	
	Na	Cl
No restriction	<115 ppm or 5 meq/liter	<100ppm or 3meg/liter
Severe restriction	>460 ppm or 20 meq/liter	<350ppm or 10 meq/liter

7.8. Excess of Water or Flooding

Most vegetables are highly sensitive to flooding and genetic variation with respect to this character is limited, particularly in tomato. In general, damage to vegetables by flooding is due to the reduction of oxygen in the root zone which inhibits aerobic processes. Flooded tomato plants accumulate endogenous ethylene that causes damage to the plants. Low oxygen levels stimulate an increased production of an ethylene precursor, 1-aminocyclopropane-1-carboxylic acid (ACC), in the roots. The rapid development of epinastic growth of leaves is a characteristic response of tomatoes to water-logged conditions and the role of ethylene accumulation has been implicated. The severity of flooding symptoms increases with rising temperatures; rapid wilting and death of tomato plants is usually observed following a short period of flooding at high temperatures.

7.9. The Need for Adaptation to Climate Change

7.9.1. Water-saving Through Drip Irrigation

Vegetable	Yield increase (%)	Water saving (%)
Tomato	50	39
Water melon	88	46
Okra	16	40
Brinjal	14	53
Bitter gourd	39	53
Ridge gourd	17	59
Beet root	7	79
Chilli	44	62
Sweet potato	39	60

7.9.2. Cultural Practices that Conserve Water and Protect Crops

Crops/Vegetables	Plastic sheet thickness(μ)	Yield increased (%)
Brinjal	25	10-27
Okra	25	48-55
Potato	50	49-50
Tomato	25	65-70
Snap bean	25	33-73.3
Cucumber	25	44-52
Cabbage/Cauliflower	50	10-71
Chilli	25	60
Carrot	50	10-50

7.9.3. Improved Stress Tolerance Through Grafting

Crop	Root stock	Tolerance to biotic and abiotic stresses
Brinjal	*Solanum torvum*	Root knot nematode
	Solanum torvum X Solanum sanitwoagsei	Bacterial wilt
Tomato	*S. habrochates*	Corky root
	Brinjal(Eg-203 and EG-195	Bacterial wilt, root knot nematode
	S. melongena, S. lycopersicum L X *S. habrochates*	Multiple disease tolerance
Hot pepper	PI201232, PBC535PPO 237-7502	Bacterial wilt, nematode
Watermelon	Bottle gourd *(Lagenaria siceraria L)*	
	Squash (*Cucurbita moschata* Duch)	Vigorous root system, fusarium wilt low temperature tolerance
	Interspecific hybrid squash (*Cucurbita maxima* Duch X *C. moschata* Duch	Vigorous root system, fusarium low temperature high temperature strong vigour
	Pumpkin (*Cucurbita pepo*L.)	Vigorous root system, fusarium wilt low temperature
	Winter melon (*Benincasa hispida* Thumb.)	Good disease resistance
	Watermelon (*Citrullus lanatus* Thumb.)	Fusarium wilt
	African horned(AH) cucumber (*Cucumis metuliferus*)	Fusarium wilt, nematode tolernce
Cucumber	Fig leaf gourd(*Cucurbita ficifolia* Bouche)	Low temperature, good disease tolerance
	Squash (*Cucurbita moschata* Duch.)	Fusarium wilt, fruit quality modification
	Interspecific hybrid squash (*Cucurbita maxima* Duch X *C. moschata* Duch.)	Fusarium wilt, low temperature

Contd.

	Bur cucumber(*Sicyos angulatus L.)*	Fusarium wilt, Low temperature, high soil moisture, nematode
	AH cucumber (*Cucumis metuliferus*)	Fusarium wilt, nematode tolerance
Muskmelon	Squash (*Cucurbita moschata* Duch.	Fusarium wilt, Low temperature
	Interspecific hybrid squash (*Cucu bita maxima* Duch X *C. moschata* Duch.)	Fusarium wilt, Low temperature tolerance, high temperature, high soil moisture
	Pumpkin (*Cucurbita pepo* L.)	Fusarium wilt, low temperature wilt, high temperature tolerance, high soil moisture

Source: Dhall (2015).

7.9.4. Climate-Resilient Vegetables

Improved and adapted vegetable is the most cost-effective option for farmers to meet the challenges of a changing climate. These vegetables are Bird's eye chilli (*Capsicum minimum Roxb. Syn. C. fastigiatum* Bhumme), Kakrol (*Momordica cochinchinesis*), Kartoli (*M. dioica*), Chow-chow (*Sechium edule* Sw.), Indian bean (*Lablab purpureus* L.), Broad bean (*Vicia faba L*), Cowpea (*Vigna unguiculata* L. Walp.),Muccuna bean *(Muccuna pruriens),*Winged bean (*Psophocarpus tetragonolobous*), Cluster bean (*Cyamopsis tetragonolobus*), Jack bean *(Canavalia ensiformis),* Tree bean (*Parkia roxburghii),* Sword bean *(Canavalia gladiate),* Elephant foot yam *(Amorphophallus* spp.), Arbi (*Colassia esculentum*) Tapoica (*Manihot esculenta*)*,* Sweet potato, (*Ipomea batatas*),Ash gourd (*Benincasa hispida*), Pumpkin *(Cucurbita moschata),* Tree tomato *(Cyphomandra betacea),* Drumstick (*Moringa olerifera*) Curry leaf *(Murraya koenigii),* Snapmelon *(Cucumis melo momordica)*, Snake gourd (*Trichosanthes angunia*), Bathuwa (*Chenopodium* spp.).

7.9.5. Climate-Resilient Vegetable Crop Varieties/ lines (Heat)

Crops	Day temperature range(°C)	Genetic materials
Tomato	38-40	Kashi Adabhut, Kashi Topas CLN-1621, CLN-2026, EC-620419 EC-620419, EC-620421, EC- 620438, EC-538441, EC- 538-380 Suncherry, PR-161-L
French bean	30-32	Kashi Sampann (VRFBB-1), Kashi Rajhans (VRFBB-2)
Indian bean	35-38	VESEM-855 and VRSEM-860, Kashi Bounisem-3, Kashi Bounisem-18
Cowpea	35-40	Kashi Nidhi, Kashi Kanchan

7.9.6. Tolerance Moisture Deficit (drought) Vegetable Crop Varieties/lines

Vegetable crops	Drought tolerance genotypes/ species
Tomato	*S. habrochaites* (EC-520061), *S. pennelli* (IIHR 14-1, IIHR 146-2, IIHR-383, IIHR 553 , IIHR 555, K-14, EC-130042, EC-104395, Sel-28), *S.pimpinellifoloium* (PI-205009, EC- 65992, Pan American), *S. esculentum* var. *cerasiforme, S. hirsutum, S. cheesmanii, S. chilense, S. habrochaites, S. sitiens* Arka Vikas, RF- 4A *L. pennellii* (LA0716), *L. chilense* (LA1958, LA1959, LA1972), *S. sitiens* (LA1974, LA2876, LA2877, LA2878, LA2885), *S. pimpinellifolium* (LA1579)
Brinjal	*S. microcarpon, S. gilo S. macrosperma, S. integrifolium,* Bundelkhand Deshi *S. sodomaeum (syn. S. linneanum)* SM- 1, SM- 19, SM- 30, Violette Round, Supreme
Chilli	*C. chinense*, *C. baccatum* var. *pendulum*, *C. eximium* Arka Lohit, IIHR - Sel.-132
Potato	*S. acaule*, *S. demissum* and *S. stenotonum,* Alpha, Bintje *S.ajanhuiri, S.curtilobum, S.xjuzepczukii,* Kufri Sheetman *Solanum chacoense,* Kufri Sindhuri
Okra	*A. caillei, A. rugosus, A. tuberosus*
Onion	*Allium fistulosum, A. munzii,* Arka Kalyan, MST 42, MST 46
Frenchbean	*P. acutifolius,* Pinto, White Half Runner P. Acutifolius, CCGB-44, BAT-44 NEP-2, Negro Argel,
Cowpea	CB-5, IGFRI-450, IGFRI-437
Watermelon	*Citrullus colocynthis (L.) Schrad.*
Wintersquash	*Cucurbita maxima*
Cucumis Spp.	*Cucumis melo var. momordica* VRSM- 58, INGR-98015 (AHS-10),INGR-98016 (AHS-82), CU 159, CU 196,Cucumis pubescens, INGR-98013 (AHK-119),*Cucumis melo* var. *callosus,* AHK- 200, SKY/DR/RS-101,*Cucumis melo var. chat,* Arya *Cucumis melo,* SC- 15
Cassava	CE-54, CE-534, CI-260, CI-308, CI-848, 129, 7, 16, TP White, Narukku-3,Ci-4, Ci-60, Ci-17, Ci-80
Sweet potato	VLS6, IGSP 10, IGSP 14, Sree Bhadra

Source: Kumar *et al.* (2012).

7.9.7. Saline Soils tolerant Vegetable Crop Varieties/lines

Crops	Varieties/ lines
Tomato	*L. cheesmanii*, Pusa Ruby
Lettuce	Calmar, Climax
Okra	Pusa Sawani
Onion	Punjab Selection, Udaipur-102,
Pea	New Line Perfection, Market Prize
Cucumber	PI-177361
Lettuce	Calmar, Climax

7.9.8. Atmospheric Pollutant tolerant Vegetable Crop Varieties/lines

Tomato	Heinz-1439 and VF-145B(*least sensitive), L. peruvianum, L. hirsutum f. glabratum and L. glandulosum (moderately sensitive)* PI-1099835, PI-237136,PI-285663 and PI303792 *of L. esculentum resistant*
Brinjal	Blacknite
French bean	Black Turtle Soup
Onion	Downing Yellow Glove, Improved Autumn Spice (tolerant)
Potato	Superior (tolerant)
Cucumber	Polaris-135
Watermelon	Charleston Gray
Pea	Sparkle

7.9.9. Use Local Climate-Resilient Land Races

Crops/vegetables	State	Land races
Brinjal	Punjab	Sinhindi, Sanawi Red, Sonauri Yellow, Jullundar, Shokati Longi, Ludhiana Local, Batia.
	Andhra Pradesh	Mundu, Shivali, Warangal, Lanka Chilli, Seena Minapa.
	Maharastra	Manjari Gota, Bourad Local, Borgona, Local Khandesh, Khed Shivapur, Muleti, Dondicha, Achalpur, Malkapuri, Shiruri, Khandala, Khanpur, Rajangona, Songona Kagal, Tambalwadi Local, Chikalgaon Local and Dorli.
	Tamil Nadu	Wynad Gaint, Pattabiram, Annamalai, Salem, Ramananad. Samba Kodaki, Sattm Samba
	Madhya Pradesh	Nurki Round, Nurki Long, Banjari, Elichup NP-34, Japani Laungi
	Jammu & Kashmir	Javari, Javageal, Coibldanur, Gowrindnur
	Bihar	Hyderpur, Improved Muktakeshi, Rajari, Sity Patna Red, Sabour
	Gujarat	Gholar, Patta, Junagadh Bhattu, Surati Gota, Gulabi Dorla
	West Bengal	Makra, Elokeshi, Krishnanagar Purple Round, Krishnanagar Green Long, Muktakeshi, Baromashi, Kalyani Green, Nurki.

Contd.

	Assam	Suryaukhi Latabh, Tiger
Chilli	Punjab	Sinhindi, Sanawi Red, Sonauri Yellow, Jullundar, Shokati Longi.
	Andhra Pradesh	Osimilagi, Lavang Mirche, Golgonda Micle, S4, Mundi, Sadasivpet, Shivali, Nallapadu, India Dundicut, Tomato chilli, Mundu, Shivali, Warangal, Lanka Chilli, Seena Minapa, Gundu Type, Samba, Bagyalakshmi and India Long
	Maharashtra	Musalvadi, Shankeshwar, Sindhur, Seema Mirapa, DPLC, Bombay 742, Dondicha, Achalpur, Malkapuri.
	TamilNadu	Salem, Ramananad, Samba Kodaki, Sattur Samba, Kovilpatti.
	Orissa	Puri Red and Puri Orange
	Kerala	Kandhari, Achar, Vella Kadhari, Aana Mulagu, (Elephant chilli)
	Karnataka	Arsikera, Madhugiri,
	Madhya Pradesh	Elichip, Kalipeeth, NP-34, Japani Laungi.
	Jammu & Kashmir	Javari, Javageal, Coibldanur, Gowrindnur
	Bihar	Rahri, Sity Patna Red, Sabour, Angon, Sabour Anal
	Gujarat	Gholar, Patta
	Assam	Suryaukhi, Latabh, Tiger, Baghi
	Sikkim	Bird's eye
	Uttar Pradesh	Kalianpur Red, Suryamukhi, Kandhari
Muskmelon	Uttar Pradesh	Lucknow Safeda, Kanpuria, Jagia, Mathuria, Batti, Kajra, Jaunpuri, Mau, Bagpat, Mahaban, Netted (Jametha), Allahabad Kajras
	Gujarat	Sankheda, Balteshwar (Panam) and Galteswar
	Madhya Pradesh	Kharri, Jalgaon Kabri, Gurbeli, Kavita
	Rajasthan	Sanganer, Hara Gola, Motia, Tonk, Harela
	Andhra Pradesh	Sharbat-e-Anar, Bathesa, Papaya, Chiranji, Ladoo
	Karnataka	Kadapa
	Maharastra	Batti, Goose, Jam, Neel
	Haryana	Kutana, Bhagpat
	Punjab	Hardhai, Musa
Non-desert type Muskmelon	Andhra Pradesh	Nakka Dosa Kaya, Budam Kaya
	Tamil Nadu	Vellarikkai
	Kerala	Chavathakkai, Mudikode
	Maharashtra	Chibur
	UP, MP and Bihar	Kakri, Tar, Phoot
	Rajsthan	Kachri
Watermelon cucumber	Uttar Pradesh	Farrukhabadi, Moradabadi
	Maharashtra (Pune)	Poona Khira
	Uttar Pradesh (Saharanpur)	Balam Khira
	West Bengal	Darjeeling/Sikkim Type
Radish	UP (Jaunpur)	Jaunpuri
Onion	Maharashtra	Niphad, Nasik Red, Nasik White Globe, Poona Red, Bombay Red, Bombay White, Matheuwad, Shirwal, Kagar, Peth

Contd.

	Bihar	Patna Red
	Uttar Pradesh	Rampur Local, Kalyanpur Red
	Karnataka	Telgi Red, Bellari Red
	Punjab	Ludhiana Local
	Haryana	Panipat Local, Rajpur Red, Onion Karachi, Hissar Local
	Tamil Nadu	Multiplier onion, Cuddalorae
Garden pea	Madhya Pradesh	Kalangini, Khapan Kheda,
	Uttar Pradesh	Kap Bonia, Local Yellow Batri, Lucknow Bonia, Hara Bonia
	Punjab (Amritsar)	Asanji, Hoshiarpuri, Kanawari

7.10. Initiatives Taken by Government of India

Main streamed in the National Mission on Sustainable Agriculture (NMSA), one of the eight mission set up under Prime Minister,s National Action Plan on Climate Change (NAPCC), the National Initiative on climate Resilient Agriculture (NICRA) project of the ICAR has made an excellent beginning towards rendering Indian agriculture including vegetables more resilient to climate change. NICRA is a network project of the Indian Council of Agricultural Research (ICAR) launched in Feburary, 2011. The project aims to enhance resilience of Indian Agriculture to climate change and climate vulnerability through strategic research and technology demonstration. The project consists of four components *viz*; strategic research, technology demonstration, capacity building and sponsored / competitive grants. Under the strategic research, phenotyping of germplasm collections of wheat, rice, maize, pulses, vegetable crops tomato and Onion are being done for climate induced stresses like drought, heat stress and submergence, and selected lines are being used for developing stress tolerant high performing varieties. High throughput phenotyping systems and field facilities for studying the impacts of elevated temperature and carbon dioxide on crops and network of flux towers are some of the state of the art facilities already commissioned under the project at leading institutes. A comprehensive program on pest surveillance in relation to weather variables, crop simulation modeling with a systems approach for understanding impacts and designing adaptation strategies, nutritional and genetic strategies for reducing heat stress on milch animals, understanding the impact of climate variability on pollinators and flowering phenology of fruit crops are other areas of research being pursued in the project. The carbon sequestration potential of agro forestry and conservation agriculture systems is being estimated across the country for mitigation. The project is working on mechanisms of adaptation financing in the context of development planning in India.

The first ever vulnerability atlas of India at district level has been prepared which is likely to aid in prioritizing investments in vulnerable regions. The most significant contribution of the project has been the demonstration of best bet practices in 100 vulnerable districts in the form of stress tolerant varieties, water harvesting, conservation agriculture, farm mechanization through custom hiring centers which helped the farmers to cope with the annual climate variability's, yielding encouraging outcomes. The promising experiences of the Village Climate Risk Management Committees (VCRMC) and the Climate Smart Village pilots encompassing water, carbon, energy and nutrient smart technologies should be judiciously up- and out-scaled.

7.11. Future Strategies

Enhancing adaptation of tropical production systems to changing climatic conditions is a huge undertaking. It requires the combined efforts of many national and international institutions and an effective and efficient strategy to be able to deliver technologies that can mitigate the effects of climate change on the diverse crops and production systems. The scientific information and technologies developed through these initiatives must be readily accessible, consolidated and utilized in a strategic way. This can only be achieved through collaboration, complementarity, and coordinated objectives to address the consequences of climate change on the world's crop production. The future strategies are

7.11.1. Technologies and Infrastructure

- Standardize methodologies for vulnerability assessment and climate smart agriculture; enhance the density of weather observatories; establish rain gauges at block/village level; and enable access to and efficient management of weather related information by modern tools like remote sensing and GIS.
- Institutionalize a mechanism to collect and collate micro-level information continuously (climate, crops, socio-economic, natural resources etc.) and establish credible database as well as efficiently disseminate it which can be used as an input for macro-level policies.
- Invest in research and development of locally-adaptable crops, management practices, input sources etc., decision support system (DSS), and models for analysing the impact of climate change and mitigation strategies, particularly in arid and semi-arid regions in view of their greater vulnerability.
- Develop and diffuse drought, heat and submergence tolerant crop cultivars. Change planting dates to avoid terminal heat stress or cyclones at maturity stage.
- Improve techniques for water (rain water harvesting, micro-irrigation), nutrient (SSNM) and energy (reduced tillage) conservation to adapt the crops to climatic stresses and also contribute to mitigation.
- Encourage adoption of location-specific conservation techniques (cover cropping, *in situ* moisture conservation, rainwater harvesting, ground water recharge, locally adapted cropping systems etc.) for water efficient agriculture and demonstration of such technologies on farmers' fields.
- Blend farmers' traditional/indigenous knowledge on natural resource management and climate coping strategies with advanced technological interventions eg. varieties, crop management, resource conservation technologies, rainwater harvesting and storage
- Manage climate risks through weather-based agro-advisories, and affordable weather insurance products. The Government of India should move from reactive (relief payments) to practice (promoting insurance) approach in dealing with climate variability.

- Harness non-conventional energy sources in agriculture and other allied sectors which contribute to mitigation.

7.11.2. Research Priorities

- The focus should be the development of infrastructure tools for integration of high throughput data for effects of abiotic stress factors and genomics, associated with climate change.
- Development of simulation tools for further testing and application to climate change research issues ranging from plant breeding strategies to regional impact and mitigation studies.
- Generation of functional genomics, proteomics, metabolomics, and comparative genomics data
- Multidisciplinary approach to use current biological knowledge to relate genetic change to phenotypic outcome
- Incorporation of prediction of responses of phenology, plant architecture, and molecular and metabolic events related to climate change into conventional plant breeding.

7.11.3. Partnership and Capacity Building

- Create favourable environment to attract public and private funds for investment in Climate Resilient Agriculture (CRA). Much of the corporate social responsibilities funds from leading private sector players in the country should be channelized to promote CRA in vulnerable regions.
- Channelize investment in human resource development and capacity building through awareness and training among officials, extension workers and farmers, incentives to farmers for adoption of natural resource conservation practices and support to improve the existing indigenous technologies that are eco-friendly and sustainable in long-run.
- Revise and restructure university curricula and institutionalize teaching and research facilities in concerned educational institutions to develop graduates and postgraduates suitably trained in climate change management.
- Encourage role of the Non-Governmental Organizations, Civil Societies, Public and Philanthropic organizations for enhancing adaptation preparedness among the local community.
- Forge international/regional partnerships, especially with FAO, CCAFS of CGIAR, UNEP, IPCC for developing tools and technologies suited to local requirement through pooling financial and intellectual resources, and help judiciously implement the international agreements.

7.11.4. Farmer's Oriented Policies

- Increase concessional credit to small and marginal farmers for adoption of climate resilient agricultural practices. Evolve a new verification system at field level to sensitize farmers through credit and input subsidies.

- Establish efficient co-operatives, community organizations and associations/groups to tackle critical needs of farmers like resource mobilization, custom hiring, marketing their outputs and efficient natural resource management. Suitably empower Gram Panchayats to play a leading role at the grass root level in developing and implementing concerned programs.
- Evolve national policy on disaster management in agriculture when major events like cyclones and floods devastate agriculture, horticulture and livestock.
- Implement the recommendation of the National Commission on Farmers (NCF) for establishment of a National Agricultural Risk Management Fund and its need-based timely distribution.
- Identify, critically document and share most successful stories in climate change management and organise pilot demonstrations of most successful modules, and in a partnership mode scale-up and scale-out the selected ones to establish climate smart villages throughout the country.
- Introduce soil and water conservation practices on a large scale for achieving long-term sustainability of the systems, including revitalization and management of common property resources. Farmers must be given incentives to adapt CRA practices.
- Build on priority infrastructure like markets and information gateways and create opportunities in the non-farm sector in vulnerable regions to help the farmers to diversify their incomes.

8

Plant Health Management

8.1. Prevalence of Fungal Diseases of Vegetable Crops

Crop	Disease	Pathogen	Severity (%)	Average incidence (%)
Brinjal	Phomopsis blight	*Phomopsis vexans*	10-70	32.5
	White rot	*Sclerotinia sclerotiorum*	5-22	8.7
	Collar rot	*Sclerotium rolfsii*	10-30	20
	Leaf blight	*Alternaria alternata*	5-35	25.2
	Root rot	*Rhizoctonia solani*	5-20	4.2
	Rhizopus fruit rot	*Rhizopus stolonifer*	2-20	5.2
	Leaf spot	*Corynespora cassiicola*	2-10	2.5
	Wilt	*Fusarium solani*	1-2	1
	Myriothecium leaf spot	*Myriothecium roridum*	2-10	2.4
Tomato	Alternaria blight	*Alternaria solani*	15-90	40
		Alternaria. alternata f. sp. *lycopersici*	2-5	2
	Septoria leaf spot	*Septoria lycopersici*	5-20	10
	Late blight	*Phytophthora infestans*	5-80	8
	White rot	*Sclerotinia sclerotiorum*	5-10	5
	Collar rot	*Sclerotium rolfsii*	10-40	20
	Fruit rot	*Rhizoctonia, Cladosporium, Pythium*	5-20	15
	Black leaf mold	*Pseudocercospora fuligena*	0-3	<1
	Wilt	*F. oxysporum* f. sp. *lycopersici*	0-2	<1
	Leaf spot	*Myriothecium roridum*	5-20	5
Chilli/ Capsicum	Die-back	*Colletotrichum capsici*,	15-60	35
	Anthracnose	*Colletotrichum capsici*	10-30	15
	Phytophthora blight	*Phytophthora capsici*	5-10	8
	Leaf blight & fruit rot	*Alternaria alternata, Alternaria solani*	5-20	13.7
	Leaf spot	*Cercospora capsici*	10-35	20
	Collar rot	*Sclerotium rolfsii*	2-5	3
	White rot	*Sclerotinia sclerotiorum*	0-2	1
	Root rot	*Rhizoctonia solani*	2-8	5
	Myriothecium leaf spot	*Myriothecium rorridum*	0-3	1
Cucurbits	Downy mildew	*Pseudoperonospora cubensis*	10-80	30
	Anthracnose	*Colletotrichum lagenarium*	30-90	55

Contd.

	Cercospora leaf spot	*Cercospora citrullina*	20-50	30
	Gummy stem/leaf blight	*Didymella bryoniae*	2-15	5
	Wine & Fruit rot	*Sclerotium, Rhizoctonia Pythium, Sclerotinia*	10-20	15
	Powdery mildew	*Sphaerotheca fuliginea Erysiphe cichoraceaurm*	5-15	8
	Phytophthora blight	*Phytophthora cinnamomi*	25-60	35
Cowpea/ Pea/ Beans (Legumes)	Leaf blight	*Pseudocercospora cruenta Cercospora cruenta*	20-90	60
	Ascochyta blight	*Ascochyta phaseolorun*	5-15	8
	Root rot/Ashy stem rot	*Rhizoctonia bataticola*	2-15	5
		Macrophomina bataticola	5-20	10
	Web blight	*Rhizoctonia solani*	1-2	1
	Collar rot	*Sclerotium rolfsii*	2-15	5
	Phoma leaf blight	*Phoma phaseolina*	3-15	12
	Rust	*Uromyces phaseoli*	5-30	10
	Powdery mildew	*Erysiphe pisi*	10-90	50
	Downy mildew	*Peronospora pisi*	5-60	15
	White rot	*Sclerotinia sclerotiorum*	2-35	25
	Wilt	*F. solani* f. sp. *pisi*	2-5	2
	Leaf spot	*Myriothecium roridum*	5-10	5
Cole crops	Leaf spot	*Alternaria brassicae A. brassicicola*	10-40	26
	Downy mildew	*Peronospora parasitica*	5-25	10
	White rot	*Sclerotinia sclerotiorum*	2-10	5
	Root rot/wire stem	*Rhizoctonia solani*	5-15	8
	Black leg	*Phoma lingam*	2-5	2
Root crops	Leaf spot	*Alternaria raphani*	20-80	3
	Collar rot	*Sclerotium rolfsii*	2-10	4
	White rot	*Sclerotium sclerotiorum*	2-3	2
	Cercospora leaf spot	*Cercospor a dauci*	2-5	2
Okra	Leaf blight	*Cercospora abelmoschi C. hibisina*	25-95	70
	Charcoal rot	*Macrophomina phaseolina*	5-15	8
	Leaf spot	*Myriothecium roridum*	3-5	3
Onion/ Garlic	Purple blotch	*Alternaria porri*	15-80	40
	Leaf blight	*Stemphyllium vesicarium*	20-40	25
	Downy mildew	*Peronospora destructor*	10-25	10
Elephant foot yam (Suran)	Collar rot	*Sclerotium rolfsii*		
Leafy vegetables	Leaf spot	*Cercospora* sp.	5-10	5
Nursery crops	Damping off	*Rhizoctonia, Phythium Phytophthora, Colletotrichum Sclerotium, Phomopsis Alternaria, Fusarium*	30-85	50

8.2. Important Diseases of Seed Spices

Seed Spice	Disease
Cumin	Wilt, blight, powdery mildew
Coriander	Stem gall, powdery mildew, wilt, blight disease
Fennel	Leaf blight, wilt disease, powdery mildew
Fenugreek	Dumping off, leaf spot, leaf blight
Nigella/Kalongi	Root rot, powdery mildew
Ajwain	Alternaria blight, collar rot, powdery mildew
Sowa (Dill)	Powdery mildew, dill blight
Celery	Stem rot, bacterial leaf spot, early blight
Anise	Leaf blight

8.3. Label Claimed Fungicides in Vegetable Crops

Crop	Common name	Formulation (a.i.)	Target disease	Dose (% of trade)	Waiting days
Tomato	Azoxystrobin	23% SC	Early blight, powdery mildew	0.1%	3
	Mancozeb	75% WP	Early blight &late blight	0.25%	5-6
	Propineb	70% WP	Buck eye rot	0.3%	10
	Cymoxanil 8% + Mancozeb 64%	72% WP	Late blight	0.25%	10
	Famoxadone 16.6% + Cynoxanil 22.1%	38.7% SC	Early & late blight	0.1%	3
Chilli	Azoxystrobin	23% SC	Fruit rot, powdery mildew	0.1%	5
	Copper Sulphate	2.62% SC	Fruit rot, powdery mildew, Leaf spot	0.2%	3
	Captan	50% WG	Fruit rot, anthracnose	0.3%	5
	Chlorothalonil	75% WP	Fruit rot	0.1%	10
	Flusilazole	40% EC	Powdery mildew	0.02%	5
	Kitazin	48% EC	Fruit rot, dieback	0.2%	3
	Propineb	70% WP	Die back	0.5%	10
	Sulphur	80% WP	Die back	0.4%	
	Tebuconazole	25.9 EC	Fruit rot, powdery mildew	0.1%	5
	Captan+ Hexaconazole	70% + 5% WP	Fruit rot, anthracnose	0.1%	5
Cucurbits	Thiophanate methyl	70% WP	Powdery mildew, anthracnose	0.2%	1
	Cymoxanil 8%+ Mancozeb 64%	72% WP	Downy mildew	0.3%	10
Legume	Fenarimol	12% EC	Powdery mildew	0.04%	15

8.4. MRL for Fungicides in Vegetable Crops

Common name	Formulation (a.i.)	MRL in mg/kg (ppm)
Benomyl	50% WP	0.50
Carbendazim	50% WP	0.50
Captan	50% WG	15
Difenconazole	25% EC	0.002 (Chilli)
Dimethomorph	50% WP	2
Flusilazole	40% EC	0.01(Chilli Tomato)
Iprodione	50% WP	5 (Tomato)
Mancozeb	75% WP	0.02 (Cauliflower)
Metiram	70%WG	5 (Tomato)
Propineb	70%WP	2.0 (Green chilli)
Triadmefen	25%WP	0.1 (Pea)
Zineb	75% WP	3 (Tomato)

8.5. Some of Commercial Bio-Pesticides used Against Vegetables Crops Diseases

Name	Organism	Country	Application
AgriphageTM	Bacteriophages of *Xanthomonas*spp. and *Pseudomonas syringae* pv. tomato	USA	Bacterial spot in pepper and tomatoes, and bacterial speck in tomatoes
Actinovate® AG	*Streptomyces lydicus* WYEC 108	USA	Broad spectrum *Pythium*, *Fusarium*, *Rhizoctonia*, powdery mildew, downy mildew, *Botrytis*, *Alternaria* etc
Actinovate® SP	*Streptomyces lydicus* WYEC 108	USA	*Pythium*, *Fusarium*, *Rhizoctonia*, *Verticillium*, powdery mildew, downy mildew, *Botrytis*, *Alternaria* etc
Serenade® MAX™	*Bacillussubtilis* strain QST 713	USA	*Sclerotinia*, Rust, Powdery Mildew, Bacterial Spot and White Mold etc
	Bacillus subtilis	USA	Seed dressing
	B. subtilis FZB 24	Gerrmany	Seed dressing (potatoes)

8.6. Yield Losses Due to Major Insect-Pests in Vegetables in India

Crop/Pest	Yield loss (%)	Crop/Pest	Yield loss (%)
Tomato		**Cabbage**	
Fruit borer (*Helicoverpa armigera*)	24-73	Diamondback moth	17-99
		(*Plutella xylostella*)	
Brinjal		Cabbage caterpillar	69
		(*Pieris brassicae*)	
Fruit and shoot borer	11-93	Cabbage leaf webber	28-51
(*Leucinodes orbonalis*)		(*Crocidolomia binotalis*)	
Chillies		Cabbage borer (*Hellula undalis*)	30-58
Thrips (*Scirtothrips dorsalis*)	12-90	**Cucurbits**	
Mites (*Polyphagotarsonemus latus*)	34	Fruit fly	
		(*Bactrocera cucurbitae*)	
Okra		Bitter gourd	60-80
Fruit borer(*H. armigera*)	22	Cucumber	20-39
Leafhopper	54-66	Ivy gourd	63
(*Amrasca biguttula biguttula*)			
Whitefly (*Bemisia tabaci*)	54	Musk melon	76-100
Shoot and fruit borer (*Earias vittella*)	23-54	Snake gourd	63
		Sponge gourd	50

8.7. Changing Pest Scenario in Vegetable Crops in India

Insect Pest	Major pest	Presently infested
Serpentine leaf miner, (*Liriomyza trifolii* (Burgress)	Tomato	Brinjal, cow pea, French bean, squash, leafy vegetables, cucurbits
Spiraling whitefly, (*Aleurodicus dispersus* Russell)	Guava, citrus, tapioca	Bhendi, capsicum, brinjal, tomato
Mealy bug, (*Phenacoccus solenopsis* Tinsley)	Cotton	Brinjal, tomato, chilli, okra, cucumber, pumpkin
Hadda beetle, (*Henosepilachna vigintioctopunctata*) Fab. and *Epilachna dodecastigma* (Wied.)	Brinjal	Bitter gourd, cow pea
Fruit borer. (*Helicoverpa armigera* (Hubner)	Gram, cotton, tomato, cabbage	Peas, chilli, brinjal, okra
Gall midge. (*Asphondylia capparis* Rubsaman.)	Brinjal	Chilli, capsicum
Cabbage butterfly, (*Pieris brassicae* Linn.)	Cabbage, cauliflower, mustard	Knol-khol, radish
Stem fly. (*Ophiomyia phaseoli* (Tryon)	Beans	Okra
Red spider mite, (*Tetranychusurticae* Koch.)	Okra, Brinjal	Cucumber, cowpea, indian bean
Leaf-hopper (*Empoasca motti* Singh-Pruthi)		Bitter gourd
Plume moth, (*Sphenarchescaffer* Zeller)	Field bean	Bottle gourd

8.8 . Baculoviruses of Crop Pests Reported From India and Crops on Which They Can be Used

Insect	Viruses	Crops
Heliothis armigera	NPV, GV	Chickpea, pigeonpea, cotton, sunflower, groundnut, tomato, lablab, bean, sorghum
Spodoptera litura	NPV	Cotton, groundnut, banana, tobacco, blackgram
Amsacta albistriga	NPV	Groundnut
Mythimna seperata	NPV	Sorghum
Spodoptera mauritia	NPV	Rice
Spilosoma obliqua	NPV	Groundnut, cowpea, soybean, sunflower
Anadevidia peponis	NPV	Snake gourd
Agrotis segetum	NPV, GV	Potato
Eupterote cardamomi	NPV	Cardomom
Chilo infuscatellus	GV	Sugarcane
Plutella xylostella	GV	Cauliflower, cabbage, mustard
Cnaphalocrocis medinalis	GV	Rice

8.9. Bacterial Based Bio-Pesticides for Vegetable Crops

Microbial pesticide	Crops	Target pests	Recommended formulation dose/ ha
Bacillus thuringiensis var. kurstaki, 3a, 3b,SA-II WG	Cabbage	Diamond back moth	0.5 kg
Bacillus thuringiensis var. kurstaki, BMPn 123 (2x) WDG, *3a, 3b*	Brinjal	Shoot and fruit borer	0.25 – 0.5 kg
Bacillus thuringiensis var. kurstaki, HP WP	Cabbage	Diamond back moth	300-500 g
Bacillus thuringiensis var. galleriae Serotype, 3a, 3b,	Cabbage Tomato Okra	Diamond back moth fruit borer Shoot borer	0.60- 1.0 kg 1 – 1.5kg 1 – 1.5 kg
Bacillus thuringiensis var. kurstaki, strain Z-523, serotype H3a, 3b WP	Okra	Fruit and shoot borer	0.4 – 1.0 kg
Bacillus thuringiensis var. kurstaki, WP	Legumes	Pod borer	0.75 – 1.0 kg
Beauveria bassiana Strain No. IPL/BB/MI/01 ($1x10^9$ CFU/gm min)	Okra	Fruit borer and Spotted boll worm	3.75-5.0 kg
NP V of *Spodoptera litura* 0.5 % AS	Tomato	*Spodoptera litura*	1500 ml
NPV of *Helicoverpa armigera* Strain No. IBH-17268 ($1x10^9$ POB/ml min) 2.0% AS	Tomato	*Helicoverpa armigera*	250-500 ml
NPV of *Helicoverpa armigera* 0.43% AS	Tomato	*Helicoverpa armigera*	1500 ml

8.10. Biocontrol Agents Recommended in Vegetable Crops

Bioagent	Dose	Target pest
Trichogramma brassiliensis	2,50,000 parasitised eggs/ha (Inundative release)	Okra shoot and fruit borer
	50,000 parasitised eggs/ha (Weekly inoculative release)	Tomato fruit borer
Chrysoperla zastrowi arabica (weekly release)	50,000 first instar larvae/ha	Okra aphid Cabbage aphid
HaNPV	250 LE/ha (10 days interval)	Tomato fruit borer
SlNPV	250 LE/ha (10 days interval)	*Spodoptera litura*
Bacillus thuringiensis	500 g ai/ha (10 days interval)	Diamond back moth Shoot and fruit borer of brinjal and okra tomato fruit borer

8.11. Commercial Bio-insecticides Based on Pathogenic Fungi

Microorganism	Insect controlled	Product	Country
Verticillium lecanii	Aphids, scale insects, mites, thrips	Vertalec/Bioline	UK/India
Entomopthora sp.	Aphids, mites		USA
Nomurea releyi	Lepidopteran larvae, Alfafa weevil		USA
Hirsutella thompsonii	Citrus rust mite	Mycar	USA
Beauveria bassiana	Colorado potato beetle, Codling moth Coffee berry borer	Boverin Blorin	USSR India Columbia
Asohersonia aleyrodis	Citrus scale insect		USSR
Metarhizium anisopliae	Spittle bug	Metaquino	Brazil
Paecilomyces lilacinus	Nematodes	Bicon	Philippines
Metarhizium flavovirde	Locust, Grass hopper		USA
Pandora delphacis	BPH	Mycoinsecticide 70 WP, 10 dust	India (TNAU, Coimbatore)

8.12. Neem Based Insecticides for Insect-pest Control in Vegetable Crops

Sl No	Botanical Insecticide	Crops	Target pests	Recommended dose/ha Formulation (g/ml)
1.	Azadirachtin 0.03% (300 ppm)	Okra, brinjal, cabbage	Fruit borer, shoot & fruit Borer, beetles whiteflies, leaf hopper, aphids, DBM,	2500-5000 ml
2.	Azadirachtin 0.15% (500 ppm)	Okra, tomato cabbage	Aphids, jassids, DBM, fruit borer and whitefly	1 – 2 l

Contd.

3.	Azadirachtin 0.3% (3000 ppm)	Cabbage	DBM	1.67 – 3.34 l
4.	Azadirachtin 5% (50000 ppm)	Okra, tomatocabbage, brinjal	DBM, aphids, *Spodoptera litura*, whitefly, jassids, aphids and shoot and fruit borer	200 ml
5	Azadirachtin1% (10000ppm)	Tomato brinjal	Fruit borer and fruit and shoot borer	1000-1500 ml

8.13. Economic Threshold Level (ETL) for Major Insect-pests of Vegetable Crops

Crop/Pest	ETL
Tomato	
Fruit borer (*H. armigera*)	8 eggs/15 plants or 1 larva/plant or 1 damaged fruit/ plant
Whitefly (*B. tabaci*)	3 nymphs/leaf or 4 adults/leaf
Leaf miner (*Liriomyza trifolii*)	26 mines/trifoliates or 6 adults/6 rows
Brinjal	
Fruit and shoot borer (*L. orbonalis*)	0.5-5% shoot and fruit damage
Chillies	
Thrips (*S. dorsalis*)	2 thrips/leaf
Mites (*P. latus*)	1 mite/leaf
Okra	
Leafhopper (*A. biguttula biguttula*)	4.66 hoppers/leaf
Shoot and fruit bore (*Earias vittella*)	5.3% of fruit infestation
Cabbage	
Diamond back moth (*P. xylostella*)	2 larvae/plant at 1-4 weeks after transplanting or 5 larvae/ plant at 5-10 weeks after transplanting.
Cabbage leaf webber (*Crocidolomia binotalis*)	0.3 egg mass/plant
Pea	
Pea aphid (*Acyrthosiphonpisum*)	3-4 aphids/stem tip

8.14. Waiting Period/Pre-Harvest Interval (PHI) of Insecticides Recommended for Insect Control in Vegetable Crops

Insecticides	Waiting period or pre-harvest interval (Days)						
	Tomato	Brinjal	Chilli	Okra	Cabbage	Cauliflower	Cucurbits
Acetamiprid 20 SP	-	-	3	3	7	-	-
Azadirachtin 1%	3	3	-	-	-	-	-
Azadirachtin0.03%	-	7	-	7	7	-	-
Azadirachtin 5 %	5	-	-	5	5	-	-
Buprofezin	-	-	5	5	-	-	-
Carbaryl 5DP	-	-	-	8	8	-	-
Carbaryl 50 WP	8	5	-	3	8	5	-
Carbosulfan	-	-	8	-	-	-	-
Chlorantranilprole	3	22	3	5	3	-	7 (Bittergourd)
Chlorfenpyre	-	-	5	-	7	-	-
Chlorfluazoron	-	-	-	-	7	-	-
Cyantraniliprole	3	-	3	-	5	-	5 (Gherkins)
Cypermethrin 0.25DP	-	3	-	-	-	-	-
Cypermethrin 10 EC	-	3	-	3	7	-	-
Cypermethrin 25 EC	-	1	-	3	-	-	-
Deltamethrin 2.8 EC	-	3	5	1	-	-	-
Dicofol	-	15-20	-	15-20	-	-	-
Difenthiuron 50 WP	-	3	3	-	7	-	-
Emamectin benzoate	-	3	3	5	3	-	-
Ethion	-	-	5	-	-	-	-
Etoxazole	-	5		-	-	-	-
Fenazaquin	7	7	10	7	-	-	-
Fenpropathrin	-	10	7	7	-	-	-
Fenpyroximate	-	-	7		-	-	-
Fenvalrate	-	5	-	7	-	7	-
Fipronil	-	-	7	-	7	-	-
Flubendamide 20WG	5	-		-	7	-	-
Flubendamide 40 SC	-	-	7	-	7	-	-

Contd.

Insecticides	Waiting period or pre-harvest interval (Days)						
	Tomato	Brinjal	Chilli	Okra	Cabbage	Cauliflower	Cucurbits
Flufenoxuron	-	-	-	-	7	-	-
Flumite/ Flufenzine	-	5	-	-	-	-	-
Hexythiazox	-	-	3	-	-	-	-
Imidacloprid 70 WG	-	-	-	3	-	-	5(Cucumber)
Imidacloprid 17.8 SL	3	-	40	3	-	-	-
Indoxacarb 14.5 SC	5	-	5	-	7	-	-
Indoxacarb 15.8 EC	-	-	-	-	5	-	-
λ-Cyhalothrin 4.9 CS	5	5	5	5	-	-	-
λ-Cyhalothrin 5 EC	4	4	5	4	-	-	-
Lufenuron	-	-	5	-	14	5	-
Metaflumizone	-	-		-	3	-	-
Methomyl	5-6	-	5-6	-	-	-	-
Milibectin	-	-	7	-	-	-	-
Novaluron	1-3	-	3	-	5	-	-
Phosphamidon	-	10	-	-	-	-	-
Propergite	-	6	7	-	-	-	-
Pyridalyl	-	-	-	3	3	-	-
Quinalphos 20 AF	7	-	-	7	-	-	-
Spinosad 2.5 SC	-	-	-	-	3	3	-
Spinosad 45 SC	-	-	3	-	-	-	-
Spiromesifen	3	5	7	3	-	-	-
Thiacloprid	-	5	5	-	-	-	-
Thiodicarb	-	6	6	-	7	-	-
Thiamethoxam25WG	5	5	-	5	-	-	-
Tolfenpyrad	-	-	-	3	5	-	-
Betacyfluthrin 8.49 + Imidacloprid19.81OD	-	7	-	-	-	-	-
Cypermethrin 3+ Quinalphos 20 EC	-	7	-	-	-	-	-
Deltamethrin 1 + Trizophos 35 EC	-	21	-	-	-	-	-
Indoxacarb 14.5 + Acetamiprid 7.7 SC	-	-	5	-	-	-	-
Novaluron 5.25 + Indoxacarb 4.5 SC	5	-	-	-	-	-	-
Pyriproxyfen 5 + Fenpropathrin 15 EC	-	7	7	7	-	-	-

8.15. Approved Bio-rational Insecticides for use in Vegetable Crops

Common name	Crop	Target pest	Dose/ha (g a.i.)
Imidacloprid 17.8% SL	Chilli	Jassid, aphid, thrips	25-20
	Okra	Jassid, aphid, thrips	20
Thiamethoxam 25% WG	Okra	Jassid, aphid, whitefly	25
	Tomato	Whitefly	50
	Brinjal	Whitefly	50
Thiacloprid 21.7% SC	Chilli	Thrips	54-72
Fipronil 5% SC	Cabbage	DBM	40-50
	Chillies	Thrips, aphid, fruit borer	40-50
Indoxacarb 14.5% SC	Cabbage	DBM	30-40
	Chilli	Fruit borer	50-60
	Tomato	Fruit borer	60-75
Spinosad 2.5% SC	Cabbage/ cauliflower	DBM	15.0-17.5
Spinosad 45% SC	Chillies	Fruit borer	73
Chlorantranilprole 18.5% SC	Cabbage	DBM	10
	Okra	Fruit and shoot borer	9.5-11.0
Emamectin benzoate	Cabbage	DBM	7.5-10.0
	Chilli	Fruit borer, thrips, mite	10
	Brinjal	Fruit and shoot borer	10
Chlorfenopyre 10% SC	Chilli	Mite	75-100
Spiromesifen 22.9% SC	Brinjal	Red spider mite	96
	Chilli	Yellow mite	96
Diafenthiuron 50% WP	Cabbage	DBM	300
	Chilli	Mite	300
	Brinjal	Whitefly	300
Lufenuron 5.4% EC	Cabbage/ cauliflower	DBM	30
Novaluron 10% EC	Cabbage	DBM	75
	Tomato	Fruit borer	75
	Chilli	Fruit borer, tobacco caterpillar	33.5
Buprofezin 25% SC	Chillies	Yellow mite	75-100
Flufenoxuron 10% DC	Cabbage	DBM	40

8.16. The Indian MRL for Pesticides Recommended for Insect Control in Vegetable Crops

Insecticides	MRL or Tolerance Limits in mg/kg (ppm)						
	Tomato	Brinjal	Chilli	Okra	Cabbage	Cauli-flower	Cucurbits
Acetamiprid 20SP	-	—	0.1	-	0.1	-	-
Buprofezin	-	-	0.01	-	-	-	-
Carbaryl 5 DP	-	-	-	10.0	-	-	-
Carbaryl 50 WP	-	-	5.0	-	-	-	-
Carbosulfan	-	-	0.2	-	-	-	-
Chlorantranilprole	-	-	-	-	0.03	-	-
Chlorfenpyre	-	-	0.05	-	0.05	-	-
Cypermethrin0.25 DP	-	0.20	-	-	-	-	-
Cypermethrin10EC	-	2.0	-	-	-	-	-
Cypermethrin 25 EC	-	0.20	-	-	-	-	-
Deltamethrin2.8EC	0.05	-	-	0.05	-	-	-
Dicofol	-	-	1.0	-	-	-	-
Difenthiuron 50 WP	-	1.0	0.05	-	1.0	-	-
Emamectin benzoate	-	-	-	0.05	-	-	-
Ethion	-	-	-	-	-	-	0.5
Etoxazole	-	-	-	-	-	-	-
Fenazaquin	-	-	0.5	-	-	-	-
Fenpropathrin	-	0.2	0.2	0.5	-	-	-
Fenpyroximate	-	-	1.0	-	-	-	-
Fenvalrate	-	2.0	-	2.0	-	2.0	-
Fipronil	-	-	0.001	-	0.001	-	-
Flumite/ Flufenzine	-	0.5	-	-	-	-	-
Hexythiazox	-	-	0.01	-	-	-	-
Indoxacarb 14.5% SC	0.05	-	0.01	-	0.1	-	-
ë - Cyhalothrin 4.9 CS	0.1	0.2	0.5	2.0		-	-
Lufenuron	-	-	-	-	0.3	0.1	-
Methomyl	0.05	-	0.05	-	-	-	-
Milibectin	-	-	0.01	-	-	-	-
Novaluron	0.01	-	0.01	-	0.01	-	-
Phosphamidon	-	-	2.0	-	-	-	-
Propargite	-	-	2.0	-	-	-	-
Pyridalyl	-	-	0.2	0.02	0.02	-	-
Quinalphos 20AF	-	-	0.2	-	-	-	-
Spinosad 2.5 SC	-	-	-	0.02	0.02	-	-
Spinosad 45 SC			0.001	-	-	-	
Spiromesifen			-	-	-	-	-
Thiacloprid			0.02	-	-	-	-
Thiodicarb			0.01	-	-	-	-
Thiamethoxam 25 WG	0.01	0.3	0.01	0.5	-	-	-
Tolfenpyrad			-	0.7	0.01	-	-

8.17. Dissipation Half Life of Pesticides in/on Vegetables

Commodity	Pesticide	Half life (Days)
Tomato	Flubendiamide Thiacloprid	0.72-1.32
	Flubendiamide	1.64 - 1.98
	Bifenthrin	1.83-2.32
	Chlorpyrifos	4.38- 4.43
	Mancozeb Metalaxyl	3.76 and 4.14
Cabbage	Emamectin Benzoate	1.34–1.72
	Fipronil	3.21 -3.43
	Trichlorfon	1.80
	Quinalphos Fubendiamide	4.8 - 5.3
	Flubendiamide	3.4 to 3.6
	Thiacloprid	12.3–13.1
	Spinosad	1.4 and 1.5
	Metaflumizone	1.7–2.1
	Emamectin Benzoate	<5
Okra	Flubendiamide	4.7 to 5.1
	Spiromesifen	1.68 and 1.65
	Imidacloprid Beta-	1.07 and 2.41
	Cyfluthrin	1.98 and 3.30
	Chlorpyriphos	0.6
Cauliflower	Chlorantraniliprole	1.36
	Cypermethrin	1.5–2.1
	Deltamethrin	2.9–3.3
	Profenofos	2.6–3.0
	Triazophos	2.2–2.6
Chilli	Chlorpyriphos	4.43 and 2.01
	Cypermethrin	2.51 and 2.64
	Trifloxystrobin	1.81 and 1.58
	Tebuconazole	1.37 and 1.41
	Deltamethrin	0.36 to 1.99
	Acetamiprid	2.24–4.84
	Chlorfenapyr	2.93 to 2.96
Brinjal	Thiacloprid	0.47 and 0.50
	Profenofos	2.15–2.31
	Cypermethrin	0.91–1.86
	Chlorpyrifos	3.27–3.10
	Cypermethrin	2.19 to 3.27
	Quinalphos	2-3
	Flubendiamide	0.62 and 0.54

8.18. Insecticides with New Chemistries for Control of Vegetable Insect-pests

Insecticide group	Target site	Mode of action	Active ingredients
Neonicotinoids	Nerve	Agonists of nicotinic acetylcholine receptor (nAChR)	Imidacloprid, Acetamiprid, Thiamethoxam, Thiacloprid
Pyridine-carboxamide	Nerve	Modulators of chordontal organs	Flonicamid
Diamide	Nerve and Muscle action	Ryanodine receptor modulators	Flubendamide Cyantraniliprole Chlorantraniliprole
Tetronic and tetramic acid derivatives	Lipid synthesis	Inhibitors of acetyl CoA carboxylase	Spiromesifen
Pyrrole Insecticides	Energy metabolism	Uncouplers of oxidative phosphorylation via disruption of proton gradient	Chlorfenapyr
Thiourea Insecticides	Energy metabolism	Inhibitors of mitochondrial ATP synthase	Diafentiuron
Avermectins	Nerve	Glutamate-gated chloride channel modulators	Emamectin Benzoate Milbemectin
Spinosyns	Nerve	Nicotinic acetylcholine receptor (nAChR) allosteric activators	Spinosad
Phenylpyrazoles	Nerve	GABA gated chloride channels antagonists	Fipronil
Benzoylureas	Growth regulation	Chitin biosynthesis Inhibitors type 0	Flufenoxuron
Chitin Synthesis Inhibitors	Energy metabolism	Chitin biosynthesis Inhibitors type I	Buprofezin, Novaluron
METI Acarcides	Energy metabolism	Mitochondrial complex I electron transport inhibitors.	Fenpyroximate, Fenzaquin, Tolfenpyrad
Mite Growth Inhibitor	Growth regulation	Regulates the growth of mite	Hexthiazox, Etoxazole, Flufenzine
Sulfite Ester Acaricides	Energy metabolism	Inhibitors of mitochondrial ATP synthase	Propargite

8.19. List of Pesticides Restricted or Banned in India

a. Pesticides restricted for use

1. Aluminium phosphide
2. Captafol
3. Carbaryl
4. Dieldrin
5. Ethylene dibromide (EDB)
6. Methyl bromide
7. Sodium cyanide
8. Lindane
9. Methyl parathion

b. Pesticides Banned for Use in Agriculture in India

1. Dibromochloropropane
2. Endrin (DBCP)
3. Pentachloronitrolbenzene (PCNB)
4. Pentachlorophenol (PCP)
5. Toxaphene
6. Ethyl parathion
7. Chlordane
8. Heptachlor
9. Aldrin
10. Paraquat-di-methyl sulphate
11. Nitrogen
12. Nicotene sulphate
13. Phenyl mercury acetate
14. Tetradifern
15. Calcium cyanide
16. Copper Acotoarsenite
17. Ethyl mercury chloride
18. Menazon
19. Sodium methane arsonate
20. BHC (HCH)
21. Phenyl mercury acetate (PMA)
22. Nichotine sulphate
23. DDT
24. Chlorobenzilate

8.20. Natural Enemies of Insect-pests of Some Important Vegetable Crops

Pest	Parasitoid/Predator
Crucifers	
Plutella xylostella	*Apanteles plutellae* *Diadegme semiclausum*
Brachymeria excarinata	
Crocidolomia binotalis	*Alanteles crocidolomea*
Hellula undalis	*Bracon spp.*
Tomato	
Helicoverpa armigera	*Trichogramma spp*
Okra	
Earias spp.	*Trichogramma spp*
Spodoptera litura	*Telenomus rowani*
Aphis spp.	*Coccinella septempuctata* *Chrysopela zastrowi sillemi*

8.21. Different Carriers used to Develop Bio-Formulations

Carrier (s)	Bio-control agent (s)	Shelf-life
Talc	*P. fluorescens* (P7NF, TL3)	12 months
	P. fluorescens (Pf1)	8 months
	B. subtilis	1.5 months
	P. putida	1.5 months
Lignite	*P. fluorescens* (Pf1)	4 months
Peat	*P. fluorescens* (Pf1)	8 months
Peat+chitin	*B. subtilis*	6 months
Peat	*P. chlororaphis B. subtilis*	6 months
Vermiculite	*P. fluorescens* (Pf1)	8 months
	B. Subtilis	1.5 months
	P. putida	1.5 months
FYM	*P. fluorescens* (Pf1)	8 months
	P. fluorescens (Pf1)	4 months

8.22. Plant Products used for Management of Insect-pests in Vegetable Crops

Pest	Plant products	Mode of action
Leucinodes orbonalis	Oil (2%) of *Pongamia pinnata*, *Madhuca indica* and *A. indica*	Contact
	Neem Azal (0.03%), Neem oil (0.3%)	Antifeedant and contact
Epilachna vignitioctopunctata	Leaf extract (1%) of *Lantana camara*	Antifeedant
	Leaf extract (6%) of *Ageratum* haustriarum *Melia azedarach*	Contact
Bemesia tabaci	Neemal (0.5%), Replin (Neem based formulation)	Mortality
Pieris brassicae	Achook, Neem oil and Nimbicidene	Insect growth regulator (IGR), antifeedancy
Spodoptera litura	Leaf extract of Persa *americara*	Antifeedant and contact

Earias vittela	NSKE (5%)	Contact and ovicidal
Pest complex of okra	NSKE (5%), Mltineem (2.5 l/ha)	Contact
Pest complex of crucifers	Nimbecidine (7.5 ml/l)	Contact
Pest complex of tomato	NSKE/Melia seed extract (5%)	Contact
Pest complex of eggplant	Nimbecidine/Neemgold/ Neem Azal (0.1%)	Contact

8.23. Safer Insectisides to Natural Enemies of Vegetable Crops

Insecticides	Target insect pest	Safe for natural enemies
Sulphur	Mite	*Amblyseius tetranychivorus*
NSKE, Phosalone	Tobacco caterpillar	*Telenomus remus*
Phosalone, Permethrin, Deltamethrin, NSKE, Fenvalerate, Cypermethrine, Fluvalinate	Diamond back moth	*Cotesia plutellae*
Acephate, Phosalone	Fruit borer	*Camploetis chloridiae*
Fenvalerate		*Trichogramma brassiliensis*
Endosulfan, phosalone, Rynaxpyre, Flubendamide	Neonate larvae	*Coccinella septempunctata*

9

Post-harvest and Value Addition

9.1. Post-harvest Losses of Vegetables (mean range of all the regions and seasons)

Vegetables	Post-harvest losses(per cent)	Remarks
Onion	6.01-40.0	Storage & transportation
Potato	30.0-40.0	Harvesting & storage
Garlic	0.9-2.7	Storage
Tomato	6.7-33.5	Transportation & marketing
Brinjal	3.7-13.4	Marketing
Cabbage	3.0-15.0	Marketing
Cauliflower	10.0-13.2	Transportation & marketing
Bottle gourd	7.0-10.0	Transportation & marketing
Okra	5.0-10.0	Marketing
Chilli	4.0-35.0	Farm and storage
Beet root	10.0-15.0	Marketing
Radish	3.0-5.0	Marketing
Carrot	5.9	-
Pointed gourd	19.81	Marketing storage
Garlic	0.9-2.7	Marketing storage

9.2. Causes of Post-Harvest Losses

(A) Primary Causes:

- Mechanical injury.
- Physio-biochemical losses.
- Microbial losses.
- Physical losses.

(B) Secondary Causes:

- State of maturity.
- Time of harvesting.
- Storage facilities.
- Bruishing caused due to transportation and distribution.

9.3. Control of Post-Harvest Losses

The extent of post harvest losses in vegetables can be minimized by

- Careful harvesting.
- Harvesting of vegetables at the right stage of maturity.
- Proper sorting, grading and packing.
- Careful transportation and distribution.
- Adequate and suitable storage facilities.
- Pre and post harvest treatment.

9.4. Standards for Grading of Vegetables for Marketing

Vegetables	General Grade	Commercial Grade
Arvi	Diameter 25 mm and above, length minimum 50 mm	Diameter 25 mm and above, length 30-45 mm.
Brinjal (long)	No shrivelling, free from brown patches, green stalk.	Shrivelling and brown spots, <20 per cent surface area, dull appearance.
Brinjal (round)	No shrivelling, proper shaped, no mechanical damage, lustrous, with green stalk, 65-150 mm diameter and more than 5-10 per cent packing/pressure damage, greenish brown area <10 per cent (January-March) and <25 per cent (September-October).	Up to 20 per cent shrivelling, mis shaped, dull look dry or without stalk, up to 20 per cent packing/pressure damage, greenish brown area <25 per cent (January-March) and <50 per cent (September-October).
Coriander leaves	Should not be yellowish, tender stems.	Slight yellow colour.
Capsicum (Bell pepper)	Diameter 46-85 mm, length minimum 70 mm.	Diameter 30-45 mm (From stem end) length minimum 50 mm.
Capsicum	Firm diameter 50 mm and above, length 50 mm and above.	Slightly soft, diameter 30-49 mm, no length ranges.
Cabbage	Puffiness not allowed, compact, light green colour, 25-800 g without cuts.	Slight puffy with light weight, whitish colour, open head, no weight specification, with clean cuts upto 50 mm long, 20 mm wide and deep.
Cauliflower	Riceynes <10 per cent surface area, snow white cream in colour, compact curd with no curd injury<1 s. cm, with no insect damage, with weight 200-1000 g.	Riceyness >10 per cent surface area, loose curd with dull look, upto 2 sq. cm injury, with insect damage <2 sq. cm bt insect not visible, with weight up to 1.5 kg.
Carrot	Fresh red colour, well tapered, max. 3 nodes on the surface with no cuts, up to 10mm long green top with diameter 25-40 mm and length 150 mm.	Pale look, mis-shaped, not properly tapered, up to 5 nodes on the surface, with cuts, 70 mm long and 3-5 mm wide and, deep, 11-30 mm long green top, with diameter 11-25 mm or above.
Cucumber	Green or slightly brown colour, firm straight, unshrivelled diameter 35-50 mm and length 125-180 mm.	Yellowish, curved, slightly shrivelled at end diameter 30-34 mm, length minimum 75 mm.
Ginger	Thick, shiny, firm, dry, pieces weighing 0.50 g.	Slightly dry with small pieces but weighing not less than 20 g each.
Garlic	White or with violet exterior, compact, diameter 30-35 mm.	Bulbs of sizes smaller than general grade but less than 25 mm length or single cloves with minimum length 8 mm and length 15 mm.
Bitter gourd	Green or up to 10 per cent colour, tender and firm, should not have bruising, length 25-55mm, and length 60-200 mm.	Slightly yellow colour (up to 20 per centsurface area) slightly poor look with slight bruising, size specification same as general grade.

Contd.

Kakri	Green colour, tender should not be matured, length 10-30 mm.	Slightly yellow (up to 10 per cent), dia 31-40.
Okra	Green light green in colour, tender and turgid, with no visible seeds, lustrous, with no black edges, dia <18 mm (at stalk end), length 50-130 mm (excluding stem).	With visible seeds but finger not mature, less lusturous, with slight black edges, with no length limitation and dia < 20 mm.
Bottle gourd	Green/light green, tender uniform profile, without cut or maximum two cuts of < 50 mm length, brown colour/scaling < 10 per cent of surface area, with no ruptured skin and black tip, with packing/ pressure damage not more than 10 per cent surface area, weight 300-800 g.	Slightly puffy, with any number of cuts upto 50 mm length or maximum three cuts 50 mm long, brown colour, scaling 11-75 per cent, with ruptured skin upto 75 per cent surface area, black tip < 30mm, shrivelled tip, packing/ pressure damage up to 25 per cent, no weight restriction but without any defect.
Methi and Spinach	Green, preferably small leaves and should be clean.	Slightly, yellow/turning yellow leaves slightly dropping leaves.
Onion	Colour characteristic to the variety, well cured, cut not more than one layer deep and 10 mm long, with skin atleast at 25 per cent of the surface area, no sprouting, with no sun burning, black powdery spots < 25 per cent, with no mechanical injury, with no discolouration diameter 40-60 mm.	With cuts not more than 3 layers deep and length 50 per cent of bulb diameter, sprouted, without skin and sun burning, 50 per cent area of the bulb, black powdery spots < 50 per cent with double/split neck > 15 mm diameter, mechanical injury not covering > 1 squre cm area, discolouration up to 90 per cent of surface, diameter 25-80 mm.
Potatoes	Colour characteristics to the variety, should be without mud, with no green spot, with no cut or maximum cut not more than 2 mm deep and length maximum 25 per cent of tuber diameter, with no natural cracks and properly shaped. Brown colour, without surface skin not exceeding 15 per cent, with no mechanical injury and blemishes, diameter 40-60 mm.	With green spots, with maximum of 3 cuts not more than 2 mm deep and length maximum 50 per cent of tuber diameter, upto maximum of three natural cracks, mis shaped and twins allowed, brown colour without surface skin upto 75 per cent of area, with slight (upto 20 mm diameter) injury, blemished. Tuber of any size.
Peas	Green, lustrous, dry skin not exceeding 10 per cent surface area, with no split skin, with no brown/ black spots on pod, no black tip.	Dry skin > 10 per cent surface area. With split skin, brown/black spots not exceeding 20 per cent surface area and with black tips.
Sweet potato	Colour according to variety but free from cuts and damage, having proper shape, diameter 40-80 mm, length up to 60 mm.	Pieces broken from both ends but free from fungal infection, slight cuts allowed, diameter 25-90 mm, length 60 mm and above.

Contd.

Radish	White/snow white colour, clean turgid and proper shape, secondly roots trimmed, with brown/black spots < 5 to surface area, with green leaves but not more than 50 per cent of the total weight, diameter 25-50 mm and length minimum 150 mm.	Mis-shaped/twisted/twins allowed, with brown/black spots < 10 per cent surface area, leaves yellow/wilted that are to be removed, diameter 20-60 mm and length minimum 150 mm.
Tinda	Green colour, tender, should be from diameter 25-60 mm	Without excessive black spots, diameter 60-70 mm
Tomato	Colour typical of variety (Partly Red coloured) with no dry cracks and insect damage, with no white/yellow hard sun burn patches, properly shaped, with packing/pressure damage < 10 per cent surface area, with green/yellow colour < 25 per cent of surface area, with no black/brown spot, diameter 45-59 mm (desi) and 30-45 mm (oval) and length minimum 55 mm	With maximum of 4 dry cracks, with insect damage not more than the diameter of pin head, sun burn patches not exceeding 210 mm diameter, mis-shaped, with pressure damage < 50 per cent surface area, with green/yellow colour upto 75 per cent, with black brown spots covering < 1 sq. cm surface area, if 30-44 mm (desi), 25-29 mm (oval) and length 30-54 mm of 35-45 mm round variety
Turnip	Diameter 45-80 mm (round variety)	Diameter 35-45 mm (round variety)

9.5. Acid- fermented Vegetables Produced in Different Regions of the World

Product name	Country	Major ingredients	Microorganisms	Usage
Sauerkraut	Germany	Cabbage, salt	*Leuconostoc mesenteroides*, *Lactobacillus brevis*, *Lactobacillus plantarum*	Salad, side dish
Kimchi	Korea	Korean cabbage, radish, various vegetables, salt	*L. mesenteroides*, *Lb. brevis*, *Lb. plantarum*	Salad, side dish
Dhamuoi	Vietnam	Cabbage, various vegetables	*L. mesenteroides*, *Lb. plantarum*	Salad, side dish
Dakguadong	Thailand	Mustard leaf, salt	*Lb. plantarum*	Salad, side dish
Burong mustasa	Philippines	Mustard	*Lb. brevis*, *Pediococcus cerevisiae*	Salad, side dish

Source: Breidt *et al.* (2013).

9.6. Osmotic Dehydration of Vegetables

Vegetables	Osmotic agent and concentration	Temperature °C	Sample to solution ration	Agitation	Sample size (mm)
Carrot	Sucrose 54+ salt 10 %	29	-	-	2
	Sucrose 40+ salt 10 %	RT	-	Yes	-
	Sucrose 10%	20	NK	NK	NK
	Salt and ethanol	NK	NK	NK	NK
	Sucrose + salt	30	1:5	–	5
	Sucrose	–	–	–	–
	NaCl 5–15%+ sucrose 50 °B	35–55	4–6	–	–
Cantaloupe	Sucrose 45–55 °B	40–50	–	–	–
Onion	Sucrose 54+ salt 10%	29	–	–	6–7
Pepper red, sweet	Sucrose 54+ salt 10%	29	–	–	–
Potato	NaCl, 10–18%	25–55	–	–	10
Sugar beet	Sucrose 30–70%+ salt 0–8%	30–50	–	–	–
Tomato	Salt 10%	29	–	–	10
	Sucrose 65–80%	49	4	Yes	–
	NaCl	–	–	–	–
	Salt 5%+ sucrose 35%	60	–	–	–

Note: NK= Not known; RT= Room temperature;°C= Degree celcius °B= degree brix; NaCl = Sodium chloride

9.7. Osmotic Agents Used in Osmotic Dehydration Process

Osmotic agent	Remark
Calcium chloride	Increase firmness of apple pieces, preserve the texture during storage. Prevents browning because of synergistic effect with ascorbic acid or sulfur di oxide.
Ethanol	Decrease the viscosity and freezing point of osmotic solutionin the de-hydro cooling process.
Fructose	Solute penetration rate is higher than sucrose, sucrose ispreferred over fructose.
Invert sugar	More effective than sucrose on sameconcentration because when completely inverted, it has twice as many molecules per unit volume. Practically a little difference in osmotic dehydration rate.
Lactose	Much lower level of sweetness than sucrose. Low solubility in aqueous solution
Maltodextrin	Can be used at higher total solids concentration or in mixed system.
Sodium chloride	Excellent osmotic agent for vegetables. Retards oxidative and non-enzymatic browning. Sometime bleaching effects on colored products, can be prevented using mixtures e.g. salt and sugar. Concentration should be around 10%. Hinders shrinkage
Sucrose/sugar	Dry sugar is unsuitable due to oxidative browning. Difficulty in disposing the sugar syrup formed. Sweetness prevents it for vegetable processing.
Mixture of invert sugar and salt, sucrose and salt, ethanol and salt	More effective than sucrose alone due to combination of properties of both the solutes.

9.8. Effect of osmo- air Dehydration on Quality of Vegetable Crops and Their Uses

Name of vegetables	Effect on quality attributes	Uses of osmo- dehydrated product
Okra	• Retention of vitamin C (6-8mg/100g). • Rehydration ratio (3-3.5 in boiling water for 4-5 min. • Recovery of dried okra slices (6.5-7.25%).	Dried okra is fried in refined oil along with spices followed by addition of water for rehydration during curry preparation.
Bitter gourd	• Good overall acceptability sensory score of 7.5 0n 9- point Hedonic scale of rehydrated bitter gourd slices during six months of storage. • Vitamin C (20-27mg/100g). • Rehydration ratio (5.0-5.8). • Recovery of dried bitter gourd slices (6.5-7.2%).	Dried bitter gourd slices are fried in refined oil along with spices followed by addition of water for rehydration.
Cauliflower	• Final moisture content 1-2%. • Retention of ascorbic acid (16-18 mg/100g). and total carotenoids (1.5-1.75 mg/100g). • Sensory overall acceptability score of 8.0 on 9-point Hedonic scale. • Recovery of dried cauliflower (9.5-10.8%).	Dried cauliflower pieces are fried in refined oil along with spices followed by addition of water for rehydration.
Indian bean	• Sensory overall acceptability score of 7.5 on 9- point Hedonic scale moisture (1-1.25%). • Vitamin C content (14-17 mg/100g) during storage. • Decrease in green colour (a) value from – 4.56 to -3.94 during storage. • Recovery of dried Indian beans pieces (7.5-8.5%).	Dried Indian bean pieces are fried in refined oil along with spices followed by addition of water for rehydration.
Carrot	• Overall sensory acceptability score of 8.5 on 9-point Hedonic scale. • Vitamin A content (800-1000 IU). • Recovery of dried carrot slices (10.5-11.75%).	Osmo-air dried carrot slices is directly consumed as sweet meat.

Contd.

Name of vegetables	Effect on quality attributes	Uses of osmo- dehydrated product
Ivy gourd	• Moisture (1.5-2.0%). • Ascorbic acid (5.0-6.0 mg/100g). • Rehydration ratio (3.0-3.5). • Recovery of dried ivy gourd slices (2.8-3.0%).	Dried ivy gourd is fried in refined oil along with spices followed by addition of water for rehydration during curry preparation.
Parwal	• Good rehydration ratio of 2.5-3.0 in boiling water for 4 min. • Overall acceptability score of 8.0 on 9-point Hedonic scale • Ascorbic acid (10-12 mg/100g). • Recovery of dried pointed gourd slices (8.5-9.25%).	Dried pointed gourd is fried in refined oil along with spices followed by addition of water for rehydration during curry preparation.
Green chilli	• Retention of 48 mg/100 vitamin C, 1.363 mg/l chlorophyll and 0.4% capsaicin in green chilli powder. • Retention of 80-85% green colour in dried green chilli powder. • Overall acceptability score of 8.0 on 9-point Hedonic scale. • Recovery of dried green chilli powder (7.5-8.5%).	Green chilli powder can be preferred in place of red chilli powder.
Tomato	• Ascorbic acid (8-10 mg/100g). • Lycopene (3-3.5 mg/100g). • Rehydration ratio (1.5-2.0). • Overall acceptability score of 7.5 on 9-point Hedonic scale. • Recovery of dried tomato powder (2.5-3.25%).	Tomato powder can be used in place of tomato in curry preparation.
Cabbage	• Vitamin C (15.5-17.0 mg/100 g) in dried cabbage leaves. • Overall acceptability score of 8.0 on 9-point Hedonic scale. • Recovery of dried cabbage leaves (6.8-7.5%).	Dried cabbage leaves are fried in refined oil along with spices followed by addition of water for rehydration during curry preparation.

9.9. Effect of Osmo- freeze Drying on Quality of Vegetable Crops and Their Uses

Name of vegetables	Effect on quality attributes	Uses of osmo- dehydrated products
Carrot	• Decrease (10.75%) of initial sugar content of carrot shreds in freeze dried samples during storage. • Decrease in red colour intensity in terms of a value (25.6%) in dried carrot shreds during storage. • Overall sensory acceptability of 8.0 on 9-point Hedonic scale.	Freeze dried carrot shreds after rehydration in boiling water for 1-2 min can be used in soup or curry preparation.
Bottle gourd	• Good rehydration ratio of 3.0-3.5 after rehydration in boiling water for 4-5 min. • Good overall acceptability score of 8.0 on 9-point Hedonic scale.	Freeze dried bottle bottle gourd pieces can be used in milk-based sweets.
Curry leaf	• Good rehydration quality with rehydration ratio of 2.5 -3.0 in boiling water for 2-3 min. • Good sensory qualities with overall acceptability score of 8.0 on 9-point Hedonic scale during storage. • Decrease in green colour in terms of a value from -7.67 to -5.87 after 5 months of ambient storage of 20-25oC.	Dried curry leaves are fried with seasoning to give desired aroma in food.
Onion Flakes	• Overall sensory acceptability score of 8.5 on 9-point Hedonic scale during storage. • Rehydration ratio of 1.5-2.0 in boiling water for 1-2 min.	Freeze dried onion flakes can be used as seasoning for increasing flavour in food.
Garlic pieces	• Overall sensory acceptability score of 8.5 on 9-point Hedonic scale during storage. • Rehydration ratio of 2.5-3.0 in boiling water for 4-5 min.	Freeze dried garlic pieces can be used as seasoning for increasing flavour in food.

Source: Information collected from Singh and Singh (2016).

9.10. Blanching Media and Time Required for Vegetables

Name of the vegetables	Blanching medium	Blanching time (minutes)
Potatoes	1. Boiling water	3
	2. Water at 200 ^{0}F	4
	3. 3 per cent boiling salt solution	3
Carrot	1. Boiling water	5
	2. Water at 200 ^{0}F	5
	3. 3 per cent boiling salt solution	6
Turnip	1. Boiling water	4
	2. Water at 200 ^{0}F	5
	3. 3 per cent boiling salt solution	3
Squash	1. Boiling water	2
	2. Water at 200 ^{0}F	4
	3. 3 per cent boiling salt solution	2
Bitter gourd	1. Boiling water	2
	2. Water at 200 ^{0}F	3
	3. 3 per cent boiling salt solution	2
Pumpkin	1. Boiling water	3
	2. Water at 200 ^{0}F	2
	3. 3 per cent boiling salt solution	6
Cabbage	1. Boiling water	6
	2. Water at 200 ^{0}F	8
	3. 3 per cent boiling salt solution	6

9.11. Canning Time for Non-acid Vegetables

Vegetables	Type of can	Strength of brine	Exhaust	Processing time min. at 0.7 kg per cm^2 steam pressure				
				No. 2Can	No.2½ can	No. 10 can	Pint jar	Quart jar
Asparagus	Plain	2.25 per cent Common salt solution	Exhaust the can at 192-212 ^{0} F (90-100^0 C) for 7-10 min. or until the temperature in the centre of the can reaches at least 170 ^{0} F (77^0 C)	20	24	40	30	35
Bean	Plain	2.25 per cent common salt solution	-do-	40	40	75	35	60
Beet root	Sulphur resistant	Water or 1.5 per cent common salt solution	-do-	30	30	40	25	25
Cabbage	Plain	2 per cent common salt solution	-do-	-	40	60	-	-
Carrot	Plain	-do-	-do-	20	25	50	35	40
Cauliflower	Plain	-do-	-do-	20	20	-	25	30
Green gram	Plain	-do-	-do-	40	45	-	40	40
Mushroom	Plain	-do-	-do-	25	25	40	30	40
Okra	Plain	-do-	-do-	25	35	-	25	50
Pea	Sulphur resistant	2 per cent common salt & 2.5 per cent sugar solution	-do-	40	45	60	40	40
Potato	Plain	-do-	-do-	40	45	-	-	-
Turnip	Plain	-do-	-do-	30	35	50	35	40

9.12. Effect of Steeping Preservation on Quality of Vegetable Crops and Their Uses

Name of vegetables	Effect on quality attributes	Uses of steeping preserved products
Cauliflower	• Overall acceptability score of 8.0 on 9-point Hedonic scale after 8 months of storage. • Maximum decrease in pH of curd pieces from pH 6.3 to 3.68 after 15 days of storage in steeped cauliflower samples with 4% sodium chloride, 1% acetic acid and 350 ppm sulphur dioxide. • Maximum decrease in hardness value of curd pieces (15.20N-10.12N) during 120 days of storage with steeped solution of 6% sodium chloride, 2% acetic acid and 350 ppm sulphurdioxide. • Decrease in extent of browning, ascorbic acid and total carotenoids content in steeped cauliflower samples of 2-6% sodium chloride, 1-2% acetic acid and 350 ppm sulphur dioxide, respectively during storage.	Steeped cauliflower is washed in water and it is used for pickle or curry preparation.
Carrot	• Overall acceptability score of 8.02 on 9-point Hedonic scale after 6 months of storage at ambient temperature. • Reduction of reducing sugar, total carotenoids and ascorbic acid to the level of 30-26.45%, 44-48% and 48–58%, respectively during storage. • Suitable for carrot based *halwa* even after 6 months of ambient storage.	Steeped carrot is washed in water and it is consumed for salad or for the preparation of carrot based *halwa*
Parwal	• Overall acceptability score of 7.0 on 9-point Hedonic scale after 4 months of storage. • Maximum decrease in pH from 6.94 to 3.84 after 4 months of storage. • Maximum decrease in green colour in terms of a value (-9.94 to -6.67) after 4 months of storage.	Steeped pointed gourd is washed in water and it is used for pickle or curry preparation.
French bean	• Decrease in pH from 6.3 to 4.8 during storage. • Decrease in green colour in terms of a value from -3.2 to -2.4 during storage. • Decrease in hardness value from 4.3N to 2.8N during storage.	Steeped French bean is washed in water and it is used for pickle or curry preparation.
Bitter gourd	• Good sensory overall acceptability score of 7.5 on 9-point Hedonic scale after 5 months ofambient storage. • Decrease in ascorbic acid to 18-20 mg/100g after storage.	Steeped bitter gourd slices is washed in water and it is used for pickle or curry preparation.

Contd.

	• Decrease in hardness value of bitter gourd slices from 3.8N -1.5 N after storage. • Decrease in green colour in terms of a value from -5.5 to -3.5 after storage	
Onion	• Significant reduction in microbial load (98-99%) after acetic acid steeping (pH 2.5-2.75) and 2% sodium chloride solution. • Overall acceptability score of 7.5-8.0 on 9-point Hedonic scale after 75 days of ambient storage. • Reduction in D value (1.58 min-1.0 min) in onion bulb at pH 2.5-2.75 after 2% sodium chloride steeping solution, 300 ppm sulphur dioxide and heat treatment at 100°C for 3 min.	Steeped onion after washing is preferred as salad in food.

Source: Information collected from Singh and Singh (2016).

9.13. Effect of Intermediate Moisture Preservation on Quality of Vegetable Crops and Their Uses

Name of vegetables	Effect on quality attributes	Uses of intermediate moisture preserved products
Amaranth	• Good overall acceptability score of 8.0 on 9-point Hedonic scale after 50 days of storage at 10-15°C. • Decrease in ascorbic acid from 45.58 mg/ 100 g to 30.23 mg/100g after 50 days of storage. • Moisture content varied from 18.5- 15.75% during storage.	Dried amaranth leaves are fried in refined oil along with spices followed by addition of water for rehydration during curry preparation
Spinach	• Good overall acceptability score of 7.5 on 9-point Hedonic scale after 50 days of storage at 10- 15°C. • Decrease in ascorbic acid to the extent of 45-50% during 50 days of storage. • Increase in moisture content from 16.4-17.3% during storage.	Dried spinach leaves are fried in refined oil along with spices followed by addition of waterfor rehydration during curry preparation.

Source: Information collected from Singh and Singh (2016).

9.14. Convenience Processed Food / Vegetables

Convenience food or tertiary processed food, is food that is commercially prepared (often through processing) to optimize ease of consumption. Such food is usually ready to eat without further preparation. It may also be easily portable, have a long shelf life, or offer a combination of such convenient traits. Although restaurant meals meet this definition, the term is seldom applied to them. Convenience foods include ready-to-eat dry products, frozen foods such as TV dinners, shelf-stable foods, prepared mixes such as cake mix, and snack foods.

9.14.1. Advantages of Convenience Foods: These are;

- Preparation time is reduced to a great extent.
- No storing, buying or planning of ingredients.
- Can hardly get any leftovers.
- Could have a variety of items especially for inexperienced cooks.
- Faster presentation and easy cleaning up.
- Less spoilage and waste occur with packaged convenience foods.
- Transportation of packaged foods is cheaper especially in concentrated form.
- Cost efficient for mass production and distribution.
- Ready to eat cereal and instant breakfast difficult to prepare at home because of its expensive product technology used in preparation.

9.14.2. Disadvantages: These are;

- Cooking time is sometimes increased for thawing or longer baking time.
- Harder to control fat, salt and sugar levels.
- Cost per serving may be higher than homemade.
- Convenience foods are typically high in calories, fat, saturated fat, sugar, salt, and trans-fats.
- They tend to lack freshness in fruits and vegetables.
- Convenience foods allow little recipe modification.
- Convenience foods are often processed.

9.14.3. Effect of on Convenience Processed Vegetables on Quality and Their Uses

Name of vegetables	Effect on quality attributes	Uses of convenience processed products
Bitter gourd chips	• Moisture (1.0%) • Good overall acceptability sensory score of 8.0 on 9-point Hedonic scale during storage • Vitamin C (20-22 mg/100g) • Rehydration ratio (5.0-6.0) • Dehydration ratio (5.8-6.0) • Extent of browning (0.12-0.16) • Recovery of dried bitter gourd slices (5.5-6.8%)	Dried bitter gourd slices are fried in refined oil and are consumed as snack food.
Ivy gourd chips	• Moisture (1.0-1.50%) • Ascorbic acid (5.0-6.0 mg/100g) • Rehydration ratio (2.5-3.0) • Recovery of dried ivy gourd slices (2.4-2.6%).	Dried ivy gourd slices are fried in refined oil and are consumed as snack food.

Contd.

Pointed gourd chips	• Good rehydration ratio of 2.5-3.0 in boiling water for 4 min. • Overall acceptability score of 8.0 on 9-point Hedonic scale. • Ascorbic acid (10-12 mg/100g). • Recovery of dried pointed gourd slices (8.0-8.25%).	Dried pointed gourd slices are fried in refined oil and are consumed as snack food.
Fennugreek leaves	• Rehydration ratio (3.0-3.5). • Overall acceptability score of 8.0 on 9-point Hedonic scale. • Vitamin C (35-40 mg/100g). • Recovery of dried fenugreek leaves (6.8-7.5%).	Dried fenugreek leaves are fried in refined oil along with spices followed by addition of water for rehydration during curry preparation.
Bathuwa leaves	• Rehydration ratio (1.5-2.0). • Vitamin C (20-25 mg/100g). • Overall acceptability score of 8.0 on 9 –point Hedonic scale. • Recovery of dried bathua leaves (6.5-6.75%).	Dried bathua leaves are fried in refined oil along with spices followed by addition of water for rehydration during curry preparation.
Spinach leaves	• Rehydration ratio (4.0 - 4.5). • Sensory overall acceptability score of 8.0 on 9-point hedonic scale. • Vitamin C (10-12 mg/100g). • Recovery of dried spinach leaves (6.0-6.25%).	Dried spinach leaves are fried in refined oil along with spices followed by addition of water for rehydration during curry preparation.
Amranth leaves	• Rehydration ratio (4.5-5.0). • Sensory overall acceptability score of 8.0 on 9-point Hedonic scale. • Vitamin C (10.0 – 12.0 mg/100g).	Dried amaranth leaves are fried in refined oil along with spices followed by addition of water for rehydration during curry preparation.
Cabbage leaves	• Vitamin C (13.0-15.5 mg/100 g) in dried cabbage leaves. • Overall acceptability score of 7.5 on 9-point Hedonic scale. • Rehydration ratio (4.5-5.0). • Recovery of dried cabbage leaves (6.8-7.5%).	Dried cabbage leaves are fried in refined oil along with spices followed by addition of water for rehydration during curry preparation.

Source: Information collected from Singh and Singh (2016).

9.15. Vegetable Based Sweets

The demand of vegetable-based sweets is increasing because of many nutritional and functional attributes from vegetables in sweets. Among vegetable-based sweets, petha is very popular dish of western parts of Uttar Pradesh such as Mathura, Agra and Kanpur. Many petha based industries at small cottage scale as well as big established petha manufacturing industries are located to produce variety of sweets from ash gourd. The delicacy of sweet can be judged that it can be prepared and served in many forms depending upon the choice of consumers. The variation in the variety of sweets from petha is reflected towards crystallized or glazed petha or dipping of cooked ash gourd in concentrated sugar syrup along with flavouring and colouring material for increasing the aesthetic quality. On composition basis, petha based sweets contain on an average 0.4% of fat, 65% of total carbohydrate, 3% of dietary fibre, 0.6% protein and 40% sugar content. Food Safety and Standards Act, 2006 limits the maximum permissible limit of 150 ppm of sulphur dioxide or 500 ppm sorbic acid in finished crystallized or glazed petha.

9.16. Packaging

After grading, it is essential to put the vegetables into suitable containers of required and desired sizes. In India, vegetable marketing is not so sophisticated. Many vegetables are transported in gunny bags or bamboo baskets or loose. The characteristics of vegetables packaging are:

- It serves as an efficient handling unit for customers and dealers.
- It serves as convenient ware house or storage unit.
- It should protect vegetables from mechanical injury.
- It should reduce the wastage of moisture loss.
- It should keep vegetables in clean and hygienic manner.
- It should be convenient for transportation and service.
- It should be attractive to customers in different modes.
- It should be economical in every respect.
- It should have height adjustment in such a way that upper stack doesn't press vegetables of lower stack.
- It should provide adequate ventilation to vegetables to avoid storage and transportation loss.
- It should be acceptable in all marketing areas.
- It should fulfill Goverment compliance problem, manufactures responsibility for safety and regard of consumer health, welfare and essential interest.

9.16.1. Purposes of Packaging: These are;

- **Packaging for distant markets:** For sending vegetables to distant markets, they are packed in bamboo baskets for vegetables like okra, guar, chillies, cabbage and cauliflower. Dry grasses and leaves are used as lining material inside the containers. Potato, sweet potato, onion and garlic are packed in gunny bags and paper cutting are used as packing materials. The top of basket or gunny bags is stitched.
- **Packaging for local markets:** Practically, vegetables are not packed for selling in local markets. Vegetables are carried in full of baskets and gunny bags. These are taken out and arranged properly for sale.
- **Packaging for consumers:** In India, no packing is done for consumers. People go to market for purchasing vegetables along with handbag. But recently vegetable sellers have started giving vegetables in polythene bags.

9.16.2. Merits of Packaging: These are

- Packed vegetables are not subjected to immediate losses.
- They maintain their freshness for considerable period.
- Packed vegetables have good demand and fetch comparatively high prices.
- Packed vegetables are conveniently transported.
- Packed vegetables are protected from dust and dirt and wilting.
- Packing avoids much of the labour cost and wastage during handling.

9.16.3. Characteristics of Good Packaging: These are

- Good packing is designed to deliver the contents conveniently and cheaply with quality unimpaired.
- It should have provision for aeration.
- A good packing is economical and easy in handling.
- A good packing attracts consumer which may result in good sale.
- A good packing is suitable for distant transportation, loading and stacking with security and economy of space.
- A good packing is neither loose nor too light because both are harmful and may result in bruising.

9.16.4. Kindof Packaging

In India, much attention is not given on packing of vegetables for home consumption. However, for export marketing it is done in proper manner because good packing carry good impression on good quality. Most common in India, packing is done in (i) gunny bags, (ii) baskets made of bamboo and or arhar sticks, (iii) wooden boxes, (iv) plastic containers, (v) polythene bags and (vi) cartons made of cardboard.

9.17. Labelling

Labelling is done for identification of the item without opening the packet. It indicates, the weight, price, date of packing, name and the address of producer. Some precautions and warnings are also included wherever they are applicable. Labelling is accomplished by (i) printing directly on packing, (ii) pasting a printed label on the package and (iii) wrapping with material or using printed bags. Both colour and design make labelling impressive and informative.

9.18. Precooling

Precooling is a method of removing field heat from harvested vegetables especially during hot weather which prevents decay, retard the ripening and senescence, and loss in quality. Precooling is done particularly when vegetables are transported to long distance or stored for a long time. Precooling is done after harvesting and prior to storage. It is economical to do precooling with cold water. Vegetables like tomato, runner bean, lettuce, carrot, celery, asparagus, okra, artichokes etc. respond well to precooling in terms of less physiological weight loss during storage.

9.18.1. Methods of Precooling

- Placing the produce in refrigerated trucks with forced humified air circulation.
- Placing ice in package.
- Placing ice in water and passing the produce through spray of cold water and
- Vacuum cooling: Leafy vegetables respond well to vacuum cooling.

9.19. Storage of Vegetables

9.19.1. Reasons for Storage of Vegetables

The following reasons are given for storing vegetables;

- Storing of vegetables ensures confirmed supply of fresh vegetable off-season.
- It helps fetching high prices, which are not available at the time of production due to glut in the market.
- Storage protects vegetables from fluctuating weather condition, and help in precision planning.
- Stored vegetables can be used economically for making various products.

9.19.2. Morphological Structure of Vegetables for Storage

Basic morphological structure	Example
Underground structure	
Bulb	Onion, garlic
Stem tuber	Potato, jerusalem artichoke, yam
Root	Carrot, radish, beet, turnip, sweet potato, cassava
Corm	Colocasia, elephant foot yam
Rhizome	Lotus, mango zinger
Above ground vegetative structure and flower	
Flowers	Drumstick, sesbania, pumpkin, artichoke (floral bud)
Buds	Cabbage, brussels sprout, lettuce
Stem	Asparagus, amaranthus
Leaves	Leafy vegetables
Reproductive structure	
Legume	Pea, dolichos bean, cluster beans
Berry	Solanaceous vegetables, cucurbitaceous vegetables
Pepo	Pumpkin, watermelon
Capsule	Vendi

9.19.3. Classification of Vegetables According to Respiratory Behavior

Climacteric vegetables	Non climacteric vegetables
Tomato, water melon, musk-melon	Brinjal, capsicum, cucumber, tomatillo, cabbage, chinese cabbage, lettuce, beans

9.19.4. Respiration Rates of Vegetables

Class	Range at 5 °C (mg CO2 kg-1 h-1)	Vegetables
Very low	<5	—-
Low	5 to 10	Onion, potato
Moderate	10 to 20	Cabbage, carrot, lettuce, pepper, tomato
High	20 to 40	Cauliflower, lima bean
Very high	40-60	Artichoke, snap bean, Brussels sprouts,
Extremely high	> 60	Asparagus, broccoli, pea, spinach, sweet corn

9.19.5. Detrimental Effect of Ethylene on Post- harvest Quality of Vegetables

Vegetables	Symptom of ethylene injury
Asparagus	Increase toughness of spears.
Snap beans	Loss of green colour.
Broccoli	Yellowing, abscission of floret, development of off flavor
Cabbage, Chinese cabbage	Yellowing and leaf abscission.
Carrot	Development of bitter flavor.
Cauliflower	Leaf abscission and yellowing, brown discoloration of remaining portions of leaves.
Cucumber, summer squash	Accelerated softening, yellowing.
Brinjal	Calyx abscission, browning of pulp and seeds, accelerated decay.
Lettuce	Russet spotting.
Potato	Sprouting.
Sweet potato	Brown discoloration and off flavor detectable upon cooking
Turnip	Increase toughness.
Water melon	Reduced firmness, flesh tissue maceration resulting in thinner rind, poor flavor.

9.19.6. Storage Temperature and Relative Humidity of Different Vegetables

Vegetables	Temperature (^{0}C)	RH (per cent)	Storage life (weeks)
Asparagus	0.0	95	3-4
Brinjal	10.0-11.1	92	3-4
Indian bean pod	0.6-1.7	90	3
Beet, topped	0.0-1.7	90-95	8-14
Beet, bunched	0.0	92	1-5
Bitter gourd	0.6-1.7	85-90	4
Cabbage, early	0.0-1.7	92-95	4-6
Cabbage, late	0.0-1.7	92-95	12
Carrot, topped	0.0	95	20-24
Cauliflower (Snow ball)	0.0-1.7	85-95	7
Celery	0.6-0.0	92-95	8

Contd.

Colocasia	11.1-12.8	85-90	21
Coriander, leaves	0.0-1.7	90	5
Cucumber	10.0-11.7	92	2
Garlic	0.0	65	28-36
Ginger	7.2-10.0	75	16-24
Lettuce, head	0.0	90-95	3
Lettuce, leaves	0.0	95	1
Lima bean, pods	4.4-7.2	90-95	1.5-2.0
Musk melon (Cantaloupe) (Honey dew)	1.7-3.37.2	90-9585	1.5-4.5
Okra	8.9	90	2
Onion, leaves	0.0	90-95	2
Onion, bulbs	0.0	70-75	20-24
Pea, green	0.0	88-92	2-3
Pepper green	7.2	85-90	3-5
Pepper, ripe	5.6-7.2	90-95	2
Potato	3.0-4.4	85	34
Pumpkin	1.7-11.6	70-75	24-36
Radish, topped	0.0	88-92	3-5
Squash, winter	12.8-15.6	70-75	24-36
Sweet corn	0.6-1.7	90-95	1
Sweet potato	10.0-12.8	80-90	13-20
Tapioca, root	0.0-1.7	85	23
Tomato, unripe	8.9-10.0	85-90	4-5
Tomato, ripe	7.2	90	1
Turnip	0.0	90-95	8-16
Water melon	7.2-15.6	80-90	2
Yam	26.7	66-70	3.5

9.19.7. Shelf- life and Physiological Loss in Weight (P.L.W.) of Vegetables

Vegetables	Storage months	Outside		Evaporative Cool Chamber	
		P.L.W. (per cent)	Shelf life (days)	P.L.W. (per cent)	Shelf life (days)
Mint	May-June	58.5 (73.1)	< 1	18.6	3
Coriander	May-June	30.0 (44.00)	< 1	13.0	3
Amaranthus	May-June	49.8 (63.8)	< 1	10.9	3
Spinach	Feb.-March	16.0 (31.5)	3	7.3	8
Methi	Feb.-March	18.0 (43.5)	3	10.8	10
Lettuce	Feb.-March	9.5 (29.6)	5	2.3	10
Okra	May-June	14.0 (32.5)	1	5.0	6
Bitter gourd	May-June	18.2 (38.1)	2	5.6	6
Chilli	May-June	23.3 (32.2)	3	8.8	6
Tinda	May-June	17.8 (35.0)	2	5.4	6
Pointed gourd	May-June	32.8 (89.5)	2	3.8	5
Cucumber	May-June	19.4 (35.6)	3	5.5	8

Contd.

Kakri	May-June	31.4 (63.0)	1	5.2	3
Carrot	Feb.-March	29.0 (46.6)	5	9.0	12
Beet	Feb.-March	14.5 (29.2)	5	2.3	12
Radish	Feb.-March	24.7 (58.4)	5	4.1	10
Turnip	Feb.-March	16.0 (35.4)	5	3.4	10
Peas	Feb.-March	29.8 (51.7)	5	9.2	10
Cauliflower	Feb.-March	16.9 (27.3)	7	3.4	12

Figures in parentheses are P.L.W. at the end of storage in cool chamber.

9.20. Effect of on Shellac Coating Quality of Vegetable Crops and Their Uses

Name of vegetables	Effect on quality attributes	Uses of Shellac coated products
Capsicum	• Shelf life extension of 30-35 days after storage at 10°C. • Decrease in ascorbic acid content from 102 mg/100g to 70 mg/100g after 35 days of storage at 10°C Decrease in green colour in terms of a value from -12.1 to - 8.1 after 35 days of storage at 10°C. • Decrease in hardness in terms of force 4.02N to 2.8N during storage. • Overall sensory acceptability score of 7.5 on 9 – point Hedonic scale.	Capsicum is washed thoroughly in running water and consumed for preparation curry as fresh vegetable.
Pointed gourd	• Shelf life extension of 15 days after storage at 10°C. • Increase in physiological loss in weight to 8.5% after 15 days of storage at 10°C. • Increase in total soluble solids from 3.85% to 5.8% after 15 days of storage at 10°C. • Decrease in ascorbic acid (40-44%) after 15 days of storage at 10°C.	Pointed gourd is washed thoroughly in running water and consumed for preparation curry as fresh vegetable.
Brinjal	• Shelf life extension of 7 days at ambient storage temperature (20-22°C). • Increase in physiological loss in weight from 6.0 – 25.7% after 7 days of storage. • Increase in total solids from 8.5-11.9% during storage. • Decrease in texture from 89.24 N to 55.7N during storage. • Decrease in antioxidant activity from 389.7 to 182.8 µM gallic acid/g.	Brinjal is washed thoroughly in running water and consumed for preparation curry as fresh vegetable.
Carrot	• Overall sensory acceptability score of 7.5	Carrot is washed thoroughly

Contd.

	on 9-point Hedonic scale after 20 days of storage at10°C. • Physiological loss in weight increased from 2.64% to 14.8% during storage. • Total solids increased from 9.67% to 12.4% during storage. • Red colour in terms of a value increased from 4.38 to 6.67 during storage. • Antioxidant activity in terms of FRAP decreased from 7.18 to 5.96 µM/g.	in running water and consumed for preparation curry as fresh vegetable.

Source: Information collected from Singh and Singh (2016).

Section-II

10

Vegetable Breeding

10.1. Floral Biology of Vegetable Crops

Common Name	Botanical name	Time of anthesis	Time of dehiscence	Duration of pollen fertility	Duration of stigma receptivity
Tomato	*Lycopersicon esculentum*	7.00-8.00 hr	9.00-11.00 hr	On day of the anthesis	16 hr before anthesis to the day of anthesis
Potato	*Solanum tuberosum*	5.00-6.00 hr	5.30-7.00 hr next day early morning	On the day of anthesis to	On the day of anthesis to next day afternoon
Chilli	*Capsicum annuum*	5.00-6.00 hr	8.00-11.00 hr	On day of the anthesis	On day of the anthesis
Brinjal	*Solanum melongena*	6.00-11.30 hr next morning also	4.15-11.00 hron the 2 days after anthesis	On day of the anthesis to anthesis	2-3 hr before anthesis to 2 days after
Okra	*Abelmoschus esculentus*	8.00-10.30 hr	6.00-11.30 hr	6.00-12.00	One day before 6to the day of anthesis
Pea	*Pisum sativum*	5.45-6.30 hr	5.45-7.30 hr 24 hr thereafter	One day of the anthesis to	48 hr before and 24 hr after anthesis
Sem	*Dolichos lablab*	9.00-17.00 hr	5.00-14.00 hr	On day of the anthesis	On day of the anthesis
Beans	*Phaseolus* spp.	5.00-7.00 hr	5.30-7.30 hr	On day of the anthesis	On day of the anthesis with maximum peak between 7.00-8.00 hr
Goar	*Cyamopsis tetragonoloba*	9.00-16.00 hr	1-2 hr before anthesis hr after anthesis	2 hr before to 11	On day of the anthesis
	Psophocarpus tetragonolobus	8.00-9.00 hr (i.e. before anthesis)	20.00-6.00 hr	On day of the anthesis	24 hr before to 34 hr after anthesis
Sweet	*Apium graveolens* var. *duece*				
Potato	*Ipomea batatas*	4.00-14.00 hr 2 hr after anthesis	Simultaneously or	On day of the anthesis	On day of the anthesis
Radish	*Raphanus sativus*	9.00-10.00 hr	9.00-10.00 hr when stored at 3 °C the pollen is viable for 60 days	On the day of antheis	Most receptive at the time of anthesis and last till 4 days after anthesis
	Brassica oleracea (Capitata Group)	8.00 to 10.00 hr	8.00 to 10.30 hr	On the day of anthesis	2-3 days before to the the day of anthesis

Contd.

Common Name	Botanical name	Time of anthesis	Time of dehiscence	Duration of pollen fertility	Duration of stigma receptivity
	Brassica oleracea (Gongylodes Group)	8.00-10.00 hr	8.00-10.30 hr	On day of the anthesis	On day of the anthesis
Beet root	*Beta vulgaris* var. *bengalensis*	7.00-17.00	8.30-18.30	On day of the anthesis	6 hr before to 8 hr after anthesis
Muskmelon	*Cucumis melo*	5.30-6.30 hr	5.00-6.00 hr	5.00-14.00 hr	2 hr before to 2-3 hr after anthesis
Watermelon	*Cittrullus lanatus*	6.00-7.30	5.00-6.30 hr	5.00-11.00 hr	2 hr before to 3 hr after anthesis
Bonlegourd	*Laganaria siceraria*	17.00-20.00 hr	13.00-14.30 hr till next morning	On the day of anthesis	36 hr before to 60 hr after anthesis
Bittergourd	*Momordica charantia*	9.00-10.30 hr	7.00-8.00 hr	5.00-12.00 hr	One day before and one day after anthesis
Parwal	*Trichosanthes anguina*	18.00-21.00 hr anthesis	Shortly before dehiscence	10 hr before to 49 hr after	7 hr before to 51 hr after anthesis
Ridge gourd	*Luffa acutangula*	17.00-20.00 hr	17.00-20.00 hr	On the day of anthesis to till 2-3 days after anthesis in winter and 18 hours in rainy season	6 hr before to 84 hr after anthesis
Waxgourd	*Benincasa hispida*	6.00-7.00 hr	3.00-4.00 hr	7.00-16.00 hr	12 hr before to 36 hr after anthesis
Cucumber	*Cucumis sativus*	5.30-7.00 hr	4.30-5.00 hr	Up to 14 hr	12 hr before to 6-7 hr after anthesis
Pumpkin	*Cucurbita pepo*	3.30-6.00 hr	21.00-3.00 hr	16 hr after anthesis	2 hr before to 10 hr after anthesis

10.2. Breeding Objectives

10.2.1. Tomato

- To develop early , high yielding and consumer preference varieties / hybrids.
- Large round fruit with adequate firmness and shelf-life, uniform fruit sizes shape, red colour and freedom from external blemishes or abnormalities for fresh market.
- Large fruit size, high fruit quality and continuous production for home garden tomatoes.
- Deep, uniformly red coloured tomatoes , pH below 4.4, high total soluble solid (4.5-7) and high alcohol solids (AIS) in processing tomatoes.
- To evolve varieties / hybrid resistant to diseases like fusarium wilt, verticillum wilt, late blight, early blight, septoria leaf spot, anthracnose, bacterial wilt, bacterial canker and tomato leaf curl virus.
- To develop varieties/ hybrids resistant to root-knot nematodes.
- To breed varieties/ hybrids suitable for abiotic stresses like low Day (K10°C) and high temperatures (day 35+2°C) excess and moisture deficient, salt etc.
- To develop varieties/ hybrids for prolonged storage and transportation.
- To develop multi – disease and insect resistant varieties / hybrids.
- To develop varieties hybrids suited for protected cultivation.
- To develop varieties/hybrids suited for mechanical harvesting.
- To development varieties/hybrids suited for vertical gardening.
- To develop varieties / hybrids suited for export.
- To develop varieties/hybrids for nutritional rich (high TSS, lycopene / beta carotene, ascorbic acid, acidity and low in oxalate content)

10.2.2. Brinjal

- To develop early with high yielding varieties/ hybrids.
- To develop varieties / hybrids on the basis of fruit shape, size and colour as per consumer preference.
- To develop varieties / hybrids suited for bhartha preparation.
- To develop varieties/ hybrids of upright sturdy plant free from lodging.
- To develop varieties/ hybrids resistant to bacterial wilt, phomopsois blight, little leaf, root-knot nematodes, shoot and fruit borer, jassid and epilachna beetle.
- To develop varieties hybrids tolerant to high temperature (day 35-40°C)

10.2.3. Bell pepper and Chilli

- To develop varieties / hybrids having earliness with high yield.
- To develop varieties/ hybrids should have desirable fruit shape and size (Oblate or round fruit in bell peper and long fruits in chilli).
- To develop varieties / hybrids have superior fruit quality (Pleasing Flavour, high vitamin c in bell pepper and high capsaicin in chilli.

- To develop varieties/hybrids having high oleoresin content.
- To develop varieties/hybrids tolerance to diseases like fruit rot, cercospora leaf spot, powdery mildew, bacterial leaf spot, phytophthora, root rot, root-knot nematode and common tobacco mosaic virus.
- To develop varieties/hybrids tolerance to insects viz; thrips, mite, aphids and fruit borer .
- To develop varieties/hybrids resistant/tolerant to abiotic stresses like high temperature (day 35-40°C), moisture deficiet and salinity.
- To develop varieties hybrids suited for protected cultivation.
- To develop varieties/hybrids suited for export purposes
- To develop varieties/hybrids for pickles and powder.

10.2.4. Okra

- To develp high yielding varieties/hybrids capable of giving more marketable yield having dark green, tender, thin, medium long, smooth, 4-5 ridged-pods.
- To breed early maturing varieties with prolonged harvest.
- To evolve varietie/hybrids resistant to yellow vein mosaic virus and enation leaf curl virus; fungal diseases like fusarium wilt, cercospora leaf spot, powdery mildew and alternaria leaf spot, and insects like white fly, jassids alongwith root knot nematodes.
- To develop multiple disease and pest resistant varieties/hybrids.
- To develop most suitable ideiotype. Short plants with more number of nodes with short internodal length would be more productive than a tall plant with long internodal length. Plants and fruits should be devoid of conspicuous hairs. Fruits should not snap easily from the stalk for facilitating easy and economic harvest.
- To breed varieties/hybrids with optimum seed setting ability for their rapid multiplication.
- To evolve varieties/hybrids tolerant to abiotic stresses especially tolerance to low temperature (day 15-20 °C), excessive rains, saline and alkaline soils
- To develop varieties suitable for export purposes.
- To evolve varieties/hybrids suitable for processing purposes.

10.2.5. Muskmelon

- To develop varieties/hybrids having early in maturity with high total marketable yield.
- To develop varieties/hybrids of attractive and shapesphorical. Thick flesh with a attractive colour, small seed cavity and attractive colour.
- To develop varieties/hybrids with sweet, juicy and musky flavoursome fruits. The sugar content in muskmelon is a premium attribute. It should vary from 11 to 13 per cent or higher not less than 10 per cent.
- Tough netted skin of fruit.

- To develop varieties/hybrids resistant to common diseases like powdery mildew, downey mildew and viruses.
- To develop varieties/hybrids resistant/ tolerant to insect- pests like red pumpkin beetle, fruit fly and aphids.
- To develop varieties suited for protected cultivation.
- To develop varieties/hybrids for export purposes.

10.2.6. Watermelon

- To develop varieties/hybrids having plant type bearing first pistillate or hermaphordite flower at early node number. It gives fair indication of earliness.
- To develop varieties/hybrids having tough skinned fruits, better suited for long distance transportation.
- To develop varieties/hybrids possessed with 10 per cent or higher TSS content so as to meet consumer acceptance.
- To develop varieties/hybrids having fruit with fewer and smaller seeds and attractive deep red flesh.
- To develop varieties/hybrids of high fruit yield in terms of weight and number of fruits of marketable quality.
- To develop varieties/hybrids resistant/ tolerant to major diseases like virus, fusarium wilt, anthracnose and powdery mildew.

10.2.7. Cucumber

- To develop varieties/hybrids having minimum node number at which first pistillate or hermaphordite flower appears.
- To develop varieties/hybrids of high female to male sex ratio especially in monoecious plant types.
- To develop varieties/hybrids of attractive green or dark green fruits with smooth fruit surface and without prominent spines or prickles.
- To develop varieties/hybrids having uniformaly long cylindrical shape without crook – neck. Fruits should be free from carpel sepration showing hollow spots.
- Fruits should be free from bitterness.
- To develop varieties/hybrids for export purposes
- To development varieties/hybrids for low temperature tolerance.
- To develop varieties/hybrids which do not produce, mature seeds at edible maturity.
- To develop varieties/hybrids resistant/ tolerant to unfavourable conditions and major diseases and insect- pest.
- To develop varieties/hybrids having parthenocarpic feature which suited for protected cultivation.

10.2.8. Bitter gourd

- To develop self stalked varieties/hybrids with high yielding and early bearing.
- To develop varieties/hybrids resistant to major diseases and insect-pest
- To develop varieties/hybrids suited for protected cultivation.
- To develop gynoecious lines for minimizing cost of hybrid seed production.
- To develop varieties/hybrids suited for processing purposes.
- To develop varieties/hybrids for export purposes

10.2.9. Bottle gourd

- To develop varieties/hybrids of higher yield desirable fruit shape (straight long having blunt end), size (40-50 cm in length), light green in colour, soft skin with tender flesh.
- To develop varieties/resistant/tolerant to common diseses and insect-pest.
- To develop varieties suited for protected cultivation.
- To develop varieties/hybrids suited for winter season cultivation.
- To develop varities/hybrids for export and processing purposes.

10.2.10. Summer squash

- To develop varieties/hybrids with plant type of bearing first pistillate flower at early node number. It gives a fair indication of earliness.
- To develop varieties/hybrids of high female to male sex ratio as it results in higher fruit yield.
- To develop varieties/hybrids having medium vine characteristic in non- bushy types.
- To develop varieties/hybrids having fruits with attractive green colour and desirable fruit shape.
- To develop varieties/hybrids resistant/ tolerant to powdery mildew, virus and red pumpkin beetle.

10.2.11. Sponge gourd and ridge gourd

- To develop varieties/hybrids having the lowest node number at which first pistillate or hermaphordite flower appears , an indicator of earliness.
- To develop varieties/hybrids of high female to male ratio as it results in higher fruit yield.
- To develop varieties/hybrids having unformly thick cylindrical fruits free from bitterness.
- To develop varieties/hybrids having fruits which remain tender and non- fibrous in optimum, sized fruits at edible maturity.
- To develop varieties/hybrids of high fruit yield in terms of weight and number of fruits of marketable quality.
- To develop varieties/hybrids tolerant to cucumber mosaic virus and fruit fly.

10.2.12. Pumpkin

- To develop early maturing varieties/hybrids.
- To develop high yielding varieties with high female to male ratio.
- To develop varieties/hybrids with high carotenoids.
- To develop varieties fruits yellow or mottled and non- ridged rind which are more attractive.
- To develop fruits with thick flesh and narrow seed cavity.
- To develop fruit shape having a high flesh recovery per volume of fruit from yield point of view.
- To develop medium vine characteristics.
- To develop varieties/hybrids tolerant to diseseses like mildews powdery and downey and insects like fruit fly and red pumpkin bettle.
- To develop varieties/hybrids rich in betacarotene.

10.2.13. Snake gourd

- To develp varieties/hybrids having lowest number at which the first female flower apperars. It is an indication of earliness.
- To develop varieties/hybrids having high female to male ratio as it results in higher fruit yield.
- To develp green long and white long fruits which have better consumer acceptance.
- To develop varieties which fruits remains tender and non – fibrous at edible maturity.
- To develop varieties tolerant to diseases and insect- pest.

10.2.14. Tinda

- To develop varieties of early and high yielding.
- To develop varieties of high female to male ratio.
- To develop varieties which fruits remain tender and non- fibrous at edible maturity. Tenderness can be judged from fruits having sparse/hairs persisting on the skin.
- To develop light green colour of the fruit, being highly acceptable.
- To develop varieties resistance tolerant to diseases and insect-pests.

10.2.15. Onion

- There is need to develop high yielding varieties having improved quality of bulbs with longer storage life, suitable for different agro- ecological conditions.
- To develop hybrids having high productivity.
- To develop varieties / hybrids resistant/ tolerant to diseases like purple blotch, basal rot, stemphylium blight and storage rots, besides, insect- pest like thrips.

- To develop varieties/ hybrids suitable for export to the world market.
- To develop white varieties with high dry matter content suitable for dehydration industry.
- To develop varieties resistant/ tolerant to abiotic stresses like moisture stress, high temperature, soil salinity and alkalinity.
- To develop varrieties/hybrids suited for rainy season cultivation.

10.2.16. Radish

- White berg/stump roots with thin top root and non-branching habit.
- To develop varieties of short duration this could be adjusted in different cropping system.
- To develop varieties having high pungency of roots which should be as per consumer preferance
- The varieties must be slow bolting habit
- Varieties should be heat and moisture deficit tolerance
- To develop F1 hybrids with the help of CMS lines.
- To develop varieties which could stand for a longer period without becoming pithy.
- To develop varieties which could be suited for different agro- climatic conditions.
- To develop varieties / hybrid resistant/ tolerant to diseases like alternaria blight, white rust and radish mosaic virus and tolerance to insect like aphids.

10.2.17. Turnip

- To develop varieties of more uniformity
- To develop varieties with root quality of temperate types and ability to produce seed under tropical candition
- To develop varieties with variying matrity period
- To develop disease resistant varieties particularly to while rust phyllody of seed crop.

10.2.18. Carrot

- To develop varieties with high carotene content by crossing Asiatic and European types.
- To develop F_1 hybrids with the help of cytoplasmic male –sterile lines.
- To develop varieties/hybrids with good colour, size, earliness, top root ratio and resistance to cracking.
- To develop varieties/hybrids heat tolerance (30-35°C.
- To develop varieties resistant/ tolerant to diseases and insect - pest.

10.2.19. Garden Pea

- To develop high yielding varieties.
- To develop varieties having regional adaptability.

- To develop varieties resistant/ tolerant to lodging and shattering
- To develop varieties resistant/ tolerant to powdery mildew day temperature and temperature upto of 34°C.
- To develop varieties having good quality and effective nitrogen fixation.

10.2.20. French bean

- To develop varieties high pod yield with non-stringy, long pods round shape for vegetable and flat shape for pulse.
- To develop widely adaptive varieties suited to various agro-climatic regions.
- To develop photo- insensitive varieties suited for both temperate and tropical regions of the country.
- To develop pole type varieties which could suited for cultivation in both plain and hilly areas
- To develop varieties for fresh market and pod processing purposes.
- To devolvep varieties bearing pods the above the leaves being useful for easy picking and early ripening.
- Varieties free from inter-nodal space.
- To develop varieties resistant/ tolerant to major diseases particularly anthracnose, rust, angular leaf spot and mosaic both golden yellow mosaic and bean mosic.
- To develop varieties of high – fertilizer responsive.
- To develop varieties tolerant to frost, heat and herbicides.
- To formulate breeding strategy for quality improvement particularly for more protein content.
- To develop varieties of dry shelled beans with red colour, bold grain and more shelling percentage.

10.2.21. Cowpea

- To develop widely adaptable vegetable type varieties suitable for various agroclimatic conditions.
- To develop photo- insensitive varieties for successive planting during the year.
- To develop dwarf type varieties and high yielding to avoid high expenditure on staking of the crop.
- To develop varieties having short tender pods of whole pod processing.
- To develop varieties having long tender and stingless pods for fresh consumption.
- To develop varieties resistant/ tolerant to anthracnose, powdery mildew and mosaic.
- To develop varieties suited for inter cropping.
- To develop varieties for high protein content.
- To develop varieties suited for winter season cultivation.

10.2.22. Indian Bean

- Comprehinsive germplasm collection, evaluation, maintenance and conservation.
- To develop varities having bushy growth habit, high yielding, good pod qualities and resistant/tolerant to delichos yellow mosaic virus (DYMV)/commo virus.
- Identification of suitable rhizobium strain for inoculation widely differing climates.
- Identification of Rhizobium strain for inoculation, its nodulation and amount of nitrogen it can fix and transfer to the soil.
- Uniform maturing thermo-insensitive varieties tolerant to day temperature of 38°Cvarieties.
- Resistant to diseses, insect-pest adverse soil and weather conditions.
- Development of varieties for pulses purposes
- Compatability as a inter crop with food and forage legumes.
- Improvement of feeding values of seeds for human and livestock (including ploutry and pigs.).
- To develop varieties having less anti- nutritional factors.

10.2.23. Faba bean

- Stable and high yield with desirable seed size and colour as per consumers prefernace for the region.
- High seed protein content range 27-34% on dry matter basis.
- To develop varieties possessed high methionine and check with low tannins, glucosides (vicine and convicine).
- To develop varieties resistance / tolerance to chocolate spot, ascochyta blight, rust, bean leaf roll virus, bean yellow mosic virus etc.
- To develop varieties tolerance to heat, moisture dificit and salt.

10.2.24. Cabbage

- To develop self- incompatible but cross compatible lines for use in hybrid seed production programme.
- To develop cultivars and hybrids which can grow under mild winter conditions.
- To standardize the technique for hybrid seed production.
- To develop varieties resistant to black rot *(Xanthomonas campestris* and cabbage yellows *(Fusarium oxysporum* f. *conglutianans*).
- To develop varieties tolerant / resistant to cabbage butterfly caterpillar (*Pieris brassicae*), aphids (*Brevicoryne brassicae*) and diamond back moth (*Plutella oxygostella*).
- To develop varieties/hybrids which accomodates more plants per unit area.
- To breed varieties which could stay longer in the field after head formation.

10.2.25. Cauliflower

- To develop self- incompatible but cross- compatible inbred lines in the better combining parents.

- To develop varieties/hybrids which can form curds during summer and rainy season in the hills to feed the market in the plains.
- To standardize the techniques for hybrid seed production.
- To breed varieties with better seeding ability as some of the varieties could not become popular only because of their poor seeding habit.
- To develop varieties resistant to diseases like black rot , sclerotinia rot, alternaria blight , downy mildew and erwinia rot.

10.2.26.Amranths

- Collection and evaluation of germplasm to identify suitable vegetable amranth types with high yield potential coupled with nutritional qualities.
- Evaluation and identification of erect and clipping (cutting) types suited for early harvest by pulling and continued harvest by periodical cutting, respectively to suit different regions.
- Evaluation and selection of dual amranth types (grain cum leafy amranth) with high yield potential and quality attributes to replace the local types in their specific areas of cultivation .

10.2.27. Spinach

- To develop lines / varieties having high yield, good quality and resistance to diseases.
- To develop line / varieties having photo- insensitive, slow bolting, fast growing multiple cutting types so that varieties can be grown throughout the year.
- To develop male sterile lines for hybrid seed production.

10.2.28. Potato

- To develop varieties for high tuber yield, earliness, photo-period-insensitve and responsiveness to fertilizer.
- To develop varieties suited for warm humid tropics.
- To develop varieties rich in protein and vitamin.
- To develop varieties resistantce/tolerance to late blight, early blight, charcoal rot, common scab, bacterial wilt, viral diseases and nematodes.
- To develop varieties resistance / tolerance to insects like aphids, potato tuber moth
- To develop varieties better keeping quality, resistance / tolerance against storage rottage, accumulation of sugars specially reducing sugar and reasonable dormancy
- True potato seed technology needs to be refined and popularized.
- To develop varieties resistanee / tolerance to heat, moisture deficit, frost and soil salinity.

10.3. Breeding Methods Used in Vegetable Crops

S.N.	Crop groups	Breeding methods used
1.	Bulb crops (Onion and garlic)	Mass selection, heterosis breeding and interspecific hybridization.
2.	Cole crops (Cabbage, cauliflower, knol-khol, broccoli, Brussels sprouts)	Introduction, mass selection, pedigree, bulk population, heterosis breeding, double back cross, interspecific and intergeneric hybridization, mutation and polyploidy.
3.	Cucurbitaceous (Cucumber, muskmelon, watermelon, pumpkin, and squashes, bottle gourd, ridge and sponge gourds)	Single plant selection, mass selection, pedigree method, bulk population method, back cross, heterosis breeding, mutation breeding, polyploidy breeding, interspecific and intergeneric hybridization.
4.	Solanaceous vegetables (Tomato, brinjal, chilli and bellpeper)	Mass selection, single plant selection, single seed descent method, pedigree selection, back crossing method, heterosis breeding, mutation breeding, polyploidy breeding, interspecific and intergeneric hybridization.
5.	Malavaceous vegetable (Okra)	Pure line selection, mass selection, back cross method, pedigree method, bulk population, mutation breeding, polyppoidy breeding, heterosis breeding and interspecific hybridization.
6.	Leafy vegetables (Amranth and spinach)	Mass selection, bulk population method, interspecific hybridization and polyploidy.
7.	Root vegetables(Radish, carrot, turnip and beet root	Mass selection, pedigree method, heterosis breeding, interspecific and intergeneric hybridization, recurrent selection and polyploidy.
8.	Legume vegetables (Garden pea, French bean, Indian bean and cowpea)	Introduction, pure line selection, mass selection, back cross method, pedigree method, heterosis breeding, mutation breeding, interspecific hybridization, HIMSI (hybridization and mass sowing of individual selection).
9.	Vegetatively propogated vegetables (Parwal, kundru, ginger, turmeric, potato, colocassia and sweet potato etc.)	Introduction, clonal selection, modified pedigree, heterosis breeding and mutation.
10.	Tree vegetables (Curry leaf and drumstick	Single plant selection, mass selection, exploitation and maintainance of vigour observed in transgrassive segregant, polyploidy breeding and mutation breeding.

10.4. Breeding for Quality Attributes

Name of Crops	Quality parameters
Tomato	Large round fruit with adequate firmness and shelf life, uniform fruit size, shape, red colour and freedom from external blemishes or abnormalities for fresh market.Large fruit size, high fruit quality and continuous production for home garden tomatoes. Deep

	uniformally red coloured tomatoes, pH below 4.4, high total soluble solids (4.5-7%) and high alcohol insoluble solids (AIS) for processing tomatoes.
Brinjal	Fruit shape, size and colour as per consumer preference with soft flesh, low proportion of seed,soft flesh and lower olenine content
Bell pepper and Chilli	Oblete or round fruit in bell pepper and long fruit in chilli. Pleasing flavour, high sugar/acid ratio, high pigment content and vitamin C in bell pepper and high capsaicin ($C_{18}H_{27}NO_3$) and high oleoresin in chilli
Okra	Dark green, tender, thin, medium long, smooth 4-5 ridged pods at marketable stage.Pods should be free from conspicuous hairs and optimum seed setting ability.
Pea	Long, attractive green pods with more seeds/pod. Sweetness in pods with high shelling percentage.
Cauliflower	Non-ricey, compact bract free protected curds with retentive cream/ white colour.Bettter seeding quality.
Cabbage	Longer staying capacity in field after formation, narrow, short and soft core with short stem.
Knol-khol	Spherical swollen bulb like stem and it should be free from bolting.
Radish	White, long/stump roots with thin tap root and non-branching habit, nonpithy roots with slow bolting habit. Pungency of roots should be as per consumer preference.
Carrot	Scarlet/orange colour roots with uniformity in shape and size. Smooth root surface, thick flesh roots, and thin and self-coloured core in roots. Broad shouldered, cylindrical, uniformly tapering or stump rooted with non-branching habit. Early rooting with free from cracking. High sugar and dry matter content in roots.
Turnip	Root colour as per consumer's preference, white, purple types more liked in India that golden ball types. Stump rooted hybrids with thin tap root and non-branching habit. Slow bolting habit and appropriate dry matter (8-9%) in roots.
Beet root	Dark red and uniformly coloured roots alongwith uniform root shape. Absence of internal white rings in roots. Slow bolting with manogerm seeds.
Onion	High TSS is important for dehydration industry producing onion chips and powder.
Cucumber	Attractive green or darkgreen fruits with smooth surface and without prominent spines or prickles. Uniform long cylindrical shape without crookneck. Fruits should be free from carpel seperation without hollow spots with free from bitterness alongwith less seeds at edible maturity.
Muskmelon	Fruits should be attractive round/spherical in shape with thick flesh and attractive in colour. Small seed cavity, sweet, juicy musky flavoursome fruits. TSS should not less than 10% with tough netted skin of fruit.
Watermelon	Tough skinned fruits for long distance transportation. TSS content not less than 10%. Fruits with smaller and fewer seeds with attractive deep red flesh and firm flesh.
Squash and	Thick fruit flesh and small seed cavity. Round/oblong/flat round

Contd.

Pumpkin	fruit shape. Orange flesh colour, rich in beta carotene.
Bottlegourd	Attractive green fruit of round/long/club shaped with sparse hairs persisting on skin and nonfibrous flesh at edible stage. Fruits should be nonbitter.
Bittergourd	Less ridged fruit surface with thick fruits particularly suitable for stuffing. Fruit size variation as per consumer's preference (Small 7.5-10 cm long, medium long 10-15 cm, long 15-20 cm and extra long 20-40 cm). Immature seeds for longer period during green edible stage.

10.5. Vegetable Varieties Developed Through Introduction

Crop	Variety	Country
Tomato	Sious	US
	Marglobe	US
	LaBonita	US
	Roma	South America
	Dwarf Money Maker	Isreal
	Balkan	Bulgaria
	Fireball	Canada
Bellpepper	Yolo Wonder	California
	California Wonder	USA
	Chinese Giant	USA
	R-449	Russia
Pea	Early Badger	US
	Bonneville	US
	Sylvia	Sweden
	Arkel	England
	Meteor	England
	Little Marvel	England
	Dwelich Commondo	Wisconsion
French bean	Contender	US
	Kuntkey Wonder	USA
	Bountyful	USA
	Top Crop	USA
	Wates	USA
	Premier	Sweden
	Giant Stringless	Sweden
	BKW-74	Sweden
	Jampa	Mexico
Cowpea	Phillippine Early	Phillippine
Watermelon	Asahi Yamato	Japan
	New Hampshire Midget	USA
	Suger Baby	USA
	Shipper	USA
Summer Squash	Australian Green	Australia
Onion	Early Grano	USA
	Burmedo Yellow	Phillipines

Contd.

	Red Granno	America
Radish	Pusa Chetki	Denmark
Sweet potato	FA 17 White	China
Okra	Ghana	Ghana (Africa
Cauliflower	Snowball -16	Holland
	Improved Japani	Isreal
Cabbage	September	Jerman Democratic Republic
	Pride of India	UK
	Copenhagen Market	UK
Cucumber	Poinsett	USA
Summer squash	Pattypan	USA
Carrot	Jeno	Jerman Democratic Republic

10.6. Promising Lines Introduced in Vegetable Crops for Different Traits

Crop/ varieties	Accession number	Salient feature	Country
High yielding and desirable fruit type			
Tomato	EC-391024	Long shelf line	Australia
	EC-3100299	Slow ripening	USA
	EC-321425-26	Paste type	Taiwan
Cucumber	EC-398030	Early and determinate type	China
Chillies	EC-391073	Pungent type	Taiwan
	EC-391089-92	Early maturity and bunch type	Taiwan
	EC-347363	High pungent type	Taiwan
Watermelon	EC-380989-92	Yellow flesh and early maturity	USA
	EC-393240-43	Red flesh/ round/ early maturity	USA
Cauliflower	EC-348166	High yielding / early type	USA
Onion	EC-30802-11	High bulb yielding	USA
	EC-378476-77	High TSS and long shelf life	UK
Garlic	EC-367655-58	High yielding and bold clove	Isreal
French bean	EC-29490	High yield	Russia
	EC-24958	High yield	Russia
	EC-30021	High yield	Russia
	EC-595960	High yield	Canada
Male sterile/ restorer lines / hybrids			
Tomato	EC-347359-68	Hybrids (F_1)	Taiwan
	EC-343391-95	F1 hybrids (Cherry tomato	Taiwan
	EC-346011	Stamen less line (F_2)	USA
	EC-346013	Corolla & stamen line (F_2)	USA
	EC-346014	Green Pistillate type	USA
Cucumber	EC-382737-39	Gynoecious lines	USA
	EC -329300	Gynoecious (G4)	USA
Muskmelon	EC- 48140-43	F_1 Hybrid (Early & Sweet)	USA
	EC-382726-36	Male sterile gene (Ms2 to Ms5)	France
Cabbage	EC-304718-25	Cytoplasmic male sterile and restorer lines	USA
	EC-187228-30	Male fertile lines	Canada

Contd.

Germplasm for abiotic tolerance			
Tomato	EC -399828-38	Heat tolerance	USA
	EC -347359-69	Heat tolerance	Taiwan
	EC -321425-26	Heat tolerance	Taiwan
	EC -37868-83	Low irrigation	Australia
Chinese Cabbage	EC -345978	Heat tolerance	Taiwan
Cabbage	EC -350918-28	Heat tolerance	USA
	EC -168041-42	Heat tolerance	USA
Cauliflower	EC -164414-16	Heat tolerance	USA
Capsicum	EC -334206	Water submergence	Taiwan
Muskmelon	EC -350603	Sulphur tolerance	USA
	EC -342751-54	Heat tolerance	Japan
	EC -319095-96	Salt tolerance	Austarlia
Germplasm for biotic tolerance / resistance			
Tomato	EC- 399828-38	Multiple disease	USA
	EC- 347369-90	Tomato mosaic virus and bacterial wilt	Taiwan
	E -321890-928	Viral disease	Taiwan
Watermelon	EC -383809	Fusarium wilt	USA
	EC -378523-24	Fusarium wilt	USA
	EC- 333659-69	Wilt	USA
	EC -217073-74	Fusarium and gummy stem blight	USA
Muskmelon	EC -350602	Aphid	USA
	EC- 350603	WMB	USA
	EC -330956	Multiple disease	USA
Chinese cabbage	EC -345978	Multiple disease	Taiwan
Cabbage	EC -168041-42	Club root & black root	Taiwan
Cauliflower	EC- 175800-06	Multiple disease	USA
Cucumber	EC -320526	Multiple disease	USA
Chilli	EC -323333	Multiple disease	USA
Okra	EC- 305616	YVMV	Bangladesh
Garlic	EC -378476-77	Pink rot	UK

10.7. Varieties Developed through Pure Line Selection Followed by Single Plant Selection.

Crop	Varieties
Tomato	Improved Meeruti, CO2, Arka Vikas and Arka Saurabh.
Brinjal	Pusa Purple Long, Pusa Purple Round, Arka Sheel, Arka Shirish, Arka Kushumaker, MDU and PKM-1.
Chilli	K-1, Co.1, CO.2 and PLR-1.
Bell pepper	Arka Mohani, Arka Gaurav and Arka Basant.
Okra	Co.1.
Amranth	Co.1 Co.2 Co.3 and Co.4.
Cowpea	Pusa Phalguni.
French bean	Arka Komal and YCD-1.
Muskmelon	Arka Jeet, Arka Rajhans, MH-1.
Bottle gourd	Pusa Summer Prolific Long, Pusa Summer Prolific Round and Arka Bahar.

Bitter gourd	Pusa Do-mousami, Arka Harit and Co-1.
Snake gourd	Co-1.
Pumpkin	Arka Chandan, Arka Suryamukhi, Co-1 and Co-2.
Cauliflower	Hissar-1.
Cabbage	Pusa Drum Head.
Sweet potato	Pusa Safad.
Onion	Pusa Red, Punjab Selection-1, Pusa Ratnar and Hissar-2.
Turnip	Pusa Sweti .

10.8. Vegetable Varieties Developed through Hybridization

Crop	Name of the variety	Parents
Tomato	Pusa Ruby	Sioux X Improved Meeruti
	Pusa Early Dwarf	Improved Meeruti X Red Cloud
	HS-101	Sel.2-3 X Exotic cultivar
	HS-102	Sel-12 X Pusa Early Dwarf
	Punjab Chhuhara	Punjab Tropic X EC 55055
	Punjab Kesari	Punjab Tropic X EC 55055
	Hisar Lalima	Pusa Early Dwarf X HS-101
	Hisar Lalit	HS-101 X Resistant Banglore
	Hisar Anmol	Hisar Arun X *Lycopersicon hirsutum* f. *glabratum*
	Hisar Arun	Pusa Early Dwarf X K-1
	Sel.1	Pusa Early Dwarf X HS-101
	Sel.2	(HS-101 x Punjab Tropic) X (H-14 x Punjab Tropic)
	Arka Meghali	Arka Vikas X IIHR-554
	Azad T-2	HB-5 X Kuber
	DVRT-1(Kashi Amrit)	Hisar Arun X *Lycopersicon hirsutum* f. *glabratum* B6013
	DVRT-2(Kashi Anupam)	Hisar Arun X *Lycopersicon hirsutum* f. *glabratum* B6013
	IIVR SEL-2(Kashi Sarad)	MTH-6X Kalyani Eunish
	IIVRSEL-1(Kashi Hemant)	Sel-18 X FloraDade
	Junagarh Ruby	Big Silari X Pusa Ruby
	Gujarat Tomato -2 (GT-2)	Anguar Lata X Punjab Chhuhara
	Keckruth	Kecki Methi X Ruthger
	Keckruth Ageti	Keckruth X Ruthger
	Sweet - 72	Pusa Red Plum X LE- 79
	Utkal Kumari	Selection -22 X BT-2
	Utkal Urbasi	Punjab Chhuhara X LE-79
	Paiyur	Pusa Ruby X Marutham
	Narendra Tomato-3	Resistant Banglore X Kalyan Kuber
	Narendra Tomato-4	Pusa Ruby X Kalyan Kuber
	NDTS-2001-3	H-24 X NDT-120
	Kashi Chayan	Meghalaya Local XH-88-78-2
Brinjal	Arka Keshav(IIHR-21)	Dingrass Multiple Purple X Arka Sheel
	Arka Nidhi(BWR-12)	Dingrass Multiple Purple X Arka Sheel

Contd.

	Azad Karanti	Banarasi Giant Long X Pusa Purple Long
	Arka Navneet	IIHR-22-1 X Supreme
	Azad B-2	Banarasi Giant Round X 7103
	KS-224	Pusa Purple Round X Arka Sheel
	Gujarat Brinjal -6	Doli-5 X Morvi -4-2
	Hisar Pragati	R-34 X Sel- 26
	Hisar Shyamal	Aushey X BR-112
	H-4	Pusa Purple Long X Hyderpur
	H-5	Aushey X R-34
	H-9	Aushey X R-34
	Juangarh Long	Doli-5 X Inbred Panch Mahal
	Pant Rituraj	Kalyanpur T-3 X Pusa Purple Cluster
	Pusa Kranti	(Pusa Purple Long x Hyderpur) x Wynad Giant
	Pusa Anupam	Pusa Kranti X Pusa Purple Cluster
	Punjab Barsati	Pusa Purple Cluster X H-4
	Utkal Jyoti	KT-4 X BB-11
	Uttkal Kesari	BB-11 X KJ-3-1
	Uttkal Madhuri	PBR125-5 X Pipli -4
	Uttkal Tarani	Pusa Karanti X Gopa Local
	Narendra Brinjal-2	NDB-25 X NDB-2
Chill and Capsicum	Arka Suphal	Pant C-1 X IIHR-517A
	Andhra Jyoti	G-2 X Bihar Variety
	ACH-1	S-49 X CDPS- 120
	ACH-30	S-5-5 X Punjab Guchedar
	Bhaskar (LCA-235)	G-4 X Yellow Anther Mutant
	Gujarat Vegetable Chilli-121	G-4 X S-49
	Jawahar -218	Kalipeeth X Pusa Jwala
	Kashi Surkh(CCH-2)	CCA-4261 X Pusa Jwala
	PKM-1	ACNO. 1797 X C0-1
	Prakash (LCA-206-B)	G-3 X Huntaka
	Punjab Lal	Perennial X Long Red
	Pusa Sadabahar	Pusa Jwala X IC-31339
	X-235	G-4 X Anther Mutant
	KTCPH-3	Yolo Wonder X HL-201
	KTCPH-5	Yolo Wonder X EC-143570
	Pant C-1	NP-46 A X Local Cultivar
	DH-76-6	Puri Red X Byadgi Local
Okra	CO2	AE-180 X Pusa Sawani
	CO3	Parbhani Kranti X MDU- 1
	Prabhani Kranti	Pusa Sawani X *A. manihot*
	Punjab Padamani	*A. esculentus* X *A. manihot* ssp *manihot*
	Punjab-7 (P-7)	Pusa Sawani X *A. manihot* ssp *manihot*, PDIB-2 X PDIB-1
	Pusa Sawani	IC-1542 X Pusa Mukhmali
	Phule Utkarsha	Parbhani Kranti X Varsha Uphar
	Selection -2	(Pusa Sawani X Best – 1) X Pusa Sawani X IC- 7194

Contd.

	Sheetla Uphar	PDIB-2 XPDIB-1
	Varsha Uphar	Lam Selection -1 X Prabhani Kranti
Garden Pea	Azad P-1	Line 6416 X 6405
	GC 195	T-19 X Little Marvel
	PH-1	Bonneville x P-23
	Jawhar Matar -1(JM-1 or GC-141)	T-19 X Greater Progress
	Jawahar Matar –2 (JM-2 or GC-477)	Russian -2 X Greater Progress
	Jawahar Matar –3(JM-3or Early December	T-19 X Little Marvel
	Jawahar P-4 (JP-4 or JM- 6)	Local Yellow Batri X 6588X 46C
	Jawahar Pea-71 (JP-71)	(Arkel X JP-829) X (P -501 X JM-1)
	Jahahar Pea-83 (JP-83)	(Arkel X JP-829) X (46CX JP-501)
	Little Morvel	Chelsea Gem X Suttons Alska
	Kashi Nandani (VRP-5)	P-1542 X VT-2-1
	Kashi Udai (VRP-6)	Arkel X FC-1
	Kashi Mukti (VRP-22)	No.7 X PM-5
	Kashi Shakati (VRP-7)	Harabona X NDVP-8
	Madhu	6126 X Sylvia
	Matar Ageta-6	Massey Gem X Harabona
	Narendra Sabzi Matar-6	KS-123 X Arkel
	Punjab -87	Pusa-2 Morrassis-55
	PM-2	Early Badger X IP-3
	Punjab -88	Pusa-2 X Morrasis-55
	VL-3	Old Sugar X Early Wrinkled Dwarf 2-2-a
	VL-6	Pant Uphar X VL Matar -3
Cowpea	Arka Samrudhi (IIHR-16)	Arka Garima X Pusa Komal
	Arka Garima	TUV-762 X *Vigna unguiculata* spp. *sesquipedelis*
	Arka Suman	Pusa Komal X Arka Garima
	Bidhan Barbati -1	EC-243954 X EC- 305827
	Bidhan Barbati -2	V-70 X Sel Tm -3
	IIHR-16	Arka Garima X Pusa Komal
	Kashi Gauri	IIHR Sel-16x Sel. 2-1
	Kashi Unnati	Cowpea-263 X Arka Garima
	Kashi Kanchan	(Sel. 2-2 X BC-244002) X Sel. 2.2
	Kashi Nidhi	Kasni Unnati X Cowpea-263
	Narendra Lobia -2 (NDPC-13)	Sel-2-1 X Red Red Seeded
	Pusa Dofasli	Pusa Phalguni x Phillippines
	Pusa Komal	P-85-2 X PU-26
	S-203	Selection -2 X Virginia
	S-488	Virginia X Iron Grey
Cluster bean	Durga Bahar	Pusa Navbahar X ROC-401
	P-28-1-1	Pusa Navbahar X IC-11521
French Bean	IIHR-909	Blue Crop X Contender
	Lakshmi	Contender (Bush Type) X Local (pole type
	SVM-1	*Phaseolus vulgaris* var Contender X *P. multiflorous* var. PBL-257

Contd.

	Arka Anoop	IIHR-22 X Arka Komal
	Kashi Sannpann	Arka Komal X Contender
Indian Bean	Co2	Co-8 XCo-1
	Hebbal Avare -3	Hebbal Avare-1 XUS-67-13
	WalKonkan	Wal-2-K-2 X Wal-125-36
	Kashi Bounisem-3	Kashi Haritima X Arka Vijay
	Kashi Bounisem-9	Kashi Sheetal X Gomachi Green
Bitter gourd	Phule Priyanka(RHRBGH-1)	RHR-5 X RHR-5
Bottle gourd	Pant Sankar Lauki-1(PBOGH-1)	PBOG-22 X PBOG-40
	Pant Sankar Lauki-2(PBOGH-2)	PBOG-22 X PBOG-61
	Kashi Ganga	IC92465XDVBG-151
Cucumber	Pant Sankar Khira -1(PCUCH-1)	PCUC-28 X PCUC-8
	Pant Sankar Khira -3(PCUCH-3)	PCUC-15 X PCUC-25
Pumpkin	Kashi Harit (IVPK-226)	NDPK-24 X PKM
Muskmelon	Hisar Madhur	Pusa Sharabati X 75-34
	MH-10	WI-998 X Punjab Sunehri
	MHY-3	Durgapur Madhu X Pusa Madhuras
	Pusa Sharbati	Kutna (PMR-6) X American Cantaloupe
	Punjab Sunheri	Hara Madhu X Edisto
	Punjab Rasila	WMR-29 X Hara Madhu
	Punjab Hybrid-1	MS-1 X Hara Madhu
	RM-50	Durgapur Madhu X Sel-1
Watermelon	Arka Manik	IIHR-21 XCrimson Sweet
	Pusa Bedana	Tetra-2 X Pusa Rasaal
	Durgapur Lal	Sugar Baby X KS-3566
Roundmelon	Arka Tinda	T-3-4 X T-8-2
Cabbage	H-113	Sel-18 X 83-6
	Pusa Muketa	EC-24855 XEC-10109
Cauliflower	Pusa Snowball	EC-12013 X EC-12012
	Pusa Snowball-1	EC-12013 X EC-12012
Palak	Arka Anupma	IIHR-10 X IIHR-8
	Pusa Harit	Sugarbeet X Local Palak Variety
Carrot	Pusa Kesar	Local Red X Nantes
	Pusa Meghali	Pusa Kesar X Nantes
	Pusa Yamdagni	EC-9981 X Nantes
	Selection -233	Nantes X No. 29
Radish	Pusa Himani	Radish Black (Temparate type) X Japanese White
Turnip	Pusa Kanchan	Local Red Round X Golden Ball
	Pusa Chandrima	Snow Ball (European type) X Japanese White (Asiatic type)
	Pusa Swarnima	Golden Ball X Japanese White
Onion	Co-4	AC-863 X Co-3
	Phule Suvarna	RHR-200 X RHR-155
	Arka Kritiman	MS-65XSel-13-1-1
Cassava	Sree Harsha	OP-4 X H-230
	Rayong -3	MCol-1-1684 X Rayong-1
Potato	Kufri Alankar	(Kennebee X O.N. 2090) X (Majestic

		X Ekishiraju
	Kufri Anand	PJ-379 X PH/ F -1430
	Kufri Ashoka	EM/C -1020 X Allerfuii Heste Gelbe
	Kurfi Badshah	Kufri Jyoti X Kufri Alankar
	Kufri Bahar	Kufri Red X Ginek
	Kufri Chamatkar	Ekishiraju X Phulwa
	Kufri Chandrmukhi	S-4485 X Kufri Kuber
	Kufri Chipsona-1	MEX-750826 X MS/ 78-79
	Kufri Chipsona-2	F-6 X QB- B-92-4
	Kufri Giri raj	SLB/ J-132 X EX/ A 680-16
	Kufri Himalani	SLB/ H -140 X SLB/Z-389 (b)
	Kufri Jawahar	Kufri Neelamani X Kufri Jyoti
	Kufri Jeevan	M-109-3 X D-698
	Kufri Jyoti	3069 d (4) X 2814 Q (1)
	Kufri Khashigaro	Taborky X SD-698
	Kufri Lalima	Kufri Red X CP-1362
	Kufri Lauvkar	Serkoy X Adina
	Kufri Muthu	3046 (I) X M-109-C
	Kufri Naveen	D-692 X 3070d (4)
	Kufri Pukhraj	Craig, s Defiance X JEX/ B -687
	Kufri Sheetman	Craig, s Defiance X Phulwa
	Kufri Sherpa	Ultimus X Adina
	Kufri Sindhuri	Kufri Kundan X Kufri Red
	Kufri Sutlej	Kufri Bahar X Kufri Alankar
	Kufri Swarna	Kufri Jyoti X (Vin) 2 (62.33.3)
Sweet Potato	Pusa Sunehari	Porto Blanko Wannop X Australian Canner
	Gouri	H-219 X H-42
	Varsha	(ACCNo. 39 X ACCNo. 3) X (AccNo 1871 X AccNo1130)
	Sankar	H-219 X S-73
	Sree Rethna	S-187 X Sree Vardhini
Black Pepper	Panniyur -1	Uthigankotta X Cheriakaniakadan
	Panniyur -3	Uthigankotta X Cheriakaniakadan
	Shyama	Uthigankotta X Cheriakaniakadan

10.9. Varieties Developed Through Pedigree Method

Name of Crop	Variety	Parentage
Chilli	PKM-1	AC.No.1797 X Co.1
	Andhra Jyoti	G2 X Bihar Variety
	Pusa Sababahar	Pusa Jawala X IC-31339
	K-2	K1 X Satur Samba
Cassava	H-97	Manjavella X Acc. NO.300
	H-165	Chadaymangalam X Vella X Kalikalan
	H-226	M4 X Ethakkkaruppan
	Sree Visakham	Acc.No1501 X S-2312 (exotic)
	Sree Harsha	(OP-4 (2x) X H-2304(4x)
Sweet potato	H-41	Norin X Indigenous cultivar
	H-42	Vella damph X Triumph
	Varsha	(Acc.No39 X Acc. No.3) X (Acc. (No.187 X Acc.No.1103)
	Sree Rethana	S-187 X Sree Vardhani
	Gouri	H-219 X H-42
	Sankar	H-219 X S-73

10.10. Vegetable Species/varieties for Higher Nutraceuiticals

Crops	Varieties/acessions/landraces/ wild relatives	Nutrition
Tomato	*L. pimpinellifolium*, Caro Red	Vitamin A Beta carotene
	High pigment mutants (hp), Crimpson (og), Pusa Rohini	Lycopene
	L. pennelliii IL6-2, IL7-2	Phenolics
	L. pennelliii IL12-4	Ascorbic acid
	Anthocyanin fruit (Aft) from *L. chilense*, atroviolacium (atv) from *L. cheesmaniae*	Anthocyanin
Chilli	*C. annuum* var. IC: 119262(CA2), Bayadaggi Kadd	Ascorbic acid
Paprika	KTPL-19	Capsanthin
Muskmelon	Honey Dew 32	Ascorbic acid
	Canary Yellow	Flavons
Spine gourd	*Momordica dioca*	Protein
	M. chochinchinenesis	Beta carotene
Bitter gourd	DRAR-1, DVBTH-5	Beta carotene
	DRAR-1, DVBTG-5	Ascorbic acid
Sweet potato	Resisto, Zambezi, Chiwoko	Beta carotene
Cassava	UMUCASS 44, UMUCASS 45 and UMUCASS 46	Vitamin A
Carrot	Pusa Asita	Anthocyanin
	Pusa Rudhira, Pusa Vrishti, Pusa Vasudha	Lycopene
	Pusa Nayanjyoti	Beta carotene
Amaranth	Pusa Lal Chaulai	Anthocyanin
	Arka Smraksha	Antioxidant
Broccoli	PalamVichitra	Anthocyanin
Red cabbage	Red Acre	Anthocyanin
Radish	Pusa Jamuni	Anthocyanin
	Pusa Gulabi	Lycopene
Bitter gourd	Pusa Aushadi	Beta carotene
Beet leaf	Pusa Bharati	Ascorbic acid

10.11. Identified Linked Markers for Quality Improvement in Vegetable Crop

Crop	Trait	Gene	Marker
Cauliflower	High carotene	Or	SSR
	High anthocyanin	Pr	BoMYB3, BoMYB4
Broccoli	Glucosinolates	QTL	SSR
Pepper	Pungency (Punl)	Punl, CCR, KAS, HCT	SNP
Water melon	Lycopene	LCYB gene	CAPS
Tomato	Mineral content	QTLs	SSR, SNP, InDel
	Fruit traits (Soluble solid)	QTLs	InDel
	Fruit ascorbic acid	QTL	RFLP, SSR
Carrot	Alternative oxidase (AOX) enzyme	DcAOXl gene	SNP, InDel
Carotenoid	Gene DCAR 032551	DCAR 032551	
	Anthocyanin	QTLs (Cy3XG, Cy3XGG, Cy3XSGG, Cy3XFGG)	SSR
Onion	Fructon	QTLs	SSR

10.12. Tolerant/resistant genotypes of Some Vegetable Crops Against Major Diseases

Crop	Disease(s)	Genotype(s)
Tomato	Tomato leaf curl virus (carrying) Ty3gene	Kashi Chayan
Indian Bean	Yellow mosaic virus	Wal Konkan-1, Kashi Sheetal
Cauliflower	Black rot	Pusa Shubra
	Downey mildew	Pusa Hybrid-2, Pusa Kartik Sankar
Cabbage	Black rot	Pusa Mukta
	Yellowing	Sri Ganesh Gol
Carrot	Powdery mildew and leaf spot	Ooty-1
Bottle gourd	Powdery mildew and downy mildew	Narendra Rashmi
Muskmelon	Powdery mildew	Arka Rajhans, Punjab Hybrid-1
Cucumber	Downy mildew and powdery mildew	PCUCH-3
Squash	Downy mildew, powdery mildew and cucumber mosaic virus	Punjab Chappan Kaddu-1
Ridge Gourd	Downy mildew	Arka Sujat
	mosaic and downy mildew	Deepti
Watermelon	Powdery mildew, downy mildew and anthracnose	Arka Manik
	Blight and bud necrosis	Durgapura Lal
Sponge gourd	Wilt and bean mosaic virus	Phulle Prajakta
Spinach beet	Cercospora leaf spot	Arka Anupma
Cowpea	Cercospora leaf spot	Kashi Nidhi
French bean	French bean golden yellow mosaic	Kashi Rajhans

10.13. Heterosis Breeding

10.13.1. Heterosis Events

- First record to exploit hybrid vigour in vegetable crops, Cucumber: Hayes and Jones (1916)
- First commercial hybrid in vegetable crops, Brinjal: Kakizaki (1931)
- First utilization of self-incompatibility system, Cabbage: Pearson (1931)
- First utilization of cytoplasmic - genic male sterility mechanism, Onion : Jones and Clarke (1943)
- First Identification of gynoecious sex form, Cucumber: Peterson (1960)
- First identification of cytoplasmic male sterility, Radish: Ogura (1968)
- First ethylene-induced femaleness in cucurbits : Rudich et al, (1969)
- First identification of cytoplasmic - genic male sterility mechanism in carrot: Morelock et al, (1996).

10.12.2. Why are we still talking about heterosis?

- ***Unique way of translating biological science to Industry:*** Worth of vegetable seed market in India likely to increase from present 4000 crore to 8000 crore by next 5 years
- **Incredible value of the hybrid in enhancing yield and adaptability:** Vegetable production need to be enhanced by 35% in next 5 years
- ***Income and employment generation in the rural sector:*** About 3.0 million man days are generated annually and average benefit cost ratio of hybrid seed production is 2.50
- ***Earning of foreign exchange:*** Present export worth of hybrid seeds is about >500 crore

10.13.3. Wide array of hybrids in vegetable crops

Cross-pollinated crop: Cabbage, cauliflower, broccoli, Brussels sprouts, Chinese cabbage, onion, carrot, beet, turnip, watermelon, musk melon, pumpkin, summer squash, winter squash, bottle gourd, bitter gourd, ridge gourd, sponge gourd, cucumber, gherkin, sweet corn, coriander, etc.

10.13.4. Major vegetable hybrids in India by value

1. Tomato
2. Cabbage (import 100%)
3. Okra
4. Chilli (import 60%)
5. Cauliflower (import 80%)
6. Watermelon
7. Cucumber
8. Bottle gourd

9. Bitter gourd
10. Ridge gourd
11. Carrot (import 100%)
12. Coriander (import 100%)

10.13.5. Targeted Characters in the Hybrids

Hybrid	Targeted characters
Watermelon	Large, elongated melons with finely-textured, bright pink-red flesh and sweet (Jubilee pattern), resistant to watermelon bud necrosis + fusarium wiltSugar Baby and icebox type with 3 to 3.5 kg fruit weight, blackish green colour skin, very good transportability, TSS 13°Brix and above, fine texture
Cucumber	Early maturing, nice green or dark green Poinsettia type fruit, uniform long cylindrical shape without crook-neck, prolific yielder, resistant to CMV + PM + DM.
Bottle gourd	Attractive green fruit of round/cylindrical shaped with sparse hairs persisting on skin and non-fibrous flesh at edible stage, resistant to DM + PM.
Bitter gourd	Spindle shaped green fruit with medium prickle on fruit surface with extended harvest span, resistant to Mosaic + DM.
Muskmelon	Consistent yield, netted cantaloupe, honeydew, sutured melon and Galia types, better adaptability and shipping qualities, resistant to Fusarium wilt + CMV + PM + DM.
Brinjal	Round with purple and white stripes, green long, purple long, green round and large purple oval fruits, resistant to phomopsis blight + Bacterial wilt.
Tomato	Determinate growth habit, dual purpose and processing quality , good transportability, high yield, resistant to high temperature + TLCV+ early blight + bacterial wilt. Indeterminate hybrids with extended harvest span.Determinate growth habit, flattish-round, high acid fruits.
Okra	Attractive light green to green fruit, tender, thin, medium long, smooth, 4-5 ridged , free from conspicuous hairs, resistant to YVMV.
Cabbage	High temperature tolerant, firm, semi-flat heads, weighing within two kg and with good field holding capacity, resistant to black rot + diamond back moth.
Chilli	Very pungent (>70,000 Schoville Heat Units) for fresh market and as dry powder, medium pungent (30,000 SHU) for pickle making , resistant to leaf curl + thrips + mites + anthracnose. Low pungency coupled with attractive deep red colour .
Cauliflower	High temperature tolerance, non ricey, compact, bract free and self blanching curd with retentive cream/white colour, resistant to black rot.

Note: CMV= Cucumber mosaic virus, PM,= Powdery mildew DM = Downy mildew.

10.13.6. Common Mechanisms/Methods for Developing Commercial Hybrids

Mechanism/ Method	Commercially exploited crops
Hand emasculation + MP	Tomato, brinjal, okra, sweet pepper
Bagging/protection of staminate and pistillate flowers + MP	Cucurbits (bottle gourd, pumpkin, watermelon, cucumber, muskmelon, bitter gourd, ridge gourd)
Pinching of staminate flowers + MP/NP	Cucurbits (bitter gourd, bottle gourd, pumpkin, watermelon, bitter gourd, ridge gourd)
Male-sterility + MP	Tomato, sweet pepper, chilli
Male-sterility + NP	Onion, cabbage, carrot, radish, muskmelon, chilli
Self-incompatibility +NP	Cabbage, cauliflower, broccoli, radish,
Gynoeicy + NP	Cucumber
PGR and pinching of staminate flowers+ NP	Summer squash, winter squash, etc.

Note: MP: Manual pollination, NP: Natural pollination, PGR: Generally ethephon

10.13.7. Main Reasons for Rapid Growth of Vegetable Hybrid Seed Industry in Different Countries of the World

- Continuous flow of new hybrids with high product quality, better adaptability and fortified with resistance to biotic and abiotic stresses
- Continuous development of the parental lines with unique traits through marker assisted selection, utilization of crop wild relatives, mutants, etc.
- Development and utilization of different pollination control mechanisms.
- Usage of new molecular technologies in breeding like, gene insertion, gene editing, etc.
- Adoption of different seed technologies like, seed coating, priming, pelleting, etc.

10.13.8. Key to Hybrid Technology

Development of widely divergent and smart parental lines: Incorporation of traits from landraces, mutants and crop wild relatives to develop "Smart parental line" with broad gene base with a view to develop resilient hybrids.

Development of heterotic pools: As divergent as possible, because heterosis depends on the differences in allele frequency between two populations.

Built-in resistance: Incorporation of specific resistant genes in the parental lines like, tomato leaf curl virus resistant genes *Ty-1, Ty-3, Ty-4* and *Ty-6* originating from different accessions of *S. chilense* , *Ty-2* originating from *S. habrochaites* accession. First Public sector Triple Disease Resistant Tomato Hybrid in India "Arka Rakshak" resistant to tomato leaf curl virus, bacterial wilt and early blight.

Applications of "Double haploids (DH)": Effective alternative to produce homozygous parental line in the crop showing high inbreeding depression like, carrot, onion, early cauliflower, etc.

Application of Molecular biology

- Marker assisted transfer of specific genes/QTLs controlling desirable traits
- Assessment of molecular divergence of the parental lines based on a large number of markers to establish heterotic pool.
- Assessment and maintenance of genetic purity of parental lines and hybrid seed.

10.13.9. Thrust Areas of Research on Hybrid Breeding Technology

- Development of widely divergent and "Smart" parental lines with broad gene base with a view to develop climate resilient hybrids
- Marker assisted transfer of specific genes like, resistance to biotic and abiotic stress, fertility restoration in cytoplasmic-genic male-sterile lines, nutrient enhancing genes, etc
- Assessment of molecular divergence of the parental lines based on a large number of markers to establish heterotic pool
- Identification of stable self-incompatible and cytoplasmic male-sterile lines in cabbage and cauliflower for their utilization in Indian condition.
- Development of cytoplasmic-genic male-sterile lines in pink bulb cultivars of onion to develop onion hybrids with pink bulb colour, pungency, uniformity in bulb size and good storage capacity.
- Development of suitable parental lines with monoecious sex form in place of usual andromonoecious sex form in muskmelon to reduce the cost of hybrid seed production.
- Development of tropical gynoecious sex form for the production of promising hybrids of cucumber and muskmelon.
- Identification of suitable locations for maintenance of the genic-cytoplasmic male sterile lines of carrot and cytoplasmic male sterile lines of cauliflower, cabbage and subsequent hybrid seed production.

10.13.10. Hybrids: Confusion and Concern

Confusion

- It is understood that organic agriculture is an ecologically-oriented production system however, it is confusing why this sector is hesitant of using the hybrids
- It is often confused that the hybrids are less nutritious than the open-pollinated and farmers' varieties.

Concern

- Hybrids threaten agro-biodiversity because a few hybrids outcompete a broad range of farmer varieties.
- Widespread adoption of hybrids create dependency of farming communities on few big seed companies which may affects autonomy of small grower
- Various widespread disease and pest outbreaks may happen due to narrowness in biodiversity as happened in maize belts of USA due to susceptibility of the hybrids carrying T-cytoplasm to southern com blight.

10.13.11. F_1 Hybrids Developed in India by Public and Private Sector

Vegetables	Vegetable hybrids developed (Number)			Share of public sector (%)
	Total	Private	Public	
Toamto	39	16	23	41.0
Brinjal	40	27	13	32.5
Chilli	15	10	05	33.3
Sweet pepper	05	01	04	80.0
Okra	13	05	08	61.5
Cabbage	09	06	03	33.3
Cauliflower	07	03	04	57.1
Bottle gourd	05	02	03	60.0
Bitter gourd	04	02	02	50.0
Ridge gourd	02	01	01	50.0
Ash gourd	02	00	02	100.0
Cucumber	05	03	02	40.0
Watermelon	02	01	01	50.0
Muskmelon	02	00	02	100.0
Carrot	01	00	01	100.0
Total	151	77	74	49

10.13.12. Public Sector Hybrids in Vegetable Crops

Crop	Hybrids	Source
Tomato	Pusa Hybrid-1, Pusa Hybrid-2, Pusa Hybrid-4, Pusa Hybrid-8, Pusa Divya (Kt-4)	IARI, Delhi
	Arka Rakshak, Arka Anaya, Arka Samrat, Arka Shreshta, Arka Vishal, Arka Vardan, Arka Abhijit	IIHR, Bangaluru
	Kashi Abhiman	IIVR, Varanasi
	Pant Hybrid-1, Pant Hybrid-2, Pant Hybrid-10, Pant Hybrid-11	GBPUAT, Pantnagar
	Rajashree, Phule Hybrid-1	MPKV, Rahuri

Brinjal	DBHL-20, Pusa Hybrid-5 (long), Pusa Hybrid-6 (Round), Pusa Hybrid-9, Pusa Hybrid-9, Pusa Anupama (Kt-4)	IARI, Delhi
	Arka Navneet	IIHR, Bengaluru
	Kashi Sandesh	IIVR, Varanasi
Chilli	CH-1, CH-3	PAU, Ludhiana
	Arka Meghana, Arka Harit, Arka Sweta	IIHR, Bengaluru
	Kashi Early, Kashi Surkh	IIVR, Varanasi
Sweet Pepper	Pusa Deepti, KTCPH-3	IARI, Delhi
Cucumber	Pusa Sanyog	IARI, Delhi
Bitter gourd	Pusa Hybrid-1, Pusa Hybrid-2	IARI, Delhi
Bottle gourd	Pusa Hybrid-3	IARI, Delhi
	Pant Sankar Lauki 1	GBPUAT, Pantnagar
	Narendra Sankar 1	NDAUT, Faizabad
Muskmelon	Pusa Rasraj	IARI, Delhi
	Punjab Hybrid-1	PAU, Ludhiana
Pumpkin	Pusa Hybrid 1	IARI, Delhi
Watermelon	Arka Jyoti	IIHR, Bengaluru
Cauliflower	Pusa Hybrid-2, Pusa Snowball Hybrid-1	IARI, Delhi
Cabbage	Pusa Cabbage Hybrid-1	IARI, Delhi
Carrot	Pusa Vasundha, Pusa Nayanjyoti	IARI, Delhi
Onion	Arka Lalima, Arka Kirtiman, Arka Bhima	IIHR, Bengaluru
Ash gourd	Pusa Shreyali and Pusa Urmi	IARI, Delhi

11

Biotechnology, Nanotechnology and Seed Technology

11.1. Landmark in Biotechnology

Activities	Year
Animal biotechnology	
Yeast used to make wine and beer	Before 6000 BC
Yeast used for making leavened bread	About 4000BC
Copper mined with the aid of microbes (Rio Tinto. Spain)	Before 1670 AD
Sewage treatment systems using microbes developed / established	About 1910 AD
Large scale production of acetone, butanol and glycerol using bacteria	1912-1914
Large scale production of penicillin	1944
Mining of uranium with the aid of microbes (Canada)	1962
First successful genetic engineering experiments	1973
Marketing of human food of fungal origin (UK)	1980
The use of monoclonal antibodies of diagnosis approved in USA	1981
Approval for the use of insulin produced by genetically engineered microbes (GEMs) (USA and UK)	1983
Animal interferons, produced by GEMs, approved for the protection of cattle against diseases	1984
Conceptualization of human genome project .	1986
Launch of human genome project.	1990
Development of human genetic map for all 23 chromosome.	1992
Dolly, a cloned sheep produced.	1997
Drosophilla genome sequence published.	2000
Work draft of human genome sequence published.	2001
Rat genome sequence published.	2004
Plant biotechonology	
First attempt of plant tissue culture	1902
Embryo culture of selected crucifers attempted	1904
Asymbiotic germination of orchid seeds *in vitro*	1922
In vitro culture of root tips	1922
Use of embryo culture technique in interspecific crosses of *Linum*	1925
Successful culture of tomato roots	1934
In vitro culture of cambial tissues of ulmus to study adventitious shoot formation.	1940
Use of coconut milk containing a cell division factor for the first time in Datura.	1941
In vitro culture of crown gall tissues.	1941
In vitro adventitious shoot formation in tobacco.	1944

Contd.

Raising whole plants of *Lupinus* and *Tropaeolum* by shoot tip culture . 1946
Use of meristem culture to obtain virus-free dahlias. 1952
First application of micrografting . 1952
Production of haploid callus of the gymnosperm *Ginkgo biloba* from pollen. 1953
First plant from a single cell. 1954
Discovery of kinetin a cell division hormone. 1955
Discovery of the regulation of organ formation by charnging the ratio to auxin: cytokinin. 1957
Regeneration of somatic embryos *in vitro* from the nucellus of citrus ovules. 1958
Regeneration of embryos from callus clumps and cell suspensions of Daucus carota. 1959
Publication of first handbook on plant tissue culture. 1959
First successful test tube fertilization in *Papaver rhoeas.* 1960
Use of the microculture method for growing single cells in handing drops in a conditioned medium. 1960
Enzymatic degradation of cell walls to obtain large number of protoplasts. 1960
Filtration of cell suspensions and isolation of single cells by plating . 1960
Development of Murashige and Skoog nutrition medium. 1962
Production of first haploid plants from pollen grains of Datura. 1964
Restriction endonuclease term coined to a class of enzymes involved in cleaving DNA. 1968
Selection of biochemical mutants in vitro by the use of tissue culture derived variation. 1970
First achievement of protoplast fusion . 1970
Discovery of first restriction endonuclease from *Haemophillus influenzae* 1970
Rd: It was later purified and named Hind II.
Preparation of first restriction map using Hind II enzyme to cut circular DNA of SV 40 into 11 specific fragments was prepared . 1971
Regeneration of first plants from protoplasts. 1971
First report of interspecific hybridization through protoplast fusion in two species of *Nicotiana*. 1972
First recombinant DNA molecular produced using restriction enzymes . 1972
Joining of two restriction fragments regardless of their origin produced by the same restriction enzyme by the action of DNA ligase. 1972
Development of a procedure in which the appropriate enzyme can be added to fill in any single-stranded gap and the use of DNA ligase to join the two fragments thus giving rise to recombinant DNA. 1972
Discovery of reverse transcripase: In certain cancer- causing animal virus, genetic information flows in the reverse from. 1972
Use of the Lobban and Kaiser technique to develop hybrid plasmid- insertion of EcoRi fragment of DNA molecular into circular plasmid DNA of bacteria using DNA ligase. Gene from African clawed toad inserted into plasmid DNA of bacteria. 1973
Cytokinin found capable of breaking dromancy in excised capitulum explants of Gerbera. 1973
Regeneration of haploid *Petunia hybrida* plants from protoplasts. 1974
Biotransformation in plant tissue cultures. 1974
Discovery that the Ti plasmid is the tumor inducing principle of *Agrobacterium*. 1974
Positive *in vitro* selection of maize callus cultures resistant to T toxin of *Helminthosporium maydis*. 1975

Contd.

Development of the high resolution two dimensional gel electrophoresis procedure, which led to the development of proteomics.	1975
Shoot initiation from cryopreserved shoot apices of carnation.	1976
Octopine and nopaline synthesis and breakdown found to be genetically controlled by the plasmid of *A. tumefaciens*.	1976
Successful integration of the Ti plasmid DNA from *A. tumefaciens* in plants.	1977
A method of gene sequencing based on degradation of DNA chain.	1977
Discovery of split genes.	1977
Somatic hybridization of tomato and potato resulting in pomato.	1978
Cocultivation procedure developed for transformation of plant protoplasts with *Agrobacterium*.	1979
Use of immobilized whole cells for biotransformation of digitoxin into digoxin.	1980
Commercial production of human insulin through genetic engineering in bacterial cells.	1980
Restriction fragment length polymorphism (RFLP) technique developed.	1980
Studies on the structure of T-DNA by cloning the complete EcoRI digest of T37 tobacco crown gall DNA into a phage vector, thus allowing the isolation and detailed study of T-DNA border sequences.	1980
Introduction of the term somaclonal variation.	1981
Incorporation of naked DNA by protoplasm resulting in the transformation with isolated DNA.	1982
Polymerase chain reaction (PCR), a chemical DNA amplification process idea conceived.	1983
Transformation of tobacco with Agrobacterium; transgenic plants developed.	1984
Development of the genetic finger printing technique for identifying individuals by analyzing polymorphism at DNA sequence level.	1984
TMV virus- resistant tobacco and tomato of coat protein gene of TMV.	1986
Development of biolistic gene transfer method for plant transformation.	1987
Isolation of Bt gene from bacterium (*Bacillus thuringirnsis*)	1987
Formal launch of the Human Genome project.	1990
Development of the random amplified polymorphic DNA (RAPD) technique.	1990
Development of DNA microarray system using light directed chemical synthesis system.	1991
Reporting by the Institute for Genomic Research of the complete DNA sequence of *Haemophilus influenzae*	1995
Development of DNA finger printing by amplified fragment length polymorphism (AFLP) technique.	1995
Sequencing of E. coli genome.	1997
Sequencing of the genome of a multicellular organism (Caenorthabditis elegans).	1998
Sequenceing of human genome successfully completed.	2001
K. mullis and coworkers invented polymerase chain reaction (PCR).	1985
A Murray, J Szostak constructed the first artificial chromosome.	1983
Alec Jeffreys developed the technique of DNA fingerprinting	1984
KA Barton isolated Bt gene from *Bacillus thuringiensis*.	1987
JGK Williams et al. Developed the technique of RAPD.	1990
M Schena developed DNA chip "microarray" system.	1995
P Vos developed AFLP technique.	1995
Calgene released first transgenic crop (flavr savr tomato) for commercial cultivation.	1996

Contd.

'International Rice Genome sequencing project' (IRGSP) launched.	1998
Completion of a "rough draft" of the human genome in the Human Genome Project.	2000
Celera Genomics and the Human Genome Project create a draft of the human genome sequence. It is published by Science and Nature Magazine.	2001
Syngenta & BGI published draft rice genome sequences.	2002
Rice becomes the first crop to have its genome decoded.	2002
The Human Genome Project is completed, providing information on the locations and sequence of human genes on all 46 chromosomes.	2003
Japanese astronomers launch the first Medical Experiment Module called "Kibo", to be used on the International Space Station.	2008
Cedars-Sinai Heart Institute uses modified SAN heart genes to create the first viral pacemaker in guinea pigs, now known as iSANs.	2009
Thirty-one-year-old Zac Vawter successfully uses a nervous system-controlled bionic leg to climb the Chicago Willis Tower.	2012
Emergence of fast and precise new method for editing snippets of the genetic code. The so-called CRISPR Cas 9 system takes advantage of a defense strategy used by bacteria.	2013
An international team of scientists reconstructed a synthetic and fully functional yeast chromosome. A breakthrough seven year in the making, the remarkable advance could eventually lead to custom-built organisms	2014
Scientists hit a number of breakthroughs using the gene-editing technology CRISPR. Researchers in China reported modifying the DNA of a nonviable human embryo, a controversial move. Elsewhere, scientists reported using CRISPR Cas 9 to potentially modify pig organs for human transplant and modify mosquitoes to eradicate malaria.	2015
Researchers in Sweden developed a blood test that can detect cancer at an early stage from a single drop of blood.	2015
Researchers found that an ancient molecule, GK-PID, is the reason single-celled organisms started to evolve into multicellular organisms approximately 800 million years ago.	2016
First step taken toward epigenetically modified cotton.	2017
Research reveals different aspects of DNA demethylation involved in tomato ripening process.	2017
Sequencing of green alga genome provides blueprint to advance clean energy, bioproducts.	2017
Fine-tuning 'dosage' of mutant genes unleashes long-trapped yield potential in tomato plants.	2017

11.2. Tissue Culture

11.2.1. Landmark of Tissue Culture

Years	Landmark
19th century	Selective cross breeding
Early 20th century	Cell culture
Mid 20th century	Mutagenesis and selection
1930	Somaclonal variation

Contd.

1940	Embryo rescue
1950	Polyembryogenesis
1970	Anther culture
1980	Recombinant DNA technology
1980	Marker Assisted Selection
1990	Genomics
2000	Bioinformatics

11.2.2. Growth Media Used in Tissue Culture

S. N.	Medium
1	MS Medium(1962)
2.	White Medium(1963)
3.	Gamborg B5 Medium(1968)
4.	Nitch Medium(1969)
5.	Woody Plant Medium (1981)

11.3. Micropropagation Reports

11.3.1. Tomato

Explant	Medium	Response
Cotyledon	2.5μM NAA+ 1.5 μ M Kin	Normal plantlet regeneration
Seedling leaf	20μM BA+ 1μM NAA	True to type
Node / shoot/ shoot tips	MS major salt + B5	Flowering plantlets
Hypocotyl	BA	Shoot proliferation
Apical shoot	Various regulators	True to type
Cotyledon	0.1 μM Zeatin	Shoot proliferation
Hypocotyl/ cotyledon	1μ M NAA+ 1μM Seating	Normal plantlet regeneration
Cotyledon	6 μM IAA+ 5μM kin	High yielding rapid multiplication
Shoot / shoot tips	4 μM BA+ 4 μM IAA	Normal plantlet regeneration

11.3.2. Brinjal

Explant	Medium	Response
Leaf explant	2.9 μM Kin	High frequency of planlet regeneration
Cotyledon	3.5μM IAA + 0.7 μM Zeatin	Shoot formation
Cotyledon, hypocotyl, leaf	11.1μM BA+ 2.9μM IAA	Plantlet regeneration

11.3.3. Chilli

Explant	Medium	Response
Apical / axillary buds	3μ MBA + 0.9μ MIAA/ 5μ MBA+ 1.5μ M IAA	High frequency of plantlet generation
Apical / axillary buds	3μMBA+ 0.5μMIAA	Rooted plantlets
Hypocotyle	MS medium	Shoot proliferation
Immature Zygotic embryo	9μM 2,4-D+ 10% CW+ 8% sucrose	Normal plantlet generation
Cotyledon	PD+ MS inorganic salt+ ZH organic + 5 BA+ 0.2 u MIAA+ 2 $AgNO_3$	High frequency of plant-let generation
Shoot / shoot tips	B5+ 300Mg/l chloramate orB5+ 50μ M thiophnate methyl	Rooted plantlets
Node / axillary bud	Half strength MS medium	Rooted plantlets
Shoot/ shoot tips	MS basal medium	Normal plantlet generation
Cotyledon	2.5μMTDZ+0.1μMIAA+ 2μMGA$_3$	Plantlet generation
Shoot and shoot tips	5μ M BA + 0.5μM IAA	Rooted plant lets

11.3.4. Cucurbits

Explant	Medium	Response
Leaf explant	0.5 μM IAA+ 2.0 μM BA+ 1.0μM $AlCl_3$	Direct organogenesis
Cotyledon/ leaf/ nodal portion	3.0 μM BA	Field transfer of plants
Cotyledon/ leaf/ nodal portion	9.0 Sucrose	Somatic embryo
Apical meristem	0.01 μM IBA + 0.1 μM BA+ 10.0 Ascorbic acid	Regenerated plants
Pumpkin		
Shoot tip/ axillary bud	1 μM BA+ 0.5μM IAA	Direct organogenesis
Shoot tip/ nodal portion	0.01M BA+m0.1μM NAA	Field transfer of plants
Shoot tip/ nodal portion	1μM BA	Field transfer of plants
Axillary buds	2.0 μM BA+ 0.1 μM IAA	Multiple shoot
Seedling buds	3.0 μM BA	Field transfer of plants
Root explant	1.0 μM BA	Field transfer of plants
Cotyledon	2.0 μM BA	Plants with quality fruits

11.3.5. Cole Vegetables

Explant	Medium	Response
Hypocotyl, curd pieces/ branches	2.44μM BA+ 5.0μ M NAA+ 168μM Sucrose	Multiple shoot
Curd meristem	2.0 Kin Liquid	Field transfer of plants
Head explant	1.0 NAA+ 0.1 IAA (mg/l)	Plants with high survival rate
Internode and in floresence axis	5.0μM BA	Regenerated plants

Contd.

Leaf and stem	8.88 μM BA	Regenerated plants
Cotyledon	Various combinations	Shoot bud formation
Axillary buds	28.5μm IAA+ 18.58 UM Kin + 0.87μM TDZ	Regenerated plants field transfer
Shoots	0.5 μM BA+ 0.1μM IBA	Regenerated plants field transfer

11.3.6. Bulb Crops

Explant	Medium	Response
Immature flower / ovary	1.0μ M NAA+ 2.0 μM BA+ 0.02 μM TDZ	Large number of plantlets through direct organogensis
Immature flower bud	BDS+ 2.0 μMBA+ 2.0 2, 4-D+ 100 mg/l myoinositol + 10% Sucrose	High frequency plantlets
Shoot primordial	1.0 μM 2,4-D+ 0.5 μM picloram	High frequency plantlets
Sliced basal plate	4.44 μM BA	Shoot proliferation with no variation in regenerated plants
Garlic (*Allium sativum*)		
Shoot tip	0.3 μM IAA = 2.0μM2iP	Plantlet formation
Leaf explant through globular bodies	2 Kin+ 0.5 IAA μM	High frequency of plantlets
Maristems	2 μM iP+ 5μ M jasmonic acid	High frequency plantlet regeneration
Root & leaves	5μM IAA	Somatic embryogenesis
Root explant	1μM NAA+ 6μM BA	High frequency plantlets regeneration
Bud & Basal plate	B5 pH 7.5 + 15°C	Bulblet formation
Meristem	MS+ B5 basal	Microbulbils
Shoot tips	Ms + 0.5 % ascorbic acid + 12% sucrose	Commercial low cost bulbils
Clove shoot	0. 5 μM NAA	Virus free plantlet
Scale tip	0.5 μM NAA + 0.5 μM Kin	High frequency of virus free plantlets

11.3.7. Achievement of Tissue Culture

Crop	Technique applied for
Anther/Microspore/Ovule culture	
Brassica oleracea	Haploid production
Capsicum annuum	Haploid production
Lycopersicon esculentum	Haploid production
Solanum melongena	Haploid production
Cucurbita pepo	Haploid production
B. rapa	Haploid production
Embryo Rescue	
L. esculentum X *L. peruvianum*	To rescue the hybrid embryo
P.vulgaris X *P.augustissimus*	To rescue the hybrid embryo

Contd.

Vigna pubescens X *V. unguiculata*	To rescue the hybrid embryo
S. melongena X *S.torvum*	To rescue the hybrid embryo
Meristem culture	
Allium sativum	Elimination of onion yellow dwarf virus
A. ascalonicum	Elimination of leek yellow dwarf virus
Pisum sativum	Elimination of pea seed borne mosaic virus
Solanum melongena	EMCV
S. lyepersicum	Cryopreservation
P. sativum	Cryopreservation

11.4. Molecular Breeding

11.4.1. Molecular Markers

Hybridization based markers	PCR based markers
• Restricted Fragment Length Polymorphism((RFLP) (Botstein *et al;* 1980)	• RandomAmplifiedpolymorphism DNA(RAPD)(William *et al*;1990) • Amplified Fragment Length Polymorphism (AFLP) (Vos *et al*;1995) • Simple Sequence Repeat (SSR) or Microsatellite (Tuntz *et al*;1989) • Cleaved Amplified Polymorphic Sequence (CAPS) • DNA Amplification Fingerprint (DAF) • Expressed Sequence Tag (EST) • Sequence Characterized Amplified Region (SCAR) • Single Strand Confirmation Polymorphism (SSCP) • Sequence Tagged Site (STS) • Simple Sequence Length Polymorphism (SSLP) • Inter Simple Sequence Repeat (ISSR) • Derived Cleaved Amplified Polymorphism (dCAPS) • Single Nucleotide Amplified Polymorphism (SNAP) • Single Primer Amplification Reaction (SPAR) • Double Standard Conformational Polymorphism (DSCP)

11.4.2. Characteristics of DNA Markers

Characters	DNA Markers			
	RFLP	RAPD	AFLP	SSR
Inheritance	Co-dominant	Dominant	Dominant	Co-dominant
Based on	Hybridization	PCR	PCR	PCR
Degree of polymorphism	High	High	High	Very high
DNA required	2-30μg	1-100μg	100ng	50-100ng
Cost	High	Low	High	High
Reproducibility	High	Low	High	High
Obtaining data	Easy	Easy	Complex	Very easy
Number of loci	1-3	1-10	20-100	1-5

11.4.3. Genetic Segregation Ratio in Different Mapping Populations

Markers	Nature	Populations			Back crosses		
		F_2	RIL	DHs	NILs	B_1	B_2
RFLP	Co dominant	1:2:1	1:1	1:1	1:1	1:1	1:1
RAPD	Dominant	3:1	1:1	1:1	1:1	1:0	1:1
ARLP	Dominant	3:1	1:1	1:1	1:1	1:0	1:1
Microsatellite	Co-dominant	1:2:1	1:1	1:1	1:1	1:1	1:1

11.5. Gene Index in Vegetable Crops

11.5.1. Watermelon

Preferred symbol	Synonyms	Character
A		Andromonoecious, recessive to monoecious
Ar	(B) Ge	Anthracnose resistance, resistance to *Giomerella cingulata* var. *orbiculare*.
C		Canary yellow flesh, dominant to pink.
d		Dotted seed coat, black dotted seed when dominant for r, t and w.
dw-1		dwarf-1, short internodes, due to fewer shorter cells than normal.
dw-2		dwarf-2, short internodes, due to fewer cells.
e	(t)	explosive rind, thin, render rind, bursting when cut. Furrowed fruit surface, recessive to smooth.
g	(D)	Light green skin, light green fruit, recessive to dark.
gs	(ds)	Stripped green skin, recessive to dark green but dominant to light green skin.
Go*	(c)	Golden, yellow colour of older leaves and mature fruit.
Gms	(msg)	Glabrous male sterile line, foliage lacking trichomes, male sterile.
1		Long seed, long recessive to medium length of seed, interact with s.
m		Mottled skin, greenish white mottling of fruit skin.
n*		Nonlobed leaves, leaves lack lobing, dominance incomplete.
O		Oval fruit , incompletely dominant to spherical.
P		Penciled lines of skin, inconspicuous stripes, recessive to netted fruit.
Pm		Powdery mildew susceptibility, susceptibility to *Sphaerotheca fuliginea*.
r		Red seed coat, interact with w and t.
s		Short seeds, epistatic to 1.
Su*	(suBi)	Suppressor of bitterness, nonbitter fruit.
t	(bt)	Tan seed coat, interacts with r and w.
w		White seed coat, interact with r and t .
Wf*	(W)	White flesh, dominant to red
y	®	Yellow flesh, recessive to red.

*Proposed new symbol.

11.5.2. Muskmelon

Preferred symbol	Synonym	Character
a	*(M)*	Andromonoecious. Mostly staminate, fewer perfect flowers; interacts with g.
ab		Abrachiate. Lacking lateral branches; ab, a plant produce only staminate flowers.
Af*		*Aulacophora foveicollis* resiatance. Resistance to the red pumpkin beetle.
Ag		*Aphis gossypii* tolerance. Freedom from leaf curling following aphid infestation.
b		Bush. Short internodes, compact plant habit.
Fom-1*	*(Fom 1)*	*Fusarium oxysporum* f. melonis resistance. Resistance to race 1.
Fom-2*	*Fom 1.2*	*Fusarium oxysporum* f. melonis resistance. Resistance to race 1 and 2 of fusarium wilt.
g		Gynomonoecious. Mostly pistillate, fewer perfect flowers; a g plants produce perfect flowers exclusively.
gf*		Green flesh color. Recessive to salmon.
gl		Glabrous. Trichomes lacking.
gp*		Green petals. Corolla leaf-like in color and venation.
h		Halo cotyledons. Yellowcotyledons, later becoming green.
Mc		*Mycosphaerella citrullina* resistance. High degree of resistance to gummy stem blight.
Mc-2*	(Mc1)	*Mycosphaerella citrullina* resistance. High degree of resistance to gummy stem blight.
ms-1*	(ms1)	Male sterile-1. Indehiscent anthers with empty pollen walls in tetrads.
ms-2*	(ms2)	Male sterile-2. Anthers indehiscent, containing mostly empty pollen walls, growth rate reduced.
n		Nectarless. Nectaries lacking in all flowers.
O		Oval fruit shape. Dominant to round; associated with a
p*		Pentamerous. Five carpels and stamens; recessive to trimerous.
Pm-1*	(Pm1)	Powdery mildew resistance. Resistance to race 1 of *Sphaerotheca fuligenea.*
Pm-2*	(Pm2)	Powdery mildew resistance-2, Race-2 resistance, incompletely dominant.
Pm-3*	(Pm3)	Powdery mildew resistance-3. Resistance derived from PI 124111
Pm-4*	(Pm4)	Powdery mildew resistance-4. Resistance derived from cv. Seminole.
Pm-5*	(Pm5)	Powdery mildew resistance-5. Resistance derived from cv. Seminole.
r		Red stem. Red pigment under epidermis of stems, especially at nodes.
s		Sutures. Presence of vein tracts ("sutures"; recessive to ribless
So*		Sour taste. Dominant to sweet.

Contd.

sp*		Sphaerical fruit shape. Recessive to obtuse; dominance incomplete.
st*		Striped epicarp. Recessive to nonstriped fruit
v		Virescent. Chlorotic foliage.
w*		White colour of mature fruit. Recessive to dark green fruit skin.
wf*		White flesh. Recessive to orange.
wi*		White color immature fruit. Recessive to dark green fruit skin.
wt*		White testa. Dominant to yellow or tan seed coat color.
Y		Yellow epicarp. Dominant to white fruit skin.
yg*	(y)	Yellow green leaves. Reduced chlorophyll content.

* Proposed new symbol.

11.5.3. Cucumber

Gene Symbol	Character
a	Androecious, products only male flower if recessive at Acar/acr locus.
Acr (F, acrf, D)	Female, high degree of female sex expression.
Bi	Bitterfree, lacking cucurbitacin.
cp	Compact, reduced internode length, poorly developed tendrils, small flowers
de(I)	Determinate, short vines with stem terminating in flowers.
df	Delayed flowering under long photoperiod.
dvl (dl)	Divided leaf.
gy	Gynoecious, recessive gene for high degree of female sex expression.
m	Male, high degree of male expressiong, m plants are andromonoecious if recessive for F and hermaphrodite if dominant for F.
m-2	Perfect flowers-2, bisexual flowers with normal ovaries.
ms-1	Male sterile-1, male flowers abort before anthesis.
ms-2	Male sterile-2, male flowers abort.
n	Negative geotropic peduncle response, pistillate flowers upright.
ns	Numerous spines on fruits.
Pc(P)	Parthenocarpy, fruit setting without pollination.
sp	Short petiole, 20% of the normal size at first node.
T	Tall plant, incompletely dominant to short.
Tr	Trimonoeciou s, producing male, bisexual and female flowers in that sequence during plant development.
ul	Umbrella leaf, leaf margins turn down at low relative humidity giving cup shaped leaves.
Fruit quality	
B	Black or brown spines dominant to white spines on fruits.
B-2	Black spine-2, interact with B to produce an F2 of 15 black: 1 white
B-3	Black spine- 3, interact with B-4 to produce an F2 of 9 black : 7 white.
B-4	Black spine -4, interacts conversely with B-3.
c	Cream mature fruit colour, interaction with R (red mature fruit) giving an F2 ratio of 9 red (R+) : 3 orange (Rc) : 3 yellow (+ +): cream (+ c).
D	Dull skin colour, dull skin colour of American cultivars dominant to glossy skin of most European Cultivars.
gl	Glabrous, foliage lacking trichomes, fruits without spines.

Contd.

H	Heavy netting of fruit, dominant to no netting.
R	Red mature fruit, interact with c, linkerd or pleiotropic with B and H.
s	Spine size and frequency, many small fruit spines, characteristics of European cultivars, recessive to the few large spines of most American cultivars.
te	Tender skin of fruit , thin tender skin of some European cultivars recessive to thick , tough skin of most American cultivars.
Tu	Tuberculate fruit, warty fruit , characteristic ofAmerican cultivars dominant to smooth , non warty fruits of European cultivars.
u	Uniform immature fruit colour recessive ti mottled or stippled colour.
w	White immature fruit colour , recessive to green.
wf	White flesh.
yf	Yellow flesh.
Resistance genes	
Ar	Anthracnose- PI 175111, PI 175120, PI 179676 and PI 182445.
Cu	Scab- Davis Perfect.
dm	Downey mildew- Poinsett.
pm-1, pm-2 and pm-3	Powdery mildew- Natsufushnari, PI200815, PI-200818.
Foc	Fusarium wilt- Wisc. 248.
Cmv	Cucumber mosaic virus- Wisc. SMR-12, Wisc. SMR-15 and Wisc. SMR-18.

11.5.4. Onion

Gene symbol	Character
a/a	Albino seedlings
y1/ y1	Yellow seedling linked with glossy
y2/ y2	Yellow seedling not linked with glossy
Pg/pg	Pale green seedling
v/v	Virecent seedling
gl/gl	Glossy foliage
ea/ea	Exposed anther
ya/ya	Yellow anther
pr/pr	Pink root resistance
ms/ms	Male sterility
	Bulb colour
i/i C/C R/R	Homozygous red
i/i C/c R/R	Heterozygous red
i/i C/C R/r	Heterozygous red
i/i C/c R/r	Heterozygous red
i/i C/c r/r	Heterozygous yellow
i/i c/c R/R	Homozygous recessive white
i/i c/c R/r	Heterozygous recessive white
i/i c/c r/r	Homozygous recessive white
I/I—	Homozygous dominant white
I/i - -	Heterozygous dominant white (buff)

11.5.5. Cabbage

Gene Symbol	Characters
c	Anthocyaninless.
A	Basic anthocyanin colour factor.
A^{rc}	Coloured lamina.
B	Light red midrib.
M	Magenta plant colour (reddish purple)
As	Asparagoides, bizarre.
Er	Entire leaf margin.
fc	Fused cotyledons.
gl	Glossy foliage, dominant types produce wax on stems
Hr-1	Hairy first leaf hairs on margins.
sm	Smooth leaves.
Pet	Petiolate.
W	Wide vs narrow leaf.
K	Dominant factor for heading.
Ax	Axil sprouts.
T	Tall.
dw	Dwarf, short internodes, round leaves.
wh	White petal.
cp	Crinkly petal.
ms-1	Broccoli (male sterile).
2	Brussels sprouts.
4	Purple cauliflower.
5	Cauliflower.
6	Broccoli.
S	Self- incompatibility multi- allelic.
f	Major gene for resistance to black rot.

11.5.6. Cowpea

Gene symbol	Character
A	Alfaalfa like pod shape.
ax	Axillary buds, active buds of cotyledons.
B	Blue seed coat.
Bc-1	Bacterial cancker resistance -1.
Bc-2	Bacterial canker resistance-2.
bcm	Blackeye cowpea mosaic virus resistance, likely a synonym of blc
Bcy	Brown calyx colour, dominant to green.
Bk	Black pod, dominant to white pod.
Bl	Black seed coat, also conditions anthocyanin production in the pod tip, calysx and peduncle, heterozygote produces mottled seeds.
blc	Black eye cowpea mosaic virus resistance, likely a synonym of bcm.
Bp	Brown pod, dominant to straw colour.
Bpl-1	Bacterial pustule resistance-1.
Bpl-2	Bacterial pustule resistance-2.
bpl-3	Bacterial pustule resistance-3.

Contd.

bpl-4	Bacterial pustule resistance-4.
bpl-5	Bacterial pustule resistance-5.
by	Bean yellow mosaic virus resistance.
CC	Cowpea chlorotic mottle virus resistance, the recessive allele at the Mvi locus is likely a synonym.
Ci	Compound inflorescence.
Cls-1	Cercospora leaf spot resistance –1.
cls	Cercospora leaf spot resistance –2.
Cm	Cucumber mosaic virus resistance.
crpt	Crumpled petal
Cy	Cylindrical – length pod
D	Dark flower colour.
df	Dwarf (slow growth, dark green leaves , short internodes
Ef-1	Early –flowering-1.
Ef-2	Early –flowering -2.
Er	Erect pod attachment, dominant to drooping pod attachment.
Gp	Gp Green pod, dominant to cream pod.
Gr	Green pod, dominant to white pod.
La	Lanceolate leaf.
lg	Light green pod.
Llf	Long leaf.
ls	Leaf size, small leaf recessive to large leaf.
ms-1	Male sterile -1.
ms-2	Male sterile -2.
ms-3	Male sterile -3.
ms-4	Male sterile -4.
Nlf	Narrow leaf, dominant to broad leaf.
Nv	Necrotic synergistic reaction associated with cowpea stunt.
O	Hilum ring seed coat pattern.
P	Purple pod, dominant to green, also causes anthocyanin production in the calyx and penduncle.
pa-1	Pod apperarance-1 wrinkled dry pod recessive to smooth appearance.
pa-2	Pod apperarance-2 wrinkled dry pod recessive to smooth appearance.
Pb	Purple petiole base.
Pbr	Purple branch base.
Pf	Purple flower.
Pg	Pale green plant.
Pn	Penducle length, longpenduncle dominant to short.
Pu	Purple pod, stem and petiole and completely purple.
R	Red seed coat.
rh	Beetle resistance.
Rk	Root –knot resistance, allelic to rk^i
rk^i	Root –knot resistance- intermediate, allelic to Rk.
S	Spotting pattern, patches of black pigment on certain types of seed coat.
Sbm	Southern bean mosaic virus resistance.
Sh	Spindly growth habit, marked elongation of the main stem few side branches.
shp	Shrunken pericarp.

Contd.

Sr	Stem rot resistance.
St	Standard petal exhibit full expression of colour.
stx	Sesquipedalis- like texture of pod (soft).
Tr	Stem root resistance.
un	Unifoliate leaf, petiole, all stipellate, and the two lateral leaflets with their petioles and missing.
V	Seed coat mottling.
Vw	Verticillium wilt resistance.
Ymr	Cowpea yellow mosaic virus resistance, conditions resistance to cow pea mosaic virus.

11.5.7. French bean

Gene symbol	Character
Are	Resistance to anthracnose.
Da	Straight pod.
Dw1 dw2	Duplicate gene causing dwarf plant.
Ext	Interspecific gene for external stigma in *Phaseolus coccineus*.
Fa	Basic gene for pod membrane.
Fin (fin^{+})	Indetyerminat vs fin determinat plant growth.
gas	Causes both male and female sterility.
in	Determinate growth = (fin)
itor	With ram triple branched infloresence
L	Long vs 1 short internodes.
mo	Conditions resistance to bean virus.
neu^{+}	Short day flowering response.
ri	Confers resistance to bean virus 1.
St	Stringy pods.
te	Twining habitvs t non- twining
To	Cell wall fibre.
tri	Produces three cotyledons.
Uni	Unifoliate leaves.

11.5.8. Bell pepper

Gene symbol	Character
A	Anthocyanin- basic gene for purple colour in foliage, stem, flower, fruit, incompletely dominant
B	Bata carotene – high in mature fruit, interacts with t for higher level in mature fruit.
t	High beta carotene – complementary with B.
Y	Yellow or orange mature fruit colour.
Ys	Yellow spot on corolla of *C. pendulum*.
Yt_1, yt_2	Yellow top young expanding leaves are yellow and gradually turn green.
Dw_1, dw_2	Dwarf plant.
fa	Fasciculate – flowers and fruit borne in cluster or bunches, compounded nodes, bushy plants with determinate tendency.
fi_1	Filiform- thread like leaves, blossom irregularities, female sterile.

Contd.

fr	Frilly- leaf margins undulated.
H_1	Hairless- smooth stem in *C. annuum* var. minimum (Blanco) dominant over fruit shape dominant over elongate.
O	Oblate or round fruit shape dominant over elongate.
P	Ponited fruit apex incompletely dominant over blunt.
rl	Round leaf – leaf length reduced changing the length: width ratio from 1.50 to 1.24.
ru	Rugose or savoyed mature leaves.
up	Puright or erect pedicel and fruit orientation, intermediate expression in some genetic background.
fs_1	Female –sterile mutant in *C. annuum*, mature plants larger, otherwise normal, male fertile, sets parthenocarpic, seed less fruits.
ms	Male sterile.
C	Capsaicin- pungent fruit , modifiers increase or decrease capsaicin to produce a bimodal distribution of pungency in F_2.
Bs_1	Bacterial spot resistance to X. campestris pv. vesticatria race 1 in *C. chacoence* PI 260435.
Bs_2	Bacterial spot resistance to race 2.
N	Root – knot nematode resistance to *M. incognita*.

11.5.9. Tomato

Gene Symbol	Character
aa	Anthocyanin absent.
alc	alcobaca
Aps 1	Acid phosphatase 1
B	Beta carotene
bs	Brown seed
c	Potato leaf
d	dwarf
h	Hair absent.
hp	High pigmented.
j	Jointless.
ls	Lateral suppression.
ms	Male sterility.
nor	Non – ripening.
Nr	Never ripe.
rin	Ripening inhibitor
sp	Self-pruning.
tmf	Terminating flower.
u	Uniform light –green colour of fruit.
Cf, I, I-1, I-2, Mi, h_2, Ph, Py Tm-1, Tm-2, $Tm\text{-}2^2$	Genes conferring resistance to diseases.

11.5.10. Pea

Gene Symbol	Character
Plant Characters	
Cry	Influences length of internodes ands plant height along with la and ls.
La	Influences length of internodes and plant height along with cry and la.
ls	Influences length of internodes and plant height along with cry and la.
Branching	
Ram	Increases number of branches.
Leaves and stipules	
Af	Leaflets converted to tendrils.
Cri	Leaves, stipules, flowers, and pods folded and crisp.
Lat	Double leaflet and stipule area.
At	Stipules reduced to straplike structures.
Tac	Tendrils present on acacia leaves.
Tl	Leaves with extra leaflets and no tendrils.
Wax (bloom)	
Wa	Without wax on pods, upper and lower stipule surfaces, and underside of leaflets.
Was	Reduced wax as with wa.
Wb	Pods without wax, little wax on rest of plant.
Wel	Wax absent from all parts of the plant.
Wex	Extra wax on all aerial plant parts.
Colour	
A	Absence of anthocyanin.
Alb	Plans without chlorophyll, albina, lethal.
Inflorescence	
Number of flowers	
Fn	With fna determines number of flowers on the inflorescence, greatly influenced by environment.
Fna	With fn determines number of flowers on the inflorescence, greatly influenced by environment.
Pollen colour	
Yp	Yellow pollen.
Seeds	
Form	
Com	Sides of seeds flattened.
R	Seed cotyledons wrinkled.
Surface	
Gty	Surface texture gritty.
Colour	
I	Green cotyledons, I produces yellow cotyledons.
Pods	
Breadth	
It	Increases pod width 25%.
Form	
Bt	Apex of pods blunt.
Con	Affects curvature of pod.

Contd.

Fibre	
Dpo	Pods tough and lethery, readily dehisce at maturity.
Colour	
Gp	Young pod yellow.
Disease resistance:	
Enation mosaic virus	
En	Resistant to enation mosaic virus.
Fusarium wilt and near wilt	
Fnw	Resistant to *F.oxysporum* race2.
Fw	Resistant to *F. oxysporum* race1.
Pea seed borne mosaic virus	
Sbm	Resistant to pea seed-borne mosaic virus.
Powdery mildew	
Er-1	Resistant to *E. polygoni.*
Wil	Wilts quickly under moisture stress.

11.6. Gene Mapping in Vegetable Crops for Various Traits

Vegetable crops	Molecular Markers	Traits
Tomato	CAPS	*Fusarium oxysporum* resistance locus *I-2.*
	RFLP	Male sterile 14 gene and a hotspot for recombination.
	RFLP	Regulation of iron-metabolism.
	RFLP	Sequencing of cDNA clone.
	SNP	*Cf-2* gene.
	RAPD	Integration of the classical and molecular linkage maps of chromosome-6.
	RFLP	Soluble solids, fruit weight, fruit pH, fruit size and shape, fruit ripening, yield.
	SCAR and CAPS	Pathenocarpy.
	RFLP	Ripening inhibitor and non-ripening Loci.
	AFLP and RFLP	Root knot nematode resistance locus.
	RAPD	Salt tolerance.
	RFLP	Golden nematode resistance gene (*Hero*).
	RFLP	Lateral suppressor(Is) locus.
	RFLP	Tandemly repeated telomeric DNA sequences.
	RFLP	Physical location of *Cf-2* gene.
	RAPD	Integration of the classical and molecular linkage maps of tomato chromosome-6.
	RAPD and RFLP	Close linkage between the *Cf-2/Cf-5* and *Mi* resistance Loci.
	RAPD	Carotenoid loci.
	AFLP	Quantitative resistance to late blight.
	RAPD and AFLP	High resolution map of chromosome VII harbouring the nematode resistance gene.
	RFLP	Mapping of simple sequence repeat loci.
	SSR and CAPS	Senescence related QTLs.
	InDels	Fine mapping of *Ph 3* gene conferring resistance to late blight.

Contd.

	SNP and In Dels	21 SNPs and one InDel were identified in candidate genes for starch content, tuber yielc and starch yield.
	SNP	Genetic mapping and QTL analysis of agronomic traits *viz.*, total tuber yield, number of tubers or tuber set per plant, average tuber weight, specific gravity, vigor, maturity and tuber end rot.
Cabbage	RFLP	Linkage group alignment.
	RFLP	Location of the self incompatibility locus.
	RFLP	Comparative genome mapping
	RFLP	Linkage group alignment from four independent- RFLP maps.
Hot pepper	RFLP, RAPD	*Xanthomonas compestris.*
	SSR	Mapping for Bacterial wilt(*Ralstonia solanacearum*).
	RAPD, AFLP	Genetic relationship among 34 cultivars.
Egg plant	SSR	Bacterial wilt resistance.

11.7. Identified Genes with Linked Markers for Disease Resistance in Vegetable Crops

Host	Pathogen	Gene	Type of markers
Tomato	*Meloidogyne incognita*	*Mi*	CAPS
	Cladosporium fulvum	*Cf9*	SCAR
		Mi3	RAPD, RFLP
	Leveillula taurica	*Lv*	RFLP, RAPD
	Phytophthora infestans	*Ph2*	CAPS
	Verticillium dahliae	*Ve*	CAPS
	Oidium lycopersicon	*Ol1*	RAPD, RFLP
	Yellow leaf curl virus	*Ty1*	CAPS
		Ty2	SCAR
		Ty3	SCAR
		Ty4	CAPS
		Ty5	dCAPS
	Tospovirus	*SW-5*	SCAR, SNP
Potato	*Globodera rostochiensis*	*H1*	SCAR
	Phytophthora infestans	*R1* and *R3*	SCAR
Lettuce	*Bremia lactuceae*	*Dm17* and *18*	RAPD, SCAR
		Dm8 and *10*	RAPD, SCAR
	Plasmopara lactucae-radicis	*Plr*	SCAR
	Turnip mosaic virus	*Tu*	RAPD, RFLP
Bean	*Uromyces appendiculatus*	*Up2*	RAPD
	Common bean mosaic virus	*I*	CAPS, SNP
	Pseudomonas syringae pv. *phaselicola*		RAPD and AFLP
Pea	Pea seed borne mosaic virus	*Sbm1*	SNP
	Pea common mosaic virus	*Mo*	RFLP
	Erysiphe polygone	*Er*	SNP
	Fusarium oxysporum	*Fw*	CAPS
Corn	*Bipolaris maydis*	*Rhm*	SSR
Chineese cabbage	*Plasmodiophora brassicae*	*CRb*	SCAR and CAPS

11.8. Genes Conferring Abiotic Stress Tolerance and Their Mode of Action

Genes	Function	Mechanism of action
DREBs/CBFs; ABF3	Stress induced transcription factors	Enhanced expression of down stream stress related genes confers drought/cold/ salt tolerance.Constitutively over-expression can lead to stunting growth.
SNAC1	Stress induced transcription factor	SNAC1 expression reduces water loss increasing stomatal sensitivity to ABA.
ZAT12	Stress induced transcription factors	Enhanced expression of down stream stress related genes confer drought/heat/ salt tolerance.
OsCDPK7	Stress induced Ca-dependent protein kinase	Enhanced expression of stress responsive genes.
Farnesyl-transferase *(ERAI)*	Negative-regulator of ABA sensing	Down-regulation of farnesyltransferase enhances the plant's response to ABA and drought tolerance reducing stomatal conductance.
Mn-SOD	Mn-superoxide dismutase	Overe xpression improves stress tolerance also in field conditions.
AVP1	*Vacuolar* H^+ pyrophosphatase	Over expression facilitate auxin fluxes leading to increased root growth.
HVA1; OsLEA3	Stress induced LEA proteins	Over-accumulation of LEA increases. drought tolerance also in field conditions
ERECTA	A putative leucine-rich repeat receptor like kinase is a major contributor to a locus for D on *Arabidopsis* chromosome2	ERECTA acts as a regulator of transpiratione fficiency with effects on stomatal density,epidermal cell expansion, mesophyll cell proliferation and cell–cell contact.
otsA and *otsB*	*Escherichia coli* trehalose biosynthetic genes	Increased trehalose accumulation correlates with higher soluble carbohydrate levels, elevated photosynthetic capacity and increased tolerance to photo-oxidative damage.
P5CS	d-Pyrroline-5-carboxylate synthetase	Enhanced accumulation of proline leads to increased osmotolerance.
mtlD	Mannitol-1-phosphate dehydrogenase	Mannitol accumulation leads to increased osmotolerance
GF14l	14-3-3 protein	Lines over expressing GF14l have a "staygreen" phenotype, improved water stress tolerance and higher photosynthetic rates underwater deficit conditions.
NADP-Me	NADP-malic enzyme	The overe xpression decreased stomatal conductance and improves WUE.
AREB cupida dehydrine	bZIP transcription factor in tomato	Overexpression increasing dehydrin expression. Overwilting or stomatal

Contd.

	Leaf necrosis in tomato	defect.
	Increased distances from dehydrins activated by	Probably the dehydrins protect membranesduring stresses.
	abscisic acid in tomato	Dehydrins are upregulated by abscisic acid.
Chloroplast drought induced stress protein	Thiol-disulfide exchange intermediateactivity in potato	Preservation of the thiol: disulfide redox potential of chloroplastic proteins during water deficit.
CDSP 32	Thiol-disulfide exchange intermediateactivity in potato	Preserve chloroplastic structures against oxidative injury upon drought.
CDSP 34	Increases in CDSP 34 transcript andprotein abundances were also observed inpotato plants subjected to highillumination.	The CDSP 34 protein is proposed to play a structural role in stabilizing stromal lamella ethylakoids upon osmotic or oxidative stress.
Wilty	Dominant TGRC gene in tomato Leaves overwilt when drought stressed	Wilting under field or greenhouse conditions; marginal leaf narcrosis.
Wilty dwarf	Recessive TGRC gene in tomato	Grayish-green, droopy leaves; stunted plants;leaves droop when drought stressed.
Water stress induced *ER5* protein	Stress induced CaLEA6 (for *Capsicum annuum* LEA) is 709 bp long with anopen reading frame encoding 164 aminoacids	Predicted to produce a highly hydrophobic, but cytoplasmic, protein.
Abscicic acid stress ripening 2	Putative DNA binding and chaperon likeactivity	A member of the Asr gene family. It is inducedby abiotic stress such as water and is expressedin the leaf phloem companion cells.
OsWRKY45	Transcription factor	Drought tolerance.
SodERF3	Ethylene responsive factor	Increased tolerance to drought and osmotic stresses.
CAP 160 and CAP 85	Dehydrin and Lea-like	Slightly enhanced freezing tolerance.
HsfA1	Transcription factor	Heat shock tolerant/ Heat shock sensitive.
Hsf3	Transcription factor	Heat shock tolerant.
Hsp70	Heat shock protein	High temperature tolerant/ sensitive.
Hsp101	Heat shock protein	Acquired thermo tolerance.
Hsp17.7	Heat shock protein	High temperature tolerant/ sensitive.
Fad7	Fatty acid denaturation	High temperature tolerance.
Hvapx1	Active oxygen species metabolism	Heat shock tolerant.
OsHSFA2e	Transcription factor	*Arabidopsis* plants showed enhanced thermotolerance.
AtHsfA2	*A. thaliana*	Thermo tolerance as well as oxidative stress tolerance.
hal1	Protein involved in regulation of K+ transport	Salt stress tolerance.

Contd.

BADH-1	Over expression of betaine aldehyde dehydrogenase encoded by *BADH* gene catalyzes conversion of betaine aldehyde into glycine betaine	Salt stress tolerance.
NHX1	Over expressed the *NHX1* vacuolar Na^+/H^+ antiporter in tomato plants	Salt stress tolerance.
MAPK gene (*CsNMAPK)*	ROS scavenger and osmotic adjustment Transcription factor	Salt stress tolerance.

11.9. Improvement of Taste and Flavor of Vegetable Crops Through Biotechnological Interventions

Target compound	Species	Gene used
Flavonoids	*Solanum lycopersicum* *Brassica napus*	CHI, Flavone synthase, CHS, polyketide reductase, ANT1 (MYB transcription factor, DELILA (bHLH transcription factor), MYC-RP and MYC-GP (both bHLH), *Lc* (bHLH), CRYPTOCHROME2, stilbene synthase (STS), UDP-glucose:sinapate glucosyltransferase
Carotenoids (provitamin A, etc)	*Solanum lycopersicum* *Solanum tuberosum* *Solanum phureja* *Brassica napus*	PSY, β-LYC and β-carotene hydroxylase, 1-deoxy-d-xylulose-5-phosphate synthase (DXS), zeaxanthin epoxidase, EuCrtB, EuCrtI, EuCrtY, BoOr, AtZEP, PaCrtB, β-carotene ketolase, lycopene cyclise, geranylgeranyl diphosphate synthase, phytoene synthase (PSY) and phytoene desaturase (PDS) and plant or bacterial β-lycopene cyclase (β-LYC)
Tocopherols	*Solanum tuberosum* *Brassica napus*	tocopherol cyclases, *At-HPT*
Vitamin C	*Lactuca sativa* *Solanum tuberosum*	1-gulono-1,4-lactone oxidase, *StVTC2A*
Folate	*Solanum lycopersicum*	Synthetic GTP cyclohydrolase-1
Calcium	*Solanum tuberosum*	*Scax1, Cax2b* chimeric
LC-PUFAs	*Brassica juncea*	Fatty acid biosynthesis enzymes
Protein	*Solanum tuberosum*	*AmA1*, *CgS90*, StTA, AK and DHDPS

11.10: Quality Trait Improvement of Vegetable/horticultural Crops Using Genome Editing Technology

Plant	Target genes	Traits
Solanum lycopersicum	Ripening inhibitor (RIN)	Fruit ripening
	Anthocyanin 1 (ANT1)	Anthocyanin biosynthesis
	Phytoene desaturase (S1PDS)	Carotenoid biosynthesis
	Phytochrome interacting factor (S1PIF4)	Carotenoid biosynthesis
	S1IAA9	Parthenocarpy
	Slagamous-LIKE 6 (S1AGL6)	Parthenocarpy
	Phytoene synthase (PSY1)	Fruit colour
Solanum tuberosum	StMYB44	Phosphate transport
Brassica oleracea	Granule-bound starch synthase (GBSS)	Starch quality
Brassica oleracea	Gibberellin 3-beta-dioxygenase 1 (BolC.GA4.a)	Plant development
Cucumis sativus	Translation initiation	Virus resistance

11.11. Gene Sequencing

11.11.1. Gene Sequencing in Tomato

Name of the country	Chromosome number
USA group	1,10,11
Korea	2
China	3
UK	4
India	5
Netherland	6
France	7
Japan	8
Spain	9
Italy	10

11.11.2. Whole Genome Sequences in Vegetable Crops

Crops	Common name	Genome size (Mbp)	Number of genes
Amaranthus hypochondiacus	Grain amaranth	502	-
Asparagus officinalis	Garden asparagus	1188	32073
Beta vulgaris	Sugar beet	540	-
Brassica juncea	Mustard	955	9746
Brassica napus	Turnip	848	20899
Brassica oleracea	Wild cabbage	489	53670
Capsicum annuum	Pepper	2936	41504
Capsicum baccatum	Hot pepper	3216	35853

Contd.

Capsicum chinense	Pepper	3071	34974
Chenopodium pallidicaule	Chenopodium	337	-
Chenopodium quinoa	Chenopodium	1334	58734
Chenopodium suecicum	Chenopodium	537	-
Cucumis sativus	Cucumber	196	20396
Daucus carota	Carrot	422	36299
Dioscorea rotundata	White yam	457	-
Ipomea batatas	Sweet potato	837	-
Ipomea trifida	Wild sweet potato	513	-
Lactuca sativa	Lettuce	1134	-
Manihot esculenta	Cassava	582	31881
Momordica charantia	Bitter gourd	286	21623
Phaseolus vulgaris	French bean	550	-
Rapanus raphanustrum	Wild radish	254	-
Raphanus sativus	Radish	427	58031
Soalnum arcanum	Wild tomato	665	-
Solamum pimpinellifolium	Wild tomato	688	-
Solanum commersonii	Wild Potato	730	-
Solanum lycopersicum	Tomato	824	30336
Solanum melongena	Egg plant	833	-
Solanum pennelli	Wild tomato	926	32519
Solanum tuberosum	Potato	706	33410
Spinacia oleracea	Spinach	494	21539
Viccia faba	Faba bean	80	-

11.12. Transgenic in Vegetables

11.12.1. Global Area of Transgenic Crops in 2006 and 2015 (Country wise in descending order)

Country	2006	2015	Increase in area (%)	Crops (2015)
	Area (m ha)	Area (m ha)		
USA	54.6	70.09	22.1	Soybean, maize, cotton, canola, sugarbeet, alfalfa, papaya, squash
Brazil	11.5	44.2	73.9	Soybean, maize, cotton
Argentina	18.0	24.5	53.0	Soybean, maize, cotton
India	3.8	11.6	67.2	Cotton
Canada	6.1	11	44.5	Canola, maize, soybean, sugarbeet
China	3.5	3.7	5.40	Cotton, papaya, poplar, tomato, sweet pepper

Contd.

Paraguay	2.5	3.6	30.5	Soybean
Pakistan	-	2.9	-	Cotton
South Africa	1.4	2.3	39.1	Soybean, maize, cotton
Uruguay	0.4	1.4	71.4	Soybean, maize
Bolivia	-	1.1	-	Soybean
Australia	0.2	0.7	71.4	Cotton, canola
Philippines	0.2	0.7	71.4	Maize
Myanmar	-	0.3	-	Cotton
Burkina Faso	-	0.4	-	Cotton
Mexico	0.1	0.1	0	Cotton, soybean
Spain	0.1	0.1	0	Maize
Colombia	<0.1	<0.1	0	Cotton
Chile	-	<0.1	-	Maize, soybean, canola
Honduras	<0.1	<0.1	0	Maize
Portugal	<0.1	<0.1	0	Maize
Czech Republic	<0.1	<0.1	0	Maize
Poland	-	<0.1	-	Maize
Egypt	-	<0.1	-	Maize
Slovakia	<0.1	<0.1	0	Maize
Romania	0.1	<0.1	0	Maize
Sweden	-	<0.1	-	Potato
Costa Rica	-	<0.1	-	Cotton, soybean
Germany	<0.1	<0.1	0	Potato
Total		170.70	549.9	100

Source: James 2015; International Service for the Acquisition of Agro-Biotech Applications (ISAAA),

11.12.2. Examples of Successful Transgenic Vegetables for Post-harvest Traits

Purpose of genetic manipulation	Transgene product	Origin of transgene	Transformed plant
Improved storage/shelf-life	Antisense polygalacturonase	Tomato	Tomato
	α-mannosidase (α-Man) and β-D-N-acetylhexosaminidase (β-Hex) RNAi	Tomato	Tomato
Ripening	Antisense ACC oxidase	Tomato	Tomato
	Antisense ACC synthase	Tomato	Tomato
	Endo-1,4-beta-D-glucanase (EGase) CaCel1	Pepper	Tomato
	Antisense ACC oxidase	Tomato	Melon

Fruit pigmentation	Phytoene synthase gene	Tomato	Tomato
Improved flavour and aroma	*LeCCD1*	Tomato	Tomato
Modify a sour taste into a sweet taste	Miraculin	Richadellad ulcifica	Tomato

11.12.3. Successful Engineered Vegetables for Parthenocarpic Fruits

Transgenic aganist	Transgene	Origin of transgene	Transformed plants
Tomato	Rol B gene	*A. rhizogens*	Tomato
Brinjal	*Iaah gene*	*Ps. Syringae* pv. *savas*	Brinjal

11.12.4: Mechanism of Action of Different Herbicides

Active principle of herbicide	Inhibited pathway	Target product	Use	Basis of resistance
I. Amino acid biosynthesis inhibitor				
Glyphosate (Roundup)	Aromatic aminoacid biosynthesis	EPSPS	Broad spectrum	Over expression of *EPSPS* gene; bacterial *aroA* gene
Sulphonylurea and Imidazolinones	Branched chain Amino acid	ALS	Selected crops	Mutant *ALS* gene
Phosphinothricin	Glutamine biosynthesis	GS	Broad spectrum	Gene amplification *bar* gene: detoxification
II. Photosynthesis Inhibitors				
Atrazine (Lasso)	Photosystem II	Q_B (32k Da protein)	Selected crops	Mutant *PsbA* gene: *GST* gene:; detoxification
Bromoxynill (Buctril)	Photosynthesis	-	Selected crops	*bxn* gene: detoxification

11.12.5. Vegetable Transgenic Development Activities in India

Institute	Vegetable crops	Transgenic	Target
I. Public Sectors			
CPRI , Shimla	Potato	Bt cry 1 Ab	Developed plant resistant to potato tuber moth.
		Osmotin	Developed water stress tolerant plants.
		Coat protein	Developed plants resistant to potato virus Y (PVY).
Delhi University, Delhi	Tomato	Ctx- B and Tcp antigens of *Vibrio cholerae*	Edible vaccine development.
	Brinjal	Chitnase, glucanase and thaumatin encoding genes	Create disease resistant plants.
IARI, New Delhi	Brinjal	Cry 1Ab	Generate lepidopteron resistant plants.
	Tomato	Cry 1Ab	Develop lepidopteron resistant plants.
	Cauliflower	Cry 1Ab	Develop diamond back moth resistant plants.
	Cabbage	Cry 1Ab	Develop diamond back moth resistant plants.
	Tomato	ACC synthase	Controlling fruit ripening.
		Replicase gene	Develop tomato leaf curl virus resistant plants.
IIHR, Banglore	Muskmelon	Rabies glycoprotein	Double edible vaccines.
	Tomato	Leaf curl virus	Generate leaf curl virus resistant plants.
		Chitinase and glucanase	Develop plant resistant to fungal disease.
JNU, New Delhi	Tomato	OXDC	Develop fungal diseases resistant plants.
	Potato	Ama 1	Develop protein rich potatoes.
II. Private Sectors			
IAHS, Bangalore	Tomato	Alafa glucanase and tomato leaf curl virus genes	Generate plants resistant to viral and fungal diseases.
Proagro PG-S (India) Ltd; Gurgaon	Tomato	Cry1 Ab	Lepidopteran resistant plants.
	Brinjal	Cry1 Ab	Lepidopteran resistant plants.
	Cauliflower	Cry1H/ Cry 9C	Lepidopteran resistant plants.
		Bar, barnase, barstar	Superior hybrid culture.
	Cabbage	Cry1H/ Cry 9C	Lepidopteran resistant plants.

11.12.6. Transgenic Released in the Market by Seed Companies

Genetic trait	Crops	Companies
Insect resistance	Corn	Mycogen, Novartis, Monsanto, Dekalb Genetic
	Potato	Monsanto.
Herbicide resistance		Canola, Soybean Monsanto.
	Cotton	Monsanto, Calgene.
	Corn	Dekalb Genetics, Pioneer.
Virus resistance	Squash	Asgrow seeds.
Specialty oils	Canola	Calgene.
Fruit ripening	Tomato	Calgene, Monsanto, DNA Plant Technology.
Increased pectin	Tomato	Zeneca Plant Science.

Source: Biotechnology Industry Organization.

11.12.7: Committies for Release of Transgenic

S.N.	Name of Committee
1.	The Institute of Biosafety Committee(IBSC)
2.	The Review Committee on Genetic Manipulation(RCGM)
3.	The Monitoring and Evaluation Committee(MEC)
4.	The Genetic Engineering Approval Committee(GEAC)
5.	The Recombinant DNA Advisory Committee(RDAC)
6.	The State Biosafety Coordination Committee(SBCC)
7.	The District Level Committee (DLC)

11.13. Synthetic Seeds

11.13.1. Gels Used for Development of Synthetic Seeds

Gel	Conc. % w/v	Complexing agent	Conc. In mM
Sodium alginate	0.5-5.0	Calcium salts	30-100
Sodium alginate with gelatin	2.0-5.0	Calcium salts	30-100
Carrageenan with locust bean gum	0.2-0.80.4-1.0	Potassium or ammonium chloride	500
Gelrite	0.25	Temperature lowered	

11.13.2. Potential Horticultural Crops for Synthetic Seeds

Category I Strong technological basis			**Category II Strong commercial basis**		
Alfalfa	Oilpalm	Asparagus	Impatiens	Cucumber	
Sandal wood	Banana	Begonia	Cyclamen	Soybean	
Caraway	Orchard grass	Broccoli	Lettuce	Doglas fir	Spinach
Carrot	Orange	Cardamom	Loblolly pine	Garlic	
Celery	Panicum	Cauliflower	Petunia	Geranium	
Coffee	Pennisetum	Corn	Potato	Gerbera	Tomato
Eggplant	Wlanut			Grape	Watermelon

11.14. Nanotechnology

11.14.1. Concept

- Nanotechnology is science, engineering, and technology conducted at the nanoscale, which is about 1 to 100 nanometers.
- Physicist Richard Feynman is considered as father of nanotechnology. The idea and concepts behind nanoscience and nanotechnology started with a talk entitled "There *is Plenty of Room at the Bottom*" by physicist Richard Feynman at an American Physical Society Meeting at the California Institute of Technology on December 29, 1959, long before the term nanotechnology was used. In his talk, Feynman described a process in which scientists would be able to manipulate and control individual atoms and molecules. Over a decade a later, in his explorations of ultra precision machining, Professor Norio Taniguchi coined the term nanotechnology.
- It was not until 1981, with the development of the scanning tunnelling microscope that could "see" individual atoms that modern nanotechnology began. Nanotechnology has spread to almost every field. In the recent years, its potential was realised in a big way during scientific research in various fields. Developing products based on nanotechnology - be it drugs, cosmetics, paints, clothes or washing machines, is the new trend across the world. Therefore, the field of nanotechnology is here to stay with the promise of exciting and rewarding career opportunities for those interested in sciences with a penchant for research. Nanotechnology is an interdisciplinary science. It has wide applications in fields such as medicine, agriculture, energy, chemistry, environment, industry, communications and information technology (IT).
- Opportunities for nanotechnologists are galore in all these fields. Also, students from Mathematics as well as Life Sciences background can venture into this field and improve their career prospects exponentially.
- *Nanotechnology is the study of matter at atomic and molecular levels. It involves manipulation of matter at a miniature level called the nano scale. Nanotechnology research concentrates on particles less than one billionth of a meter in diameter. Little wonder then that research involving nanotechnology yields some fascinating and astonishing discoveries.* The biological properties of atoms and molecules are greatly different on a nano scale compared to their properties as constitutes of a material.

11.14.2. History

- 1959: Richarol Feyman – Father of Nano-technology
- 1974: Taniguchi used term Nano-technology
- 1984: Bucky ball dicovered
- 1991: Carbon nanotube discovered
- 1997: First company founded (Zyvex)
- 2000: USA President launched U.S. National Nanotechnology Initiative

11.14.3. Application of Nanotechnology in Agriculture

Agricultural Sciences	Brief description
Seed Science	Seed is most important input determining productivity of any crop. Conventionally, seeds are tested for germination and distributed to farmers for sowing. Synthesis of metal oxide nano-particles and carbon nanotube can be used to improve the germination of rainfed crops. These processes facilitate germination which can be exploited in rainfed agricultural system.
Crop nutrition	Nano-fertilizer technology is very innovative but scantily reported in the literature. However, some of the reports and patents strongly suggest that there is a vast scope for the formulation of nano-fertilizers. Significant increase in yields have been observed due to foliar application of nano particles as fertilizer.
Weed Management	The encapsulated nano-herbicides are relevant and are being design and produce nano-herbicide that is protected under natural environment and acts only when there is a spell of rainfall, which truly mimics the rainfed system. Developing a target specific herbicide molecule encapsulated with nanoparticle is aimed for specific receptor in the roots of target weeds, which enter into roots system and translocated to parts that inhibit glycolysis of food reserve in the root system.
Pesticides	Persistence of pesticides in the initial stage of crop growth helps in bringing down the pest population below the economic threshold level and to have an effective control for a longer period. In order to protect the active ingredient from the adverse environmental conditions and to promote persistence, a nanotechnology approach, namely "nano-encapsulation" can be used to improve the insecticidal value. Nanoencapsulation comprises nano-sized particles of the active ingredients being sealed by a thin-walled sac or shell (protective coating).
Water Management	Nanotechology, offers the potential of novel nanomaterials for the treatment of surface water, ground water and waste water contaminated by toxic metal ions, organic and inorganic solutes and microorganisms. Due to their unique activity towards recalcitrant contaminants many nanomaterials are under research and development for use for water purification.
Nano-scale carriers	Nanoscale carriers can be utilized for the efficient delivery of fertilizers, pesticides, herbicides, plant growth regulators, etc. The mechanisms involved in the efficient delivery, better storage and controlled release include: encapsulation and entrapment, polymers and dendrimers, surface ionic and weak bond attachments among others.
Biosensors	Biosensors provide high performance capabilities for use in detecting contaminants in food or environmental media. They offer high specificity and sensitivity, rapid response, user-friendly operation, and compact size at a low cost.
Agricultural Engineering	Nanotechnology has many applications in the field of agricultural machinery so as to increase their resistance against wear and corrosion and ultraviolet rays; producing strong mechanical components with use of Nano-coating and use of bio-sensors in smart machines for mechanical-chemical weed control; production of Nano-cover for bearings to reduce friction.

Animal Sciences	Nanotechnology has the ability to provide appropriate solutions for addressing the issues of food items, veterinary care and prescription medicines as well as vaccines for domesticated animals. Taking certain medications such as antibiotics, vaccines, and probiotics, would be effective in treating the infections, nutrition and metabolic disorders, when used at the nano level.
Fisheries and aquaculture	Nanotechnology has tremendous potential to revolutionize fisheries and aquaculture sector Nanotechnology tools like nano-materials, nano-sensor, DNA nano-vaccines, gene delivery and smart drug delivery have the potential of solving many puzzles related to fisheries nutrition and health production, reproduction, prevention and treatment of disease

11.14.4. Colleges Offering Nanotechnology Courses in India

S.No.	Organizations	Course	Eligibility	Admission	Contact
1.	Jawaharlal Nehru Technological University, Hyderabad	M. Tech in Nanoscience and Technology	B. Tech relevant field	GATE/entrance test	http://jntu.ac.in
2.	Amity University, Noida	M.Sc Nanoscience and M.Tech Nanotechnology, a dual degree course M.Sc Nanoscience by research B.Tech in Nanotechnology	B.Sc with minimum 55 per cent B.Tech or B.Sc (Physics/ Chemistry/ Biotechnology/ Electronics)Minimum 60 per cent marks in class X and XII and minimum 60 per cent marks in PCM/ PCB	Entrance test	www.amity.edu
3.	Vellore Institute of Technology, Tamil Nadu	M.Tech in Nanotechnology	BE/ B.Tech in ECEI VLSI/ E and I/ M.Sc Physics with Electronics as specialisation/MaterialScience/ Solid State Physics or any cquivalent with minimum 50 per cent marks	GATE/entrance test	www.vit.ac.in
4.	Sastra University, Thanjavur	M.Tech in Medical Nanotechnology M.Tech in Nanoelcctronics	M.Sc in Biochemistry/ Chemistry/ Physics or BE/ B.Tech in BiotechnologyBE/B.Tech in electronics engineering	Marks obtained in the qualifying examination	www.sastra.edu
5.	SRM University, Kancheepuram District	B.Tech in Nanotechnology	10+2 with at least 70 per cent aggregate in Mathematics, Physics and Chemistry	Entrance test	www.srmuniv.ac.in
6.	College of Engineering, Andhra University, Visakhapatnam	M.Tech in Nanotechnology of engineering	BE/ B.Tech in relevant branch	GATE orentrance test	www.andhrau niversitv.info

11.15. Seed Technology

11.15.1. Approximate Time Required for Germination in Vegetable Crops

Vegetable crops	Days
Bean	7 - 14
Beet	10 - 16
Cole crops	5 - 10
Cucumber	7 - 14
Leek	10 - 15
Onion	10 - 15
Lettuce	6 - 10
Tomato	5 - 10
Radish	4 - 7
Pea	7 - 14
Melons	4 - 8
Parsley	14 - 30
Spinach	7 - 10
Carrot	12 - 15
Brinjal	7 - 12

11.15.2. Dormancy Breaking Treatment for Some Important Vegetable Crops

Crop	Dormancy release treatment
Cabbage	Prechill, KNO_3
Cauliflower	Prechill, KNO_3, light
Chillies and pepper	KNO_3, GA_3
Cucumber	Removal of testa
Spinach & beet root	Pre wash, prechill, dryheat
Onion	Prechill
Radish	Prechill, preheat
Tomato	KNO_3, GA_3
Turnip	Prechill, KNO_3
Lettuce	Prechill, KNO_3
Bitter gourd	Acetone, seedcoat removal
Brinjal	KNO_3, GA_3

11.16. Seed Priming

11.16.1. Concept and Methods

Priming could be defined as controlling the hydration level within seeds so that the metabolic activity necessary for germination can occur but radicle emergence is prevented. Different physiological activities within the seed occur at different moisture levels. The last physiological activity in the germination process is radicle emergence. The initiation of radicle emergence requires a high seed water content. By limiting seed water content, all the metabolic steps necessary for germination can occur without the irreversible act of radicle emergence. Prior to radicle emergence, the seed is considered desiccation tolerant, thus the primed seed moisture content can be decreased by drying.

After drying, primed seeds can be stored until time of sowing.

Several priming methods have been reported to be used commercially both at liquid and vapour phase. Seed priming methods can be grouped into two categories depending upon whether the water uptake is controlled or noncontrolled. Noncontrolled water uptake includes those methods in which water is freely available and is governed by the seed to the water. The seeds may be soaked, or kept on moist blotters. Here, since the availability of water is mostly controlled the seeds will ultimately enter the 3rd phase. Therefore, limiting the duration of imbibition at proper temperature must arrest the process.

In controlled water uptake, water availability or water potential is regulated thus preventing the seeds to enter phase III stage. Among them, liquid or osmotic priming and solid matrix priming appear to have the greatest following (Khan et al., 1991).

Osmatic priming

Osmatic priming is accomplished using chemicals that lower osmatic potential in the seed environment. Polyethylene glycol is a commenly used osmatic priming material because it is readily available and has no physiological reaction with seed. Very large molecules of this substance do not pass through seed cell membranes. Other osmatic priming agents includes glycerol, manitol and agro Lig.

Matric priming

Matric seed priming substances or materials control water potential by reducing the matric potential of the water in them through adsorption on particle surfaces. Seeds are mixed with materials of high surface area with variable particle size (including colloidal) and a non-soluble solid state with low chemical reactivity. Specialized vermiculite compounds (Zonolite), celite and microcel are used. These have high matric potential and low osmatic potential.

Hydro priming (Drum priming)

This is achieved by continuous or successive addition of a limited amount of water to the seeds. A drum is used for this purpose and the water can also be applied by humid air. 'On-farm steeping' is the cheep and useful technique that is practiced by incubating seeds (cereals, legumes) for a limited time in warm water. On a commercial scale, controlled hydration by drum priming elevate the seeds to a desired moisture level by applying given amount of water at specific time. Another drum priming system controls seed hydration by the time intervals and volume of water application. The total water required is divided into different intervals and injected to the system. The prior knowledge of the water imbibition capacity of the seed should be known in advance for this technique.

11.16.2. Advantages of Seed Priming

1. In practical primed seeds emerge from the soil faster and often more uniform than nonprimed seeds. Priming accomplishes this important step in field by shortening the lag period in phase II of the germination process. Since the seed have already gone through this phase during priming germination time

requirement can be reduced to approximately 50 per cent upon subsequent dehydration.

2. Another important benefit of priming has been the germination of seeds under sub optimum temperature. From a practical standpoint, priming enables seeds of several species to germinate and emerge at supra-optimal temperatures. Examples are available in almost all temperate vegetables like tomato, pepper and lettuce.
3. Priming has also alleviated secondary dormancy mechanisms that can be imposed if exposure to supra-optimal temperatures lasts too long or in photo-sensitive lettuce varieties.
4. Priming has been commercially used to eliminate or greatly reduce the amount of seed-borne fungi and bacteria. Organisms such as *Xanthomonas campestris* in *Brassica* seeds and *Septoria* in celery have been shown to be eliminated within seed lots as a by-product of priming. In the case of *Xanthomonas campestris* in *Brassica* sp., zero infection in 50,000 seeds has been commonly reported. The mechanisms responsible for eradication may be linked to the water potentials that seeds are exposed to during priming, differential sensitivity to priming salts, and/or differential sensitivity to oxygen concentrations.

11.16.3. Seed Pelleting

Seed pelleting is the process of enclosing a seed with a small quantity of inert material just enough to produce a globular unit of standard size to facilitate precision planting. The inert material creates natural water holding media and provides small amount of nutrients to young seedlings. Seed pelleting also serves a mechanism of applying needed material in such a way that they affect the seed or soil at the seed soil interface.

The main objective of seed is precision planting with added advantage of better establishment and increased productivity.

The advantage of seed pelleting is summarized below

- Increase in size.
- Singling of seeds to prevent clogging.
- Precision planting.
- Attraction of moisture.
- Supply of growth regulators, micronutrients.
- Stimulation of germination.
- Influence of micro-environment.
- Savings of chemicals/fertilizers applied to soil.
- Supply of oxygen.
- Protects seed at aerial seedling by improving ballistic ability.
- Reduces seed rate.
- Uniform field establishment.
- Increase yield.

- Remedy for sowing at problematic soils.
- Protection from birds, animals and insects.

11.16.4. The process of Pelleting

The three basic steps are involved in pelleting are stamping, coating and rolling. The materials needed for pelleting are seed, adhesive and filler materials. The seeds are uniformly coated with adhesive in correct quantity initially. Then the filler, materials are sprinkled on the coated seeds and are rolled on the filler material for effective and uniform coating.

For increased efficiency following points be kept in mind;

- Excess adhesive should not be added. It may lead to clogging of seeds.
- The adhesive should be with required viscosity, otherwise the coating will not be perfect.
- The filler material used should be a fine powder. Then only coating will be perfect and coating also will be retained for longer duration.
- The coated seed should be spread in this layer of filler material otherwise more seed will be there in single pellet. It will also bring the pellets to a uniform size.

11.17. Selection of Materials Used for Pelleting

Adhesive materials

The materials used for coating should be perfect as the physical integrity of coating is decided by the type of adhesive and this was highly influential during handling, transport and planting operation of the pellets. The adhesives recommended are gum Arabic, methyl cellulose, gelatin, casein casemate salts, plastic rexins, polyvinyl acetate, methyl ethyl cellulose, polyurethane polyvinyl alcohol, polyvinyl acetate, poly electrolyte or dextran and ply ethylene oxide.

Some of the cheap and low coat binding materials are the rice gruel, maida gruel, sago gruel and starch (revine) gruel.

In selection of these adhesive, the concentration of the adhesive important for development of required viscosity which can fix the filler material in efficient manner without breaking and dusting on shade drying.

The concentration recommended for methyl cellulose is 3% w/v, methyl ethyl cellulose is 5% w/v, and gum Arabic is 45%. The low cost adhesive such as rice gruel, maida gruel etc., are used at a concentration of 5%, 10% depending upon filler material used for pelleting. Selection of adhesive is also based on selective purposes such as plastic resins, polyvinyl acetate and insoluble poly electrolyte complexes are used to bind pesticides to seeds; poly ethylene oxides is prevent erosion of surface sown seeds, polyurethane to bind lime in a way that resist coat abrasion, blends of polyvinyl alcohol and polyvinyl acetate to bind vermiculite and poly electrolyte or dextran to aggregate soil around the seeds, thereby improving the aeration of sown seeds.

Criteria for Selection of Coating Materials

- The coating must be porous to allow movement of air to the seed.
- The coating must be weaken or breakdown when it comes in contract with soil moisture to prevent any physical impedance to seed germination.
- Materials used must not have any toxicity to the seeds.
- It must be possible to apply the coating on commercial basis.

Filler materials

The material used for filler materials for pelleting must be beneficial and harmless to both seed and the rhizosphere.

The most common materials used are lime, gypsum, dolomite and rock phosphate. Other materials include clay minerals such as montmorillonite and vermiculite. Besides, blood, peat, poultry manure, moss and mucilage are also used.

The size of particle for filler material vary with the type of filler material. The particle size important for resistant coating on the seed material. The activated clay and lime dolomite activated and clay should pass through 300 meshs sieve, the dried blood, wood charcoal, milk powder and yeast extract should pass through 150 mesh sieve size. In case of dried blood, milk powder and yeast extract alone are used, they are used in combination with dolomite in different proportions viz.,

Dried blood -	15:85 (w/w) blood	: dolomite
Milk powder -	3:85 (w/w) milk powder	: dolomite
Yeast extract-	1: 99 (w/w) yeast powder	: dolomite

In addition to the above materials biofertilizers are also used as filler materials

For low cost investment and eco-friendly benefit, botanic leaf powders are used as filler materials. The common botanic used for pelleting are arappu (*Albizia amara*), pungam (*Pungamia pinnata*), Notchi (*vitis negunto*) prosopis (*Prosopis juliflora*), neem (*Azadirachta indica*), moringa (*Moringa pterygosperm*) and tamarind (*Tamarind indica*). These botanics are recommended @ 200-300 g/kg of seed. The fineness of the powder should be in such a way that it passes through muslin cloth. These leaf powders contain an auxin like substances which regulates the growth of seedlings in initial establishment.

The characters of filler material should be as follows

- It should be non-toxic.
- Friendly to both seed, adhesive and environment.
- Easily dissolved in water.
- Easily available for commercial production.
- Low cost.

Types of pelleting

The seed pelleting can be classified into five different types. They are

11.17.1. Inoculant pelleting

The different bio-fertilizers viz., rhizobia, phosphobacteria, Asozpirillium or Azatobactor are used as filler materials which are fixed to the seed with the help of an adhesive. This type of pelleting will help in improving the activity of microorganisms of rhizosphere and help in nitrogen fixation. The selection of biofertilizer vary with crop. Powell (1979) reported that VAM (*Vascular Arabuscular Mycorrhiza)* can also be used pelleting the seeds.

11.17.2. Protective Coating

The disease controlling biocontrol agents like *Rhizobacteria bataticola* or *bacillus* spp. or *Streptomyces* spp. can also be used for pelleting the seed. Antibiotic are also used for control of diseases through pelleting. Seed pelleting is also done with fungicides and pesticides and they are added to the adhesive and coated on the seeds. But caution should be taken in such a manner that the filler material should be compatible with the fungicides and pesticides used. For inoculants pelleting, pesticides and fungicides inclusion will not be good always. Bird repellants like mestranol and resoreinal can also be used for pelleting to protect the seed from birds and rodents. Sometimes, coating with nutrients, clays and lime itself in sufficient as they pest may not recognize the seed as good.

11.17.3. Herbicide coating

Filler antidote or absorbent coatings can be used before sowing. Herbicide antidote like 1,8 napthalic anhydride (NA) is found the best as seed pelleting. The absorbent, activated carbon can also be used as filler material which is found good in protecting the seed from 2,4-D and Alachlor herbicide damage.

11.17.4. Nutrient Coating

The nutrient coating with micro and macro nutrients enhances the germination and seedling growth and also make it less available to weed species and also avoid the wastage of nutrients. The micronutrients are required in less quantity than soil foliar application. The micronutrients used are $ZnSO_4$, $FeSO_4$, $CuSO_4$, KH_2PO_4, Kcl, Borax etc. The micronutrients are added at required quantity to (Kg DAP: 3 Kg, ZnSO4 300 mg/ Kg, Borax 100 mg/Kg) the adhesive and are filled with the filler material.

11.17.5. Hydrophilic Coating

Starch graft polymers (which can absorb upto 1000 times their own weight of water) and magnesium carbonate are capable of improving movement of air and water. The increase in germination is due to increase in the rate of imbibitions where the fine particles in the coating acting as a wick or moisture attracting material or perhaps to improve seed soil contact.

11.17.6. Oxygen supplier coating

Seeds are coated with peroxides of zinc and calcium which aids in increased oxygen supply to the germination seeds. The seeds which has got seed coats impermeable to oxygen, this treatment will be of highly beneficial for enhancing the germination.

Seed pelleting is very much useful for precision sowing. It is more beneficial in smaller seeds as singling resulted through pelleting helps in reducing the cost and wastage of seeds. It also reduces the problem of thinning and gap filling in seeds. In bigger seeds, it is preferred for addition of needed bioactive substances to the seed based on demand and requirement. This prevents the materials applied to the field for the defined purpose in any other form (soil or foliar). The requirement of chemical is also very low. It serves in most cases a solution for enhancing establishment in problem soil. Use of botanic as filler material makes this treatment as ecofriendly cost and easily adaptable technology to small as well as big entrepreneurs.

11.18. Seed Testing

11.18:1. Objectives and Procedures

The main objective of seed testing is to assess the actual planting value of the seed in terms of its germination capacity besides determination of percentage composition of the pure seeds, weed seeds, other crop species, extraneous matter and moisture content of the submitted sample.

11.18:2. Seed Testing Procedures

Registration of Seed Samples

The submitted samples should be of the specified weight. The accepted sample is registered for testing and is given a code number so as to maintain the secrecy about its identity during testing. The details of the samples such as crop, variety, class of seed, tests required etc. are entered in individual seed analysis cards. Working sample of specified size is obtained from the submitted sample by using the seed dividers.

Physical Purity Analysis

The purity analysis is done on a working sample of prescribed weight drawn from the submitted sample. The working sample is separated into different components like pure seed, other crop seed, weed seed and inert matter by physical examination and the details are recorded in the individual analysis card. The composition of different components is expressed either in percentage by weight or as numbers per kilogram.

Germination Testing

The pure seed fraction from the purity test is used for germination analysis. A minimum of four hundred seeds in replications as per convenience are tested for germination. The most important requirements for seed germination testing are substrata, moisture, temperature and light.

Substrata

The substrate serves as a moisture reservoir and acts as a medium for the seeds to germinate and the seedlings to grow. The commonly used substrates are paper and sand. The Standard Kraft paper (towel), filter paper and blotters are the widely used paper substrates. Sterilized sand with a particle size between 0.045 mm to 0.85mm is used for germination test.

11.18.3. Methods of Using Substrata

***Top of paper* (T.P)**

In this method seeds are placed directly on one or more layers of moist filter or blotter papers in Petri dishes or plastic boxes which are in turn kept for incubation. This method is used for small sized crop seeds like ragi, jute, onion, tomato etc.

***Between paper* (B.P.)**

Seeds are placed in between two moist germination papers and rolled together to look like a rolled towel. The rolled towels are placed inside the germination cabinet/room for incubation.

Sand substrata

Plastic boxes are filled with sterilized sand of recommended particle size upto 3/4th of box height. The sand is moistened upto 50% of its water holding capacity. The seeds are sown on the levelled layer of moist sand and covered with 10-20 mm of uncompressed sand depending on the size of the seed. Irrespective of the method, the substratum is made wet sufficiently and uniformly before putting the seeds for germination test and they are incubated either in a cabinet seed germinator or a walk-in germinator room where the temperature and relative humidity are regulated as per the prescribed specifications. For most of the agricultural and horticultural seeds the temperature range of 20° C to 35°C and the relative humidity level of 90% and above is maintained in the seed germinator/germinator room. Light is not very much essential for seed germination except for crops like lettuce and tobacco.

11.18.4. Duration of the Test

The duration of sample incubation varies from crop to crop. For most of the crops first 'count is taken' on the 4th or the 5th day and the final count between 7 to 10 days. The time for count is fixed in such a way that it is sufficient to allow seedlings to reach a stage of development which allows for accurate evaluation. In case of sand media tests, the first count is omitted. The test can be terminated before the end of prescribed test period, if the sample under test meets the minimum limits of germination during the first count.

11.18.5. Seedling, Evaluation

During each count, the germinated seedlings and the remaining unterminated seeds are classified in to any of the following 5 categories.

Normal seedlings

Seedlings which shows the capacity for continued development into mature plant when grown under favorable conditions and having well developed root and the shoot system.

Abnormal seedlings

Seedlings with any abnormality in their root or shoot system thus which do not have the capacity to develop into a normal plant when grow.

Hard seeds

Seeds which remain hard at the end of the prescribed test period because of the non-absorption of moisture due to the presence of impermeable seed cost. Usually hard seeds are seen in leguminous crops.

Fresh un-germinated seeds

Seeds other than hard seeds, which remain firm, fresh and apparently viable, even at the end of the test period.

Dead seeds

Seeds which at the end of the test period are neither hard nor fresh and have not produced seedlings are classified as dead seeds. Dead seeds often show the symptoms of decaying and fungal growth which can be felt by pressing the seed under test.

11.18.6. Germination Percentage

The replication wise details of all categories of seedlings / seeds observed during evaluation are recorded in the seed analysis card. The result of germination test is calculated as the average of the replicates and is expressed as percentage by number of normal seedlings. The percentage is calculated to the nearest whole number. The percentage of abnormal seedlings, hard, fresh un-germinated and dead seeds are also calculated the same manner.

Retesting

When the test results are unsatisfactory due to out of tolerance performance between replicates or : wrong evaluation of seedlings or : errors in testing conditions, a second test is conducted by the same method or by alternative method to confirm the results before they are declared.

Moisture Determination

Seed moisture content is determined by using hot air oven or moisture meter. Seed moisture content is expressed as percentage by weight.

Hot air oven method

Here the seed moisture is removed by drying the pre-weighted sample at a specified temperature. The difference in weight is taken as moisture content and is expressed as a percentage of original weight. This is the most standard and accurate method of seed moisture determination.

Moisture meter method

Here the moisture content is determined using moisture meter which is calibrated and standardized against air oven method. Moisture test is conducted in two replications and the average is recorded in the seed analysis card.

11.19. Seed Vigour

11.19.1. Concept and Importance

Seed vigour is an important quality parameter which needs to be assessed to supplement germination and viability tests to gain insight into the performance of a seed lot in the field or in storage. Several definitions have been offered to explain seed vigour. Looking into the complexity of the situation, the International Seed Testing Association (ISTA) adopted the definition of seed vigour as *" the sum total of those properties of the seed which determine the level of activity and performance of the seed or seed lot during germination and seedling emergence'"*.

However, AOSA (1975) defined *"seed vigour as those seed properties which determine the potential for rapid uniform emergence and development of normal seedlings under a wide range of field condition"*. This definition quantifies vigour in terms of rapid uniform emergence and development of normal seedlings. Although differences in physiological attributes of seed lots can be demonstrated in the laboratory'. It was recommended that the term should be used to describe the performance of seeds when sown in the field. As the germination test is conducted in an optimum condition specific to different species, it is not always possible to get an idea of the performance of a seed lot in the field on the basis of germination test in the laboratory. It is mainly because of the reason that field conditions are seldom optimum and the emerging seedling suffers from one or the other kind of stress. In many cases seed lots having similar laboratory germinations may give widely differing field emergence values. Similarly, two seed lots having the same germination percentage in the laboratory may age differently when stored under ambient condition. These two situations indicate the incompleteness of germination test in assessing the performance of a seed lot in the field or storage. This offers scope and possibility to determine vigor of a seed lot so that its field and storage performance can be assessed.

Seed vigour is still a concept rather than a specific property of a seed or seed lot. Several factors like; genetic constitution, environment and nutrition of mother plant, maturity at harvest, seed weight and size, mechanical integrity, deterioration and ageing and pathogens are known to influence seed vigour. Therefore, care has to be exercised in selecting a seed vigour test to do the job. Two criteria have been employed by the ISTA seed vigour committee to evaluate the performance of seed vigour test methods for different crops:

- Reproducibility of vigor method
- The relationship between vigor test results and seedling emergence in field soil.

11.19.2. Significance of Seed vigour

- Seed vigour differences exist in seed lots of agricultural, horticultural and silvicultual species.
- The significance of seed vigour for sowing depends mostly on seedbed and environmental conditions.
- When conditions begin, field emergence percentage will often be close to the germination percentage of the seed lot and seed vigour may not be a factor in seedling performance.
- Environmental stress (e.g. low temperature, wet soils) may result in varying field performance depending on the vigour status of the seed lot.

- High vigour seed will perform better (emergence and seedling growth) under environmentally stressed seed bed conditions than low vigor seed lots, even though the laboratory germination of the lots may not differ.

11.19.3. Factors Influencing Seed Vigour

The development of a seed encompasses a series of important ontogenetic stages from fertilization, to accumulation of nutrients, to seed dry downand, to dormancy. Each of these stages represents a change in morphological and physiological development that can alter seed performance potential. The point at which the seed achieves its maximum dry weight is called physiological maturity. At this point, it has its greatest potential for maximum germination and vigour. However, since seeds generally achieve physiological maturity at high moisture levels it is unsafe for storage, seed is typically not harvested until it attains harvest maturity, which is low enough for safe storage, but high enough to minimize mechanical injury. Between physiological maturity and harvest maturity, the seed is essentially stored on the plant where it may be exposed to severe environmental conditions that adversely affect seed quality.

11.19.4. Characteristics of a Seed Vigour Test

A vigour test should possess certain essential characteristics that can make it useful to the seed producer and consumer. These characteristics have been described by McDonald (1980) as follows:

Inexpensive

Due to limited budgets for seed testing, it is important that a vigour test be reasonably priced and require a minimum investment in labour, equipment, and supplies.

Rapid

Every seed laboratory has periods of peak activity, thus it is important that the vigour test be conducted rapidly to minimize analyst time and germinator space. Furthermore, seed producers desire a quick turn around time for samples submitted for vigour tests since such quick information on seed quality can provide them with a competitive marketing advantage.

Uncomplicated

Where possible, vigour test procedures should be simple so that they can be performed in seed laboratories without requiring additional staff with special backgrounds and training.

Objective

For a vigour test to be easily standardized, a quantitative or numerical index of quality that avoids subjective interpretations by analysts should be utilized.

Reproducible

The success of any test depends on its reproducibility. If these results can not be repeated because of intricate procedures or subjectivity of interpretation, then comparison of results among laboratories becomes meaningless.

Correlated with Field Performance

Most definitions of seed vigor emphasize the relationship between seed vigour and field performance, and many studies have demonstrated this association exists. Consequently, the ultimate value of any vigour test may be its ability to predict field performance.

11.19.5. Kind of Seed Vigour Tests

There is no universally accepted vigor test for all kinds of seeds. Following vigour tests will be useful in gaining additional information on seed quality.

11.19.5.1 Direct Vigour Tests

Hiltner Test (Brick gravel test)

Principle: The test was developed by Hiltner in Germany in 1917. He observed that the seeds of cereal crops affected by Fusarium disease were able to germinate in regular test but were not able to emerge from brick gravels of 2-3 mm size. Compared to this, healthy seeds were able to emerge from the brick gravel (Roberststs, 1972). The principle is that the weak seedlings are not able to generate enough force to overcome the pressure of brick gravels, so this method can be used to differentiate vigour levels in cereal seeds. Perry (1984b) found this method reproducible and associated with field emergence in case of wheat.

Apparatus and equipment: Germination box, aluminium tray, sand, sand marker brick gravel of 2-3 mm size, germinator, seed sample.

Procedure: The sand is sieved, moistured and filled in the germination box leaving about 3 cm empty at the top. One hundred seeds are placed in each box in the impressions made by a sand marker. After this 2-2.5 cm of porous brick gravel is spread over the seeds. The box is kept in the germinator at appropriate temperature. After the period required for germination, the box is removed and the seedlings which have emerged through the brick gravel layer are counted. The percentage of emerged seedlings are used to complete seed vigour of different lots. The test should be repeated 3-4 times to get authentic value.

Paper Piercing Test

Principle: The principle of paper piercing test is similar to that of brick gravel test. High vigour seed lots are expected to produce strong seedlings which can pierce a particular type of paper while seedlings of poor vigour lots may not be able to pierce the paper. Therefore, the seedlings which emerge by piercing the paper are more vigorous than those which are not able to emerge through the paper.

Apparatus and equipment: All the material required for conducting germination test in sand boxes or trays plus the special paper which should have the following characteristics:

(a) Basic weight =90 *g/m2*

(b) Thickness =0.4 mm

(c) Bulk =4

(d) Dry bursting strength = 0.3 kg/cm

(e) Breaking length = 1000-5000mm

(f) Filtering speed = 500 ml/minute

(g) Wet bursting strength = 150 mm

(h) Ash content = 0.1%

(i) Fibre composition = Chemical wood pulp with high alpha percentage

Procedure: The cereal seeds are placed on 1.5 cm moist sand in a tray or sand box. The seeds are covered with specially selected dry filter paper which is then covered with 2 cm of moist sand. After this, the sand boxes/trays are kept in a germinator maintained at 20°C temperature for 8 days. After 8 days sand boxes/trays are taken out and seedlings emerging above the paper are counted. A seed lot having maximum number of seedlings coming out of paper is considered to be most vigorous. The test is highly dependent on the quality of paper and should be used when such papers are available.

Cold Test

Principle: The cold test has been developed in USA to evaluate the seed vigour of maize (corn). In USA when the corn is planted in late spring, the soil is humid and cold. The weak seeds do not germinate and establish. Therefore, to simulate the actual field conditions witnessed at the time of corn planting, cold test has been developed. The test aims to differentiate between weak and vigorous seed lots by subjecting them to low temperature prior to germination at optimum temperature. The test has been criticized for using field soil which greatly varies from place to place.

Apparatus and equipment: Aluminium tray, field soil, sand markr, germinator, seed sample.

Procedure: After grinding and properly sieving the soil is field in tray upto 2 cm depth. Fifty seeds are placed over the sand and covered with another 2 cm thick layer of soil. The soil is compacted and enough water is added to make the soil saturated to 60- 80%. The temperature of the water should be 5-10° C. After watering, the trays arc covered with polythene bags and placed in the refrigerator maintained at 10° C (temperature for one week). After one week the trays are remove, and placed in the germinator at 25°C temperature. The seedlings emerged after 4 days are counted and germination percentage is computed by counting the number of normal seedlings as in germination test. Higher the germination percentage greater is the vigour.

Accelerated Ageing Test

Principle: The accelerated ageing test has been developed at the Seed Technology Laboratory, Mississippi State University, USA for determining the storage potential of seed lots. The ageing process is accelerated by subjecting the seeds to high temperature and relative humidity in a chamber before standard germination. The seed lots that show high germination in accelerated ageing test are expected to maintain high viability during ambient storage as well. Thus, ageing test gives an indication of the performance of the seed lot during ambient storage.

Tests conducted at Pantnagar with Bragg soybean seeds have shown positive relationship between days accelerated ageing test (42- 45°C temperature, 95-100% RH.) and viability after 6 months of ambient storage (Gupta, 1980). However, Pent (1984) reported inconsistency in accelerated ageing test results and not well related to field emergence of maize and soybean. The test also settlers from fungal growth on seeds at high temperature and humidity (Agrawal, 1987). This test is recommended for soybean seeds.

Apparatus and equipment: Accelerated aging chamber, equipment for germination test, seed samples, tight jar, muslin cloth, wire mesh etc.

Procedure: One hundred seeds each in four replications are tied in a fine muslin cloth. The tied seeds are placed in jar on a wire mesh. The lower part of the jar is filled with water. There should not be a direct contact between water and the seed. The jar is covered with the lid and sealed with parafin wax to make it air tight. The jar is then placed in the accelerated aging chamber maintained at 45°C temperature for 3-5 days. The jar is removed after this period and the seeds are cooled in a dessicator. The seeds are then tested in a normal germination test specific to different crops. The percent germination gives level of seed vigour. Higher the germination percentage greater is the vigor of the seed.

11.19.5.2 Indirect vigour test

Growth Tests

Principles: Growth tests are based on the principle that vigorous seeds grow at a faster rate than poor vigor seeds even under favourable environments. Vigorous seeds rapidly germinate, metabolize and establish in the field. Therefore, any method used to determine the rapidity of growth of the seedling will give an indication of seed vigour level.

Apparatus and Equipments: All the equipment and materials needed to conduct a germination test are required. Additionally, a top loading balance and an air oven are also required.

Procedure

(a) ***First count:*** The test is done along with the regular germination test. The number of normal seedlings germinated on the first count day, as specified in the germination test for each species, are counted. The number of normal seedlings gives an idea of the level of seed vigour in the sample. Higher the number of normal seedlings greater is the seed vigour.

(b) ***Seedling Growth Rate and Dry Weight:*** The seedlings are grown either in laboratory, green house or field. In laboratory, in between rolled towel paper method should be followed. Ten seeds are planted in the centre of the moist towel papers in such a way that the micropyles are oriented towards bottom to avoid root twisting. The rolled towel papers are kept in the germinator maintained at a temperature recommended for crop in reference. After a specified period of time (5-10 days) towel papers are removed and five seedlings are selected, their length is measured and mean seedling length is calculated. Seed lots producing the taller seedlings are considered more vigorous than the seed lots producing shorter seedlings. For dry weight determination, the seedlings are removed and dried in an air oven at 100°C temperature for 24 hours. The seedling dry weight provides additional information for assessing seed vigour.

(c) ***Speed of Germination:*** One hundred seeds each in four replications are planted in recommended substratum for germination. The substratum is kept in a germinator maintained at recommended temperature for the crop in reference Crable S.l). Number of seedlings emerging daily are counted from day of planting the seeds in the medium till the time germination is complete. Thereafter a Germination Index (G.I.) is computed by using the following formula:

(G.I. = n/d

where, n =number of seedlings emerging on day 'd'

d = day after planting

The seed lot having greater germination index is considered to be more vigorous.

Example

Seed lot A No. of seedlings= 0,0,0,40,30, 12,7, counted

Day of counting = 1, 2, 3, 4, 5, 6, 7

Seed lot B No. of seedlings =0, 0, 0, 0, 30, 42, 21counted

Day of counting = 1, 2, 3, 4, 5, 6, 7

G.I. of Seed lot A 0/1+ 0/2+ 0/3+ 40/4+ 30/5+ 12/6+ 7/7

=0+0+0+10+6+2+1 = 19

G.I. of Seed lot B 0/1+ 0/2+ 0/3+ 0/4+ 30/5+ 42/6+ 21/7

0 + 0 + 0 + 0 + 6 + 7 + 3 = 16

In this example seed lot A has greater G.I. (19) than seed lot B '(16), so, seed lot A is more vigorous than seed lot B.

(d) ***Seed Vigour Index (S.V. I.):*** This is calculated by determining the germination percentage and seedling length of the same seed lot. Fifty seeds each in four replications are germinated in towel papers as prescribed for the crop species in germination test. While evaluating the number of normal seedlings at the time of final count, the seedling length of 5 randomly selected seedlings are also measured.

Seed Vigor Index is calculated by multiplying germination (%) and seedling length. The seed lot showing the higher seed vigour index is considered to be more vigorous (Abdul-Baki and Anderson, 1973).

Example

Seed lot	Germination (%)	Seedling length (mm)	Vigor index
A	96	85	8160
B	95	76	7220
C	94	71	6674

In this example seed lot A is the most vigorous and seed lot C the least vigorous as they have the highest and the lowest values of seed vigour index, respectively.

Conductivity Test

Principle: Weakening of cell membrane in poor vigour seeds causes leakage of water soluble compounds like sugars, amino acid, electrolytes etc. when immersed in water. On the other hand fresh seeds having intact membrane leach less quantity of these chemicals. The measurement of electrical conductivity (EC) of the leachate by a good and sensitive conductivity meter gives an accurate estimation of membrane permeability. The EC has been positively correlated with the emergence percentage of peas and broad beans (Mathews and Bradnock, 1968). The value of this test appears to be restricted to the large seed species of the Leguminoceae (Perry, 1984).

Apparatus : Conductivity meter, beaker, 0.1% mercuric chloride, distilled water, seed sample, wash bottle and tissue paper.

Procedure:A seed sample of 2-5 g is weighed and surface sterilized with O.1'k $HgCl_2$ for 5-10 minutes. The sample is washed thoroughly in distilled water. The cleaned seed are immersed in 100 ml of water at 25°C temperature for 10-12 hours. After this, the seeds are removed with a clean forceps. The steep water left is decanted and is termed as leachate.

The conductivity meter is warmed for about 30 minutes before testing. First the conductance of distilled water is measured in a beaker. The electrode is then cleaned with a tissue paper and conductance of the leachate is read. The electrode is thoroughly washed using a wash bottle and wiped with a clean tissue paper before reusing. While recording the conductance, the lower bulb of the electrode should be fully emerged in the leachate. To get the EC of leachate the reading of distilled water is substracted from the sample reading. The value is then corrected for the temperature and multiplied by the cell constant factor. The reading is expressed as mu *mhos/cm/g* of seed. Lower the value of EC greater is the seed vigor.

Exhaustion test

This test involves germination and seedling development in complete darkness and with carefully regulated amounts of water supply. The seeds are placed on a printed line on moisted paper towel. The towel is then folded into a role and placed within a glass container that is covered to prevent evaporation. The seed vigor is evaluated on the basis of no. of seedlings crossing the pointed line.

Tetrazolium Test

This test infact involves the reddening of colourless tetrazolium due to activity of dehydrogenases in embryo. However, the amount of tetrazolium staining and its pattern could indirectly help in assessing the seed vigour differences of seed lots red colour formation is extracted in a organic solvent methyl cellusolve and quantified spectrophotometrically. Thus the absorbance and quantity of tetrazolium determine the seed vigour.

Osmotic Stress

Usually seeds when subjected to drought stress results in poor emergence. Such drought conditions can be simulated in laboratories by using soil, soil solutions and osmotic viz., PEG, mannitol, sucrose, glucose and NaCl etc.

Respiration

Seed germination and seedling growth require the use of metabolic energy acquired from respiration. A decrease in the rate of respiration of germinating seeds precede decline in the rate of seedling growth. Respiration rate measured during the first 18 hours of germination can be used to defect the seed vigor. Use of respirometer and trained personnel is essential

11.19.6. Approximate Life of Vegetable Seeds Stored Under Cool Conditions

Vegetable	Year
Asparagus	3
Bean	3
Beet	3
Cabbage	5
Carrot	3
Cauliflower	5
Celery	5
Cucumber	5
Egg plant	5
Endive	5
Kale	5
Kholrabi	5
Leek	3
Lettuce	5
Muskmelon	5
Mustard	4
Okra	2
Onion	2
Pea	1-2
Pepper	3
Pumpkin	4
Radish	5
Spinach	5
Swiss chard	4
Tomato	4
Turnip	5
Watermelon	5

11.20. Indian Minimum Seed Certification Standards

11.20.1. Fruit Vegetables

Brinjal

Isolation Distance

Contaminants	Minimum distance (meters)	
	Foundation	Certified
1	2	3
Fields of other varieties	300	150
Fields of the same variety not conforming to varietal purity requirements for certification.	300	150

Seed Standard

Factor	Foundation	Certified
Pure Seed (minimum)	98.0%	98.0%
Inert matter (maximum)	2.0%	2.0%
Other crops seeds (maximum)	None	None
Weed seeds (maximum)	None	None
Germination (minimum)	70%	70%
Moisture (maximum)	8.0%	8.0%
For vapour-proof containers (maximum)	6.0%	6.0%

Capsicum and Chilli

Isolation Distance

Contaminants	Minimum distance (meters)	
	Foundation	Certified
1	2	3
Fields of other varieties	500	250
Fields of the same variety not conforming to varietal purity requirements for certification.	500	250
Fields of Capsicum from Chilli and vice versa	500	250

Seed Standard

Factor	Foundation	Certified
Pure Seed (minimum)	98.0%	98.0%
Inert matter (maximum)	2.0%	2.0%
Other crops seeds (maximum)	5/kg	10/kg
Weed seeds (maximum)	5/kg	10/kg
Germination (minimum)	60%	60%
Moisture (maximum)	8.0%	8.0%
For vapor-proof containers (maximum)	6.0%	6.0%

Okra

Isolation Distance

Contaminants	Minimum distance (meters)	
	Foundation	Certified
1	2	3
Fields of other varieties	500	250
Fields of the same variety not conforming to varietal purity requirements for certification and wild Okra (*A. ficulneus* (L.) Wt.& Arn.	500	250

Seed Standard

Factor	Foundation	Certified
Pure Seed (minimum)	99.0%	99.0%
Inert matter (maximum)	1.0%	1.0%
Other crops seeds (maximum)	None	None
Total weed seeds (maximum)	None	None
Objectionable weed seeds (maximum)	None	None
Other distinguishable varieties (maximum)	10/kg	20/kg
Germination including hard seeds (minimum)	65%	65%
Moisture (maximum)	10.0%	10.0%
For vapour-proof containers (maximum)	8.0%	8.0%

Tomato

Isolation Distance

Contaminants	Minimum distance (meters)	
	Foundation	Certified
1	2	3
Fields of other varieties	50	25
Fields of the same variety not conforming to varietal purity requirements for certification	50	25

Seed Standard

Factor	Foundation	Certified
Pure seed (minimum)	98.0%	98.0%
Inert matter (maximum)	2.0%	2.0%
Other crop seeds (maximum)	5/kg	10/kg
Weed seeds (maximum)	None	None
Germination (minimum)	70%	70%
Moisture (maximum)	8.0%	8.0%
For vapour-proof containers (maximum)	6.0%	6.0%

11.20.2. Cucurbits

Ash gourd

Isolation Distance

Contaminants	Minimum distance (meters)	
	Foundation	Certified
1	2	3
Fields of other varieties	1000	500
Fields of the same variety not conforming to varietal purity requirements for certification	1000	500

Seed Standard

Factor	Foundation	Certified
Pure Seed (minimum)	98.0%	98.0%
Inert matter (maximum)	2.0%	2.0%
Other crops seeds (maximum)	None	None
Weed seeds (maximum)	None	None
Germination (minimum)	60%	60%
Moisture (maximum)	7.0%	7.0%
For vapour-proof containers (maximum)	6.0%	6.0%

Bitter gourd

Isolation Distance

Contaminants	Minimum distance (meters)	
	Foundation	Certified
1	2	3
Fields of other varieties including commercial hybrid of the same variety	1500	1000
Fields of the same hybrid (code designation) not conforming to varietal purity requirements for certification and from balsam apple (Mokha): *M. balsamina* L.; Bhat karela: (kakrol): *M.cochinchinensis* spreng.; Jangli karela: *M. dioica* Roxb. Ex. Willd.	1500	1000
Between blocks of the parental lines in case seed parent and pollinator are planted in separate blocks and hand pollination is to be adopted		5

Seed Standard

Factor	Foundation	Certified
Pure Seed (minimum)	98.0%	98.0%
Inert matter (maximum)	2.0%	2.0%
Other crops seeds (maximum)	None	None
Total weed seeds (maximum)	None	None
f&Objectionable weed seeds (maximum)	None	None
Other distinguishable varieties (maximum)	5/kg	10/kg
Germination (minimum)	60%	60%
Moisture (maximum)	7.0%	7.0%
For vapour-proof containers (maximum)	6.0%	6.0%

Bottle gourd

Isolation Distance

Contaminants	Minimum distance (meters)	
	Foundation	Certified
1	2	3
Fields of other varieties	1000	500
Fields of the same variety not conforming to varietal purity requirements for certification	1000	500

Seed Standard

Factor	Foundation	Certified
Pure seed (minimum)	98.0%	98.0%
Inert matter (maximum)	2.0%	2.0%
Other crops seeds (maximum)	None	None
Weed seeds (maximum)	None	None
Germination (minimum)	60%	60%
Moisture (maximum)	7.0%	7.0%
For vapor-proof containers (maximum)	6.0%	6.0%

Cucumber

Isolation Distance

Contaminants	Minimum distance (meters)	
	Foundation	Certified
1	2	3
Fields of other varieties	1000	500
Fields of the same variety not conforming to varietal purity requirements for certification	1000	500

Seed standard

Factor	Foundation	Certified
Pure seed (minimum)	98.0%	98.0%
Inert matter (maximum)	2.0%	2.0%
Other crop seeds (maximum)	5/kg	10/kg
Total weed seeds (maximum)	None	None
f&Objectionable weed seeds (maximum)	None	None
Germination (minimum)	60%	60%
Moisture (maximum)	7.0%	7.0%
For vapour-proof containers (maximum)	6.0%	6.0%

Indian squash

Isolation Distance

Contaminants	Minimum distance (meters)	
	Foundation	Certified
1	2	3
Fields of other varieties	1000	500
Fields of the same variety not conforming to varietal purity requirements for certification	1000	500

Seed Standard

Factor	Foundation	Certified
Pure seed (minimum)	98.0%	98.0%
Inert matter (maximum)	2.0%	2.0%
Other crop seeds (maximum)	None	None
Weed seeds (maximum)	None	None
Germination (minimum)	60%	60%
Moisture (maximum)	7.0%	7.0%
For vapour-proof containers (maximum)	6.0%	6.0%

Ivy gourd

Isolation Distance

	Minimum distance (meters)	
	Foundation	Certified
1	2	3
Fields of other varieties	20	20
Fields of the same variety not conforming to varietal purity requirements for certification	20	20
Between the blocks of female and male parents	20	20

Seed Standard

Factor	Foundation	Certified
Pure Seed (minimum)	98.0%	98.0%
Inert matter (maximum)	2.0%	2.0%
Other crops seeds (maximum)	5/kg	10/kg
Total weed seeds (maximum)	None	None
Objectionable weed seeds (maximum)	None	None
Germination (minimum)	60%	60%
Moisture (maximum)	7.0%	7.0%
For vapour-proof containers (maximum)	6.0%	6.0%

Muskmelon

Isolation Distance

Contaminants	Minimum distance (meters)	
	Foundation	Certified
1	2	3
Fields of other varieties	1000	500
Fields of the same variety not conforming to varietal purity requirements for certification and from longmelon *Cucumis melo* L. var. utilissimus Duth. & Full.), oriental pickling melon (*Cucumis melo* L. var. conomon Makino), snapmelon phnoot: *Cucumis melo* L. var. momordica Duth. & Full., *Cucumis prophetarum*; weedmelon (Takmek)(*Cucumis melo* (L.) var. agrestis Naud. and other non-dessert forms of *Cucumis melo* (L.) known to cross or suspected of being able to cross.	1000	500

Seed Standard

Factor	Foundation	Certified
Pure Seed (minimum)	98.0%	98.0%
Inert matter (maximum)	2.0%	2.0%
Other crops seeds (maximum)	5/kg	10/kg
Total weed seeds (maximum)	None	None
Objectionable weed seeds (maximum)	None	None
Germination (minimum)	60%	60%
Moisture (maximum)	7.0%	7.0%
For vapour-proof containers (maximum)	6.0%	6.0%

Pointed gourd

Isolation Distance

Containments	Maximum distance (meters)	
Fields of other varieties	20	20
Fields of the same variety not conforming to varietal purity requirements for certification	20	20
Between the blocks of female and male parents	20	20

Seed Standard

Factor	Foundation	Certified
Pure living planting stakes (minimum)	99.50% (by number)	98.0% (by number)
Other living plants including their stem cuttings (maximum)	0.50% (by number)	2.0%(by number)

Pumpkin

Isolation Distance

Contaminants	Minimum distance (meters)	
	Foundation	Certified
1	2	3
Fields of other varieties	1000	500
Fields of the same variety not conforming to varietal purity requirements for certification and from Winter squash (*Cucurbita maxima* Duch.), *Cucurbita pepo* Duch.) and Cushaw (*Cucurbita mixta* Pang.)	1000	500

Seed Standard

Factor	Foundation	Certified
Pure seed (minimum)	98.0%	98.0%
Inert matter (maximum)	2.0%	2.0%
Other crop seeds (maximum)	None	None
Weed seeds (maximum)	None	None
Germination (minimum)	60%	60%
Moisture (maximum)	7.0%	7.0%
For vapour-proof containers (maximum)	6.0%	6.0%

Ridge gourd

Isolation Distance

Contaminants	Minimum distance (meters)	
	Foundation	Certified
Fields of other varieties	1000	500
Fields of the same variety not conforming to varietal purity requirements for certification and from sponge gourd (*Luffa cylindrica Roem.*)	1000	500

Seed Standard

Factor	Foundation	Certified
Pure seed (minimum)	98.0%	98.0%
Inert matter (maximum)	2.0%	2.0%
Other crop seeds (maximum)	None	None
Weed seeds (maximum)	None	None
Other distinguishable varieties (maximum)	5/kg	10/kg
Germination (minimum)	60%	60%
Moisture (maximum)	7.0%	7.0%
For vapour-proof containers (maximum)	6.0%	6.0%

Snake gourd

Isolation Distance

Contaminants	Minimum distance (meters)	
	Foundation	Certified
Fields of other varieties	1000	500
Fields of the same variety not conforming to varietal purity requirements for certification and from *Trichosanthes palmata* (L.), *Trichosanthes lobata* (L.), &Jangli chachinda (Rambel): *Trichosanthes cucumerina* (L.)	1000	500

Seed Standard

Factor	Foundation	Certified
Pure seed (minimum)	98.0%	98.0%
Inert matter (maximum)	2.0%	2.0%
Other crop seeds (maximum)	None	None
Total weed seeds (maximum)	None	None
Objectionable weed seeds (maximum)	None	None
Germination (minimum)	60%	60%
Moisture (maximum)	7.0%	7.0%
For vapour-proof containers (maximum)	6.0%	6.0%

Snap melon

Isolation Distance

Contaminants	Minimum distance (meters)	
	Foundation	Certified
Fields of other varieties	1000	500
Fields of the same variety not conforming to varietal purity requirements for certification and from muskmelon (*Cucumis melo* L. var. utilissimus Duth. & Full oriental pickling melon (*Cucumis melo* (L.) var. conomon Makino), *Cucumis prophetarum*: weedmelon(Takmek) *Cucumis melo* (L.) var.agrestis Naud.) and other non-dessert forms or *Cucumis melo* (L.) known to cross or suspected of being able to cross	1000	500

Seed Standard

Factor	Foundation	Certified
Pure seed (minimum)	98.0%	98.0%
Inert matter (maximum)	2.0%	2.0%
Other crop seeds (maximum)	5/kg	10/kg
Total weed seeds (maximum)	None	None
Objectionable weed seeds (maximum)	None	None
Germination (minimum)	60%	60%
Moisture (maximum)	7.0%	7.0%
For vapour-proof containers (maximum)	6.0%	6.0%

Sponge gourd

Isolation Distance

Contaminants	Minimum distance (meters)	
	Foundation	Certified
1	2	3
Fields of other varieties	1000	500
Fields of the same variety not conforming to varietal purity requirements for certification and from muskmelon (*Cucumis melo* L. var.utilissimus Duth.&Full oriental pickling melon (*Cucumis melo* (L.)var. conomon Makino), *Cucumis prophetarum*: weedmelon(Takmek) *Cucumis melo* (L.)var.agrestis Naud.) and other non-dessert forms or Cucumis melo (L.) known to cross or suspected of being able to cross	1000	500

Seed Standard

Factor	Foundation	Certified
Pure seed (minimum)	98.0%	98.0%
Inert matter (maximum)	2.0%	2.0%
Other crop seeds (maximum)	None	None
Weed seeds (maximum)	None	None
Other distinguishable varieties (maximum)	5/kg	10/kg
Germination (minimum)	60%	60%
Moisture (maximum)	7.0%	7.0%
For vapour-proof containers (maximum)	6.0%	6.0%

Summer squash

Isolation Distance

Contaminants	Minimum distance (meters)	
	Foundation	Certified
1	2	3
Fields of other varieties	1000	500
Fields of the same variety not conforming to varietal purity requirements for certification and from (*Cucurbita moschata* (Duch. Poir) cushaw (*Cucurbita mixta* Pang.), and winter squash (*C. maxima* Duch.)	1000	500

Seed Standard

Factor	Foundation	Certified
Pure seed (minimum)	98.0%	98.0%
Inert matter (maximum)	2.0%	2.0%
Other crop seeds (maximum)	None	None
Weed seeds (maximum)	None	None
Germination (minimum)	60%	60%
Moisture (maximum)	7.0%	7.0%
For vapour-proof containers (maximum)	6.0%	6.0%

Watermelon

Isolation Distance

Contaminants	Minimum distance (meters)	
	Foundation	Certified
1	2	3
Fields of other varieties	1000	500
Fields of the same variety not conforming to varietal purity requirements for certification and wild watermelon (Indrayan) : *Citrullus colocynthis* L.	1000	500

Seed Standard

Factor	Foundation	Certified
Pure seed (minimum)	98.0%	98.0%
Inert matter (maximum)	2.0%	2.0%
Other crop seeds (maximum)	None	None
Total Weed seeds (maximum)	None	None
Objectionable weed seeds (maximum)	None	None
Other distinguishable varieties (maximum)	5/kg	10/kg
Germination (minimum)	60%	60%
Moisture (maximum)	7.0%	7.0%
For vapour-proof containers (maximum)	6.0%	6.0%

Winter squash
Isolation Distance

Contaminants	Minimum distance (meters)	
	Foundation	Certified
1	2	3
Fields of other varieties	1000	500
Fields of the same variety not conforming to varietal purity requirements for certification and from Pumpkin (*Cucurbita moschata* (Duch.) Poir.), and summer squash (C. pepo Duch.)	1000	500

Seed Standard

Factor	Foundation	Certified
Pure seed (minimum)	98.0%	98.0%
Inert matter (maximum)	2.0%	2.0%
Other crop seeds (maximum)	None	None
Weed seeds (maximum)	None	None
Germination (minimum)	60%	60%
Moisture (maximum)	7.0%	7.0%
For vapour-proof containers (maximum)	6.0%	6.0%

11.20.3. Legume Vegetables

Cowpea
Isolation Distance

Contaminants	Minimum distance (meters)	
	Foundation	Certified
Fields of other varieties	10	5
Fields of the same variety not conforming to varietal purity requirements for certification	10	5

Seed Standard

Factor	Foundation	Certified
Pure seed (minimum)	98.0%	98.0%
Inert matter (maximum)	2.0%	2.0%
Other crop seeds (maximum)	None	10/kg
Weed seeds (maximum)	None	10/kg
Other distinguishable varieties (maximum)	5/kg	10/kg
Germination including hard seeds (minimum)	75%	75%
Moisture (maximum)	9.0%	9.0%
For vapour-proof containers (maximum)	8.0%	8.0%

Indian bean
Isolation Distance

General factors	Minimum distance (meters)	
	Foundation	Certified
Fields of other varieties	10	5
Fields of the same variety not conforming to varietal purity requirements for certification	10	5
B. Specific requirements		
	Maximum permitted (%)*	
Factor	Foundation	Certified
Off-types	0.10	0.20
	0.10	0.20

**Plants affected by seed borne diseases

Seed Standard

Factor	Foundation	Certified
Pure seed (minimum)	98.0%	98.0%
Inert matter (maximum)	2.0%	2.0%
Other crop seeds (maximum)	None	None
Weed seeds (maximum)	None	None
Other distinguishable varieties (maximum)	5/kg	10/kg
Germination including hard seeds (minimum)	75%	75%
Moisture (maximum)	9.0%	9.0%
For vapour-proof containers (maximum)	8.0%	8.0%

Garden pea
Isolation Distance

Contaminants	Minimum distance (meters)	
	Foundation	Certified
Fields of other varieties	10	5
Fields of the same variety not conforming tovarietal purity requirements for certification		

B. Specific requirements

Factor	Maximum permitted (%)*	
	Foundation	Certified
Off-types	0.10	0.20

*Maximum permitted at the final inspection

Seed Standard

Factor	Foundation	Certified
Pure seed (minimum)	98.0%	98.0%
Inert matter (maximum)	2.0%	2.0%
Other crop seeds (maximum)	None	5/kg
Weed seeds (maximum)	None	None
Other distinguishable varieties (maximum)	5/kg	10/kg
Germination including hard seeds (minimum)	75%	75%
Moisture (maximum)	9.0%	9.0%
For vapour-proof containers (maximum)	8.0%	8.0%

French bean
Isolation Distance

Contaminants	Minimum distance (meters)	
	Foundation	Certified
Fields of other varieties	10	5
Fields of the same variety not conforming to varietal purity requirements for certification	10	5

B. Specific requirements

Factor	Maximum permitted (%)*	
	Foundation	Certified
Off-types	0.10	0.20
**Plants affected by seed borne diseases	0.10	0.20

Seed Standard

Factor	Foundation	Certified
Pure seed (minimum)	98.0%	98.0%
Inert matter (maximum)	2.0%	2.0%
Other crop seeds (maximum)	None	None
Weed seeds (maximum)	None	10/kg

Other distinguishable varieties (maximum)	5/kg	10/kg
Germination (minimum)	75%	75%
Moisture (maximum)	9.0%	9.0%
For vapour-proof containers (maximum)	7.0%	7.0%

Soybean
Isolation Distance

Contaminants	Minimum distance (meters)	
	Foundation	Certified
Fields of other varieties	3	3
Fields of the same variety not conforming to varietal purity requirements for certification	3	3
B. Specific requirements		
	Maximum permitted (%)*	
Factor	Foundation	Certified
Off-types	0.10	0.50

*Plants affected by seed borne diseases.

Seed Standard

Factor	Foundation	Certified
Pure seed (minimum)	98.0%	98.0%
Inert matter (maximum)	2.0%	2.0%
Other crop seeds (maximum)	None	10/kg
Weed seeds (maximum)	5/kg	10/kg
Other distinguishable varieties (maximum)	10/kg	40/kg
Germination (minimum)	70%	70%
Moisture (maximum)	12.0%	12.0%
For vapour-proof containers (maximum)	7.0%	7.0%

11.20.4. Cole Crops

Cabbage
Isolation Distance

Contaminants	Minimum distance (meters)	
	Foundation	Certified
1	2	3
Fields of other varieties	1600	1000
Fields of the same variety not conforming to varietal purity requirements for certification and from the following varieties of Brassica oleracea (L)	1600	1000

Seed Standard

Factor	Foundation	Certified
Pure seed (minimum)	98.0%	98.0%
Inert matter (maximum)	2.0%	2.0%
Other crop seeds (maximum)	5/kg	10/kg
Weed seeds (maximum)	5/kg	10/kg
Germination (minimum)	70%	70%
Moisture (maximum)	7.0%	7.0%
For vapour-proof containers (maximum)	5.0%	5.0%

Cauliflower
Isolation Distance

Contaminants	Minimum distance (meters)	
	Foundation	Certified
1	2	3
Fields of other varieties	1600	1000
Fields of the same variety not conforming to varietal purity requirements for certification and from the following varieties of Brassica oleracea (L)	1600	1000

Seed Standard

Factor	Foundation	Certified
Pure seed (minimum)	98.0%	98.0%
Inert matter (maximum)	2.0%	2.0%
Other crop seeds (maximum)	5/kg	10/kg
Weed seeds (maximum)	5/kg	10/kg
Germination (minimum)	65%	65%
Moisture (maximum)	7.0%	7.0%
For vapour-proof containers (maximum)	5.0%	5.0%

Chinese cabbage
Isolation Distance

Contaminants	Minimum distance (meters)	
	Foundation	Certified
1	2	3
Fields of other varieties of the same species	1600	1000
Fields of the same variety not conforming to varietal purity requirements for certification and from any of the other species of genus Brassica.	1600	1000

Seed Standard

Factor	Foundation	Certified
Pure seed (minimum)	98.0%	98.0%
Inert matter (maximum)	2.0%	2.0%
Other crop seeds (maximum)	5/kg	10/kg
Weed seeds (maximum)	5/kg	10/kg
Germination (minimum)	70%	70%
Moisture (maximum)	7.0%	7.0%
For vapour-proof containers (maximum)	5.0%	5.0%

Asparagus
Isolation Distance

Contaminants	Minimum distance (meters)	
	Foundation	Certified
1	2	3
Fields of other varieties	500	300
Fields of the same variety not conforming to varietal purity requirements for certification	500	300

Seed Standard

Factor	Foundation	Certified
Pure seed (minimum)	96.0%	96.0%
Inert matter (maximum)	4.0%	40%
Other crop seeds (maximum)	5/kg	10/kg
Weed seeds (maximum)	5/kg	10/kg
Germination (minimum)	70%	70%
Moisture (maximum)	8.0%	8.0%
For vapour-proof containers (maximum)	6.0%	6.0%

Fenugreek
Isolation Distance

Contaminants	Minimum distance (meters)	
	Foundation	Certified
1	2	3
Fields of other varieties	50	25
Fields of the same variety not conforming to varietal purity requirements for certification	50	25

Seed Standard

Factor	Foundation	Certified
Pure seed (minimum)	98.0%	98.0%
Inert matter (maximum)	2.0%	2.0%
Other crop seeds (maximum)	10/kg	10/kg

Total weed seeds (maximum)	10/kg	10/kg
for Objectionable weed seeds (maximum)	2/kg	5/kg
Other distinguishable varieties (maximum)	10/kg	20/kg
Germination including hard seed (minimum)	70%	70%
Moisture (maximum)	8.0%	8.0%
For vapour-proof containers (maximum)	6.0%	6.0%

11.20.5. Root Crops

Carrot

Isolation Distance

Contaminants	Minimum distance (meters)			
	Mother root production stage		Seed production stage	
	Foundation	Certified	Foundation	Certified
Fields of other varieties of the same species	5	5	1000	800
Fields of the same variety not conforming to varietal purity requirements for certification and rat-tail radish (Daucs carota L.)	5	5	1000	800

Seed Standard

Factor	Foundation	Certified
Pure seed (minimum)	95.0%	95.0%
Inert matter (maximum)	5.0%	5.0%
Other crop seeds (maximum)	5/kg	10/kg
Weed seeds (maximum)	5/kg	10/kg
Other distinguishable varieties (maximum)	5/kg	10/kg
Germination (minimum)	60%	60%
Moisture (maximum)	8.0%	8.0%
For vapour-proof containers (maximum)	7.0%	7.0%

Radish

Isolation Distance

Contaminants	Minimum distance (meters)			
	Mother root production stage		Seed production stage	
	Foundation	Certified	Foundation	Certified
Fields of other varieties of the same species	5	5	1600	1000
Fields of the same variety not conforming to varietal purity requirements for certification and rat-tail radish (*Raphanus caudatus* L.)	5	5	1600	1000

Seed Standard

Factor	Foundation	Certified
Pure Seed (minimum)	98.0%	98.0%
Inert matter (maximum)	2.0%	2.0%
Other crops seeds (maximum)	5/kg	10/kg
weed seeds (maximum)	10/kg	20/kg
Germination (minimum)	70%	70%
Moisture (maximum)	6.0%	6.0%
For vapour-proof containers (maximum)	5.0%	5.0%

11.21. Seed Production

Guidelines

- To meet the Nation's food security needs, it is important to make available to Indian farmers a wide range of seeds of superior quality, in adequate quantity on a timely basis. Public Sector Seed Institutions should be encouraged to enhance production of seed towards meeting the objective of food and nutritional security.
- The Indian seed programme adheres to the limited three generation system of seed multiplication, namely, breeder, foundation and certified seed. Breeder seed is the progeny of nucleus seed.
- Nucleus seed is the seed produced by the breeder to develop the particular variety and is directly used for multiplication as breeder seed.
- Breeder seed is the seed material directly controlled by the originating or the sponsoring breeder or Institution for the initial and recurring production of foundation seed.
- Foundation seed is the progeny of breeder seed. Foundation seed may also be produced from foundation seed. Production of foundation seed stage-I and stage-II may thus be permitted, if supervised and approved by the Certification Agency and if the production process is so handled as to maintain specific genetic purity and identity.
- Certified seed is the progeny of foundation seed or the progeny of certified seed. If the certified seed is the progeny of certified seed, then this reproduction will not exceed three generations beyond foundation stage-I and it will be ascertained by the Certification Agency that genetic identity and genetic purity has not been significantly altered.
- Public Sector Seed Production Agencies should be continued to have free access to breeder seed under the National Agriculture Research System (NARS). The State Farms Corporation (SFC) of India and National Seeds Corporation should be restructured to make productive use of these organisations in the planned growth of the Seed Sector.
- Private Seed Production Agencies should also have access to breeder seed subject to terms and conditions to be decided by Government of India.

- State Agriculture Universities/ICAR Institutes will have the primary responsibility for production of breeder seed as per the requirements of the respective States.
- Special attention should be given to the need to upgrade the quality of farmers' saved seeds through interventions such as the Seed Village Scheme.
- Seed replacement rates should be raised progressively with the objective of expanding the use of quality seeds.
- DAC, in consultation with ICAR and States, should prepare a National Seed Map to identify potential,alternative and non-traditional areas for seed production of specific crops.
- To put in place an effective seed production programme, each State should undertake advance planning and prepare a perspective plan for seed production and distribution over a rolling (five to six years) period. Seed Banks should be set up in non-traditional areas to meet demands for seeds during natural calamities.
- The 'Seed Village Scheme' should be promoted to facilitate production and timely availability of seed of desired crops/varieties at the local level. Special emphasis should be given to seed multiplication for building adequate stocks of certified/quality seeds by providing foundation seed to farmers.
- For popularising newly developed varieties and promoting seed production of these varieties, seed minikits of pioneering seed varieties should be supplied to farmers. Seed exchange among farmers and seed producers will be encouraged to popularise new/non-traditional varieties.
- Seeds of newly developed varieties must be made available to farmers with minimum time gap. Seed producing agencies will be encouraged to tie up with Research Institutions for popularization and commercialization of these varieties.
- As hybrids have the potential to improve plant vigor and increase yield, support for production of hybrid seed should be provided.
- Seed production will be extended to agro-climatic zones which are outside the traditional seed growing areas, in order to avoid unremunerative seed farming in unsuitable areas.
- Seed Banks should be established for stocking specified quantities of seed of required crops/varieties for ensuring timely and adequate supply of seeds to farmers during adverse situations such as natural calamities, shortfalls in production, etc. Seed Banks will be suitably strengthened with cold storage and pest control facilities.
- The storage of seed at the village level should be encouraged to facilitate immediate availability of seeds in the event of natural calamities and unforeseen situations. For the storage of seeds at farm level, scientific storage structures will be popularised and techniques of scientific storage of seeds will be promoted among farmers as an extension practice.
- Seed growers should be encouraged to avail of Seed Crop Insurance to cover risk factors involved in production of seeds. The Seed Crop Insurance Scheme will be reviewed so as to provide effective risk cover to seed producers and

will be extended to all traditional and non-traditional areas covered under the seed production programme.

11.22. Quality Assurance

Guidelines

- The Seeds Act should be revised to regulate the sale, import and export of seeds and planting materials of agriculture crops including fodder, green manure and horticulture and supply of quality seeds and planting materials to farmers throughout the country.
- The National Seeds Board (NSB) should be established in place of existing Central Seed Committee and Central Seed Certification Board. The NSB will have permanent existence with the responsibility of executing and implementing the provisions of the Seeds Act and advising the Government on all matters relating to seed planning and development. The NSB will function as the apex body in the seed sector.
- All varieties, both domestic and imported varieties, that are placed on the market for sale and distribution of seeds and planting materials will be registered under the Seeds Act. However, for vegetable and ornamental crops, a simple system of varietal registration based on "breeders declaration" should be adopted.
- The Board will undertake registration of kinds/varieties of seeds that are to be offered for sale in the market, on the basis of identified parameters for establishing value for cultivation and usage (VCU) through testing/trialling.
- Registration of varieties will be granted for a fixed period on the basis of multilocational trials to determine VCU over a minimum period of three seasons, or as otherwise prescribed as in the case of long duration crops and horticultural crops. Samples of the material for registration will be sent to the NBPGR for retention in the National Gene Bank.
- Varieties that are in the market at the time of coming into force of the revised Seeds Act, will have to be registered within a fixed time period, and subjected to such testing as should be notified.
- The NSB will accredit ICAR, SAUs, public/private organisations to conduct VCU trials of all varieties for the purpose of registration as per prescribed standards.
- The NSB will maintain the National Seeds Register containing details of varieties that are registered.This will help the Board to coordinate and assist activities of the States in their efforts to provide quality seeds to farmers.
- The NSB will prescribe minimum standards (of germination, genetic characteristics, physical purity, seed health, etc.) as well as suitable guidelines for registration of seed and planting materials.
- Provisional registration would be granted on the basis of information filed by the applicant relating to trials over one season to tide over the stipulation of testing over three seasons before the grant of registration.

- Government will have the right to exclude certain kinds or varieties from registration to protect public order or human, animal and plant life and health, or to avoid serious prejudice to the environment.
- The NSB will have the power to cancel the registration granted to a variety if the registration has been obtained by misrepresentation or concealment of essential data, the variety is obsolete and has outlived its utility and if the prevention of commercial exploitation of such variety is necessary in the public interest.
- Registration of Seed Processing Units should be required if such Units meet the prescribed minimum standards for processing the seed.
- Seed Certification should continue to be voluntary. The Certification tag/label will provide an assurance of quality to the farmer.
- The Board will accredit individuals or organisations to carry out seed certification including self-certification on fulfillment of criteria as prescribed.
- To meet quality assurance requirements for export of seeds, Seed Testing facilities will be established in conformity with ISTA and OECD seed certification programmes. The State Government, in conformity with guidelines and standards specified by the Board, will establish one or more State Seed Testing Laboratories or declare any Seed Testing Laboratory in the Government or non-Government Sector as a State Seed Testing Laboratory where analysis of seeds will be carried out in the prescribed manner.
- Farmers should be encouraged to use certified seeds to ensure improved performance and output.
- Farmers will retain their right to save, use, exchange, share or sell their farm seeds and planting materials without any restriction. They should be free to sell their seed on their own premises or in the local market without any hindrance provided that the seed is not branded. Farmers' right to continue using the varieties of their choice will not be infringed by the system of compulsory registration.
- Stringent measures should be taken to ensure the availability of high quality of seeds and check the sale of spurious or misbranded seeds.

11.23. Seed Distribution and Marketing

Guidelines

- The availability of high quality seeds to farmers through an improved distribution system and efficient marketing set-up should be ensured to facilitate greater security of seed supply.
- For promoting efficient and timely distribution and marketing of seed throughout the country, a supportive environment should be provided to encourage expansion of the role of the private seed sector. Efforts should be made to achieve better coordination between State Governments to facilitate free Inter-State movement of seed and planting material through exemption of duties and taxes.
- Private Seed Sector should be encouraged and motivated to restructure and reorient their activities to cater to non-traditional areas.

- A mechanism should be established for collection and dissemination of market intelligence regarding preference of consumers and farmers.
- A National Seed Grid should be established as a data-base for monitoring of information on requirement of seed, its production, distribution and preference of farmers on a district-wise basis.
- Access to term finance from Commercial Banks should be facilitated for developing efficient seed distribution and marketing facilities for growth of the seed sector.
- Distribution and marketing of seed of any variety,for the purpose of sowing and planting should be allowed only if the said variety has been registered by the National Seeds Board.
- National Seeds Board can direct a dealer to sell or distribute seeds in a specified manner in a specified area if it is considered necessary to the public interest.

11.24. Infrastructure Facilities

Guidelines

- To meet the enhanced requirement of quality/certified seeds, creation of new infrastructure facilities along with strengthening of existing facilities, should be promoted.
- National Seed Research and Training Center should be set up to impart training and build a knowledge base in various disciplines of the seed sector.
- The Central Seed Testing Laboratory should be established at the National Seed Research and Training Center to perform referral and other functions as required under the Seeds Act.
- Seed processing capacity should be augmented to meet the enhanced requirement of quality seed.
- Modernisation of seed processing facilities should be encouraged in terms of modern equipment and latest techniques, such as seed treatment for enhancement of performance of seed, etc.
- Conditioned storage for breeder and foundation seed and aerated storage for certified seed should be created in different regions.
- A computerized National Seeds Grid should be established to provide information on availability of different varieties of seeds with production agencies, their location, quality etc. This network will facilitate optimum utilisation of available seeds in every region.
- Initially, seed production agencies in the public sector would be connected with the National Seed Grid, but progressively the private sector will be encouraged to join the Grid for providing a clear assessment of demand and supply of seeds.
- State Governments, or the National Seeds Board in consultation with the concerned State Government, may establish Seed Certification Agencies.

- State Governments will establish appropriate systems for effective execution and implementation of the objectives and provisions of the Seeds Act.

11.25. Transgenic Plant Varieties

Guidelines

- Biotechnology is playing a vital role in the development of the agriculture sector. This technology can be used not only to develop new crops/varieties, which are tolerant to disease, pests and abiotic stresses, but also to improve productivity and nutritional quality of food.
- All genetically engineered crops/varieties is tested for environment and bio-safety before their commercial release, as per the regulations and guidelines of the Environment Protection Act (EPA), 1986.
- The EPA, 1986, read with the Rules, 1989 would adequately address the safety aspects of transgenic seeds/planting materials. A list is generated from Indian experience of transgenic cultivars that could be rated as environmentally safe.
- Seeds of transgenic plant varieties for research purposes is imported only through the National Bureau of Plant Genetic Resources (NBPGR) as per the EPA, 1986.
- Transgenic crops/varieties is tested to determine their agronomic value for at least two seasons under the All India Coordinated Project Trials of ICAR, in coordination with the tests for environment and bio-safety clearance as per the EPA before any variety is commercially released in the market.
- After the transgenic plant variety is commercially released, its seed will be registered and marketed in the country as per the provisions of the Seeds Act.
- After commercial release of a transgenic plant variety, its performance in the field, will be monitored for at least 3 to 5 years by the Ministry of Agriculture and State Departments of Agriculture.
- Transgenic varieties can be protected under the PVP legislation in the same manner as non-transgenic varieties after their release for commercial cultivation.
- All seeds imported into the country is required to be accompanied by a certificate from the Competent Authority of the exporting country regarding their transgenic character or otherwise.
- If the seed or planting material is a product of transgenic manipulation, it will be allowed to be imported only with the approval of the Genetic Engineering Approval Committee (GEAC), set up under the EPA, 1986.
- Packages containing transgenic seeds/planting materials, if and when placed on sale, will carry a label indicating their transgenic nature. The specific characteristics including the agronomic/yield benefits, names of the transgenes and any relevant information shall also be indicated on the label.
- Emphasis is placed on the development of infrastructure for the testing, identification and evaluation of transgenic planting materials in the country.

11.26. Import of Seeds and Planting Material

Guidelines

- The objective of the import policy is to provide the best planting material available anywhere in the world to Indian farmers, to increase productivity, farm income and export earnings, while ensuring that there is no deleterious effect on environment, health and bio-safety.
- While importing seeds and planting material, care should be taken to ensure that there is absolutely no compromise on the requirements under prevailing plant quarantine procedures, so as to prevent entry into the country of exotic pests, diseases and weeds detrimental to Indian agriculture.
- All imports of seeds will require a permit granted by the Plant Protection Advisor to the Government of India, which will be issued within the minimum possible time frame.
- All import of seeds and planting materials, etc. is allowed freely subject to EXIM Policy guidelines and the requirements of the Plants, Fruits and Seeds (Regulation of import into India) Order, 1989 as amended from time to time. Import of parental lines of newly developed varieties will also be encouraged.
- Seeds and planting materials imported for sale into the country will have to meet minimum seed standards of seed health, germination, genetic and physical purity as prescribed.
- All importers will make available a small sample of the imported seed to the Gene Bank maintained by NBPGR.
- The existing policy, which permits free import of seeds of vegetables, flowers and ornamental plants, cuttings, saplings of flowers, tubers and bulbs of flowers by certain specified categories of importers will continue. Tubers and bulbs of flowers will be subjected to post-entry quarantine.
- After the arrival of consignments at the port of entry, quarantine checks would be undertaken; which may include visual inspection, laboratory inspection, fumigation and grow-out tests. For the purpose of these checks, samples will be drawn and the tests will be conducted concurrently.

11.27. Export of Seeds

Guidelines

- Given the diversity of agro-climatic conditions, strong seed production infrastructure and market opportunities, India holds significant promise for export of seeds.
- Government is evolved a long-term policy for export of seeds with a view to raise India's share of global seed export.
- The export policy will specifically encourage custom production of seeds for export and will be based on long term perspective, dispensing with case to case consideration of proposals.

- Establishment and strengthening of Seeds Export Promotion Zones with special incentives from the Government will be facilitated.
- A data bank is created to provide information on the International Market and on export potential of Indian varieties in different parts of the world.
- A data base on availability of seeds of different crops to assess impact of exports on domestic availability of seeds is created.
- Promotional programmes to improve the quality of Indian seeds to enhance its acceptability in the International Market is be taken up.
- Testing and certification facilities is established in conformity with international requirements.

11.28. Promotion of Domestic Seed Industry

Guidelines

- Incentives is provided to the domestic seed industry to enable it to produce seeds of high yielding varieties and hybrid seeds at a faster pace to meet the challenges of domestic requirements.
- Seed Industry is be provided with a congenial and liberalized climate for increasing seed production and marketing, both domestic and international.
- Membership to International Organisations and Seed Associations like ISTA, OECD, UPOV, ASSINSEL, WIPO, at the National level or at the level of individual seed producing agencies, will be encouraged.
- Emphasis is given for improving the quality of seed produced and special efforts will be directed towards improving the quality of farmers' saved seeds.
- Financial support for capital investment, working capital and infrastructure strengthening is be facilitated through NABARD/ Commercial Banks/ Cooperative Banks.
- Tax rebate/concessions is considered on the expenditure incurred on in-house research and development of new varieties and other seed related research aspects. In order to develop a competitive seed market, the States are encouraged to remove unnecessary local taxation on sales of seeds.
- To encourage seed production in non-traditional areas including backward areas, special incentives such as transport subsidy is provided to seed producing agencies operating in these marginalised areas.
- Reduction of import duty is considered on machines and equipment used for seed production and processing which are otherwise not manufactured in the country.

11.29. Strengthening of Monitoring System

Guidelines

- The Department of Agriculture & Cooperation (DAC) will supervise the overall implementation and monitoring of the National Seeds Policy.
- The physical infrastructure in terms of office automation, communication facilities, etc., in DAC will be augmented in a time bound manner.
- The technical capacity of DAC need to be augmented and strengthened to undertake the additional work relating to implementation of National Seeds Policy, implementation of PVP&FR Bill, Seeds Act, Import and Export of Seeds, etc.
- Capacity building, including National and International training and participation in Seminars/Workshops will be organized for concerned officials.

11.30. Policy Initiatives in Seed Sector

11.30.1. Important Events & Regulatory Secenario in Indian Seed Sector

Year	Events
1924	International Seed Testing Agency.
1955	Essential Commodities Act.
1960	Central Seed Testing Laboratory established at 1960 and presently located at NSRTC, Varanasi.
1963	National Seed Corporation started.
1966	Seed Act passed. Varieties Notified under section 5.
1968	Seed Review Team submitted report
1969	SFCI created, UP Seeds & Tarai Development Corporation established
1970	The Patents Act (with amendments in 1999, 2002, 2005).
1971	National Commission on Agriculture constituted Indian Society of Seed Technology formulated Indian Minimum Seed Certification Standards adopted.
1972	National Commission on Agriculture's Seed Group.
1975	National Commission on Agriculture submitted report Project report on NSP was submitted.
1977-78	NSP I launched with World Bank assistance of US$ 52.7 million.
1978-79	NSP II launched with World Bank assistance of US$ 34.9 million.
1979-80	All India Coordinated 'National Seed Project' launchedAll India Coordinated Project on 'Seed Borne Diseases' launched.
1981	First workshop on Seed Technology under NSP was held.
1975-85	Launching of the World Bank aided National Seeds Programme in three phases leading to the creation of State Seeds Corporations, State Seed Certification Agencies, State Seed Testing Laboratories, Breeder Seed Programmes etc.
1983	Seed Control Order.

1986	Consumer Protection Act enacted.
1987	Seed Transport Subsidy Scheme.
1988	Separate seed divisions at ICAR created, New Seed Policy Implemented.
1989-90	Special Project on Hybrids in nine selected crops and seed technology launched,Research started by ICAR more aggressively.
1990-91	NSP III launched.
1991	AICRP on Seed Borne Disease merged with NSP (Crops).
1994	GOI signed GATT agreement.
1999	Geographical indication of goods (Registration and Protection Act).
2000	Seed Bank Scheme.
2001	PPV & FR Act 2001 passed.
2002	National Seeds Policy.
2004	New Seed Bill proposed, by amalgamating the provisions of Seeds Act, 1966 & Seeds Control Order 1983 as a single enactment.
2005	National Seed Plan.
2006	ICAR Mega Seed Project on Seed production in agricultural crops, horticulture and fisheries launched.
2007	National Food Security Mission, Rashtriya Krishi Vikas Yojna.
2007-08	Formation of Expert committee to suggest measures for improvement of thefunctioning of the state seed corporations by DoAC.
2007-12	Formulation of National Seed Technology Mission.
2019	New Seed Bill proposed.

11.30.2. National Seeds Policy, 2002: Thrust Areas

- Variety development
- Plant variety protection
- Seed production
- Quality assurance
- Seed distribution and marketing
- Infrastructure facilities
- Transgenic plant varieties
- Import of seeds and planting materials seed export
- Promotion of domestic private sector seed industry
- Strengthening of the monitoring system

11.30.3. Seed Bill, 2004

- Governemnt, of India has proposed a New Seed Bill, 2004 regulating seeds trade and in registration of all varieties of seeds to be marketed for production, processing, quality control & law enforcement. This Bill was proposed by amalgamating the provisions of the varietal notification and release mechanism.

Salient Features

- Registration of kinds and varieties of seeds etc.
- Evaluation of performance.
- Compensation to framers.
- Registration of seed producers and processing units.
- Seed dealers to be registered.
- Regulation of Sale of seed and seed certification.
- Seed analysis and seed testing.
- Export and import of seeds and planting material.
- Offences and punishment.

11.30.4. Proposed Seed Bill 2019

- The Ministry of Agriculture and Farmers' Welfare released the revised draft Seeds Bill 2019 in the public domain on October 28, 2019 for views and comments.
- Draft Seed Bill has 10 Chapters and 53 Clauses.

The Bill seeks to:

(a) repeal the Seeds Act, 1966;

(b) establish the Central Seed Committee; and

(c) maintain a National Register of Seeds for all varieties of seed.

Chapter -1: Preliminary

Short title, extent, application and commencement

Section: 1

- This Act may be called the Seeds Act, 2019; extends to the whole of India and shall apply to (a) every dealer; and (b) every producer of seed, other than farmer, except when the seed is produced by him for his own use and not for sale.
- Provided that nothing contained in this Act shall restrict the right of the farmer to grow, sow, re-sow, save, use, exchange, share or sell his farm seeds and planting materials except when he sells such seeds or planting material under a brand name.

Section 2: Definitions

"Agriculture" includes horticulture, forestry and cultivation of plantation, medicinal and aromatic plants. "Farmer" means any persons who owns cultivable land or any other category of farmers who are doing the agricultural work as may be notified by the Central/State Govt.

"Seed" means any type of living embryo or propagule including seedlings, tubers, bulbs, rhizomes, roots, cuttings, all types of grafts, tissue culture plantlets, synthetic seeds and other vegetatively propagated material capable of regeneration and giving rise to a plant of agriculture which is true to such type.

Other Definitions

Certification Agency; Chairperson, Committee, container, dealer, essential derived varieties (ED Vs), extant variety, farmer, horticulture nursery, kind, notification, registered kind or variety, Seed Analyst, spurious seed, transgenic variety, producer, registration sub-committee, seed quality monitoring officer, seed inspector.

Chapter II: The Central Seed Committee, Registration and Other Sub-Committees

Section 3: The Central Government shall, constitute a Committee to be called the Central Seed Committee for the purpose of this Act at New Delhi.

Section 4: Composition of the Committee

- The Secretary, DAC&FW, MoA&FW - Chairman (Ex-officio) Members- Agric. Commissioner (DAC&FW), DDG (Crop Sci. & Hort. Sci.); Jt. Secy (Seeds), Hort. Comm.; representatives of DBT; Min. of Env., Forest and Climate Change, Director (National Centre for Aromatic and Med. Plants), Chairperson (PPF&RA), Chairperson (NBA) "[ex-officio]"; And, Secretary (Agric.) from 5 States (on rotation basis from the Five Geographical zones); Director, State Seed Cert. Agency (from one state); Managing Director, State Seeds Corporation (from one state); two representatives of farmers; two representatives of seed industry; two specialists or experts in the field of seed development (nominated by Central Govt.).Geographical Zones

Zone-I: AP, Telangana, Karnataka, Kerala, Lakshadeep, Puducherry and Tamil Nadu

Zone-II: Andoman & Nicobar Island, Bihar, Chhattisgarh, Jharkhand, MP, Odisha and West Bengal

Zone-III: Arunachal Pradesh, Assam, Manipur, Meghalaya, Mizoram, Nagaland, Sikkim and Tripura

Zone-IV: Dadar and Nagar Haveli, Daman and Diu, Goa, Gujarat, Rajasthan and Maharashtra

Zone-V: Chandigarh, Haryana, H.P., J&K, NCR of Delhi, Punjab, Uttarakhand and Uttar Pradesh

- The Committee may associate any person whose assistance or advice it may desire in complying with any of the provisions of the Act- the person shall have the right to take part in discussion but NO right to vote (entitled for two years; eligible for re-nomination)
- The Central Government may, at any time, remove from office any member other than ex-officio member, after giving him a reasonable opportunity of showing cause against the proposed removal.

Section 5: Powers and functions of the committee

The Committee shall be responsible and shall have the powers for the effective implementation of this Act and shall advise the Central Government and the State

Governments on matters relating to-

a) seed programming and planning
b) seed development and production
c) export and import of seeds
d) standards for registration, certification and seed testing
e) seed registration and its enforcement
f) such other matters, as may be prescribed

Section 6: Powers of Committee to Specify Minimum Limits of Germination, Purity, Seed health, etc.

On the recommendation of the Committee, the Central Government, may, by notification, specify

a) The minimum limits of germination, genetic and physical purity, seed health and additional standards including transgenic events and corresponding traits for transgenic seeds, with respect to any kind or variety;
b) The mark or label on the packet or container to indicate that such seeds conforms to the specifications mentioned above in Clause (a) and other particulars such as expected performance of the seed in accordance with information provided by the producer under Sec. 15.

Section 7: Registration and Other Sub-Committees of the Committee and Their Functions

- The duty of the Registration Sub-Committee shall be to register kinds and varieties of seeds after scrutinizing their claims as made in the application and to perform such other functions as are assigned to it by the Committee.
- The Committee may appoint as many other Sub-Committees including a Sub-Committee on Seed Certification to exercise such powers and perform such duties as may be delegated to them.

Section 8: Procedure of the Committee and its Sub- Committees

- The Committee may, subject to the previous approval of the Central Government, make regulations for the purpose of regulating its own procedure and procedure of any Sub-Committee thereof.

Section 9: Secretary and other Officers of the Committee

The Central Government, shall

(a) Appoint a person to be the Secretary of the Committee,
(b) Provide the committee with technical and other officers and employees for the efficient performance of the functions of the Committee under this Act.

Section 10: Meetings of the Committee

- The Committee shall meet as and when necessary as per the provisions of the regulations.
- The Chairperson or, in his absence, the Agri. Commissioner or, in the absence of both, any member chosen by the members present from amongst themselves, shall preside meeting of the Committee.
- All questions at a meeting of the Committee shall be decided by a majority of votes of the members present and voting, and in the case of an equality of votes, the Chairperson or the person presiding, shall have and exercise a second or casting vote.

Section 11: State Seed Committee

- Register *State seed varieties*
- Keep a register of State seed varieties to be called as State Register of Seeds;
- Advise the State Government, on registration of seed producing units, seed processing units, seed dealers and fruit (horticulture) nurseries;
- Maintain, in each district, a list of seed dealers, seed producers, seed processing units and fruit nurseries;
- Seek information from persons engaged in the production, supply, distribution, trade or commerce in seeds of any kind or variety regarding stocks, prices, sales and other information;
- Advise the State Govt, and the Committee on all matters arising out of the administration and implementation of this Act; and
- Carry out other functions assigned to, by, or under this Act.

Chapter III: Registration of Kinds and Varieties of Seeds, etc

Section 12: Maintenance of National Register of Seeds of Kinds and Varieties

- For the purposes of this Act, a National Register of Seeds, for all kinds and varieties of seed shall be kept by the Registration Sub-Committee wherein all specifications shall be maintained (provided that the farmers shall not be required to register the farmers' varieties of seeds in the said register)
- Subject to the directions of the Committee, the Register shall be kept under the control and management of the Registration Sub-Committee.
- The Registration Sub-Committee shall, publish the list of kinds and varieties of seed which have been registered during that interval.

Section 13: Registration of National Seed Varieties and State Seed Varieties

- The national seed varieties shall be registered by the Registration Sub-Committee and State seed varieties shall be registered by the State Seed Committee.

- The State Seed Committee shall furnish the information regarding the State seed varieties registered by it to the Registration Sub-Committee for maintenance of the National Register of Seeds.

Section 14: Registration of any Kind or Varieties of Seed

- No seed of any kind or variety, except farmers' variety, shall, for the purpose of sowing or planting by any person, be sold unless such seed is registered by the Registration Sub-Committee.
- The seed varieties which are available in the market on the date of the commencement of this Act shall be deemed to be registered under this Act and the information related to those varieties shall be furnished by the concerned person to the registration Sub-Committee or the State Seed Committee, as the case may be, within the period of two years from the date of commencement.
- Registration made under this Act shall be valid for a period of 10 years in the case of annual and biennial crops, and 12 years for long duration perennials.
- At the expiry, the kind or variety of seed may be re-registered for a like period by the Registration Sub-committee or the State Seed Committee, on the basis of the results of such trials as may be prescribed to re-establish the performance of the kind or variety of seed.

Section 15: Procedure for Registration

- On receipt of application for the registration of a kind or variety of seed, the Registration Sub-Committee or the State Seed Committee, as the case may be, shall after enquiry and satisfying itself that the seed to which the application relates conforms to the claims, with regards to the efficacy of the kind or variety of seed and its safety to human and animals, register the seed on such conditions as may be specified by it and allot a registration number and issue a certificate of registration.
- The Registration Sub-Committee may, having regard to the efficacy of the seeds and its safety to human beings and animals, vary the conditions subject to which a certificate of registration has been granted and may, for that purpose, require the certificate holder by notice to deliver the certificate to it, within specified time.

Section 16: Special Provision for Registration of Transgenic Varieties

- No seed of any transgenic variety shall be registered unless the applicant has obtained clearance in respect of the same as required by or under the provisions of the Environment (Protection) Act, 1986:
- Provided that the Registration Sub-Committee has granted provisional registration, for a period of two years on the basis of information furnished by the producer on the results of multilocation testing (MLT) conducted in prescribed manner.

Section 17: Cancellation of Registration of Seeds of Kinds and Varieties

The Registration Sub-Committee or the State Seed Committee, may cancel any registration granted on following grounds, namely:

- That the holder of the certificate has violated any of the terms and conditions of the registration; or
- That the registration has been obtained by misrepresentation or concealment of essential data; or
- That the variety is not performing in accordance with the information furnished or has become obsolete or has outlived its utility; or
- That prevention of commercial exploitation of such variety of seeds is necessary' in the public interest. No order of cancellation of registration under this section shall be made unless the holder thereof or the affected person concerned has been given a reasonable opportunity of showing cause in respect of the grounds for such cancellation.

Section 18: Notification of Cancellation of Registration of Any Kinds and Varieties Seeds

- The Registration Sub-Committee or the State Seed Committee, shall notify the cancellation of registration of any kind or variety of seed made in the Official Gazette and also publish the said cancellation of registration in prescribed name.

Section 19: Exclusion of Certain Kinds or Varieties of Seeds from Registration

- No registration of any kind or variety of seed shall be made under this Act, if prevention of commercial exploitation of such kind or variety is necessary to protect public order or public morality or human, animal or plant life and health, or to avoid serious prejudice to the environment; and
- A kind or variety of seed containing any technology (GURT or Terminator), which is harmful, or potentially harmful, shall not be registered.

Section 20: Evaluation of Performance

- The Committee may, for conducting trials to assess the performance, accredit centers of the Indian Council of Agricultural Research, State Agricultural Universities and such other organizations fulfilling the eligibility requirements as may be prescribed, to conduct trials to evaluate the performance of any kind or variety of seed.

Section 21: Compensation to Farmer

- Where the seed of any registered kind or variety is sold to a farmer, the producer, distributor or vendor, as the case may be, shall disclose the expected performance of such kind or variety to the farmer under given conditions, and if, such registered seed fails to provide the expected performance under such given conditions, the farmer may claim compensation from the producer, dealer, distributor or vendor under the Consumer Protection Act, 1986.

Section 22: Seed Producers and Seed Processing Units to be Registered

- No producer or his sponsor shall grow or organize the production of seed or maintain a seed processing unit, unless he is registered under this Act by the respective State Government under this Act.
- Every seed producing unit and every seed processing unit shall furnish periodic returns on the quantity of seeds of different kinds or varieties produced or processed by it, to the State Government, in prescribed format.
- The State Government may, after giving the holder of certificate of registration, suspend or cancel the registration if -

(a) such registration has been obtained by misrepresentation as to a material particular relating to the specification in terms of infrastructure, equipment or availability of qualified manpower; or

(b) any of the provisions of this Act or the rules made thereunder has been contravened.

Section 23: Seed Dealers to be Registered

- Every person who desires to carry on the business of selling, keeping for sale, offering to sell, import or export or otherwise supply any seed by himself, or by any other person on his behalf, shall obtain a registration certificate as a dealer in seeds from the State Government.
- Every dealer registered under this section shall furnish to the State Government such information and returns regarding seed stocks, seed lots, expiry date of seed lots and other related information at such interval, as may be prescribed.
- The State Government may, after giving the dealer an opportunity of being heard, suspend or cancel a certificate granted under this Act if-
- such registration had been obtained by misrepresentation of any material fact
- contravenes any of the provisions of this Act or the rules made thereunder.

Section 24: Fruit Nursery to be Registered

- No person shall conduct or carry on the business of fruit nursery in area exceeding one hectare for any of the purposes of this Act unless such nursery is registered with the State Government.

Section 25: Duties of Registration Holders of Fruit Nursery Every Holder of a Registration of a Fruit Nursery shall-

- Keep a complete record of the origin or source of every planting material and performance record of mother trees in the nursery;
- Keep a layout plan showing the position of the root-stocks and scions used in raising the horticulture plants;
- Keep the nursery plants and parent trees used for the propagation of fruit plants free from infectious or contagious insects, pests or diseases affecting plants; and

- Furnish prescribed information to the State Government, on the production, stocks, sales and prices of planting material in the nursery.

CHAPTER- IV

Section 26: Regulation of Sale of Seeds of Registered Kinds and Varieties

No person shall himself, or by any other person on his behalf carry on the business of selling, keeping for sale,offering to sell, import or export or otherwise supply any kind of seed of any registered kind or variety unless-

- Such seed is identifiable as to its kind or variety.
- Such seed conforms to the minimum standards of germination and genetic, physical purity, seed health, transgenic traits.
- The container of such seed bears in the prescribed manner, the mark or label bearing the correct particulars thereof.
- The container of such seed, in the case of transgenic varieties, bears a declaration to this effect.

Section 27: Regulation of Sale Price in Emergent Conditions

In emergent situations like scarcity of seeds, abnormal rise in prices, monopolistic pricing or profiteering in respect of a particular variety:

- The Central Government, may regulate the sale price of such variety of seeds in prescribed manner (National seed varieties).
- The State Govt, may, in respect of Sate Seed varieties, regulate the sale price of such varieties in such manner as may be prescribed.

Section 28: State Seed Certification Agency

- The State Government, or the Central Govt, may, in consultation with the State Government, establish a State Seed Certification Agency for the State to carry out the functions entrusted to the State Seed Certification Agency under this Act.

Section 29: Accreditation of Seed Certification Agencies

- The State Government, may, with previous approval of the Central Govt, accredit - organizations of the Central Government, or State Government, to carry out certification, in the prescribed criteria.
- The accredited organizations shall be subject to prescribed inspection and control of the concerned State Government, and State Seed Certification Agency.
- The accreditation may be withdrawn by the State Govt., for reasons to be recorded in writing and after giving to the concerned organization a reasonable opportunity of being heard.

Section 30: Grant of Certificate by the State Seed Certification Agency

- Any person selling, keeping for sale, offering to sell, or otherwise supplying any seed of any registered kind or variety, desires to have such seed certified by the SSCA, may apply to that Agency for grant of a certificate for the purpose.
- The SSCA, after enquiry and satisfying itself that the seed to which the application relates conforms to the prescribed standards, grant a certificate in prescribed conditions : provided that the seed meet the minimum limit of standards.

Section 31: Revocation of Certificate

The State Seed Certification Agency may, after giving the holder of the certificate an opportunity of showing cause, revoke the certificate -

- If the certificate granted by it has been obtained by misrepresentation of essential fact; or
- The holder of the certificate has failed to comply the conditions subject to which the certificate has been granted or has contravened any of the provisions of this Act.

Section 32: Recognition of Seed Certification Agencies in Territory Outside India

- The Central Government may, on the recommendation of the Committee, and by notification, recognize any seed certification agency established in a country other than India , for the purposes of this Act.

Chapter V

- Any person aggrieved by a decision of the Registration Sub- Committee or State Seed Comm, or the State Seed Certification Agency may appeal in prescribed format to the appellate authority (constituted by the Central Govt.) within thirty days from the date of decision communicated to him.
- An appellate authority shall consist of a single person or three persons as the Central Government may think fit, to be appointed by that Government.
- On receipt of an appeal, the appellate authority shall, after giving the appellant and the other party an opportunity of being heard, dispose of the appeal as early as possible

CHAPTER VI

Section 34: Central and State Seed Testing Laboratories (CSTL)

- The Central Government may, by notification, establish a CSTL or declare any seed-testing laboratory as the CSTL to carry out the functions entrusted to the CSTL in the prescribed manner.
- The State Govt, may, by notification, establish one or more State Seed Testing Laboratories (SSTL) or declare any seed testing laboratory in the Government or

Non-govemment sector as a SSTL, where analysis of seed of any kind or variety shall be carried out under this Act in the prescribed manner.

- Every CSTL or SSTL shall have as many Seed Analysts as the Central Govt, or the State Govt, may consider necessary.

Section 35-37: Seed Analysts

- The concerned Government (Central or State) may appoint a person having the prescribed qualifications to be Seed Analysts and define the local limits of their jurisdiction.
- Every CSTL and SSTL may have as many Seed Analysts as the Central Govt, or the State Government, consider necessary.
- In case, the report of SSTL and CSTL vary, the report of CSTL shall prevail over the SSTL report.
- Where the report sent by the CSTL is produced in any proceedings, it shall not be necessary to produce the sample or part thereof taken for analysis.

Section 38: Seed Quality Monitoring Officer and Seed Inspectors

- The Central Government may, by notification, appoint such person having prescribed qualifications, to be Seed Quality Monitoring Officer and define their jurisdiction.
- The State Government may appoint a person having the prescribed qualifications, to be Seed Inspectors and define the areas within which they shall exercise jurisdiction.
- Every Seed Inspector shall be subordinate to such authority as the State Govt, may specify in this behalf.

Section 39: Powers of Seed Quality Monitoring Officer and Seed Inspectors

- Take samples of any seed of any kind or variety from - any person selling such seed; or any person who is in the course of conveying, delivering such seed to a purchaser or a consignee; or a purchaser or a consignee after delivery of such seed to him.
- Send such sample for analysis to the Seed Analyst of that area.
- Enter and search (with prior permission), at all reasonable times, with such assistance, if any, as he considers necessary, any place in which he has reason to believe that an offence under this Act has been or is being committed and order in writing the person, not to dispose of any stock of such seed for a specific period not exceeding 15 days or, unless the alleged offence is such that the defect may be removed by the possessor of the seed and seize the stock of such seed.
- The Inspectors may examine any record, register, documenter any other material found and seize the same if he has reason to believe that it may furnish evidence of the commission of an offence punishable under this Act; and exercise powers

for carrying out the purposes of this Act or any rule or regulation made thereunder.

- The power of this section includes the power to break-open any container in which any seed of any kind or variety may be contained or to break-open the door of any premises where any such seed may be kept for sale [if the owner is present and refuses to open]. Presence of two independent person from same localityjs required and take their signature on a prescribed manner.
- The provisions of the Code of Criminal Procedure, 1973, shall apply to any search or seizure as they apply to any search or seizure made under the authority of a warrant issued under section 94 of the said Code, or under the corresponding provisions of the said law.

CHAPTER VII: Import and Export of Seeds

Section 40: Import of Seeds-

- All import of seeds shall be subject to the provisions of the Plant Quarantine (Regulation of Import into India) Order, 2003, or any corresponding order made under section 3 of the DIP Act, 1914.
- Shall conform to minimum limits of germination, genetic and physical purity, and seed health, transgenic traits; and
- Shall be subject to registration on the basis of information furnished by the importer on the results of MLT for prescribed period.
- All import of Transgenic varieties shall also be subject to EPA, 1986.
- The Central Government may, by notification, permit to import an unregistered variety in such quantity and subject to fulfilling conditions specified in notification for research purposes.

Section 41: Export of Seeds

- The Central Government may, on the advice of the Committee, restrict the export of seeds of any kind or variety if it is deemed that such export may adversely affect the food security of the country, or if it is felt that the reasonable requirements of the public will not be met, or on such other grounds as may be prescribed.

CHAPTER VIII

Section 42: Offences and Punishment

If any person -

Contravenes any provision of this Act or any rule made thereunder; or imports, sells, stocks, or exhibits for sale, or supplies any misbranded seed or without having a certificate of registration; or obstructs the State Seed Committe or Seed Certification Agency or SQMO, or Seed Inspector or Seed Analyst or any other authority in the exercise of its powers or discharge of their duties under this Act or the rules made thereunder.

The person shall, on conviction, be punishable - with fine which shall not be less than 25 thousand rupees but which may extend to one lakh rupees.

The above shall also apply to the person selling any seed which does not conform to the minimum prescribed standards.

If any person furnishes any false information relating to the standards of genetic purity, misbrands any seed or supplies any spurious seed or spurious transgenic variety, sells any non-registered seeds he shall be punishable with imprisonment for a term which may extend to One Year or with fine which may extend to Five Lakh Rupees or with both.

Section 43: Forfeiture of Property

- When any person has been convicted under this Act for the contravention of any of the provisions of this Act or the rules made, the seed in respect of which the contravention has been committed shall be forfeited to the Central Government.
- Where an offence has been committed by a company, every person who was in charge of, and was responsible to the company as well as the company, shall be deemed to be guilty of the offence and shall be liable to be punished accordingly; provided that
- Any person liable to any punishment shall be rendered if he proves that the offence was committed without his knowledge and that he exercised all due diligence to prevent the commission of such offence.

Chapter: IX

Section 45: Power of Central Government

- The Central Government may give such directions to any State Govt, as necessary for carrying into execution in the State any of the provisions of this Act or of any rule made thereunder.

Section 46

- The Central Govt, may give such directions to any State Government as necessary for carrying into execution in the State any of the provisions of this Act or of any rule made thereunder.

Section 47: Exemption from Provision of Act

- The Central Government, may, by notification, and subject to such conditions as it may specify therein, exempt any educational, scientific or research or extension organization from all or any of the provisions of this Act or rules made thereunder.

Chapter X: Miscellaneous

Section 48

- No suit, prosecution or other legal proceeding shall lie against the Government or any person for anything which is done or intended to be done in provisions of this Act, the Central Government, may make section good faith under this Act.

Section 49

- If any difficulty arises during execution of the after the expiry of two years from the date of necessary provisions for removing the difficulty:
- Provided that no order shall be made under this commencement of this Act.

Section 50: Power of Central Government to Make Rules:

- The Central Government may by notification, make rules and regulations to carry out the provisions of this Act in all or any of the matters related in the Act.

Section 51: Power of Committee to Make Regulations:

- The Committee may, with the previous approval of the Central Government by notification, make regulations in consistent with the provision of this Act.

Section 52: Notification, rule, etc. to be laid before Parliament

- Every rule and every regulation made under this Act shall be laid before each House of Parliament, while it is in session, for a total period of thirty days which may be comprised in one session or in two or more successive sessions.

Section 53: Repeal and Savings

- The Seeds Act, 1966 is hereby Repealed.

No such repeal shall affect -

- the previous operation of the repealed law; or
- any right, privilege, obligation or liability acquired, accrued or incurred under the repealed law; or
- any penalty, forfeiture or punishment incurred in respect of any offence committed against the repealed Act, or
- any investigation, proceeding, legal proceeding or remedy in respect of any right, privilege, obligation, liability, penalty, forfeiture or punishment shall continue as if this Act had not been passed.· Seeds registered, Agencies established under the Seeds Act 1966, shall be deemed to be have been registered and established or recognized under this Act.

Expected Benefits from the Revised Legislation

- Availability of true to type seeds to Indian farmers and check on sale of spurious and poor quality seeds;

- Increase in the proportion of quality seed available for sowing and increase in the seed replacement rate resulting in higher productivity;
- Increased private participation in seed production, distribution, certification and seed testing; Establishment of Central Seed Committee (CSC) as a permanent body for effective monitoring of the seed development programme in the country;
- Regulation of import and sale of transgenic seed and planting material;
- Liberalized import of seeds and planting materials;
- Provision of farmers' exemption for registration, etc.
- Provide compulsory registration based on agronomic performance data thereby regulating quality and genetic purity of seeds; Establish Central Seed Committee (CSC);
- Provision for compensation.

11.30.5 Comparison of Seeds Act, 1966 and Seeds Bill, 2004

Title	Seeds Bill, 2004	Seeds Act, 1966
1. Definitions	"Agriculture" includes horticulture, forestry, cultivation of plantation, medicinal and aromatic plants. Definitions of "Seed" and "Variety" have been changed to make them more specific and technical.	"Agriculture" includes horticulture.
	Defines terms such as "Dealer", "Essentially Derived Variety", "Extant Variety", "Farmer", "Horticulture Nursery", "Misbranded", "Spurious Seed", and "Transgenic Variety".	Does not define these terms
2. Registration	All seeds for sale must be registered.	Only varieties notified by the government need to be registered.
3. Seed Committee	Constitutes Central and State Seed Committees. A Registration Sub-Committee would register seeds of all varieties.	Constitutes Central Seed Committee. The central government, after consulting with the CSC, may notify a seed in order to regulate the quality of seed.
4. Transgenic Varieties	Special provisions for registration of transgenic varieties of seeds.	No provision for transgenic varieties of seeds.
Compens-ation to Farmers	Provides for compensation to farmers under the Consumer Protection Act, 1986 in the event of under performance of seeds.	No specific provision for compensation mentioned in the Act.
5. Export and Import	All seed imports are regulated by the Plant Quarantine (Regulation of Import into India) Order, 2003 or any corresponding order of the	A person is restricted from exporting or importing notified variety of seed unless it conforms to

	Destructive Insects and Pests Act, 1914; shall conform to minimum limits of germination etc. Exports can be restricted if it adversely affects the food security of the country.	minimum limits of germination etc.
6. Penalties	Any person who contravenes any provisions of the Act or imports, sells or stocks seeds deemed to be misbranded or not registered, can be punishable by a fine of Rs 5,000 to Rs 25,000. The penalty for giving false information is a prison term up to six months and/or a fine up to Rs 50,000.	Any person who contravenes any provisions of the Act, prevents a Seed Inspector from taking samples etc. shall be punished for the first offence with a fine which may extend to Rs 500. If the offence is repeated he may be imprisoned for a maximum term of six months and/or fined up to Rs 1,000.

11.30.6. Comparison of Seeds Act, 1966 & Seeds Bill, 2019

Title	Seeds Act, 1966	Seeds Bill, 2019
1. Definitions	Agriculture" includes horticulture.	Agriculture" includes horticulture, forestry, cultivation of plantation, medicinal and aromatic plants. Definitions of "Seed" and "Variety" have been changed to make them more specific and technical.
	Does not define these terms (as in 2019).	Defines terms such as "Dealer", "Essentially Derived Variety", "Extant Variety", "Farmer", "Horticulture Nursery", "Misbranded", "Spurious Seed", and "Transgenic Variety."
2. Registration	Only varieties notified by the government need to be registered.	All seeds for sale must be registered.
3. Seed Committee	Constitutes Central Seed Committee. The central government, after consulting with the CSC, may notify a seed in order to regulate the quality of seed.	Constitutes Central and State Seed Committees. A Registration Sub-Committee would register seeds of all varieties.
4. Transgenic Varieties	No provision for transgenic varieties of seeds.	Special provisions for registration of transgenic varieties of seeds.
5. Export and Import	A person is restricted from exporting or importing notified variety of seed unless it conforms to minimum limits of germination etc.	All seed imports are regulated by the Plant Quarantine (Regulation of Import into India) Order, 2003 or any corresponding order of the Destructive Insects and Pests Act, 1914; shall conform to minimum limits of germination etc. Exports can be restricted if it adversely affects the food security of the country.
6. Compensation to Farmers	No specific provision for compensation mentioned in the Act.	Provides for compensation to farmers under the Consumer Protection Act, 1986 in the event of underperformance of seeds.
Penalties	Any person who contravenes any provisions of the Act, prevents a Seed Inspector from taking samples etc. shall be punished for the first offence with a fine which may extend to Rs 500. If the offence is repeated he may be imprisoned for a maximum term of six months and/or fined up to Rs 1,000.	Any person who contravenes any provisions of the Act or imports, sells or stocks seeds deemed to be misbranded or not registered, can be punishable by a fine of Rs 25,000 to Rs One Lakh. The penalty for giving false information is a prison term up to One Year and/or a fine up to Rs 5 Lakhs

11.30.7 Comparison of Seeds Bill, 2004 and PPV & FR Act, 2001

Title	Seeds Bill, 2004	PPV & FR Act, 2001
1. Definitions	"Farmer" means any person who cultivates crops either by cultivating the land himself or through any other person but does not include any individual, company, trader or dealer who engages in the procurement and sale of seeds on a commercial basis.	"Farmer" means any person who cultivates crops by cultivating the land himself or cultivates crops by directly supervising the cultivation or land through any other person; or conserves and preserves, severally or jointly, with any other person any wild species or traditional varieties or adds value to such wild species or traditional varieties through selection and identification of their useful properties.
2. Registration	Establishes a Registration Sub- Committee, which would maintain a National Register of Seeds.	Establishes a Plant Varieties Registry, which would maintain a National Register of Plant Varieties.
	No specifications regarding parentage of variety.	Specifies details under which a variety may be registered such as a complete passport data of the parental lines from which a variety has been derived.
	Registration is for 15 years for annual/biennial crops and 18 years for long duration perennials. On expiry, registration can be renewed for a similar period.	Registration is for 15 years for annual/biennial crops and 18 years for long duration perennials. Registration cannot be renewed.
3. Farmers'Rights	A farmer can save, use, exchange, share or sell his farm seeds and planting material. He cannot sell seeds under a brand name. Seeds sold have to conform to the minimum limit of germination, physical purity, genetic purity prescribed by the Act.	A farmer is entitled to save, use, sow, resow, exchange, share or sell his farm produce including seed of a variety protected under the Act in the same manner before this Act came into force. He cannot sell branded seed of a variety protected under the Act.
4. Compensation	The seed producer, distributor or vendor will have to disclose the expected performance of a particular variety of seed under certain given conditions. If the seed fails to perform to expected standards, the farmer can claim compensation from the dealer, distributor or vendor under the Consumer Protection Act, 1986.	If a breeder of a propagating material of a variety registered under the Act sells his product to a farmer, he has to disclose the expected performance under given conditions. If the propagating material fails to perform, the farmer can claim compensation in the prescribed manner before the Protection of Plant Varieties and Farmers' Rights Authority.

5. Penalties	Any person who contravenes any provisions of the Act or imports, sells or stocks seeds deemed to be misbranded or not registered, can be punishable between Rs one lakh and Rs five lakh or both. Penalty giving false information is a prison term up to six months and/or a fine up to Rs 50,000.	Penalty for applying false denomination to a variety is imprisonment up to two years and/or a fine between Rs 50,000 and Rs five lakh. Penalty for falsely representing a variety as registered is imprisonment up to three by a fine of Rs 5,000 to Rs 25,000. The penalty for years and/or a fine for subsequent offence is imprisonment up to three years and/or a fine between Rs two lakh and Rs 20 lakh.

11.30.8. Comparison of Seeds Bill, 2019 & PPV & FR Act, 2001

Title	PPV & FR Act, 2001	Seeds Bill, 2019
1. Definitions	Farmer" means any person who cultivates crops by cultivating the land himself or cultivates crops by directly supervising the cultivation or land through any other person; or conserves and preserves, severally or jointly, with any other person any wild species or traditional varicties or adds value to such wild species or traditional varieties through selection and identification of their useful properties.	Farmer" means any person who cultivates crops by cultivating the land himself or cultivates crops by directly supervising the cultivation or land through any other person; or conserves and preserves, severally or jointly, with any other person any wild species or traditional varieties or adds value to such wild species or traditional varieties through selection and identification of their useful properties.
2. Registration	Establishes a Plant Varieties Registry, which would maintain a National Register of Plant Varieties.	Establishes a Registration Sub- Committee, which would maintain a National Register of Seeds.
	Specifies details under which a variety may be regis tered such as a complete passport data of the parental lines from which a variety has been derived.	No specifications regarding parentage of variety.
	Registration is for 15 years for annual/biennial crops and 18 years for long duration perennials. Registration cannot be renewed.	Registration is for 10 years for annual/biennial crops and 12 years for long duration perennials. On expiry, registration can be renewed for a similar period.

3. Compensation	If a breeder of a propagating material or a variety registered under the Act sells his product to a farmer, he has to disclose the expected performance under given conditions. If the propagating material fails to perform, the farmer can claim compensation in the prescribed manner before the Protection of Plant Varieties and Farmers' Rights Authority.	The seed producer, distributor or vendor will have to disclose the expected performance of a particular variety of seed under certain given conditions. If the seed fails to perform to expected standards, the farmer can claim compensation from the dealer, distributor or vendor under the Consumer Protection Act, 1986.
4. Penalties	Penalty for applying false denomination to a variety is imprisonment up to two years and/or a fine between Rs 50,000 and Rs Five lakh. Penalty for falsely representing a variety as registered is imprisonment up to three years and/or a fine between Rs one lakh and Rs five lakh or both. Penalty for subsequent offence is imprisonment up to three years and/or a fine between Rs two lakh and Rs 20 lakh.	Any person, who contravenes any provisions of the Act, prevents a Seed Inspector from taking samples etc. shall be punished for the offence with a fine up to Rs 5 lakhs or imprisonment of one year or both.

11.30.9. Tag colour for different category of Seeds

- For breeder seed- golden yellow
- Foundation seed - white
- Certified seed- Azure blue

Public Private Partnership (PPP) in Seed Science

- Past experience has shown that healthy competition brings the best out of the public sectors like banking, telecom and airline.
- Globally sustainable food and Nutritional security is possible when resources in both public and private are pooled and synergised.
- So we need to to change the mindset: The perceived threat can become an opportunity.
- There is enough space for both public and private seed industries.
- Joint planning & execution of activities while sharing the costs risks and benefits.

PPP Models

- AVRDC Model.
- Cornell & Wisconsin University -VBI Model.
- NCSU model.
- ICRISAT Hybrid Parent Research Consortium.
- IRRI hybrid rice R & D consortium.
- ICAR-SAU partnership.
- KVK
- NGO's

Benefits of Public Private Partnership (PPP)

- Advanced research.
- Ideal to combine strengths/synergies.
- Delivering new products to millions of marginal, small & medium size growers.
- Mutual benefits.
- Participation of small & medium sized companies.
- First phase-non-competitive.
- IPR issues.

For successful PPP

- Goals to be clearly defined.
- Responsibilities to be defined.
- Communications clear & good.
- Project frame work based on goals set.
- Investments to be economically profitable.

- Sharing risks & responsibilities.
- High degree of complementarity.

11.30.10. Difference in between Public and Private Partnership

Title	Public	Private
Requirements for partnerships.	• Cooperation contract • Germplasm exchange • Bilateral research from both parties	• Restriction with partners that had breeding programs • Cooperation contract
Benefits Offered	• Co-ownership • Sharing of royalties • Indication of partnership in the cultivar's patent register/copyright	• Exclusive license to multiply and commercialize cultivars resulting from the partnership, subject to the royalties agreed upon (on a range from 3% to 10%). • The exclusivity can be for 5 or 10 years according to the initial stage of development.

11.30.11. Tasks to be Handled Through PPP

I Crop Improvement

- Genetic improvement
- Conventional breeding including mutation breeding-varieties, composites, populations and hybrids.
- Biotechnology tools - Marker assisted selection, Transgenics,
- DNA recombinant technology and genomics etc.
- Build crop based/Institution based technology parks/ incubators.
- Both public & private scientists work from the beginning.

II Seed Technology Research

- Seed production enhancement techniques.
- Ultra modem seed processing and storage technologies.
- Seed quality enhancement technologies - seed priming, coating, pelleting etc.

III Meeting Seed Production Demands of the Country

- Germplasm exchange - parting of parental material, Genes and Genes constructs; joint product development; testing; release and commercialization - including multiplication and distribution.
- To check break in seed chain-PPP.
- Development of effective diagnostic system, quality testing developing seed buffer stock to meet during natural calamites.

IV Establishment of Infrastructure Facilities and Capacity Building

- For basic/parental seed production (vis-a-vis self/cross/hybrids/vegetatively propagated) planning should be done jointly by both public and private sectors based on domestic and export demand - required infrastructure facilities and funding support needs to be provided

Advantages of Synergy Between Private and Public Sector under IPR Regime

- Product development & deployment will be faster and better.
- Better management of financial resources.
- Encouragement/motivation to the developer .
- Farmers get better and genetically improved seed.
- More investments in agri-research.
- Better human resource development.

11.30.12. Examples of PPP in Agriculture

- Sorghum and millet research between ICRISAT, India and consortium of private seed companies.
- UAS, Bangalore - IFSSA (Indian Foundation seed & Sen ices Association) MoA for promotion of rice hybrid KRH 2.
- LARI - IFSSA MoA for promotion of rice hybrid Pusa RH 10.
- DRR, Hyderabad - IFSSA MoA for promotion of DRRH 2.
- IIVR, Varanasi, following vegetable crops and varieties are under PPP model.

Crop & Variety	Name of the Company
Cowpea- Kashi Kanchan	M/S Sadhan Seeds, Nagpur, Maharashtra M/S VNR Seeds, Raipur, Chattisgarh M/S Taikojin Seeds Kolkata, West Bengal M/S Mali Agri Tech PVT Ltd. Nadia West Bengal M/S Haldighati Seed Croportion Kankroli Rajasthan M/S Pure Line Agri Pro, Bareilly, U.P. M/S Agri-Asi Seeds Pvt. Ltd. Jalna Maharashtra
Cowpea- Kashi Nidhi	M/S Sadhan Seeds, Nagpur M/S DNA Agri Seeds Pvt. Ltd. Komapally Rangareddy, Telangana M/S Dinikar Seeds Pvt. Ltd. Sabarkantha Gujarat M/S Mahi Agri TechPvt. Ltd. Nadi, West Bengal
Cowpea- Kashi Gauri	M/S Ravi Hybrid Seeds Hyderabad
Cowpea- Kashi Unnati	M/S Ravi Hybrid Seeds Hyderabad
Pea-Kashi Uday	M/S Bundelkhand Seeds Pvt. Ltd. Kalaun U.P.

Pea-Kashi Nandani	M/S DNA Agri Seeds Pvt. Ltd. Komapally Rangareddy, Telangana
Tomato-Kashi Aman	M/S Suraj Crop Sciences Ltd. Gandhi Nagar Gujarat
	M/S DNA Agri Seeds Pvt. Ltd. Komapally Rangareddy, Telangana
	M/S Dinikar Seeds Pvt. Ltd. Sabarkantha Gujarat
	M/S Ananya Agri Genetics (India) Pvt. Ltd. Kukatpally, Rangareddy, Telangana
	M/S RR Seeds Agri- Tech Pvt. Ltd. Davengere, Karnataka

12

Intellectual Property Rights

12.1. Common Term Used

- GATT (General Agreements on Tariffs & Trade)
- WTO (World Trade Organization)
- TRIPS (Trade Related Intellectual Property Right)/IPR/Pateni/Copy right/ Trademark */G.I./Sui generis* system etc.
- UPOV/PVP/PBR/Farmer's Right
- CBD (Convention on Biodiversity)

What is GATT?

- Established in 1948 (after 2nd World War)
- For the smooth conduct of trade by 22 countries *(India was the party)*
- Several negotiations
- Usually trades related to industries
- Eight round at Uruguay in 1986
- First time issues on agricultural trade, textile, investment, IPR were discussed
- (moral victory for the developing world especially county like India)

What is WTO?

- WTO is the only international organization dealing with global rule of trade (through revised GATT agreement; also called as GATT Rule Book)
- On 15th April 1994 (1986-194) in Mexico, 125 countries signed the agreement
- On 1 January 1995, came in force as WTO
- HQ: Geneva; —140 members; wwwAvto.org

Function of WTO

- Administrating trade agreements.
- Providing forum for trade negotiations.
- Settling trade disputes (DSC).
- Reviewing national trade policies.
- Technical assistance (training).
- Cooperating with other institions organizations.

Trademark

- A trademark is a distinctive sign which identifies certain goods or services as those produced or provided by a specific person or enterprise.
- Over the years these marks evolved into today's system of *trademark registration and protection.*
- The system *helps consumers identify and purchase a* product or service because its nature and quality, indicated by its unique trademark, meets their needs.

Trade-related Intellectual Property Rights (TRIPS) & their Protection Rationale or *Sui-generis* System

- **Need to incorporate equity concerns:**
  - Rights of farmers
  - Rights of village community
  - Rights of researchers
- **Greater flexibility in regard to:**
  - Protected genera/species of varieties
  - Level and period of protection
  - Sustainable development of Agro- biodiversity
- **Benefit sharing arrangement**

Copyright: Copyright is a legal term describing rights given to creators for their literary and artistic works. The kinds of works covered by copyright include: literary works such as novels, poems, plays, reference works, newspapers and computer programs; databases; films, musical compositions, and choreography; artistic works such as paintings, drawings, photographs and sculpture; architecture; and advertisements, maps and technical drawings

What is Patent?

Patent is a legal monopoly that is granted to the owner of a new invention that is capable of industrial use, for a specific period of time. It empowers the owner of an invention to prevent others from manufacturing, using, importing or selling the patented invention. Patent Act, 1970 as amended in the years 1998 and 1999 along with Patent Rules, 1972 govern patents in India.

Why Patents?

- To enjoy monopoly of marketing rights.
- To avoid reinvention.
- To know the latest trend and technology.
- Patents can be obtained for products, processes or joint.

12.2. Intellectual Propriety Right (IPR)

- It is intangible
- It can be inherited and transferred
- It can be protected by registering under laws

12.2.1. Requirements of Patent Vs Plant Variety Protection

Patents

- Novelty
- Inventive step
- Marketability

Plant Variety Protection

- Novelty
- Distinctness
- Uniformity
- Stability

Definitions

- Invention" means a new product or process involving an inventive step capable of industrial application.
- Inventive step" means a feature of an invention that involves technical advance as compared to the existing knowledge that makes the invention not obvious to a person skilled in the art.

Not patentable (General Rules)

- The mere discovery of a new form of a known substance which does not result in the enhancement of the known efficiency of that substance or the mere discovery of any new property or new use for a known substance.

12.2.2. Methods

Not patentable under Indian Law

- The living entities of natural origin such as animals, plants, in whole or any part thereof, plant varieties, seeds, species, genes and microorganisms are not patentable.
- Any process of manufacture or production relating to such living entities is also not patentable
- Any method of treatment such as medicinal, surgical, curative, prophylactic, diagnostic and therapeutic of humans and animals or other treatments of similar nature are not patentable.

- Any living entity of artificial origin such as transgenic animals and plants, any part thereof are not patentable.
- The biological materials such as organs, tissues, cells, viruses etc. and process of preparing thereof are not patentable under Section 3(c).
- Essentially biological processes for the production of plants and animals such as method of crossing or breeding etc. are not patentable.
- Any biological material and method of making the same which is capable of causing serious prejudice to human, animal or plant lives or health or to the environment including the use of those would be contrary to public order and morality are not patentable such as terminator gene technology
- The living entity of artificial origin such as microorganisms, vaccines are patentable.

Provisional and Complete Specifications

- When provisional specification is provided, a complete specification shall be filed within twelve months from the date of filing of the application.
- If the complete specification is not so filed the application shall be deemed to be abandoned.
- Within fifteen months from the date aforesaid, if a request to that effect is made to the Controller and the prescribed fee is paid on or before the date on which the complete specification is filed.
- Fully and particularly describe the invention and its operation or use and the method by which it is to be performed.
- Disclose the best method of performing the invention.
- Define the scope of the invention for which protection is claimed.

Examination of Application

- Whether the application and the specification are in accordance with the requirements of this Act and of any rules made thereunder.
- Whether there is any lawful ground of objection to the grant of the patent under this Act in pursuance of the application.
- Any other matter which may be prescribed.

Advertisement of Acceptance of Complete Specification

- On the acceptance of a complete specification, the Controller shall advertise in the Official Gazette the fact that the specification has been accepted.
- The application and the specification with the drawings (if any) filed shall be open to public inspection.

Effect of Acceptance of Complete Specification

- On and from the date of advertisement of the acceptance of a complete specification and until the date of sealing of a patent.

- The applicant shall have the like privileges and rights as if a patent for the invention had been sealed on the date of advertisement of acceptance of the complete specification.
- Provided that the applicant shall not be entitled to institute any proceedings for infringement until the patent has been sealed.

Opposition to Grant of Patent

- At any time within four months from the date of advertisement of the acceptance of a complete specification.
- The applicant for the patent has wrongfully obtained the invention or any part thereof.
- The invention has been published before the priority date of the claim.
- The invention should be publicly known.

Grant and Sealing of Patents

- Where a complete specification of an application for a patent has been accepted and either the application has not been opposed and the time for the filing of the opposition has expired; or the application has been opposed and the opposition has been finally decided in favour of the applicant.
- On request made by the applicant in the prescribed form, the patent will be granted to the applicant.

Compulsory Licences

- At any time after three years from the date of the sealing of a patent.
- Availability of the product is limited or that the patented invention is not available to the public at a reasonable price.

Special Provision for Selling or Distribution

- If the Central Government is satisfied that it is necessary in public interest to sell or distribute the substance.
- It may, by itself or through any person authorized in writing by it in this behalf, sell or distribute the article or substance.

12.2.3. Indian Patents: Examples

- Khurpa for gardening and sowing.
- Underground subsoil irrigation.
- Automatic drip irrigation system.
- Improved dripper.
- Tractor for use in horticulture operation.
- Rain guard for a latex yielding tree.
- Implements for gardening and sowing.

- Device for supporting latex collection receptacle.
- Cutting and gripping device.
- Secateur.
- Water candle for automatic watering of plant and apparatus for irrigating plants.

12.2.4. What is Geographical Indications (GI)?

GI is an indication that the good which is being commercialized under that indication has originated from a definite geographical territory either as agricultural produce (e.g. Nagpur orange) or natural produce (e.g. Mussourie Rock Phosphate) or Manufactured/ handicrafts (e.g. *Banarasi saree*) or some specific local brews of tribal areas or Food product (e.g. *Agre ka petha)*

Features of GI

- GI is used in product marketing.
- Applications of GI can be moved by registered societies or NGO's or Government organizations.
- Registered GI's can not be assigned, transferred or licensed.
- Unauthorized user can not use GI for trade.
- It essentially governs a collective rather than individual right (collective intellectual property of the entire community or society).
- A trade mark which infringes GI shall be invalidated.
- Services are not covered under GI.
- Initially granted for 10 years.

Certain GI's are not Registerable

- Which are likely to hurt religious sentiments?
- Which are determined to be *generic names* of the goods in common use *(Petha)*.
- Which represents homonymous GI (e.g. Basmati rice)?
- For which trade mark is already obtained five years before the application of GI.

Possible Indian GI in Horticulture

- Darjeeling Tea (already obtained), Alleppey Green Extra Bold, Alphanso Mango/ Chelan Mango, Cardamom, Cochin Ginger, Nagpur Orange , Malabar Pepper, Rajapuri Turmeric, Ambakadan Tapioca, Alleppey Turmeric, Lakadong Turmeric, Monsoon Coffee, Mattu Gulla '-Brinjal from Uduppi, Guntur Sannam-Chilli and 'Naga Jolokia' (Naga chilli)

12.2.5. Why Biodiversity Act (BDA)?

- To protect traditional knowledge.
- To conserve biodiversity.

- Protect India's rich biodiversity and associated knowledge against their use by foreign.
- Individuals and organizations without sharing benefits

Requirements to Use Bioresources

- Indian citizens including *Vaids* and *Hakims,* growers and cultivators of biodiversity to have free access.
- Indian industries need prior intimation to SBB to obtain bioresource.
- SBB may restrict if found to violate conservation and sustainable and benefit sharing.
- All Foreign Nationals/Organizations require prior approval of National Biodiversity Act (NBA) for obtaining Biological Resources and/or Associated Knowledge (AK) for use.

12.2.6. BDA Vs PPV&FRA

Role of BDA

- Regulatory authority to protect and conserve.
- Biodiversity of all kind.
- To ensure benefit sharing to the conservers of biodiversity.

Role of PPV & FRA

- Regulatory authority to provide breeder's right.
- To protect farmers' right and ensure benefit sharing.
- To conserve genetic diversity of crops & Agro-forestry.
- To recognize and protect the rights of farmers in respect of the contribution made at any time in conserving, improving and making available plant genetic resources for the development of new plant varieties.
- To accelerate agricultural development in the country, protect plant breeders' rights, stimulate investment for research and development in public/ private sector for development of plant variety.
- Facilitate the growth of seed industry which will ensure the availability of high quality seeds and planting material to the farmers.

12.2.7. Protection of Plant Varieties and Farmers Right Act

- This act has provisions for establishment of an effective system for protection of plant varieties, right of farmers & plant breeders and to encourage development of novel plant varieties for accelerated agricultural growth & development in the country. The act was passed in 2001, implemented in 2005 and has become effective from 2007. In the first phase, 14 major crops were taken, where the process of DUS testing and grant of protection have been started & DUS testing Guidelines for 35 crops developed by ICAR have been finalised by the authority. At present registration more than 70 crops are undergoing.

Definition Related to PPV&FRA

Farmer"

- Cultivates crops by cultivating the land himself; or
- Cultivates crops by directly supervising the cultivation of land through any other person ; or
- Conserves and preserves, separately or jointly, with any person any wild species or traditional varieties, or adds value to such wild species or traditional varieties through selection and identification of their useful properties. *(Tribal people).*

Farmers' Variety

- Has been traditionally cultivated and evolved by the farmers in their fields ; or
- Is a wild relative or land race of a variety about which the farmers possess the common knowledge

Examples of Farmers' Variety

- Bikaneri Lerma Cotton of Punjab
- Taravdi local rice of Haryana
- Pissi Local Soft Wheat of MP
- Bellary Onion of AP
- East Coast Tall Coconut of TN &AP
- Nendran Banana of Kerala
- Desari Mango of UP
- Ganesh Pomegranate of Maharashtra
- Ambri Apple of Jammu & Kashmir etc.

Variety of Common knowledge

- A publicly known variety shall be considered as a matter of common knowledge.
- The variety of common knowledge covers: those marketed for cultivation as truthfully labeled, all denotified varieties, introduced foreign materials with exotic collection numbers, varieties developed prior to the Seed Act, 1965

Essentially Derived Variety (EDV)

A variety is deemed to be essentially derived from an initial variety (IV) when it is:

- predominantly derived from the IV, or from a variety that is itself predominantly derived from the IV,
- while retaining the expression of the essential characteristics that result from the genotype or combination of genotypes of the initial variety,
- it is clearly distinguishable from the IV, and
- except for differences, which result from the act of derivation, it conforms to the initial variety in the expression of essential characteristics that result from the genotype or combination of genotypes of the initial variety.

Examples of EDV's

- Transgenic
- Mutant
- Tissue culture derived
- Back cross derivatives
- Others (Ploidy change)

Breeders

As per law a person or a group of persons or a farmer or a group of farmers or any institution who has bred or evolved or developed any variety.

12.2.8. Rights Provided to a Registered Variety Under PPV&FRA

- Plant Breeders' Rights
- Researchers' Rights
- Farmers' Rights

Plant Breeders' Rights

- Produce or reproduce the material.
- Condition the material for propagation.
- Offer the material for sale.
- Market the material.
- Distribute the material.
- Import the material (Seed is produced in foreign country).
- Export the material.
- Stock the material for any of the purposes described above.
- In case of extent varieties- if breeder does not stake claim then rights will go to Central/State Government.

Researchers' Rights

- Can use any of the variety registered under this Act by any person using such variety for conducting experiment or research.
- The use of a variety by any person as an initial source variety for the purpose of creating other varieties.
- Provided that: authorization of the breeder of a registered variety is required where repeated use of such variety as parental line is necessary for commercial production of such other newly developed variety.

Farmers Rights

- Right to save, use, exchange, share and sell farm produce of a protected variety, except sell of branded seed.
- Farmers' recognized as breeders, conservers, preservers and cultivator of traditional varieties.

- Farmers' varieties can also be registered.
- Farmers exempted from payment of fees in any proceedings.
- Protected from acts of innocent infringement.
- To be compensated for lower yields than the claims made .

Community Rights

- Recognition of the role of traditional communities in conserving and preserving genetic resources of land races and wild relatives.
- Compensation for contribution of village or local communities in evolution of a variety.
- Compensation to be determined by Plant Variety Protection (PVP) authority and deposited in gene fund.
- Breeder must inform about the use of genetic material conserved by tribal/ rural families.

Duration of protection

- The registration issued under section 23 shall be valid for nine years in case of trees and vines.
- It will be valid for six years in the case of other crops.
- They can be reviewed and renewed for the remaining period on payment of such fees that will be fixed subject to a maximum of 18 years (9+9) from registration for trees and vines 15 years (6+9) from registration for crop plants.

Registration of Plant Varieties

What can be registered?

- Extent varieties
- New varieties
- Any Farmers' variety
- Any genera or species notified by GOI's official gazette

Extent variety

- Means a variety available in India which is notified under section 5 of the Seed Act, 1966; or
- Farmers' variety; or a variety about which there is common knowledge; or any other variety which is in public domain;

Requirement for Registration

A new variety shall be registered under this Act if it conforms to the criteria

- Novelty
- Distinctness

- Uniformity
- Stability

Novelty

- If, at the date of filing of the application the propagating or harvested material of such variety has not been sold in India, earlier than one year outside India, in the case of trees or vines earlier than six years, or, in any other case, earlier than four years before the date of filing such application.
- Trial of a new variety will not effect novelty (but seeds should not be sold or disposed off)
- If the variety become a matter of common knowledge other than the aforesaid reason it will loose its novelty.

Distinctness

- If a variety is clearly distinguishable by at least one essential characteristic from any other variety whose existence is a matter of common knowledge in any country at the time of filing the application.

Uniformity

- If, subject to the variation that may be expected from the particular features of its propagation it is sufficiently uniform in its essential characteristics.

Stability

- If, its essential characteristics remain unchanged after repeated propagation or, in the case of a particular cycle of propagation, at the end of each such cycle

12.2.9. Denomination is Compulsory for Registration

What is denomination?

Expressed by means of letters or a combination of letters and figures written in any language

- Should not be the trademark .
- It should be known by the same name if registered under common knowledge.
- If the variety is an introduction then the same name used in the country of its original registration should be used.

Filing of Applications

- Applications should be made in respect of a variety which has a denomination.
- An affidavit that it does not contain terminator technology.
- Complete passport data of parental lines.
- Brief description of the variety to prove novelty, distinctness, uniformity and stability.

- Declaration that the genetic material for breeding/evolving/developing the variety was lawfully acquired.

Requirements for Transgenics

- For Transgenic Varieties a copy of the Genetic Engineering Approval Committee (GEAC) approval will be required.
- Approval for bio-safety clearance from Ministry of Environment and permission for commercial seed production will be required.
- If required, special test in the laboratories will be conducted for establishing the distinctiveness of the Essentially Derived Variety (EDV).

Acceptance of Application

- Application may be accepted absolutely or subject to conditions.
- It may require amendments.
- It may be rejected only after reasonable opportunity of defending it.

Advertisement of Application for Opposition

- The application will be published in the official publication of PP & VFRA for inviting oppositions.
- Any person, with in 3 months of the date of advertisement, on payment of prescribed fee, in written format in a prescribed manner.

Grounds for Opposition

- Entitled to breeder's right.
- The variety is not registerable under this act.
- Registration may not be in public interest.
- Variety may have adverse effect on environment.

Compulsory License

- At any time after 3 years from the grant of certificate
- Ground for appeal.
- Reasonable quantity of propagating material is not available at reasonable price.
- Any person can appeal for the grant of licence.
- Authority will ensure: nature of variety, price of seed and measures taken by the breeder to meet the public requirement capability of the applicant in marketability of propagule.

Fees Associated with Plant Variety Registration

- Application Fee
- DUS testing fee
- Annual maintenance fee

The annual fee shall be uniform for the extended period of the registration and be payable in advance in single installment.

Benefit Sharing

After registration of a variety,authority will publish the contents of certificate and invite claims of benefit sharing.

Who can claim?

- Any person who is Indian citizen, GI or NGO.
- Opposition for counter claim by the breeder.
- Disposal is must: either grant or reject benefit money.

How much benefit share?

- Authority will decide benefit share depending on: extent & nature of use of genetic resources in the derivation of new variety

12.2.10. PPV&FRA vs GI Registration

1. Most relevant to plant breeders and seed industry.	Most relevant to traditional growers producers/ commodity traders.
2. Protection of a variety for its commercialization (sell of seed).	Protection for marketing of produce.
3. Breeder/licensee can market.	Only registered growers can market.
No such specificity.	Related to specific qualities of a geographic location.
For a plant variety which is associated with GI, GI registration and variety protection is equally important	
1. Seed of basmati rice can be sold by anybody.	Any person can sell anything as basmati.
2. Seed of basmati rice can be sold by anybody.	Any person can sell anything as basmati.
3. No liability for benefit sharing.	A basmati rice grown in non basmati area can be sold as basmati.
4. For exploitation of useful genes, no royalty to be paid.	Synonym can be used for trade (dehradun rice, Tarawadi rice etc..

12.2.11. Future Issues

- A coordination will be required among the agencies implementing PPV&FR Act, 2001, Environmental Protection Act, Biodiversity Act, Seed Act, Patent Act and Bio-Safety Regulations.
- What are the possibilities and procedures if a gene or event or step of biotechnological research is patented and transferred to a plant variety and submitted for Plant Breeder Rights under PPV&FRA?.
- For such transgenic varieties how the Researchers Rights will work?.
- How infringement will work if accidentally or naturally gene escape to the neighbouring crop variety?.

- For essentially derived variety what shall be the minimum genetical difference required to establish distinctiveness.
- The methods for special tests are to be standardized which should be repeatable, reliable and reproducible.
- Weather the transgenic variety will affect on Farmers' Rights in respect of conservation, preservation of plant genetic resources and on farm biodiversity?.

12.2.12. Biosafety and IPR

What is Biosafety: The policies and procedures adopted to ensure the safe application of modem biotechnology for human welfare.

Biosafety Concerns:

Food safety and nutrition

- Allergenic reaction (product of transgene)
- Resistance to antibiotic (product of marker gene)

Environmental safety

- Transgene escape
- Genetic erosion
- Development of resistance in insect-pest
- *Evolution of super weeds* Social and ethical issues

Competent Authorities

- The Institute Biosafety Committee (IBSC)
- The Review Committee on Genetic Manipulation (RCGM)
- The Monitoring and Evaluation Committee (MEC)
- The Genetic Engineering Approval Committee (GEAC)
- The Recombinant DNA Advisory Committee (RDAC)
- The State Biosafety Coordination Committee (SBCC)
- The District Level Committee (DLC)

Guidelines for Toxicity Evaluation of Transgenic Seeds

- Acute oral toxicity test in Rat
- Sub-chronic (90) days oral toxicity test in Rat
- Primary skin irritation test in Rabbit
- Irritation of mucous membrane test in Rabbit
- Skin sensitization test in Guinea Pigs
- Sub-chronic oral toxicity test in Goats (90 days)

12.2.13. Information's Related to Patenting

A book "Patenting in Biotechnology: Patent information on Internet" by Biotechnology Patent Cell, Department of Biotechnology, Ministry of Science & Technology, New Delhi, India contains several useful sites. Important web sites are:

- www.uspto.gov (US)
- www.euoropean-patent-office.org (European)
- www.patent.gov.uk fUKJ www.ipo-miti.go.jp (Japan)
- www.wipo.org (IPO)
- www.pctgazette.wipo.int (PCT)

12.3. US Patents Awarded for Selected Vegetable Crop

Crop/year	Patent no.	Brief description about invention (product/process)
Asparagus		
2006	6994874	A skin whitening composition includes an extract of asparagus obtained by sequentially exposing the asparagus to two or more solvents.
2006	7025995	Herbal synergistic formulation comprises plant extracts for treatment of acute and chronic stomach ulcers.
2006	7014872	Disease preventive nutraceutical herbal formulation(s) for diabetics. Formulation comprises seed powders mixture from selected genus including *Asparagus*.
2005	6914075	The invention provides cystine derivatives, which may be in a free form, a salt form, a solvate form.
2005	6881425	Neutraceutical herbal formulation for women, and lactating mothers. Formulation comprises roasted seed powders mixture from selected genus including *Asparagus*.
2002	6386778	A dispensing system for a multi-component product.
1990	4963370	A process for producing a proteinous material.
1951	2559625	Isolation of an organic sulfur compound from asparagus.
1936	2052219	Isolation of vitamin concentrates and process of making the same.
Bittergourd		
2006	7014872	Health protective, promotive and disease preventive nutraceutical herbal formulation(s) for diabetics and a process for its preparation.
2005	6964786	Novel oil extracted from the seeds for topical application to a body of mammal and used as anti-inflammatory, anti-arthritic, vasculodilatory and wound healing agent.
2005	6852695	A water soluble extract (MC6), methods for its preparation and methods for its use in the treatment of hyperglycemic disorders.
2005	6911577	Methods and compositions for modulating development and defense responses and nucleotide sequences encoding defense in proteins.
2005	6960348	A novel cosmetic preparation can be obtained by incorporating bitter gourd fruit and leaves into generic paraffin and cosmetic clay.
2004	6831162	A novel and highly effective hypoglycemic protein called polypeptide-k, extracted, which is useful in the treatment of diabetes mellitus.

2004	-	The invention is directed to secreted and transmembrane polypeptides and to nucleic acid molecules encoding those polypeptides.
2004	-	Novel nucleic acids, novel cathepsin V-like polypeptide sequences encoded by these nucleic acids and their uses.
2004	6800726	Isolation of nucleic acids and their encoded polypeptides that are involved in enhancing the essential amino acid content.
2004	6673988	Isolation of nucleic acid fragment encoding a lipase.
2003	-	Pharmaceutical products are provided comprising EC progenitors for use in methods for regulating angiogenesis.
2003	-	Variant immunoglobulins, particularly humanized antibody polypeptides along with methods for their preparation and use.
2003	6593514	The preparation and use of nucleic acid fragments encoding plant fatty acid modifying enzymes associated with modification of the delta-9 position of fatty acids, in particular, formation of conjugated double bonds are disclosed.
2003	6562379	Methods of inducing weight loss and treating adult-onset diabetes in a mammal by administering to isolated lectin. Lectin pharmaceutical compositions are also disclosed.
2002	6379718	Novel herbal extracts provide potent efficacy in the treatment of acne and furuncle. The formulated extracts are from either the whole plant or parts of the plant.
2000	6042829	Cytotoxic biotherapeutic agents effective for treating certain types of cancer in humans. This comprises the TP-3 murine monoclonal antibody chemically conjugated to pokeweed antiviral protein.
1999	5900240	An edible composition comprising a mixture of at least two herbs selected from the bitter gourd and eggplant. The herbal mixtures are useful as dietary supplements including humans suffering from diabetes mellitus.
1999	5929047	An anti-viral agent comprising as the effective component, an alkali extract of mangroves, bitter gourd and *Aspalathus linearis* belonging to *Leguminosae* family.
1996	-	Baits for diabroticine beetles are microspherical particles containing a homogeneous mixture of a toxicant for diabroticine beetles and a feeding stimulant in a binder containing a gelatin and a gum.
1996	5484889	A protein, in particular MAP 30, obtainable from both the fruit and seeds or produced by recombinant means useful for treating tumors and HIV infections is disclosed.
1990	4958009	Immunotoxins comprising a cytotoxic moiety and monoclonal antibodies, which bind to human ovarian cancer tissue. Methods of killing human ovarian cancer cells, retarding the growth of human ovarian cancer tumors in mammals or extending the survival of mammals carrying human ovarian cancer tumors are claimed.
1989	4795739	A method of inhibiting expression of HIV antigens in human blood cells infected with HIV. The infected cells are exposed to a plant protein or glycoprotein, such as trichosanthin or momorcharin.
1989	4869903	A method of inhibiting HIV replication in and cellular proliferation of HIV-infected cells.
1983	4368149	A protein hybrid having cytotoxicity obtained by covalently bonding an immunoglobulin or its fragment, which is capable of binding

		selectively to an antigen possessed by a cell to be destroyed, to a protein.
Cabbage		
2004	6825321	Invention of thermogenic genes (*SfUCPa* and *SfUCPb*) derived from skunk cabbage.
1994	5288626	A method for increasing the proportion of mutants in a first plant species having a recognized and established phenotype.
Pepper		
2005	6919095	A method of providing an essential oil extracts (capsaicinoid and terpene).
2004	6689399	An anti-inflammatory composition for treatment of joint and muscle pain through transdermnal delivery of a capsacinoid in conjunction with glucosamine.
2003	6,517,832	A prophylactic treatment for the human malady clinically (migraine headache) by daily prescribed dosage of a first formulation, which is derivatives from beet root, powder, watercress, celery, dandelion, capsicum and artichoke extract.
2003	6632839	A method and formulation for sterilizing and disinfecting surfaces, and for killing bacteria on contact, particularly adapted for sterilization and disinfecting food and meat stuffs, and for food and meat processing equipment and facilities.
2003	6523298	A method for exterminating existing infestations of ants, termites, insects or other living organisms in structures, soils and other materials using a *Capsicum*-containing killing solution in either a liquid or vapor form.
-	7097867	A process for obtaining oleoresin of improved color and pungency.
2002	7097867	A cancer cell growth suppressor or a cell differentiation inducer, which contains as an effective component a water-soluble component from *Capsicum*.
2001	-	This invention relates to the novel improvements of pungency factors of *Capsicum* in particular the capsaicinoids and intermediates of phenyl propanoid pathway leading to capsaicinoid biosynthesis.
2000	6143349	Distinct and stable cultivars of no-heat Jalapeno peppers are disclosed. Non-pungent Jalapeno cultivars in which substantially all the fruits produce no capsaicin.
2000	6074687	Principal components of paprika, red pepper, pungent chili, or other plants of the genus *Capsicum* containing carotenoid pigments are simultaneously extracted and concentrated with an edible solvent in a series of mixing and high temperature and pressure mechanical pressing steps.
2000	6159474	A repellant composition for repelling both domesticated and wild animals which comprises between 0.05% and 2% by weight of an essential oil of either black pepper or *Capsicum*.
2000	6069173	Insecticidal compositions comprising a synthetic surfactant and capsaicin or other capsaicinoid exhibit synergistic effects against numerous insects.
2000	6060060	Analgesic compositions obtained from the fruit and therapeutic uses of this analgesic composition.
1999	5945580	Polynucleotides of hemicellulase gene and compositions and its uses in controlling plant development and other characteristics.

1999	5910512	A water-based topical analgesic and method of application wherein the analgesic contains capsicum, capsicum oleoresin and/or capsaicin. This analgesic is applied to the skin to provide relief for rheumatoid arthritis and osteoarthritis.
1998	5773075	Principal components of paprika, red pepper, pungent chili, or other plants of the genus *Capsicum* containing carotenoid pigments are simultaneously extracted and concentrated with an edible solvent.
1998	5811640	The novel variety (JZA) of *Capsicumchinense* is the product of an organized pedigree breeding program.
1997	5599803	Insecticidal compositions, comprising normally-employed insecticides but comprising also an effective activity-enhancing amount of capsaicin or other capsaicinoid.
1997	5698191	Non-lethal bio-repellent composition comprising a carrier, a bio-repellent amount of capsicum oleoresin, and an amount of a saponin.
1990	4931277	Medicaments for treatment of alcoholic toxicomania comprise at least one extract of vegetable origin, particularly those obtained by maceration, decoction and/or infusion in an aqueous alcoholic solvent of *Capsicum* and/or bark or wood of *Populus poplars*.
1986	4592912	A composition for the prevention and relief of muscular aches and pains, aches caused by tension such as headaches and backaches and aches and pain caused by inflamed muscles and inflammation surrounding muscles.
1953	2636824	Spice substance and method of its preparation.
Cauliflower		
1998	5710364	A novel cruciferous plant containing a large quantity of carotene even in those parts where a conventional cruciferous plant contains little carotene.
1997	5629175	Novel constructs are provided for expression of physiologically active mammalian proteins in plant cells, either in culture or under cultivation.
1971	3578466	Pickled vegetable product.
Coccinia		
2006	7014872	A health protective and disease preventive nutraceutical herbal formulation(s) for diabetics. The formulation comprises the base product of microwave roasted seed powders mixture from selected genus including *Coccinia*.
1999	5856487	A process for isolating berberine from plants.
1995	5466455	Processes for polyphase fluid extraction, active therapeutic components from parts of selected medicinal plants, which have been identified as chemotaxonomically.
Coriander		
2003	6579543	A composition for topical application to an animal's skin for relief from a variety of symptoms caused by medical conditions or physical injuries.
2002	6365175	Edible compositions containing petroselinic acid are used for the preparation of food compositions or food supplements and used as anti-inflammatory compositions.

2000	6017373	An artificial firelog which contain 2% to about 6% sub. weight coriander seed added to create a crackling sound that mimics the sounds produced during the burning of natural logs.
1999	5959131	A nutritionally superior fat for food compositions, which comprises triglycerides containing cis-asymmetric monounsaturated fatty acids.
1995	5430134	A process for producing lipids containing the fatty acid namely, petroselinic acid.
1993	5256405	A stick deodorant composition that has active antibacterial constituents consisting essentially of natural materials. The active antibacterial constituents include coriander oil.
1972	3637859	The coriander oil has been used for the fragrance.
1970	3527827	The monocyclic terpenes were made by this process from the seeds of coriander.
1963	3082095	Method for dust proving of an edible, dry, finely divided product and the resulting product.
1925	1523840	The oil is used in preparation of tooth pest.
1879	222187	Coriander seeds are used in preparation of medicated herbal beverages.
Cucumber		
2004	527165	Cucumber sandwich.
2004	6765130	Seeds of inbred line (8D-5079) and to methods for producing a cucumber plant, either inbred or hybrid.
2000	6084152	A transgenic plant that produces high levels of superoxide dismutase (SOD) and to a method for producing the transgenic plant.
1997	5623066	A DNA fragment which encodes the coat protein of cucumber mosaic virus strain c (CMV-C), the method of preparing it, its use to develop transgenic plants.
1997	5654414	Chemically regulatable DNA sequences capable of regulating transcription of an associated DNA sequence in plants or plant tissues.
1989	4822949	Production of F_1 hybrid seeds and a method wherein the pollen-parent bears only male flowers and thus lacks the capability to bear fruits.
1909	915186	Pickles from fruits.
Eggplant		
2006	6984725	A method for the separation of a triglycoalkaloid from roots.
2006	7078063	A water-soluble extract from *Solanum* genus consists essentially of at least 60%-90% of solamargine and solasonine.
2006	7012172	Methods for interfering with expression of the genes in plant cells by using replicating recombinant viral vectors.
2004	6753462	Transgenic plants over-expressing a transgene encoding a calcium-binding protein or peptide (CaBP).
2003	6639050	A new approach in the field of plant gums is described which presents a new solution to the production of hydroxyproline (Hyp)-rich glycoproteins (HRGPs), repetitive proline-rich proteins (RPRPs) and arabinogalactan-proteins (AGPs).
2002	6369296	Nucleic acid vectors may be used as expression vectors or for achieving viral induced gene silencing (VIGS) of a target gene.
2002	453238	Eggplant soap.

2002	6483012	Use of the promoter region of the *DefH9* gene of *Anthirrhinum majus* or of a promoter of a homologous gene displaying the same expression pattern and characteristics for the establishment of parthenocarpy or female sterility in plants.
2001	6207881	Control of fruit ripening through genetic control of ACC synthase synthesis.
2001	6225528	Pathogen-resistant transgenic plants and methods of making the plants.
2000	6072105	Transgenic plants along with improved culture media and methods enabling efficient regeneration of shoots from cultured explants.
2000	6043409	The cDNA and genomic DNA encoding the ACC oxidase of broccoli are provided along with recombinant materials containing antisense constructs of these DNA sequences to permit control of the level of ACC oxidase.
2000	6133505	Nucleotide sequences produced by mutation of C1 nucleotide sequences present in a pathogenic geminivirus genome in plants with one or more mutations capable of producing a dominant negative phenotype for the replication of the pathogenic virus.
2000	6023013	Transgenic plants and transformed host cells, which express modified *cry3B* genes with enhanced toxicity to Coleopteran insects.
1999	5955652	Nucleic acid sequences for ethylene insensitive, *EIN* loci and corresponding amino acid sequences.
1999	5900240	An edible composition comprising a mixture of at least two herbs selected from the group consisting of *Syzygium cumini*, *Gymnema sylvestre*, *Momordica charantia* and *Solanum melongena*. The herbal mixtures are useful as dietary supplements, particularly humans suffering from diabetes mellitus.
2000	6156956	ACC synthase of higher plants are coded by multigene families; only certain members of these families are responsible for various plant development characteristics affected by ethylene.
1998	5723766	ACC synthases of higher plants are coded by multigene families; only certain members of these families are responsible for various plant development characteristics effected by ethylene.
1998	5744334	A *Blec* plant promoter sequence and a method of transforming plants with a *Blec* promoter-gene.
1997	5614408	A hybridoma cell line produces and secretes a monoclonal antibody, which selectively binds to the glycoalkaloids of potatoes, tomatoes, and eggplants, as well as their corresponding aglycones.
1997	5627216	A composition for the treatment of hemorrhoids. The composition effectively reduces swelling and pain in the anal area is formed by mixing powdered eggplant leaves and boiling virgin olive oil in a covered container for approximately 30 minutes.
1997	5674701	A process for identifying a plant having disease tolerance, comprising administering to a plant an inhibitory amount of ethylene and screening for ethylene insensitivity.
1996	5589623	A method for control of ethylene biosynthesis in plants, comprising a vector containing codons for a functional heterologous polypeptide having AdoMetase activity.
1990	4921804	An enzyme preparation having specific bilirubin degrading activity. Specific plant sources include eggplant, tomato and potato.

Garlic		
2003	6511674	A composition of a garlic extract solution having a concentration greater than 10% by weight of a garlic extract.
2003	6641836	A dietary composition and method for enhancing immune response and improving the overall health of canines.
2002	6468571	A method for processing fresh garlic, which will not leave an unpleasant odor.
2002	12761	A cultivar (Melany), characterized by early harvesting of the plant, high yield of bulbs, disease-free vegetation.
2001	12272	A cultivar (Angelique), characterized by the presence of flower escape, bigger-sized bulbs, vigorous foliage.
2001	6270803	An orally administrable formulation for the controlled release of granulated garlic.
1999	5913729	Efficient methods for cultivating garlic plants.
1998	5746024	Large quantities of true seeds are obtained from garlic using a process that involves the growing of a garlic parent plant from a virus-free garlic propagule under virus-free conditions.
1977	4022923	A method of processing garlic to form a composition of matter effected by a stable emulsion for the retention of flavor thereof and to permit freezing of the same.
1966	3258343	The process of dry and powdered garlic from row garlic.
1951	2554088	A process by which the cloves of garlic are treated in such a manner that this servers as a very good antibiotic toward both gram positive and gram negative bacteria.
1949	2490424	The extract of garlic is an ingredient of carminatives.
Moringa		
2006	7070817	An herbal composition comprising extract of plant, for treating or alleviating of vascular headaches, neurological conditions and neurodegenerative diseases.
2005	6858588	A novel nitrile glycoside of Formula I named NIAZIRIDIN and to analogues and derivatives.
2005	6890565	A process for preparing proteins that can act as effective coagulants in the treatment and purification of contaminated water.
2004	6780441	A pharmaceutical or medicinal preparation, which comprises a mixture of herbs including moringa.
2004	6750256	Methods and compositions based upon natural aromatic aldehydes, which may be used as pesticides.
2003	6667047	Cosmetic compositions with enhanced slip and/or break strength are described, said compositions comprising ultra-stable moringa oils, or its derivatives.
2003	6517861	An herbal dietary supplement composition for lactating mothers, comprising the required quantum of one or more herbs.
2002	6440437	A skin health enhancing soft wet wipe or wipe-type product, such as a baby wipe, hand wipe or faces wipe.
2002	6383495	A novel herbal formulation useful for the treatment of skin disorders and comprising two or more plant extracts including from moringa.
2001	6217874	A fat composition for cosmetic or pharmaceutical emulsion products.
2001	6271001	Certain cultured plant cell gums, including those produced in suspension culture.

2001	6287581	A superior skin barrier enhancing body facing material, such as a body side-liner.
2000	6080401	The curative action of drugs, including herbal remedies, allopathic remedies, and periodontal remedies, is enhanced and accelerated by administering such drugs.
1999	5994404	A baby or infant composition, which comprises one or more nutrient materials and, as a supplement, nervonic acid.
Okra		
2002	6379719	Use of at least one protein fraction extracted from *Hibiscus esculentus* seeds and to a cosmetic composition containing such a fraction.
2000	6124248	Mucilages and their extracts those are effective as water-soluble, non-toxic, biodegradable, environmentally benign lubricants and/or coolants for a variety of industrial and machining purposes.
1998	5851963	A new organic lubricant for lubricating and cooling tools.
1980	4233075	A food base preservative solution made from okra, water and a food preservative agent. Useful for material surfaces such as finished furniture surfaces, painted surfaces, glass surfaces, vinyl plastic surfaces.
1979	4154822	Polysaccharide substances-essentially consisting of rhamnose, galactose and galacturonic acid and preferably derived by extraction and purification of okra plant.
1960	2932610	Brightening material of plant origin for electroplating
1936	2060336	Composition of matter containing mucilaginous extracts from plants
1865	51251	Improvement in the manufacture of paper.
1951	8184	Making hemp from okra
Onion		
2002	6468565	A cycloalliin-enriched onion extract.
1926	1612255	Hair lotion and its method of preparation.
1924	1492823	The ointment made with the onion extract.
Pea		
2005	6916787	A method for producing haemin proteins.
2002	6344600	A method for producing human hemoglobin proteins.
1987	4677065	Seeds of a grain legume of relatively low lipid content are processed under conditions found to yield an improved protein isolate, which is well suited for human consumption.
Radish		
2004	6686517	Plants containing increased levels of anthocyanins.
2002	6428822	A mixed substance extracted from carrot and whole radish for treating hypertension, constipation, detoxification and boosting immune system.
1998	5736144	A medicinal extract from boiling radish leaves for increasing fertility in mammalian males and for use as an anti-microbial or anti-inflammatory agent
1997	5650559	Male sterile plants possessing Ogura cytoplasms derived from a Japanese radish with plants having pure nuclei of genus *Brassica*.
1994	5324707	A method for the *in vitro* application of bioregulator compounds.

Tomato		
2006	015277	Materials and methods for providing genetically engineered resistance in plants to geminivirus, using polynucleotides containing all or a portion of a replication associated protein (*Rep*) gene of TYLCV.
2004	6806399	A genotype-independent method for efficiently carrying out pollen-mediated transformation of maize, tomato or melon is described.
2002	6429299	Nucleotide sequences *TDET1* (*HP-2*) gene. The sequences, if modified, result in a light hypersensitive phenotype. Vectors and uses for the production of transgenic plants.
2002	6340748	A tomato promoter (*LeExp-1*), which can direct a high level of fruit-specific expression.
2001	6252141	An isolated complementary and genomic DNA segment encoding lycopene cyclase of the *B* locus of tomato.
2001	6239331	A method for enhancing the expression of a tomato phytoene synthese gene in a plant, while avoiding or reducing co-suppression.
2001	6180854	Determinate, delayed-ripening hybrids cherry tomato plants, derived from a determinate, non-ripening parental line.
2001	6207881	Recombinant materials for the production of tomato ACC synthase.
2000	6060648	Seed-less tomatoes developed by crossing a tomato plant containing at least one parthenocarpic gene as the male parent with a male sterile tomato plant containing at least one parthenocarpic gene as the female parent.
2000	069389	A method for breeding tomato plants that produce tomatoes with reduced fruit water content.
1999	5871574	A tomato pigment is obtained by centrifuging a treated mass of tomato.
1997	845539	A protein expansion (*Ex1*) from tomato, melon and strawberry that is highly abundant and specifically expressed in ripening fruit.
1999	6414226	A new and distinct inbred tomato line (FDR 16-2045).
1999	5952546	Tomato plants exhibiting a delayed ripening phenotype, comprise of a T-DNA insert comprising a tomato *Acc* synthase gene.
1998	5821398	An isolated nucleotide sequence encoding an inducible soft fruit promoter, particularly the alcohol dehydrogenase-2 promoter.
1998	5824873	A method for modifying fruit ripening characteristics in plants and is particularly suitable for modification of tomato plants.
1998	5817913	A method for breeding tomato plants that produce tomatoes having superior taste characteristics including the step
1997	5614408	Hybridoma cell lines, which produces and secretes a monoclonal antibody that selectively binds to the glycoalkaloids of potatoes, tomatoes, and eggplants and their corresponding aglycones.
1997	5656474	Two osmotic stress- and ABA-responsive members of the endochitinase gene family has been isolated and identified from leaves of drought-stressed *Lycopersicon chilense* plants.
1997	5700506	A method by which the shelf life of fresh tomato pieces can be substantially increased.
1996	5585542	An isolated DNA sequence encodes at least part of the tomato enzyme endopolygalacturonase PG1 beta-subunit, which may be used to produce genetically engineered tomato plants with modified ripening characteristics.

1996	5495071	A method for producing genetically transformed plants exhibiting toxicity to Coleopteran insects.
1996	5489745	Novel tomato lines having disease resistance, and producing a fruits having a weight of at least 140 g with high pigment and reduced blossom end scar.
1996	5536653	Promoters isolated from potato, which cause expression of a gene of choice in tomato; tomato plant cells and plants containing them.
1996	5569831	Methods of creating transgenic tomatoes containing a lowered level of polygalacturonase (beta-subunit) isoform 1.
1996	4835339	A method for forming haploid male sterile tomato plants and doubled haploid true breeding lines.
1996	5569829	A method for making fruit (particularly tomatoes) having increased solids content, comprises cultivating fruit-bearing plants in which expression of genes homologous to pTOM36 is partially inhibited.
1995	479384, 5413937	A process for the inhibition of the production of a gene product in a plant cell.
1995	479384	Fertile hybrid seed or hybrid seed comprising fertile and sterile seed using male-sterile plants created by employing molecular techniques to manipulate anti-sense gene and other genes that are capable of controlling the production of fertile pollen in plants.
1995	5387757	Fruit, especially tomatoes, having lowered expression of fruit-softening enzymes caused by antisense gene expression.
1995	-	Chimeric isopentenyl transferase (*ipt*) gene constructs were prepared and introduced into tomato plants via *Agrobacterium* mediated transformation.
1993	5254800	DNA constructs comprise a DNA sequence homologous to some of the gene encoded by the clone pTOM36. Fruit from the transformed plants are expected to have modified ripening properties.
1991	5073676	The antisense mRNA produced delays softening of fruit, in particular tomatoes.
1990	509673	A new tomato cultivar with homozygous recessive genetic factor, which confers the ability to bear fruit that accumulate sucrose.
1990	4940839	A method for producing a hybrid plant of a wild species and a cultivated species of *Lycopersicon* using protoplast fusion of the wild and cultivated species.
1980	PP4539	A new hybrid tomato plant characterized as novel when compared to Walter, the most similar variety to it, by uniform crop characteristics, low grading loss, early maturity and multiple disease resistance and tolerance.
1974	3826851	Process for enhancing fresh tomato flavor in tomato products.

Section-III

13

Vegetable Crop Varieties/Hybrids

13.1. Bulb Vegetables

13.1.1. Garlic

Name	Remarks
Agrifound Parvati	Developed through selection from an exotic collection obtained from Hong Kong market. The variety is long day type and suitable for cultivation in mid and high hill of northern states. It has medium storability and suitable for export.
Agrifound White	This variety has been developed from local collection obtained from Sharif area of Bihar from NHRDF, Nasik. It is recommended for cultivation in the areas where there is not much problem of purple blotch or *Stemphylium* blight in *rabi* season. This variety is recommended for the cultivation in Punjab, tarai region of Uttaranchal, Bihar, Madhya Pradesh (excluding Eastern areas) and Maharashtra.
Bhima Omkar	This variety has been developed through clonal selection of the local material obtained from Nalanda, Bihar. The bulbs are medium in size, compact and white in colour, 18-20 cloves per bulb having 41.2 %TSS. An Average yield is 10.76 t/ha. This variety has been recommended for cultivation in Gujarat, Haryana, Rajasthan and Delhi.
Bhima Purple	It has been developed through clonal selection of the local material obtained from Angul, Orissa. The bulbs are medium in size, compact and purple in colour having 16-20 cloves per bulb, TSS 33.6% and allicin @ 2.9 mg/g (fresh weight basis) and 9.6 mg/g (dry weight basis). An average yield is 6.89 t/ha. This variety has been identified for commercial cultivation in Delhi, UP, Haryana, Bihar and Punjab, Maharashtra, Karnataka and Andhra Pradesh.
GODAVARI	This variety has been developed by MPKV, Rahuri in the year 1987. Bulbs are of medium size with pinkish white colour and have 22-25 cloves per bulb. It matures in 140-145 days after planting and average yield is 10.0-10.5 t/ha.
Gujarat Garlic-4	This variety has been recommended for release in 2009 for Zone IV. The material has been developed through clonal selection of a local clonal selection from the local material. The bulbs of this variety are medium in size, compact and white in colour.
Jamnagar	It is popular in Gujarat, Maharastra, Andhra Pradesh and Madhya Pradesh.

Ooty-1	This variety has been developed at Horticultural Research Station, Ooty of Tamil Nadu Agricultural University, and Coimbatore. The bulbs are bigger in size with dull white colour. Each bulb on an average possesses 20 –25 cloves. It potential yield is 17 t/ha in crop duration of 120 – 130 days.
Rajalle Gaddi	This is slightly bigger size variety grown in south India.
Sheta	This variety has been developed by MPKV, Rahuri. The bulbs are bigger in size and silvery white in colour with an average of 25-26 cloves per bulb. It matures with 130-135 days and average yield is 10.0-10.5 t/ha.
Yamuna Safed	It is developed from local collection obtained from Delhi (Azadpur) and developed from NHRDF, Nasik. The variety is tolerant to insect- pests and diseases like purple blotch, *Stemphylium* blight and onion thrips.
Yamuna Safed-2	It is developed from local collection obtained from Karnal area of Haryana, and developed from National Horticulture and Developed Foundation (NHRDF), Nasik. It is recommended for northern India.
Yamuna Safed-3	The variety has been developed by mass selection from a local collection obtained from Tamil Nadu. Bulbs are creamy-white and big sized (5-6 cm diameter), having 15-16 cloves/bulb. It contains total soluble solids 38-42% and dry matter 39-43%. The average yield is 17.5-20 t/ha. It is suitable for export purposes and is medium store. It performs very well in northern and central India. The variety has been released in 1999 by Central Varietal Release Committee for growing all over the country.
Yamuna Safed-4	This variety is developed by mass selection from local collection obtained from Badlapur, Jaunpur district of U.P. by NHRDF. The plants are vigorous with wider green leaves. The bulbs are silvery white, bigger sized (3.5-4 cm) and have 25-30 cloves per bulb, TSS is 40-42% and dry matter is 41-42%. An average yield is 17.5-20.0 t/ha. The variety is recommended for growing in North India.
Yamuna Safed-5	Selection made from the collection maintained at NHRDF Salaru, Karnal. Recommended for release and cultivation in the States of Delhi, Uttar Pradesh, Haryana, Bihar, Punjab, Rajasthan, Gujarat, Maharashtra, Karnataka and Andhra Pradesh conditions. Suitable for processing through dehydration. Tolerant to environmental stress conditions. Tolerance to stemphylium blight and purple blotch disease. An average yield is 17.0-17.5 t/ha.

13.1.2. Onion

Name	Remarks
Agrifound Red	The variety has been developed by National Horticultural Research and Development Foundation (NHRDF), Nasik. This variety comes in multiplier onion group.
Agrifound Rose	This is small onion of pickling type. It is widely grown in Andhra Pradesh and Karnataka for export. It is grown in *kharif* in Andhra Pradesh and in all the three seasons in Karnataka.

Agrifound Dark Red	The variety has also been developed by National Horticultural Research and Development Foundation (NHRDF), Nasik from a local stock of kharif onion. It is moderately pungent and suitable for growing in kharif season.
Agrifound Light Red	It is also developed by National Horticultural Research and Development Foundation (NHRDF), Nasik and most suited for rabi season.
Agrifound White	This variety has been developed by National Horticultural Research and Development Foundation, Nasik. It is a selection from local stock of white onion grown during Rabi season in Nimad area of M.P. The bulbs are globular, 4-6 cm in diameter with tight skin, silvery attractive white colour. TSS is 14-15% and good for dehydration. Crop matures in 125-130 days. An average yield is 20.0-25.0t/ha.
Arka Bindu	It is developed from local rose onion collection 'IHR 402' through mass selection and released from IIHR, Bangalore for cultivation in Karnataka region. It exclusively meets our export requirement.
Arka Kalyan	This variety was developed through mass selection at the IIHR, Bangalore from a local collection (IIHR 145) from Kalawana Taluka in Maharashtra. The variety is moderately resistant to purple blotch disease and performs very well in *kharif* season. This variety is widely grown in Bihar, Punjab, Gujarat, Haryana, Maharashtra, Karnataka and Tamil Nadu.
Arka Niketan	It was developed through mass selection from a local collection (IIHR 153) at IIHR, Bangalore It can be grown both in *rabi* and *kharif* seasons. This variety is widely grown in Maharashtra, Madya Pradesh, Karnataka and Tamil Nadu.
Arka Kirtiman	It was released from IIHR, Bangalore and developed through hybridization. Parentage is MS 65 x Sel 13-1-1. Bulbs are attractive red, uniform, globose and firm. Stores well for 4-5 months. Can be grown in both kharif and rabi seasons. TSS is 8.10%. Maturity 130 DAT. Yield potential is 40 – 45 t/ha. Identified for cultivation in southern dry zone of Karnataka.
Arka Lalima	It was released from IIHR Bangalore and developed through hybridization. Its parentage is MS 48 x Sel 14-1-1. Bulbs are attractive deep red, uniform, globose and firm. Stores well for 4-5 months. Can be grown in both kharif and rabi. TSS is10-12%. Maturity is 140 DAT. Yield is 45 – 50 t/ha. This variety is identified for southern dry zone of Karnataka.
Arka Pitamber	This is a short-day, medium-sized bulb, yellow onion and released for cultivation in Karnataka. Bulbs are uniformly yellow in colour with perfect globe shape. It is suitable for the export to the European countries, the USA and Japan. Arka Pitamber is expected to meet about 10 per cent of the requirement of yellow onion market.
Arka Pragati	It is developed at IIHR, Bangalore from a local collection IIHR-149 from Nasik and released for Karnataka state in 1984. Bulbs are attractive red, globe shaped, uniform size, thin neck, highly pungent and early maturing. It can be grown successfully during *rabi* and *kharif* seasons.

Bangalore Rose — It is a popular variety grown near Bangalore exclusively for export. Bulbs are small (2-2.5 cm), flatish round with deep red colour.

Baswant-780 — This is common big size onion grown in *Rabi* season. Bulbs are attractive red in colour, globular in shape and mildly pungent, less bolting with twins. This variety is suitable for export purposes. It is grown in *Kharif* season in Maharashtra.

Bermunda Yellow — This is yellow skin variety introduced from Philippines. It is an excellent yielder and suitable for both marketing as well as fresh consumption. This variety has no bolting but poor storability.

Brown Spanish — This variety has been developed from IARI Regional Station, Katrain (Kullu Valley), Himachal Pradesh. Bulbs are solid, attractive, reddish-brown with less pungent. It is a medium long day variety.

Bhima Raj — A dark red onion variety identified by DOGR Pune for *kharif* and late *kharif* season in the states of Maharashtra, Karnataka and Gujarat. In can be cultivated in *rabi* for immediate market in states of Rajasthan, Gujarat, Haryana and Delhi. The variety matures within 120-125 days after transplanting with absolutely no bolters with average yield ranges from 25-30 t/ha. It produces single centered bulbs with thin neck.

Bhima Red — This variety has been recommended for *rabi* season in Maharashtra and Madhya Pradesh. It has recommended for *kharif* season in Delhi, Gujarat, Haryana, Karnataka, Maharashtra, Punjab, Rajasthan and Tamil Nadu. It can also be grown in late *kharif*. Maturity is 105-110 days after transplanting during *kharif* and 110-120 DAT during late *kharif* and *rabi* seasons. The average marketable yield in *kharif* season is 19-21 t/ha, in late *kharif* season is 48-52 t/ha and it is 30-32 t/ha in *rabi* season. It can be stored up to 3 months *rabi* harvesting crop.

Bhima Super — This variety was developed from DOGR Pune which has been recommended for *kharif* season in Chhattisgarh, Delhi, Gujarat, Haryana, Karnataka, Madhya Pradesh, Maharashtra, Odisha, Punjab, Rajasthan and Tamil Nadu. It can also be grown in late *kharif* season. It is reported to have an average yield of 20-22 t/ha in *kharif* and 40 - 45 t/ha in late *kharif*. Bulbs attain maturity within 100-105 days after transplanting (DAT) in *kharif* and 110-120 days after transplanting in late *kharif*. It produces mostly single centered bulbs.

Bhima Shweta — It was identified in 2011 for commercial cultivation in Delhi, UP, Haryana, Bihar and Punjab, MP, Chhattisgarh, Orissa, Maharashtra, Karnataka and Andhra Pradesh for *rabi* season. It is also recommended for *kharif* in Chhattisgarh, Gujarat, Karnataka, Madhya Pradesh, Maharashtra, Odisha, Rajasthan and Tamil Nadu. TSS is around 11-12^{0}B and it matures within 110-20 DAT. Average marketable yield during *kharif* season is 18-20 t/ha and in *rabi* is 26-30 t/ha. Bulbs are attractive white in colour, round in shape, very less number of bolters and doubles less than 3% in *rabi* season, thin neck, TSS 11.5%. It is tolerant to thrips.

Bhima Shubra — This white onion variety has been recommended for Chhattisgarh, Gujarat, Karnataka, Madhya Pradesh, Maharashtra, Odisha, Rajasthan and Tamil Nadu for *kharif* season. It is also recommended

	for late *kharif* in Maharashtra. It matures in 110-115 DAT during *kharif* and 120-130 DAT in late *kharif*. TSS is 10-12^{0}B. It is a medium storer with a capacity to tolerate environmental fluctuation. Average marketable yield during *kharif* is 18 - 20 t/ha and during late *kharif* 36-42 t/ha.
Bhima Kiran	A light red onion variety developed from DOGR Pune identified for *rabi* season in the states of Maharashtra, Karnataka, Andhra Pradesh, Delhi, UP, Haryana, Bihar and Punjab. The variety matures in 130 days after transplanting and the average marketable yield is up to 41.5 t/ha. This variety has better storage up to 5-6 months.
Bhima Shakti	A red onion variety developed from DOGR for late *kharif* as well as *rabi* seasons in the states of Maharashtra, Karnataka, Andhra Pradesh, Delhi, UP, Haryana, Bihar, Punjab, Rajasthan, Gujarat, MP, Chhattisgarh and Orissa. Bulbs mature in 130 days after transplanting during late *kharif* and *rabi* seasons. Marketable yield during late *kharif* is 45.9 t/ha and during *rabi* 42.7 t/ha. This variety has better storage for 5-6 months.
Early Grano	It is an American variety, which produces globular bulb of yellow colour and mild pungency. It is most suitable for salad purposes. The bulb attains full size in about 95 days after transplanting compared with the bulbs of the local red varieties, which take more than 100 days to attain a reasonable size.
Hisar-2	It is developed at CCSHAU, Hisar by mass selection from indigenous material. Bulbs are bronze red and flatish globular shapes. This variety is tolerant to salinity. The variety has been recommended for cultivation in Haryana and Punjab.
Hisar Onion-3	A Selection from the local material collected from Bahadurgarh area developed at CCSHAU, Hisar. Bulb light bronze in colour with off white flesh, globular in shape, thin neck and hearting single. Leaves green and erect in habit. Moderately resistant to purple blotch and also susceptible to onion yellow dwarf virus than checks susceptible to thrips. Average yield is 31.61t/ha.
Kalyanpur Red Round	It is a popular variety of Uttar Pradesh, developed at CSAUA&T, Kalyanpur and released for the state of Uttar Pradesh. Bulbs are bonze red globular moderately pungent.
NHRDF Red-2	This variety was developed through selection made from materials collected from NBPGR, New Delhi in 1982 and improved through mass selection. Bulbs are attractive red colour, 5-6 cm diameter, size index 22-24 cm2, TSS 13-14% and dry matter 14-15%. Leaves are straight, green colored, 9-11/plant. An average yield is 30-40 t/ha.
Niphad-53	It is an improved strain of onion which has a bright scarlet red colour, developed at Nasik/Pimalgaon (Maharashtra). It is quite popular for *kharif* season cultivation.
Patna Red	Bulbs are of bronze red colour, flat to slightly flatish globular and very pungent.
Phule Samarth	This selection was made by MPKV, Rahuri for cultivation during *Kharif* and early *Rabi (Rangeda)* seasons, and has been recently released by the state government. The bulbs have dark red colour, globular round shape and thin neck. Bolting as well as double bulb per cent are less in this variety compared to other varieties.

Phule Survarna	It was developed by MPKV, Rahuri, Maharashtra and recommended during 1997. Year-round planting of this variety is possible. Bulbs are medium to big size, yellow coloured, less pungent with 11.5% TSS and suitable for export in Europe, Australia and America. Bulbs can be stored for long period (4-6 months). An average yield is 24.0 t/ha.
Phule Safed	It was developed by MPKV, Rahuri through selection from local material of Kagal and released in 1994. Bulbs are globular in shape and white colour. TSS is about 13% and bulbs are suitable for dehydration. An average yield ranged 25.0-30.0t/ha.
Punjab Naroya	It has been developed at PAU, Ludhiana, derived through selection from a line collected from Maharashtra. Bulbs are red, medium to large, round with thin neck. This variety is tolerant to purple blotch and thrips. This variety is suited for cultivation for Rajasthan, Gujarat, Haryana and Delhi.
Punjab Red Round	It is an early maturing variety, developed at PAU, Ludhiana. Bulbs are shining red, globular, medium with thin neck. This variety is suaitable in cultivations during *rabi* season for Punjab, Uttar Pradesh. and Bihar.
Pusa Madhvi	It was developed at IARI, New Delhi from a local collection, obtained from Muzaffarnagar for Indo-Gangetic plains.
Pusa Ratnar	It is selected from a hybrid cultivar introduced from the USA under the name of Granex and released from NBPGR, New Delhi. Bulbs are generally more exposed above the ground at maturity. Bulbs are bronze deep red, obovate to flat globular, less pungent and drooping neck with good storage qualities.
Pusa Red	Developed at IARI, New Delhi from an indigenous collection. Bulb is red, medium size, firm with good keeping quality. It is one of the most popular high yielding variety grown throughout the country for *rabi* season.
Pusa White Flat	This variety was developed at the IARI, New Delhi for onion growing areas of Uttar Pradesh, Bihar, Punjab, Rajasthan, Gujarat, Haryana and Maharashtra. Bulbs are attractive white, flat, medium to large and good storability.
Pusa White Round	It was developed from a local collection Line 106 at IARI, New Delhi and for onion growing areas in Uttar Pradesh, Bihar, Punjab, Rajasthan, Gujarat, Haryana and Maharashtra. The bulbs are white, roundish flat and medium size.
Spanish Brown	This is long day onion suitable for growing in hills. Bulbs are attractive brown in colour with mild pungency and good keeping quality.
Udaipur 101	This variety was developed at RAU, Rajasthan and recommended for cultivation in Rajasthan and adjoining states. Bulbs are deep red, flatish globe, TSS 12-14 per cent and sweet with less pungency. It is good for salad purpose.
Udaipur 102	This variety was developed at RAU, Rajasthan and recommended for cultivation in Rajasthan and adjoining states. Bulbs are medium to large in size and white in colour.
Udaipur 103	This variety was developed at RAU, Rajasthan and recommended for cultivation in Rajasthan and adjoining states. Bulbs are red but

	lighter than Udaipur101, oblate, globular, sweet but slightly more pungent

13.2. Cole Crops

13.2.1. Brocoli

Name	Remarks
Palam Haritia	It has been developed and released from HPKV, Palampur by mass selection. It is a sprouting broccoli with dark green upright leaves having purple reddish tinge. The heads are attain marketable stage in about 145-150 days. This variety has yield potential of 23.0-25.0 t/ha.
Palam Kanchan	It has been developed and released from HPKV, Palampur by mass selection. It is a heading broccoli with long, broad, bluish green upright leaves having prominent white midrib and veins. The head is large in size, compact, attractive yellowish green in colour. It is rich in vitamin A.
Palam Samridhi	It has been developed and released from HPKV, Palampur by mass selection. Green sprouting broccoli is tender, fresh and full of flavour, It can be consumed raw as salad, in cooked form and also be pickled. Terminal head weight is 300-400 g each.
Palam Vichitra	It has been developed and released from HPKV, Palampur by mass selection. It is a heading broccoli, medium-sized, open dark green leaves. Purple tinge is prominent on stem at seedling stage and on leaf margins at full growing stage. The head is purple and compact. The variety is rich in nutrients especially vitamins.
Pusa Broccoli KTS1	It has been developed and released from the IARI Regional Station Katrain and developed through recurrent & selection from exotic material. Heads are compact, light green with small buds weighing 250-400 g; maturity 85 95 days; Yield is 12.5 t/ha.
Punjab Broccoli-1	This variety has been identified from PAU, Ludhiana. It is suitable for salad and cooking purposes. Sprouts are compact and attractive. An average yield is 7.0 t/ha.

13.2.2. Brussels Sprouts

Name	Remarks
Hilfd Ideal	This is an introduction and recommended by IARI Regional Station, Katrain, Kullu Valley.
Jade Cross (F_1 hybrid)	Sprouts are firm, dark green, closely packed on long stems, can be grown under wide range of growing conditions.

13.2.3. Cabbage

Name	Remarks
Bajrang (BSS-50)	The hybrid has been developed at Beejo Sheetal Seeds Pvt. Ltd., Jalna. It is tolerate high temperature (up to 36°C) and resistant to fusarium wilt.

BSS-44	The hybrid has been developed at Beejo Sheetal Seeds Pvt. Ltd, Jalna. This hybrid can grow well both in cold and hot weather conditions. This hybrid is resistant to fusarium wilt.
Hari Rani Gole	It is a good hybrid for medium late maturity. It produces medium sized ball shaped dark blackish green, solid head with good wrapper leaves.
Pride of India	This variety is an introduction recommended by Dr. Y.S. Parmar University of Horticulture and Forestry, Solan. The plant type of this variety is similar to 'Golden Acre'. But it is about a week later in maturity.
Mitra	It is an early hybrid with excellent head to plant ratio. It has good field retention ability.
Pusa Drum Head	It is an important variety selected and released by IARI, Regional Station, Katrain (Kullu Valley). It is probably the earliest variety among the Drum Head Group. It also possesses field resistant to black leg.
Pusa Muketa	This is a new variety developed at IARI Regional Station, Katrain (Kullu Valley) by hybridization between EC 24855 x EC 10109. It is resistant to black rot (*Xanthomonas campestris*) and has been specially identified for the areas where this disease is a problem.
Pusa Synthetic	This variety has been developed from IARI, Regional Station, Katrain (Kullu Valley). It is an early synthetic variety.
Red Cabbage	This variety is tolerant to diamond back moth insect, which is serious pest of cabbage.
Pusa Cabbage Hybrid-1	This hybrid was developed by female parent: '83-1' –a self-incompatible inbred line male parent: an inbred line of 'Golden Acre' from IARI, Regional Station, Katrain. Heads are round, waxy and slightly serrated leaves, very compact head, covered with outer leaf. Bursting of head is very late hence very good staying capacity. This hybrid is tasty, vitamin C content 51.38 mg/100g, dry matter 7.59% and total carotenoids 0.114mg/100g. This variety is suitable for growing under low to high temperature conditions, Field resistance to black rot. An average yield is 58.8 t/ha
September	This variety is an introduction from German Democratic Republic and most popular in the Nilgiri hills. This variety is recommended for cultivation by Tamil Nadu State Department of Horticulture. It has very good keeping quality.
Sri Ganesh Gol	The hybrid has been developed at Maharashtra Hybrid Seeds Co. Ltd., Jalna and recommended for cultivation in Andhra Pradesh, Eastern Part of Madhya Pradesh and Orissa. It is resistant to yellowing. It is good transport quality.
Sudha (BSS115)	The hybrid has been developed at Beejo Sheetal Seeds Pvt. Ltd., Jalna. This hybrid is resistant to fusarium wilt.
Suvarna (BSS32)	The hybrid has been developed at Beejo Sheetal Seeds Pvt. Ltd., Jalna. This hybrid has strong smooth outer leaves.
Quisto	It is a high yielder hybrid and has ability to stand over severe hot conditions. It is good for tropical climate.

13.2.4. Cauliflower

Name	Remarks
Dania	It is developed from IARI Regional Station, Kalimpong for eastern hilly area. This variety is tolerant to the stress conditions.
Early Kunwari	It is an early variety suitable for growing in Punjab, Haryana, Himachal Pradesh and Delhi, selected by PAU, Ludhiana. This variety has been recommended for sowing from middle to the end of May.
Improved Japanese	It is an introduction form Israel. It can not tolerate hot season. It is recommended for sowing in north Indian plains from July end to early August.
Kashi Agahani	It is developed by parentage gene pool maintained at IIVR, Varanasi collected from Hazipur, Bihar. This variety has white, medium sized and compact curd. Curd shape is semi-dome intermediate stalk, petiole and leaf lamina and vigorous growing habit. Tolerant to high temperature and humid condition during vegetative growth.The variety belongs to mid maturity group. It is moderately resistant to downy mildew. An average yield is 21.5 t./ha
Kashi Kunwari	This variety is developed through family selection. This variety is characterized by semi erect, plant semi-dome shaped curd white colour, medium size curd compact, curd length 10.5-13.5 cm, curd width 10.25-12.50 curd weight (Individual) 425-500 g, curd texture fine, blanching not covered. An average yield is 20.0 t/ha.
Pusa Deepali	This has been developed through inbreeding from the local material at IARI, New Delhi and recommended for general cultivation in entire north India particularly Delhi and Punjab.Uniform curds are well protected by leaves and raciness almost absent. It is recommended for sowing from May end to early June.
Pusa Early Synthetic	It was released in 1990 by IARI, New Delhi. Plants are erect with bluish green leaves. It is suitable for early cultivation in northern and southern states. It is resistant to raciness.
Pusa Him Jyoti	It is released from IARI, New Delhi and suitable for transplanting in hill tract in the month of May and August.
Pusa Hybrid-2	It is recommended for cultivation in 1993 from IARI, New Delhi. It is resistant to downy mildew. This variety is recommended for cultivation in humid Bengal-Assam basin and Sub-humid Satluj Ganga-Alluvial Plains.
Pusa Katki	This was one of the earliest variety released from IARI, New Delhi which maturing in October-November. It is suitable for sowing the middle of May.
Pusa Sharad	The IARI Variety Release Committee had released this variety in 1999. It is suitable for cultivation in Uttar Pradesh, Punjab, Haryana, Bihar, Rajasthan and West Bengal.
Pusa Shubra	It is highly tolerant to raciness. This variety is also resistant to black rot in both field and artificial conditions.
Pusa Snowball-1	It is a derivative of the cross between EC 12013 and EC 12012 and released from IARI, Regional Station, Katrain (Kullu Valley) in 1977 by the Central Sub-Committee on Varietal Release for growing

	throughout the country where Snowball groups are grown. It is a late variety and suitable for cool season.
Pusa Snoball-2	Central Sub-committee on Varietal Release Committee, New Delhi, releases it in 1977 for general cultivation throughout the country. It is suitable for late sown conditions. This variety could not become popular because of its poor seeding ability.
Pusa Snoball K-1	This is also developed at IARI Regional Station, Katrain (Kullu Valley) and is tolerant to black rot caused by *Xanthomonas campestris*. Amongst the Snowball types, it has best quality curds which are snow white in colour and retain it even if the harvesting is delayed. It is also late by a week than Pusa Snowball 1 and 2, which will further extend the cauliflower availability period.
Pusa Synthetic	It is a mid-season variety, synthesized from 7 inbred lines with good combining ability released from IARI, New Delhi. It is suitable for planting from mid-September to late September in North India.
Pusa Meghna	This variety developed from IARI Pusa, New Delhi. This variety is extra early (September maturity), white compact medium sized curd (350-400 g). Maturity is 95 days. An average yield is 12.5 t/ha, an increase of 20% over check Pusa Early Synthetic.
Pusa Sharad	This variety is developed from IARI, Pusa New Delhi. Compact curd weight is 900 g. Crop maturity is 80 days. An average yield is 24.0 t/ha, an increase of 40% over check Pusa Synthetic.
Pusa Paushja	This variety is developed from IARI, Pusa New Delhi. This is December -January maturity group variety. Curds are compact and white. Crop maturity is 75days. An average yield is 40.0 t/ha. This variety is recommended for cultivation in Punjab, UP, Uttaranchal and Bihar.
Pusa Shukti	This variety is developed from IARI Pusa, New Delhi. This variety belongs December –January maturity group. Curds are compact and white. Crop maturity is 75days. An average yield is 44.0 t/ha.
Swarna	It can be grown from September to December in plain and around the year in the hills.
Summer King	It can be grown during summer season in northern plain.

13.2.5. Knol Khol

Name	Remarks
Early Purple Vienna	The knobs are globular round large, purple skin with light green flesh.
Early White Vienna	It is an early variety.
King of North	This variety possess flatish round knobs, large leaf sheath which well spread over the knob.
Large Green Purple	It is a late variety. It is adapted to Himachal Pradesh.
Vienna	It is a late group variety. Knobs are big in size with purple colour spot.
White Vienna	It is an early variety possessing dwarf plant.

13.3. Cucurbitaceous Vegetables

13.3.1. Bitter Gourd

Name	Remarks
Arka Harit	It is a selection from Rajasthan collection and released by IIHR, Bangalore.
Coimbatore Long	It is selection by National Seeds Corporation, New Delhi. Suitable for rainy season.
Kalyanpur Baramasi	This variety has been developed from Vegetable Research Centre, Kalyanpur (Kanpur) and suitable for cultivation throughout the year.
MDU-1	It is an induced mutant developed by gamma irradiation of local cultivar MC 103. It is early in flowering (60 days) with a sex ratio of 1:20 of female and male flowers, respectively . Fruits also contain less seed.
Priya	It is a selection from Kerala Agricultural University Vellanikkara.
Preeethi	It is a high yielding variety developed at the College of Horticulture, Vellanikkara, Kerala and recommended for release and cultivation in 1996 for Madhya Pradesh, Maharashtra, Karnataka, Tamil Nadu and Kerala.
Punjab-14	This variety has been developed through selection from local material and released by the PAU, Ludhiana. It is suitable for spring summer and rainy seasons. It has good nutritive value.
Pusa-do-Mausami	It is a selection from local collection, suitable for spring-summer and rainy seasons and released from IARI, New Delhi.
Pusa Hybrid-1	This hybrid has been developed and released from IARI, New Delhi. Fruits are suitable for making vegetable, pickles and also for dehydration purposes.
Pusa Hybrid-2	This hybrid has been developed and released from IARI, Pusa, New Delhi. Fruits are dark green medium long and medium thick, suitable for vegetable pickle, dehydration and export. Fruits are mature in 52 days after seed sowing. An average yield is 18.0 t/ha. This hybrid is recommended for cultivation in Punjab, Delhi, Haryana, Rajasthan, Gujarat, Uttranchal, Bihar, Chattisgarh, Orissa and Andhra Pradesh.
Pusa Vishesh	It is a dwarf vine variety suitable for higher plant density. This is suitable as vegetable for pickling and dehydration. It is released by IARI, New Delhi.

13.3.2. Bottle Gourd

Name	Remarks
Anand Bottle Gourd-1	This variety was selected from germplasm BGM-9 collected from adjoining area of Borsad, District Anand and developed from Main Vegetable Research Station Anand Agricultural University, Anand. Fruits are long, tender and slightly round at stem and as well as blossom end. Fruit skin is non- hairy, smooth and attractive with

	light green colour and fine luster. This is medium maturity group variety and an average yield is 23.3t/ha.
Arka Bahar	It is an improvement over a local collection from Karnataka and released by IIHR, Bangalore. It is very good for cooking along with good keeping quality.
Kashi Bahar	This variety has been developed through heterosis breeding. Plants are prostrate viny, fruit shape straight, fruit colour light green and fruit size medium. Number of fruits per plant is 10-12, fruit length 30-32 cm, fruit diameter 7.5-8 cm and fruit weight (Individual) 800-900 g . An average yield is 52.5 t/ha.
Kashi Ganga	This variety has been developed through pedigree selection of cross IC 92465 x DVBG-151 at IIVR, Varanasi. Plants are prostrate viny, fruit shape straight cylindrical, fruit colour light green and fruit size medium.Number of fruits per plant is 18-22, fruit length 25-32 cm and fruit diameter 5-7 cm. An average yield is 52.8 t/ha in June-July sown crop and 43.5 t/ha in February sown crop.
Narendra Reshmi	It has been developed at NDUA&T Faizabad. It is derived through selection from a local collection. Plants are moderately tolerant to red pumkin beetle, powdery mildew and downey mildew. This is suited for cultivation for Punjab, Uttar Pradesh and Bihar.
Punjab Komal	It is an early maturity variety and released by PAU, Ludhiana. It is tolerant to cucumber mosaic virus (CMV).
Punjab Long	It is also improved stock and selected from the locally grown material. It is recommended for cultivation in Punjab.
Punjab Round	This variety is an improved of local type. It is recommended for cultivation in Punjab.
Pusa Samridhi	This variety has been developed is in from IARI, Pusa New Delhi. Fruits long without neck. Maturity 50-55 days. An Average yield is 27.2 t/ha in spring-summer and 30.8 t/ha in *kharif* season cultivation.
Pusa Santushti	This variety has been developed from IARI, Pusa, New Delhi and recommended for commercial cultivation in states like Delhi, Punjab, Uttaranchal, Bihar, MP and Maharashtra. Fruits are pear shaped. This variety has an ability to set fruits under low temperature (10-12 °C) as well as high temperature (35-40 °C). Fruits can be harvested 55-60 days after seed sowing. An average yield is 26.0 t/ha in spring-summer and 29.0 t/ha in *kharif* season.
Pusa Hybrid-3	This hybrid has been developed and released from IARI, New Delhi.The fruits are highly suitable for easy packaging in card board boxes for distant market. It can successfully be grown both spring-summer (February-June) and *kharif* seasons (July-November) in northern plains.
Pusa Manjari	It is a F_1 hybrid between Pusa Summer Prolific Round and Selection-11and released by IARI, New Delhi.
Pusa Meghdoot	It is high yielding F_1 hybrid between 'Pusa Summer Prolific Long' and Selection-2, released by IARI, New Delhi. It is early and suitable to both spring and summer seasons cultivation.
Pusa Naveen	It is suitable for planting in spring summer as well as in rainy season in northern plains. It is free from crook-necked fruits.
Pus Summer Prolific Long	It is a selection from a local material particularly suited for growing as a summer crop. This variety can also be grown in rainy season. It

	has been released by IARI, New Delhi.
Pusa Summer Prolific Round	It is a local selection. It was released by IARI, New Delhi.
Pusa Sandesh	It was released from IARI, New Delhi. It is recommended for commercial cultivation as well as home gardening. It can successfully be grown both in spring summer (February-June) and in *kharif* seasons (July-November) in northern plains of the country.

13.3.3. Cucumber

Name	Remarks
Japanese Long Green	It is a temperate variety released by IARI, Regional Station, Katrain and suited to hills and lower hills.
Pule Priyanka	This hybrid is suitable for cultivation under rainy and summer seasons. It is tolerant to downy mildew.
Poinsette	This variety was originally developed at Charleston (South Carolina), USA and multiplied by National Seeds Corporation, New Delhi. It is tolerant to downy mildew, powdery mildew, anthracnose and angular leaf spot.
Pusa Sanyog	This hybrid is cross between Japanese gynoecious line and Green Long Naples and released by IARI, Regional Station, Katrain.
Pusa Uday	This was released from IARI Pusa, New Delhi. This variety is suitable for cultivation both in spring-summer and rainy seasons. Maturity is 50-55 days. An average yield is 15.5 t/ha.
Pusa Barkha	This variety has been developed from IARI, Pusa, New Delhi. This variety is an extra early for *Kharif* season cultivation in north India plains. This variety is field tolerant to high humidity, high temperature and downy mildew disease. An average fruit yield is 18.8 t/ha during *kharif* season.
Shalimar Cucumber Hybrid-1	This hybrid is derivative of cross SH-K-1 x SH-K-11 and developed from SKUAST – Kashmir. Plants are long vine vigorous having medium to large leaves, monoecism with medium to dark yellow flowers, females starts from 2nd or 3rd node. Fruits are long cylindrical uniform with sparse spines, light yellowish green stripes and pointed blossom end. This variety is tolerant to drought and low temperature conditions and also tolerance to angular leaf spot and moderately tolerant to powdery mildew, downy mildew and mosaic.
Shalimar Cucumber Hybrid-2	This hybrid has been developed by single cross between SH-K-1 x SH-K-12 from SKUAST – Kashmir. Plants are long viny vigorous leaves medium to large, monoecious with medium to yellow flowers and female flowers starts from 2nd or 3rd node and long fruiting period. Fruits are medium green, long cylindrical uniform with sparse spines light yellowish green stripes and pointed blossom end. This variety is suitable for salad and export and rich in vitamin C (8.2 mg/100g), TSS (3.5^{0}B) and dry matter (6.15%). This variety is tolerant to drought and low temperature and also tolerance to angular leaf spot and moderately tolerant to powdery mildew, downy mildew and mosaic.

Sheetal	This variety has been developed from Konkan Krishi Vidyapeeth, Dapoli (Maharashtra). This variety is suitable for high rainfall area.
Straight Eight	It is released by IARI Regional Station, Katrain. It is an early maturing, high yielding variety and suited for hills.

13.3.4. Muskmelon

Name	Remarks
Arka Jeet	It is a selection from 'Bati' strain of Uttar Pradesh and released from IIHR, Bangalore.
Arka Rajhans	It is selection from a local collection (IIHR-107) from Rajasthan and released by IIHR, Bangalore. It is recommended for cultivation in southern region of India. It is a mid-season variety. This variety possesses good keeping and transport qualities. It is resistant to powdery mildew.
Durgapura Madhu	It is a selection from local material of Rajasthan.
Gujarat Muskmelon-1	It is a selection from a local collection from Sabarkantha district in Gujarat.
Gujarat Muskmelon-2	It is a selection from the local germplasm collected from Nagpur area of Maharashtra.
Hara Madhu	This is an inbred selection from the local material of Kutana type (a local collection of Uttar Pradesh), released by PAU, Ludhiana. It matures late. Its post-harvest life is short and poor transportability.It is susceptible to powdery and downy mildews.
Hisar Madhur	This is a cross of Pusa Sharbati and 75-34, developed from pedigree selection at CCSHAU, Hisar.
Kashi Madhu	This variety has been developed through selection from IIVR, Varanasi. Plants are long vine, fruit shape roundish, fruit colour yellow, fruit size medium, number of fruits per plant 2.34, fruit length 9.51 cm, fruit diameter 10.83 cm, fruit weight (Individual) 785 g and fruit flesh colour orange. This variety possesses 13-14 %TSS. An average yield is 20.0 t/ha.
Lucknow Safeda	It is a very early variety with medium vine growth. Less juicy and sweet with good keeping quality.
Punjab Hybrid	This is an F_1 hybrid variety recommended for cultivation in 1981 and released from PAU, Ludhiana. Its parents are a male sterile line (MS-1) and Hara Madhu. It is moderately resistant to powdery mildew and fruit fly.
Punjab Rasila	It a cross between WMR-29 and Hara Madhu and released from PAU, Ludhiana.
Punjab Sunehri	It is a derivative from the cross-Hara Madhu x Edisto and released by the PAU, Ludhiana. It has a long post-harvest life and has on excellent transportability. It is tolerant to powdery and downy mildews.
Pusa Madhuras	It is released for northern India by IARI, New Delhi. Keeping quality of fruit is poor.
Pusa Rasraj	This variety has been developed from IARI, New Delhi by crossing of monoecious lines M-3 and Durgapur Madhu.
Pusa Sharbati	This variety has been developed from the cross between Kutana and PM Resistant No. 6 of the USA and released by IARI, New Delhi. It

	is suitable for riverbed cultivation and other field conditions in Northern India. Keeping quality of this variety is good.

13.3.5. Pointed Gourd

Name	Remarks
Kashi Alankar	This variety has been developed through clonal selection from IIVR, Varanasi. Plant is medium viney and, fruits are spindle shape, light green in colour and medium in size, number of fruits per plant 120-130, fruit length 6-7 cm, fruit diameter 2-3 cm, fruit weight (individual) 25-27 g, strips at distal end. An average yield is19.0 t/ha.
Kashi Suphal	This variety was developed from IIVR, Varanasi. Plant spread of this variety is 3.5-4.0 meter. Harvesting starts 90-95 days after transplanting. Fruits are attractive light green in colour, less seeded and good flesh than other variety with better keeping quality. This variety yielded18.0-21.5 t/ha. This variety is suitable for cultivation in Uttar Pradesh, Bihar, Jharkhand and West Bengal.

13.3.6. Pumpkin and Squashes

Name	Remarks
Anand Pumpkin – 1 (AP – 1)	This is medium maturity variety developed by selection from the germplasm collected from local area of Anand district from Anand Agricultural University, Anand. Fruit shape is globular with light mottled fruit skin colour pattern. Fruit shin colour of immature fruit is light green and mature fruit is creamish. Stem end and blossom end fruit shape are depressed. Mature flesh colour of the variety is deep yellow. An average yield is 24.39 t/ha.
Arka Chandan	It is an improvement over a local collection from Rajasthan (IIHR-105) and released by IIHR. It has pleasant aroma. Cooking and keeping quality is good.
Arka Suryamukhi	It is an improvement over a local collection (IIHR-79) from Bangalore and released during 1970. This variety belongs to *Cucurbita maxima* and a selection from a foreign introduction. Keeping and transportation quality is good. It is resistant to fruit fly.
Australian Green	It is an introduction from Australia and released by IARI, Regional Station, Katrain. It belongs to *Cucurbita pepo.*
Early Yellow Prolific	It belongs to *Cucurbita pepo* and released by IARI Regional Station, Katrain. It is early and bush type. Skin is light yellow turning orange-yellow on maturity.
Kashi Harit	This variety is developed through pedigree selection. Plant is short viny, fruit shape round flat, fruit colour light green with white splash and fruit size small. Number of fruits per plant is 3.63-4.78 and polar circumference of fruit 51-52 cm, equatorial circumference of fruit 52-53cm, fruit weight (Individual) 2.13-2.5 kg and , fruit flesh colour light yellow, total caroteoid content 3.14 mg/100g of edible fruit part. An average yield is 30.0 t/ha.

Kashi Subhangi	This is summer squash variety developed from IIVR, Varanasi. This variety is suitable for winter (2nd fort night of September) season. Plant is bushy with silvery patches on leaf. Plant height is 35-45cm. Flowering and fruiting starts after 36-46 days of sowing and starts after 36-46 days of sowing and first harvesting can be done within 46-58 days. Individual fruit weight is 800-900g. Yield potential is 30-35 t/ha.
Pattypan	It belongs to *Cucurbita pepo* and released by IIHR, Bangalore. It is a short duration cultivar of 85 days.
Pusa Alankar	It belongs to *Cucurbita pepo* and released by IARI Regional Station, Katrain. It is an F_1 hybrid between EC 207050 and 15-1-8 (a derivative cross between Chappan Kaddu and Early Yellow Prolific). It is early maturing having uniform dark green fruit with light coloured stripes.
Pusa Biswas	This is a local selection of line 'SM 107' from IARI, New Delhi. Fruits are light brown, spherical with thick golden yellow flesh.
Pusa Hybrid-1	It is first hybrid of pumpkin available for commercial cultivation. The fruits are round-flat and medium in size. The flesh is deep golden-yellow in colour. It is ready for picking 100 days after sowing in spring-summer season.
Pusa Vikas	It is developed from IARI, New Delhi. Flesh is yellow. It is suitable for growing in spring-summer season (February-March to June) in northern plains of India.

13.3.7.: Roundmelon

Name	Remarks
Arka Tinda	This variety has been developed by crossing a local selection T-3-4 (Rajasthan) with T-8-2 (Punjab) followed by pedigree selection and released by IIHR, Bangalore. It is an early summer season variety. It is tolerant to fruit fly.

13.3.8. Snake Gourd

Name	Remarks
CO-1	It is a pure line selection collected from Alangulam, Tirunelveli district and released from TNAU, Coimbatore. It is an early maturing variety. Fruits are dark green with white stripes
CO-2	It is a pure line selection from Coimbatore district and released in 1986 from TNAU, Coimbatore. The fruits are short and stout, light greenish white in colour. The variety does not require pandal.
CO-4	It is an early maturing variety released from TNAU, Coimbatore. The first marketable fruit comes to harvest in 70 days after seed sowing.
MDU-I	It is a F_1 hybrid between Panripudal and Selection-1 from Thaniyamangalam and released in 1981 from TNAU, Coimbatore. It is an early flowering type (84 days) with a sex ratio of 1:38. The fruits are fairly rich in vitamin A (44.4 mg/100g) and very low in fiber content (0.6 per cent).
PKM-1	It is an induced mutant from H-375 and suitable for growing throughout the year. Fruit is dark green in colour with white stripes on outer side and light green on inside.

13.3.9. Sponage Gourd

Name	Remarks
Kalyanpur Chikni	This variety has been developed from Vegetable Research Centre, Kalyanpur (Kanpur).
Kashi Divya	It is open pollinated variety and suitable for summer and rainy season and recommended for commercial cultivation in Uttar Pradesh, Bihar, Jharkhand and Punjab. Plant bears 14-16 fruits/ plant. Fruits are attractive cylindrical, straight 20-25 cm long with fruit circumference of 8.0-8.72 cm, fruit weight is 125-150 g with light green &white colour flesh. Yield potential is around 20 t/ ha.
Pusa Chikni	It is a selection from Bihar collection and released by IARI, New Delhi. It is an early, smooth and dark colour fruits. This variety is suitable for both spring-summer and rainy seasons.
Pusa Sneha	This variety has been developed and released from IARI, New Delhi. Inflorescence is racemose, unisexual flowers, monoecious and campanulate. It is suitable for growing in both spring-summer and *kharif* seasons.
Pusa Supriya	It is released from IARI, New Delhi. Flowers are monoecious, campanulate. Fruits become ready for picking 50-55 days after sowing in spring-summer and 44-48 days after in *kharif* season.

13.3.10. Ridge Gourd

Name	Remarks
Arka Sujata	It is a selection from a cross between 'IIHR54' and 'IIHR18'. It has inherited desirable characters of both parents. It is also suitable for growing round the year in Karnataka. It bears first female flower at 13-15th node 40 days after sowing. It is moderately resistant to downy mildew.
Arka Sumeet	It has been selected from a cross between 'IIHR-54' and 'IIHR-24'. It bears first female flower on 15th node onwards and takes 52 days for first picking. It is suitable for cultivation round the year in Karnataka.
Kalyanpur Dharidar	It is an early variety developed from Vegetable Research Centre, Kalyanpur (Kanpur). Plants bear maximum number of female flowers rather than male.
Kashi Khushi	This variety has been developed from IIVR, Varanasi. Plant bearing light green fruits with 10 dark green superficial & continuous longitudinal ridges. Single plant bears 140 fruits/ plant in cluster of 5-6 fruits. An average yield is 5.24 -6.27 kg/ plant.
Pusa Nasadar	It is a selection from Neemuch, Madhya Pradesh Collection and released from IARI, New Delhi. It is suitable for summer and rainy season.
Punjab Sadabahar	This variety is released from PAU, Ludhiana.Fruits are rich in protein. This variety can be sown from May to July.
Pusa Nutan	This variety is released from IARI, New Delhi. Fruits are 25-30 cm long, straight and attractive green, An average fruit weight is 105 g, flesh tender, suitable for spring summer and *kharif* season. Maturity is 45-50 days after seed sowing. An average yield is 16.0 t/ha.

13.3.11. Watermelon

Name	Remarks
Arka Jyoti	It is a mid-season F_1 hybrid developed by crossing a local watermelon selection (IIHR-20) from Rajasthan with Crimson Sweet from USA and released by IIHR, Bangalore. It is an early variety with good keeping quality.
Arka Manik	This variety was evolved by crossing IIHR-21 with cv. 'Crimson Sweet 'and released by IIHR, Bangalore. This variety possesses good storage and transport qualities.This variety is resistant to powdery mildew and tolerant to anthracnose.
Asahi Yamato	It is mid-season Japanese introduction and released by IARI, New Delhi.
Durgapura Kesar	It is a late variety released by Agricultural Research Station, Durgapura, Rajasthan. The flesh is yellow and moderately sweet.
Durgapura Meetha	It is a late maturing (125 days) variety released from Agricultural Research Station, Durgapura, Rajasthan. Rind is thick with good keeping quality. Flesh is dark red colour and black seed.
Shipper	This variety is an American introduction and released by PAU, Ludhiana. Fruits have characteristic tripartite blossom end.
Sugar Baby	It is an early season American introduction, which is released by IARI, New Delhi. The fruits are slightly smaller weighing 3 to 5 kg per fruit, round in shape with bluish black rind and pink flesh.

13.3.12. Wax or Ash Gourd

Name	Remarks
Kashi Dhawal	This variety was developed through selection from IIVR, Varanasi. Plant is long vine growth, fruit shape oblong, fruit colour white, fruit size large, number of fruits per plant 2.5-3.0, equatorial circumference of fruit 79-81 cm, polar circumference of fruit 89.20-89.50 cm, fruit weight (Individual) 11-12 kg fruit and pulp colour white. An average yield is 57.5t/ha.
Kashi Surabhi	This is open pollinated variety developed from IIVR, Varanasi and recommended for cultivation in Uttar Pradesh, Bihar, Jharkhand and Punjab. This variety is suitable for petha preparation. Fruits can be stored up to 4 months after harvesting at ambient temperature. Plant is tolerant to leaf minor& resistance to anthracnose disease. An average yield 70 t/ ha.
Kashi Ujwal	This variety has been developed from IIVR, Varanasi through selection. Plant is long vine growth, fruit shape round, fruit colour white, fruit size medium, number of fruits per plant 2.6-3.0, equatorial circumference of fruit 74.33-76.76 cm, polar circumference of fruit 77.76-80.00 cm, fruit weight (Individual) 7.0-9.0 kg, fruit pulp colour whitish. An average yield is 50.0 t/ha.
Mudliar	This is a popular variety of Tamil Nadu, whose fruits are big with light green colour.
Pusa Ujwal	This variety has been released from IARI Pusa, New Delhi and recommended for commercial cultivation in Delhi, Punjab, and Haryana.

	Fruits are green in immature stage and white in full mature stage. Fruits are cylindrical and rind colour green. Immature fruits are pubescent, cylindrical (Average length-23.50 cm and girth-55.0 cm). Mature fruits have a dense pelt of minute hairs and covered with a white waxy bloom. The average fruits weight is 7 kg and average number of fruits per plant is 3. The fruit flesh is white and seeds are creamy white in colour. Fruits ellipsoid, ideal for packing and long-distance transportation. This variety is resistant to cucumber mosaic virus and water melon mosaic virus. An average yield is 45.0 t/ha.

13.4. Fruit Vegetables

13.4.1. Brinjal

Name	Remarks
Annamalai	This variety is selection from AC-49A and released in 1971 from TNAU, Coimbatore for winter season cultivation. Fruits are deep purple, whereas, lighter in summer and suitable for ratooning. This variety is resistant to aphids.
Arka Anand	This F_1 derived from cross IIHR-3 x IIHR-322 and developed at IIHR Bangalore. Plant habit is tall & spreading. Foliage colour- green stem and green foliage (leaves). Fruits are green, long and average weight 50-55 g. This variety has been found resistant to bacterial wilt and less incidence of shoot & fruit borer. An average yield is 65.00 t/ha.
Arka Keshav	This variety has been released from IIHR, Bangalore.Fruits are purple in colour measuring 18-20 cm in length and 5-6 cm in diameter.
Arka Kusmkar	It is an improvement over a local collection IIHR '93' in Karnataka state and identified in 1981 for cultivation. The fruits are borne in cluster of 5 to 7 and contain less seeds. It has good flesh texture and cooking quality. It is very high yielding.
Arka Navneet	It is a cross between IIHR 22-1 x Supreme development from IIHR, Bangalore and identified in 1981 for cultivation. This is a very high yielding round-fruited hybrid with shining deep purple colour and green calyx.
Arka Nidhi	This variety has been developed at IIHR, Bangalore. Fruits are medium in length and bearing occurs in cluster.Fruit colour is black purple. It is resistant to bacterial wilt.
Arka Sheel	This is improved over Purple Long cultivar of brinjal developed at Coorg in Karnataka and released from IIHR, Bangalore. The fruit contains more edible part and less number of seeds. This is very high yielding variety.
Arka Shirish	It is an improvement over the Irangeri brinjal of Karnataka and released from IIHR, Bangalore. The fruits are very tender and extra-long. The flesh texture is good with better cooking quality. It is very high yielding
Aruna	This variety has been developed at MPKV, Akola, derived through selection from a local cultivar. Plants are prolific bearers. It was recommended for cultivation in 1988 for Madhya Pradesh and Maharashtra.

Azad Kranti	This variety was identified in 1983 from Kalyanpur. Fruits are dark purple with shining green colour and less seeded.
Barahmasi	This is long duration fruiting variety. It is a cross of Punjab Neelam and Punjab Barsati and developed at PAU, Ludhiana. Fruits are oblong, shining deep purple, large (237.2 g average weight) with 6.55 mm pericarp thickness.
Bhagyamati	A selection from a TUNI and was released from Andhra Pradesh in 1980.Fruits are oblong in shape of varying size from 6-8 cm in length at edible stage with deep shining purple colour that does not fade even at harvest for 2-3 days. Calyx firms and has a green to purplish due in different seasons.
Black Beauty	It is an introduction from USA. Fruits are roundish oblong, 10-12 cm long of dark purplish black colour.
Dudhia	This variety is famous for its milk like white colour fruits and suitable for winter season cultivation. It is suitable for bhartha preparation.
Green Long	This variety has been bred at RAU, Sabour. Plant bears 18 fruits. Fruits are long, green and 135 g of an average per weight. This variety is for commercial cultivation in Punjab, Uttar Pradesh and Bihar.
Gujarat Brinjal-6	It is a derivative of the cross between Doli-5 x Morvi-4-2 and was released from Gujarat in 1976. Fruits are 10.1 cm long and 9 cm in girth of dull violet black colour.
Gulabi	It is developed at APAU, Hyderabad and recommended for cultivation in Chhattisgarh, Orissa and Andhra Pradesh. Fruits are medium-long, light purple, bear in cluster of 3-5.This variety is suitable for long distance transportation.
Hisar Pragati	This variety was developed at CCSHAU, Hisar, derived through pedigree method from the cross R-34 x Sel-26 and recommended for cultivation in Punjab, Uttar Pradesh, Bihar, Rajasthan, Gujarat, Haryana and Delhi.Fruits are long, dark bright purple with creamish white flesh It is tolerant to little leaf and high temperature.
Hisar Jamuni	It is an oblong brinjal suitable for growing in Haryana.It is a cross of Aushey (a round brinjal) and R 34 (a long brinjal). It is suitable for autumn and spring seasons as well as ratoon crop in early spring.
Hisar Shyamal	It is developed at CCSHAU, Hisar; derived through backross-pedigree method from the cross Aushey x BR-112 and recommended for cultivation in West Bengal, Assam, Punjab, Uttar Pradesh, Bihar, Chhattisgarh, Orissa, Andhra Pradesh, Rajasthan, Gujarat, Haryana, Delhi, Madhya Pradesh and Maharashtra, Karnataka, Tamil Nadu and Kerala. Fruits are round, dark bright purple with creamish white flesh.
Jamuni Gola	This variety has been developed at Ludhiana and was identified in 1986 for cultivation. Fruits are plump and shining purple colored. It is an early in maturing whose first harvesting starts 65 days after transplanting.
Junagarh Long	This variety is derivative of the cross Doli-5 x Inbred Panch Mahal released in 1981 in Gujarat State. Fruits are tapering at the distal end and 20-25 pickings can be taken at short intervals for edible purposes. This variety is free from collar rot disease under field condition.
Kashi Komal	This variety has been developed from IIVR, Varanasi. Plant is tall and erect (80-90 cm height), fruit shape small long, fruit colour purple, number of fruits per plant 25-30, fruit length 6.5-7.5 cm, fruit diameter

	3.4-4.5 cm and fruit weight (Individual) 60-65 g. An average yield is 40.0 t/ha.
Kashi Prakash	This variety has been developed through mass selection at IIVR, Varanasi and recommended for cultivation in Bihar, Uttar Pradesh and Jharkhand. Plant is semi-erect, fruit shape oblong, fruit colour purple with light green spots. Number of fruits per plant is 14-17, fruit length 5.8 cm, fruit diameter 4.2 cm, fruit weight (Individual) and 190 g. An average yield is 60.0 t/ha.
Kashi Sandesh	This hybrid has been developed from IIVR, Varanasi. Plants are semi-erect (71.0 cm height), fruit shape oval round, fruit color purple, fruit size large, number of fruits per plant 50-60 and fruit weight (Individual) 350-400 g. An average yield is 70.0 t/ha.
Kashi Taru	Its variety has been developed by mass selection from IIVR, Varanasi and recommended for commercial cultivation in Uttar Pradesh, Bihar and Jharkhand. Plant is tall and erect, fruit shape long, fruit colour dark purple, fruit size medium, number of fruits per plant 20-25, fruit length 14-16 cm, fruit diameter 4-5 cm and fruit weight (Individual) 75-85 g. An average yield is 37.5 t/ha.
Kashi Uttam	This is round fruited high yielding variety developed from IIVR, Varanasi. Fruits are round, purple, shiny with less suitable for bharta making. Plants are tolerant to fruit and shoot borer and, resistant to lodging. An average yield is 50 t/ ha.
Kalpataru	It has been developed at Maharashtra Hybrid Seeds Co. Ltd., Jalna. An average fruit weight is 60-70 g.
Narendra Hybrid Brinjal-1	It has been developed at NDUAT, Faizabad and was recommended for commercial cultivation in Punjab, Bihar and Uttar Pradesh plains in the year 1995. Fruiting occurs in clusters.
Neelam	This variety has been developed from PAU, Ludhiana. It is an early variety having attractive round purple colour fruits. This variety has least infestation of shoot and fruit borer.
Pant Rituraj	It is derivative of Kalyanpur T-3 x Pusa Purple Cluster and released for cultivation throughout the country. It is suitable for *kharif* and summer seasons. Fruits are almost round with slight tapering towards fruit bottom and dark purple in colour. Fruit is soft in texture, less seeded with good flavour and keeping quality. This variety is resistance to bacterial wilt.
Pant Samrat	It is developed through pure line selection and was released by Central Sub-Committee on Crop Standards, Notification and Release of Varieties in 1984 for the entire country. Fruits are medium long, borne in small clusters, attractive purple colour with soft texture .This variety is resistant to phomopsis blight and bacterial wilt under field condition and less affected by shoot fruit borer and jassids.
Punjab Bahar	It is a selection from local material from Punjab and developed from PAU, Ludhiana. Fruits are suitable for bhartha making.
Punjab Barsati	It is released from PAU, Ludhiana. Fruits are medium long, shining purple and suitable for rainy season. This variety is tolerant to shoot and fruit borer.
Punjab Chamkila	It is released from PAU, Ludhiana. Fruits are long, thin and dark purple. This variety is good for summer and autumn seasons.

Punjab Haryana Brinjal-4	It is a derivative of the cross Hyderpur x Pusa Purple Long for general cultivation for Punjab, Haryana, Uttar Pradesh, Delhi, Rajasthan and Gujarat States. This variety has been named as Punjab Haryana Brinjal-4 for the derivative of the cross Hyderpur x Pusa Purple Long under the selection No. S-4 done at Punjab Agricultural University, Ludhiana and selection No.H-4 done at Haryana Agricultural University, Hisar. Fruits are long to medium, thin, dark purple in colour with light green flesh.
Punjab Moti	It is a small-fruited variety developed from PAU, Ludhiana. Fruits are round shining, dark purple and suitable for autumn and spring seasons.
Punjab Neelam	This variety is developed from PAU, Ludhiana. Fruits are oval-round, medium, shining dark purple and suitable for February and August transplanting.
Punjab Sadabahar	It is developed from PAU, Ludhiana. Fruits are long, thin and deep purple in colour. It is tolerant to shoot and fruit borer and suitable for rainy season.
Pusa Ankur	This variety has been developed at IARI, New Delhi.It is recommended for cultivation in Gujarat, Maharashtra and Central plains of India. It is an early bearing and becomes ready for first-picking in 45 days after transplanting. Its fruits do not loose colour and tenderness even on delayed pickings.
Pusa Anmol	It is hybrid cultivar evolved from a cross between Pusa Purple Long and Hyderpur at IARI, New Delhi.
Pusa Anupam	This variety has been developed at Regional Station of the IARI, Katrain through hybridization of 'Pusa Kranti' and 'Pusa Purple Cluster'.Fruits are borne in cluster of 3-5 and purple in colour. The fruit is also suitable for pickle making. It is available from August to November in the hilly regions.
Pusa Bindu	This variety has been developed from IARI, New Delhi. Plants are pigmented, uprights with moderate branching habit and free from spines. Fruit is pendent, small, oval-round and glossy. Bearing habit is solitary to partial cluster.
Pusa Hybrid-5	This is an early and long-fruited hybrid developed and released from IARI, New Delhi. Fruits are long, glossy, attractive, dark purple with partially pigmented peduncle.
Pusa Hybrid-6	This is an early-bearing and round-fruited hybrid developed and released from IARI New Delhi. Fruit are round, glossy, attractive, purple with partially pigmented peduncle.
Pusa Hybrid-9	It is a round-fruited hybrid.Fruits are big, oval-round, glossy, highly attractive, dark purple with partially pigmented stalk.
Pusa Kranti	The variety has been developed from the cross of PPL x Hyderpur x Wynd Giant. Fruits are oblong (15-20 cm), dark purple with shining green calyx, less seeded and do not touch the ground. This variety is suitable for growing both the spring and autumn seasons.
Pusa Purple Cluster	It is an early variety and developed at IARI, Regional Research Station, Katrain after purification from indigenously collected material.Fruits borne in clusters (4-9), 10-12 cm long and deep purple in colour. It is suitable for southern and northern hills and moderately resistant to bacterial wilt.

Pusa Purple Long	It is an old variety developed and released from IARI, New Delhi. This is a selection from the mixed Batia cultivar grown in Punjab, Delhi and Western Uttar Pradesh. Fruits are long (20-25 cm), purple, glossy and tender. It is suitable for summer and autumn seasons. It performed extremely well in north India.
Pusa Purple Round	This cultivar has been evolved at IARI, New Delhi. This cultivar was found resistant to shoot and fruit borer and little leaf disease.
Pusa Shyamla	This variety has been developed from IARI Pusa, New Delhi and recommended for cultivation in Punjab, Uttranchal and Bihar. Fruits are long, glossy, dark purple and weighing 80-90 g. Maturity is 50-55 days.An average yield is 39.0 t/ha.
Pusa Upkar	Plants are semi-vigorous with moderate branching and free from spines. Fruits are medium-sized, glossy, dark purple and 200 g single fruit weight.
Pusa Uttam	Plants are semi-upright, vigorous, well branched and free from spines. Fruits are pendent, oval, medium, large-sized and glossy with dark purple skin and green peduncle.The bearing habit is solitary.
Ram Nagar Giant	This variety is very much popular in the Varanasi region and it's surrounding areas. Fruits are light green in colour, very big size (1.5-2.5 kg) about 15-20 cm long and 12-15 cm in diameter, soft, very less seed and used mostly for Bharta preparation.
Rajendra Baingan	Fruits are long, light green colour with slight curve, heavy bearer, less seeded and smooth. This variety is suitable for growing in rainy and winter seasons. It is less affected by wilting and phomopsis blight.
Ravaiyya	It has been developed at Maharashtra Hybrid Seeds Co. Ltd., Jalna. Fruits are oval, shining, reddish purple with non-spiny calyx. Fruiting occurs in cluster (4 -6). It is an early bearing hybrid.
RHRBH-1	It is a cross of RHRB-1 and JB-16 developed at MPKV, Rahuri. Fruits are purple with non-spiny and green calyx, purple having white stripes, 8.5 cm length, and 6.4 cm diameter. It gives an average yield of 57.6 t/ha.
RHRBH-2	It is a cross of RHRB-1 and RB-25 developed at MPKV, Rahuri. Plants are short and spreading type. Fruits are purple with white stripes, 5.5 cm length, 4.5 cm diameter with spiny calyx.
RHRBH-3	It is a cross of RHRB-1 and Vaishali developed at MPKV, Rahuri. Fruits are purple with white stripes, 7.5 cm length, 5.5 cm diameter with spiny calyx.
Shalimar Brinjal Hybrid – 1	This hybrid is derivative of SH-B-4 x SH-B-12. Plant is tall and compact. Fruits are medium long and cylindrical. Colour of fruit (edible) is uniform pink and yellowish brown at mature fruit (ripe) stage. Flesh is medium compact, less seedy with high TSS and dry matter content. This hybrid is highly tolerant to early blight, wilt and phomopsis fruit rot. An average yield is 87.8t /ha.
Shalimar Brinjal Hybrid – 2	This hybrid is derived by single cross hybrid between SH-B-11x SH-B-12. Plants are tall and compact born 1-4 light violet flowers on leaf axil. Fruits are medium long purple and cylindrical in shape. This hybrid is highly tolerant to early blight, wilt and tolerant to phomopsis fruit rot under field conditions. An average yield is 68.8t /ha.
Shyamal	This hybrid has been developed at Ankur Seeds Pvt. Ltd., Nagpur and recommended for commercial cultivation in Punjab, Bihar, Uttar

	Pradesh plains, Andhra Pradesh, and eastern part of Madhya Pradesh, Orissa, Haryana, Rajasthan, Gujarat and Maharashtra for cultivation. Fruits are purple and oblong with milky-white flesh.The shelf life of fruit is 4-5 days at room temperature, hence, good for long distance transportation. It is tolerant to sucking borer.
Surya	It is a bacterial wilt resistant variety, developed at College of Horticulture, Vellanikkara, Kerala. Plants are non-prickly and spreading. Fruits are oval and purple. It is recommended for cultivation in Karnataka, Tamil Nadu and Kerala.
Swetha	It is a bacterial wilt resistant variety, developed at College of Horticulture, Vellanikkara, Kerala.Fruits are medium-long, light green, solitary (Occasionally in cluster). It is recommended for cultivation in Jammu & Kashmir, Himachal Pradesh, Uttaranchal, Rajasthan, Gujarat, Haryana, Delhi, Karnataka, Tamil Nadu and Kerala.
Utkal Jyoti	This variety has been developed at OUA & T, Bhubaneshwar, derived through pedigree method from cross KT-4 x BB-11. Fruits are long, small medium, purple with white flesh. Fruits have good shelf life. It is tolerant to bacterial wilt. It is recommended for cultivation in Karnataka, Tamil Nadu and Kerala.
Utkal Keshari	This variety has been developed at OUA&T, Bhubaneshwar derived through pedigree method from the cross BB-11 x KJ-3-1 and recommended for commercial cultivation in Rajasthan, Gujarat, Haryana, Delhi, Madhya Pradesh and Maharashtra. Fruits are long, medium-large, uniform thick, basal portion slightly broad, deep purple and 5-6 days shelf life. This variety is tolerant to bacterial wilt and *fusarium* wilt.
Utkal Madhuri	This bacterial wilt resistant variety has been developed at OUA & T, Bhubaneshwar, derived through pedigree method from the cross PBR 125-5 x Pipli-4 (local collection). It is resistant to fusarium wilt and drought. It has prolonged fruiting period. It is recommended for cultivation in Chhattisgarh, Orissa, Andhra Pradesh, Madhya Pradesh and Maharashtra.
Utkal Tarini	This is a bacterial wilt resistant variety, developed at OUA & T, Bhubaneshwar, derived through pedigree method from the cross Pusa Kranti x Gopa Local.Fruits are oblong, medium sized, deep purple with cremish white flesh, 6-7 days shelf life. It is recommended for cultivation West Bengal, Assam, Chhattisgarh, Orissa and Andhra Pradesh.
Vijay Hybrid	It is a very high yielding hybrid having oval to oblong shaped fruits. The fruits are purple colour with green calyx. It is developed from Indo-American Hybrid Seeds Ltd., Bangalore.
VRBHR-1	It is a cross of Pant Rituraj and BR-SPS-14 developed at IIVR, Varanasi. Fruits are round, light purple with 10.28 cm diameter, 11.6 cm length, average weight of 569 g with green calyx.

13.4.2. Chilli

Name	Remarks
Andhra Jyoti	This is evolved from a cross between G-2 and a Bihar variety and released from Agricultural Research Station, Lam, Guntur. The fruits of this cultivar are short and 'gundu' types. The fruits are bright red measuring 5.1 cm in length and 6.3 cm in girth.
Aparna	It is selection from local material, released from Agricultural Research Station, Lam, Guntur. Fruits attain yellow colour on ripening and retain colour in storage.It is highly pungent variety. It is moderately tolerant to major pest and diseases under field condition.
Arch-236	It has been developed at Ankur Seeds Pvt. Ltd., Nagpur. Fruits are elongated, undulated, pointed and green, turns red at maturity with good self-life and good for fresh market. It has high capsaicin content reommended for cultivation in Punjab, Bihar and Uttar Pradesh plains.
Arka Harita	This variety has been developed by cross between MS3 (A line) & IC 296665 (B line) x IHR3312 (PMR 14) (INGR No. 04054) from IIHR Bangalore and recommended for commercial cultivation eastern dry zone of Karnataka. Plants are erect and spreading having in intermediate in growth. Fruit is green in edible stage and turning red on maturity stage. Fruits are medium length and width with pointed tip. This variety is tolerance to powdery mildew and viruses (CHVMV). Green chilli yield is 30 t/ha whereas, dry chilli 3 t/ha.
Arka Lohit	This is a pure line selection and released from IIHR, Bangalore. Fruits are dark green colour in immature and dark red colour in mature. Highly pungent variety contains 0.21 per cent capsaicin.
Bhaskar	It is an early maturing variety developed at Agricultural Research Station (RARS), Lam Farm and recommended for commercial cultivation in Punjab, Uttar Pradesh, Bihar, Chhattisgarh, Orissa, Andhra Pradesh, Rajasthan, Gujarat, Haryana, Delhi, Karnataka, Tamil Nadu and Kerala., Guntur, derived from the cross G-4 x Yellow Anther Mutant. Fruits are thin, medium-long, thick red with red-flesh and 45 per cent seed content, pungent with high oleoresin and suitable for export. This variety possesses good shelf life and transport quality. It is fairly tolerant to mites, thrips and aphids.
Bhagyalakshmi	It is selection from Thohian chillies from Sri Lanka and was released at State (1968) as well as national level (1977). Fruit is green and turning dark red on ripening. It is fairly tolerant to diseases and insects.
Bharni	This variety is widely cultivated in Bilaspur of Chhattisgarh. Immature fruits are green in colour and 10 cm in length.
BSS-141	This hybrid has been developed at Beejo Sheetal Pvt. Ltd. Jalna. Fruits are dark green, highly pungent turns bright red at maturity gives very high yield.
Chanchal	It is selection from local germplasm and was released from Uttar Pradesh in 1973. Fruits are 25-30 cm long, 6-7 cm thick, erect, highly pungent, dark green when fresh and shining red on maturity. This variety is suitable for kitchen gardening. It can grow leaf curl disease infested area.

Gayatri	It has been developed at Beejo Sheetal Pvt. Ltd., Jalna. Plants are spreading type and 70-80 cm tall. Fruits are dark red, attractive, thick skin and medium pungent.
Gujarat Chillies	It is a selection from germplasm material of Reshampatta group of chillies and has been released by Gujarat State.
Guchhedar	This variety fruit is small (4.68 cm), erect and borne in bunches. Fruit colour is deep red and suitable for drying and processing.
Gujarat Anand Vegetable Chilli Hybrid-1	This variety is derived of female CMS line (A-line) CCA-4759 and male R-(line) ACR-1. Fruits are elongated, pointed blossom end having semi-wrinkle surface and light green colour.Medium maturity group. low incidence of anthracnose. Low incidence of thrips and fruit borer damage. An average yield is 23.7t/ha. (Green fruit yield)
Gujarat Anand Vegetable Chilli-112	It has been developed by cross of ACS-97-1 x RHRC-16-5. Growth habit is interminate.Fruits are pungent, elongated straight and Plant compact, Fruits surface is semi-wrinkle with light green shining colour. An average yield is 9.8t/ha.
HC-44	It is originated as single plant selections from the open pollinated segregating material collected from the north-eastern Haryana. This variety is highly suitable for dry powder production. It is resistant to TMV, CUV, PVY and leaf curl diseases and moderately resistant to fruit rot, powdery mildew and dieback diseases. It is free from the attack of thrips, mites, pod-borers, whiteflies and aphids. It is capable of setting fruit at comparatively higher and lower temperatures, hence, highly suited to rainy and spring seasons. As ratoon crop, it provides fruits in the early spring.
H-28	It is originated as single plant selections from the open pollinated segregating material collected from the north-eastern Haryana. It is highly pungent. Fruits carry slight blackish tinge on surface under low temperature, which is a marker character. It is suitable for dry powder production. This variety is highly resistant to TMV, CMV, PVY and leaf curl diseases. It is free from fruit rot, powdery mildew and dieback diseases. It is most suitable for rainy and spring seasons. It may be grown as ratoon crop during the early spring.
IVPBC-535	This variety is selected from introduced population of AVRDC. This variety is paprika type. Plant is determinate, semi-dwarf. Fruit shape is long and pendent, dull shaped wrinkled. Fruit colour is green. Number of of fruits per plant is 50-55, fruit length 11.5-12.0 cm, fruit diameter 1.3 -1.5 cm and individual fruit weight 6-7 g. An average yield is 20.0 t/ha (green).
Japani Laungi	This is popular variety of Chhattisgarh and can be grown throughout the year. Fruiting occurs in clusters with 10-20 fruits per cluster. This variety is tolerant to most of the diseases and insect- pest.
JCA-154	This is a pickling cultivar from JNKVV, Jabalpur, Madhya Pradesh. Fruits are dark green when unripe and bright red when ripe.
Jawahar-218	It is selection from a cross between Kalipeeth and Pusa Jwala and was released at State level from JNKVV, Jabalpur (MP) in 1984. Fruit is green turned rosy red at maturity.It is early and high yielding. It is suited for green and red chilli production. It is tolerant to leaf curl and fruit rot.

Jawahar-283	It has been developed by selection made from local genotype collected from the adjoining areas of Jabalpur. The fruits are straight, firm, medium in length, thin (2.5- 3.5 cm girth in the middle) and dark green in the colour. Fruits are very attractive with high consumer preference. The red ripe fruits are bright red and pungent.
Kalyanpur Mohini	This variety has been developed from Vegetable Research Station Kalyanpur of CSAUAT, Kanpur. In this variety fruits bear upright.
Kashi Anmol	This variety is selection from base population (KA-2) - introduced from Sri Lanka and developed in IIVR, Varanasi .Plant is determinate, dwarf, umbrella shape, fruit shape straight and smooth. Fruit colour is dark green at immature stage. Fruit size is medium long and number of fruits per plant 250-350, fruit length 5.5-7.5 cm, fruit diameter 0.7-1.0 cm, fruit weight (Individual) 4-5 g, capsaicin 0.5% and vitamin 'C' content found 40 mg / 100 g of edible portion at green fruit stage. An average yield is 25.0 t/ha (Green fruit) .
Kashi Early	This variety is developed at IIVR, Varanasi. Plant is indeterminate (80-100 cm height). Fruit shape pendent, smooth, fruit colour green and fruit size medium long. Number of fruits per plant is 100-125, fruit length 9 -10 cm, fruit diameter 1.0-1.1 cm, fruit weight (Individual)8-10 g, capsaicin 0.7 % and vitamin 'C' 45 mg/100 g of edible portion measured at green fruit stage. An average yield is 25t/ha (Green fruit).
Kashi Gaurav	This is open-pollinated mild pungent variety developed at IIVR, Varanasi and suitable for table purpose. Fruit size is 9-11cm long and1.1-1.2 cm thick. Highly tolerant to thrips, mites and anthracnose. An average yield is 12 t/ha.
Kashi Sinduri	Plant are spreading type and recommended for commercial cultivation J&K, HP, Uttaranchal, Punjab, Bihar& Jharkhand, Karnataka, Tamil Nadu & Kerala. This is open-pollinated paparika type variety. Fruits are green and deep red at ripe stage (90-95 days after transplanting). Fruits size is 10-12 cm long and1-1.3 cm thick with high oleoresin content with no pungency suitable for oleoresin (Colour) extraction. An average yield of red ripe fruit is11 t/ha
Kashi Surkh	Plant type is tall indeterminate (110-120 cm height). Fruit shape is straight, slightly wrinkled, fruit colour light green, fruit size medium long, number of fruits per plant 85-90, fruit length 10-12 cm, fruit diameter 1.0-1.2 cm, fruit weight (Individual): 10-12 g with capsaicin 0.5 % and vitamin 'C' 23 mg/100 g of edible portion at green fruit stage. An average yield is 20.0 t/ha(Green chilli).
Kashi Tez	This variety is CMS based early maturating, dual purpose, tolerant to anthracnose disease& thirps but susceptible to mites developed at IIVR, Varanasi. Single plant produces 150-175 parrot green fruits/ plant. An average yield is 14-15 t/ha.
Kiran	Fruits are long and thin with light green pericarp turning to rosy red color on ripening. This variety is fairly tolerant to thrips, mites and aphids.
Local Kashmiri	Fruit surface is smooth to sunken. Fruit is 7-15 cm long, light to dark green when unripe and blood red on ripening. Fruits are pungent and containing 10-15 fruits/ plant.

MDU-1	It is an induced mutant from K-1 chilli by using 30 kr of gamma rays and release in 1978 from TNAU, Coimbatore. The fruits are bore in cluster of 4 to 9 at nodes as against single fruit borne at nodes as in K-1 or K-2 varieties. The fruits are long with dark shiny red colour.
Musalabadi	This is local selection, released at state level from Mahatma Phule Agricultural University, Rahuri (Maharashtra).Fruit is small, dark green with black patches and used as green as well as dry purposes. It has been found tolerant to die back and powdery mildew.
NP46 A	Plants are dwarf dense and spreading. This is a 'Samba' type variety. Released at national level from IARI, New Delhi. Fruit is 8 to 9 cm long, thin, wrinkled, light green color turned light red on ripening. It is tolerant to thrips and susceptible to viral diseases. This variety is less seeded and contains 0.53 mg capsaicin/g of fruit.
Numex	This is imported variety having medium tall in stature. Leaves are light green in color having two to three branches per plant. Fruits are small and capsule in shape. Per plant bears 80 to 100 fruits.
Pant C-1	It is an advanced generation selection from a cross between NP46A and a Local cultivar and released from state level by GBPUA&T, Pantnagar. Fruit is erect, small size, highly pungent, light green and turning light red at maturity. It is tolerant to mosaic and leaf curl virus.
Pant C-2	It is also selection from a cross involving the same parents as that of Pant C-1 and released from GBPU&T, Pant Nagar at state level. Fruit is pendent. It is tolerant to mosaic and leaf curl virus.
Pant Chilli-4	This is developed by cross combination PS-3-4 x AC-515 and suitable for spring, summer& rainy seasons. Plants are dark green foliage having fruit long (8-10 cm), thick, solitary, dark green at immature stage &deep red at maturity and cylindrical & pointed and bulging base in fruit shape. This is tolerance against leaf curl virus, nematode and anthracnose diseases under field conditions. It is less affected with mites. An average yield is 13.5 t/ha.
PKM-1	This is a hybrid derivative of cross between AC.No.1797 x Co.1 and was released in 1990 from TNAU, Coimbatore. It is suitable for cultivation under irrigated conditions. It has very bold fruits, which are dark red in colour.The number of fruits/ plant is 204 with 85 seeds/ fruit.
Prakash	It has been developed at RARS, Lam Farm, Guntur, derived from the cross G-3 x Huntaka. Fruits are long, thin, bright red at maturity with red flesh. This variety possessing good shelf life and transport quality. First picking starts about 135 days after sowing.This variety is moderately tolerant to sucking pests, bacterial leaf spot and fruit rot. This variety is suitable for rainfed condition. It is recommended for cultivation in Chhattisgarh, Orissa, Andhra Pradesh, Madhya Pradesh, Maharashtra, Karnataka, Tamil Nadu and Kerala.
Punjab Lal	This variety is derived from a cross between Perennial x Long Red and was released at state level from PAU, Ludhiana in 1985.Fruit is erect medium size (4.25 x 0.79 cm) dark green and turning dark red at maturity. This variety is resistant to CMV and leaf curl virus and moderately resistant to fruit rot and die back.
Punjab Surkh	Fruit is long (6.68 m) and deep red on maturity. It is very good for drying. It is tolerant to fruit rot and resistant to viral diseases

Pusa Jwala	This is an early cultivar of 'Samba' type. This is derived form a cross between NP46 A and Puri Red and released at national level from IARI, New Delhi in 1974. Fruit is 9 to 10 cm long and thin, light green turning light red at maturity. Dry fruits are wrinkled and liable to break during packing and transport. This variety has been also spread to Australia and Europe. Pungency is high. It is fairly tolerant to thrips, mites and aphids.
Pusa Sadabahar	This is evolved from a cross between Pusa Jwala x IC31339 (*C. fruitescens*) and was released at state level from IARI, New Delhi in 1989. Fruit is erect 6 to 8-cm length in cluster (6 to 14/cluster). Ripe fruit is bright red. It is resistant to CMV, TMV and leaf curl viruses.
Sankeshwar-32	It is selection from Sankeshwar type and released from MPAU, Rahuri, and Maharashtra. Fruit is longe (25-30 cm), thin wirely and highly wrinkled.Immature fruit is light green and turn red on maturity. It retains red colour in storage. It is mostly grown for dry fruit.
Sindhur	It is a dual-purpose chilli selected from Hot Portugal (CA960) and was released at state level from ARS, Lam, and Guntur in 1978. Fruits have deep red thick pericarp. Pericarp of fruit is light green turning deep red on maturity with smooth surface. Top is blunt. Fruit has mild pungency.
Solan Yellow	This variety has been developed from Y.S. Rao Parmer University of Horticulture and Forestry by local germplasm. The fruits of this variety are four to five cm in length having good pungency.
Sweet Banana	The fruits of this variety are thick pulpy light yellow colour having less pungency. This variety is suitable for salad and pickle purposes.
Surya Rekha	The plants of this variety are 50 cm tall with 15 to 20 branches. This variety is suitable in both seasons *Rabi* and *Kharif*.

13.4.3. Capsicum

Name	Remarks
Arka Basant	This variety has been developed from IIHR, Bangalore.It is an improvement over a Hungarian variety Soroksari. It is having good aroma and crisp texture. The variety is suitable for both *kharif* and *rabi* seasons as well as under protected covers. It has got good export value of the fruits.
Arka Gaurav	It is a pure line selection from Golden Calwonder from USA and released from IIHR, Bangalore.Fruits turn to orange yellow on maturity. It is good for both *kharif* and *rabi* seasons. Foliage covers the fruits to avoid sunscald. Plants are tolerant to bacterial wilt disease.
Arka Mohini	It is a selection from variety Titan from USA and released from IIHR, Bangalore. Plant is determinate with medium to large blocky fruits. Fruit is dark green surface, thick fleshed, 3-4 lobed and becomes red on ripening.This variety is suitable for both *kharif* and *rabi* seasons. Foliage covers the fruits avoiding the sunscald.Tipping of initial flowers is advocated to get higher yield.
Bharat	This hybrid has been released from Indo-Amercian Hybrid Seeds Ltd., Bangalore. Plants are vigorous. Fruits are dark green, blocky, four lobed and large sized (150 g).

Bull Nose	Plant is 50-60 cm tall, erect and sturdy. Fruits are 8-10 cm long, thick walled with three lobed and deep green. Flesh is thick with non-pungent. Fruit becomes scarlet red on maturity.
California Wonder	It is an introduction from USA. Fruits are smooth, 3-4 lobed with medium thick flesh. This variety can be used for market gardening.
Punjab-27	This variety is developed and released from PAU, Ludhiana. Fruits are light yellows, sweet and elongated.
Pusa Deepti	This variety has been released at IARI Regional Station Katrain for zone-1 comprising temperate and subtropical regions of northern India. It is early to medium in maturity.Since, it is tolerant to bacterial leaf spot and anthracnose under field conditions, it is more suitable for commercial production. It can be grown successfully in spring-summer (February-June) in hills and northern plains of India. It can be grown in the plains of western and southern parts of the country in *kharif* and *rabi* seasons.
Sel-2 (Nishant-1)	This variety has been developed at Shalimar Campus, Jammu & Kashmir. Fruits are dark green, turn yellow at physiological maturity, 3-4 lobed, non-pungent and bell shaped. It is recommended for cultivation in Jammu and Kashmir, Himachal Pradesh, and Uttaranchal
Shalimar Capsicum Hybrid - 1	This hybrid is developed by single cross hybrid between two lines (SH-SP-2x SH-SP-461) from Division of Olericulture, SKUAST – Kashmir, Shalimar. Plants are compact, foliage dark green, fruits large, blocky 3-4 lobed, dark green, uniform and yellow on ripening, rich in ascorbic acid, total chlorophyll, dry matter and TSS with good shelf life, salad and export qualities. This variety is tolerant to fusarium wilt, leaf spot and fruit rot. Maturity early with an average yield is 57.3t /ha.
Shalimar Capsicum Hybrid-2	This hybrid derived by single cross hybrid between two lines (SH-SP-2x SH-SP-11) from Division of Olericulture, SKUAST - Kashmir, Shalimar. Plants are compact with dark green foliage, fruit large to medium, blocky 3-4 lobed, dark green, thick fleshed and become red on ripening. This variety tolerant to fusarium wilt leaf spot and fruit rot under natural field conditions. An average yield is 48.6t /ha.
VL Shimla Mirch-2	It is developed by an introduction and selection from AVRDC line 9955-36 at (VPKAS), Almora, (Uttarakhand). Plants are vigorous and tall. Stems are strong with green foliage. Branching is just like chilli plant. The fruits are medium, bell shape and dark green in colour with smooth surface. Mature fruits are dark red. Fruits are slightly narrow in shape towards distal end. Fruit length and diameter ratio is > 1(1.21 %). This variety is resistant to fruit, wilt and powdery mildew.
Yolo Wonder	Plant of this variety is dwarf, prolific bearer and late with green. Fruits are blocky, drooping, medium flesh thickness with 3-4 lobes.
World Beater	Fruit is four lobed with medium thick flesh and mild sweet.

13.4.4. Okra

Name	Remarks
Arka Abhaya	It is released from IIHR Bangalore. Fruits are having 5-6 ridges, dark green in colour with good keeping quality. It is resistant to yellow vein mosaic virus.

Arka Anamika	It has been identified for general cultivation under the All India Coordinated Vegetable Improvement Project in 1990. It is earlier yellow vein mosaic virus resistant variety but at present it has become susceptifle to yellow vein mosaic virus. It is of inter specific origin between *Abelmoschus esculentus* and a wild species *A. manihot* spp tetraphyllus. Fruits are medium, green, rough, 5-ridged and start after 5-6th node onward.
Kashi Bhairav	This variety is developed at IIVR, Varanasi. Plant is medium tall with 2-3 branches. Number of ridges on fruit 5, fruit colour dark green, no. of fruits per plant 20-28, fruit length 11-14 cm, fruit diameter: 1.2-1.4 cm and fruit weight (Individual) 10-12 g. An average yield is 19.0 t/ha.
Gujarat Bhindi-1	It is a pure line selection from an unknown bulk seed sample received from IARI, New Delhi and was released from, GAU, Ahmedabad in 1983. Fruiting starts from 4-5th node. Fruits are 5-ridged, tender, 14-15 cm long and 6-7 cm girth in the center at marketable stage.
Gujarat Okra Hybrid-2	This hybrid has been developed at Junagadh from cross combination of KS-404 x HRB-108-2. Stem colour at seedling stage is green, whereas at maturity stage reddish. Leaves are deeply lobbed and serrated, smooth, green tender and attractive in colour. Less incidence of YVMV. Less infection of Jassids and pod borer. An average yield is 13.8t/ha.
Gujarat Anand Okra – 5	This hybrid is derived by VRO6 x AOL 00-6 and developed from Anand Agricultural University, Anand. Stem leaf and pod colour are dark green. The leaf tips are obtuse. The calyx colour of the flower is dark green. This is medium maturity group. In this variety there is low incidence of YVMV, jassids and white fly. An average yield is 14.1t/ha (Green pods).
Harbhajan	It is recommended by the Dr. Saini and his group at the College of Agriculture, Solan, Himachal Pradesh in 1983-84. The original 'Perkins Long Green' or Sel-6 has been named as Harbhajan to propagate the memory of the most dedicated vegetable scientist, Dr. Harbhajan Singh of Plant Introduction Division, IARI, and New Delhi. It is a main season variety. Fruits are very long, tapered, bright green, spine less and mostly 8-edged.
Hisar Unnat	It is developed and released from CCSHAU, Hisar.This variety is moderately tolerant to leaf hopper. It is loterant to yellow vein-mosaic virus.
Kashi Kranti	It is early and medium tall (100-115cm). Fruit colour is dark green & 8-10 cm long at marketable stage, Harvesting of pods can be done at crop after 45-95 days after seed sowing.An average yield is 14-15 t/ha and recommended for commercial cultivation in the States of Uttar Pradesh, Bihar, Jharkhand and Punjab suitable for warm humid climate.
Kashi Lila	This variety is suitable both rainy & summer season. Plant height is110-130cm. Fruits are five ridges, fruits size 3-15 long, 9-11 g in weight at marketable stage. An average yield is 19 t/ ha. This variety is recommended for cultivation in Andhara Pradesh, Odisha, Chhattisgarh and Maharashtra & MP.
Kashi Mahima	This variety is developed at IIVR, Varanasi. Plant is tall (130-170 cm). Fruits have five ridges (sometimes 6), colour dark green, number of fruits per plant 20-25, fruit length 11-13 cm, fruit diameter 1.15-1.4 cm, fruit weight (Individual) 10-12 g. An average yield is 20.0 t/ha.

Kashi Mohini	This is a YVMV resistant variety developed at IIVR, Varanasi by pedigree method of selection. Plants are tall and resistant to ELCV. Fruits are green with five ridges.
Kashi Mangali	This variety was developed at IIVR, Varanasi by pure line selection. Fruits are green with five ridges. It is suitable for cultivation under summer as well as for rainy season. This variety has been recommended for cultivation in Punjab, Uttar Pradesh, Bihar, Chhattisgarh, Orissa and Andhra Pradesh.
Kashi Pragati	This variety has been developed through pedigree selection of cross combination NIC 9303 x PK 20 at IIVR, Varanasi. Plant is tall, short internode (120-140 cm height), fruit color dark green, no of ridges on fruit 5, number of fruits per plant 20-25, fruit length 11-13 cm, fruit diameter 1.15-1.40 cm, fruit weight (Individual) 10-12 g. An average green pod yield is 16.0 t/ha
Kashi Satdhari	It is seven ridges fruited variety. Fruit length is 13-15 cm at marketable stage. On an average, it bears 18 fruits per plant.
Kashi Vardhan	It is early maturing and medium tall (120-125 cm) variety. An average yield is 15-15.5 t/ ha.This variety is recommended for cultivation in Uttar Pradesh, Bihar, Jharkhand and Punjab.
Kashi Vibhuti	This variety has been developed through pedigree selection of cross (NIC 9303 x IC111547) x IIVR 20). Plant type is dwarf (60-70 cm height), fruit shape long, fruit colour dark green, number of ridges on fruit 5, number of fruits per plant 20-25, fruit length 11-14 cm fruit diameter 1.3-1.5 cm and fruit weight (Individual) 10-13 g. An average yield is 10.0 t/ha.
P-7	This was yellow vein mosaic virus resistant variety developed by Thakur and Arora in 1988 at PAU, Ludhiana from a cross between *A. esculentus* cv. 'Pusa Sawani' and *A. manihot* ssp. *manihot*, a related species from Ghana carrying resistance to yellow vein mosaic virus. The F_1 was back crossed to 'Pusa Sawani' four times and selection was followed in the selfing generation upto F_8. Fruits are medium long, green, tender and 5-ridged. The top of the fruit is blunt and slightly furrowed.
Parbhani Kranti	This was yellow vein mosaic resistant variety evolved at MPAU, Parbhani, from interspecific cross between *A. esculentus* cv. Pusa Sawani and *A. manihot*, a Japanese species carrying resistance to yellow vein mosaic virus. F_1 was twice back crossed to 'Pusa Sawani' and followed by selection in subsequent generation upto F_8. The fruits are extremely dark green, smooth, tender, slender, 5-ridged with long and narrow top. It was notified by the Central Seed Committee in 1986 for general cultivation in throughout the country.
PUSA A-4	The plants have single stem with short internode (2-5 cm) and the fruits are 5-ridged, attractive dark green, 10-12 cm long having low mucillage and excellent shelf life. This variety was resistant to yellow vein mosaic virus and tolerant to aphids, jassids and least preferred by shoot and fruit borer. Plants have good adaptability.
Pusa Makhmali	This variety was developed through plant introduction at IARI, New Delhi. It was selected from the material collected from West Bengal. It is an early maturing variety. It is highly susceptible to yellow vein mosaic virus. This is considered good for yellow vein mosic virus free

	period, i.e., in spring-summer in northern India and rainy season in southern India.
Perking Long Green	It is a mid season variety. Fruit is long, tapered, bright green, spineless and mostly eight edged. It is especially suitable of hilly areas.
Punjab Padmini	It is a cross between *Abelmoschus esculentus* and *A. manihot* ssp. *manihot*. F_1 plant of *A. esculentus* cv. Reshmi x *A. manihot* ssp. manihot cv. Ghana was hybridized with F_2 (OP) plants of *A. esculentus* cv. Pusa Sawani x *A. manihot* ssp. manihot cv. Ghana. Fruits are quick growing, dark green, shining smooth, thin, 15-20 cm long, weighing 20-21 g, 5-ridged and remain tender for a long period (3-4 days). This variety was possessed field resistance to yellow vein mosaic virus and tolerance to jassids and cotton boll worm. It is recommended for cultivation during spring, summer and rainy seasons under north Indian conditions and also during winter in the south.
PUSA SAWANI	It was evolved by H.B. Singh in 1957-58 at the Plant Introduction Section, Division of Botany, IARI, New Delhi. It is derived from an intervarietal hybridization between IC-1542, a field resistance to yellow vein mosaic virus and Pusa Mukhmali a commercial cultivar. The fruits are smooth (slightly hairy on the edges), 5-edged, dark green and 18-20 cm long when fully developed. It is distinguished by the presence of a purple patch at the base of the yellow petal on both the sides (a character of the parent IC 1542), whereas, in most of the okra varieties, the patch is present only on the inner side. It was reported to free from the yellow vein mosaic virus under field conditions all over the country. But at present, it behaves as susceptible. The variety is still suitable for growing in the plains of northern India in virus free period (spring-summer season). In the hills, it can be sown form April to May depending on the altitude. It has very wide adaptability and can be successfully grown almost all over the country.
Varsha Uphar	This variety is a cross between 'Lam Selection 1' and 'Parbhani Kranti' which was developed and released at CCSHAU, Hisar.The fruits are smooth, dark green with 5 ridges and are ready for first picking 47 days after sowing. It is resistant to yellow vein mosaic virus.

13.4.5. Tomato

Name	Remarks
Arka Abha	This variety has been developed from IIHR Bangalore. Plants are indeterminate in growth. Fruits are flat, round, green shoulder and average fruit weight is 70-80 g. This variety is resistant to bacterial wilt.
Arka Abhijit	This is semi- determinate growth habit variety having 75 cm plant height and takes 55-60 days to first fruit maturity. Fruits are round having 70 g average fruit weight with green shoulder.TSS is 4.3 per cent and 17 days keeping quality at room temperature (from breaker to softening). It is resistant to bacterial wilt and suitable for fresh marketing.
Anand Tomato	This variety is developed through selection from F_7 progeny of cross Mahabaleshwar-2 x Sel.-7 from Anand Agricultural University, Anand. Plant growth habit is determinate type. Foliage is dark green colour

	with thick and big size leaves. At mature stage fruits have attractive dark red colour and thick pericarp .Fruits are round shaped and big size. This is medium maturity group variety and tolerant to leaf curl virus. An average yield is 32.6t/ha.
Arka Ahuti	It is pure line selection of variety Otwa-60 and released from IIHR' Bangalore. Plants are indeterminate in growth habit. Fruits are oval in shape, pulpy, tough skin and uniform ripening.
Arka Alok	This variety has been developed from IIHR, Bangalore. Fruits are determinate. Fruits are large in size (100 g), round in shape having green shoulder. It is resistant to bacterial wilt.
Arka Meghali	This variety is cross of Arka Vikas x IIHR-554 and developed through pedigree method of selection which released from IIHR, Bangalore. Plants are semi-determinate. Fruits are superior to Pusa Ruby variety in size (63 g), flesh thickness and fruit firmness. This variety is suitable for rainfed condition.
Arka Saurbh	It is an improvement over breeding line V-685 from Canada and released from IIHR, Bangalore. Plants are semi- determinate.Fruits are firm, fleshy, deep red and weighing about 70 g. This is a dual purpose variety suitable for both fresh market and processing purposes. It is resistant to fruit cracking.
Arka Shreshtha	It is developed and released from IIHR, Bangalore. Plants are semi-determinate. Fruits are round having light green shoulder and 75 g an average fruit weight. Fruits can be stored for 17 days (from breaker to softening stage) at room temperature. It is resistance to bacterial wilt and suitable for both fresh marketing and processing purposes.
Arka Vardan	It has been developed at IIHR, Bangalore. Plants are indeterminate in growth. Fruits are flat round, firm deep red with green shoulder with average weight of 140 g. It is resistant to nematodes and recommended for cultivation in Jammu and Kashmir, Himachal Pradesh, Uttranchal, Punjab, Bihar, Uttar Pradesh plains, Karnataka, Tamil Nadu and Kerala.
Arka Vikas	It is a selection from American variety TipTop and released from IIHR, Bangalore. Plants are semi-determinate in growth habit. Fruit is oblate, deep red in colour. It is suitable for fresh market purposes.
Arka Vishal	It has been developed at IIHR, Bangalore. Plants are indeterminate. Fruits are round, firm, deep red with green shoulder and average fruit weight of 140 g. It is tolerant to fruit cracking. It is recommended for cultivation in Punjab, Bihar and Uttar Pradesh plains.
ARTH-3	It has been developed at Ankur Seeds Pvt. Ltd., Nagpur. Plants are determinate. It is moderately tolerant to drought. It is recommended for cultivation in Assam, West Bengal, Maharashtra, western part of Madhya Pradesh, Karnataka, Tamil Nadu and Kerala.
ARTH-4	It has been developed by Ankur Seeds Pvt. Ltd., Nagpur. Plants are semi-spreading and indeterminate. Fruits are deep red and flat round. Flesh is red. It is moderately tolerant to drought. It is recommended for cultivation in Punjab, Bihar, Uttar Pradesh plains, Karnataka, Tamil Nadu and Kerala.
AZAD T-2	It is a derivative of the cross between HB-5 x Kuber, released in 1983 from CSAUA&T, Kanpur. Plants are determinate. Fruits are round, green when unripe and red on maturity with light green netting on dorsal side. Fruits are in clusters consisting of 6-8 fruits/ truss and 50-

	60-fruits/ plant. It is resistant to root knot nematode and moderately resistant to leaf curl virus. It is suitable for processing purposes.
Balkan	This is cluster bearing variety introduced from Bulgaria. Fruits are dark red with no greening or spot and medium to small in size. Plants can withstand in considerable cold. Due to its dwarf, compact and erect habit, more plants/unit area can be accommodated. Though, the fruits are medium small but attractive and firm, hence suitable for transportation. It is good for cultivation in early winter (rabi). It can be used in hybridization for developing cold and frost tolerant varieties.
Best Of All	It is indeterminate and mid season variety. Fruits are medium in size, scarlet red in colour, round, juicy, small scar, thin skin, three loculed with green shoulder and borne in clusters of four to five fruits.
CO-1	It was developed and released from TNAU, Coimbatore. Plant is determinate and suitable for growing in southern India. Fruits are round with yellow stem end, uniform ripening.
CO-2	It is a pure line isolated from USSR type and adopted in Tamil Nadu State. Plant is 70 cm tall, semi-dwarf, erect in growth habit with moderate branching, well spread and needs no staking. Fruits are ovate, medium in size, smooth, green when unripe and bright red on ripening. Fruits are devoid of cracking. Plant contains 4-5 fruits/truss and 20-25 fruits/ plant.
CO-3	It is a mutant of Co.1 variety and released in 1981 from TNAU, Coimbatore. Plants are dwarf, erect and determinate in growth habit. Fruits are medium in size, borne in clusters (4-5-fruits/truss), roundish, globular in shape, parrot green when unripe and attractive red on ripening. It is susceptible to mosaic, leaf curl virus and leaf spot diseases.
COTH-1	It is a cross between IIHR-709 and LE-812 and developed at TNAU, Coimbatore. Plants are determinate. Fruits are round to slightly oblong, medium sized (average weight 60 g) and bright red at maturity. First picking starts after 88-94 days.
Gulmohar	It has been develop at Maharashtra Hybrid Seeds Co. Ltd; Jalna. Plants are determinate. Fruits are red, square shape with average weight of 90 g. It is recommended for Maharashtra, western part of Madhya Pradesh, Karnataka, Tamil Nadu and Kerala.
Hisar Anmol	It is a determinate variety resistant to TLCV, derived through backcross-pedigree method from an inter-specific cross *L. esculentum* cv. Sel-7 x L. *hirsutum* f. *glabratum*. Fruits are flatish-round, fleshy, medium and red. This variety has been most widely utilized as a source of TLCV resistant for developing resistant varieties world-wide. This variety is recommended for release and cultivation in 1997 for Chhattishgarh, Orissa and Andhra Pradesh.
H.S.101	This variety was released by Central Sub-Committee on Release of Varieties in 1977 for commercial cultivation in Haryana, Uttar Pradesh, Gujarat and Tamil Nadu states. It is suitable for winter season. Plants are determinate in growth habit. Fruits borne in clusters (2-3 fruits/ truss), round small to medium in size, 3-4 loculed and uniform red on ripening.
Flora-Dade	This variety was brought from Florida. Plants are determinate.Fruits are big in size weighing 150-175 g/ fruit. This variety is tolerant to early blight.

HS-102	It is suitable for both winter and summer seasons and adopted to Haryana state. Plants are determinate in growth habit.Fruits are borne in cluster (3-4-fruits/truss), small to medium in size, and 3-4 loculed and uniform red on ripening.
HS-110	It is a selection from an exotic line and recommended for cultivation in Haryana. Plants are determinate having potato leaf type. It is suitable for table purposes.
Hisar Gaurav	It is developed and released from CCSHAU, Hissar. Fruits are large size, flat orange and fleshy. It is recommended for cultivation in leaf curl virus infested area.
Hisar Lalima	This variety has been developed through hybridization of Pusa Early Dwarf x HS-101 at CCS HAU, Hissar. It is an early maturing and large fruited variety. Fruits are round, flat attractive red, fleshy with 4-6 locules, a thick pericarp, less prune to cracking and suitable for both the tomato seasons (autumn and spring) in the north India. Harvest index is very high. Because foliage is less and fruit more in number.
Hisar Lalit	It is a derivative of HS-101 x Resistant Bangalore. Plant is semi-determinate. Fruits are round and medium too large. It is resistant to root knot nematode and recommended for cultivation in root knot nematode infested areas.
Jawahar Tamatar- 99	This variety has been developed from JNKV, Jabalpur by a germplasm collected from USA. Plants are determinate. It is an early variety. Fruits are round, hard and medium size with attractive yellow colour after ripening. This variety is suited for processing due to high TSS (5.3%).
Junagarh Ruby	It is a derivative of the cross between Inbred Big Silari x Pusa Ruby, released in 1981 from Gujarat state. Semi-spreading in growth habit. Four loculed and orange red on ripening with pinkish red flesh. It does not possess complete resistance against any disease and insect/pests.
Kalianpur Angoorlata	It is a selection from local germplasm at Kanpur, released in 1982. Plants are indeterminate growth habit. Fruits are small. Immature fruits are yellowish green and red on ripening. It is moderately resistant to leaf curl mosaic and resistant to root knot nematode.
Kalianpur T-1	It is a selection from local germplasm made at Kanpur and released in 1982. Plants are indeterminate in growth habit. Fruit is round, slightly pointed at the stigmatic end, 4-5 loculed, 4-5 fruits/ truss, non-cracking, light green when unripe and red on ripening. It is susceptible to tomato mosaic virus.
Kashi Abhiman	This is derived by VRT-04/010 x VRT-04/011. Plants are determinate in growth. Fruits are deep red in colour. Pericarp thickness is 0.6 cm and suitable for long distance transportation.Average fruits weight ranges from 75-95 g .TSS content is 4.2-4.6 brix. This is tolerant to tomato leaf curl virus disease as it carries Ty2 gene. Planting is late October. This variety is recommended for cultivation in Jammu & Kashmir, HP, Uttaranchal, Punjab, Uttar Pradesh, Bihar and Jharkhand in autumn-winter season. An average yield is 75.0 t/ ha.
Kashi Aman	Plant of this variety is determinate in growth. Fruits are round with high pericarp thickness. An average fruit weight ranges from 80-100 g with 4 locules..TSS content is 4.6 brix at fruits ripe stage. This variety is recommended for cultivation in Punjab, Bihar & Jharkhand. An average yield is 55.0 t/ ha.

Kashi Anupam	This variety has been developed through backcross pedigree selection. Plant type is determinate. Fruits are round in shape of red in colour. Fruits are large in size and borne an average 21.7 fruits/plants. Number of locules per fruit is 5.4 having T.S.S 4.4 % and consisting vitamin 'C' content 24 mg/100g edible fresh weight. First harvesting starts 75-85 days after transplanting. An average yield is 59.0 t/ha.
Kashi Amrit	This variety is derived from backcross selection (Sel.7×B-6013). Plant type is determinate. Fruit shape is round with red in colour. Fruit size is medium to large. Number of fruits per plant is 40-50 measured 5.5-6.5 cm in length, 5-6 cm in diameter and 90-100g (individual) fruit weight. Fruit pulp colour is red consisting T.S.S of 4.2 %. Vitamin 'C' content is 24 mg/100g edible fresh weight. First harvesting starts 75-80 days after transplanting. An average yield is 60.0 t/ha.
Kashi Hemant	This variety is developed through pedigree selection (Sel. -7 × Flora-Dade). Plant type is determinate in growth. Fruit shape is spherical round, fruit colour red, fruit size medium and fruit weight (Individual) 90-100 g. T.S.S is 4.1-4.2 % .Vitamin 'C' content is 22 mg/100g edible fruit weight. This variety is recommended for commercial cultivation in Chhattisgarh, Orissa, Andhra Pradesh, Madhya Pradesh and Maharastra. An average yield is 41.5 t/ha.
Kashi Sharad	This variety is derived through pedigree selection. Plant type is indeterminate. Fruits are slightly oval in medium size with red in colour. An average number of fruits per plant is 35-40 of 80-90 g (Individual) weight. T.S.S is 5.0-5.2. Vitamin 'C' content is 20 mg/100g edible fresh weight. Recommended for cultivation in Jammu & Kashmir, Himanchal Pradesh and Uttar Pradesh. An average yield is 60.0 t/ha.
Kashi Chayan	This variety was developed through hybridization followed by single plant selection. Plants are indeterminate in growth and resistant to tomato leaf curl virus carrying Ty_3 gene. An average yield is 60t/ha. This variety is scitable for juice prepation.
Kashi Vishesh	This variety has been developed through back-cross pedigree selection. Plant is determinate in growth habit. Fruits are round in shape and medium to large in size.Plants bear an average 30-40 fruit/plant and measured 90-100 g (individual) fruit weight. This variety was resistant to ToLCV. T.S.S is 4.4 % and vitamin 'C' content 25 mg/100g edible fresh weight.This variety has been recommended for cultivation in Uttaranchal, Jammu & Kashmir, Himanchal Pradesh, Punjab, Uttar Pradesh, Bihar, Jharkhand, Chhattisgarh,Orissa, Andhra Pradesh, Karnataka, Tamilnadu and Kerala. An Average yield is 42.5 t/ha.
Keckruth	It is a derivative of the cross Kecki Methi x Ruthger. Fruits are round, medium to large (70-80 gm), deep red on maturity, 3-4 locules and pericarp 0.3 cm thick.
Kechruth Ageti	It is a derivative of Keckruth x Ruthger. Plant is 100 cm tall. Fruits are round, medium in size (40-50 g) with green shoulder, which disappears on ripening, 3-4 loculed and pericarp 0.24 cm thick.
Labonita	It is an introduction from USA. Plants are determinate in growth habit. Fruits are plum shaped. This variety is suitable for spring summer season. It is resistant to fusarium wilt.
Shakati	It was developed through pure line selection at College of Horticulture, Vellanikkara, Kerala.Plants are determinate in growth with pubescent stem and normal leaf. Fruits are round, white and of medium size. It is

	resistant to bacterial wilt and fruit cracking. This variety is recommended for cultivation in Jammu & Kashmir, Himachal Pradesh, Uttaranchal, Chhattisgarh, Orissa and Andhra Pradesh, Madhya Pradesh, Maharashtra, Karnataka, Tamil Nadu and Kerala.
Madhuri	It has been developed at Beejo Sheetal Seed Pvt. Ltd., Jalna. This variety is determinate in growth and early in maturity. Fruits are dark red, flat round with thick skin, crack resistant and can with stand long transportation.
Manikhamnu	Plant is dwarf (34.5 cm), early maturing, determinate and multibranched. Fruits are medium size, round, smooth with 2-3 locules, uniform red at maturity.It is suitable for processing as well as fresh consumption purposes. It is resistance to fruit cracking and tolerant to leaf curl virus.
Manileima	It is an early maturing, determinate and multibranched variety. Fruits are medium size, oval, nipple shaped and bilocular. It is suitable for processing and long distance transportation. It is resistance to fruit cracking and tolerance to leaf curl virus. It is also tolerant to moisture stress and suitable for spring summer season.
Manithoibi	The plants are dwarf (35 cm), determinate and multibranched. It is an early maturing variety and capacity to withstand in moisture stress condition. Fruits are oval, medium, bilocular, good shelf life and uniform ripening.
Manisha	It has been developed from Beejo Sheetal Seed Pvt. Ltd. It has good shelf-life and transport quality.
Marglobe	It is a mid season variety and indeterminate in growth habit. Fruits are nearly round, deep scarlet colour on ripening. Fruits have dark green shoulder.
Meenakshi	This hybrid has been developed at Beejo Sheetal Seeds Pvt. Ltd., Jalna. Fruits are dark red, round global. It is resistant to fusarium wilt.
Megha	It has been developed at Beejo Sheetal Seed Pvt. Ltd., Jalna. Plants are determinate in growth. Fruits are red with thick skin, good shelf life and transport quality.
NDTR-1	It is a derivative from the multiple crosses between *Lycopersicon esculentum* x *L. peruvianum.* Plants are indeterminate growth habit. Fruits are medium to large (70-80 g), round, 4-6 loculed, 3-4 mm flesh thickness and bright red on ripening.
OX Heart	Foliage is dark green in colour. Fruit is heart shaped, pink in colour and each weighing 300-400 g. Interior of the fruit is extremely solid with thick firm walls and small seed cavities with few seeds.
Pant Bahar	It is a selection from germplasm lines maintained at Pantnagar and released by Central Sub Committee on Crop Standards, Notification and Release of varieties in 1985 for cultivation in both autumn- winter as well as spring- summer season in the plains. Plants are interminate in growth and branched. Fruits are flatish round, slightly ridged and red on maturity. It is resistant to verticillum wilt and fusarium wilt under field conditions. Fruits are good for processing purposes.
Punjab Chhuhara	It is derivative of the cross Punjab Tropic x EC55055, released in 1975 from PAU, Ludhiana. It is suitable for summer season. Plants are dwarf (60 cm), bushy and determinate growth habit. Fruits are pear shaped, thick pericarp, and well protected under foliage.It has good

	keeping quality and sets fruits under high temperature conditions. It is good for processing purposes.
Punjab Kesari	It is a derivative of the cross Punjab Tropic x EC55055, released from PAU, Ludhiana. Fruits are oval round, medium in size (55 g), three loculed and red on maturity.
Punjab Tropic	It is a selection from the introduction of USA and released from PAU, Ludhiana. Plants are indeterminate growth habit with luxuriant growth. Fruits are large (100 g), round, red on maturity). It has late fruit setting with slow development of fruits.
Pusa Divya	This hybrid has been developed by utilizing closed anther mutant with potato leaf marker gene (functional male sterility) as female parent. This hybrid is especially suitable for cultivation in Uttar Pradesh, Punjab and Bihar. Plants are indeterminate in growth with profuse branching. Fruits are firm, thick, skinned, round to oval shaped, green with dark green stem end and turn dark red on ripening. Due to thick skin, fruits have longer shelf life with suitability for long distance transportation. This hybrid has less infestation to late blight and buckey rot.
Pusa Early Dwarf	It is a derivative of the cross Meeruti x Red Cloud and widely adopted. It is suitable for rainy season in plains and for spring-summer sowing in hills. Plants are dwarf with determinate growth. Fruits are roundish, slightly flattish, medium large, uniform red, ribbed and obscure furrows.
Pusa Gaurav	It has been developed from the exotic segregating generation of a cross between Galmour and 'Watch' and released by the IARI, New Delhi. Plants are dwarf, bushy with moderate foliage cover. The fruits are smooth, elliptical (egg shaped) and borne in clusters. The unripe fruits are firm with thick flesh (0.6 cm) and two well-filled locules that facilitate easy transportation over long distances. Whole fruit is suitable for processing and canning because it is without neck constriction and has higher TSS (6 per cent) and better keeping quality at room temperature.
Pusa Hybrid-1	Plant is determinate in growth habit.Fruits are round, smooth and attractive. It is ready for market from late May to mid July. Pusa Hybrid-1 has an added advantage of providing tomatoes form June to mid July, the lean period for tomato in north India. It can set fruit upto a temperature of 28 ^{0}C during night.
Pusa Hybrid-2	It has developed by combining desirable commercial characters and recommended it for cultivation in humid western Himalayan regions, sub-humid Sutluj-Ganga alluvial plains and Western plains, semi-arid plateau. Plants are semi-determinate.Fruits are round to flatish round, firm, smooth, attractive and develop a uniform red colour on maturily. This hybrid is highly tolerant to root knot nematode.
Pusa Hybrid-4	Plants are determinate in growth. Fruits are attractive, round, smooth, medium-sized (70-80 g). This hybrid is highly tolerant to root knot nematodes under field condition.
Pusa Red Plum	It is a selection from a cross between the dwarf variety Red Cloud and Merruti. This variety does well in summer and in winter growing seasons.
Pusa Ruby	It is a derivative of Improved Meeruti x Sioux. This is early maturing very old and wider adoptable variety having indeterminate growth

	habit. Fruits are flattened, grooved, firm and medium size. It is suitable for rainy season for all over the country.
Pusa Sadabahar	This variety has been released by IARI, New Delhi. It is highly suitable for growing under wide range of 8-30 ^{0}Cnight temperature. Plant is determinate in growth habit. This variety can be accommodated more number of plants per unit area. This variety is very prolific bearer with smooth oval to round attractive fruits. This variety can be grown throughout the year in north Indian plains except rainy season (July to early September).
Pusa Sheetal	It has been developed by combining the desired attributes of two cold set lines Balkan from Bulgaria and Temnorrosnij from USSR by hybridization and selection of plants to set fruit at very low temperature in segregating generation. Fruits are flatish round, smooth, attractive and developed uniformly red colour on maturity. This cultivar is very suitable for raising as an additional early crop in northern India.
Pusa Uphar	It is indeterminate and having higher fruit setting with desirable quality attributes in slightly adverse temperature. It is developed form IARI, New Delhi and released by the Central Variety Release Committee in 1999. Fruits are attractive round, medium sized (60 g), thick-skinned and uniform in ripening. This variety is slightly tolerant to fruit borer under field conditions. It is suitable for cultivation in Ganga alluvial and western plains.
PUSA-120	It is well-adopted very old variety and released from IARI, New Delhi. Plants are semi-indeterminate. Fruits are attractive, round to flatish round, medium to large in size, smooth, uniform red in colour, less acidic and less seeded. It is resistant to nematodes and does well in both summer and winter seasons.
Roma	It is an introduction form USA. Plants are semi-dwarf. Fruits are pear shaped with thick pericarp, red in colour on ripening, free from green shoulder, bilocular, small seed cavity and less seeded. This variety possesses good keeping quality and good for processing.
Shalimar Tomato Hybrid-1	This hybrid is developed by Single cross hybrid between a male sterile and apollen parent (SH-FMS-1 x SH-T-11) from SKUAST - Kashmir, Shalimar. Plants are determinate with excellent light green foliage cover, flowers light yellow, fruits uniform red oval round, firm with smooth fruit surface pulpy, rich in vitamin C, TSS, dry matter content and tolerant to cold and fruit cracking. An average yield is 110.4t/ha.
Sioux	It is an exotic variety introduced from USA. It is indeterminate type and produce yellowish green, medium large fruit, which becomes uniform red at ripening. It has ability to set the fruits in spring and summer seasons.
Solan Gola	This variety has been developed from YS Parmar University of Forestry and Horticulture, Solan. Plants are indeterminate in growth habit. Fruits are round attractive, medium size, red colour and thick pericarp. This variety is suited for transportation to distant market.
Sonali	It is a high yielding bacterial wilt resistant variety evolved from an exotic collection and recommended for the bacterial wilt prone southern district of Konkan.
Sweet-72	It is cross of Pusa Red Plum x Sioux and developed at the Regional Agricultural Research Institute, Gwalior. The fruits of Sweet-72 are

	round oval and somewhat flattened in shape. They are attractive and scarlet red in colour. Vitamin-C content of tomato Sweet-72 is very high (20.91 mg per 100 ml). It is very sweet in taste with sugar percentage of 1.62.
Utkal Kumari	This is a bacterial wilt resistant and indeterminate variety, developed at OUA& T, Bhubaneshwar. It is derived from the cross Selection 22 x BT-2. Fruits are round, red, medium-large with 5-6 days shelf-life. This variety is recommended for cultivation in Chhattisgarh, Orissa, Andhra Pradesh, Rajasthan, Gujarat, Haryana and Delhi.
Utkal Urbasi	This variety has been developed at OUA&T, Bhubaneshwar. It is derived from the cross Punjab Chhuhara x LE-79. Plants are indeterminate in growth. Fruits are pear shaped, red with green shoulder, 2-3 locules, low seed content and thick skin. This variety is resistant to bacterial wilt and tolerant to early blight. This variety has been recommended for cultivation in 1996 for Jammu &Kashmir, Himachal Pradesh, Uttaranchal, Punjab, Uttar Pradesh and Bihar.
Vl Tamatar-4	It is developed by an introduction and selection from AVRDC line CL 5915-206 at VPKAS, Almora. Plants are indeterminate vigorous in growth with standard leaf type. The immature fruits are light green coluor. The mature fruits are medium large, smooth round shape and dark red in colour with slight locular impression. Resistant to fruit rot & seedling rot.
Yashwant-2	This variety has been developed from YS Parmar University of Forestry and Horticulture, Solan. Plants are indeterminate growth habit. Fruits are uniform red in color with thick pericarp. This variety is resistant to buckeye rot.

13.5. Leafy and Salad Vegetables

13.5.1. Amranths

Name	Remarks
Annapurna	It is a pure line selection from a bulk collected from Pauri district of Uttar Pradesh hills and identified for hills of Uttaranchal, Himachal Pradesh, and North-East Hill Zone. The variety has multipurpose used in early stages. It is resistant to lodging, highly resistant to drought and hardy to frost. It is also highly resistant to leaf spot diseases and *Alternaria* spp.
Arka Arunima	It is developed through pure line selection from IIHR-49 and released from IIHR, Bangalore. It is a multi-cut variety. The leaves are rich in Ca and Fe and low in anti-nutrient factors like oxillate and nitrates. It is resistant to white rust.
Arka Suguna	It provides highly succulent stems along with attractive broad and green leaves. This is an ideal for multicut without becoming fibrous and generates at the fast rate, which becomes ready for first cutting at 24 days after sowing.
CO.1	It belongs *Amaranthus dubius* Linn. Inflorescence is terminal, thinly fingered green at emergence and yellow green at maturity. It is especially suited for late harvest at 30-35 days after sowing.

CO.2	It is a local selection belongs *Amaranthus tricolor* L. The leaves contain 1.3 per cent crude fibre with 19.0 mg of iron and 20.0 mg of calcium per 100 g.
CO.3	It is a selection from local types A.83. This variety belongs *Amaranthus tricolor* var. *tristis*. The variety is suitable for green purpose. The leaves contain 25.2 mg vitamin 'C' per 100 g of edible part, 1.74 per cent crude fibre, 0.8 per cent iron and 2.48 per cent calcium.
CO.4	It is also selection from local type belongs *Amaranthus hypochondiacus* L. The grains are rich in protein (15.9 per cent) and other essential amino acids. The popped grains mixed with jaggery can be made in to sweet meat, balls and other snacks. This variety is tasty and nutritious 'Amranths malt' can also be made from the grains.
Pusa Badi Chauli	This variety belongs to *Amaranthus tricolour*. It is suitable for summer and crop may prolong up to the end of rainy season.
Pusa Chhoti Chauli	This variety belongs to *Amaranthus blitum*. It is suitable for both summer and rains.
Pusa Kiran	It is a cross of *Amaranthus tricolour* and *A. tristis*, this variety is suitable for rainy season cultivation.
Pusa Kirti	This variety belongs *A. tricolor* group develop by local material S-21-4, collected from Tamil Nadu. This variety is suitable for summer season cultivation.
Pusa Lal Chauli	The upper surface of leaves is deep red or magenta, whereas lower surface is purplish red. It is suitable for both summer and *kharif* season in the plains.

13.5.2. Celery

Name	Remarks
Standard Bearer	It is an early variety. Stem is medium pink with white longitudinal streaks. Stalk is solid with good size and flavor.
Wrigt Grove Giant	Plant is tall which produces large white, stalks of fine quality.

13.5.3. Lettuce

Name	Remarks
Crisp Head	The cultivars are New York 515, Imperial 44, Imperial 152, Imperial 456 or Cornell 456, Imperial 615 and Imperial 847, Imperial 859, Great Lakes and Pennlake.
Butterhead	Important cultivars are: Big Boston. White Boston, May King, Salamandar and Wayahed. Bibb type is small and dark green with reddish margins and also known as Limestone, popular in USA. The English cultivars like Borough Wonder, Cobham Green and Avondefiance, Dutch cultivars Reskia, Wonder Van Voorbing and May King and Belgian cultivar Hilde are adapted to warm weather.
Cos or Romainer	The important cultivars are: Effel Tower, Paris Island, Paris White and Dark Green Valmaine.
Leaf or Bunching	The important cultivars are: Black - seeded Simpson, Prizehead, Australian and Salad Bowl for outdoor growing and Grand Rapids for

	green house production. This type is grown in the United State of America, Australia, Europe and also in India.
Stem	The cultivars have thick stem, which is peeled and eaten raw or cooked as vegetable. The leaves are edible but inferior in quality to the leaves of the other types.
Latin	The important cultivars are Gallega (mosaic resistance), Criolla, Verde, Criolla Blenca and Madrilene.

13.5.4. Spinch Beet (Palak)

Name	Remarks
All Green	This is an early variety suitable for growing in September.
Arka Anupama	It has been developed through cross of IIHR-10 and IIHR-8 followed by pedigree method of selection and released from IIHR, Bangalore. It is a late bolter with vigorous initial growth and regenerates at a faster rate. Leaves are rich in chlorophyll, vitamin C and iron content. It is resistant to cercospora leaf spot under field condition.
Banerjee Giant	It is a very popular cultivar evolved by SP Banerjee in West Bengal. This cultivar has been developed from a cross between Local Palak and Beet Root. It produces large thick leaves with very succulent stem and fleshy root.
Jobner Green	This cultivar was evolved at Department of Horticulture, University of Udaipur at Jobner Campus during 1964 as a result of spontaneous mutation detected from the population of a local collection Serial No. 5. It produces uniform green large thick succulent tender leaves with strong flavour having entire margin. Leaves are easily cooked and taste is comparable to cv. 'All Green'.
Pusa Bharti	The leaves are pure green without any red pigmentation. It can be grown in summer and *kharif* season also. For a regular supply, periodical sowing is recommended from March onwards upto mid-September .
Pusa Harit	This cultivar has been developed by hybridization between sugar beet and local palak at IARI, Regional Station, Katrain (Himachal Pradesh). This cultivar is suitable for cultivation in the hills throughout the year mainly because of its chilling requirements.This character has been inherited from its sugar beet. It has late bolting habit and wide range of adaptability to varying climate. It can also tolerate alkaline soil.
Pusa Jyoti	It is evolved through an induced polyploid of cultivar All Green with two per cent colchicine for 24 hrs and selection. The variety is quick growing and generated quickly after each cutting.It is a giant-leaved strain and produces large, green, thick, tender, succulent, crisp leaves of good taste even when eaten as salad. When cooked, they develop nice flavour and colour. It is rich in potash, calcium, sodium, iron and ascorbic acid and can be grown throughout the year.
Pusa Palak	The cultivar was released by IARI, New Delhi in 1967. It is selection from a cross between Swish Chard and Local Palak. It produces uniform green leaves without any purple pigmentation. It is a late bolting cultivar.
Round Leaves	Leaves are round, pointed and green. Average yield is 5.0 t/ha in 50-60 days crop duration.
Ooty-1	It is a tasty green leafy vegetable released during 1995 from TNAU, Coimbatore through selection of Local type in which cutting starts 45

	days after sowing and continued at 15 days intervals for a period of two years. Leaves are green and rich in vitamin 'A'. It yields 15.0t q/ha of leaves. They contain higher carotene content. It can be grown throughout the year and can withstand frost.
Virginia Savoy	It is suitable for September-October sowing. Plants are upright and vigorous, leaves blistered, crimpled, thick and dark green and late bolting type. Five-six cuttings can be done at 15-20 days interval. It is a good yielder and smooth seeded variety.

13.6. Legume Vegetables

13.6.1. Broad Bean

Name	Remarks
Pusa Sumeet	It has attractive dark green pods and borne in cluster.
Pusa Udit	Pods are extra-long, flattish and light green. This is a dual purpose broad bean variety. This variety is suitable for packaging and transport. The variety gave 88.52% higher yield than the earlier released variety Pusa Sumeet.

13.6.2. Cluster Bean

Name	Remarks
Durga Bahar	It is a derivative of the cross between Pusa Navbahar and ROC 401 released in 1984 from Rajasthan. Plants are photosensitive. Pods are 13-14 cm long, fleshy, borne in cluster with 3-4 pods/cluster at every node. It is moderately susceptible to bacterial blight and suitable for *kharif* as well as summer seasons.
Pusa Mausami	It is a selection from Local cultivar of North India. It is good for rainy season. Plants are short stature, photosensitive and sparsely branched. Pods are 9-10 cm long, smooth, light green, glossy surface, tender and sweetish.
Pusa Navbahar	It combines the good traits of both Pusa Mausami and Pusa Sadabahar cultivars. The disadvantages of this variety are single-stemmed nature, susceptibility to bacterial blight and lodging.
Pusa Sadabahar	It is a selection from a local cultivar 'Jaipuri' of Rajasthan. It is a non-branching type suitable for both summer and rainy seasons. The disadvantage with this cultivar is poor quality of pods
Sharad Bahar	It is evolved on the basis of single plant selection form IC11704 (a local collection from Maharashtra).

13.6.3. Cowpea

Name	Remarks
Arka Garima	This popular variety has been bred at IIHR, Bangalore derived through back cross and pure line selection from the cross TUV-762 x *Vigna unguiculata* spp. *sesquipedelis*. Pods are light green, long thick, round,

	fleshy and stringless. It is tolerant to heat and drought. This variety is recommended for cultivation in Madhya Pradesh, Maharashtra, Karnataka, Tamil Nadu and Kerala.
Bidhan Barbati-1	It is an advance generation collection of cross EC-243954 of culti group, *unguiculata* and EC-305827 of culti group *sesquipedalis*. Plants are determinate in growth habit. Pods are tender. It shows resistant to cow pea mosaic and cowpea golden mosaic virus.
Bidhan Barbati-2	It is an advance generation collection of cross V-70 of culti group, *biflora* and Sel Tm-3 of culti group *sesquipedalis*. Plants are semi-determinate. The tender pod contains high protein (0.4 per cent crude protein). It shows very low incidence of cowpea mosaic and cowpea golden mosaic virus.
Birsa Sweta	It is selection from local material collected from Bihar. It is suitable for rainy season. Plants are indeterminate in growth habit.
Cowpea-263	It is a selection form Bangalore local, a germplasm collected from the IIHR, Bangalore and developed by PAU, Ludhiana for the commercial cultivation in Punjab. This variety is suitable for both spring and rainy seasons. Plants are dwarf. It is an early maturity variety. It is free from the golden mosaic and comparatively resistant to other mosaics.
Kashi Gauri	It is developed from a cross of IIHR Sel. 16 × Sel. 2-1. It is bush type and dwarf (70-75 cm height), photo-insensitive and early variety suitable for sowing in both spring-summer and rainy seasons. It flowers in 35-40 days and pods get ready for harvest in 45-50 days. It produces 35-40 pods per plant of 25-30 cm long. The pods are green, tender, fleshy with less fibrous and free from parchment layer. The variety is resistant to cowpea golden mosaic virus and produces 10.0-12.5t/ha^{-1} green pods.
Kashi Kanchan	It is developed from a back cross selection (Sel. 2-2 × BC-244002) × Sel. 2-2. It is bush type and dwarf (50-60 cm height), photo-insensitive and early variety suitable for sowing in both spring-summer and rainy seasons. It flowers in 40-45 days and pods get ready for harvest in 50-55 days. It produces 40-45 pods per plant of 30-35 cm long. The pods are dark green, tender, pulpy with less fibrous and free from parchment layer. The variety is resistant to cowpea golden mosaic virus and produces about 15.0-17.5 t/ha^{-1} green pods.
Kashi Nidhi	It is developed from a cross of Kashi Unnati × Cowpea-263. It is dwarf & bush type (45-50 cm), photoperiod-insensitive, early variety suitable for sowing in both spring-summer and rainy seasons. It flowers in 40-45 days after sowing and pods get ready for harvest in 50-55 days. It produces 30-35 pods per plant of 30-35 cm long. The pods are dark green, thin, pulpy, cylindrical and parchment free. The variety is resistant to Golden Mosaic Virus and *Cercospora cruenta*, and produces 12.5-15.0t/ha^{-1} green pods.
Kashi Shyamal	It is developed through the selection from local collection (Kala Jhalma). It is an early, dwarf and bush type variety (70-75 cm height) suitable for sowing in both spring-summer and rainy seasons. It flowers in 30-35 days and pods become ready for harvest in 40-45 days. It produces 35-40 pods per plant with average pod length of 30-33 cm. The pods are light green with reddish tip, soft and pulpy. The average pod yield is ranged 7.5-10.0t q/ha^{-1}. It was released and notified by CVRC vide

	DAC notification No. 597(E) dated 25.4.2006.
Kashi Sudha	It is developed from a cross of Kashi Shyamal × NDCP-13. It is a photo-insensitive, dwarf and bushy type (50-60 cm height) early variety suitable for sowing in both spring-summer and rainy seasons. It flowers in 40-45 days and pods get ready for harvest in 50-55 days. It produces 20-25 pods per plant with average pod length of 35-40 cm. The average pod yield is ranged 10.0-12.0t q/ha^{-1}. It has been identified & recommended by XXVI Group Meeting of AICRP (VC) held at OUA&T, Bhubaneswar from 23-27 Feb. 2008 for Zone IV, V and VII (Punjab, U.P., Bihar, Jharkhand, Chhattisgarh, Orissa, A.P., M.P. and Maharashtra States).
Kashi Unnati	It is developed from a cross of Cowpea-263 × Arka Garima. It is a photo-insensitive, dwarf and bushy type (40-45 cm height) early variety suitable for sowing in both spring-summer and rainy seasons. It flowers in 30-35 days and pods get ready for harvest in 40-45 days. It produces 40-45 pods per plant with average pod length of 30-35 cm. The average pod yield is ranged 12.5-15.0t q/ha^{-1} and it was resistant to cowpea golden mosaic virus. It is released by State Variety Release Committee of Uttar Pradesh and notified by CVRC for entire Uttar Pradesh.
Pusa Barsati	It is an exotic selection from Philippines introduction. It is an early cultivar suitable for growing during the rainy season.
Pusa Do-Fasli	It has been evolved by crossing Pusa Phalguni with a cultivar from the Philippines. It is a bushy cultivar suitable for sowing in both spring-summer and rainy seasons.
Pusa Phalguni	It has been selected from a Canadian cultivar. It is a bushy type dwarf variety and suitable for sowing in February-March in northern India. It gives dark green erect pods of 12.5 cm length.
Pusa Komal	It is a cross of P85-2 and PU26 cowpea strains. The pods are bright green, non-fibrous, cylindrical, soft and meaty.
Pusa Rituraj	It is a selection developed by NPBGR, New Delhi. Due to high photo-thermo-insensitive nature, this variety can be grown in summer as well as in rainy seasons. It gives comparatively better performance even under severe summer conditions. The plant is bushy. It is a dual-purpose variety as pods and seeds (brown) can be used for cooking.
Pusa Sukomal	This variety is developed from IARI Pusa New Delhi. This variety is resistant to golden yellow mosaic virus and leaf spot diseases. Maturity is 55-60 days. An average yield is 6.0 and 6.5 t/ha during summer and *kharif* seasons, respectively.

13.6.4. French bean

Name	Remarks
Arka Komal	It is an improvement over Australian collection IIHR - 60. Plant is bushy. The pods are green, straight, flat and tender. It is very good in cooking and transport purposes.

Arka Anoop	This variety has been developed through hybridization between IIHR 220 and Arka Komal. Plant height is 55-60 cm. Plants are bushy, photo insensitive, with white flowers. Pods are straight, long (17-18), light green and fleshy.This variety is suitable for sowing in both early &late. The variety has fleshy, green smooth pods and suitable for fresh market. This variety is resistant to rust and bacterial blight diseases. An average green yield is 17.1t/ha. This variety is recommended for cultivation in Himachal Pradesh, J&K, Uttaranchal, Chhattisgarh, Orissa, Andhra Pradesh, Karnataka, Tamil Nadu and Kerala.
Bayo	Plant is medium, semi-trailing and foliage medium green. It is medium to late maturity variety. It is susceptible to red spider injury.
Blue Pod Medium	It is a white seeded variety. The pods are medium having bluish blacking spot on pods. It is susceptible to all common diseases of beans.
Bountiful	It is an introduction from USA. Plants are bushy type and coming up well during September to February in south India. Pods are borne in clusters on the main stem.
Brown Sweedish	Plant is dwarf, upright and foliage dark green. It is susceptible to blight and anthracnose.
California Cream	Plants are dwarf. It is an early maturing variety. It is resistant to common diseases.
Contender	It is an introduction from USA.It is bush type. Pods are round, green, 13-14 cm long, stringless, meaty and slightly curved. It is tolerant to powdery mildew and mosaic.
Crane Berry	It is a late season variety and sensitive to extreme heat.
Gaint Stringless	It is an introduced variety with early and bush habit. The pod is green, medium-large, long, slightly cured, tender, meaty and stringless.
Jampa	It is a Mexican variety having outstanding performance in Maharashtra. The plant has a slight trailing habit. The pods are round, smooth, and become fibrous when mature and hence should be harvested at tender stage. It is highly resistant to wilt diseases and can withstand warmer conditions.
Kashi Param	This variety was developed through pedigree selection. Plant is bushy, pod color dark green and pod size medium. Number of pods per plant is 12-14, pod length 10.5-11.6 cm, pod diameter 0.65-0.85 cm, pod weight (10 pods) 40-50 g, and 3-4 pickings. An average green pod yield is 15.0 t/ha.
Kashi Sampann	This variety was developed through hybridization (Arka Komal X Contender) at IIVR, Varanasi. Plants are bushy and multi- branched. Flowering occurs in axial of the leaf. Pods are light green in round shape. Sometimes 75 pods are harvested in one plant. Pods are 11.2-14.0 cm in length, 0.7-1.0 cm width and 0.6-0.9 cm in thickness consisting 5-7 seeds per pod. Per plant yield harvested 400 g green pods in 4-5 pickings. Flowering-fruiting continue in day temperature upto 32-34°C. Seeds are bright
Kashi Rajhans	This variety was developed at IIVR, Varanasi from a Canadian line EC- 595960 exclusively for vegetable type. This has ability to give flowering – fruiting at temperature of day temperature 32-34 °C in Varanasi condition (heat tolerance). Peak fruiting period is second week of February and continue up to first week of April. An average green pod yield is 23.8t/ha. This variety yielded33.09% more pod yield with national check Arka Komal.

Kentucky Wonder	It is an introduction from USA. A pole type variety which pods are ready in 60-65 days for picking.
Lakshmi	It has been bred from a cross between Contenders (bush) x Local (pole) varieties. It has been adopted in mid hill areas. Plants are indeterminate. Pods are formed in cluster of three, stringless, green, round and are quite attractive. It is the tolerant to angular leaf spot disease.
Michigan Robust	It is immune to mosaic and resistant to anthracnose and blight.
Pant Anupama	This is bushy type and early bearing variety. Pods are round, smooth, tender, stingless and green. It is resistant to angular leaf spot and moderately resistant to common mosaic virus.
Peary Marrow	It is cross between Wells Red Kidney and White Marrow. It is resistant to anthracnose and mosaic but susceptible to blight.
Pink	Seeds are somewhat square ended and fairly resistant to heat and disease.
Pinto	Seeds are greyish, strapped and flattened with greenish to pink colours. It is susceptible to bean rust.
Premier	This is a bushy variety with black seeds bearing profusely and more hardy than Bountiful. This variety is suitable for late sowing and less susceptible to wilt and mosaic diseases.
Pusa Himlata	It has been developed through pure line selection of an exotic introduction at the IARI Regional Station, Katrain. It is climbing or pole type. Pods are light green. The seeds are white and suitable for processing as green-shelled bean. Mature seeds also have good cooking quality and are suitable for use as dry bean (rajmah). Besides, high yield, it is also superior in other pod characters to 'Kentucky Wonder'.
Pusa Parvati	This variety was is developed through X-ray irradiation of an American variety, 'Wax Pod' at the IARI, New Delhi.It is an early bush type with attractive round, meaty with light green pods, which matures in 40-45 days. It is resistant to mosaic and powdery mildew diseases.
Red Kidney	Seeds are pink when newly harvested and dark red when old. This variety is resistant to mosaic but susceptible to anthracnose and blight.
Red Mexican	This variety is resistant to heat and drought.
Seminole	This variety was evolved in Florida. Pods are smooth and round. It is highly resistant to rust, mildew and mosaic diseases.
SVM-1	It is pole type variety evolved by interspecific hybridization between *Phaseolus vulgaris* var. Contender and *P. multiflorus* var. PBL257, where the latter is resistant to angular leaf spot disease. It has been recommended for mild hill areas. Pods are green, round, stringless, 13-14 cm long, 8-10 seeds/pod, and brown shining in colour with black scar. Protein content is 22 per cent.This variety is resistant to angular leaf spot both in leaf and pods. It is a dual-purpose variety, thus can be used for vegetable and seeds as pulse.

13.6.5. Garden Pea

Name	Remarks
Alaska	This is an early smooth seeded canning cultivar with bluish green seeds. Pods are borne singly, light green in colour, 7 x 1.25 cm, contain 5-6 small green seeds and shelling percentage 42.

Alderman	This is an excellent cultivar for home garden, shipment and freezing. This cultivar is suitable for hills.
Arkel	It is an early wrinkled-seeded, most popular exotic variety introduced from England and tested by IARI, New Delhi, occupies large area almost in northern and central India. Pods are dark green, sweet, sickle shaped, incurved towards the sutures having pointed distal end and with 7 to 8 green ovules per pod. The variety is highly susceptible to collar rot if sown very early especially under high temperature conditions. It is suitable for fresh market and dehydration.
Asauji	The selection of this variety has been made from the material collected from Amritsar and released from IARI New Delhi. It is a dwarf, early, green and smooth seeded cultivar suitable for early sowing. The pods are produced singly, about 8 cm long, curved, dark green, narrow and appear round when fully developed having 7 seeds /pod.
AZAD P-1	It is a derivative of the cross 6416 x 6405 and released in 1983 from Uttar Pradesh. Pods are smooth, dark green, 8-10 cm long, narrow (1.2 - 1.4 cm), very tightly filled, 8-10 seeds / pod and 30-40 pods / plant. Pods are slightly curved at the distal end. Mature seed is wrinkled. This variety escapes powdery mildew and rust.
AZAD P-2	It is a powdery mildew resistant variety, developed at Vegetable Research Station, CSAU & T, Kanpur, derived from the cross-Bonneville x 6587. Pods are medium with 6-7 ovules, nearly straight, light green, smooth and firm. Seeds are wrinkled and brown seed; suitable for cultivation in late sown condition and powdery mildew prone areas cultivation in 1990 for Punjab, Uttar Pradesh, Bihar, Rajasthan, Gujarat, Haryana, Delhi, Madhya Pradesh and Maharashtra.
Bonneville	This is a wrinkled-seeded mid-season most popular variety and introduced from USA. Pods are light green, 8 cm in length with 8 bigger green sweet ovules. This variety is highly susceptible to powdery mildew.
Early Badger	It is a dwarf early wrinkled-seeded cultivar evolved at Wisconsin. It is suitable for sowing in early October. The plant flower in 40-45 days and first blossom appears at 10-11th node and ready for harvesting in 60 to 65 days. The yellowish green pods are borne singly, 7.5 cm long, well filled, 5-6 seeded and sweet. It is a good canning cultivar having a shelling percentage of 36. It is resistant to fusarium wilt and tolerate heat and drought.
Early Giant	It is a late variety suited to hills of Himachal Pradesh. Plants are tall and need staking. Pods are 9-10 cm long, dark green with 9-10 bold grains. Seeds are wrinkled.
Early Supperb	It is an English dwarf cultivar with yellowish green foliage. The plants are branched from base. It is an early smooth-seeded variety. It flowers in about 45 days and first blossom appears at 8-10th node. The pods are borne singly, dark green and curved with 6-7 seeds. The shelling percentage is 40.
Harbhajan	It is an introduction and suitable for all dry areas of north India. Pods are green and long. Seeds are small (13 g/100 seeds), round, wrinkled and yellow in colour. Flowering starts from 6th nodes. It is susceptible to powdery mildew.

Hisar Harit	The variety is semi-dwarf and early. Pods are single to double, large, green, well filled, and dimpled after drying.
Hara Bona	It is developed through pure line selection from the local field pea variety and released in 1980 from Punjab. Pods are 7.8 cm long, dark green and 5-6 seeds per pod with 40 per cent of shelling. Mature seeds are bold, round, dimpled both sides and green in colour. This variety escapes powdery mildew and pea rust.
Jawahar Matar-1	It is a derivative of the cross T-19 x Greater for all pea growing areas of the country. Pod setting begins from 11th node and usually two pods per axil. Pods are straight with bead like out growth at the lower end, green colour, medium thick pod wall and 8-9 seeds/pod.
Jawahar Matar-2	This is a derivative of the cross Russian 2 and 'Greater Progress'. It has bigger pods having 9 green bigger sweet ovules. Shells are comparatively thicker and have better keeping quality suitable for transportation.
Jawahar Matar-3	A very early variety developed from a cross of 'T19' and 'Early Badger'. It is a dwarf cultivar. This variety produces light pods, roundish oval, with a length of 5-7 cm and width of 1 cm having 4-5 ovules/pod.
Jawahar Matar 4	It has been developed from the cross 'T19' x 'Little Marvel'. Plants are 55-60 cm tall and possess medium size green pods (7.0 cm), having 5 or 6 ovules/pod.
Jawahar Matar-5	It was released in 1980 from Madhya Pradesh. Plants are 1.5 - 2.0 meters in length with large inter nodes, greenish yellow foliage, two pods/ axil and 5-6 seeds per pod. Pods are comparatively thin walled. Mature seeds are yellow and wrinkled. This variety is immune to powdery mildew.
Jawahar Peas-4	It is a cross of 'Local Yellow Batri' x ('6588' x '46c'). The variety possesses medium size pods with 5-6 bigger size green ovules. This variety is most suitable to hilly areas and can be planted in August.
Jawahar Peas-83	It is a mid-season powdery mildew resistant garden pea developed from a double cross (Arkel x JP-829) x (46-C x JP-501). Pods are bigger in size curved with 8 green sweet ovules.
Kashi Ageti	The plant height is 50-55 cm. Pods are green colour and slightly curved. Fruit length is 9-9.5 cm with 9-8 seed/ pod. An average yield is12.0 t/ha Green pods. This variety is recommended for commercial cultivation in Uttar Pradesh, Bihar, Jharkhand and Punjab.
Kashi Mukti	This variety is developed through pedigree selection (No.7 x PM-5). Plants are determinate (50-60 cm height). Pod shape is straight, pod color light green, number of pods per plant 9-10,pod length 8.5-9.0 cm, pod diameter 3.4-4.5 cm, pod weight (single pod) 6.0-6.5 g, number of seeds seeds/pod 8.4-9.4, and shelling percent 43-45 %. This variety possessed reducing sugar 0.256 %, total sugar 4.713 % and protein 24.46 %.This variety is resistant to powdery mildew. An average yield is 9.5 t/ha (Green pods).
Kashi Nandini	This variety has been developed through pedigree selection (P-1542 x VT-2-1). Plant is determinate, erect, pod shape straight and slightly curved at tip, pod colour dark green, number of pods per plant 8-10, pod length 8.5-9.0 cm, pod weight (Individual) 8-8.5 g, number of seeds/pod 7.8-8.1 and shelling percent 43-45 %. This variety possesses reducing sugar 0.27 %, total sugar 5.032 % and protein 29.43 %. An average yield is 11.0 t/ha (Green pods).

Kashi Samridhi	Plant type is semi-determinate 60-63cm height bears attractive and well filled green smooth pods and 13-14 pods /plant. Fruits are straight and slightly curved at tip. An average pod weight is 5-6 g with round shaped 7-8 bold seeds /pod. This variety has minimum shattering at the time of maturity. This variety is resistant to powdery mildew disease and tolerant to leaf minor & pod borer. An average yield is 13.0 t/ha (Green pods). This variety is recommended for cultivation in Uttar Pradesh, Bihar and Punjab.
Kashi Shakti	This variety is developed through pedigree selection (Hara Bona x NDVP-8). Plant is semi-determinate (80-100 cm height), pod shape slightly curved, pod colour dark green, number of pods per plant 11-12, pod length 10.0-10.5 cm, pod diameter 3.2-4.2 cm, number of seeds/pod 7.8-8.1, pod weight (Individual) 10-11 g and shelling percent 43-45 %.The pod has reducing sugar 0.27 %, total sugar 4.91 % and protein 25.96 %. An average yield is 13.5 t/ha (Green pods).
Kashi Udai	This variety has been developed through pedigree selection (Arkel x FC-1). Plant is determinate, pod shape curved, pod colour dark green, number of pods per plant 8-10, pod length 9-10 cm, number of seeds/ pod7-9, pod weight (Individual) 8.5-9.2 g and shelling percent 43-45 %.This variety has reducing sugar 0.27 %, total sugar 4.726 %, protein 26.7 %. Average yield is 10.5 t/ha (Green pods).
Knawari	It is a smooth-seeded main season variety. This is a tall-growing double-podded cultivar. Pods are about 8.5 cm long, yellowish green and 5-6 seeded with 40 per cent shelling.
Khapar Kheda	It is tall growing double podded cultivar. Pods are 5.5 to 6 cm long and 4-5 seeded with 50 per cent shelling. It is very popular in Madhya Pradesh.
Kelvedon Wonder	It is having dwarf plant. Pods are curved, borne singly, green, about 9 cm long and 6-seeded.
Lincoln	It is a dwarf to medium-tall, single podded cultivar. Pods are dark green, 9.5 - 10 cm long, 6-7 seeds pod with shelling percentage 45. It is suitable for late sowing. Pods retain good colour after harvesting and are good for canning.
Little Marvel	This cultivar has been bred in England from the cross-Chelsea Gem x Suttons Alaska. Plants are dwarf with dark green foliage. Pods are about 8 cm long, borne singly thick- skinned dark green, straight and broad containing 5-6 seeds/pod. It gives shelling percentage of 40. The green seeds are very sweet and fine in quality.
Lucknow Boniya	It is early smooth-seeded cultivar of in the plains. It is dwarf white seeded cultivar flowers in 40 days and first blossom appears at 8-9th node. The pods bear singly, small, narrow, green and 4-5 seeded.
Madhu	It is derivative of the cross 6126 x Sylvia, released in 1973 in Uttar Pradesh. Pods are 12-15 cm long, light green, smooth, membrane less, straight, 2 - 2.5 cm broad, 20-25 pods per plant and 5-6 seeds per pod. Mature seeds are smooth, round and of grey colour. This variety is susceptible to powdery mildew.
Matar Agata 6	It is an improvement over 'Arkel' and 'Harabona' and released by PAU, Ludhiana. It can withstand high temperature, prevalent at the time of planting in northern India. Plants are dwarf. Pods are long, 12-15 in number, bears singly and in pairs, well filled and containing six

	seeds/pod. The seeds are not as sweet as that of 'Arkel' but taste better than those of Harabana.
Metor	It is a round smooth seeded early variety and introduced from England. Plants are 35-40 cm tall, dark green and flowers bear generally singly. Pods are dark green, 8.7 cm long, well filled with 7 seeds/pods, having shelling percentage of 45.
Pant Uphar	It is a medium tall variety (70 cm), relatively thin stem, leaflet small in size and foliage light green. Pods are medium size, 7.5 cm long having 7 seeds/pod. This variety is susceptible to powdery mildew.
Punjab-87	It is a derivative of the cross Pusa-2 x Morrasis-55 and released from Punjab. Pod is 9.3 cm in length, 1-2 pods/axil, green ovules, sweet, mature seed bold and wrinkled, 7-6 seeds/pod and 48.3 per cent shelling.
Punjab-88	It is developed by selection from the cross 'Pusa-2' and 'Morassis 55'. Plants are tall with medium size pods and having 7 green ovules per pod. The seeds are green, wrinkled and bold. This variety is also susceptible to powdery mildew.
Sylvia	It is an edible-podded and tall growing variety. Pods are about 8.5-cm long, yellowish green and 5-6 seed/pod with a shelling percentage 40.
Thomas Laxton	Pods are of excellent quality, broad, and blunt, 8.25 cm long having cream and green coloured seed and suitable for freezing.
Vivek-6	It is a cross between Pant Upahar and VL Matar 3. The plants are dwarf. The pods are smooth, straight, medium sized (6-7 cm), light green and completely filled. It is tolerant to cold and moisture stress conditions. It is recommended for cultivation in Uttaranchal, Himachal Pradesh, Jammu & Kashmir, Haryana, Delhi and Rajasthan.
VL Ageti Matar-7	It is an early maturing and high yielding variety and developed from VPKAS, Almora. The green seeds are dimpled bold, very sweet with high T.S.S. (16.8 per cent). It is free from the incidence of powdery mildew.
Vivek Matar-11	This variety is an indigenous collection, the seed sample was collected from Srirampur village, Agra developed at Vivekananda Parvatiya Krishi Anusandhan Sansthan (ICAR), Almora, Uttarakhand. Plants are dwarf, vigorous in growth with green foliage. Pods are long, dark green and curved.Seed is wrinkled and greenish in colour.This variety is resistant to powdery mildew and wilt (5-8% incidence), white rot (2-3% incidence) and leaf blight. Less incidence of pod borer has also been recorded. An average yield is 11. 0 t/ha (Green pods).

13.6.6. Indian Bean

Name	Remarks
Arka Jay	Plants photo-insensitive. Fruits are long and curved.
Arka Vijay	Plants are dwarf and photo-insensitive. Pods are pulpy, short and green in colour.
Hebbal Avare-3	It is a derivative of the cross Hebbal Avare-1 x US-67-13 and released from Karnataka in 1978. Plants are 65-75 cm tall, erect, determinate and photo-insensitive.
Kashi Khushhal	This is cluster bearing semi-pole type promising line collected from Ramana village of Varanasi from farmer field. As per discussion with farmer, the line was collected from Uttrakhand. It is the earliest variety

	which flowering starts in 66 days and pods are ready for harvesting in 95-100 days after seed sowing. Fruiting starts from last week of September and continued second week February in agro climatic condition of Varanasi. Fruits are dark green in colour measured12.5-14.6cm in length, 1.3-2.4cm in width with 07-1.0cm thickness containing 4-6 seeds per pod. Pod yield is 6.6 kg/plant green pods. Seeds are brown in colour measured 1.16-1.23cm and 0.78-0.84cm in length and width, respectively.
Kashi Haritima	Pods are attractive darkgreen (13-16 cm) in length and 3.1-3.4 cm width) free from prachrnent layer laving 12-16 pods/plant/ An average yield is 38.0 t/ha (Green pods).
Kashi Sheetal	An average pod yield is about 35.9 t/ha (Green pods) which was 30.6% green pod yield in compare with national check Swarn Utkrist.
Konkan Bhushan	It is a bush type variety having 60.75-cm height. Pods are tender, green and stringless.The pod is 10 cm long and 1.5 cm wide. It has proved to be adaptable in varying soil and climate with fairly economic yield.
Pusa Early Prolific	It bears early and pods are long and thin in bunches. It is suitable for sowing in early autumn and early spring in the Northern Plains.
Pusa Sem-2	It has been developed through intensive breeding programme at the IARI, New Delhi. Pods are available from mid-November to mid-March. Pods are semi-flat, 15-17 cm in length, dark green, 11-13-pods/ cluster and 5-6-seeds/ pod. This variety is highly resistant to anthracnose & virus and tolerant to aphids, jassids and pod-borers. It is also tolerant to frost.
Pusa Sem-3	This variety was developed through intensive breeding programme at the IARI, New Delhi. Pods are flat, 15-16 cm length, green in colour, 5-6 seeds/pod and 10-12-pods/ cluster. This variety is tolerant to anthracnose, virus, aphids, jassids and pod borers but susceptible to frost.
Rajani	This is a popular variety of Uttar Pradesh. Plants are indeterminate in growth having purple colour stem in early stage of growth, which turns green later.
Wal Konkan-1	It is a derivative of the cross Wal 2 K2 x Wal 125-36 and released from Maharashtra for Konkan Region. It is resistant to yellow mosaic virus.

13.7. Perennial Vegetables

13.7.1. Drumstick

Name	Remarks
PKM-1	It belongs to *Moringa pterigosperma* and released from TNAU, Tamil Nadu by pure line selection from the population generated by continuous selfing of seed moringa types for six generations. The fruits are long, fleshy and tasty. This variety can be grown as an intercrop in orchards and coconut gardens during the pre-bearing period. Chillies, onion and groundnut can be grown as intercrops in annual moringa.

13.8. Root Vegetables

13.8.1. Beet Root

Name	Remarks
Crimson Globe	Roots are round to flatten round and medium red with indistinct zones. It is non-corrosive in taste when taken raw.
Crosby Egypitian	Roots are flat globes with a small taproot and a smooth exterior. The internal colour is dark purplish red with some indistinct zoning. This cultivar shows pronounced white zoning when grown in warm weather.
Detroit Dark Red	Roots are smooth, uniform, and attractive with small collar and perfectly round with deep red skin.Flesh is very dark, blood red with light zoning, tender, round, fine grains and corrosive in taste when taken raw.
Early Wonder	The roots are flattened globe with rounded shoulders and smooth dark red skin. The interior is dark red with some lighter red zoning.
OOTY-1	It is a selection from the local type and released from TNAU, Coimbatore. The roots are blood red colour with thin skin and good quality. It can be used as a salad. It can be grown throughout south Indian hills.

13.8.2. Carrot

Name	Remarks
Chantenay	It is European type and an excellent cultivar for canning and storage. It is having attractive roots with deep reddish orange colour. The flesh is beautiful rich orange, tender, sweet and fine textured with indistinct core.
Danvers	It is a European type variety. The roots are yellow in colour. This variety is suitable for both fresh as well as processing purposes.
Early Nantes	It has almost cylindrical roots terminating abruptly in small thin tail, 12-15 cm long and fine textured. Flesh is orange with self-coloured core.
Hisar Gairic	It has been developed through mass selection and released from CCSHAU, Hisar. Roots are long (18.1 cm long and 3.9 cm across), tapering, attractive, light brick red, thin self-core, less fibre and forking. It is good for early sowing. It contains 96.2 mg carotene in 100g of fresh weight. This variety is free from insect and pest.
Imperator	It is a cross between Nantes and Chanteny and extensively grown for fresh market. It is a mid-season to late maturing cultivar with large and strong foliage. Roots are 15 - 17.5 cm long and 2.5 - 4.5 cm in diameter with short tapered end, deep orange cortex and slightly less pigmented core.
Jeno	This is a popular variety of Nilgiri hills, which was brought from Germany and recommended for cultivation in Tamil Nadu. Roots are 15-17 cm long with conical shape in lower portion.
Nantes	It is a European cultivar, which can be grown in the plains of India for root production but not for seed production. Seeds are produced in the hills of India. The roots are half-long, slim, well-shaped, cylindrical

	with stumped end forming a small thin tail, deep orange-red cortex and core. It ranks first in quality but has a week, brittle top that makes difficult in pulling. It does not keep well because of its thin skin and fine texture. This cultivar is suitable for cultivation in cooler months.
Nantes Half Long	It is temperate variety, suitable for sowing during winter months and released from IARI Regional Station, Katrain. Roots are cylindrical, stumpy, well-shaped with abrupt tail, orange scarlet with self-coloured core. Flesh is sweet, fine grained with good flavour and orange scarlet in colour.
Pusa Asita	This variety was released from IARI, Pusa New Delhi. It has self-black coloured and is late bolter. Maturity is 95-100 days. Average yield is 30.0 t/ha.
Pusa Kesar	This is a selection from a cross between Local Red and Nantes Half Long and released by IARI, New Delhi. The leaf top is markedly shorter than Local Red. The roots develop with narrow central core, which is also sufficiently red coloured. It contains higher amount of carotene (38mg/100 g edible protein) than Local Red (26mg/100 g). The roots of this variety can stay about a month longer in the field than Local Red without showing any sign of bloting. The forking percentage is also less. It sets seed freely in the plains, suitable for sowing from early September to early November and takes 80-90 days from sowing to root formation. It can tolerate high temperature than Nantes.
Pusa Meghali	It is an advance generation selection from a cross between Pusa Kesar and Nantes. It was identified and released as improved tropical carrot from IARI Variety Release Committee, New Delhi. It has a short top, smooth roots, orange flesh, self-coloured core and stumpy to slightly tapering roots. It is suitable for sowing as early (August-September) as well as late (October-November) crop. It is preferred for early sowing and can be marketed in 110-120 days. The variety is capable of setting in the plains.
Pusa Rudhira	This variety has been developed from IARI, Pusa New Delhi. It has self-core red coloured with delayed bolting. Maturity is 85-90 days. An average yield is 33t /ha.
Pusa Vasuda	This hybrid has been developed from IARI, Pusa, New Delhi. This is first public sector tropical carrot hybrid developed using CMS system. Self-red coloured carrot hybrid. High in total carotenoids, lycopene, TSS and minerals.
Pusa Vrishti	This variety was released from IARI, Pusa, New Delhi. It is a new heat tolerant tropical carrot variety. It is suitable for early sowing beginning in July under north Indian plains. Maturity is 85-90 days. An average yield is 25.0 t/ha.
Pusa Yamdagni	It is developed by hybridization between EC-9981 x Nantes and released by IARI Regional Station, Katrain. It combines the earliness of EC-9981 and self-colored core character of Nantes. Roots are 15-16 cm long, orange, self-colored core and slightly tapering stumpy to semi-stumpy ending. Top is medium size and quick growing in comparison with other temperate types. It is high yielder and richer in carotene content.
Royal Chantenay	This is widely adopted cultivar and is primarily grown for processing, but is well suited for home garden.

Red-Cored Chantenay	It is similar to Chanteny variety, quite popular and extensively grown.
Zeno	This is very popular variety for the Nigiris hills, introduced from German Democratic Republic and recommended by the State Department of Horticulture, Tamil Nadu. The roots are 15-17 cm long, slightly tapering toward the end. The exposed portion of the root becomes pinkish green, medium top and self-coloured.

13.8.3. Radish

Name	Remarks
Arka Nishant	It is an improvement over a collection (IIHR-72) from Singapore, developed after 10 cycles of mass selection and released for commercial cultivation in 1980 by IIHR, Bangalore. It is Asiatic variety and matures within 45-55 days. Roots are medium-sized (25 cm x 3-4 cm), marble white, crisp texture, pleasant aroma, free from early bolting, pithiness, splitting and forking and each root weighing 300-400 g.
Chinese Pink	It is an introduction identified by Dr. YS Parmar University of Horticulture and Forestry, Nauni (Solan). Roots are 12-15 cm long, semi-stumpy to stumpy roots, pink with white colour towards the tip and takes about 50-55 days from sowing to root formation. It is a good cultivar for the hills but does well in plains with mild climate. It requires low temperature for seed production.
Kashi Sweta	It is developed through selection from Japanese materials suitable for growing in spring, summer, autumn and winter seasons. It is ready for harvesting in 30-35 days after sowing. Roots are 25-30 cm long, 3.5-4 cm in diameter straight, tapering with blunt tip.
Kashi Hans	It is suitable for planting from September to February and harvesting within 40-50 days after sowing. Due to late pithiness, it can stand the field up to 10-15 days after ready for harvesting. Its foliage is soft and smooth. Roots are straight and tapering types, 35-40 cm long and 3.5-4.2 cm diameter.
Japanese White	It was originally named as Shiroaguri-Kyo and released by IARI, New Delhi under the name Japanese White. Roots are 25-30 cm long, 5 cm in diameter, cylindrical and blunt at the tip. Skin is pure white and smooth. Flesh is snow white, crisp, solid and mild pungent. Tops are medium large with deeply cut leaves. It is suitable for growing between October-December in the plains and July-September in the hills.
Kalianpur No.1	It is a selection from local material released in 1982. Stem and foliage is green, smooth, top heavy, leaves long, broad and less lobed. Roots are 22-23 cm long, smooth, crispy, and white with green shoulder, thick and tapering. It is free from mustard sawfly, aphids and white rust.
Nadauni	This is developed from a local material and very popular in Himachal Pradesh. The roots are long, tapering, smooth and light pink in colour. The tops are dark green with cut leaves.
Punjab Ageti	It is suitable for April to August sowing. Roots are long, thin with lower half-white and upper red.
Punjab Pasand	It is suitable for main season. Roots are long and white semi-stumped.
Punjab Safed	It is a derivative of cross White5 x Japanese White. Roots are white,

	tapering smooth, mild in taste, free of forking, 30-40 cm in length and 3.5 cm thick. It is a quick growing type with roots remaining edible for 10 days after attaining full size.
Pusa Chetki	It is a selection made from a material collected from Denmark. Roots are medium large and stumpy, pure white, tender and smooth and mildly pungent. Since, it can tolerate high temperature, therefore, it has been found suitable for sowing from the middle of March to the middle of August.
Pusa Desi	It is a tropical and subtropical cultivar, suitable for sowing from middle of August to early October in the northern plains. It is selection from local material. Roots are pure white, 30-35 cm long, tapering with green stem end, pungent and heavy yielder, tolerant to slightly higher temperature, medium light green top with cut leaves.
Pusa Gulabi	This variety has been developed from IARI, Pusa, New Delhi. Roots are entire pink fleshed unique trait nutritional rich radish variety. Medium root size, cylindrical shape, optimal yield and consumer preference over the existing varieties. High total carotenoids, anthocyanins and optimal ascorbic acid.
Pusa Himani	It is developed through hybridization between a temperate type (Black) and a popular Asiatic Type (Japanese White) and released from IARI, Regional Station Katrain. It is suitable for December to February sowing in the plains when no other variety can form such good roots. It is the only variety, which can be grown throughout the year in the hills farming. The roots are 30-35 cm in length and 10-12 cm in girth with green stem and they are semi-stump to tapering with short tops. The skin is pure white. The flesh is crisp and sweet-flavored with mild pungency.
Pusa Jamuni	This variety has been developed from IARI, Pusa, New Delhi. Roots are purple fleshed unique trait nutritionally rich. This variety contains higher anthocyanins and ascorbic acid.
Pusa Mridula	This variety has been developed at IARI, Pusa New Delhi. Roots are globular with bright red skin, mildly pungent. Maturity is within 25 days. An average yield is 13.0 t/ha.
Pusa Reshmi	It is a main season variety in Asiatic group and suitable for mid-September to early October sowing. Roots are 30-35 cm long, tapering white with green shoulder, mildly pungent, tolerant to slightly higher temperatures medium light green top with cut leaves.
Rapid Red White Tipped	It is an extra early European variety, which matures in 25-30 days. It is bunching and table type. Roots are small, globular, bright red with white tip. Flesh is pure white, crisp and snappy. Tops are short, mildly pungent in flavor and suitable for November-December sowing in the plains.
Scarlet Globe	Root is round small, two cm in diameter and bright red. Flesh is crisp and white.
Scarlet Long	It is an early variety having light green foliage with 15-20 cm length. Roots are long and tapering to a point. Flesh is white and crisp.
White Icicle	It is a medium-short European variety that matures in 30 days. The skin is pure white, thin and tender, whereas, the flesh is white icy, crisp, juicy, mild and sweet flavor with juicy enough pungency to appeal the appetite. The root is solid Icile -shaped straight and tapered

13.8.4. Turnip

Name	Remarks
Early Milan Top	It is very shy seeder and highly susceptible to turnip malformation. It takes about 65-70 days from sowing to root formation. A temperate variety recommended by IARI Regional Station, Katrain (Kullu Valley) Himachal Pradesh.
Golden Ball	This is a temperate type variety and developed from IARI Regional Station, Katrain (Kullu Valley) Himachal Pradesh. Roots are globe shape, soft with medium size. Roots are ready for harvesting in 70-75 days after seed sowing.
Pusa Chandrima	This is a temperate type and has been developed through hybridization between Asiatic and European types and released by IARI Regional Station Katrain, (Kullu Valley) Himachal Pradesh. It is an early maturing and high yielding cultivar, which possesses all the good qualities of the European type. It is particularly suitable for the areas where growing period is very short. Roots are medium to large in size, 8-9 cm long, smooth, pure white, fine grained with sweet and tender flesh. It is a temperate or biennial cultivar and does not produce seeds in the plains of India.
Pusa Kanchan	It has been developed through hybridization between Asiatic type (Local Red Round) and European type (Golden Ball) and released by IARI, New Delhi. It is an Asiatic early maturing and high yielding cultivar, which possesses all the good qualities of the European type and Asiatic type. The skin is red but the flesh is creamy yellow. It has excellent flavor and taste. The leaf top is shorter than the Local Red Round. It becomes ready for harvesting about 10 days later than Local Red Round but the roots can be kept longer in the field without being spongy. It produces seeds satisfactory in the plains.Seed crop is harvested about a fortnight later than the Local Red Round and produces seeds under tropical conditions. Under late sown conditions, it produces seeds stalks directly without the enlargement of roots. Therefore, late sowing should be avoided.
Punjab Safed-4	This is an early Asiatic variety and commonly grown in Punjab and Haryana. The roots are pure white round and medium sized having mild taste.
Pusa Swarnima	It is temperate variety released by IARI Regional Station, Katrain (Kullu valley).This cultivar has been developed by hybridization between Asiatic type (Japanese White) and European type (Golden Ball) followed by selection. It is earlier than Golden Ball by about a fortnight and gives 40 per cent higher yield. The roots are flattish round, 6-7 cm long and 7-8 cm in diameter with creamy yellow skin. Flesh is amber colored, fine-textured and mild-flavored. The tops are medium and not very deeply cut. It is superior to 'Golden Ball' in seed yield and less susceptible to turnip malformation, a mycoplasma disease.
Pusa Sweti	It is an Asiatic cultivar suitable for sowing from August to October. The roots are attractive white and mature 45 to 50 days from sowing. It was released from IARI.
Purple Top	It is an introduction and recommended by IARI Regional Station,

White Globe	Katrain. It is suitable for cooler months. It is a heavy yielding and large rooted cultivar. The roots are nearly round, upper part purple and lower portion creamy. Flesh is white, firm, crisp and mildly sweet flavored. The top is small, erect with cut leaves.
Snowball	It is ready in 55 days. Leaves are small and light green. Roots are round and medium sized with light yellow flesh.

13.9. Tuber and Rhizomatous Crops

13.9.1. Cassava

Name	Remarks
ADIRA-1	It is a sweet cultivar with only 50 ppm HCN in the tuber and yield of 25.0-30.0 t/ha. It is recommended for small scale farms, where cassava is intercropped with other food crops. It can be harvested in 7-8 months.
ADIRA-2	It is high yielding cultivar. Tuber is medium in starch content and high in HCN. It is tolerant to cassava bacterial blight (CBB).
ADIRA-4	It is a bitter cultivar with approximately 90 ppm HCN, but capable of producing high yield and widely adopted. It is suitable for large planting of industrial use.
Faroka	This cultivar has yielded of 19.0 t/ha and is adopted for dry areas. The tubers are low in HCN with good table qualities.
Golden Yellow	This cultivar gives yield both under open and partially shaded conditions prevent in coconut garden. Tubers are low in HCN and suitable for table purpose. It is an early maturing (8-10 months) cultivar.
H-97	It is a hybrid between an indigenous cultivar 'Manjavella' and an Exotic selection of Brazilian origin. The variety is characterized by light sepia color of three-merging leaf and conical medium sized tuber with 27-29 per cent starch on fresh weight basis. This hybrid is tolerant to CMD.
H-165	This is a hybrid between two indigenous cultivars 'Chadayamangalam Vella' and 'Kalikalan'. Generally, it is non-branching with pinking petiole and light brown emerging leaves. Tuber skin is golden brown and the flesh is creamy with starch content of 23-25 per cent. This variety is tolerant to CMD.This variety is cultivated in large areas of Tamil Nadu and Andhra Pradesh for industrial use. It is suitable cultivar for Tamil Nadu, Kerala, Karnataka and Andhra Pradesh.
H-226	It is cross between M-4 introduced from Malaya and a local cultivar 'Ethakkakuruppan'.The hybrid is occasionally branching with characteristic green color of leaves and tuber with purple rind and white flesh. Due to very high starch content (28.30 per cent), it is very popular for industrial use in Tamil Nadu and Andhra Pradesh.
Kadabao	This cultivar also performs well under open and partial shade. This cultivar has high starch content and fairly low HCN.
Kalikalan	It is early maturing cultivar with good table quality of tubers. It is highly susceptible to CMD. It is well adapted to low fertility conditions.
Karuthakaliyan	This cultivar is spreading type with 10 months duration. It produces non-bitter tuber with an average yield of 32.0 t/ha. It is susceptible to

CMD, bacterial leaf spot (BLS) and mites.

Rayong-1 — It is widely adopted bitter cultivar. Since tuber has high dry matter and starch content, it is well accepted as an industrial cultivar.

Rayong-2 — It was selected from hybrid seeds of CM305 introduced from CIAT, Colombia. Its fresh root yield dry matter content and starch content are similar to Rayong-1. This cultivar is table type, good for making fried chips and other convenient foods. It has yellow flesh content, high carotene and very low HCN.

Rayong-3 — It is a selection from CM407 cross which was introduced from CIAT, Colombia. In tuber dry matter and starch content are superior to Rayong-1. These qualities fetch higher price for Rayong-3. The tuber yield of this cultivar is on at par with Rayong-1.

Rayong-60 — It is a cross between CIAT and Thai clones (MCol-1684 x Rayong-1). This cultivar is superior to Rayong-1 in fresh root yield and root dry matter content. It is early maturity and adapted to low fertility.

Sree Harha — This is cross of triploid {OP-4 (2x) X H-230 (4x)} released from CTCRI, Trivandrum in 1996. Plants are tall, erect branching and stout stem. Mature stem is grayish and green with purple tinge colour of shoots. Leaves are thick broad with acuminate tip having light purple colour of emerging leaf. Tubers are conical in shape and light brown in colour. It is drought tolerance, robust plant, high starch content acceptable especially for industrial use. This variety is adoptable for the area of Kerala and Tamil Nadu. The yield potential of this variety is 35.0-40.0t/ha in 10 months of crop duration. It is susceptible to cassava mosaic disease and field tolerant to cercospora leaf spot, spider mite and scale insect.

Sree Jaya — It is a selection from indigenous germplasm collection of cassava from Kottayam district, Kerala State, released from State Variety Release Committee, Kerala in 1998. It is early maturing (6-7 months) variety. This variety is especially suitable for low land cultivation as a rotation crop in paddy based cropping system This variety is moderately susceptible to cassava mosaic disease and field resistant to scale insect.

Sree Prakash — It is a short duration cultivar selected from the indigenous collections in 1987. The plants are relatively dwarfed and non-branching. The cooking quality of the tuber is fairly good without bitter. It is suitable for single cropped rice fields of Kerala.

Sree Prabha — This variety has been developed through pedigree method of breeding and released in 2000. Tubers are conical in shape with brown in colour. This variety is susceptible to cassava mosaic disease, field tolerant to cercospora leaf spot and field resistant to scale insect. This variety is adoptable for Kerala, Tamil Nadu, Karnataka and Andhra Pradesh.

Sree Rekha — This variety has been developed through pedigree methods of breeding and released in 2000. Tubers are long conical with light brown skin colour. This variety is suitable for cultivation of both under upland and low land conditions and in non-traditional areas of Tamil Nadu, Karnataka and Andhra Pradesh.This variety is susceptible to cassava mosaic disease and field resistant to scale insect.

Sree Sahya — This is a hybrid developed from multiple crossing of five parents of which two are exotic and three are indigenous. Plants are tall predominantly non-branching, producing long necked tubers. Tuber

	skin is light brown and the flesh is white with a starch content of 29-31 per cent. The tubers are non-bitter and fair in cooking quality. The plants are tolerant to CMD.
Sree Vijaya	It is a selection from indigenous collection of cassava from Thiruvananthapuram district, released for area of Kerala State 1998. Plants are erect branching having greenish brown mature stem with green colour shoot. Tubers are conical in shape with brown skin colour.This variety is field tolerant to cercospora leaf spot and moderately susceptible to cassava mosaic disease. It is susceptible to spider mite and scale insect.
SreeVisakham	This is a hybrid resulted from crossing an indigenous cultivar and an accession from Madagascar. The hybrid is non-branching with light brown emerging leaf and tuber having brown rind and cream colored flesh. The tuber is low in HCN contains 25-27 per cent starch and 466 IU carotene /g fresh tuber. The tuber yield is 350-380 q/ha in 8-10 months of crop duration with reasonably good culinary qualities. It is tolerant to CMD.
TMS-30001	It is early maturing and sweet cultivar. Tubers contain low HCN and well accepted by consumers. It is resistant to CMD but susceptible to root rot and insect pest.
TMS-30555	It is high yielding and widely adopted cultivar. It is resistant to CMD and CBB.
TMS-30572	It is widely adopted cultivar because of high yield (40.0 t/ha) and good quality of tubers. It is resistant to CMD and CBB. It is susceptible to cassava mealy bug and cassava green mites.
TMS-50395:	This cultivar is resistant to CMD, CBB and tolerant to cassava green mite. It is widely adopted though the tubers are high in HCN.

13.9.2. Colocasia

Name	Remarks
Apra Kochai	It is grown in Madhya Pradesh mainly in Bilaspur region. The yield potential of this cultivar is 15.0-30.0 t/ha.
Bangau Banda	It is very common on north India having dark purple leaves and petioles.
Ban Kachu	This is wild variety commonly known in Bengal as Bay Kachu. It is more important for their leaves and stalks than their tubers.
Char Kachu	It is wild variety commonly important for their leaves and stalk than their tubers.
Dasheen	This kind of colocasia produces only one main corms are elongated and fleshy having nodes and internodes and only one growing but at the top.
Deshi Banda	It is very common in north India.
Indra Arvi-1	It has been developed and released from IGAU, Raipur, Chhattisgarh in 2003. It is a good table variety having good cooking quality and taste. It is suitable for cultivation in both irrigated and rainfed areas. This variety has wider adaptability, high yielding capacity and disease and pest tolerance. This variety is suitable for cultivation in whole Chhattisgarh.
Kaka Kachu	It is a promising variety, which produces side corms and is fleshy with better taste.

Kalla Kachu	It is wild variety more valued for their leaves and stalks than for their tubers.
Khasi Bagga	It contains more acridity as compared to other varieties.
Koni Kachu	This variety belongs in eddoe group. This variety produces many daughter tubers very similar to poultry eggs. It is very good for currying and has a good cooking quality.
Munshikuntla Kachu	It is just like wooden pegs in shape and size. It is very soft and highly palatable.
Naga Kaju	This is famous variety of Nagaland having bigger sized mother tubers and small daughter tubers
Punch Mukhi	This variety belongs in eddoe group. The word Punch Mukhi means a type of colocasia with five-mouth or five tubers attached together. It can be kept for more than a year after harvest. It is grown successfully in the hills above an elevation of 1200 m and has very good cooking quality.
Sar Kachu	It is very good variety for aquatic situation and recommended for Bengal.
Satmukhi	Its tuber shape is rectangular, medium in size, brown skin, pulp (flesh) white in colour and matures in 175-190 days. It is widely grown in Andhra Pradesh, Kerala and Karnataka.
Sahasramukhi	It is a collection from Maharashtra.
Sree Rashmi	This accession is a natural triploid and released for cultivation from Kerala State by Varietal Release Committee. The cormela are medium size, conical and have bluish and mucilaginous pulp. Leaves are free form acridity thus rendering all vegetative parts edible. Cormels contain 15.25 per cent starch and 2.5 per cent protein.
Sree Pallavi	It is also a triploid. This accession is from Meghalaya and released for cultivation on Kerala by the State Varietal Release Committee. This is also late maturing (29-30 weeks) with yield of (14.0 to 18.0 t/ha). Cormel is small (8.85 g means weight), club shaped and edible. Cormels alone are found edible.
Thamarannah	It is a popular variety cultivated locally in Kerala for the mainly big cormels (20-40 g).
Thamgri	It is suitable for rainfed crop in Orissa for local cultivation.

13.9.3. Elephant Foot Yam

Name	Remarks
Dholi	It is grown in Bihar.
Dorada Kanda	It is suitable for upland condition and arid variety. It is popular in Tamil Nadu. Its size is much smaller.
Gajendra	This is a selection from 'Kovur', a local variety from West Godavari district at Andhra Pradesh and released by APAU, Kerala.
Gajendra-5	It is acrid free variety. It is released from APAU, University, Kerala.
Kovur	It is mainly grown in south India. It is high yielding variety. Tubers are smooth, acrid free and good flesh quality. It has uniform tuber.
Rough Skinned Corm	This type at elephant foot good in comparatively not high yielder but corms having no acidity. Therefore, its demand in market is very high. The yield is compensated by high prices. This type is propagated by whole corm.

Santragachi	It is mainly grown in north India. Plant has good gravity tuber with acridity. Tuber is rough and light buttery colour. It develops many tubers. It becomes ready 3-4 seasons for harvesting.
Smooth Corm	This is high yielder. The corms having acidity. The planting is done by cutting the corm into piece (weight at least 20 to 30 g / piece). This variety possessing reduced acridity.
Sree Padama	It is a selection from indigenous germplasm collection, released from Kerala in 1998.The variety is characterized by light green with typical green ornamentations of petiole. This variety fairly tolerant to mosaic disease and collar rot.
Thiya Kanda	It is suitable for unirrigated condition and popular in Tamil Nadu. The size and shape are much smaller.

13.9.4. Potato

Name	Remarks
Kufri Alankar	It is a derivative of the cross (Kennebee x O.N.2090) x (Majestic x Ekishiraju), released for plains of Punjab, Haryana and Western Uttar Pradesh and especially suited for sandy soils.Tubers are oblong, tapering towards end, flesh dull white eyes and medium deep to fleet. It shows slow rate of degeneration. Tubers develop crack if allowed to remain till full maturity. It is a rapid bulking variety keeping quality not good. It matures 75 days in plains and 140 days in hills. This variety is moderate field resistance to late blight with immunity to Race 'O' susceptible to common scab.
Kufri Anand	A derivative of PJ376 x PH/F 1430, released from CPRI, Shimla. Tubers are white, large oval long, flattened, smooth skin, fleet eyes, white flesh having red purple sprouts. It is a medium maturing variety (100-110 days). This variety is adaptable to plains of Uttar Pradesh and neighboring states. This variety is resistant to late blight. The tubers are ideal in shape for French fries.
Kufri Ashoka	It is a wider adaptable variety released from CPRI, Shimla. It is a derivative of (EM/C-1020 x Allerfruii Heste Gelbe). Tubers are white, large, oval long, smooth skin and fleet eyes with white flesh having purple sprouts. It is an early maturing (70-80 days), suited in Bihar, Haryana, Punjab, Uttar Pradesh and West Bengal for cultivation. It is susceptible to late blight and not suitable for processing.
Kufri Badshah	It is a cross of Kufri Jyoti and Kufri Alankar and released in 1980 by Central Sub Committee on release in varieties for Indo-gangatic plains of North India, including Punjab, Haryana, Uttar Pradesh, Bihar, West Bengal, Madhya Pradesh and Plateau region. Tubers are mostly large to medium, oval, shining white, smooth, regular with shallow eyes, flesh dull white, sprouts stout, thick, bulbous white with light red pigmentation at the base. Stolens are thick, short and white. Flowers are scanty, white, and medium in size, fully stretching wings, pollen fertility 50-60 per cent and frequently set berries in the hills. This variety possesses medium dormancy. It shows slow rate of degeneration. Tubers are tasty with good flavour. It contains 13.6 g/100 g starch and 18.6 per cent dry matter content. It matures in plains 90-100 days. It is tolerant to frost, resistant to late blight, early blight and potato virus 'X' but susceptible to soft.

Kufri Bahar	It is a derivative of the cross Kufri Red x Ginek and released by Central Sub-Committee on Release of Varieties for the plains of Haryana, Punjab and Western Uttar Pradesh. Tubers are large, white, round to oval, skin smooth with medium deep eyes, flesh white. Sprouts are bulbous and red. Stolens are medium long. Keeping quality is average with medium dormancy. It is mid maturity variety (90-100 days). Resistant to late blight, early blight and potato virus 'X', 'Y' and leaf roll. It is susceptible to insect pests, drought and frost.
Kufri Chamatkar	A derivative of the cross Ekishiraju x Phulwa and released for the plains of Uttar Pradesh, Madhya Pradesh, Haryana, Punjab where one crop of long duration is raised. Tubers are round and white, eyes medium deep, flesh yellow and red sprouts.Degeneration is slow and quick tuberization. It is late maturing variety, which matures 110-120 days in plains and 150 days in hills. It is resistant to early blight but susceptible to viruses, late blight, brown rot, charcoal rot, wilts and common scab.
Kufri Chandramukhi	It is a derivative of the cross S.4485 x Kufri Kuber and released in 1967 in Central Variety Release Committee for the plains of Punjab, Haryana, Uttar Pradesh, Madhya Pradesh, Rajasthan, Bihar, West Bengal and Maharashtra. It also grows well in Himachal Pradesh hills and Jammu regions. Plants are medium tall with open foliage habit and free from secondary growth. Foliage is grass green and glossy.Tubers are oval, white, flesh dull white, eye fleet, and sprouts light red and pubescent. This variety has slow rate of degeneration and early bulking. It possesses good keeping quality. It is mid-season variety, matures 80-90 days in plains and 120 days in hills. An average yield is 20.0 t/ha in plains and 7.5 t/ha in hills. It is susceptible to common scab, late blight, brown rot, nematodes, charcoal rot and wilts.
Kufri Chipsona-1	It is a cross of MEX.750826 x MS/78-79 and released from CPRI, Shimla in 1998. Tubers are white medium to large oval, smooth skin, fleet eyes, dull white flesh having green sprouts. It is medium maturing variety (90-110 days) It is suitable for cultivation in Bihar and Uttar Pradesh. It is resistant to late blight. The variety is highly suitable for making chips and French fries.
Kufri Chipsona-2	It is a derivative of F-6 x QB/B-92-4 and released from CPRI, Shimla. Tubers are white, medium, round oval, smooth skin, fleet eyes, and yellow flesh having reddish brown sprouts. It is medium maturing variety yielded 35.0 t/ha. This variety is resistant to late blight and tolerant to frost. Due to high dry matter content, low reducing sugars and low phenols, the variety is highly suitable for making chips and French Fries.
Kufri Dewa	It is a derivative of the cross Craigs Defiance x Phulwa and released by Central Sub-Committee on Release of Varieties in 1973 for Tarai area of Uttaranchal and Shimla agro-climatic conditions. It is also suitable for Bihar and Orissa. Tubers are erratic round with purple splashes, eye deep and pigmented and sprout light red with white flesh. Tubers develop brown spots after harvest. It is highly susceptible to late blight, possesses good resistance to frost and drought.

Kufri Frysona	Its plant is medium tall, semi-erect, plant canopy, semi-compact and vigorous growth. Tuber size is medium, long oblong, white cream, smooth, eyes shallow, normal eyebrows, flesh white, texture mealy. This variety is field resistant to late blight. An average yield is 35.0 t/ ha.
Kufri Garima	Plant height is 55-60 cm and medium growth, plant canopy compact. Tubers are ovoid, skin light yellow, eyes shallow, eyebrows normal, flesh light yellow, texture mealy. This variety is recommended for Indo-gangetic plains and plateau regions as main season cultivation . This variety is field resistant to late blight. An average yield is 32.5 t/ ha.
Kufri Gaurav	Plant height is 75 cm medium tall, erect, compact &vigorous. Tubers are oval shape, white skin, large sized, fleet eyes &creamy flesh colour. Good keeping quality. Perform well under low nutrient condition. Moderately resistant to late blight and susceptible to early blight in both field and controlled conditions. Average yield is 27.0-29.0 t/ha. This variety is recommended for cultivation in Punjab, Haryana, Uttaranchal plains and Western Uttar Pradesh as main season crop.
Kufri Giriraj	It is north and south India adaptable variety. It is a cross of SLB/J-132 x EX/A 680-16.Tubers are white, medium to large, oval smooth skin, fleet eyes, and white flesh and sprout light purple. This variety is resistant to late blight (both foliage and tubers). It is not suitable for processing.
Kufri Himalini	It is a derivative of cross SLB/H-140 x SLB/Z-389 (b). This recommended for Hilly regions (hills of Northern India and Nigiris in South) in the country. Tubers are medium to large, oval, slightly flattened, skin white, eyes shallow to medium deep, flesh dull white and mealy texture. Tubers possess medium dormancy (2 - 2½ months). Keeping quality is good and does not show shrinkage on five months storage in hills. It is highly resistant to late blight but susceptible to early blight, phoma leaf spot, brown rot, common scab and moderately susceptible to powdery scab and leaf blotch. Planting is done in March-April as summer crop in Nilgiris in northern hills, August-September for autumn crop in the southern hills.
Kufri Jawahar	It is a derivative of Kufri Neelamani x Kufri Jyoti and released from Central Potato Research Institute, Shimla in 1996.Tubers are creamy white, medium sized, round-oval smooth skin, eyes fleet, pale yellow fleshes having purple sprouts. It is an early maturing variety (80-90 days). This variety is resistant to late blight.It is not suitable for processing.It is widely adaptability in Haryana and Punjab, plateau region of Gujarat, Karnataka and Madhya Pradesh. It is suitable for intensive cropping.
Kufri Jeevan	It is a derivative of the cross M-109-3 x D-698 and adopted for northwest hills of Himachal Pradesh and Uttar Pradesh. Tubers are medium, white skin, oval shaped, eyes fleet, faint red picked, flesh waxy and pale yellow. It matures 150-160 days in hills and 120 days in plains. It is resistant to wart, highly resistant to late blight and in moderately resistant to early blight.

Kufri Jyoti	It is a derivative of the cross 3069d (4) x 2814 Q (1) and released in 1968 by the Central Variety Release Committee for Himachal Pradesh and Kumaon Hills of Uttaranchal and also plains where late blight is a limiting factor.Tubers are oval, white, eye fleet. Flesh is light white and waxy. Sprouts are blue purple and medium thick. It has good keeping quality if given proper post-harvest treatment. It is field resistant to late blight with immunity to race 'O'. It is resistant to early blight and wrat. It matures 100 days in plains and 120 days in Hills.
Kufri Khashigaro	It is popular variety of hilly region and a derivative of the cross Taborky x SD 698 D. It is adapted to hilly regions of Assam. Tubers are medium, attractive white, round with deep eyes and waxy, pale yellow flesh and rapid bulking. It possesses short dormancy.
Kufri Khyati	It is developed by cross between MS/82-638 x Kufri Pukhraj from CPRI Shimla. Plants are tall, erect, medium-compact and vigorous Stem many, thick, not coloured at base, well developed straight wings. are Leaves open and rachis green. Tubers are oval, pale yellow, medium sized, fleet eyes and light yellow flesh. This variety is moderately resistance to late blight and resistant to early blight. An average yield is 25-28 t/ha under early (75 days) harvest.
Kufri Lalima	It is a fast bulking variety and a derivative of the cross Kufri Red x CP 1362 which released in 1982 by Central Sub-Committee on Release of Varieties for the plains of Uttar Pradesh, Bihar, West Bengal, Orissa and Karnataka States. Tuber is uniformly red, medium to large, round, regular, smooth with fleet to medium deep eyes. Flesh is white colour with mealy texture. It is susceptible to late blight wart, powdery, scab, leaf blotch, phoma leaf spot, brown rot, charcoal rot and common scab. It is susceptible to virus 'Y'. It possesses slow rate of degeneration and medium dormancy (about 2½ months).
Kufri Lauvkar	It is a derivative of cross Serkoy x Adina released in 1973 by Central Sub-Committee on Release of Varieties for Decan Peninsula (Maharashtra). It is an early variety. Tuber is round, white, flesh white, sprouts beet root red colour, cooking and peeling easy. Cooked flesh is white and good in taste. It has slow rate of degeneration. It is susceptible to late blight, leaf blotch, potato virus 'Y' and leaf roll. This variety escapes attack to tuber moth. It is susceptible to early blight.
Kufri Muthu	It is a derivative of the cross 3046(I) x M-109-C and released for Nilgiri Hills for summer and autumn seasons. Tubers are large, white, roundish, oval, smooth eyes medium deep and flesh white. Sprouts are of blue purple colour. It is resistant to late blight but susceptible to early blight.
Kufri Naveen	It is a derivative of the cross D-692 x 3070d (4) and adapted to northeast hills of Assam and high attitude of Himachal Pradesh. Tubers are medium, white and oval with fleet eyes.Flesh is waxy and pale yellow. It is susceptible to early blight and resistant to wart. It possesses high degree of field resistant/immunity to race 0, 1 and 4 of late blight.
Kufri Pukhraj	It is a wider adaptable variety and a cross of Craig's Defiance x JEX/B-687 which released in 1998 from CPRI, Shimla. Tubers are white, large, oval, slightly tapered, smooth skin, fleet eyes, yellow flesh having blue purple sprouts.It is an early maturing variety (70-90 days). It is

resistant to early blight and moderately resistant to late blight. This variety is suitable in Bihar, Gujarat, Haryana, Himachal Pradesh, Karnataka, Madhya Pradesh, Maharashtra, Orissa, Punjab, Uttar Pradesh and West Bengal. It is not suitable for processing.

Kufri Sheetman — It is a derivative of the cross-Craig Defiance x Phulwa, released in 1968 by Central Variety Release Committee for plains especially frost affected areas of Punjab, Rajasthan, Haryana and Western Uttar Pradesh. Plants are tall open erect and vigorous, stem thick, firm and erect. Leaflets are rough dull green with waxy margins. Tubers are oval and white with fleet eyes. It is resistant to frost and drought. It is susceptible to late blight and leaf roll.

Kufri Sherpa — It is a derivative of the cross Ultimus x Adina and recommended for cultivation in the hills to West Bengal State. Tubers are medium in size, round flattened, skin smooth, medium thick, white, eyes medium deep and flesh of pale yellow colour. Sprouts are conical, blue purple and medium thick, white, eyes medium deep and flesh of pale yellow colour. Tuber dormancy is medium (2-2½) months with good keeping quality. It matures 135 and 100 days in hill and plains, respectively. It is susceptible to frost, brown rot and leaf roll and resistant to late blight (both in foliage and tubers) and phoma leaf spot but moderately resistant to early blight and highly immune to wart.

Kufri Sindhuri — It is derivative of the cross Kufri Kundan x Kufri Red and released by Central Variety Release Committee in 1966 for plains of Punjab, Jammu, Orissa, Bihar, Haryana, Uttar Pradesh, Madhya Pradesh and West Bengal. Tubers are round, light red, with medium deep eyes. Flesh is dull white. Tubers are moderate in number, skin firm, not prone to brushing, bigger tubers having tendency to develop hollow heart. Keeping quality is good. It is late variety and matures in 120 days in plains and 165 days in hills.It is slightly resistance to frost.It is susceptible to late blight, common scab charcoal rot and wilts, moderately resistant to early blight and possesses field resistance to viral disease.

Kufri Sutlej — It is a derivative of Kufri Bahar x Kufri Alankar. Tubers are white, large, oval, smooth skin, fleet eyes, and white flesh and sprouts light red. It is medium maturing (90-100 days) variety. This variety is moderately resistant to late blight. It is recommended for cultivation in Bihar, Haryana, Madhya Pradesh, Punjab and Uttar Pradesh. This variety has good consumer quality because of easy to cook, waxy texture, and mild flavor and free from discoloration after cooking. It possesses medium dry matter. It is not suitable for processing.

Kufri Swarna — It is a cross of Kufri Jyoti x (VIn)^2 (62.33.3).Tubers are white, medium, round oval, smooth skin, fleet eyes, and white flesh having blue purple sprouts. This variety is widely adaptable for south India hills. It matures 130-135 days in summer while 100-110 days in autumn. This variety is highly resistant to both the species of cyst nematodes (*Globodera rostochiensis* and *G. palida*) and resistant to early and late blight. This variety is not suitable for processing.

Shalimar Potato – 1 — This is medium maturing developed by clonal selection from heterogeneous white skinned population from SKUAST - Kashmir, Shalimar. Plants are green, medium tall semi compact, flowers white,

	semi stellate with long style and yellow anthers, tubers medium to large, round to irregular, white with yellowish white flesh and shallow eyes. This variety produces good chips and French fries and have excellent cooking and keeping quality. Tubers are rich in vitamin C, proteins, dry matter and average in TSS. This variety is tolerance to frost, drought, early blight, late blight and soft rot. An average yield is 36.4t/ha.
Shalimar Potato – 2	This is medium maturing variety derived by Clonal selection from heterogeneous red skinned population from SKUAST – Kashmir, Shalimar. Plants are medium tall, dark green semi-compact, flowers light pink, semi-stellate with long style and yellow anthers, tubers medium round to irregular, pink with creamy flesh and shallow to medium eyes. Tubers have firm flesh on cooking with excellent keeping quality.Chip and French fries' qualities are average to good. Tubers are rich in vitamin C, proteins, dry matter content and average in TSS. This variety is tolerant to frost & drought and highly tolerant to early blight, moderately tolerant to late blight and rot. An average yield is 24.7t/ha.

13.9.5. Sweet Potato

Name	Remarks
CO-1	It is a clonal selection of IB3 collected from Tiruchirapalli district and released from TNAU, Coimbatore. Raw tuber taste is saltish sweet while it is sweet on cooking with firm consistency. Tubers contain 10.6 per cent TSS, 1.2 per cent acidity, 1.6 per cent reducing sugars, 9.7 per cent total sugars and 20 mg per 100 g of ascorbic acid. The clone is tolerant to root weevil which infestation has been registered only 11 to 15 per cent.
CO-2	It is also clonal selection (IB8) from seedling progeny obtained form open pollinated seeds of a type (IB37) in germplasm bank. Tubers are medium sized with light pink skin and white flesh containing a high starch content of 29.5 per cent and carotenoids of 3.2 mg per 100 g. The variety has better consumer's appeal and grower preference. The root weevil incidence is only 10 to 15 per cent.
CO-3	It is a seedling clone (IB2837) obtained from the seeds of random mating population of IB758 and released from TNAU, Coimbatore. The tubers are medium sized with red skin and deep orange flesh. Tubers are markedly rich in carotenoids (13.28 mg/100 g), starch (30.72 per cent), ascorbic acid (21.1 mg/100g) and amylopectin (81.31 per cent). The clone has better consumers preference than the other clones. The root weevil (*Cylas formicarius*) incidence ranges from zero to 3 per cent.
GOURI	It is cross of H-219 x H-42, released in 1998. This is a medium duration variety with high carotene content, can tolerate mid-season stress. This variety is suitable for kharif and rabi seasons.This variety is widely adopted for orissa region.
H-41	It is released in 1971 by Central Sub-committee on Release of Varieties for Cultivation in the States of Tamil Nadu, Kerala and Karnataka. Tubers are sweet with excellent cooking quality. It is responsive to fertilizers. It is resistant to sweet potato weevil.

H-42	It is released by Central Sub-Committee on Release of Varieties for Tamil Nadu and Kerala states. Tubers are sweet with excellent cooking quality. It is responsive to fertilizers. It is resistant to sweet potato weevil.
Varsha	This is a double hybrid involving four cultivars viz., ACC No.99 x ACC No.3 (Hybrid-74) x ACC No.1871 x ACC No.1130 (Hybrid-42). The tubers of the variety are 14-20 cm long and 6-8 cm in diameter. The tubers are fusiform in shape. The tubers skin colour is red, rind colour pink and flesh colour light yellow. Tuber cooks well and is sweet in taste. This variety has been found highly tolerant to sweet potato weevil.
Kalmegh	This is an extra early variety developed from RAU, Dholi (Bihar). Tubers are round with light brown colour.
Kiran	This variety has been recommended for cultivation in Andhra Pradesh States.
Pusa Safed	It is a selection of Taiwan variety FA-17. The tubers are medium size with good cooking quality.
Pusa Lal	It is a selection of Japani variety Norin. Tubers are medium size with red colour skin and white flesh. This variety has good keeping quality.
Pusa Sundheri	The variety has high carotene content, imported from USA and selected at IARI, New Delhi. Flesh colour of tuber is orange.
Rajendra Sakarkand-5	It is a derivative of cross between Cross-4 x H-5and released by Central Sub- Committee on Crop Standards, Notification and Release of Varieties in 1985 for Bihar State. It is suitable for rabi season. Tubers are cylindrical with thin rind, tubers skin and flesh both whites, tubers (4-6) per plant with average tuber weight is 595 g. It is tolerant to frost, water-logging for a week period and sweet potato weevil.
Rajendra Sakarkand-35	This variety is recommended for cultivation in Assam, Karnataka and West Bengal. The tubers are dark brown colour with white flesh.
Rajendra Sakarkand-43	This variety has been recommended for cultivation in Assam, Karnataka, Maharashtra and Kerala states.
Samrat	This is a selection from the open pollinated seedling progeny. The tubers are fusiform with light pink skin and white flesh. It is an early maturing variety. The variety is resistant to sweet potato weevil.
Sankar	It is a progeny of H-219 X S-73 released in 1998. Plants are spreading type with green vine colour. Emerging leaves are green with purple in colour. Tubers are elliptic shape with red skin colour. It is medium duration variety with goood yield and excellent cooking quality.
Sree Bhadra	It is a seedling selection from the introduced seed population from Nigeria, released from 1996. Tuber is spherical in shape with light pink tuber skin colour. This variety is susceptible to sweet potato weevil. It is an early maturing with excellent cooking quality.
Sree Nandini	It is a selection made from the open pollinated progeny. The tubers are fusiform with light cream skin and white flesh. The tubers cook well and are tasty. The variety is highly tolerant to sweet potato weevil.
Sree Rethna	This hybrid is cross of S-187 x Sree Vardhini released in 1998 from Kerala state. Tuber is spherical in shape with purple tuber skin. It is susceptible to sweet potato weevil. This variety possessing excellent cooking quality.

Sree Vardhini	It is a selected from the open pollinated progeny seeds. The tubers of the variety are somewhat round with pink skin and light orange tuber flesh. The tubers cook well and have good acceptable taste. The crop is highly tolerant to sweet potato weevil and nematode.
V.L Sakarkand-6	It is an introduction from USA under the name B-129, released in 1974 from Uttar Pradesh for hilly areas. Length of the tuber is 15-18 cm and girth of the tuber is 12-14 cm. Crop duration is 135-140 days.

13.9.6. Yams

Name	Remarks
Sree Latha	This is the first cultivar of edible yam released through selection from CTCRI, Thiruvananthapuram and belongs to *Dioscorea esculenta*. Tubers are oblong to fusiform with greyish brown skin, which is partly hairy. The cultivar produces about 20-25 medium to large tubers/ plant. The average tuber length is about 13.5 cm and girth is 12.2 cm. They have good cooking quality and taste.
Sree Priya	This cultivar is related to *D. rotundata* sp. and having cylindrical, dark brown and smooth tubers. The flesh is white.
Sree Roopa	It belongs to *D. alata* species.
Sree Subhra	This belongs to *D. rotundata*. Tubers are cylindrical, brown, partial hairy with white flesh.

13.10. Spices and Condiments

13.10.1. Black Pepper

Name	Remarks
Sakthi	Its variety is open pollinated progeny of Perambramundi. It is tolerant to *Phytophthora capsici*. An average yield is 22.53t/ha and contains 3.7% essential oil.
Thevam	Developed through Clonal selection of Thevamundi. It is tolerant to *Phytophthora*. An average yield is 2.4t/ha and contains 3.1% essential oil.
Girimunda	This variety is developed through cross between Narayakodi x Neelamundi and recommended in rainfed conditions for high elevation. An average yield is 2.88t/ha and contains 3.4% essential oil.
Malabar Excel	This variety is derived from cross between Cholamundi x Panniyur-1 and suitable for cultivation in high elevation of plains. An average yield is 1.44t / ha and contains 2.8% essential oil.
Krishna	It is developed from Pepper Research Station (KAU), Panniyur, Kerala. It is an open pollinated line from cultivar Balamcotta and suitable for all pepper growing tracts. It has 10.89 per cent oleoresin and 35.7 per cent dry recovery.
Panchami	This variety was released from NRCS, Calicut. This is a high yielding clone already in cultivation and locally known as Aimperian.
Panniyur-1	This is a hybrid between Uthigankotta x Cheriakaniakadan and released in 1966 from Pepper Research Station, Panniyur, Kerala. High productivity of this variety was due to the recombination of favorable and complementary yield components from the diverse parents. Chief attributes of this variety are vigorous growth, large cordate leaves, non-pigmented growing tip, long spikes and bold berries. It performs well only under adequate sunlight.

Panniyur-2	This is a clone from the open pollinated progeny of cultivar Balankotta and released for high yield. This cultivar is popular in the northern districts of Kerala and south Canara of Karnataka. It has vigorous in growth and non-pigmented growing tip. It is tolerant to shade compared to other cultivars.
Panniyur-3	This is one of progeny in the cross Uthirankotta x Cherianiakadan and released for its high yields. Its characteristics are similar to Panniyur-1 but have faint pigmentation on growing tip.
Panniyur-4	It was released in 1989 from Kerala.It comes to harvest later in the season than most other cultivars. This variety has long and curved baracts in it or the basal flowers (at fruiting stage) in same spikes that can be used as a varietal character.
Panniyur -5	This variety is developed by open-pollinated progeny of Perumkodi and suitable for cultivation in both mono cropping & mixed crop in coconut/arecanut gardens. It has long spikes. An average yield is1.10t/ha and contains essential oil 3.8%.
Panniyur- 6	This variety is developed through Clonal selection from Karimunda steady and stable yielder, tolerant to drought and adverse climatic conditions. It is suitable for open condition as well as partial shade.
Panniyur -7	This variety is open pollinated progeny of Kalluvally. Plants are vigorous, hardy and a regular bearer, long spike and contain high piperine (5.6%). Tolerates to adverse climatic condition and suitable for cultivation in open and shaded conditions. An average yield is1.41t/ ha and contains 1.5% essential oil.
Panchami	Its variety is clonal selection from Aimpiriyan.It is late maturing variety have an excellent fruit set. An average yield is 2.82t/ ha and contains 3.4% essential oil.
Pournami	This variety was released in 1991 from NRCS, Calicut. It possesses tolerance to nematode as well as high yield. It had been tested under the name Ottaplackal-1.
PLD -2	This variety is clonal selection of Kottanadan. It is late maturity variety having high quality and recommended for cultivation in Trivandrum and Quilon districts of Kerala. An average yield is 2.47t/ha and contains 4.8% essential oil.
Shyma	It was developed from Pepper Research Station (KAU), Panniyur, Kerala. It is a hybrid between Uthigankotta x Cheriakaniakadan and suitable for all pepper growing tracts of country. It gives 12.6 per cent oleoresin and 27.8 per cent dry recovery.
Sreekara	This is a high yielding variety selected from Karimunda clones. The vines are slender and have characteristics of dark green leaves and berries. Like other cultivars, these varieties also produced off-season flowers. It is suitable for all pepper growing regions. An average yield is 2.67t/ ha and contains 7% essential oil.
Subhakara	This is a clonal selection from Karimunda.The variety contains12.4% oleoresin and 6 % essential oil. It has wider adaptability to all pepper growing tracts. An average yield is 2.35 t/ha.

13.10.2. Small Cardamom

Name	Remarks
Appangala-1	This variety is developed by selection of Malabar and suitable for intensive cultivation of both under mono crop and mixed crop cultivation. This is early maturing variety, highly adaptive and produces 89% bold capsules. It is recommended for cultivation in cardamom growing tracts of Karnataka and Wayanad of Kerala. The potential yield is 1.32 t/ha dry capsules.
Appangala-2	This is high yielding and resistant to *Cardamom mosaic virus*/Katte. Recommended for cultivation in All cardamom growing tracts of Karnataka and Wayanad of Kerala. An average yield is 0.9t/ha.
CCS-1	Capsules are parrot green and round shaped which is suitable for Karnataka.
CEYLON	The leaves are smooth, panicles are erect and the pods elongated loosely arranged in the panicle
CL-37	Selection from Malabar clone produces bold capsules on long panicles, high recovery.
ICRI-1	Dark green round shaped capsule is suitable for Kerala and Tamil Nadu cultivation.
ICRI-2	It is a small cardamom cultivar. The capsules are parrot green and long shaped. This variety is suitable for Tamil Nadu and Kerala.
ICRI-3	Its variety is developed through selection of Malabar. It is tolerant to rhizome rot and recommended for cultivation in all growing tracts of Karnataka. An average yield is 0.59 t/ha.
ICRI-4	This variety is derived from selection of Malabar cultivar.This variety is suitable for cultivation in low regions and adapted to lower Palani hills. An average yield is 0.96t/ha.
ICRI-5	This variety is developed from selection of Malabar. This variety contains high oil content. It is recommended for cultivation in Kerala and some parts of Tamil Nadu. An average yield is 1.54 t/ha.
ICRI-6	This variety is moderately tolerant to rot, thrips, borer and drought. It is recommended for cultivation in Kerala and some parts of Tamil Nadu. An average yield is 1.9t/ha.
Nithyashree	It is a superior open pollinated selection from elite tree from Anjarkandy, Cannanose. The young flushes of this variety are purple in colour, which turn in to green in two days. Regeneration capacity is 4-5 shoot/year. This variety possesses 2.7 per cent bark oil and 3 per cent leaf oil.
Avinash	This variety is resistant to rhizome rot with high yielding and suitable for planting in valleys and produces 51% bold and dark green capsules. This variety suited for cultivation in hotspot of rhizome rot prone areas. Potential yield is 1.48t/ha dry capsules.
Vijetha	This variety is cardamom mosaic virus resistant (Katte) and recommended for cultivation in moderate to high shaded mosaic disease prone areas of Kodagu, Hassan, Chikmagalur and North Wayanad. Adapted to moderate rainfall and moderate to high shade areas. Potential yield is 0.97t/ha dry capsules.
Suvasini	This variety is selection from open pollinated progeny of CL-37 from RRS Mudigere. This is Malabar type and early maturing variety.This variety is suitable for high density planting having long panicle. This variety is tolerant to rhizome rot, thrips, and shoot/panicle/capsule borer.

Malabar	The plant is medium in size which attains a height of 2-3 meters. Pods are light green, angular, 20-25 black seeds and closely packed. Tillers are 10-30 in well-grown clumps and 20-25 spikelets. It is the most common variety widely cultivated on the Travancore hills and south western ghats. It is drought resistant and is mostly suitable for lower elevations.
MCC-61	This is clonal selection from Mysore type, suited for higher elevations, produces long bold parrot green capsules, tolerant to azhukal disease.
MCC-49	It is also a selection from Malabar type, suited for both irrigated and rainfed conditions, bold dark green capsules, suitable for medium elevation.
MHC-10	Presence of angular bold and deep green capsules is an important feature of this hybrid. The percentage of 7 mm and above sized capsule is above 41. Capsule possess an essential oil content of 6.4 per cent. This variety is highly suited to Idukki and Malliamputhy hill of Kerala and Nilgiris of Tamil Nadu.
MHC-13	This hybrid is characterized by medium long capsules above 44 per cent of the capsules are having 7 mm and above size. Essential oil content is 7.2 per cent under moderate management and it can yield up to 600 kg/ha. This hybrid is well suited to Milliampathy and Idukki hill of Kerala and Nilgiris of Tamil Nadu.
MHG-18	This hybrid is characterized by deep green, angular bold, capsular, more than 80 per cent of the capsule are 7 mm and above size. This variety can be given a yield of 470 kg/ha under rainfed condition. Essential oil content is 6.6 per cent. The hybrid is well adapted to Idukki and Melliampathy hills of Kerala.
Mudigere-1	This is developed through selection of Malabar cultivar. Its capsules are parrot green and round shaped pubescent type, oval medium. It is tolerant to shoot borer and thrips. This is recommended for cultivation in traditional cardamom growing Malanad areas of Karnataka under rainfed conditions. An average yield is 2.75 t/ha.
Mudigere -2	Its variety is derived through selection of Malabar. It is suited for cultivation in valleys and cardamom growing tracts of Karnataka. An average yield is 4.75 t/ha.
Mudigere 3	It is developed by selection of clone Malabar. It is tolerant to thrips and borers. This variety is recommended for cardamom growing tracts of Karnataka. An average yield is 0.40t/ha.
Munzerabad	The plants are sturdier than Malabar. The panicles are prostrate and pods are round and closely arranged. It is a good yielder. The variety is grown at lower elevations in the north Wynad area.
Mysore	Pods are longer and globose with dark green colour and 25-30 spikelets. This is a high yielding variety suited to higher elevations and withstands exposure and wind better. It is suitable for areas from 900 to 1200 m.
PV-1	It is selected through Malabar cultivar. It has an early maturing variety with elongated, long green colour capsule. It is adaptable in Kerala and Tamil Nadu. This variety is tolerant to thrips infestation. An average yield is 0.50 t/ha.
PV 2	This variety is derived from selection of Vazhukka cultivar. It has green bold capsules. This variety is reserve for cultivation in cardamom growing area of Idukki. An average yield is 0.98 t/ha.
VAZHUKKA	This variety is a hybrid of Mysore and Malabar as plants exhibit intermediate characters. It shows adaptability too fairly wide range of environmental conditions.

13.10.3. Large Cardamom

Name	Remarks
Ramshai Or Ramsey	It is derived from two Bhutia words 'Ram' meaning mother and 'Sey' for gold. The variety is suited to higher altitudes as well as on steep slopes. This variety occupies a major area under the large cardamom both in Sikkim and Darjeeling district (West Bengal). Capsule size is smaller with less number of seeds (16-30). The capsule wall colour content of the seed ranges between 1.0 per cent and 1.8 per cent on volume by weight basis.The variety is susceptible to both the viral infection i.e. Chirkey and Foorkey, especially at lower altitudes. The variety is known for its irregular performance and easily affected by environmental fluctuations. This variety requires deep shade conditions for its thriving.
Golshai or Golsey	It is derived from both Hindi and Bhutia words, 'Gol' meaning round and 'Sey' for gold. The variety is mostly found grown at low and mid elevations and a larger area has been covered under this variety near 'Dzongu' in north-Sikkim. The clump size is medium to small with less number of tillers and hence suited to close spacing and also to less shaded conditions, because of its upright self-shading canopy. The leafy stem is greenish to maroonish depending upon the strains. The capsules are bold, roundish with reddish brown to dark-pinkinsh in colour and slightly echinated. On an average, the capsules contain about 40-55 seeds and the volatile oil content of the seeds is estimated in between 2-3.5 per cent on volume by weight basis (v/w). The variety is known for its consistent performance though not a heavy yielder. It is also found tolerant to 'Chirkey' and to some extent to 'Foorkey' viral diseses, but is susceptible to leaf spot diseases caused by fungi.
Sawney	A Nepalese term derived from, 'Sawan' for the month during August, in which the capsules of this variety become ready for harvest at low and mid altitudes. The variety is mostly adapted to mid altitutes of south, east and west districts of Sikkim. The capsules are reddish-brown to maroonish, medium too bold in size and having seeds of about 30-40 per capsule. The volatile oil content of the seed ranges between 1.8 to 2.5 per cent (weight basis). The plants are susceptible to both the viral diseases and also to leaf spot and spot rot diseases. Moderate deep shade condition is necessary for its thriving.
Ramla	At present the area under this cultivar is limited to a few mid-high-altitude plantations in north Sikkim. The capsules are dark pinkish, uniform and medium blold in size. The volatile oil content of seeds ranges between 2.2-3.0 per cent (weight basis). It needs moderate to deep shade conditions for its thriving. This seems to be a natural hybrid between the two cultivars 'Dz Glosey' and 'Ramsey'. The plants are found susceptible to 'foorkey' but moderatley tolerant to 'chirkey'.

13.10.4. Cinnamon

Name	Remarks
Konkan Tej	This variety is developed through seedling selection from progenies of Sri Lankan accessions. It has 3.2% bark oil with 29.16% bark recovery, 70.23% cinnamaldehyde in bark oil, 6.93%, eugenol in bark oil and 75.5% eugenol in leaf oil. Average yield is 0.33 t/ ha.

Navashree	It is a selection from open-pollinated seedling progenies of Sri Lanka introduction. The important distinguishing morphological character is purple in colour of young flush and they turn green in 7-10 days. It has high and stable generation capacity (6 to 7 shoots per year), high bark recovery (40.6 per cent) and high yield (average yield 56 kg/ha at the first harvest). It has excellent quality attributes viz; bark oil 2.7 per cent, cinnamaldehyde content 73 per cent, bark oleoresin 8.7 per cent and leaf oil 2.8 per cent. It is recommended for all cinnamon growing areas both in plains and hills.
Nithyashree	It is another selection from germplasm. The important character is that the young flushes are purple in colour and they turn green in two days. It has good and stable generation capacity (4 to 5 shoots per year). It has high yield (average 54 kg/ha in first four harvests) coupled with excellent quality (bark oil 2.7 per cent, bark oleoresin 10 per cent, leaf oil 3 per cent and eugenol content 78 per cent. It is recommended for all the cinnamon growing places, both in plains and hills.
PPI (C) -1	It is selection from open pollinated seedling progeny introduced from Sri Lanka. This cultivar is suitable for cultivation in high rainfall zones and hill regions of Tamil Nadu at an altitude range of 100-500 m MSL. An average yield is 0.980 t/ha.
RRL(B) C-6	This is developed through selection from germplasm collection open pollinated seedling progenies. Plants are spreading and branching in nature. This is high quality variety, sweet and pungent bark with 83% cinnaldehyde content in bark oil and 94.0% eugenol in leaf oil. An average yield is 0.25t/ ha.
Sugandhini	This is a Sri Lankan type variety developed through single tree selection from Wayanadu local collection and recommended for cultivation for leaf oil production and contains 45% cinnamaldehyde in bark oil and 93.7% eugenol in leaf oil. This variety is released mainly for leaf oil purpose. This variety has densely foliage. An average yield is 0.640 t/ha.
YCD-1	This is clonal selection from opening seedling progenies of Sri Lankan type having good bark recovery and adopted for cultivation in wide range of soil and rainfed conditions. This variety is recommended for high ranges at 500-1000m above MSL. An average yield is 0.36 t/ ha.

13.10.5. Coriander

Name	Remarks
ACR- 01-256	It is developed by reselection from EC-467683 from Russia. It is dual purpose variety, long duration, resistant to stem gall and wilt. An average yield is1.10t/ ha.
ACr-1	It is developed through reselection from EC-467683 from Russia. Grains are medium to small, having essential oil content up to 0.5 %. Resistant to stem gall and have tolerance to powdery mildew. An average seed yield is 1.25t/ ha.
APHU-Dhania-1	This variety was a selection made from the landrace collected from Koilakuntla village of Kumool district by practicing mass selection developed at A.P Horticultural University, Horticultural Research Station, Lam, Guntur. Plants are semi-erect with 6-9 primary branches and 10 to 16 secondary branches. Leaves rose with an arcus of 45° longest basal. Leaf is deeply incised with 3 lobes, upper leaves more than twice pinnate. Plants have medium foliage with greenish stem. An average yield is 0.85 to1.0 t/ha under rainfed cultivation and 1.2 to1.5t/ha under irrigated cultivation.

Ajmer Coriander-1	This is dual purpose variety suitable for leaves & seed production.
Azad Dhania-1	This is developed by mass selection from Kalyanpur germplasm collection. Plants are erect, early branching, 5 umbellate/ umbel and tolerant to moisture stress, powdery mildew and aphids. An average yield is 1.0 t/ha.
CHIMPA S-33	This variety is introduced from Bulgaria. Plants are tall having late maturity. Seeds are fine.
CIMPOS-33	This is selection from germplasm introduced from Bulgaria. Plants are tall erect, compact, profused branching and flowering, grains small and bold. This variety is mainly recommended for oil production. An average yield is 2.1 t/ ha.
CO-1	It is developed by TNAU, Coimbatore through selection and released in 1972. It is suitable for rainfed conditions of southern district of Tamil Nadu.
CO-2	It is developed by TNAU, Coimbatore through selection from P_2 cultivar of Gujarat and released in 1985. It is dual-purpose cultivar suited for use as greens and for production of grains. It can be grown in water logged, drought, saline and alkaline conditions.
CO-3	It is developed by TNAU, Coimbatore through selection from ACC-695 of IARI and released for irrigation and rainfed conditions.The plants are dwarf. It is tolerant to wilt, powdery mildew and grey mould.
CO-4	This variety was developed through reselection from germplasm ATP77 Guntur collection. This is an early maturing variety suitable for both rainfed and irrigated condition. Grains are oblong and medium.This variety is field tolerant to wilt and grain mould. An average yield is 0.6t/ ha.
CS-287	This is an early maturing variety which matures in79-87 days. It has field tolerance to wilt and grain mould and gives an average yield 0.6t/ha.
DH-5	It is developed by CCSHAU, Hisar through selection from a local collection and identified in 1993 for irrigated conditions. The plants are medium-tall and bushy.
DH-209	Seeds are medium sized, maturity 130-140 days, average yield18-20 q/ha.
GC-1	It is developed by GAU, Gujarat through selection in local material and released in 1974 for early sowing conditions.The plants are erect. It matures in 112 days and produces an average yield of 1.1t/ha. Seeds are medium size (13.2 g/1000 grains), round and yellow. It is moderately tolerant to wilt and powdery mildew.
Hisar Anand	Its variety is developed from HAU Hisar. Its variety is grown irrigated and unirrigated condition. An average yield is 1.4t/ha.
Hisar Sugandh	This is dual purpose variety suitable for both as leaves and seeds. It belongs to medium maturity group. An average yield is 1.4 t/ha.
Hisar Surubhi	This variety is developed from HAU Hisar. Its variety is tolerance to frost and less affected by aphid, having volatile oili 0.42 %. An average yield is 1.9t/ha.
Katwan type	It is recommended for Madhya Pradesh. It is very popular among the farmers due to maximum green leaf cutting, late maturity and taller growth habit.
Kiran	It is a recommended variety for irrigated conditions of Rajasthan. This variety is resistant to stem gall.
Merrocan	This variety has high oil content. It is recommended for Madhya Pradesh.
Narnaul Selection	It is released from CCSHAU, Hisar.

Pant Haritama	This variety was released from GBPUA&T, Pantnagar, Uttaranchal. It is a fine seeded variety having late maturity. It is a dual-purpose variety and resistant to stem gall of coriander.
Rajendra Swathi	It is developed by RAU, Bihar through selection from Muzaffarpur Local and released in 1987. The plants are medium-sized with fine round aromatic grains (12.5 g/1000 grains). It is resistant to stem gall and moderately resistant to wilt, aphid and weevil.
Rajendra Sonia	This variety is medium tall high yielding variety, resistant to wilt, aphid's, weevil and tolerant to fruit fly. Average yield of1.2t/ha and maturesin110 days.
RCR-20	It is developed by RAU, Rajasthan through recurrent half-sib selection from a local collection of Jaipur and released in 1997 from limited moisture conditions and heavier soils of southern Rajasthan. The plants are bushy-spreading with medium height. It is moderately tolerant to powdery mildew, wilt and stem gall.
RCR-41	It is also developed by RAU, Rajasthan through recurrent half-sib selection from a local collection of Kota and released in 1988 for irrigated conditions. The cultivar is highly resistant to stem gall and wilt but moderately tolerant to powdery mildew.
RCR-435	The cultivar is developed by RAU, Rajasthan through half-sib selection from a local collection of Jalore district and identified for release in 1995 for irrigated conditions.The plants are bushy with quick early growth.
RCR-436	The cultivar is developed by RAU, Rajasthan through half-sib recurrent selection from a local collection of Kota and identified for limited moisture conditions. Plants are bushy with quick early growth and bold grains (16.0 g/1000). It matures in 90-100 days and produces average yield of 1.1t /ha under limited moisture conditions.
RCR-446	It is also developed by RAU, Rajasthan through half-sib selection from a local collection of Jaipur district and identified for release for irrigated conditions. .
RCR-684	This variety is suitable for Rajasthan in irrigated condition. Seeds are large and bold. Maturity of crop is130 days. An average yield is 1.0 t/ha. This variety is resistant to stem gall.
RCR-728	The variety has been developed through recurrent selection based on individual plant progeny (half sib) performance in UD- 728 which was a local collection from Garoth, Mandsaur (MP) developed at S.K.N. college of Agriculture, (Rajasthan Agricultural University) Campus – Jobner. Plants are bushy ,erect and vigorous growth. This variety is free from stem gall &powdery mildew and moderately resistant to wilt &root knot nematode. An average yield is 1.37 t/ha.
Sadhna	It is developed by APAU, Kerala through mass selection from Alur collection and released for rainfed conditions. The cultivar is tolerant to white fly and mites.
Sindhu	It is developed by APAU, Kerala through mass selection from Warrangal Local and released for rainfed conditions. The cultivar is tolerant to wilt and powdery mildew and resistant to aphids.

13.10.6. Cumin

Name	Remarks
Ac-01-167	It is developed through reselection from EC-243373. Seeds are bold. This is resistant to wilt. An average yield is 6.50 t/ha.
GC-1	It is developed by GAU, Gujarat through recurrent single plant selection. The cultivar is tolerant to wilt disease.
GC-2	It is also developed by GAU, Gujarat through pure line selection. The cultivar is moderately tolerant to wilt, blight and powdery mildew. .
GC- 3	It is developed through recurrent selection derived from West German entry EC-232689.This is characterized as bushy dwarf plant, fruit medium sized, resistant to frost and suitable for winter season in limited irrigation. This has high essential oil content, seed pungent with good aroma. An average yield is 6.20 t/ha.
GC-4	It is resistant to fusarium wilt. An average yield is 8.75 t/ha.
MC-43	This is selection from germplasm pool. Plants are plant semi spreading, grains bold lustering withstands lodging and shattering, moderately tolerant resistant to Fusarium wilt, Alternaria blight & powdery mildew. An average yield is 5.80 t/ ha.
RZ-19	It is developed by RAU, Rajasthan through recurrent single plant progeny selection from a collection of Kepri (Ajmer). The cultivar is more tolerant to wilt as well as blight.
RZ-209	It is also developed by RAU, Rajasthan through recurrent single plant progeny selection from a local collection of Ahore (Jalore) and identified in 1995. The cultivar has shown high resistance to wilt and blight diseases.
RZ-223	This is tolerance to wilt. It has 3.23 % essential oil content. An average seed yield is 0.6 t/ha.
RZ-345	This is medium maturity group(120-130 days) variety suitable for Rajasthan and Gujarat. Seeds are bold. attractive having high volatile oil content. This is moderately resistant to wilt.
Topolka	It is a high yielding variety introduced from Bulgaria and resistant to *Pseudomonas cumini.*
UC-198	It is highly tolerant to wilt and having very high quantity of volatile oil (5-6 per cent). The grain of this variety is somewhat fragile.
5-404	It is selection from local germplasm. Plants are erect having medium sized fruits. This is moderately tolerant to powdery mildew. An average yield is3.50 t/ha.

13.10.7. Fennel

Name	Remarks
AF-01-119	It is recurrent selection from individual plant progeny. This is medium maturity variety. Seeds are bold. This variety is tolerant to blight. An average yield is1.95t / ha.
Ajmer Fennel -1	This variety is suitable for growing for both early sowing as rabi crop. Seeds are attractive, bold, medium sized and fragrant with volatile oil content up to 1.65%. An average yield is 1.95 t/ha during rabi season and 2.51 t/ha when grown as an early crop.

Apsheronskji	It is a variety of Azortai Jan regions with vigorous high green leaves. The yield of this variety is very low.
Azad Sanuf-1	It is selection from germplasm . Plants are medium in height. Seeds are bold green. This is resistant to blight and root rot diseases, escapes attack of aphids due to early maturity. An average yield is 1.5 t/ ha.
Co-1	It is developed by TNAU, Coimbatore through reselection from PF-35. It is suitable for drought-prone,waterlogged, saline and alkaline conditions. It is suitable for hilly areas as well as for intercropping and border cropping.
Funnel S-7-9	This is a dwarf variety seeds are bold .
Gujarat Fennel-1	It is developed by GAU Gujarat through selection from Vijapur Local and released in 1985.It is suitable for early sowing and reasonably tolerant to drought. It is moderately tolerant to sugary disease and leaf spot.
GF-2	It is long duration variety and plants are tall in height. An average yield is 1.8t/ha
GF-11	This is suitable for rabi season under irrigated condition. An average yield is 2.4 t/ha. Seed are containing 1.80% oil content.
GF-12	This variety is recommended for Gujarat and other states under irrigated condition. Crop maturity is 150-160 days. It has 1.9-2.2 % volatile oil content. Seed yield is1.87 t/ha,
Hisar Swarup	This variety acquiring an average height of 132 cm, spreading and late in maturity. Yield potential is 1.7 t/ha. This variety is resistant to lodging and shattering of grains.
Mutant-1	Before opening, flowers of this mutant are seemed normal flowers but soon leaf-like tips appeared which eventually developed into leaf-like appendages.
Mutant-2	Plants of this mutant are of the same height as Mutant-1. This Mutant-2 did not form any seed because the pollens are completely sterile.
Mutant-3	This was isolated from a market sample collected at Delhi. This is characterized by the complete absence of corolla. Unlike in Mutant-1 and Mutant-2, no other plant part appeared to be affected in this mutant.
Pant Madhurika	This medium maturity variety has been developed through pure line selection from local germplasm. Plants are tall robust, erect with big umbels having bold seeds with green fine ridges and sweet in taste.
Pf-35	It is developed by GAU, Gujarat through selection from local germplasm and released in 1973. It is moderately tolerant to sugary disease, leaf spot and leaf blight.
Pomorje	This is a variety from Bulgaria by several cycles of recurrent individual and family selection within a local population. This is a perennial winter hardy drought resistant and has high resistant to fungal diseases.
RF-101	It is developed by RAU, Rajasthan through recurrent half-sib selection from a local collection of Tank.
RF-125	It is developed by RAU, Rajasthan through recurrent half-sib selection from an exotic collection, EC-243380 from Italy. The plants are early, short with compact umbels and long bold grains.
RF-143	This variety is medium maturity group. An average yield is 1.2 t/ha and having 1.87 % oil content in seed.
RF-205	The variety has been developed through recurrent selection based on individual plant progeny (half sib) from F_2 generation of a cross between JF-25x RF-125. Plants are erect and medium tall plant. Seeds are long,

	attractive and bold with high volatile oil content (2.48%).This is resistant to rumularia blight. An average yield is 1.6t /ha.
SEL-32	Plants are moderate in vigour with high seed yields.
UF-31	This is a variety from Jobner.
UF-32	This is a variety from Jobner. It has higher number of umbellets / plants that are the main yield attributing characters in this crop.
UF-90	It is a promising cultivar and well suited to Jobner of Rajasthan.

13.10.8. Fenugreek

Name	Remarks
APHU Methi-1	This variety is suitable for Andhra Pradesh Crop matures in 80-90 days after seed sowing. Seeds are flat shaped medium sized. An average yield is 0.7 to0.9 t/ha in rainfed condition,1.2-1.5 t/ha irrigated condition.
Ajmer Fenugreek-1	Plant height is medium, bears broad leaves with less bitterness seed are bold in size with 17-20 g test weight, seed per pod ranges from17-20. An average seed yield is 2.72 t/ha and matures in 137 days.
Ajmer Fenugreek-2	Seed are small in size, seeds per pod ranges from16-18. An average seed yield is 1.8-2.0 t/ha.
Ajmer Fenugreek-3	This variety is moderately resistant to powdery mildew and root rot.It has1.79% disogenin and 0.97% hydroxyisocinen in seed.
AM-01-35	This is developed through selection from local germplasm. This variety is dual purpose, tolerant to powdery mildew. An average yield is 1.72t / ha.
Barbara	It is having erect plants, yellow seeded and high trigonellin content in seeds.
CO-1	A reselection from TG-2336. It is moderately tolerant to root rot.
CO-2	This is selection from CF 390. This is short duration dual purpose variety and field tolerant to *Rhizoctonia* root rot disease. This is suitable for both kharif and rabi seasons.
Hissar Sonali	It is developed by HAU, Hisar through pure-line selection from local germplasm. It is moderately resistant to leaf spot and root rot complex diseases.
Hisar Suvarna	This is dual purpose variety suitable for cultivation in Haryana, Rajasthan and Gujarat. It is resistant to powdery mildew and moderately resistant to downey mildew. An average yield is 2.0 t/ha
Hisar Mukta	It is developed through natural green seed coat mutant selected from IL-335-1. An average yield is 2.3 t/ha. It is resistant to downey mildew and moderately resistant to powdery mildew.
Hisar Madhavi	This variety is medium in maturity and having average yield of 2.0 t/ha. This variety is resistant to powdery mildew and moderately resistant to downey mildew.
HM-103	It is developed by CCSHAU, Hisar through pure-line selection from local germplasm. It is moderately resistant to leaf spot disease.
IC-74	It is local cultivar having erect green, more branching and good green as well as seeds.
Kasuri Selection	It is a late cultivar of Kasuri methi and selected at IARI, New Delhi. Leaves are small. Pods are sickle shaped. It is commonly grown in Punjab, Rajasthan, Haryana, Delhi and Uttar Pradesh.
Lam Selection	Plants are medium in height and bushy with better yield potential.
-1	It is developed by APAU, Kerala through selection from germplasm

	collected from Madhya Pradesh. It is tolerant to root rot, powdery mildew, caterpillars and aphids.
Pant Ragini	This medium maturity variety has been developed through selection from local germplasm. This is dual purpose, bushy in growth and resistant to downy mildew and root rots, Seed contains 2-2.5% essential oil. An average yield is 1.2t / ha.
Prabha	It is a pure line selection from a local collection of Nagpur district. It has semi-erect growth habit with pest and disease resistance.
Pusa Early Bunching	This variety is suitable for sowing in October-November. Pods have bold seed.
Pusa Kasuri	This is small seeded kasuri type variety cultivated for leaf purpose. An average yield of green leaves is 0.8 t/ha.
Rajendra Kranti	It is developed by RAU, Bihar through mass selection from Raghunathpur germplasm and released in 1987.The plants are tall and bushy with medium-sized golden yellow seeds. It matures in 120 days and produces an average yield of 1.25 t/ha. It is moderately resistant to powdery mildew, caterpillar and aphids.
Rajasthan Methi	It is developed by RAU, Rajasthan through pure-line selection from a local collection. It is moderately resistant to root rot and tolerant to powdery mildew disease.
RMT-143	It is developed through pure-line selection in a local collection from Jodhpur area. The grains of this variety are bold with typical yellow color. It is moderately resistant to powdery mildew. It is especially suitable for heavier soils of Chittor, Bhilwara, Jhalwa and Jodhpur areas in Rajasthan.
RMT 303	It is medium maturity variety (145- 150 days) developed through mutation breeding from variety RMt 1. Seeds are bold with typical yellow colour. This variety has less incidence of powdery mildew.
RMT-305	This is developed through mutation breeding from variety RMT-1. Plants are determinate in growth and fenugreek type. Plants are resistant to powdery mildew and root knot nematode.
RMT-361	This is medium maturity group variety and suitable for cultivation in all fenugreek growing area of India. Seeds are bold and attractive yellow in color. An average yield is 1.84t/ha.

13.10.9. Ginger

End use	Varieties
(i) For dry ginger	Karakkal, Nadia, Maran, Wynad, Manantody, Valluvanad, Emad and Kuruppampalli.
(ii) For green ginger	Rio-De Janerio (preferable for extraction of oleoresin), China, Wynad Local and Tabengiya.
(iii) For high volatile oil	Sleeva Local, Narasapattam, Emad, Chemad and Himachal Pradesh.
(iv) For high oleoresin	Emad, Chemad, China, Kuruppampali and Rio-De Janeiro.

Some of the area wise commonly cultivated varieties of ginger in India

Area of cultivation	Cultivars
Assam	Thingpui, Jorhat, Nadia, Thinladium, Maran
West Bengal	Burdwan
Kerala	Wynad Local, Wynad Manantody, Emad, Thodupuzha
Karnataka	Kurappampadi, Karakkal
Andhra Pradesh	Narasapattam

Name	Remarks
Athira	This clone is a selection form soma clones of cultivar Maran.
China	It is an exotic high yielding variety and well adapted to Indian conditions.
Himgiri	It is a clonal selection developed from local ginger of Dharjar village in Solan district, released from Dr. YS Parmar University of Horticulture, Solan. It is suitable for low to mid hills. It bears bold rhizomes. It is tolerant to rhizome rot.
Maran	It is a popular variety of Assam and least affected by *Phythium aphanidermatum.*
Mahima	This is selection from germplasm pool . This is high yielder and rhizomes are plumpy and extra bold. Plants are resistant to root knot nematode species *M. incognita and M. javanica.* This variety possess1.72% essential oil.
Nadia	It is high yielding variety of West Bengal and can be grown throughout the ginger growing area in the country.
Rio- De-Janerio	It is an exotic variety but well adopted to ginger growing areas of India.
Rejatha	This variety is developed through selection from germplasm pool. This is high yielding variety which rhizome is plumpy and bold. This variety possesses 2.36% essential oil.
Surabhi	This is clonal selection from X-ray mutant of local cultivar (V_1K_{1-3}). Rhizomes are cylindrical and dark glazy in skin colour.
Suruchi	This is a local selection from Kunduli Local (PGS-35). It is less susceptible to diseases.
Suravi	This variety is developed through induced mutant of Rudrapur Local. Rhizomes are plumpy, dark skinned and yellow fleshed. This variety is suitable for cultivation in both irrigated and rainfed conditions. This variety possesses 2.1% essential oil.
Thinglai	It is a germplam collection from Mizoram and its cultivation is mainly confined to North Eastern Region of India.
Thingpui	This is also a germplasm collection from Mizoram and extensively grown in the North-Eastern Region of India. It is also popular in other ginger growing areas of the country.
Wynad	This is a popular variety of Kerala and also known as Calicut ginger.
Vareda	This variety has been released from IISR, Calicut, Kerala. This variety is having very low fibre content (3.2 per cent).

13.10.10. Turmeric

Name	Remarks
Alleppey	It is one of the popular varieties of Indian market and is appreciated for its superior quality.Rhizomes are thick, cylindrical, toper at both the ends with tubercle like protruberances and emit pepper like colour.
Armoar	It is susceptible to leaf spot and rhizome rot. It is commonly grown in northern district of Telangana (Andhra Pradesh).
Avanigadda	This clone is grown in Krishna district of Andhra Pradesh and has a good curing quality (23.0 per cent), volatile oils (4 per cent) and curcumin (3.8 per cent) content.
BSR-1	It is a mutant selected from a local cultivar of Bhavnisagar and released by TNAU, Coimbatore. The colour of the rhizomes is bright yellow with a shorter internodal length.
BSR-2	It is an induced mutant from Erode Local type. The plants are medium statured, high yielding and resistant to scale insects. The variety is adaptable to Periyar, Coimbatore, Solem, Dharmapuri, Trichirapalli, Thanjavur, North Arcot and South Arcot districts.
Chayapasupu	It is popular in areas of Godavari, Visakhapatnam and Srikakulam district in small pockets and are liked for the good colour and aroma of the rhizomes.
China Scented	It is a very good variety having 98 per cent germination. The interior of the rhizome is deep orange, very attractive and well developed.
Duggirala	It is one of the popular and superior cultivar of turmeric in trade and is extensively grown in Krishna and Guntur districts of Andhra Pradesh. It is susceptible to leaf spot and rhizome rot.
Erode	It is one of the popular cultivars of Tamil Nadu with good market acceptability.
Evaigon	It is less vigorous and gives high yield of green turmeric (45 t/ha).
G.L.Puram	It is recommended for cultivation in North Eastern Region.
Gorakhpur	This belongs to *Curcuma longa* and is grown in central parts of Uttar Pradesh.
Prabha	This variety is open pollinated progeny selection. This is a high yielding variety and rhizome matures 205 days after planting. This variety possess 6.5% essential oil.
Kedaram	This is a clonal selection from germplasm pool. Plants are resistant to leaf blotch. Crop maturity is 210 days.
Alleppeysupreme	This is a selection from Alleppey finger turmeric.Plants are tolerant to leaf blotch. Crop maturity is 210days.
Jobedi	The rhizomes are moderate in volatile oils (3 per cent) and low in curcumin content (1.2 per cent).
Kanthi	This is clonal selection from Mydukur variety of Andhra Pradesh. Plants have erect leaf with broad lamina, big mother rhizome, medium bold fingers having closer internodes. Crop maturity is 240-270 days.
Katingia	It is poor yielder (0.8 q/ha) variety of Orissa having high curing percentage (36 per cent).
Kasturi Amalapura	It is a popular cultivar of Central Delta in East Godavari district.
Kasturi Kothapeta	This is a popular cultivar grown in East Godavari district of Andhra Pradesh and distinguished by its pleasing aroma.
Kasturi Pasupa	It is popular variety of Andhra Pradesh.

Kasturi Tanuka	This is also common of west Godavari district. Foliage is dark green and having normal flowering.
Kesari Duvur	It is cultivated in a limited extent in Cuddapah district. It is susceptible to leaf blotch with moderate yields and curing percentage.
Krishna	It is a selection made from the cultivar Tekurpet and released by Turmeric Research Station Digraj, Maharashtra. It is tolerant to leaf spot and blotch diseases.
Lakadong	It is a famous variety of northeastern hill region for its high curcumin content (6.8-7.2 per cent).
Lokhandi	It is a popular variety of Maharashtra.
Local Haldi	The internal colour of rhizome is deep yellow.
Mannuthy Local	It is a popular variety of Kerala.
Megha Turmeric 1	It is suitable for growing under mid hills of Meghalaya. The variety is highly tolerant to leaf spot and leaf blotch diseases.
Mydukur	It is a popular variety of Cuddapoh district. It is highly susceptible to leaf spot and rhizome rot.
Nijamabad	It is an important variety of Andhra Pradesh.
Patana	It is famous for its deep colour and cultivated in Bihar.
Pant Peetabh	Its variety is developed through clonal selection from local type and resistant to rhizome rot.
Rajapuri	It is a popular cultivar of Maharashtra and Gujarat. It has moderate resistance to leaf spot and is susceptible to leaf blotch and rhizome rot.
Ranga	These are clonal selection from Rajpuri Local. Rhizomes are bold having spindle shaped mother rhizome. This variety is suitable for late sown condition and low lying areas. It is moderately resistant to leaf blotch and scales. Crop maturity is 250 days. This variety possess 4.4 % essential oil.
Rasmi	Its variety is developed through clonal selection from Rajpuri local. Rhizomes are bold and suitable for cultivation in both rainfed and irrigated condition in both early and late. Crop maturity is 240 days. This variety possesses 4.4% essential oil.
Rajendra Sonia	This is selection from local germplasm. Rhizomes are bold and plumpy. Crop maturity is 225 days.This variety possess 5% essential oil .
Roma	It is selection from the local cultivar Sunder released as a national variety by the Pottangi centre of the All India Coordinated Research Project on Spices (Orissa). Fingers have a blunt tip with vertical growth nodes covered with brown scales and orange yellow in colour. Rhizome quality is excellent recording a very high curcumin (9.3 per cent), oleoresins (13.2 per cent) and essential oils (4.27 per cent). It is best suited for hilly areas under irrigated dry and rainfed condition and mature in 8 months. The clone is tolerant to leaf blotch and scales.
Shillong	It is a popular cultivar of Assam that matures in 8 months. It is tolerant to leaf blotch and rhizome rot, while resistant to leaf spot.
Sonia	This variety has been developed from RAU, Dholi, Bihar. It is resistant to leaf blotch.
Sobha	It is developed through clonal selection from local type. This is high yielding variety possess high curcumin content (7.39%). Plants have erect leaves with narrow lamina. Mother rhizome is big with medium bold figures and closer internodes. Inner core of rhizomes is dark orange like Alleppey. Crop maturity is 240-270 days. Essential oil is 4.24%.

Sudharshana	It has good appeal in the local market as well as export trade. It has high oleoresin (15.0 per cent) and higher draige percentage (25.3 per cent). It is tolerant to leaf disease and rhizome rot.
Sugandham	It is clonal selection from germplasm confined to certain areas in Cuddapoh district. It is susceptible to leaf blotch and rhizome rot. This variety is thick, round rhizomes with short internodes. It is moderately tolerant to pest and diseases.
Suguna	It is short duration cultivar with an efficient driage percentage (24.6 per cent).
Suroma	This variety has been developed through Clonal selection by X- ray irradiation at Pottangi, Orissa.Rhizomes are round and plumpy. This variety is field tolerance to leaf blotch, leaf spot and rhizome scales.
Suvarna	It is an improved culture selected from Peruvannamozhi collection turmeric series and released by CPCRI, NRC for Spices, and Calicut for large-scale cultivation in Kerala, Karnataka and Andhra Pradesh. It is tolerant to leaf diseases and rhizome rot.
Suranjana	It is developed through clonal selection from local types of West Bengal. It is suitable for open and shaded condition. Crop maturity is 235days and having essential oil of 4.1%.
Tall Karbi	It is grown Karbi region of Assam and matures in 7 months. It exhibits tolerance to leaf spot and rhizome rot but susceptible to leaf blotch.
Tekurpeta	It is a popular variety grown in Rayalaseema region. It has also good curing percentage (22.3 per cent). Fingers are hard on drying giving a metallic sound and have longer storage life. It is susceptible to leaf spot diseases.
Thodopuza	It is a fairly good variety. This variety has small rhizome and fairly deep orange colour.
Varna	It is clonal selection from local germplasm. Rhizomes are bright orange yellow, medium bold with closer internodes and territory fingers present.This variety is suitable for cultivation in central zone of Kerala. This variety is field tolerant to leaf blotch.Crop maturity is 240-270 days. Essential oil is 4.56%.
Vontimitta	It is grown around Cuddapoh.

13.10.11. Dill (Sowa)

Ajmer Dill-1	Its variety is European type dill. Crop maturity is 142 days. Seeds contain3.5 % essential oil. An average yield is1.47 t/ ha
Ajmer Dill-2	This variety is Indian type dill. Crop maturity is 135 days. An average yield is 1.46 t/ ha.

13.10.12. Caron Seed (Ajwain)

Ajmer Ajwain-1 (AA-1)	This variety is suitable for cultivation under irrigated and rainfed conditions. It is late maturing variety which takes 165 days for seed harvesting. An average yield is1.42 t/ ha. This variety possess3.4% essential oil.
Ajmer Ajwain-2 (AA-2)	This variety is also suitable for cultivation under rainfed and irrigated conditions. Under irrigated condition this variety yielded 1.28t/ ha while in rainfed condition it yielded 0.52 t/ ha. Crop maturity is 147 days. This variety is resistant to powdery mildew.

GA-1	Crop maturing of this variety is 175-180 days and produces 25% more yield than local type.
Lam Selection-1	Plants are medium tall on average yield is 0.8 t/ha at 135 days of crop duration.
Lam Selection-2	Plants are busy type and produce 40-45 branches /plant. An average yield is1.0 t/ha.
Pratap Ajwain-1	Seeds of this variety are bold and greenish in colour. This variety is resistant to leaf blight and powdery mildew. An average yield is 0.8-1.0 t/ ha.

13.10.13 Nigella (Kalongi)

Ajmer Kalongi-1	This variety are suitable for cultivation under both semi-arid and irrigated conditions. Crop maturity is 135 days. An average yield is 0.8t/ha.

13.10.14 Anise (Vilyati Saunf)

Ajmer Vilayati Saunf-1	This is high yielding variety which bears attractive seeds and high volatile oil content (3.2 %). This variety is suitable for cultivation in semi-arid and irrigated conditions. An average yield 1.15 t/ha.

14
Agrotechniques

14.1. Bulb Vegetables

14.1.1. Garlic

Title	Description	
Climatic Requirements	It is cool season crop. It prefers moderate temperature in summer as well as winter. Extremely hot or long dry periods are very favourable for the formation of bulbs. Short days promote secondary growth and suppressed bulbing. The average temperature of 25 to 30 ^{0}C is most conductive for bulb initiation.	
Soil Conditions	It can be grown on variety of soils but thrives better on fertile, well-drained loamy soils, rich in nutrients, friable and rich in organic matter. It can tolerate salinity between 5.60 and 7.80 dsm^{-1}EC depending on cultivars.	
Sowing Time	North India (Plains)	September-October
	North India (Hills)	March-April
	South India	August-November
	Gujarat, Assam, West Bengal, *parts of Orissa*	October-November
	Maharashtra	November-December
	North Bihar	October-December
	Northern district of West Bengal	2nd week of November
Clove Requirements	About 300-500 kg cloves are required for planting of a hectare land. The planting cloves should be a weight of 3.6 to 5.8g.	
Methods of Planting	Dibbling: Cloves are dibbled 5 to 7.5 cm deep keeping their sprouting ends upwards. The spacing for sowing of the clove varies from place to place. A light irrigation is given immediately after sowing. Furrow Planting: The furrows are made 15 cm apart with the hand hoe or a cotton drill. In these furrows, cloves are dropped by hand 7.5 to 10 cm apart. Broadcasting: Cloves are scattered evenly over a levelled field by hand. They are, then covered by harrowing and the field is divided into convenient size of beds for irrigation. Transplanting: Nursery has also been prepared and the transplanting of plantlets. Flat Vs. Ridge Planting: Ridges are prepared at 35 cm spacing and planting of cloves are done on both sides of ridges at 7.5 cm distance. In flat beds, the plant spacing is kept at 15 x 7.5 cm.	
Spacing	Recommended spacing (cm)	Place
	15 x 18	Punjab

	15 x 8	-
	10 x 20	Chaubattia (Uttranchal)
	20 x 15	Allahabad (UttarPradesh)
	20 x 15	Jeolikot (Nainital)
	10 x 15	Haryana
Nutritional Requirements	Application of 100 kg N + 80 kg P_2O_5 + 60 K_2O kg/ha has been recommended for getting maximum economic yield.	
Intercultural Operations	First weeding is done one month after sowing and second weeding one month after first weeding. Hoeing the crop just before the formation of bulbs (about two and a half months from sowing) loosen the soil and helps in setting of bigger compact bulbs. Hoeing in the later stage of bulb formation should be avoided to improve the quality of bulbs. Weedicides Tribunal @ 1.5 kg a.i./ha, nitrofen @ 2.0 kg a.i./ha or basalin @ 2-2.5 kg a.i./ha diluted in 625 liter of water may be sprayed after 7 to 15 days of planting of cloves.	

Use of Plant Growth	Name of PGRs	Concentrations (mg/l)	Method of application	Attributes affected
	Ethephon Alar	500	Foliar spray at 20-25 days after sowing	Increases clove size and yield
	Cycocel (CCC)	1000	Twenty four hours before planting	Increased yield and storability of bulbs
	NAA	50	Sixty and ninety days after planting	Increased bulb yield.
	MH	2500	Foliar spray on foliage a fortnight before harvesting	Sprouting during storage can be controlled
	GA_3	200-400	Foliar spray	Stimulated formation of lateral buds

Water Management	First irrigation is given soon after sowing and later field is irrigated after 10 to 15 days until bulbs begin to develop. There should not be scarcity of moisture in the growing season to have best bulb development. The last irrigation should be given three days before harvesting for making it easy without damaging the bulbs.
Harvesting	Garlic is ready for harvesting in 130 to 180 days after planting depending upon cultivars, soil, season etc. Early harvest results in poor quality of bulbs, which can not be stored for longer period. After harvesting, bulbs are left for curing. Curing of bulbs is done for about a week in the fields to dry the bulbs thoroughly.
Yield	Normally, 5.0 to 11.0 tonnes per hectare bulb is obtained with the recovery of clove in the bulbs 86 to 96 per cent.
Storage	Bulbs alongwith their dried leaves are bunched and are hanged in a well-ventilated shed or room. In this way they can be stored for a longer period of time. The storage-life of bulb can further be increased in cold storage at 32 to 35^{0}F (0 ^{0}-1.6 ^{0}C) and 65 to 75 per cent relative humidity.

14.1.2. Onion

Title	Description		
Climatic Requirements	It grows well under mild climate without extreme heat or cold or excessive rainfall. A temperature range of 10 °C to 15.6 °C check bulb formation, whereas, it speeds up at 21.1 °C to 26.7 °C. At relatively low temperature of 10°C to 15.6 °C under short day of 9 to 12 hours, onion plants go for seed formation steadily, while under higher temperature of 21.1°C to 26.7°C, they do not seed either under short day or under long day of 15 hours length.		
Soil Conditions	Soils should be deep friable loam and alluvial where a free drainage, absence of persistent weeds and presence of organic matter favour the production of good crop. The optimum range of pH is 5.8 to 6.5.		
Sowing/Transplanting	Region	Sowing time of nursery	Transplanting time of seedlings
	North India	October to the middle of November *(rabi)* May to June *(kharif)*	Middle of December to JanuaryJuly to August
	Pune and Niphad area in Maharastra	October	November
	Madras and Andhra Pradesh	June to July (Mansoon crop) October to November (Winter crop) January- February (Summer crop)	August to September December to January February to March
	Madhya Pradesh and Vidarbha	Middle of December	End of January
	West Bengal	September to November	October to December
Nursery Raising	Seeds are generally sown in raised bed in the nursery. The nursery bed size should keep 10 -15 cm raised bed of about 3-6 m length and 1 m width are prepared. About 70 cm distance is kept between two beds for irrigation and intercultural operation. The top surface upto 2-3 cm should be enriched with fine, sieved well-decomposed farm yard manure before sowing. Before sowing the seed, seeds are treated with difolton or monosan @ 2.5 g/kg seed for checking pre- emergence death of seedlings as caused by damping off. To check post emergence damping off, drenching of nursery with 0.1 per cent brassicol/copper oxychloride should be done. Seeds are sown in lines at the distance of 4 to 5 cm in *rabi* and 5 to 7 cm apart in *kharif*. After sowing, the seeds are mulched with dry grass or straw or any other material. If there is lack of moisture in the bed, it should be watered by watering cane.		
Seed Rate	About 10-12 kg seed in *rabi* and 12-15 kg seed in *kharif* are required to raise seedlings for planting in one hectare.		
Methods of Sowing and Transplanting Distance	Onion crop can be grown in three methods (1) By raising seedlings (2) By planting bulbs directly in the field (green onion) and (3) By broadcasting or drilling seeds directly in the field (green onion).In nursery raising method of planting, the seedlings are ready for transplanting in		

about 6 to 7 weeks for *kharif* planting and in 8 weeks for *rabi* planting. Seedlings of 0.8-0.9 cm in diameter and about 20-35 cm in height are ready for transplanting. Over aged seedlings result in bolting and take longer time to start new growth, whereas under aged seedlings do not establish well after transplanting and withstand adverse weather conditions. The spacing of 15 cm between rows and 8 to 10 cm between plants has been found to be most conducive for high yield. In bulb method of planting, bulbs are dibbled 15 cm on the side of 45 cm wide ridges or in beds. To plant one hectare, 750 kg of medium sized bulbs is required. Large sized bulbs, if planted, tend to flower early and result in low yield. In direct sowing by broadcasting method of planting, soil is thoroughly pulverized and made free of clods. About 12-15 kg/ha seed is sown by broadcasting in band 30 cm apart.

Nutritional Requirements In general, nitrogen at 60 -80 kg phosphorus 40 -50 kg and potassium 60-80 kg per hectare alongwith 300q/ha FYM are required for high yield.

Intercultural Operations Onion exhibits greater susceptibility to weed competition than other crops. Due to shallow rooted crop, shallow hoeing once or twice will helpful in plant growth and keeping down the weeds. Generally, hand weeding is in practice. Pre-plant increporation of basalin @ 2 kg a.i./ha along with one hand weeding at 45 days after transplanting (DAT) have been recommended for weed control. Application of ranstar @ 1 kg a.i./ ha has been recommended for effective weed control. Application of fluchloralin @ 1.0 kg (PPI) + one hand weeding at 45 days has been found effective for weed control

(VGR)	Name of PGR(s) (mg/l)	Concentrations	Methods of applications	Attributes affected
	NAA	100-200	Seed Treatment	Improved bulb growth and yield
	IAA	10		
	GA	40	Seedling Treatment	Improved bulb growth and yield
	MH	2500	Foliar spray at one week before bulb digging	Check the sprouting during storage

Water Management Frequent irrigation is required at early in the growth and more frequent irrigations at the of bulb formation. The irrigation schedule should be 13 days interval during November-December, 10 days interval during January and 7 days interval during February-March. The most common method of applying to the onion crops to irrigate with basin or border strip flooding or furrow irrigation.

Harvesting Onion crop is ready for harvesting in five months for dry onion. However, for marketing green onion, the crop becomes ready in three months after transplanting. Onion should be pulled out by hand or with help of khurpi and should be immediately lifted to shade of curing. After curing, roots and tops are removed by leaving about 2 to 2.5 cm above the bulbs. Usually, 10-15 days or so will be sufficient for curing the onion bulbs.

Yield	Average yield of onion bulbs is ranged 30.0 to 40.0 t/ha in *rabi* season and about 20.0 to 25.0 t/ha in *kharif* season.
Storage	Onion bulbs store well at 0°C to 1°C temperature and 64 per cent relative humidity. The chances of sprouting of bulbs in storage will be negligible if pre-harvest foliage sprays of maleic hydrazide (MH) at 2500 ppm can be used. Another traditional methods are: **Onion on a string:** With the help of rope onion bulbs are tied on their neck arranged in spirally manner around the rope and hanged in the well-ventilated shed. **Spread onion on floor:** The onion bulbs are spread on floor in the shed-making layer of 10 to 15 cm thick. **Onion bulbs in trays:** Onion bulbs are kept in tray or tiers containing 2 to 3 layers of bulbs. These trays are arranged in well-ventilated room or shed.

14.2. Cole Crops

14.2.1. Broccoli

Title	Description
Climate Requirements	It requires cool climate and can tolerate frosty conditions. The best quality spouts are produced in the sunny weather and light frosts during nights. In warm weather, the little leaves of the buds may fail to form hard compact cabbage like heads. Suitable temperature for good crop is 10-25 °C.
Soil Conditions	Fertile soil rich in organic matter is suitable for obtaining good yield. Soils of fairly good moisture retentive have proper growth and development of plants. Soil pH should be 6.0-6.8 for better growth.
Sowing Time	In high hills, seeds are sown in May-June for summer/autumn crop. In the hilly areas, sowing is done in autumn. In the plains of northern India, sowing starts from early August and continue till November for the late cultivars.
Seed Rate, Methods of Transplanting and Spacing	Seed rate per hectare varies from 500-700 g, if crop is raised by transplanting, whereas 2-2.5 kg seeds per hectare are required for direct sowing. The seedlings are raised as methods described in cauliflower and cabbage. The seedlings when becomes 6-8 weeks old, it should be transplanted. The planting is done on the flat land, ridges or in furrows depending on climate and soil conditions. Planting distances are recommended on the basis of maturity of cultivars *viz.*; for early 45 X 45 cm or 60 X 30 cm; mid 60 X 45 cm; late: 60 X 60 cm.
Nutritional Requirements	The requirements for manure and fertilizers for broccoli are similar to cauliflower. It is advisable to top dressed the nitrogen into three splitted doses which is not commonly done in case of cabbage and cauliflower because broccoli is comparatively require long growing period.
Intercultural Operations	Weak and closer growing seedlings should be thinned to provide desired distance. In order to provide good aeration, a hoeing is done at early stage of growing crop. Hoeing however will destroy a good percentage of weeds, if some weeds left it can be pull out by hand those weddicides recommended in cauliflower and cabbage may also be used for controlling of weeds in broccoli.

Water Management	As soon as transplanting of seedling is over, irrigation water is allowed to let into the field. As broccoli requires moist conditions, subsequent irrigations should be given at frequent intervals depending upon soil condition.
Harvesting and Yield	The heads is cut along with a few leaves and stems (10-15 cm). The yield of broccoli ranges from 12.5-17.5 t/ha in open pollinated variety, however, hybrids yielded upto 40t/ha
Storage	Just after harvesting heads and shoots should be kept iced until they are sold otherwise the buds and leaves become yellowish and give an unattractive appearance. The yellowing could be delayed by storing the broccoli in an oxygen free atmosphere. Since fresh broccoli continues to develop and the flower being to open or turn yellow, the bunches are hydro cooled to 4.4 ^{0}C, packed with ice and stored under refrigeration. Broccoli can be stored at 32 ^{0}F for 8-10 days.

14.2.2. Brussels Sprouts

Title	Description
Climatic Requirements	It requires a cool climate. It can also tolerate frosty conditions. However, the best quality spouts are produced in the sunny weather and light frost during nights. Suitable temperature for good crop is 10-25 ^{0}C.
Soil Conditions	Sandy and silt loam soils are most suited. Soils must have capability for retention of good moisture. Soil pH should be 5.8 to 7.2 for better growth.
Sowing Time	Crops are sown in June- July and seedlings are planted from July to September (for early crop) and October to middle of November (for late crop) in northern parts of the India. In the hilly areas, sowing is done in autumn to harvest them in late spring in early summer.
Seed Rate, Methods of Transplanting and Spacing	Seedlings are raised similar to cauliflower and cabbage. About 200-500 g seed/ha is required. Planting distance is for early 45 x 45 cm or 60 x 30 cm; mid 60 x 45 cm; late: 60 x 60 cm. The planting is done on the flat land, ridges or in furrows depending on climate and soil conditions.
Nutritional Requirements	It requires more manure and fertilizers than cauliflower and cabbage because it comparatively requires long growing period. It is advisable to top dress the nitrogen into three splitt doses, which is not commonly done in case of cabbage and cauliflower.
Intercultural Operations	In order to provide good aeration to the root zone, one or two hoeing may be done. However, if growing weeds are very close to the plants, should be pulled out by the hands.
Water Management	First irrigation should be given just after completing the transplanting. As Brussel sprouts require moist conditions, subsequent irrigations should be given at frequent intervals.
Harvesting, Yield and Storage	The sprouts are harvested when they are firm and well developed usually 1-2" in diameter. The sprouts become ready for harvesting in 120 days after transplanting. Sprouts should be harvested at frequent interval otherwise these will open and become yellow. Regular harvesting at right stage enhances further growth of the plants and formation of new more heads. The average yield is about 10.0 t/ha. The recommended storage conditions are 0 to 1^{0}C and 90-95 per cent RH for 3-5 weeks.

14.2.3 Cabbage

Title	Description
Climatic Requirements	Cool moist climate is most suitable. The optimum soil temperature for seed germination is 21.2-26.2 °C. The optimum temperature for growth is between 25.2 to 34.2 °C. Above 43.2 °C growth is arrested in most of the cultivars.
Soil Conditions	Early cultivars grow well in light soils whereas late maturing ones perform better on heavy soils. Well-drained soils produced larger yields. Optimum pH is between 6.0-6.5. In saline soils, the plants show die back of leaf margins and dark foliage and it become more susceptible to diseases like black leg.
Sowing Time	In hills, especially in high hills, seeds are sown in May-June for summer/ autumn crop. In the hilly areas, sowing is undertaken in autumn to harvest them in late spring in early summer by over watering them. In the plains of northern India sowing starts from early August and continue till November for the late cultivars.
Seed Rate, Nursery Raising, Methods of Sowing and Transplanting Distance	About 200-500g /ha seed are required. Seeds are generally sown in a seedbed. Soil of nursery bed should be well prepared and free from disease organisms. The sieved well rotten farm yard manure or compost @ 2-3 kg/m^2 must be added in the seedbed. Before sowing, the seed should be treated with fungicide like or bavistin @ 3 g/kg seeds. Trichoderma @5g/kg seeds may also be used for seed treatment. The optimum spacing between rows in the nursery bed is 10 cm and the depth of sowing should be 1.5-2.5 cm. For planting one hectare 200-300 m^2 seedbed at the rate of 1 to 2 g per square meter is required. After sowing, the seed is properly covered with a thin layer of mixture of fine manure and soil. A regular and good moisture supply is needed for rapid germination of seed and the optimum growth of seedlings. To keep the upper soil of seedbed moist a thin layer of dry grass is spread on the beds and watering is done in the form of shower either with watering cane or with the help of a sprinkler. But the seed bed cover should be removed as soon as the emergence of young seedlings above the ground starts. The spray of blitox-50 @ 0.3 per cent is effective against 'damping off disease. Aliet @ 0.5/litre may salso be used for control of fungal at nursery diseases. Generally, 4-6 weeks old seedlings are ready for transplanting. The planting distances are generally recommended on the basis of maturity of cultivars *viz;* for early 45 x 45 cm or 60 x 30 cm, mid 60 x45 cm, late 60 x 60 cm. The planting is done on the flat land, ridges or in furrows depending on climate and soil conditions.
Nutritional Requirements	About 200-250 q/ha farm yard manure is mixed in the soil before 15-20 days of transplanting. The NPK ratios are guven below:

State	Nutrients (kg/ha)			Variety
	N	P	K	
Madhya Pradesh (Jabalpur)	180	50	50	Pride of India
Uttar Pradesh (Kanpur)	180	60	60	Pride of India
Bihar (Sabour)	150	-	-	Pride of India

	Half quantity of nitrogen and full quantity of each phosphorus and potash should be applied at the time of transplanting. Remaining quantity of nitrogen is applied at 30-45 days of transplanting.
Intercultural Operations	Two-three manual weedings are required. The weedicides like trifluralin @ 0.5 kg/ha (Soil incorporation) and fluchloralin @ 0.5 kg/ha (soil incorporation) can be used for weed control in cabbage.

Use of Plant Growth Regulators

Name of PGRs	Concentration (mg/l)	Method of application	Attribute affected
NAA IBA GA_3	0.1 0.4 5-10	Seed treatment Foliar spray	Improve head size and yield
NAA + chelated Zn	100 + 0.2 (per cent)	Foliar spray at 45 days after transplanting	Increased yield

Water Management	First irrigation is given just after transplanting of seedlings and thereafter irrigation may be done at 10-15 days interval according to season and soil conditions. But optimum soil moisture is maintained regularly.
Harvesting, Yield and Storage	Harvesting is done when the heads reach at marketable size. The early cultivars take 60-80 days, medium 80-100 days and late 100-130 days for harvesting after transplanting. The yield of open pollinated early cabbage ranges between 30-40 q/ha, whereas, medium and late cabbage variety 40-60 q/ha in northern plain. Cabbage can be stored at 0 ^{0}C and 90-95 per cent RH for about 2 to 8 months.

14.2.4. Cauliflower

Title	Description
Climatic Requirements	The optimum temperature for growth of young plants is around 23 ^{0}C but in later stage 17-20 ^{0}C are most favourable. Lower temperatures ranging from 5 ^{0}C to 28-30 ^{0}C are needed for transition from vegetative to curding phase.
Soil Conditions	Cauliflower is grown in good fertile soil. For early crops, the light soils are preferred while loamy and clay loam soils are more suitable for mid season and late maturing varieties/hybrids. Cauliflower is relatively more sensitive to deficiency of boron and molybdenum and it has also high requirement of magnesium.

Sowing Time

Groups	Time of sowing of seeds	Time of curd maturity
Early group	May-June	September
I (a) I (b)	First fortnight of July	October to mid November
Mid season group II	July-August	Late November to Mid December
Mid late group III	September	Late December to mid January
Late group (Snowball type)	October	Mid January onwards

Seed Rate, Methods of Sowing and Translanting Distance	For one hectare, 200-500 g seed would be needed. The seedlings are raised in the nursery as in cabbage. Seedlings are ready for transplanting in 3-6 weeks after seed sowing. In case of early crop, 5-6 weeks old seedlings have better establishment and less mortality in the field while in mid-season and late varieties 3-4 weeks old seedlings may be transplanted. The seedlings of early varieties are planted to 60 cm row to row and 30-45 cm plant to plant distance. The main season and late varieties are planted at spacing of 60-75 cm between rows and 45-60 cm between plants.
Nutritional Requirements	About 15-20 t/ha farm yard manure is applied in the soil before 15-20 days after transplanting. The NPK are applied in the ratio of 100-150 kg N, 80-100 kg P_2O_5 and 60-80 kg K_2O per hectare, respectively. Methods of application is same as mentioned in cabbage.
Intercultural Operations	The intercultural operations are done regularly to keep the crop free from weeds and aeration of the root system. Hoeing should not be deep to avoid injury to the roots. Usually in medium heavy and clay soils, there is crust formation soon after transplanting. These crust must be broken otherwise water and air penetration in root system are hindered which affect plant growth. For getting quality curd, blanching is an important operation to protect the curds from yellowing due to direct exposure to sun.

Use of Plant Growth Regulators (PGR)

Name of PGRs	Concentrations (mg/l)	Method of application	Attributes affected
IBA	10	Seedling treatment	Increases yield
GA + NAA + Molybdenum	100 +120 + 0.2 per cent	Foliar spray	Increases yield
GA + Urea	50 +1 per cent	Foliar spray	Increases yield
GA_3	50	Foliar spray twice at 20 and 40 days of transplanting	Increased yield

Water Management	First irrigation is given just after transplanting. Regular maintenance of optimum moisture supply is essential during both growth and curd development stage.
Harvesting, Yield and Storage	The harvesting is done as soon as the curd attains right maturity and they are compact. The white colour of the curds is maintained. If the harvesting is delayed, the curds become over mature whose quality is deteriorate. Such curds may turn loose, leafy, ricey or fuzzy. Early maturing open pollinated variety has an average yield of 15 t/ha. The main season cauliflower produces 30t/ha while Snowball group and other late maturing varieties gave 40t/ha. Cauliflower can be stored successfully at 0 °C and 90-95 per cent RH for 2-4 weeks.

14.2.5 Knol-khol

Title	Description
Climatic Requirements	Early maturing varieties have problem of premature bolting at 12 to 14ºC and these require above 15ºC temperatures for cultivation. The temperature of 20–25 ºC is considered optimum. If low temperature occurs at early stage of plant growth for considerable time, the plants will start to bolt quickly.
Soil Conditions	Fertile soils produce good quality uniform sized knobs.
Sowing Time	Seed sowing is done in September while in regions having mild winter, October is best month for planting. Sowing in hills is done in March–April and seedlings are transplanted from April onwards.
Seed Rate, Methods of Sowing and Spacing	About one kg seed will be required for cultivation of one-hectare area. The seedlings are raised as described in cabbage. Seedlings become ready for transplanting in 5-6 weeks after seed sowing. The planting distance may be 30-40 cm row to row and 20–25cm plant to plant.
Nutritional Requirements and their Management	About 10–15 t/ha farm yard manure is thoroughly mixed in the soil at 10-15 days before transplanting. The nitrogen, phosphorous and potash are applied in the ratio of 80:60:60 kg/ha, respectively. Half quantity of nitrogen and full quantity of each phosphorous and potash are applied at the time of transplanting. Remaining quantity of nitrogen should be applied 30 days after transplanting.
Intercultural Operations	Two-three weedings are required. Weeds can also be controlled by application of pre-emergence of lasso @ 1.5–2 kg/ha a.i.
Water Management	Adequate supply of water is essential during the period of stem swelling irrespective of time of planting. This crop required six irrigations amounting to 300-mm water in whole crop cultivation in whole crop duration.
Harvesting, Yield and Storage	The harvesting should be done before the knobs get over mature. The over grown knobs have poor edible quality because of more fibres content. Usually knobs may be harvested when they are of 6-8 cm diameters. For harvesting, stem can be cut just above the ground or can be pulled easily by hand. Yield per hectare varies from 12.0 to 25.0t/h. It can be stored successfully at 95-100 per cent RH for 25-30 days.

14.3. Cucurbitaceous Vegetables

14.3.1. Bittergourd

Title	Description
Climatic Requirements	It requires 20-30 ºC optimum temperature for growth and development of plant. Short days help in increasing female flower production.
Soil Conditions	It requires sandy-to-sandy loam soil. Soil should be rich in organic manure with proper drainage facility. The soil pH should be 5.5 to 6.7.
Sowing Time	(i) Summer crop is sown in February-March in Northern plains but January-February in North-west India. (ii) In West Bengal and in South India, it is sown in October November. (iii) The rainy season crop is sown in April in West Bengal, but during June-July in the rest of India and (iv) In hills of North India, it is sown in April and May.

Seed Rate, Methods of Sowing and Spacing	Seed rate is 4.5-6 kg/ha. In North India, sowing is done on raised beds or in furrow or trenches whereas in South India, it is sown in pits. In West Bengal, pits of size 60 x 60 cm and 45 cm deep are dug and filled with farmyard manure and topsoil of pits. Two seeds per hill are sown in both sides of the raised beds. The spacing is 1.5-2.0 m between rows and 60-120 cm between plants.
Nutritional Requirements	Farm yard manure @ 20-25 t/ha is applied 15-20 days before sowing of seeds in pits/furrows. The NPK is applied in the ratio as given below

Nutrients (kg/ha)		
N	P	K
100	50	50

Half quantity of nitrogen and full quantity of each phosphorus and potash are applied in the pits or furrows at the time of sowing. Remaining quantity of nitrogen may apply 30-40 days after sowing or just before flowering.

Intercultural Operations	Vines are trained on bamboo with rope or wire on bower system. In bower system, plant height should be 2.55 cm and spacing is maintained at 1.5 meter and 0.6 meter row to row and plant to plant, respectively. The variety Pusa Do Mausami is suited for bower system of training. The field should be free from weeds throughout cropping season. Avoid herbicides for controlling weeds.

Use of Plant Growth Regulators (PGR)

Name of PGRs	Concentrations (mg/l)	Method of application	Attributes affected
MH	150-250	Foliar spray at two to four leaves stage	Improves fruit yield
Paclobutrazol	100	Foliar spray at two to four true leaf stage	Improves fruit yield
NAA	100	Foliar spray at two to four true leaf stage	Increases number of female flower
CCC	50 or 100	Foliar spray at two to four true leaf stage	Increases female: male ratio
Ethrel	25	Foliar spray at two to four true leaf stage	Increases female flowers

Water Management	Rainy season crop normally does not require much irrigation except dry spells. During summer, crop is irrigated immediately after planting. Subsequently light irrigation are given every 4th or 5th day until flowering.
Harvesting, Yield and Storage	It will take 55 to 110 days from seed sowing to reach first harvest. The picking is mainly done when fruits are still tender and green. Pickings should be done at an interval of 2-3 days. The yield of open pollinated variety from 10-15 t/ha, while 20-30 t/ha of hybrids. To make fruits clean, it is advisable to wash them with water and allow drying under shade. Fruits are arranged properly in the bamboo basket on newspapers. Fruits in the basket can be kept for 2 to 3 days.

143.2. Bottle gourd

Title	Description
Climatic Requirements	It is a warm season crop. It is highly sensitive to photoperiod. Short days and humid climate promote femaleness. It requires 20-30°C optimum temperature for growth and development of plant.
Soil Conditions	Sandy to sandy loam soil with high content of organic matter is considered best for good crop. The soil p^H should be 5.5 to 6.7.
Sowing Time	(i) For plain areas: *kharif* crop: 15 June to 15 July; *rabi* crop: October-November; spring-summer crop: 15 February to 15 March, (ii) For hilly areas: March to June and (iii) River beds sowing: November-December.
Seed Rate, Methods of Sowing and Spacing	Seed rate is 3-6 kg/ha. Two seeds per hill are sown in sides to raised bed or furrows. The spacing is 1.8-3 m row to row and 0.6 -1.5 m plant to plant.
Nutritional Requirements and their Management	Farm yard manures @ 15-20 t/ha is given 15-20 days before sowing the seeds in pits/furrow. The NPK ration is given as below.

Nutrients (kg/ha)		
N	P	K
100	75	50

Half quantity of nitrogen and full quantity of each phosphorus and potash are applied in the pits or furrows at the time of sowing. Remaining quantity 30-45 days of sowing or just before flowering.

Title	Description
Intercultural Operations	Vines are trained on bamboo with rope or wire or in bower system. In bower system of training, plant height should be 2.25 meter and planting distance is kept at 2.5 x 0.6 meter. Pre- sowing incorporation of fluchloralin @ 3.0 l/ha or butachlor @ 2.5 l/ha can also be used for weed control.

Use of Plant Growth Regulators

Name of PGR (s)	Concentrations (mg/l)	Method of application	Attributes affected
NAA	25-50	Foliar spray at two and four leaves stages	Increased fruit yield
TIBA	50	Foliar spray at two and four leaves stages	Increased fruit yield
Ethephon	500	Foliar spray at two and four leaves stages	Increased fruit yield
Paclobutrazol	175	Drenching in soil at two leaf stage	Increased fruit yield

Title	Description
Water Management	Summer crop requires frequent irrigation after every 3rd or 4th day while the crop sown in rainy season, is irrigated whenever required. Winter sown crop is irrigated sparingly once in 10 days. Soil moisture deficit

	during fruit development greatly reduces fruit size and yield.
Harvesting, Yield and Storage	Crop will be ready for harvesting in about 60 to 100 days after seed sowing depending upon the variety and seasons. The fruit of bottle gourd takes about 12-15 days after fruit setting to reach marketable stage. The fruit should be tender and medium in size and still dark green. Yield ranges 20-35 t/ha in open pollinated varieties and 50-60 t/ha in hybrids. It can be stored for few weeks under 10 ^{0}C and 60-70 per cent relative humidity.

14.3.3. Cucumber

Title	Description
Climatic Requirements	It is a warm season crop. High humidity and short day length promote female flower production. It requires 18 ^{0}C minimum temperature for seed germination and 20-30 ^{0}C for growth and development of plant.
Soil Conditions	It requires sandy to sandy loam soil for early and good crop whereas heavy soils are good for high yields. The soil pH should be 5.5 to 6.7. For higher production, the soil should be rich in organic manure with proper drainage facility.
Sowing Time	(see table below)

Region	Optimum sowing time
North India	
a. Plains	February to March
b. Hills	April to May
South and Central India	October to November
Western region	September to February
West Bengal	
a. Summer crop	March to April
b. Rainy season	June to July

Seed Rate, Methods of Sowing and Spacing	Three to five kilogram seeds are sufficient for sowing in one hectare. Sowing is done on raised beds, in furrows or in pits according to system followed. Two seeds per hill are generally sown on both sides of the bed. In case of pit system, prepare pits of size 45 x 45 cm about 60 cm deep and filled with farm yard manure and soil in equal proportion up to 30 cm above ground level. Three to four seeds per pits are sown. Plant spacing is be kept 1.5-3 m row to row and 60-90 cm plant to plant.
Nutritional Requirements	About 25.0-30t/ha farm yard manure, which may be mixed with the soil 10-15 days before seeds sowing. The ration of NPK is as given below

Nutrients (kg/ha)		
N	P	K
100	50	50

Half quantity of nitrogen and full quantity of each phosphorus and potash should be applied in the pits or furrows at the time of sowing. Remaining quantity of nitrogen may be applied 30 days after sowing or just before flowering.

Intercultural Operations	For higher production and increasing the quality of fruit, vines should be trained on bamboo with rope or wire. In bower system of training, the method is described in bottlegourd. First weeding is done 15-20 days after seed sowing. Two more weedings are given at 25-30 days intervals.

Use of Plant Growth Regulators

Name of PGRs	Concentrations (mg/l)	Method of application	Attributes affected
TIBA	50	Foliar spray at two to four leaf stages	Increased yield
GA	40		
MH	100		
Ethephon	150-500	Foliar spray at two to four leaf stages	Increased yield
Paclobutrazol	75	Foliar spray at two and four leaf stages	Increased yield

Water Management	Over irrigation should be avoided, as cucumber can not withstand under water logging conditions. In dry weather, the crop is irrigated fourth or fifth day but during rainy season, the interval may be increased depending on rainfall distribution. Irrigation from start of flowering and at full bloom is particularly beneficial. Fruit enlargement also requires large supply of water. Drought during flowering results in deformed, non-viable pollen grains leading to poor yield. During irrigation, care should be taken to see that water from the basin or furrows do not overflow and inundate the plants because if they stand in water for any length of time, the foliage becomes chlorotic or yellow and the growth is retarded.
Harvesting, Yield and Storage	The crop will be ready to harvest in about 60-70 days after sowing. The fruit takes about 7-10 days from setting to reach marketable stage. The fruit is harvested when it is still tender and green. The over mature fruit would be fetch less price in the market. The fruits should be picked at an interval of 2 days. The fruit yield of open pollinated variety will vary from 20-25 t/ha. Whereas, some hybrids produces up to 60t/ha. Generally, cucumber is not stored for long time.

14.3.4. Muskmelon

Title	Description
Climatic Requirements	The crop requires a hot and dry climate. Optimum temperature requirement is 27 to 30 °C. The seed does not germinate at temperature lower than 18 °C. Short day length promotes female flower production. High temperature, low humidity and plenty of sunshine are essential for proper ripening and high sugar content. Plants are sensitive to low temperature and frost.
Soil Conditions	It requires sandy soils for early crop while loam soils are good for high yield potential. The soil pH should be 6.0 to 6.8. For higher production soil should be rich in organic good with matter drainage facility.
Sowing Time	Seed sowing time of muskmelon is (i) In northern plains, best time of sowing is February-March but if the crop is to be transplanted sowing can be done in the end of January. (ii) In north eastern region, sowing is done in month of November to March. (iii) In western region, sowing is

done in month of September-October. (iv) In south India, best sowing time is October to November and (v) In north India, sowing is done in April-May.

Seed Rate, Methods of Sowing and Spacing

Four to six kilogram seeds will be sufficient to sow one hectare. However, in case of transplanting technique only one kg seed would be sufficient for one hectare. Seed can be sown directly in the field or in the polythene bags, for raising of transplants of muskmelon. Polythene bags of 15 x 10 cm size 100 gauge thickness punched at the base are filled with mixture of field soil, silt and farm yard manure in equal proportions and placed on the eastern side of a boundary wall or other structure. Two seeds are sown in each bag and bags are watered daily with the help of sprinkler cane. The transplants will be ready in about 25 to 30 days and at the time of transplanting polythene bags are cut with a razor and removed. In case of riverbeds, trenches about 0.5-1 m deep are dug at recommended row spacing and sowing is done on spot specially fertilized with farmyard manure and fertilizers. In pit method of sowing, pit of size 60 x 60 x 60 cm are dug at recommended row and plant spacing and filled with mixture of farm yard manure. Three or four seeds are sown per pit. The recommended spacing is 1.5-2.5 m between rows and 0.5-1.0 m between plants.

Nutritional Requirements

Farm Yard manure @ 25.0-45.0 t/ha have been recommended for muskmelon. It is mixed in soil at the time of last ploughing or applied 10-15 days before sowing the seeds. The NPK ratio is as given below

Nutrients (kg/ha)		
N	P	K
100	75	50

Half quantity of nitrogen and full quantity of each phosphorus and potash should be applied in the pits or furrow at the time of sowing. Remaining quantity is applied 30 days after seed sowing or just before flowering.

Intercultural Operations

Removal of all secondary growth up to 7th node in "Hara Madhu", 3rd node in "Punjab Sunehri", 4th node in "Punjab Hybrid" and "Pusa Madhuras" and 6th node in "Pusa Sarbati" have been found to enhance fruit yield in all varieties when compared to unpruned. First weeding should be done in 15 to 20 days after seed sowing or transplanting. Two to four weddings are required before the vine covers the whole area. Weedicides like fluchloralin (pre-sowing) @1.2 kg a.i./ha or fluchloralin @ 0.48 kg/ha + nitrofen @ 0.5 kg/ha (pre emergence) or nitrofen @ 1.25 kg/ha (pre emergence) may be used for weed control.

Use of Plant Growth Regulators

Name of PGRs	Concentrations (mg/l)	Method of application	Attributes affected
NAA	25	Foliar spray at two to four true leaf stages	Increases fruit yield
GA	10		
MH	50-200		

Water Management

Pre-irrigation should be done before sowing, if there is insufficient moisture in soil. Muskmelon plants require an abundance of moisture during the period when the vines are developing most rapidly. This crop required 11 irrigations and a total of 550 mm water at 4 to 9 days intervals.

Harvesting, Yield and Storage	Crop is ready for harvest in 70-90 days after seed sowing depending upon the variety and season. The fruits will take about 25 to 30 days from fruit setting to reach to maturity stage. The maturity in muskmelon can be determined from the change in outer colour to yellow, yellow-green or brown. The fruit will also slip from the vine. This is due to the development of an abscission layer resulting in automatic detachment of the fruit from the vine when fully mature. In some varieties like "Hara Madhu", there is no development of slip. Only sign in such case is the change in outer colour. For local market fruit may be harvested at full slip stage whereas for distant markets fruits are harvested at half-slip stage or even earlier. The fruit yield varies from 10-25 t/ha. Fruits can be stored at room temperature (32+ 8 ºC) for upto eight days while 25 days at 1°C

14.3.5. Pumpkin

Title	Description
Climatic Requirements	It can be grown in relatively cooler climate than other cucurbits. Optimum temperature requirement is 18-24 ºC. Short days, cool night temperature and high relative humidity is best for production of pumpkin.
Soil Conditions	Clay and loam soils are good for yield. Soil should be well drained and with ample organic matter contents and pH should be in the range of 5.5-6.8. It can be grown on slightly acidic soils also.
Sowing Time	Summer crop is sown during February-March in north Indian plains but in December-January in rest of India. The rainy season crop is sown in April-May in West Bengal but June-July in other parts. In Tamil Nadu, optimum sowing time of rainy season crop is July-August. The crop is sown in April-May in hills of north India.
Seed Rate, Methods of Sowing and Spacing	The recommended seed rate is 6 to 8 kg/ha. Seeds are directly sown in the field on raised beds or in furrows or trenches or pits. Two seeds per hill are sown on both sides of raised bed. In case of pit method, pit of size 60 x 60 cm is dug and filled with farm yard manure and top soil of the pits. Four to five seeds per pit are sown. The recommended spacing is 3 m x 75 to 90 cm.
Nutritional Requirements and Their Management	Farm yard manure @ 150-200 q/ha should be applied 15-20 days before sowing the seeds or at the time of digging the pits or furrows. The NPK is given in the ratio of as give below

States	Nutrients (kg/ha)		
	N	P	K
Punjab	100	50	50
Himachal Pradesh	150	100	50
Karnataka	100	100	40
Madhya Pradesh	60	50	50
Tamil Nadu	32	24	24
Assam	75	80	80

Half quantity of nitrogen and full quantity of each phosphorus and potash should be applied in the pits or furrows at the time of sowing.

	Remaining quantity of nitrogen may be applied at 30-45 days after seed sowing.
Intercultural Operations	First weeding is done at 15-20 days after seed sowing. A total of three weeding operations required in order to keep the field weeds free. Herbicides like pre plant incorporation of bensulide @ 4-6 kg/ha or @ 2.5 kg/ha as pre emergence can also be used for weed control in pumpkin.

Use of Plant Growth Regulators

Name of PGRs	Concentrations (mg/l)	Method of application	Attributes affected
Ethephon	250	Foliar spray at two and four true leaf stages	Increases fruit yield

Water Management	For rainy season crop, normally no irrigation is required. The summer season sown crop, field is irrigated immediately after sowing. The second irrigation is given after a week or so. Pumpkin plants are and it should be irrigated every 4th or 5th day in dry weather.
Harvesting, Yield and Storage	The pumpkin may be harvested in 75-180 days after seed sowing depending upon variety, season and other conditions. The mature fruit will have a brown colour but in some varieties the mature fruit may not have brown. Fruit yield varies from 30 t/ha in open pollinated variety. However, potential some hybrids 60t/ha gave Pumpkin can be stored more than six month at temperature of 10 ^{0}C and relative humidity of 85 per cent. Lower temperature is harmful which may cause blemishes.

14.4. Fruit Vegetables

14.4.1. Brinjal

Title	Description
Climatic Requirements	Brinjal is a warm season crop and susceptible to severe frost. It requires long warm season during growth and fruit maturation. The optimum growing temperature is 22 to 30 ^{0}C and growth stop at temperature below 17 ^{0}C. It is observed that pollen deformity increases at temperatures of 15-16 ^{0}C. Elevation upto 1200 meter is satisfactory for brinjal cultivation.
Soil Conditions	The brinjal can be grown practically on all soils from light sandy to heavy clay. The soil pH should not more than 5.5 to 6.0 for its better growth and development.
Sowing Time	On hills, the seeds are sown in April and the seedlings are transplanted in May. In the plains, the crop is grown in three seasons viz. February-March, May-June and October-November.
Seed Rate, Methods of Sowing and Transplanting Distance	Seed rate varies from 200 to 500 g/ha. Seedlings at 8 to 10 cm in height with two to three true leaves are ready for transplanting. The seedlings should be hardened before lifting for transplanting. The planting is done on flat beds of convenient size. In high rainfall regions, brinjal plants are grown on raised bed for proper drainage. The spring-summer crop may be raised on ridges and furrow system for efficient use of water. Generally, long fruited varieties are transplanted at spacing of 60 x 60 cm and round fruited at 75 x 75 cm in open pollinated varieties. In

	case of hybrids spacing should be 90.0cm row to row and 75.0 cm in plant to plant.
Nutritional Requirements and Their Management	Farm yard manure @25-30t/ha is incorporated in the soil before 15-20 days transplanting. Nitrogen, phosphrous and potash should be applied the ratio of 100:80:60 kg/ha, respectively for open pollinated variety and potentiality of a hybrid. In case of hybrids this ratio will be 150:100:80 kg/ha depending upon soil condition. Half quantity of nitrogen and full quantities of each phosphorus and potash should be applied at the time of transplanting. While remaining quantity of nitrogen may be applied either twice or thrice depending upon the soil conditions at 30 days and 45 days after transplanting.
Intercultural Operations	• An application of fluchloralin @1.5 kg a.i./ha or pre-emergence spray of alachlor @ 2.0 kg a.i./ha + one hand weeding 30 days after transplanting (DAT) has been recommended under Pantnagar of Uttrakhand conditions. This treatment gave a cost benefit ratio of 1:1.17. • Pre-emergence application of pendimethalin @ 1.0 kg a.i./ha + one hand weeding at 30 DAT has been recommended for effective weed control under Sabour of Bihar conditions. • Application of fluchloralin @ 1.5 kg a.i./ha + one hand weeding 30 DAT has been recommended for Hyderabad areas.

Use of Plant Growth Regulators

Name of PGRs	Concentrations (mg/l)	Methods of application	Attribute affected
IAA	50	Seed treatment	Increased fruit yield
GA	40	Seedling treatment	Increased fruit yield
IAA	20	Foliar spray	Increased fruit yield
Mixtallol	4	Foliar spray 4 weeks after transplanting	Increased fruit yield

Water Management	Irrigation is essential for brinjal cultivation in regions where there is little or no rain during the growing season. Brinjal being shallow rooted crops needs irrigation at frequent intervals. Timely irrigation is very important for high yield. It is recommended to irrigate brinjal after every third or fourth day during summer season and after 12 to 15 days during winter season. Irrigation should be given according to the local need taking into consideration soil type, stage of crop growth and weather conditions. When there is danger of frost, irrigation should be given more regularly, so that the soil is always kept moist. Brinjal is generally raised with furrow system of irrigation. However drip irrigation has been found beneficial for reducing water use and weed growth as compared to conventional surface irrigation.
Harvesting, Yield and Storage	The harvesting of the fruits should be done as soon as it attains a good size and colour. A heavier crop can be produced if the fruits are harvested before they reach full size. The fruit should not loose its bright and glossy appearance. When a fruit looks dull, it is an indication of over maturity and loss of quality. Pressing the thumb against the side of the fruit can test the maturity of the fruit. If the pressed portion springs back to its original shape, the fruit is too immature. The average yield varies from 20.0 to 50.0t q/ha of open pollinated varieties. While, in

	hybrids, it ranged from 40.0-70.0 t/ha. Brinjal fruit can be stored for 1-2 days in summer and 3-4 days in winter season provided they are kept in shade under ordinary conditions. Fruits can also be stored for 7-10 days in fairly good conditions at 7.2 ^{0}C with 85-95 per cent RH.

14.4.2. Chilll and Capsicum

Title	Description
Climatic Requirements	Chilli is grown in both tropical and sub-tropical areas ranging from sea level to 2000 meter altitudes in Indian condition. A warm humid climate favors growth while warm and dry weather enhances fruit maturity. In a frost-free period of four months with maximum temperature ranging from 20-30 ^{0}C and minimum temperature not below 10 ^{0}C, is optimum for raising the crop. A soil temperature of 10 ^{0}C retards plant development, whereas 17 ^{0}C causes normal development. High temperature associated with low relative humidity at the time of flowering increases the transpiration resulting in abscission of buds, flowers and small fruit. In general, capsicum is grown under low temperature conditions than chillies.
Soil Conditions	Chilli can be grown successfully in sandy loam soil provided adequate irrigation and manuring are carried out. Black soils are also suitable for chilli as rainfed crops. An ideal soil for both crops is light loamy or sandy loam rich in lime and organic matter. Strongly acid soils and alkaline soils are not suitable for its cultivation. Both can be grown successfully with soil pH of 6-7.
Sowing Time	In north India, seeds of chilli are sown in nursery beds during May-July depending upon onset of monsoon. In the North Eastern region of India sowing is little earlier due to early monsoon arrival. In the Southern states where rainfed cultivation is in vogue, both are best grown in the south east and north east monsoon season coinciding with May-June and September-October. In Tamil Nadu, there are three seasons for growing viz. June-July, September-October and March-April. The capsicum is generally sown in August for the autumn-winter crop and in November for the spring-summer crop. In the hills of North Bengal, sowing of seeds is done in the month of March-April (Under cover) and September-October.
Seed Rate, Methods of Sowing and Transplanting Distance	One to two kilograms seed will be required to raise seedlings for one hectare. Seedlings become ready for transplanting in 35-45 days, when they are about 12-16 cm in height. Short and thick stemmed seedlings are preferred for better establishment. In older seedlings, topping has to be done one week prior to transplanting on a bright day. In chilli single healthy seedlings are transplanted at 45 x 30cm or 45 x 45cm spacing. In capsicum, if it grown in polyhense spacing may be 60x45cm or 75 x 60cm depending upon varieties/hybrids. However for open field cultivation it may at 45 x 45cm.
Nutritional Requirements and their Management Intercultural Operations	Chilli and capscium initially slow growing crops, incapable of offering any competition to the aggressive weeds. Infestation of weeds also increases insect-pests. Hence, the weeds should be controlled as soon as they are seen, either by hand weeding and hoeing or by the application of herbicides. Frequent shallow cultivation should be undertaken at

	regular intervals so as to keep the field free from weeds and to facilitate soil aeration and proper root development. Weedicides like nitrofen at 1.5 kg/ha or alachlor at 2.5 kg /ha can also be used for control of weeds.
Use of Plant Growth Regulators	Foliar spray of GA at 50 mg/l at fruit setting or planofix (NAA 10 mg/l) double sprays (at flowering and 5 week later) decreased flower dropping and gave best fruit yield in chilli. Foliar spray of triacontanol @ 2 mg/l or atonic (0.08 per cent) 30 days after transplanting and again at bloom have been also effectve in checking flower drop in chillies and enhancing fruit yield. Foliar sprays fo ethephon at 500 mg/l when about 90 per cent of fruits start turning colour, give increased in yield.
Water Management	The first light irrigation is given just after transplanting for better establishment in the soil, if there is no rain. Gap filling is done during the second irrigation after 10 days of transplanting. Generally, 8 to 9 irrigations are required depending on the rainfall, soil type, humidity and prevailing temperature. Furrow irrigation is generally practiced.
Havesting, Yield and Storage	The flowering begins 35-60 days after transplanting depending upon variety, climate, and nutritional status of land. The fruits of vegetable type of bell pepper are picked as soon as they attain marketable size. The fruits start ripening about three months after transplanting and the picking may go on for two to three months. Commercial chilli varieties yield 1.0-1.5t q/ha dry pods in rainfed conditions and 2.0-2.5 t/ha dry pods in irrigated conditions. Improved capsicum varieties yield 20-30 t/ha of green fruits, while the hybrids can yield up to 40-50 t/ha. Green chillies and capsicum can be stored for about 40 days at 0 C and 95 to 98% relative humidity. Dried chillies can be kept for month together in dry places well protected from insect-pest.

14.4.3. Okra

Title	Description
Climatic Requirements	Okra does best long warm season. It is sensitive to frost and thus requires frost tree growing period. Optimum temperature requirement is 24 to 27 ^{0}C. Seed does not germinate when temperature is below 20 ^{0}C. There is not problem of seed germination during rainy season but there is problem of poor germination in north Indian plains when it is sown in February. The plant growth is greater in rainy season as compared to spring-summer and so also the yields. Temperature higher than 42 ^{0}C may cause flower dorp.
Soil Conditions	Sandy loam soils are considered best for early crop in spring where as clay loam gives good yield potential. Soil should contain medium to high organic matter. The soil should be well drained as roots of okra are sensitive to water stagnation. The pH of soil should be 6.0 to 6.8.
Sowing Time	In north Indian plains, spring/summer crop is sown in February-March, whereas, in eastern and western, India, optimum-sowing time is January-February. In West Bengal, the sowing of okra starts in February and continued up to month of June at an interval of three or four weeks. In South India, the summer season crop is sown in November. The rainy season crop is sown in the month of June-July through out India. In north Indian Hills, the crop in sown in April-June.

Seed Rate, Methods of Sowing and Planting Distance

Sowing time	Seed rate (kg/ha)
February	40–45
March	20–25
June–July	12–15

During summer season sowing, the seed should be soaked in water for 12 to 24 hr. Okra can be sown on ridges or flat feds. If soil is heavy, sowing should be is on ridges. Okra can be sown by broadcasting method, line sowing or hand-dibbled. On commercial scale, a seed drill can also be used. In West Bengal, sowing of okra is done in pits. The recommended spacing for summer season crop is 30 x 30 cm whereas for rainy season, it 60 x 30 cm.

The requirement of Farm yard manure and ratio of NPK in Okra are given below

Nutritional Requirements and Their Management

State	Nutrients (Kg/ha)			FYM(t/ha)
	N	P	K	
Andhra Pradesh	100	50	50	20-30
Arunachal Pradesh	120	70	60	20
Assam	50	50	50	10
Bihar	140	64	75	15
Gujarat	60	30	-	10-15
Haryana	100	50	25	25
Himachal Pradesh	75	50	50	-
Karnataka	125	75	62	25
Kerla	50	8	30	12
Madhya Pradesh	80	60	60	10
Maharashtra	100	50	50	50
Orissa	112	60	90	-
Punjab	90	0	0	25
Rajasthan	60	32	30	15
Tamil Nadu	40	50	30	25
Uttar Pradesh	60	30	30	20
West Bengal	50	25	25	15

A quantity of 150 kg each nitrogen, phosphrus and potash with spacing 60 × 45 cm during *kharif* season for variety Pusa Sawani has been recommended for Jabalpur of Madhya Pradesh. Farm Yard Manure is mixed thoroughly in soil at 15-20 days before sowing the seeds. Half quantity of nitrogen and full quantity of each phosphorus and potash are applied at the time of sowing. Remaining quality of nitrogen is applied to 30–45 days after sowing the seed as top dressing. Foliar sprays of Zn at 20 mg/l or Mo at 20 mg/l or Cu at 0.2 per cent can also be used for getting high yield in okra.

Intercultural Operations

First weeding is done at 15 to 20 days after seed sowing. Total three to four weddings are needed. Following herbicides have been recommended for weed control in okra.

Herbicide/Active ingredients	Rate(kg/ha)	Time of spraying

	Basalin 48 EC (Florchloralin)	2.5 Liter (1.2 kg)	Pre-plant incorporation
	Lasso 50 EC (Alachlor)	5 liter (2.5 Kg)	Pre-emergence
	Stamp 30 EC (Pendimethalin)	2.5 liter 0.75 (kg)	Pre-emergence

Use of Plant Growth Regulators	Name of PGR (s)	Concentrations (mg/l)	Method of application	Attributes Affected
	GA_3	250	Seed treatment	Increases fruit yield even on salt affected soil
	NAA	15	Foliar spray at 20-25 days after sowing	Increase Fruit yield
	GA_3	10-20	Foliar spray at 20-25 days after sowing	Increase Fruit yield
	MH	800	Foliar spray at 20-25 days after sowing	Increase Fruit yield
	CCC	500-750	Foliar spray at 20–25 days after sowing	Induces Flowering and increase fruit yield

Water Management	There should be enough moisture in the soil at the time of seed sowing. First irrigation is given after the seed has germinated. Subsequent irrigations may be given at an interval of 4 to 5 days during summer season. In case of rainy season crop, there is no requirement of extra irrigation. Drip irrigation has given higher yield than furrow irrigation. But it is not commercially practiced due to higher initial costs.
Harvesting, Yield and Storage	The pods are ready for harvesting in about 45-60 days after seed sowing depending upon variety and season. Only tender fruits is picked. In case of Pusa Sawani variety, the fruits will reach 10-cm length in about 6 days after anthesis, whereas in case of Punjab Padmani, fruit will gain 10-cm length in about 5 days after anthesis. Frequent pickings are necessary so those pods do not grow to large for marketing. Picking should be done at an interval four days in order to get highest pod yield. An average fruit yield varies from 10.0-12.5 t/ha in summer season but 10.0-12.5 t/h during rainy season in caseof open pollinated variety whereas, incase of hybrids pod yield goes upto 40t/ha. Okra fruit can be stored at 2-3 days under room temperature (32 ± 2 °C) and 7-75 per cent RH.

14.4.4. Tomato

Title	Description
Cimatic Requirements	Tomato is a warm season vegetable and requires long season to produce. The optimum range of temperature is 21–24 °C. The mean temperatures below 16 °C and above 27 °C are not desirable. The minimum and optimum soil temperatures for seed germination are 10 °C, 30 °C and 35 °C, respectively. Seed germination maximum occurs at 24 °C. Maximum fruit setting occurs at night temperature of 15-20 °C. Flowers

fails to set fruit below at 13 °C and beyond at 38 °C. Temperature exceeds 32 °C, the formation of lycopene is inhibited. Lycopene is the highest at 21-24 °C while the production of this pigment drop off rapidly above at 27 °C night temperature. Tomato plants are highly susceptible water logging, hence an areas of high rainfall, if proper drainage is not available, its cultivation is not possible.

Soil Conditions

Tomato is grown in many type of soil from sandy to heavy clay. A well-drained fairly fertile loam with a fair moisture holding capacity is ideal for cultivation of tomato. Tomato crop prefers a soil reaction of ranging from pH 6.0 to 7.0. In acidic soil, liming will be beneficial.

Sowing Time

It can be grown almost all the year round. The planting seasons vary from place to place of the country. In northern India, for spring summer crop, the seeds are sown in November and transplanting is second fortnight of January. In area where frost does occur only one sowing is in July – August with transplanting in August – September. For autumn crop in north India, seeds are sown in July–August and transplanting in August–September. In hilly areas, the seeds are sown in March–April with transplants in April–May.

Seed Rate, Methods of Sowing and Transplanting Distance

Seeds of tomato are very light in weight. The seed rate varies from size and weight of seeds. The requirement of seed is 200 – 500 g/ha. Seedlings are ready for transplanting between 4 and 5 weeks depending upon raising of nursery in open condition or polyhouse. In polyhouse, nursery becomes ready very early as compare to open condition. The area where rainfall is limiting factor for raising nursery, it should be raised in polyhouse. The seedlings should be hardened before setting them in the field. In sunny day, transplanting is done in evening hours, while, in cloudy weather whole day transplanting can be done. At some places tomato seeds are directly sown in the field rather than transplanting. In heavy rainfall areas of Chotanagpur in Bihar, this system is some times in practice to avoid delay in transplanting due to continous rains. It has been the advantage of saving labour for transplanting and often reduces loss from "damping off". In areas where bacterial wilt and root knot nematode (*Meloidgyne* spp.) are endemic, direct sowing and the yield of in prepared beds or planting holes has sometimes been recommended as a means of reducing infection. In these areas grafted plants may also be used Planting distance is varying with growth habit. Indeterminate varieties/hybrids, the row to row distance varies from 60-120 cm and plant to plant 45-75 cm. However, determinate varieties/ hybrids are planted at spacing of 45-60 cm x 30-45 cm row to row and plant to plant, respectively.

The nutritional requirement is tomato is summerized below:

Nutritional Requirements and Their Management

- The application of NPK @ 150:60:60 kg/ha under Sabour conditions to achieve maximum net return per hectare.
- Application of NPK @ 150:60: 60 kg/ha has been recommended for the variety Pusa Ruby, Sioux and K–2, to get maximum return and the highest cost/benefit ratio under Kanpur conditions.
- Application of NPK @ 150:60: 60 kg/ha has been recommended for obtaining the most economical yield from Pusa Ruby, Pusa Early Dwarf and Arka Vikas varieties under the agro–clmatic conditions of Bhubaneswar.

- Application of NPK @ 75:60: 60 kg/ha has been recommended for the varieties Pusa Ruby, Punjab Chhuhara and Pusa Early Dwarf under Jorhat conditions.
- Application of N @ 180 kg/ha and $P_2 05$ @ 120 kg/ha showed the maximum C: B ratio (1:2.99) in determinate hybrid ARTH–3 under Sabour conditions.
- Application of N @ 40 kg/ha as basal dressing + 20 kg/ha as top dressing gave the highest yield with the C: B ratio of 1:3.09 under Kanpur Conditions.
- Application of N as 40 kg/ha as basal dressing +20 kg/ha through top dressing and 20 kg/ha as foliar spray was found conducive and gave the highest yield (413 q/ha) and C: B ratio (1:4.96) in variety Sel–7. under Varanasi conditions of eastern Uttar Pradesh.
- For variety Shakti, application of 40 kg N/ha as basal application along with 20 kg/ha as foliar spray gave a C: B ratio of 1:2.8 under Kerala conditions.

Intrcultural Operations

The surface of soil should be loosened by hoeing as soon as it is dry enough, after every irrigation or shower. The weeds should be removed in this process. Recommendation of weedicides as summerized below;

- Pre-emergence application of oxyflurofen @ 0.25 kg a.i./ha, combined with one hand weeding at 45 DAT (days after transplanting) has been recommended for Tamil Nadu conditions.
- The pre-planting in corporation of goal @ 0.25 kg a.i. and basalin @ 1.0 kg a.i/ha have been recommended for weed control and getting economic yield under Sabour conditions.
- For weed control, goal @ 0.25 @ kg a.i./ha as pre planting incorporation and sencor @ 0.75 kg/ha as pre-emergence application followed by post-emergenc spray of sencor @ 0.50 kg/ha, were found to be most effective and economical.
- The next best herbicide was basalin@1kg a.i. /ha as pre-planting incorporation. These treatments have been recommended for Sabour and Pantnagar regions.
- Application of pendimethalin @ 1.0 kg a.i./ha (PE) +one hand weeding at 45 DAT has been recommended for effective weed control under mid hill conditions of Almora. Application of this treatment gave 114.68-q/ha yield with C: B ratio of 1:1.68.

Staking is very essential operation in indeterminate group of open pollinated varieties/hybrids for getting high yield and good quality fruits. Staking may be done either by using bamboo stick or trained on wire. The beneficial effects of staking are: (i) It improves plant yield and quality. (ii) Protection of fruits from insects pest and diseases. (iii) Easy in harvesting and (iv) Easy in spraying of any chemicals.

Use of Plant Growth Regulators

Name of plant growth regulators	Concentr-ations(mg/l)	Method of application	Attributes affected
NAA	25–50	Seed treatment for 8 hr.	Increases fruit yield TSS and sugar
GA	5–20		
CIPA	10–20		
2–4.D	0.50		

NAA	100	Foliar spray	Increase fruit field
PCPA	50		
GA_3	10		
2,4-D	0.50		
CCC	200	Foliar spray	Increase fruit yield
Ethephon	250	Foliar spray	Increase fruit yield
Paclobutrazol	40	Foliar spray	Increase yield and improved fruit quality
Mixtallol	2	Foliar spray	Increased yield

Water Management

Tomato is a deep rooted crop and its root grow to a depth of 120–150 cm. Plants can withstand drought fairly well, especially on heavier or high humus soil. Plants require adequate moisture throughtout their growth period. Excess moisture is a determental as insufficient moisture. The crop required seven irrigations when 50 mm rainfall is received. The first irrigation should be done at the time of transplanting. Too much water after transplanting and before the first fruit set causes the plants to run vines and drops the blossom. Those areas where tomato cultivation is done through artificial irrigation source, the irrigation should be 3–4 days during summer and 10–15 days during winter, so as to maintain the moderately wet. Furrow irrigation is most widely used to irrigate tomato crop in India. In this method, it is essential to plant the seedling halfway down the ridges to maintain an optimum air water balance. Irrigation through drip system resulted 43.4 per cent more yield and 78.4 per cent water saving as compared furrow method of irrigation.

Harvesting, Yield and Storage

The stage of maturity at which tomato should be harvested, depends upon the purpose for which they are used and distance over which they are to be transported. The following stages of maturity for harvesting have been recognized:

(a) **Immature:** Before the seeds have fully developed and before the jelly like substance sorrounding the seeds have formed.

(b) **Mature green:** The fully grown fruit shows a brownish ring at stem scar, removal of calyx, light green colour at blossom end has change to yellowish green and seeds are sorrounded by jelly like sustancesfilling the seed cavity.

(c) **Turning:** 1/4 of the surface at blossom end shows pink (breaker stage).

(d) **Pink:** ¾ of the surface shows pink.

(e) **Hard ripe:** Nearly all red or pink but flesh is firm.

(f) **Over ripe:** Fully coloured and soft

The yield depends upon various agroclimatic factors, region and cultivars. On an average, a normal open pollinated varieties yields 40-60 t/ha. Where as, hybrids give some times more than 100.0 t/ha. Tomato can be stored either in mature green or breaker stage of maturity. Storage temperature has been reported to influence the fruit firmness in cultivars like Florida MH-1 and Flora-dade, fruit remained firm up to 21 days when kept at room temperature more than 30^{0}C.

14.5. Leafy and Salad Vegetables

14.5.1. Amranths

Title	Description
Climatic Requirements	In India, it is grown throughout the year. However, it is mainly grown in summer and rainy seasons. Severe winters are not desirable for its cultivation. It is reported that a few species as *A. caudatus, A. cruentus* and *A. edulis* are short day, and *A. hypochondriacus* is day neutral. Heavy rainfall with high winds is unfavourable conditions, particularly for production of grain type Amaranths.
Soil Conditions	Leafy types require fertile soils of sandy loam in nature with well drained and slightly acidic. It grows well only on the soil, which is thoroughly cultivated up to good tilth. The soil should be well pulverized.
Sowing Time	The seeds are sown directly in the field or beds of 2.0 x 1.5 m or by transplanting. Generally, sowing is done during March to July in the plains and May to July in the hills. In Gujarat and Maharashtra where as special type of Amranth is known as Rajgarh, the crop is taken as a *rabi* crop, and usually mixed along with cereals, pulses and vegetables. The mixed cropping is also common in the hills and plains of north India and hills of south India.
Seed Rate, Methods of Sowing and Planting Distance	The seed rate per hectare is two kilogram in case of bari chauli and about three kilogram for chhoti chauli. However, for cultivation of Amaranths for grain purpose, one and half kilogram seed will be sufficient for a hectare area because it is sown at wider spacing. The seeds are sown thinly in lines. The distances between plant to plant 10 to 15 cm and row to row distance 45 cm. The distance between plant to plant is maintained by thinning particularly when it is grown for grain purposes. For vegetable purpose, if thinning is not done, will not affect the yield adversely. As far as possible, sowing of the seeds should be done at the depth of 1 to 2 cm. The seeds are very small (thousand grain weight 0.4-1.2 g) therefore, some quantity of sand or fine powder or leaf mould or soil is mixed to get uniform distributions. It will also help in maintaining seed rate per unit area.
Nutritional Requirements	Application of 20 to 30 tonnes farm yard manure per hectare is advisable during the last ploughing. Besides, 30 to 40 kg/ha nitrogen, 40 to 50 kg/ha each phosphorus and potassium are applied. The nitrogen is applied in three or four splits. Generally, nitrogen is top-dressed after each cutting. The whole quantity of phosphorus and potassium should be applied as basal dose just before sowing.
Intercultural Operations	Hoeing at early stage of crop growth will ensure good aeration and weed free crop. Being a short duration crop weeds do not pose a problem.
Water Management	Since the seeds are very small, if irrigation is done after sowing there is risk for soil crust formation, which will result in slow and poor emergence of seedlings. Therefore, it is advisable to do pre-irrigation so that sufficient moisture is made available for rapid and uniform germination. The leaf types require irrigation at frequent interval, better if each

	cutting follows irrigation. The grain types of Amaranths are drought resistant and hence crop can easily grown as rainfed crops.
Harvesting, Yield and Storage	Usually, after 25 to 30 days plants are pulled as a whole and washed properly. The root portion along with hard portion of stem is removed. Instead of uprooting whole plants, clipping of full-grown side leaves is done. Many times tops of the plants may also be cut. The first cutting is done 25 to 30 days after planting and thereafter at 6 to 8 days intervals. Crop is over in six to eight cuttings or so. The average yield of green is 6.0 to 8.0 tonnes per hectare (Green leaves) depending upon climatic conditions and management of the crop. Amaranth leaves are very perishable in nature. They can not store for more than few hours under ordinary conditions.

14.5.2. Basella

Title	Description
Climatic Requirements	The Basella can be grown on a wide range of climatic conditions. Frost is harmful and so also extremes of hot climate. However, the crop is usually grown during warm and moist seasons. It can be grown successfully under partial shade with the advantage of better growth of the plant and getting broad succulent leaves.
Soil Conditions	It can be grown on wide range of soils. However, heavy soils are not suitable. The crop grows luxuriantly in well-manured sandy loam soil provided it is well-drained and aeration.
Sowing Time	In the northern and eastern plains of India, seeds are sown from March to May, while in the southern parts; it is grown twice, once in June and again in October to November. In the hills, Basella is sown in March to April when it is raised by stem or root cutting, planting is restricted to only monsoon season or early summer when success is high.
Seed Rate, Methods of Sowing and Planting Distance	In order to raise one hectare crop of Basella 12 to 15 kg seed per hectare will require. Basella can be raised directly sowing of seeds in the main fields or transplanting them in the main field. Seeds or seedlings of basella are spaced in beds 45 cm apart each way and the plants are allowed to sprawl over the ground. The crop is also raised on bamboo stakes or trained in trellis. In such cases, seeds are sown 20-25 cm apart in rows at the base of bamboo stake or trellis.
Nutritional Requirements and Their Management	For getting good yield, application of 20-30 tonnes well rotten farm yard manure or compost is spread in the soil well in advance to planting. Besides, nitrogen 60 to 80 kg, phosphorus 60 to 80 kg and potassium 40 to 60 kg per hectare are required for getting high yield. Application of nitrogen is done in two to three splits. Phosphorus and potassium are applied as basal dose.
Intercultural Operations	In order to provide good environment for plant growth, light intercultural operation is essential. Besides, it will also help in keeping down the weeds. Hoeing is best which is done with *khurpi*. It is advisable to put some soil very near to the base of the plant, which will prevent plants from the direct contact with water. Water stagnation should always be avoided, and aeration in the root zone helps better growth of vines.

Use of Plant Growth Regulators	In long day condition, CCC suppressed flowering, whereas, MH has been found to inhibit flowering under short days.
Water Management	Sufficient moisture is needed to produce rapid and succulent growth. Inadequate moisture may lead to thin, wing stems and small leaves. The crop in general requires five to six irrigations when grown in summer and the frequency of irrigation depends on the soil type. However, rainy season crop does not require irrigation except when there is long spell of drought.
Harvesting and Yield	Crop raised from the seeds will produce edible leaves and stem after 8-10 weeks from sowing. The plants raised from root or stem cutting will be ready for harvest in about six weeks after planting. The yield varies from 15-20 t/ha.

14.5.3. Celery

Title	Description
Climatic Requirements	Celery requires cool season. The temperature 15 to 21 ^{0}C is suitable. High temperature may result in bolting and also bitterness developed in leaves. In the higher altitude of southern states of India, its production is confined in areas where there is a mild winter or a relatively cool growing season.
Soil Conditions	Celery needs deep, fertile, well-drained loam and silt loam soil. Heavy and sandy types of soil are avoided for commercial cultivation. The crop does well on a soil having pH range of 5.5 to 6.7.
Sowing Time	Celery sowing time in the plains of India is between August and September. In temperate region, seeds are sown during January-March.
Seed Rate, Methods of Sowing and Transplanting Distance	One to two kilogram seeds are needed for raising the seedlings which can be transplanted in one hectare area. For raising seedlings, nursery bed should be thoroughly prepared. Three nursery beds of 10 x 15 meters will be sufficient for providing seedling for raising one-hectare celery crop. Seeds are slow in germination, which takes about 4-6 weeks in spring. Soaking of seeds prior to sowing hastens germination especially for the late crop. Seeds may be sown in rows or broadcasted, but sowing in rows gives an advantage in watering, thinning and weeding.Celery is transplanted at a distance of 75-90 cm row to row and 15-20 cm between the plant to plant. It has been found that 10 cm spacing between the plants gave better yield of marketable celery than in wider spacing. Just after transplanting, irrigation or water supply is essential to save the newly planted seedlings from becoming dry.
Nutritional Requirements and Their Management	Celery requires heavy manuring specially nitrogen because the major portion of plant nutrients is drawn from the top soil. In general, 20.0 to 25 t/ha of well rotten farm yard manure should be incorporated in the soil during field preparation. Besides, 100-120 kg nitrogen, 40-60 kg phosphorus and 30 to 40 kg potash per hectare are also required for good yield. Calcium deficiency causes a disorder known as 'black heart' and can be prevented by foliar application of 0.10 molar solution of calcium nitrate or calcium chloride. A chlorsis resulting from the deficiency of magnesium can be prevented by application of magnesium sulphate at 12 kg per hectare at the time of planting. Boron deficiency

	results in cracked stem with lesions on both surface of petiole, which can be controlled by the application of lime, has been advocated.
Intercultural Operations	Two to three hoeings will keep the crop in proper growth and development. Not only this, weeds will also be controlled effectively. Besides hand weeding (mostly twice), herbicides like Trefflan at 1.0 liter per hectare or basalin at 1.0 liter per hectare (applied as pre emergence) will help in controlling weeds. Blanching is usually done when plants attain height about 40 cm. It is reported that blanching in celery reduces its nutritional value particularly of vitamin A, therefore, it is advisable to grow cultivars, which are self-blanching type viz. Giant Pascal, Emperor of Jeen and Golden.
Water Management	Celery requires frequent irrigation with good drainage for its successful production. The crop is irrigated immediately after transplanting. Sprinkler method of irrigation is better for celery growth and better yield.
Harvesting, Yield and Storage	The plants are ready for harvest in plains by the middle of May and on hills on November. In general, the crop is ready for harvest within 75-90 days after transplant. In harvesting, plants are cut just below the soil surface. Cuts are given low and hand trimming is necessary. If it is cut too high, there is danger of shattering of the outer leaves. Yield varies between 35.0 to 60.0 t/ha. Celery is generally stored in trenches and cold storage. The optimum temperature in the cold storage is required 0 ^{0}C at 95-98 per cent relative humidity, where it remains in good conditions for two to three months.

14.5.4. Lettuce

Title	Description
Climatic Requirements	It is a cool season crop and requires similar climate as that of cool crops. It thrives well in a relatively cool growing season with monthly mean temperatures of 12.8 to 15.6 ^{0}C. Higher temperature (above 22 ^{0}C) induces bolting and cause bitter taste in the leaves and accelerates the disorder 'tip burn'. The seed germinate quickly at 70 to 75 ^{0}F. Both lower and higher temperatures are harmful for germination. Seeds tend to loose their viability rather rapidly in the tropics.
Soil Conditions	Lettuce grown well in light, well manured, well-drained soils with adequate watering. It is slightly tolerant to acid soils (pH 6.8 to 6.0), but highly susceptible to high acidic soils.
Sowing Time	The seeds are sown in nursery beds in the month of September to October.
Seed Rate, Methods of Sowing and Transplanting Distance	Lettuce can be grown by sowing the seeds directly in the field or by raising seedlings first in the nursery beds and then transplanting in the field. When it is grown by transplanting, thinning operations are not required because seedlings are set at desired distance. Prior to sowing, the seeds are treated with fungicide like bavistin (2 g/kg seed). About 400-500 g of seeds is required for raising one hectare crop. One gram of seeds produces about 900 to 1000 plants. Care should be taken for sufficient moisture for proper germination. Sowing of the seeds are done in rows 15 to 20 cm apart at 1 cm deep. Seedlings are thinned to

	5 cm for their proper growth. Once or twice seedlings are sprayed with fungicide like diathane M-45 or difolatan at 0.2 per cent. The lettuce seeds germinate 6 to 10 days after sowing under suitable conditions. The poor germination of lettuce seed may be due to inadequate soil moisture, soil crusting and soil temperature. Five to six weeks old seedlings are transplanted. Before transplanting, seedlings are hardened by withholding water for a week. Seedlings are transplanted at the spacing of 45 x 45 or 45 x 30 or 60 x 30 cm depending on planting season, cultivars, management practices etc.
Nutritional Requirements and Their Management	For getting good yield 10 to 15 t/ha of farm yard manure is incorporated during land preparation. Besides, 85 kg of nitrogen and 60 kg each of phosphorus and potash per hectare are applied. The one-third quantity of nitrogen along with full quantity of both phosphorus and potash are applied at the time of planting. The remaining two-third quantity of nitrogen is applied just during head formation or when leaves growing profusely.
Intercultural Operations	First hoeing is done after 15 to 21 days of planting which may also be repeated at the same interval. If weeds become a problem, weedicides like propyzamide at 1.5 kg /ha and chlorpropham + sulfallate at 1.4 kg per hectare when applied as preplanting proved effective for control weeds.
Use of Plant Growth Regulators	Plant fresh weight has been found increased with IBA and NAA at 50 or 100 ppm. The use of GA_3 at 10 mg per litre stimulates respiration in lettuce seedlings
Water Management	When sufficient moisture is not available in the soil, pre-sowing irrigation is done for seed germination in case of direct sowing. Soon after transplanting, the lettuce crop should be irrigated, it will help in establishment of newly planted seedlings. In sufficient soil moisture during or just after transplanting of seedlings will affect survival rate of the seedlings, which may also lead to gapy crop for which gap filling will have to be done to maintain desirable plant stand. Subsequent irrigations are done at 8 to 12 days interval.
Harvesting, Yield and Storage	Harvesting of lettuce depends on the type and the purpose for which it is grown. Head lettuce for market is allowed to develop a solid head, for home it is harvested before the head is well formed and leaf lettuce for home use is harvested at any time. But for market, it is allowed to develop a full size. The yield of lettuce varies due to climatic conditions, soil types and kind of lettuce cultivars. However, in Indian condition the average yield varied from 10.0 to 40.0 t/ha. Lettuce can be stored for a period of three to four weeks under refrigeration. For storage, it is packed as for market and is placed in cold storage at about 32 ^{0}F (0 ^{0}C) and 90-95 per cent RH. The freshness of the lettuce is maintained with the pre-harvest spray of BA at 5 to 10 ppm.

14.5.5. Spinach Beet (Palak)

Title	Description
Climatic Requirements	Spinach beet is a cool season crop. It can withstand frost better than other vegetable crops. High temperature, especially long days cause bolting, thus reducing its market value. It is a short-season crop. Higher

	yields are obtained under short day and mild temperature, succulency and tenderness of the leaves increase under high atmospheric humidity.
Soil Conditions	Spinach beet can be grown on a wide range of soils. It thrives best in well-drained loamy soil of which pH should be in the range 6 to 6.5. Low soil pH is harmful for growth and development of crop.
Sowing Time	In the plains, desi cultivars are sown in June to November and imported cultivars in October to December. In the hills, desi cultivars are sown in March to May and imported one in July to August.
Seed Rate, Methods of Sowing and Spacing	In general, 25 to 35 kg seeds per hectare would be enough. Spinach beet can be seeded (sown) by broadcasting or by row sowing method. In the row sowing method, rows should be 25 to 35 cm apart, Distance within rows should be 10 to 12 cm, which is only possible after thinning. Seeding should be done one and a half to two and a half centimeters deep, otherwise, there may be poor germination.
Nutritional Requirements	About 20.0 to 25.0 t/ha per hectare of farm yard manure would be enough during field preparation. Besides, application of 80 to 100 kg nitrogen, 60 kg phosphorus, and 60 kg potash per hectare are also required. The entire quantities of phosphorus and potash along with one-fourth quantity of nitrogen are applied at the time of sowing. The remaining amount of nitrogen is top dressed into three splits (20-25 kg nitrogen each) after each cutting.
Intercultural Operations	Thinning, if essential should be done to provide space for accommodation and development of large uniform plants. Shallow hoeing is essential because the spinach beet plant can not complete well with the weeds. Harvesting is made more difficult where weeds are present. Avoid weedicides for controlling weeds in palak.
Use of Plant Growth Regulators	In spinach, GA at 10 ml/l in combination with 1 per cent urea has been reported to give high yield.
Water Management	There should be sufficient soil moisture for proper germination of seed. If soil moisture is not sufficient at the time of sowing, pre-irrigation is advisable. Irrigation may also be done after sowing if soil is not too heavy because formation of soil crust may delay the germination. Later irrigation's in summer and in winter should be at 4 to 5 and 8 to 10 days of interval, respectively. However, the rainy season crop does not require any irrigation except during the long dry spell.
Harvesting, Yield and Storage	Spinach beet leaves become ready for harvesting 25 to 30 days after sowing. The successive cuttings may be done at 15 to 20 days interval. In 4 to 6 cuttings, the crop is over. On an average, yield is 12.5t/ha green leaves. Varieties of broad leaves are usually high yielding than those of a short leafed. Palak is highly perishable vegetable. Just after harvesting, it should be sent to the market. Rotting starts soon when leaves are lost within 24 hours of harvesting. Palak can not be stored at room temperature but at low temperature (0 °C) and high relative humidity (90-95 per cent) , leaves can be stored for about 10 to 14 days.

14.6. Legume Vegetables

14.6.1. Broad bean

Title	Description
Climatic Requirements	Broad bean is a hardy plant. It is grown mainly at higher altitudes where the climate is relatively cool. It is the only bean, which can withstand cold (up to 4 ^{0}C), therefore, it is grown as winter crop.
Soil Conditions	Broad bean do well in rich heavy loam soil free from water logging. Acidic soils are not good for broad bean. Liming may improve the soil reaction. It can tolerate salinity up to some extent. Land should be prepared thoroughly by digging the soil deeply.
Sowing Time	Sowing is done in the month of September-October and February-March.
Seed Rate, Methods of Sowing and Spacing	About 70 to 100 kg of seed will be needed to sow one hectare area. The best method is to prepare shallow drills 5-6 cm deep and 15 cm wide, then place the seeds in a double row with one row down each side of the drill. The spacing between two beans should be 25 cm in a row. Place the beans in one row opposite the gaps in other row. The distance between two sets of rows should be 60 to 75 cm, so that they do not over-shadow one another. In single row system, row to row distance is kept 45 cm and plant to plant 10-15 cm. The germination of broad bean is less than 75 per cent. It is advisable to sow some extra seeds at a place and transplant them to fill in gaps. The seeds germinate in 10-15 days after sowing. It is advisable to soak the seeds for overnight prior to sowing.
Nutritional Requirements and Their Management	For getting good yield, 10.0 to 15.0 t per hectare of farm yard manure is incorporated during field preparation. Besides, 15-20 kg /ha nitrogen, 40-50 kg/ha phosphorus and 30-40 kg/ha potassium should also be given in furrows at the time of sowing.
Intercultural Operations	Regular hoeing is done around the plants, especially when they are small. These operations will also helpful in keeping down the weeds besides providing good environment for plant growth. Tall varieties may be given support with wooden sticks or twigs against wind. Place stakes or canes at one meter interval down both sides of the double rows close to the beans. Then tie around the stakes with twine 30 cm to 60 cm above the ground. Sometimes, side shoots from the base of the stems are removed. When plants having 5-6 flowers, pinch out the growing points at the top of the stems. This operation encourages the formation of pods and discourages aphids (black fly) which like to feed on the growing points and youngest leaves.
Water Management	Broad bean is a hardy crop and can withstand drought. Therefore, light irrigations are given at regular intervals of 12-15 days.
Harvesting Yield and Storage	The pods are ready for harvesting in 3-4 months for spring sowing and 6-7 months for autumn sowing. Very young pods are preferred by most people. The pods are harvested at the green-shell stage as needed for home use, or for market, and those remaining on the plant are used as dry-shell beans. Pods are picked by a quick downward movement of the hand. The average yield varies from 7.0 to 10.0 tonnes of green pods per hectare.

14.6.2. Cluster bean

Title	Description
Climatic Requirements	The cluster bean is a hardy plant tolerant to drought conditions. It is grown widely in subtropical and tropical regions of India. It prefers long day conditions for growth and short day conditions for induction of flowering.
Soil Conditions	Cluster bean grows nicely on alluvial and sandy loam soils. It can tolerate 7.5 to 8 soil pH. Preparation of soil is done up to good tilth for better plant growth and higher yields.
Sowing Time	Cluster bean is grown twice in a year as a spring-summer and rainy season crop. However, under mild winter, a third crop can be taken.
Seed Rate, Methods of Sowing and Planting Distance	The seed rate varies due to cultivar, planting season etc. However, in general, 30-40 kg/ha seeds of cluster bean are required. The seeds may be sown at the spacing of 45 X 15 cm. However, for Shard Bahar cultivar, a spacing of 60 cm between rows and 12-15 within rows proved better yield.
Nutritional Requirements and Their Management	Cluster bean is a leguminous crop, the requirement of manure and fertilizers are very less. However, for getting good yield, farm yard manure 15.0-20.0 tonnes per hectare should be applied during field preparation. Inorganic fertilizers *viz.*, nitrogen 10-20 kg/ha, 50-70 kg/ha of each phosphorus and potash should be applied. Nitrogen may be applied in two splits. First half quantity of nitrogen should be given at the time of sowing along with whole quantity of phosphorus and potash. The remaining half quantiy of nitrogen should be given at flowering stage.
Intercultural Operations	Cluster bean is a shallow rooted crop. Therefore, shallow intercultural operations are done to provide good condition for crop growth and to keep down the weeds. Weeds like *Parthenium* can also be controlled by the application of 2, 4-D and DSMA (disodium methane arsonate) each at 2.0 kg per hectare.
Water Management	Rainy season crop is grown as rainfed. However, spring-summer season crop is given irrigation as per need of the crop.
Harvesting and Yield	It is a quick growing crop. It starts bearing pods in 40 days after sowing depend upon the variety. The pods are picked at tender stage for cooking as vegetable. The average yield of green pods is 5.0 t/ha and 1.0-1.2 t/ha of dry seeds.

14.6.3. Cowpea

Title	Description
Climatic Requirements	Cowpea is a warm season crop. It is more tolerant to heavy rainfall than other pulses but suffers from water stagnation on own hand and from drought on other. It thrives best between 21-35 ^{0}C temperatures. It is grown in rainy season as a pure crop or mixed with jowar, bajara or ragi. It can serve as a good summer catch crop if suitable variety is grown.
Soil Conditions	Cowpea grows well on all types of well-drained soils, but good yield can be achieved on loamy soil.

Sowing Time	In the plains especially in northern India, there are two main cropping seasons for vegetable cowpea. The summer crop is generally sown towards the end of February and the sowing can be continued till the middle of April. The sowing for the monsoon crop commences from about the middle of June and extends up to the end of August. It is sown in December-January in southern plains. In the hills, the crop is sown during April-May. The vegetable varieties which are photo-insensitive, are sown both in July and in February-March.
Seed Rate, Methods of Sowing and Planting Distance	About 30-35 kg seed during spring season and 15-20 kg seed during rainy season are required per hectare. When, it is sown mixed with other crops, the seed rate would be reduced according to the proportion. The row spacing of 40 to 60 cm and plant to plant spacing of 10-15 cm is maintained for *kharif* sowing. The row spacing in the summer and spring planting is kept between 25 to 30 cm, as the plants do not make much growth. Seeds should be treated with carbendazim at the rate of 3.5 to 4 g per kg of seed. Grain drills can be ideal for seeding.
Nutritional Requirements and Their Managements	Cowpea requires less nitrogen. However, 10-20 kg/ha nitrogen is incorporated in the soil before sowing. Application of phosphorus is very important as it promotes vegetative growth and multiplication of *Rhizobium*, and, thus fixation of atmospheric nitrogen. Phosphorus and potassium 50 to 70 kg per hectare each should be drilled in the soil before sowing. Cowpea is highly susceptible to zinc deficiency. Where zinc deficiency is known, application of 10 to 15 kg zinc sulphate per hectare would be beneficial. Inoculation of cowpea with culture of *Rhizobium* (legume bacteria) has proved beneficial in several areas. Therefore, where the culture is available, it should be used in treating the seed before sowing. This would ensure adequate nitrogen supply to the crop from atmosphere.
Intercultural Operations	Effective control of weeds in the first 20-25 days of the crop season is essential. Two to three weedings and hoeings would be required to check the weed growth. Incorporating one-kilogram active ingredient of treflin per hectare in the soil before sowing can be used as chemical control of weeds.
Use of Plant Growth Regulators	The spraying of maleic hydrazide at 15 ppm just before flowering stage increases pod set by 30 to 35 per cent. This suppresses apical dominance and causing lateral shoots, makes the plants bushy and produces more pods per plant. By using higher concentration, the plant becomes more bushy which affects the yield adversely.
Water Management	Cowpea is a shallow-rooted crop, and therefore, light irrigations are advisable. The rainy season crop does not need any irrigation but in the absence of timely rain supplemental irrigation is essential. The summer crop would need irrigation once a week during March and April and later on every fourth or fifth day. The early sown rainy season crop would need one or two irrigations in the pre-monsoon period. In any case water logging is avoided, as cowpea is sensitive to it.
Harvesting, Yield and Storage	The pods are ready for harvesting after 40 to 50 days of sowing. It is very desirable that the pods are picked up when they are tender and half-grown. The cowpea pods develop very quickly, and if not picked up at the right stage, they tend to become "puffy" unlike peas; picking of green pods in cowpea has to done more frequently. The grain crop

matures in 75 to 125 days, depending upon the season and the variety. In case of *kharif* sowing fully matured crop is harvested, left in the field for further drying and then threshed. The spring and summer crops might retain sufficient green foliage when the pods mature. Therefore, if possible, the mature pods should be picked up first and then plants should be harvested separately for the use of green forage. Cowpea produces about 15.0-20.0 tonnes of green pod per hectare. Those pods which are left for harvesting should be dried and threshed. The threshed grains should be dried in the sun so that the moisture content is around 10 per cent before the grains are stored in cool and dry place.

14.6.4. French Bean

Title	Description
Climatic Requirements	French bean is a cool weather crop but it requires mild warm season for good yield. It is sensitive both to frost and to very high temperature. French bean having cultivars of long day, short day and day neutral types but most of them are day neutral. The seeds will not germinate in cold climate. The optimum soil temperature for growth and yield are 25-30 ^{0}C. During hot weather, blossoms and pods may be dropped. Similarly, heavy and continuous rains result in dropping of blossoms and pods.
Soil Conditions	French bean can be grown on a wide range of soil types but sandy loam soil is best. Good yields are seldom obtained from heavy soils. The suitable soil reaction for French bean growing is between 5.5 and 6.0 pH.
Sowing Time	In the plains of India, French bean is sown twice in a year, first sowing is done in July to September and the second in January to February. In hills, sowing is done from March to June.
Seed Rate, Methods of Sowing and Spacing	The seed rate for the bush type of cultivars may be about 85 to 95 kg per hectare. The seed rate for pole type of cultivars is 25 to 30 kg per hectare. The bush types of French bean are planted at the spacing of 45-60 cm row to row and 10-15 cm plant to plant. Pole types are sown to one meter row to row distance between two sets of rows 60-75 cm and between the two rows 30 cm. The seeds are sown 5 cm deep. The two seeds are sown at one place and one week seedlings are removed after germination is completed. The seeds germinate slowly at a soil temperature about 15 ^{0}C, and at lower temperature they may rot in the soil. Under favourable conditions, seeds germinate in 10 days after sowing.
Nutritional Requirements and Their Management	Being a leguminous crop, this has poor nodule formation capability. Hence, the requirement of manure and fertilizers are more as compared to other legume vegetables. However, for good yield 20.0 to 30.0 tonnes per hectare well rotten farm yard manure should be incorporated at the time of land preparation. Besides it, apply 60kg nitrogen, 40kg phosphorus and 40kg potassium per hectare. Nitrogen is applied in two splits. First at the time of sowing with whole quantity of phophrous and potash, second at flowering stage.
Intercultural Operations	Very shallow cultivation is done at early stages of crop growth. Deep cultivation will disturb plant growth due to root pruning. Because

	roots are growing shallow near the surface. Cultivation during early stages will also help in keeping down weeds. Once plant growth is well, the large leaves form a dense canopy, which acts as a weed suppressor. The thick foliage completely shades the soil beneath, and weeds, starved sunlight, and are unable to compete with.Weedicides like sodium salts of pentachlorophenol may be applied at the rate of 4.5 kg per hectare as pre-emergence. Other herbicide like alachlor (losso) at 3.0 kg per hectare may be applied as pre-emergence. Usually, dwarf varieties do not require support, but climbing varieties do not grow well without support. The bamboo sticks or other wooden sticks or branches which are locally available, can be used for the support. Single stick is fixed near each plant. The length of the stick should be about 1.8 to 2.0 m. The framework consists of a line of pairs of canes stradling the axis of the row, not less than 42 cm apart at ground level. Alternatively, use twiggy branches for support or large mesh netting. Earthing up around the base of the plant, up to the first set of leaves gives additional support to the stem and encourages root growth.
Use of Plant Growth Regulators	Paclobutrazol at 150 mg/l can be used for enhancing yield and suppressing vegetative growth of pole type variety of French bean.
Water Management	Irrigation is required in the early phases of crop growth and during bloom and pod development period. Plants are susceptible to water stress, therefore, irrigation at regular intervals are necessary. Lack of adequate soil moisture may result in reduced percentage of pod setting, length of pod and number of seeds per pod. Inadequate soil moisture may also result in high fiber content in pods.
Harvesting, Yield and Storage	The pods are usually ready for harvest 2-3 weeks after the first blossom. The harvesting of French bean depends on the ways that are used. The pods are harvested when they are young, tender and delicate. They are cooked as whole. When they are little mature and seeds start forming, these are cooked after cutting into pieces. Mature pods contain developed seeds are picked and seeds are shelled, while, green seeds are cooked as vegetable. The harvesting of tender pods should be done at frequent intervals otherwise it will suppress the formation and development of new pods. For obtaining dry beans, harvesting is done when pods are fully ripe and about to shatter. In this case, whole plants are harvested either by hands or by machine. The harvested plants are staked for 7-10 days and then they are threshed either by bullocks or by machine. All possible care should be taken that seeds are not injured. The pod and grain yields of French bean varies considerably with locality, fertility of soil, variety and management practices. The yield of green pods in the bush varieties may be varied in range of 10.0-15.0 t/ha while pole varieties from 15.0 to 20.0 t/ha. The yield of dry seed varies from 1.5 to 2.0 t/ha. Completely dried seeds are stored in glass containers with tight fitting lids or polyethylene bags.

14.6.5. Garden Pea

Title	Description
Climatic Requirements	Pea crop grows best in areas having temperature for at least five months. Pea seed can be germinated up to the minimum temperature of 5 ^{0}C but the germination rate is low. The optimum temperature for germination is about 22 ^{0}C. Pea is not susceptible to cold, but severe frost causes considerable injury to the freshly opened flowers and young developing pods. In fact, pods grow best in those regions where there is a slow transition from cool to warm weather in spring.
Soil Conditions	Pea can be grown on many types of soil from light sandy to clay soil. The highly organic soils are unsuitable for pea as their moisture reserve leads to excessive vegetative growth and poor pod formation. It is very sensitive to saline and alkaline conditions. The most favourable range of pH is between 6.0 to 7.5 and when it is lower than 6.0, liming is practiced to improve the soil conditions.
Sowing Time	Pea is grown as a *rabi* crop and sown from the beginning of October to middle of November in the plains and from the middle of March to end of May on the hills. In Darjeeling, this crop is sown from June to August. In Southern states, pea is cultivated mainly in the hills whereas in North India, three sowings are done during March-April, August-September and November-December.
Seed Rate, Methods of Sowing and Spacing	When sowing is done in furrows, seed rate varies from 50-60 kg/ha. When early varieties are sown which have generally best growth, seed rate of 100-120 kg/ha are required but in case of mid late varieties only 80-90 kg seed per hectare are enough. The pea seed of good quality with 95 per cent seed germination is enough for sowing. Seeds can be sown on flat or raised beds either by broadcasting or behind deshi plough in furrows, which are covered by usual planking. Some farmers drill the seed through pora (tube) attached to deshi plough and there is no need of planking. When the seed is sown too deep, it results in slow germination and poor stand. A depth of 5-7.5 cm is optimum according soil moisture and texture. Pea can be sown at a row to row spacing of 22.5-30 cm and plant to plant spacing of 3.75-5 cm.
Nutritional Requirements and Their Management	For getting good yield, farm yard manure is applied in quantity of 8.0-10.0 t/ha at 15 days before sowing the seeds. The nitrogen, phosphorous and potassium are applied in ratio of 30:50:25 kg/ha, respectively. This nutrition is given at the time of sowing of seeds as basal dose. Foliar application of 0.1 per cent ammonium molybdate can be used for increasing number of root nodules, yield, TSS and number of seeds/pod in pea .
Intercultural Operations	• Lasso @ 0.75 kg a.i./ha pre-emergence spray or tribunil @ 1.5 kg a.i./ha pre emergence or basalin @ 2 kg a.i./ha pre plant incorporation along with one hand weeding at 45 days after sowing (DAS) have been found to be most effective for weed control under Pantnagar conditions. • Application of tribunil @ 1.87 kg a.i./ha as pre emergence spray has been recommended for controlling under agro-climatic conditions of Punjab. • Application of stomp (pendimethalin) @ 0.5 kg a.i./ha or lasso (alachlor) @ 1.5 kg a.i./ha as pre-emergence incorporation in the field followed by

	one hand weeding at 25 DAS have been recommended under Sabour conditions.
Use of Plant Growth Regulators	Floliar spray of MH at 25 mg/l or CCC at 500 mg/l before flowering has given best pod yield in pea . Seed treatment with cytozyme at 1 per cent has also been reported to improve fresh pod yield in pea.
Water Management	Two or three irrigations are required for good yield. First irrigation should be given at pre bloom stage at 40 days of sowing and second on bloom stage at 60 days after sowing. Furrow irrigation is normally adopted for irrigation. Basins are also sometimes used.
Harvesting, Yield and Storage	Generally, three to four pickings are done during the season. To maintain the quality of produce, harvesting should be done either early in the morning or late in the afternoon. The quality is ascertained by tendrometer or motovometer reading. In Indian conditions, usually periodical pickings (at 6-8 days intervals) from the same crop is done. Care is taken that not to tear or jerk the plants so that they are not injured and get partially dried up or stop bearing pods. For harvesting, it needs adequate labour and sometimes the standing crop are given to contractors who engage their own pickers. It is observed that female pickers are more efficient as compared to male pickers. Green pods are generally packed in gunny bags and baskets are also used for this purpose. About 3.0 to 4.0 tonnes of quintals of green pods per hectare are obtained in case of early varieties and 6.0-7.0 tonnes/ha in case of mid season and late varieties. The shelling percentage varies from 35-50 depending upon variety, agroclimatic conditions, management practices etc. The grain yield is about 1.5-2.0 tonnes per hectare. Peas are very perishable and heat easily, a shallow container is desirable. Fresh unshelled peas may be kept for two weeks at 32 ^{0}F (0 ^{0}C) at relative humidity of 85-90 per cent. Peas can also be stored in crushed ice for about 2-3 weeks. The pods will freeze at –10 ^{0}C.

14.6.6. Indian Bean

Title	Description
Climatic Requirements	Indian bean can be grown in both sub-tropical and tropical climatic conditions. It is susceptible to frost and extreme hot weather. Relatively cool-season is favourable.
Soil Conditions	Like other beans, Indian bean can also be grown on a wide range of soils of average fertility. Growing on soil which is of higher fertility status will cause luxuriant vegetative growth on the cost of a pod yields.
Sowing Time	Poly type varieties are sown in the month of July-August. It can be sown early also in the areas where rains come early. However, bush types varieties may be shown in last week of October in the areas where heavy rains in July-August.
Seed Rate, Methods of Sowing and Spacing	For raising one-hectare crop of Indian bean, 20-30 kg seeds are required. Indian bean is raised as monoculture and also mixed with ragi or sorghum. Sometimes, it is grown with castor crop, in this way vine types of Indian beans also get support. It is sown at the spacing of 200 x 100 cm or 75 x 75 cm as a pure crop. When it is raised as mixed crop, it is drilled between two rows of ragi or sorghum at 100 cm distance. Usually 2-3

	seeds are sown per hill, which later thinned to two or one healthy plant. When it is grown as mixed crop with sorghum, it twines on the sorghum stalk. The ear heads of sorghum are harvested and then stalks are cut for animal fodder, Indian bean increases high fodder value. The bush type varieties are sown at distance of 60x45 cm depending upon variety.
Nutritional Requirements and Their Management	For getting good yield, per hectare 10 to 15 tonnes of well rotten farm yard manure. About 20-30 kg nitrogen are required, 40-50 kg phosphorus and 30-40 kg potassium per hectare are required. Organic manure is applied during land preparation and half quantity of nitrogen and whole quantity quantities of phosphorus and potassium are applied at the time of sowing. Remaining half quantity of nitrogen is top dressed at 30-35 days after seed sowing.
Intercultural Operations	Before vining, once or twice hoeing are done. It will control weeds and will enhance crop growth.
Water Management	Only occasional light irrigation may be given. Indian bean can tolerate well comparatively dry conditions. However, during flowering, optimum moisture may be reduced flower drop. Varietal character is necessary which may also be one of the important reason of flower drop and pod set.
Harvesting, Yield and Storage	The green pod stages are available during winter till spring. Usually, they are harvested at tender. When pods are left unplucked their tenderness from such pods, the seeds are taken out and are used as vegetable. Pods may also be left till fully ripened stage. The seeds from such pods are extracted and dried and used as pulse. Average green pod yield of Indian bean is 25 tonnes per hectare. Like pea, pods of Indian bean can also be kept for two weeks at 0 °C at relative humidity of 85-90 per cent.

14.7. Perennial Vegetables

14.7.1. Asparagus

Title	Description
Climatic Requirements	Asparagus, being a broadly adopted cool season plant, is grown in most temperate and some sub-tropical regions. Mean day temperature of 25-30 °C and 15-20 °C at night are ideal for spear and fern growth. Above ground plant parts are injured or killed by frost. For areas with below freezing temperature, crown is protected from freezing by mulching. It can also be grown in plains of sub-tropical region if correct management practices are followed.
Soil Conditions	Friable, deep, well drained and fertile soils are conducive to longevity as well as productivity. A neutral pH (6.5 to 7.5) is ideal. Asparagus plants are tolerant to slightly alkaline or acidic soils. Mature plants have a high tolerance to salinity, but seedlings are very sensitive to salt.
Sowing Time	The time of sowing of seed in the nursery is March to May in the hills and July to November in the plains. Crowns are planted in the spring season or may also be planted when they are dormant during winter.

Seed Rate, Methods of Sowing and Transplanting Distance	On well-prepared nursery beds, seeds are sown at the rate of three to four kg per hectare. Asparagus can be raised by seeds either through direct seedlings or raising the seedlings first in the nursery bed and then transplant. It can be well planted with crowns, preferably one year old. Only well grown crowns of good size containing large buds, should be planted. Plant spacing ranges from 20 to 50 cm in row and 100 to 200 cm between rows.
Nutritional Requirements and Their Management	In order to improve the physical condition of the soil, about 30.0-40.0 t/ha well rotten farm yard manure or compost should be incorporated at the time of field preparation. Just before planting of seeds, crowns or seedlings, phosphorous @ 80 to 100 kg/ha and potassium @ 60 to 80 kg/ha are applied. Nitrogen @ 80 to 120 kg/ha is also needed. Nitrogen should be applied in split doses of three to four. At least one-fourth quantity of the total amount should be applied after 20 to 25 days of planting the second quantity of nitrogen is applied just before first cutting and the third and fourth quantity should be followed by second and third cuttings.
Intercultural Operations	Asparagus responds to cultivation' in standing crop. They provide favourable conditions for plant growth and keep down the weeds. Care is taken that 'spears' should not get injured during cultivation. In morning hours, spears remain turgid and brittle, therefore, planting is done in the afternoon. Asparagus fields should be kept weed free for obtaining maximum yield by proper shallow cultivation, hand weeding or by using pre-emergence application of metribuzin @ 1 kg/ha.During severe winter, usually spears are not formed crowns go under dormancy. The foliage may be cut and composted. This foliage may also be disced in between rows, which in turn add organic matter. Blanching is done for having white asparagus spears, for this keep the soil around the plant up to a 25 to 30 cm.
Use of Plant Growth Regulators	Several plant growth regulators influence bud breaks and spear growth and may be useful in asparagus production. Abscisic acid appears to promote sink strength or encourage phloem unloading in areas where assimilates are needed for growth. It is reported that gibberellic acid (GA) promotes growth of asparagus buds. Apical dominance can be controlled by additions of GA_3, which increased harvested spear number and promoted spear growth. Other plant growth regulators like chloroflurenol increases spear growth but causes spear deformation. Benzyladenine (BA) has also been found to stimulate spear emergence when applied to healthy fern. This could be useful where summer or autumn harvesting regimes are practiced or when mother fern technique is used.
Water Management	Being a deep-rooted crop, asparagus is required more frequent irrigation water during summer. The interval of irrigation in summer should not go beyond one week. Besides climatic conditions, soil types also determined the quantity and frequency of irrigations.
Harvesting, Yield and Storage	Spears are usually harvested before excessive elongation occurs. Large spear diameter and length with compact tip and spear tenderness are quality factors. Spears of 10-15 cm are generally harvested. Male plants produce large total yield while female plants produce large individual spears. Yield of 25 to 40 t/ha has been reported. Since, white asparagus

	spear subjected to greater depth of soil cover, hence have large diameter.Mostly asparagus are hand harvested for green production, spears are hand snapped or cut below soil level with a long handle narrow blade knife. Damage to young spears and latent buds below are possible, so careful insertion of knife is important. White or blanched spear harvesting is more difficult. Spears are harvested when tip is about to emerge or just protrudes through the soil surface. Even a slight amount of tip greening of white asparagus diminishes, its perceived market quality. Hence, the difficult and costly production of white asparagus is steadily being displaced by green production. Finally, the longevity of an asparagus planting varies from as little as three to four years and more than 15 years. Asparagus can be stored at two to three weeks at 95 per cent RH and 0-2 ^{0}C temperature. Spears stored in wet tissue paper looked more fresh and firm, after 13-16 days of storage.

14.7.2. Chow-Chow

Title	Description
Climatic Requirements	Chow-chow can be grown in tropical and subtropical to moderately temperate areas up to 2000 m elevations. However, it is a warm season crop. The plants require a day length of slightly over twelve hours before flowering. Hence, in temperate climate plants do not flowers until the autumn. Extremes of climate (freezing and intense heat) kill the vines. Plant growth and development has been reported from northern parts of India and from the place situated near the Arabian Sea proved that this plant is tolerant to wide climatic conditions.
Soil Conditions	Chow-chow can be grown on a wide range of soil. However, soil rich in organic matter, deep, moist, sandy loam and well drained is most suitable.
Planting Time	Fruits are generally available late in the monsoon to early winter and crop is over before chilling cold starts. This is the time when planting can be done.
Planting Requirements, Method of Planting and Planting Distance	Chow-chow is generally raised by planting entire fruits. It can also be propagated by tuberous roots. Planting fruits or tuberous roots directly in field raises the crop or first it is planted in nursery and then transplanted in the main field. In chow-chow, the seed is not separated from the fruit and hence whole fruit is planted in polyethylene bag containing a good planting medium of topsoil and manure (3:1 ratio). The fruit is buried horizontally in the soil exposing the sprout end. An adequate moisture is provided for early sprouting. The sprouts come out within a week and bear 3 to 4 leaves. When plants grew up to the height of 30 cm, they are transplanted at main site. The fruits and tuberous roots are also planted on raised nursery beds and they are lifted at transplantable age. Prior to transplanting, the pits of 45 cm^3 are dug and filled with a mixture of topsoil and well rotten farmyard manure or compost (3:1) ratio. As far as possible, two gram of furadan granules should also be mixed in the planting mixture, this will check any insect-cut worms present during the planting on the next day. The plants are taken out from the polyethylene bags without disturbing ball of soil and transplanted individually in pit by burying whole ball of the soil

and pressing well around. After that basin is irrigated. The raising of nursery in the polyethylene is necessary in the areas performed very conveniently during frost-free season. Under mild temperature, the whole fruit is planted directly in the field. The pits are dug as described above and fruits are placed horizontally and covered with soil thinly and provided with light irrigation. Since, it is a perennial vine crop, distance between two rows 2-3m, one to two meters between two vines have been recommended. Planting distance may be increased when soil is fertile.

Nutritional Requirements and Their Management Due to profuse vine growth and formation of tuberous roots, plant needs more nutrients. Application of 10 to 15 kg farm yard manure, 100 g urea, 100 g single super phosphate and 50 g muriate of potash per plant will fulfil the need of the crop year to year. Sometimes, additional application of 100 g urea per plant may be required during rainy season when plant shows poor growth. Application of neem cake at 1.5 kg per plant per year has also been reported for good yield.

Intercultural Operations Intercultural operation will help in keeping down the weeds. This is done in the early growth of the vines and can be followed twice or thrice in a year in the plot when the vines are trained on pandal or trellis. When they are allowed to grow all over the field, will suppress the weed growth, and there will be no need of any cultivation. Chow- chow is a climber with large tendrils, grows well when vines are trained on a trellis or over a fence, porch, tree etc. The planting site should be away from wind or it is protected well from heavy winds. Healthy fruits and higher yields are obtained when vines are trained as compared to vines when allowed to sprawl on the ground. However, when vines are allowed to grow on a layer much consisted of dry grasses, they found growing happily and fruits were also escaped from the direct contact of soil but insects where getting hiding places . Putting soil around the base of the vine will provide support for the proper extension of the root system and also it will prevent vine from water stagnation season.

Use of Plant Growth Regulators It has been reported that effect of inclusion of coconut milk, kinetin, indole-3 acetic acid or 2,4-dichlorophenoxy acetic acid as the growth media for promoting the growth of plant tissues. It is also observed that occurrence in plant extracts of kinetin like factors, retard the chlorophyll degradation in rice leaves and also in seeds of chow-chow. More than twenty neutral and water soluble gibberellins like substances occurring in developing seeds of chow-chow.

Water Management Light irrigation just after transplanting is required. Though, it is grown as a rainfed crop but irrigations may be done when rains are delayed in the month of May to June. Further, irrigations are done as and when required, particular during long dry spell.

Harvesting, Yield and Storage Generally, vines bear fruits in abundance during October to November. The fruits become ready for harvesting within 120 days or so and continue for 2 to 3 months. It has been observed that out of four female flowers in an inflorescence, usually single fruit is set. Sometimes, there is a setting of two fruits but three fruits also. Retention of all the fruits are rare. Fruits are picked when they are tender. Fruits are easily harvested by cutting them from peduncle. For planting mature fruits are harvested. Crop grown under good management, yields about 40 to

	50 tonnes of fruits per hectare. Sometimes more than 100 fruits per vine can easily be obtained from good cared crop. After harvesting, healthy fruits are marketed. The keeping quality of fruits is very good. Fruits can be stored for about three to four weeks without much loss under ordinary conditions.

14.7.3. Drumstick

Title	Description
Climatic Requirements	It has been known to attain the best growth and record a good performance only in tropical and peninsular climates in the plains of south India. However, it can successfully grown in northen India also.
Soil Conditions	It has been found to grow and yield satisfactory in all types of soil having stiff clays and extremely sandy soils. But sandy loams containing a good amount of lime are said to be preferable.
Planting Time	Generally, drumstick is planted on onset of monsoon. It can be planted from June to August.
Planting Requirements, Methods of Planting and Planting Distance	The drumstick can be propagated by seeds or vegetatively by limb cuttings. The method generally followed is vegetative, through limb cuttings. Budding has also been reported in Kanyakumari district. It has also reported that it is propagated by planting limb cuttings of one to two meter long and about 15 to 20 cm in circumference. The cuttings are planted in pits of 60 cm cube at a spacing of about 3 to 5 m preferably in the months of June to August.
Nutritional Requirements and Their Management	Manuring of drumstick is rarely practised, being a hardy tree capable of growing with very little attention. But in Kerala, ring trenches are dug around the trees and green leaves, farm yard manure and ash are put in the trenches, about 60 to 90 cm a way from the tree during the rainy season and covered. Research work done at the Agricultural College, Coimbatore has shown that application of 75 kg of farm yard manure and 0.037g of ammonium sulphate per tree (in December) gave a three-fold increase in yield over the unmanured trees.
Intercultural Operations	The tree basin may have to be cleared of weeds once in a year and slight hoeing of the soil under the trees will be beneficial.
Water Management	The growing plants may not require watering except during the hot weather when they may be irrigated once in about eight days.
Harvesting, Yield and Storage	The plants established from cuttings will begin to bear in the sixth to eight months producing 80 to 90 fruits per tree in the first two or three seasons. After two years of growth, yield may go up to 500 to 600 fruits per tree. In South India, the drumstick generally bears in two seasons though fruit will be found sometimes in the tree almost throughout the year, the two distinct crops are borne in July-August and March-April. The trees start bearing pods in six to eight months after planting, but regular bearing commences after the second year. There is no storage method, since the fruit is consumed immediately after harvest or it may be used after one or two days.

14.7.4. Ivy Gourd

Title	Description
Climatic Requirements	Ivy gourd thrives well under hot or moderately warm and humid climate. It remains under dormancy when temperatures go down during December-January. When temperature rises in February-March new flushes come. Due to this, they can only produce fruits once in a year. Whereas, under south and central India, where winter is not distinct and plant growth remains continue and thus plant produces fruits in two to three flushes. However there are two fruiting peaks that are during summer and rainy seasons. The average temperature for growth would be around 30-35 ^{0}C with maximum ranging around 40 ^{0}C and minimum between 20-25 ^{0}C. It performs reasonably well in high rainfall areas.
Soil Conditions	A well-drained sandy loam and fertile soil is ideal for it. It performs well in light soils if provided with adequate nutrient supply. Its cultivation in saline alkali or sodic soils is not remunerative.
Sowing Time	Planting of Ivy gourd is preferably done during June to July and or February to March.
Seed Rate, Methods of Planting and Planting Distance	Ivy gourd is propagated vegetatively through vine cuttings and tuberous roots. For planting, semi-hardwood cuttings, 25-30 cm long vine having pencil thickness (1.5-2.0 cm) are collected. Leaf cuttings having 5 to 6 leaves are desirable. It attains heavy vegetative growth and needs a permanent bower system or mandap for training vines. It is planted in pits at a distance of 3 m x 3m. Pits of 30 cm x 30 cm x 30 cm size are filled with a mixture of soil and 5 kg well rotten farm yard manure. Half-kg neem cake in each pot can be mixed to avoid insect-pest damage to its roots.
Nutritional Requirements and Their Management	Amount of fertilizers to be applied depends on type of soil and nutrient status of the soil. However, in general 60kg nitrogen, 40 kg phosphorous and 40 kg potash per hectare should be applied to get good yield. Half quantity of nitrogen is given at monthly interval in four splits from June to July. Whole quantities of phosporus and potash are applied at the time of planting as basal does. Well rotten farm yard manure @ 10 kg/plant should also be applied just after pruning.
Intercultural Operations	Ivy gourd does not require much attention for interculture. In the early stages before they start vining, it require to be kept free from weeds around the pits. At the time of top dressing of nitrogenous fertilizers weeding and earthing up are done. Vines have to be trained over trellies or supports, weeding of the pits are alone necessary under the canopy of vine growth in pandals, weed growth down below, and are nearly arrested. The only attention is that big weeds have to be manually pulled out, without disturbing the vines at later stages.
Water Management	In spring-summer crop, frequent irrigation is required, while in rainy season crop irrigation may not be necessary at all, if rainfall is well distributed between July and September. During rooting of the cuttings adequate soil moisture is necessary. Excess moisture will affect rooting and further sprouting and plant growth. Proper moisture should be supplied during flowering and fruit setting stages.
Harvesting, Yield and Storage	Ivy gourd gives a continuous harvest of vegetables for about 9-10 months of the year. Picking should be done at 3-4 days interval when

fruits are tender. Picking should not be delayed as flesh around the seeds become pink and such fruits fetch less price in the market. Heavy fruiting is obtained from July to September. Ivy gourd gives an average yield of 20.0 t/ha but higher yield of about 30.0-40.0 t/ha can be obtained with intensive management practices. The fruits can easily be kept in good quality for one to two weeks under ordinary room conditions.

14.8 Root Vegetables

14. 8.1 Beet root

Title	Description
Climatic Requirements	It is essentially a cool weather crop and hence it grows best in winter in plains of India. The optimum temperature for root growth is obtained always in cool (18.3 ^{0}C to 21 ^{0}C). At a temperature below 10 ^{0}C for couple of weeks results in bolting which affect root development. Mild climatic condition is suitable for beet root growing under warmer conditions. Beet root shows alternates white and colour circles when sliced.
Soil Conditions	Beet root can be grown on a wide range of soil. However, light sandy soils are best. Beet root is sensitive to high acidity as it is slightly tolerant to acidity (pH as low 6.0 only). This is only vegetable which can successfully be grown in saline and alkaline soils up to 9 to 10 pH. However, on alkaline soil, scab may be problem. Open and sunny site should be selected for its cultivation.
Sowing Time	The sowing should be such that there should not be heavy frost and also dry or hot conditions. Under both these conditions, beet root bolts on the expense of root development. The sowing can be done from August to November or earlier in the plains, and in the hills it is sown in the months of March to May. However, it will be better to sow the seeds at monthly interval up to January for regular supply.
Seed Rate, Methods of Sowing and Planting Distance	About 7 to 9 kg of seed per hectare are required. Seeds are sown in narrow furrow dug 2 to 3 cm deep at 5 cm apart keeping row to row distance of 30 cm. Just after sowing, furrows are covered with soil and raked properly. It will be better if adequate soil moisture is available at the time of sowing, if not, then light irrigation may be done. Prior to sowing, seeds are soaked in water for overnight, which stimulate germination.
Nutritional Requirements and their Management	For getting good yield, 20.0 to 25.0 tonnes per hectare of well rotten farm yard manure is applied during field preparation. Besides, the soil having average fertility, 60 to 70 kg nitrogen, 100 to 120 kg phosphorus and 60 to 70 kg potash per hectare should also be applied. Further, light sandy soils require more nitrogen and potassium. Application of half-to-two-third of the total nitrogen along with whole quantity each of phosphorus and potash is given as a basal dose. The remaining half-to-one-third quantity of nitrogen are applied after three to four weeks of sowing. Beet root is susceptible to boron deficiency, so it is necessary to apply borax 20 to 25 kg per hectare depending upon soil test at the time of sowing.

Intercultural Operations	At least twice thinnings are required to maintain finally 10 to 15 cm of distance between two plants depending upon type of varieties. Round and short varieties require close spacing whereas long and tall varieties is sown in wider spacing.Gap filling is done in case where germination is poor. This will maintain desired plant population.Shallow cultivation at early stage of crop growth between the rows may be done. Care is taken not to cut/damage any root while hoeing. Generally, hoeing at early stage of crop will keep down the weeds. Later, when plants get established well, they produce thick foliage, which suppress the weeds. Hand pulling of tall weeds is advisable. Earthing up is usually done to cover the swollen roots. Weeds can also be controlled by using weedicides. Pre-emergence application of alachlor or butachlor at 1.5 kg a.i./ha or fluchloralin 1.0 kg a.i./ha has been found effective herbicides for controlling weeds in beetroot for a period of 60 days
Water Management	Beet root is very sensitive to soil moisture at all stages of growth. Stress near harvest increases sugar percentage and reduces fresh weight of roots. With adequate soil moisture supply during growth, the tissues of the beet root remain tender and succulent tops. When crop is grown for seed, an adequate supply of moisture must be provided during flowering and seed development. This crop required about six irrigations with an irrigation requirement of 225 mm water. However, where there are winter rains, only three irrigations are required. Generally, planted on ridges with furrow irrigation is applied for beet root in India.
Harvesting Yield and Storage	Beet root becomes ready for final harvesting within 8 to 10 weeks. Less developed roots are also used which are available at last thinning. When such roots are uprooted, the remaining beet roots get more space for development. Harvesting is performed by pulling the roots with hands or with the help of *khurpi* or shovels. Harvesting may also be performed mechanically depending on availability, but it is applicable only on commercial scale. The yield varies from 25.0 to 30.0 t/ha. Beets can be stored well at temperature 0 °C and 90 per cent relative humidity.

14.8.2: Carrot

Title	Description
Climatic Requirements	It is a cool season crop. But some Asiatic types can tolerate higher temperature. The optimum temperature for seed germination is 7.2 to 23.9 °C. Carrot produced largest roots between 10 and 15.6 °C with poor root colour and between 15.6 and 21.1 °C with good root colour. Climate is considered much more often as a limiting factor than soil. Plants grown continuously at a temperature of 21.1–26.7 °C fail to develop flower primordial. It is reason that seeds of European types of carrot are produced only in the hills of India, where the winter is severe. At higher temperatures, the roots become shorter, thicker and non-juicy and also brightness of colour is reduced. At lower temperature (10 to 15 °C), the roots become longer and develop poor colour.
Soil Conditions	Carrots grow well in many soil types, preferably on well drained, deep loose and neutral soil (pH 5.5–7.0). Sandy loam soils rich in humus free of clods and rocks are preferred for smooth straight roots. Soil

compaction affect root growth and length, very loose or highly compact soils are detrimental to growth of roots.

Sowing Time

In the region where climatic conditions are mild, carrot can be sown almost all the year round. Several successive sowings may be done every fortnight to obtain a continuous supply of roots. In the northern plains of India, carrot is sown from the middle of August to the beginning of December. It is grown from March to August in hills.

Seed Rate, Methods of Sowing and Planting Distance

The seed rate varies from 8 to 10 kg per hectare. For better yield, carrot seed soaked for 12 hours in 50 ppm IBA solution. The seed is usually sown either by broadcasting or by drilling in rows 15-20 cm apart. The seeds are sown on ridges in flat beds. In flat bed method of planting, on one side of ridges 5 cm space between ridges and on both side such ridges 50 cm space between ridges.

Nutritional Requirements and Their Management

For getting good yield, 20.0 t/ha well rotten farm yard manure is thoroughly mixed in the soil 15-20 days before sowing the seeds. Application of 80 kg/ha nitrogen, 60 kg/ha phosphorous and 60 kg/ha potash per hectare have also been recommended as inorganic fertilizers. Half quantity of nitrogen and full quantity of each phosphorous and potash is applied at the time of sowing. The remaining quantity of nitrogen may be given 30-45 days after seed sowing.

Intercultureal Operation

Within a week of seed sowing, the seedlings start emerging through the ground. In line-sown crop, these are thinned to space 4 to 5 cm apart as soon as they are well established and have produced 3 to 4 leaves. In broadcast sown crop, thinning is done twice, once earlier to remove surplus plants from the clump leaving only one seedling at a hill. The second thinning is done at a later stage by removing the larger roots for table use, leaving the smaller one to develop. This operation should be done when soil is adequately moist. During weeding and hoeing, the crown of the root is often exposed to light. This causes greening and lowering the quality of roots. Hence, for preventing discolouration of roots, earthing up is necessary.

Water Management

Carrot is a medium rooted crop and roots are mostly confined in the depth of 120 cm. Carrot is a cool season crop, although some of the tropical types tolerate very high temperatures. It requires well-drained soil and is very sensitive to fluctuation of soil moisture. Insufficient moisture for carrot increases roughness, decreases root size and yield. Low moisture grown carrot has strong and pungent flavour. Final stages of root development are very sensitive to moisture stress. Dryness of soil followed by rain or irrigation is likely to cause growth cracks in carrot roots. First irrigation is done soon after sowing followed by another in winter and fortnight when the weather is dry. During spring and summer seasons, it may be necessary to irrigates once in 3 to 8 days depending on soil type, weather conditions and stage of development of crop. Carrot is irrigated before any wilting of leaves appears, since they may be able to obtain enough water to keep the leaves erect without having enough moisture to make the desired growth. Carrot is generally irrigated by furrow system in India. Basin irrigation is also followed occasionally.

Harvesting, Yield and Storage	Carrot should be harvested at proper stage of maturity. Otherwise, it will be puffy and unfit for consumption. The Asiatic varieties attain the marketable stage of maturity at 2.5 to 4 cm diameters at upper end. Processing carrots are left in the ground longer. Both the dry matter and colour increase with maturity. In India, harvesting is done manually, while mechanical harvesting is the rule in advanced countries. Usually light irrigation is given 20 days before harvesting. The carrots grown on ridges can be easily pulled out. Then the tops are cut. In the flat beds the green tops are first cut and roots are then dug out with kudali or a wooden plough. Generally, Asiatic types produce higher yield of 25.0 to 30.0 t/ha, while European cultivars produce around 10.0 to 15.0 t/ha.Carrot can be stored for 3-4 days under ambient conditions. However, at temperature of 0 to 4 ^{0}C with 93 to 98 per cent relative humidity, it can be stored for 6 months.

14.8.3. Radish

Title	Description
Climatic Requirements	Radish is best adapted to cool or moderate climate. Asiatic radish can tolerate higher temperatures than European varieties. It develops best flavour, texture and size at cooler temperature between 10 and 15 ^{0}C. A long day as well as high temperature results in bolting before proper root development. The roots become hard, pithy and pungent during the hot weather. Photoperiod also influenced root development in radish. The root development under 12 hour photoperiod is more as compared to 8 hours and 16 hours. Low temperature is a critical factor causing flowering, which is accelerated by long photo period.
Soil Conditions	Radish can be grown nearly all types of soils, but best results are obtained on light, friable soil that contains ample humus. Since, it is a short duration crop, it can be grown in soil that is not suitable satisfactory for other root crops. For early crop, sandy or sandy loam soils are preferred; however, for summer crop a cool moist soil gives best result. Usually heavy soils produce rough, misshapen roots with a number of small fibrous laterals, and such soils should be avoided.

Sowing Time

Varieties	Period of sowing of seeds	Period of harvesting
Pusa Desi	Mid August to mid October	Last week of September to early December
Pusa Reshmi	Mid September to mid November.	Late October to early January
Japanese White	Mid October to mid December	Mid December to early March
Pusa Himani	Mid December to mid February.	Mid February to mid April
White Icicle	Late October to February end	Late November to March
Pusa Chetki	Early April to mid August	Early May to September

Seed Rate, Methods of Sowing and Spacing

A seed rate of 10 kg and 12 kg/ha is recommended for tropical and temperate varieties, respectively. Radish is a usually grown on ridge to facilitate good root development. In order to obtain higher yield of radish, a closer spacing of 25x15 cm and 30x10 cm can be used. The spacing of 45 x 8 cm for tropical varieties is recommended, while temperate varieties can be grown in rows about 20-30 cm apart.

Nutritional Requirements and Their Management

Radish is a short duration crop, hence judicious and proper use of manure's and fertilisers are essential for getting good yield and excellent root quality. Fresh undecomposed manure should be avoided to prevent forking or branching of edible roots. A quantity of 10.0 t/ha farm yard manure, 75-100 kg/ha nitrogen, 50 kg/ha phosphorus and 50 kg/ha potash are most economical for cultivation of radish. Full quantity of farmyard manure is applied 20 days before sowing of seeds. One and half quantity of nitrogen and full quantity of both phosphorus and potash should be applied at the time of seed sowing. Remaining quantity of nitrogen is applied 20 days after seed germination. The root growth of radish is severely checked under boron deficiency conditions, hence, soil application of boron in the form of disodium tetraborate at the rate of 10 kg/ha may also applied at the time of sowing which will give high yield and best root quality. A study showed that the effect of copper application on yield and nutrient uptake by radish cv. Japanese White in acid soils of Nagaland. It has also reported that maximum yield and profitability are obtained with spray and basal application of $CuSO_4$ at 2.0 and 5.0 kg/ha, respectively.

Intercultural Operations

Intercultural operations like weeding and hoeing are necessary to check the weed growth and provide soil aeration for better growth and yield. In radish, the growing roots tend to push out the soil surface. Therefore, proper earthing up is essential to get well-developed quality roots. Since, all the parts of radish is consumed, hence, chemical weed control is avoided.

Use of Plant Growth Regulators

Soaking of seeds in NAA at 10 and 20 ppm for sowing was not effective in stimulating germination of radish seeds.

Water Management

Radish requires plenty of water from sowing time until the roots is large enough to be pulled out. The first irrigation is given immediately after sowing if soil moisture is not adequate and subsequent irrigation may be given once every 6 to 7 days. It can not withstand water logging and over watering may result in tops that are too large and succulent. Care is taken to irrigate adequately so that field may not become dry and compact and the root development may not be hindered. Dryness of soil followed by rain or irrigation is likely to cause growth cracks. In India, radish is raised both basin and furrow system of irrigations. However, for higher yield and good quality roots, it cultivation may be under sub-surface drip system of irrigation.

Harvesting, Yield and Storage

Harvesting depends on cultivars, the roots become ready for harvesting in about 25-55 days after sowing. European cultivars reach harvest maturity in 25-30 days after sowing. They become bitter and pithy if the harvesting is delayed. In India, harvesting is done manually. A light irrigation may be given before harvesting to facilitate lifting of roots. The roots are washed, graded and tied in bunches. The average yield of Indian cultivars varies from 20.0 to 30.0 tonnes per hectare, whereas

	the European cultivars produce 15.0-20.0 tonnes per hectare. However, some high yielding varieties may be as high as 40.0-50.0 tonnes per hectare both in spring-summer and winter sowings. Radish root can not store more than 2-3 days under temperature without impairing its quality. However, it can be stored for about two months in cold storage at 0^{0}C and 90-95 per cent relative humidity.

14.8.4. Turnip

Title	Description
Climatic Requirements	Turnip is best adapted to a cool or moderate climate. It is hardy crop and can tolerate mild freezing temperature. The best quality turnips are successfully grown in the northern plains and hilly tracts of India. Asiatic varieties required warmer climatic conditions and are sown earlier than European types. High ascorbic acid content is obtained at greater light intensity. The most favourable temperature for the development of the root and the ratio of root/greens are 10-13 ^{0}C air temperature and 18-23 ^{0}C root temperature.
Soil Conditions	As far as possible, turnip should be grown in open sunny place. Under shade, foliage grows in the expense of root development. Wide ranges of soils are suitable for turnip cultivation provided that these soils supplied adequate organic matter. However, rich sandy loam soil having good soil moisture retention capacity is best. The soil reaction should be neutral to slightly alkaline. However, turnip is moderately tolerant to acid soils (pH 6.8 to 5.5).
Sowing Time	In the plains of India, the seeds of Asiatic types are sown from the end of July to September and the European types from September-October to December. In the hills, they are sown from March to May.
Seed Rate, Methods of Sowing and Spacing	The seed rate per hectare is 3 to 4 kg. Turnip does not transplant well. The seeds are sown directly in the main field. The seeds are sown thinly, 1-1.5 cm deep in drills 30 to 40 cm apart and plants are thinned to space them at 10-15 cm within rows. When the plants are 10 to 15 days old, thinning is done to keep them at 10 to 15 cm in the row. Sowing is also done on ridges by opening shallow furrows on the ridges, and seeds are sown as per method mentioned above. In normal cases, seeds germinate after 4 to 6 days of sowing.
Nutritional Requirements and Their Management	The recommended quantities of manure and fertilizers for cultivation of turnip is 25.0 t/ha farm yard manure supplemented with 60-70 kg/ha nitrogen and 40-50 kg/ha each phosphorus and potash. The farm yard manure should be given 20 days before sowing. While, phosphorus and potash should be given at the time of sowing and placed 7-8 cm below the seed. The nitrogenous fertilizer should be given in two split doses, half before sowing and the rest at the time of root formation with the second and third irrigations.
Intercultural Operations	It is an essential operation for maintaining desired distance between plants and for providing better conditions for plant growth and development of roots. The first thinning is done when the seedlings are large enough to handle (4-5 cm). Thinning for weak and feeble seedlings are preferably done. Since, this much distance is very less and also in

	the first thinning all the plants may not be judge for taking out. Therefore, after about 7 to 10 days or so, the second thinning is done. The distance between plants come to 10 to 15 cm or so. Shallow hoeings at least twice are advisable for providing good environment and keeping down the weeds.In order to provide good conditions for root development, earthing up is usually done 20-25 days after sowing by putting some soil around the base of the turnip plant, so that roots are covered. Sometimes, side shoots are developed which should be removed periodically. Earthing up and top-dressing of nitrogenous fertilizer are done simultaneously.
Water Management	Usually seed is sown when there is sufficient moisture in the soil. First irrigation is given soon after germination completed. Alternatively, seed is sown in dry soil and then field is irrigated immediately. In general, the crop needs irrigation at an interval of 10-15 days. In order to obtain early and higher percentage of germination, there should be adequate soil moisture at the time of sowing. If field is dry, pre-sowing irrigation should be done. Sometimes, even after sowing when seeds are not germinating owing to lack of moisture, it is advisable to provide light irrigation. Usually, rainy season crop does not require any irrigation except during the long spells of drought. On the other hand, summer season crop requires irrigation at 5 to 6 days interval. Both basin and furrow methods of irrigation are adopted to irrigate turnip in India. High moisture at the beginning of root swelling depresses the yield, which is attributed to changes in nitrogen utilization within the plant. The crop should be supplied with plenty of water from root enlargement to harvest as it is the most sensitive critical stage and any stress will drastically lower the yields.
Harvesting, Yield and Storage	The turnip roots should be harvested as soon as they attain marketable size of 5-10 cm in diameter. If harvesting is delayed, the roots soon become fibrous and hard, and the quality deteriorates very rapidly. Harvested roots are cleaned, tops are cut and roots are graded according to size and tenderness. The average yield of turnip varies from 20.0-25.0 tonnes per hectare. Turnip does not store well. Application of wax emulsion to the roots neither improved nor retarded weight loss, but dipping in hot paraffin reduced shrinkage and improved the appearance of roots.

14.9. Tuber Crops

14.9.1. Cassava

Title	Description
Climatic Requirements	Cassava is a crop best suited to the low land tropics a warm, moist climate where mean temperature range from 25-29 °C. Cold climate is detrimental to its growth, and at temperatures below 10 °C, growth of the plant is arrested. It can not withstand frost during its active growing period, so that it can only be profitably grown in regions, which are frost free for at least the time required for the crop to mature. Sprouting of the cutting requires a minimum temperature of 10 °C, an optimum of

29 °C and a maximum of 34-38 °C. The optimum soil temperature for growing cassava is about 30 °C, while the optimum air temperature for the season as a whole is 24-28 °C. Altitude affects cassava production, through its moderating effect on temperature. The upper altitudinal limit for cassava production is 1800 m and this corresponds to a mean soil temperature of about 18 °C. The optimum rainfall for cassava is 100-150 cm per year and well distributed. Tuber formation in cassava is under photoperiodic control. Under short day conditions, tuberisation occurs readily, but when the day-length is greater than 10-12 hours, tuberisation is delayed and subsequent yields are lower.

Soil Conditions

In India, most of the cassava is in the central lateritic belt (ultisols) of Kerala and the red soils (alfisols) of Thiruvanathapuram (Kerala) and Kanyakumari and south Arcot (Tamil Nadu) districts. It is also grown in black soils (vertisols) in around Salem districts (Tamil Nadu), the coastal sandy loam (entisols) of Kerala and alluvial soils (entisols) of Godavari district in Andhra Pradesh. The best soil for cassava cultivation is a light, sandy loam soil of medium fertility. Good drainage is important in clay or poorly drained soil, root growth is poor, so that the tuber to shoot ratio is considerably decreased. Under conditions of very high fertility, cassava tends to produce excessive vegetation at the expanse of tuber formation.

Planting Time

Name of the States	Time of planting
Trivendrum (Kerala)	April-May
Tamil Nadu	September
Andhra Pradesh	June
Hyderabad	March
North Eastern States	February-April

Cutting Requirements, Methods of Planting and Spacing

Cassava is propagated vegetatively through stem cuttings taken from the previous season crop and so the stems are often to be stored for two to three months. Stems are kept in vertical position gave better sprouting as compared to those in horizontal position. Among the different portions of stem used as planting material, the lower part has been found more suitable. Planting 20 cm long setts at a depth of 5 cm resulted in higher yield. For gap filling 40 cm long setts are ideal. The optimum spacing for cassava planting is 90 x 90 cm for branching types and 75x75 cm for non-branching types. The optimum planting density for cassava may range from 14,000 to 17,000 plants/ha.

Nutritional Requirements and Their Management

For good yield, it requires 25.0-30.0 t/ha farm yard manure, 125-180 kg/ha nitrogen, 90 kg/ha phosphorus, and 100-150 kg/ha potash per hectare. The farm yard manure should be applied 20 days before transplanting. Full quantity of phosphorous and potash and half quantity of nitrogen should be applied at the time of planting. Remaining quantity of nitrogen is applied at 30-45 days after planting.

Intercultural Operations

Intercultivation to suppress weed growth in the initial stages and to encourage tuber development is an essential requirement in cassava production. Light raking of soil, followed by earthing up twice at one and two months after planting had significant beneficial effect on cassava yield as compared to no inter cultivation or only one inter cultivation. For herbicidal weed control in cassava, diuran at 1.6 kg active ingredient per hectare, atrazine (2 kg/ha) or fluometuron (2 kg/ha) have been found

	effective. The herbicide are applied before emergence and keeps the weeds in check for two months or so.
Water Management	In India, cassava is raised under irrigation only in parts of Tamil Nadu and some other non traditional areas where cassava cultivation is spreading in the recent past. Usually, one irrigation is given on the day of planting followed by two irrigations at an interval of 3-5 days till the plants established. Further irrigations are given depending on the distribution of rainfall.
Harvesting, Yield and Storage	The tuber formation in cassava commences by the end of the second month after planting. With time the tuber continues to increase in size, due to the deposit of large amounts of starch within the tuber tissues. For most cultivars, this occurs 12-18 months after planting, although some recent released early - maturing cultivars ready for harvest in 8-9 months. The yield of cassava varies from 30-50 t/ha depending upon varieties, agrotechniques adopted and condition of growing.

14.9.2. Colocasia (Taro)

Title	Description
Climatic Requirements	Colocasia requires a tropical climate but can be grown in the sub tropics and to certain extent in the warmer parts of the temperate region. It also can not withstand cooler climate where frost is a problem, but grows even under subtropical climate where temperature averages around 21 ^{0}C. Rainfall in colocasia growing areas is highly variable. It ranges from 1000 mm in parts of Burma to over 5000 mm annually in some regions of India.
Soil Conditions	Colocasia is a tropical crop prefering abundant supply of water. It can be grown in almost all types of soil except clayey soil. However, a sandy loam, well-drained and friable soils are ideally suited. The optimum soil pH range is between 5.5 to 7.0.
Planting Time	In northern parts of the country, planting of colocasia is done in February-March (summer crop), and in June-July (for raising rainy season crop) whereas in the southern parts and in Gujarat State, September-October would be ideal planting time.
Planting Requirements, Methods of Planting and Spacing	Corms, cormels or head sets are used as planting materials. The cormels are preferred in places where winter is severe for the convenience of storing till the next planting season, Corms or cormels should be planted in rows 30 to 45 cm apart with a row to row spacing of 45 to 60 cm and 6 to 8 cm in depth. The 56 g seed size gave the highest yield but the seed size of 28 g has been found to most economical. Planting should be done either in flat beds or on ridges. While planting, care should be taken that planting depth is not exceeded 8 cm; otherwise germination would not be up to the mark.
Nutritional Requirements and Their Management	During field preparation 10.0 to 15.0 tonnes of farm yard manure or compost is incorporated in the soil. Applications of 100 kg nitrogen, 60 to 80 kg phosphorus and 80 to 100 kg potassium per hectare have been found to give good yield. Three-fourth of total nitrogen is applied along with whole quantity of phosphorus and potassium at the time of planting. Remaining quantity of nitrogen is applied in the form of top-dressing at the time of earthing.

Intercultural Operations	Colocasia requires shallow hoeing for better development of corms and cormels. Generally, two earthings would be sufficient. At the time of earthing, additional shoots should be pruned off, leaving one or two main shoots in order to increase more number of cormels. Top dressing of nitrogen should also be done at this stage.
Water Management	Colocasia performs well only under moist situation. When rainfall is not enough to retain soil moisture near field capacity, supplementary irrigation is required. At the time of planting, presence of adequate soil moisture is needed. The subsequent irrigation would depend on the growing season and soil type. As such, colocasia needs lot of water, crop grown during summer should be irrigated at short intervals, atleast once in a week. Whereas in rainy season, if rains are fairly distributed, no need to irrigate the crop. Irrigation during rainy season is only needed when long dry spell is occurred. Irrigation after mansoon season may be given at 10 to 12 days interval.
Harvesting, Yield and Storage	The crop matures in about 130 to 140 days after sowing. It is common practice in our country to take out some side cormels twice or so before final harvesting or partial harvesting. The practice helps grower to get a premium price during the period when there is acute shortage of colocasia tubers in the market. In some parts of the country (Gujarat, Kerala, Karnataka, Tamil Nadu etc.) where only leaves of colocasia are preferred to cook as vegetables and tuber as propagating materials for next year crop. The leaves become ready for harvesting in 45 to 60 days after planting.About 20.0 to 25.0 t/ha tuber yield is an average where leaves are usually not plucked. This yield may come down to 15.0 to 20.0 t/ha, if leaves are plucked occasionally. In case of the type of colocasia from which leaves are harvested frequently in that type 6.0 to 8.0 t/ha of corms and cormels are obtained.

14.9.3. Elephant Foot Yam

Title	Description
Climatic Requirements	It can be grown in tropical and sub-tropical climatic conditions with mean annual temperature of 30-35 ^{0}C and elevation of 800 meters from mean sea level. It requires a well-distributed rainfall, humid and warm weather during vegetative growth. During sprouting high temperature is beneficial. For the formation and enlargement of corms, cool and dry weather condition favour. As a rainfed crop, it requires a well distributed rainfall of 1000-1500 mm spread over a period of 6 to 8 months. Water stagnation is detrimental during any phase of growth.
Soil Conditions	It is grown successfully on sandy loam, alluvial and medium black cotton soils having good provision of water drainage. Since food material is accumulated in the form of underground corm, therefore soil should be friable. The growth of corms in heavy soil is very much restricted and is reflected on the production.

Planting Requirements, Planting Time, Methods of planting and spacing

About 6,000 kg/ha of seed tubers is needed.

Types of crop	Planting time	Size of planting materials	Spacing	Duration of crop	Atmospheric rest period
First year crop	May	25-40 g (Obtained from four year's corms)	30 x30cm	8 months	3-4 months
Second year crop	May	125-150 g (Obtained from first year's corms)	60 x 30 cm	8 months	3-4 months
Third year crop	May	1 kg (Obtained from second year's corms)	60 x 60 cm	8 months	3-4 months
Fourth year crop	May	2-4 kg (Obtained from third year's corms)	150 x 50 cm	8 months	3-4 months

Nutritional Requirements and Their Management

Soil is heavily manured with bulky organic manure at 20.0 to 25.0 tonnes per hectare. Besides, application of nitrogen 40 to 60 kg/ha, phosphorus 60 to 80 kg/ha and potassium 40 to 60 kg/ha are required per hectare. From the results of experiments at CTCRI, Trivendram, recommended 25.0 tonnes of farmyard manure and 80, 60 and 100 kg/ha of N, P and K, respectively.The first application at planting with full amount of phosphorous and half of nitrogen and potash in the pits along with farmyard manure helps in the rapid development at the early stage. The second application of remaining quantity of nitrogen and potash should be done 60-70 days after emergence of shoot. It should be followed by earthing up for better bulking of the corm and good drainage.

Intercultural Operations

Occassional hoeing is beneficial for plant growth and for corm development. The weeds are kept down by hoeing. Being a perennial crop, weeds may pose problem. Therefore, intercultivation is always preferred. Two interculture operations, first at 45 days after planting and second one month after the first have been recommended.

Water Management

The crop is irrigated first during the emergence of shoot and subsequent irrigation is done if soil becomes dry before the onset of monsoon. When the crop approaches maturity, irrigation should be light and at long intervals in the absence of optimum moisture in the soil. Care should be taken to prevent stagnation of water during the rainy season.

Harvesting, Yield and Storage	The crop is harvested after 7-10 months from planting. Yellowing and drooping down of the leaves are the signs of maturity of the crop. The crop can be harvested earlier before full maturity for early market and higher price. The corm yield ranges from 50.0 to 100.0 t/ha depending upon the weight of seed corm used at planting. The corms can be retained in the soil even after full maturity. It can be stored for several months in well-ventilated rooms without any damage. It is better to harvest crop at right stage, as the rate of loss of moisture from the corms for the first four days is about 3-4 per cent per day, the total extending to even 25 per cent or more in the first month of storage.

14.9.4. Potato

Title	Description
Climatic Requirements	It requires favourable environmental conditions such as low temperature and short day conditions at the time of tuberization for rapid bulking rate. About 20 ^{0}C temperature is good for tuber formation and it reduces as the temperature increases. Tuberization is badly affected at about 30 ^{0}C temperature. At higher temperature, the respiration rate increases and the carbohydrates produced by photosynthesis are consumed rather than stored in tuber. High temperatures at any part of growing period affect the size of leaflets, thereby reducing the tuber formation. It grows best under long day conditions sunshine alongwith cooler nights are essential for reducing the spread of diseases.
Soil Conditions	Potato can be produced on a wide range of soils, ranging from sandy loam, silt loam, loam and clay soil. Soil for potato should be friable, well arrated, fairly deep and well supplied with organic matter. Well-drained sandy loam and medium loam soils, are most suitable for potato cultivation. Alkaline or saline soil is not suitable for potato cultivation. They are well suited to acidic soils (pH 5.0 to 6.5) as acidic conditions tend to limit scab diseases.
Planting Time	In plains: Early crop: Third week of September to first week of October.Main crop: End of first week to beginning of third week of October. Late crop: End of third week of October to first week of November II. In hills: Potato is planted in hills from the third week of February to second week of April. In the southern hills near Ootacamund and in Nilgiris, planting is done three times in a year, i.e. in the month of February, April and September. In the plateau regions of Maharashtra, Bihar and Madhya Pradesh, potato is raised in rainy and winter seasons. In the Mysore plateau, the summer and winter crops are planted in April-June and in October-December, respectively.
Seed Rate, Methods of Sowing and Spacing	The seed requirements for a hectare on the basis of seed size are given below: Large size- 25-30 q/ha; Medium size- 15-20 q/ha; Small size- 10-15 q/ha; Out tubers- 8-12 q/ha. Potato is planted mainly by two methods: 1. Ridge and Furrow Method: In this method, the ridges are prepared. The length of the ridges depends on slope of the plot. Too long ridges and furrows are not supplied with irrigation water conveniently. The potato tubers are planted on ridges and irrigation water is let into the furrows.

2. Flat Bed Method: In this method, the whole plot is divided into beds of convenient length and width. The shallow furrows are opened and potato tubers are planted at recommended distance. The tubers are covered with the original soil of furrows. When the germination is completed and plants become 10 to 12 cm height, earthing should be done. Suitable plant spacing in relation to potato seed grades are given in the below:

Diameter of tuber from longer axis	Planting distance (row x seed)
2.5-3.5 cm	50 x 20 cm or 60 x 15 cm
3.5-5.0 cm	60 x 25 cm
60 x 40 cm	5.0-6.0 cm

Nutritional Requirements and Their Management

Soils poor in organic matter content should be supplied with 25.0 to 50.0 t/ha of farm yard manure or compost during land preparation, preferably a fortnight before planting. Potato plant is a heavy surface feeder. When it is grown in medium type of soils, it needs 100 to 150 kg nitrogen, 80 to 100 kg phosphorus and 80 to 100 kg potassium per hectare. Two-third to three fourth quantity of nitrogen along with whole quantity of phosphorus and potassium should be applied at the time of planting. Remaining one fourth to one third nitrogen should be applied 30 to 35 days after planting i.e. at the time of first earthing up or when plants become 25 to 30 cm in hight in the form of top dressing.

Intercultural Operations

In potato crop, both types of weeds are found i.e. broad-leaved weeds as well as narrow leaved weeds. The use of weedicides in potato crop in general is not essential because earthing up operation destroy almost all weeds, if some how, weed plants are growing on ridges, they may be pulled out by hands. Pre-emergence application of nitrofen @ 1.0 kg a.i./ha or alachlor @ 2.0 kg a.i./ha or post-emergence application of propanil @ 1.0 kg a.i./ha may be used in solution form (800-1000 litre/ ha). Care is taken while spraying of post- emergence herbicides that they should not come in the contact to potato plants. Earthing is done when the plants are 15 to 22 cm in height. Generally, earthing is done at the time of top dressing of nitrogenous fertilizer. The ridges should be broad, loose and high enough to cover up tubers. If necessary, a second earthing may be done after two week of the first one. A mould board plough or a ridger may be used for earthing up in large area.

Use of Plant Growth Regulators

Soaking of potato seed tuber in CCC at 500 mg/l, sodium ascorbate at 100 mg/l , cytozyme at 5 per cent or foliar sparys with ethephon at 400 mg/l increased tuber yield.

Water Management

Pre-irrigation or just after planting may be given. The first irrigation is essentially done within 30-35 days after planting. However, when soil moisture seems insufficient for sprouting, intervals of first irrigation should be reduced. Further irrigation is done as and when crop needs. As regards method of irrigation in potato, the furrow method is commonly followed.

Harvesting, Yield and Storage

Harvested potatoes are heaped under shade for a couple of days so that their skin become hard and soil adhering with them is also separated out. Under good crop management, 35.0-45.0 tonnes of marketable potatoes of good quality can be produced from one hectare land. The sorting operation is the most important, in that all cut tubers, bruished, injured by insect-pests and diseases are removed. Sorted healthy tubers are graded in to different grades based on diameter of the tubers reduce the prices in the market. Therefore, such tubers should be sorted and marked seperately. Over sized tubers are great in demand for chip making. Very small sized tubers are also not remaining unsold. These tubers are purchased by poor people for making vegetable by partially cushing them before cooking. However, both the over sized and under sized are quite unsuiatable for seed purposes. Potatoes can be stored in the cold storage at the temeperatures of 34 to 37 ^{0}F and relative hunidity of 90-95 per cent.

14.9.5. Sweet Potato

Title	Description
Climatic Requirements	Sweet potato is essentially a worm weather crop. Growth is best at temperatures above 24 °C. When temperatures fall below 10 °C, growth is severely retarded. The crop is damaged by frost and this fact restricts its cultivation in the temperate regions to areas with a minimum frost-free period of 4-6 months. The optimum temperature for tuber growth is about 25 °C. Sweet potato is a sun-loving crop, and does best where the light intensity is relatively high. Shading of the crop under cultivation should therefore be avoided. Optimal conditions for sweet potato are found in regions with 75-100 cm of rainfall per annum, with about 50 cm falling during the non-growing season, makes it relatively easy to propagate and maintain vine growth that will be used as planting material during the next season. Although, the crop can withstand drought conditions, it appears that yields are considerably reduced if the drought occurs within the first six weeks after planting or at the time of tuber initiation.
Soil Conditions	The best soil for sweet potato is sandy loam and clay sub soil. It can be grown in loamy to clay loam soil also. Laterite soils of good depth and better fertility can also be considered suitable for its cultivation. Sweet potato is very tolerant to acid soils (pH as below as 5.0). The soil pH between 5.2 and 6.7 is appropriated for sweet potato. Highly fertile soil favours luxuriant growth of vines and unfavourable for tuber development. Heavy clay is undesirable and causes harvest problem. It is important that soil should be well drained.
Planting Time	In India, the time of planting varies from state to state, as given below:

States	Planting time
1. Bihar	1. February-March 2. September-October
2. Uttar Pradesh	1. October -November 2. June-July 3. September-October
3. Punjab	1. February-March 2. July-August
4. Haryana	1. February-March 2. July-August

5. Madhya Pradesh	1. June-July 2. September-October
6. Maharashtra	May-June
7. Andhra Pradesh	October-November
8. Karnataka	October-November
9. Tamil Nadu	1. September 2. May
10. Kerala	September-December
11. West Bengal	September-October
12. Orissa	September-October
13. Gujarat	1. October-November 2. May-June

Planting Reguirements, Methods of Planting and Spacing

Sweet potato is mainly planted by vine cuttings and sometimes by sprouts, which are obtained from tubers. Vines are obtained from previous crop. For obtaining sprouts, healthy tubers of medium size are planted in well-prepared nursery bed at 25 cm in rows of 60 cm apart. For obtaining planting both primary and secondary nurseries are prepared. For primary nursery preparation, the nursery preparation starts three months prior to planting in the main field. For one hectare of land, about 100 m^2 of primary nursery area and about 100 kg of medium size weevil free seed tubers (125-150 g each) are required. The tubers are planted at a spacing of 20 cm in ridges formed 60 cm apart. To ensure quick growth of vines, it is top-dressed with 1.5kg urea/100 m^2 at 15th days after planting. The nursery is irrigated on every alternate day for first 10 days and thrice a week thereafter. At 45th day, the vines are cut in a length of 20-30 cm for further multiplication in the second nursery.

For secondary nursery, to produce enough planting material to plant one hectare of land, vines obtained from the primary nursery are further multiplied in the second nursery to an extent of 500m^2. About 500kg farm yard manure or compost is applied at the time of preparation of nursery and ridges are formed at a spacing of 60 cm apart. Vines obtained from primary nursery or from freshly harvested crop are planted in the secondary nursery at a spacing of 20 cm within ridges. To ensure enough vegetative growth, 5 kg urea is applied in two splits, at 15th day and 30th day after planting. For better establishment of vines in the nursery, irrigations are provided every alternate day for the first 10 days and thrice a week, thereafter. The vines will be ready for planting in the main field within 45 days. The depth of planting of tubers is 5 to 10 cm. The planting of tubers is done about 90 to 100 days in advance of planting in the main field. Care for irrigation should be taken for proper sprouting and further growth. The sprouts are separated after 40 to 50 days from the mother tubers of planting, and planted in secondary nursery for growth. The cuttings, 20-30 cm in length having 3 to 5 nodes is found optimum for tuber production in different parts of India. Vines are planted at the distance of 20 to 30 cm in rows 45 to 60 cm apart. Generally, two methods are adopted for sweet potato planting in different seasons.

- Planting on ridges: This method of planting of sweet potato is followed usually during rainy season. Ridge planting facilitates to better drainage of water from the field and hence escapes the crop from any water stagnation as sweet potato affected adversely by water logging conditions.

- Planting on flat bed: This method can be followed during rabi season where water stagnation is no problem. Also places where rains are not so heavy and continuous, flat bed system of planting is followed even during *kharif* season.

Nutritional Requirements and Their Management

In order to provide better conditions for tuber development, about 10.0 to 15.0 tonnes of farm yard manure per hectare are incorporated during field preparation. Besides, application of nitrogen 50 to 75 kg, 40 to 60 kg phosphorus and 60 to 100 kg potassium per hectare are also required. Fertilizer for sweet potato is best given in splits. Usually two applications are sufficient. The first one is applied at or immediately after planting while the second application is done one month later. Where mechanical transplanter is used for planting, the first fertilizer application is in the form of the starter solution, given to the plants as they set in the field. Where starter solutions are not used, the first fertilizer application may be:

(i) Broadcast and incorporated into the soil at the time of soil preparation.
(ii) Given as a spot application after planting, or
(iii) Applied as a continuous or discontinuous band beside the ridges.

Biofertilizers have also been effective for increasing yield in sweet potato. On the basis of experimentation, it has been observed that 1/3 to 2/3 recommended dose of nitrogen + 10 kg Azospirillum/ha soil application alone with 2 kg Azospirillum per hectare vine dipping increased nitrogen efficiency and reduced nitrogen application. In acidic soil, liming is helpful in neutralizing soil acidity and application of 2000 kg Cao/ha increased the yield and improved the quality of sweet potato. Scurf injury was found to be checked in slightly acid soils.

Intercultural Operations

In order to provide favourable conditions for vine growth intercultural operations are done. First, it should be done 30 days after planting when some weeds have grown. This operation will keep down the weeds. The second intercultivation is done at about 70 to 75 days after planting. This is also high time for earthing up which is simultaneously done. The earthing up is usually done in the crop planted on ridges. Earthing up has been found to increase tuber yield. For controlling weeds, herbicides can also be applied in time. Application of chlorbromuron at 2 to 3 kg per hectare pre emergence has been found best selective weedicide in sweet potato. It controlled 85 per cent weeds upto 60 days after planting. In sweet potato, vines have tendency to from nodes which results in diversion of same quantity of nutrients for the development of such roots. To save nutrient losses, it is essential to lift and turn the vines. So that they are disconnected from the soil. This operation helps in increasing tuber yield, which is done during early stage of vine growth. However, it is not necessary to disturb the vines when they have grown to a considerable length. Though, pruning of vines is not usually done and also it is not advisable to add cost of cultivation for this operation. However, the extraordinary long vines should be taken up simultaneously when turning of vines or earthing up of is done. The pruned vines are feed to animal, which is a good green fodder.

Use of Plant Growth Regulators	Treatment with growth substances has proved effective in increasing the tuber yield in sweet potato. Foliar applications of CCC at 250, 500 and 100 ppm have been found to increase the yield. Higher tuber yield by treatment with 50 to 150 ppm CCC has been reported. Larger number of tubers and higher yield by the application of ethephon at 250 ppm is also one of the report for enhancing yield of sweet potato.
Water Management	Generally, kharif crop does not require irrigation. However, rabi crop can not be grown without irrigation. In the initial stages of crop growth when vines have not covered the soil properly more water is needed and that is about 35 to 40 days after planting. After, growing vines cover soil nearly entire ground surface results in less loss of moisture through evapo-transpiration. However, this does not mean that water requirement is less. It is used by growing vines and developing roots. For better development of root and higher yields, sufficient soil moisture supply should be ensured with the assured irrigation facilities, especially during rabi season.
Harvesting, Yield and Storage	In north India, sweet potato takes about 5-6 months for maturity, while it matures with in four months in the south. With in limits, the yield/ha will increase if the crop remains in the ground longer, but the tubers become less palatable and weevil damage and rots become more noticeable with age. The maturity of tubers can be determined by cutting fresh tubers. The cut surface of the immature tubers gives a dark greenish colour while in mature tubers, the cut ends dry clearly. Besides this, as soon as leaves start showing pale yellow colour and soil near the base of the plant shows cracks, the harvesting should be started. Sweet potato matures in 120 to 180 days depending on cultivars, climatic conditions, soil type etc. The maturity of the sweet potato tuber can be judged by cutting tubers, when the latex dries up without becoming black. Irrigate the field four to six days prior to harvest is helpful. While digging out tubers, care should be taken to avoid mechanical injuries, which would affect the storage and quality. The yield fluctuates with cultivars, seasons of planting, soil types and fertility. Under good management paractices, yield can range from 35.0-40.0 t/ha in irrigated and 8.0-10.0 t/ha under rainfed conditions. After harvesting, tubers are allowed to curing for four to five days. After curing, sorting is done. Healthy tubers can be stored at 55 to 60 ^{0}F with a relative humidity of 85 to 90 per cent. Curing of tubers is rapid and satisfactory when they are kept for 3 to 4 days at 45 to 50 ^{0}C at 85 per cent relative humidity.

14.9.6. Yams

Title	Description
Climatic Requirements	The optimum range of temperature is between 25 to 30 ^{0}C. Yams can not tolerate frost and growth as affected at a temperature below 20 ^{0}C. High rainfall is beneficial for obtaining higher yield of tuber. Yams require a well distributed rainy days for 7-10 months. Low moisture supply at the early stage may kill the young shoots, which have exhausted reserve food of the old set. Day length more than 12 hours at

the early stages promotes vine growth, while short photo period favours tuber development. Yams are relatively tolerant to dry conditions, but thrives best when supplied with ample moisture. The white yam (*D. rotundifolia*) requires a rainfall of 100-150 cm evenly distributed over six or seven-months period for optimum yield. But lesser yam (*D. esculenta*) comes well in areas experiencing a rainfall of 90-100 cm.

Soil Conditions

Tuber growth and development largely depend on the texture and preparation of the soil. Some Dioscorea go deep into soil and some spread on the upper strata. For better development, it requires a deep, rich, friable and well-drained sandy loam soil. Heavy soils require much cultivation to ensure friability and good aeration.

Planting Time

The best time of planting is June-July i.e. just beginning of monsoon season. It may be some variation from region to region.

Planting Requirements, Methods of Planting and Spacing

Yams are mainly propagated vegetatively and the material commonly used for planting is tuber piece or small whole tubers. The tubers are cut into seed pieces consisting of head, middle and tail. Planting is done mainly by three methods:

(i) The tubers are planted on the flat bed.
(ii) They are planted on mounds or ridges or on raised beds.
(iii) They are planted in trenches.

When soil is light, soft and deep, flat bed method is followed, otherwise planting on mounds or ridges or on raised beds is most common. Mounds are prepared by drawing the top soil up to 40 to 50 cm high and wide at the base. The size of mounds depends on local practices. Tubers are planted deeply. In case of planting in trenches, they are first opened and filled with rich soil and compost into which the tubers are planted. The cutting of large tubers in to setts is done 1-2 days before the envisaged date of planting, this helps the cut surface to heal over before placing in the ground. While pertaining the set, care must be taken to keep the skin – cut surface ratio as high as possible. Dusting the cut surface with ash is a common traditonal practices. Treating with pesticides to avoid damage of the sett is also under certain conditon. The distance of planting between two hill 50 cm and between two row 150 cm. With this spacing about 13,300 tubers or sets will be needed to raise the crop on one-hectare area.

Nutritional Requirements and Their Management

Yams require plenty of organic manure. About 15.0 to 20.0 tonnes of farm yard manure or compost per hectare incorporated during the preparation of field or during ridging and mounding. Application of nitrogen, phosphorous and potash at the rate of 80:60:80 kg/ha, respectively have been recommended for *D. esculenta* and *D. alata*. The first dose of nitrogen is applied in two months after planting by that time germination is completed. The second dose of nitrogen is top-dressed or applied in a ring round the base of the vine at a radius of 15 cm and at a depth of 3 to 5 cm. The rate of application depends on the soil type and previous cropping.

Intercultural Operations

Shallow hoeings are done to provide better aeration for good plant growth and for keeping down the weed. Sometimes, earthing is also done which help in giving support to the vines and also prevent water stagnation very near to the base of the vines. It has been reported that yams are particularly sensitive to competition of weeds during the early parts of their growth. The critical stages for weed interference in yams synchronises with growth phaese when leaf development and tuber bulking are maximum. Pre- emergence application of any one of the weedicide like simazine , atrazine and telvar @ 3 kg /ha has been found effective for controlling weeds in yams.

Yams must be staked for getting good yield. Available reports show that staking in yams is beneficial. But staking is costly and laborious. However, staking exposes a greater leaf area to insulation and this encourages greater photosynthesis. These are several methods of staking and grouped them as indivdual staking, pyramidal staking and trellising. Some of the important prevailing in various yams growing are (a) Stakes of bamboo or weed 2 to 5 m long and 2-10 cm thick, are used separetely for individual plants. (ii) Support of stem residuces of crops or live crops like sorghum, pegion pea, cotton, maize, castor etc. This is usually followed in intercropping and mixed cropping systems. Dioscorea species like *D. esculenta* having comparetively weak vines can be grown on such live supports (iii) In homestead farming, perennial trees such as jackfruit, mango, tamarind etc. are tied by which one such tree can provide support to many yam vines. In Kerala state, vines are usually trailes on ropes tied with coconut and other tall trees and (iv) Pyramidal staking is a practice where few adjacent stakes each carrying separate yam vines are scanted and tied at the top from a pyramidal structure.

Use of Plant Growth Regulators

Yam tubers undergo a period of dormancy at the end of the season, usually for 2-3 months. Early sprouting causes considerable shrinkage and damages to seed tubers, hence sprouts are frequently removed. Treatment with 4-8 per cent solution of ethylene chlorohydrin by quick dip breaks the dormancy of yam. Soaking of tubers in 1 per cent solution of maleic hydrazide (MH) on the other hand, delayed the sprouting in storage, pre harvest application of MH also proved effective in this respect.

Water Management

It requires regular supply of water through rains or artificial irrigation. Irregularities in the supply of moisture will affect the tuber development adversely.

Harvesting, Yield and Storage

When the leaves turn yellow and the vines completely dry up, the crop is ready for lifting, which will be in about 8-9 months after planting. For convenient harvesting, the soil around the plant is dug with the help of the spade carefully avoiding any injury to the tuber and then tubers are removed from the soil. To produce seed yams, harvesting is done by cutting the tubers from the crown, which is planted. About 20.0 to 35.0 tonnes of tubers are obtained under good crop management. The yams can easily be stored for long time. The tubers may be stored (i) by tying them on vertical states in shaded area (barn storage), (ii) by heaping the tubers pyramid-shape in well ventilated room or under shade, and (iii) by placing the tubers in a layer or in racks under shade. There is considerable loss in weight during storage. The losses are due to evaporation of water from the tubers and due to respiration.

14.10. Spices and Condiments

14.10.1. Black Pepper

Title	Description
Climatic Requirements	Pepper is a tropical plant and prefers a warm-humid climate for commercial production. It has been successfully grown from sea level to about 100 m on the inner slopes of Western Ghats from Kanyakumari to northern border of north Kanara and between latitudes of 20 ^{0}N and 20 ^{0}S. Being a tropical plant, black pepper requires an optimum temperature range of 25 – 35^{0}C. The crop tolerates temperatures between 10^{0} C and 40^{0} C. Black pepper requires a heavy rainfall, though a dry season of some duration does not appear to harm it. However, too long an exposure to sun or a very prolonged dry period certainly affects it adversely. Long continuous droughts stop the vegetation of the vines. A well distributed rainfall of 125–200 cm is considered ideal. Spells of dry weather followed by fairly heavy showers are conductive for the successful cultivation of pepper.
Soil Conditions	It is observed that flat land is more suitable for pepper cultivation than hilly slopes. If the hills are too steep, they are most to suffer from the heavy loss of surface soil during the monsoons, and in the dry seasons are liable to suffer from drought due to rapid drainage of moisture. However, level land should not be too swampy and free from flooding. Saline soil or soil containing an excess of salt is to be avoided. Virgin forest land is preferable being naturally richer in organic matter content for successful plantation. Rich friable loam with high humus and good drainage are best suited for its cultivation. Though, it thrives well in comparatively soil with an admixture of gravel and low humus content on poorer drained soil in coastal areas of Kerala. Heavy clay and sandy soils should be avoided. Alluvial soil and red laterite soils free from water stagnation are also considered excellent for growing pepper. Top soil is more important for black pepper, since a number of roots (67-85 per cent) are reported to be found in 0-30 cm deep even in 42 month old plants. The pH of soil should be 40.5 to 6.0.
Planting Time	Black pepper is generally planted with the onset of the monsoon. In traditional pepper growing areas like Kerala and Tamil Nadu rooted or unrooted cuttings are planted in June–July. Normally with the onset of monsoon 2-3 rooted cuttings of pepper are planted individually in the pits on the northen side of each standard. However, in case of unrooted cuttings, 4-5 cuttings per pit are planted and the number of nodes in this case may be 4-5. At least one node of the cuttings should go below the soil for proper rooting.
Seed Rate, Methods of Sowing and Planting Distance	Black pepper develops three types of aerial shoots viz. (1) Primary stem with long internodes and adventitious roots which cling to standard (2) Runners roots which originate from the base of the vines also have long internode which strike roots at each node and (3) Fruit bearing lateral branches with limited growth. Cuttings are raised mainly from the runner shoots, though terminal shoots can also be used. Cuttings from the lateral branches are seldom used since in addition to reduction

in the number of fruiting shoots, the vines raised from them are generally short lived and bushy in habit. However, rooted lateral branches are useful in raising pepper in pots (bush pepper).

Pits of 30 cubic cm are made on the side of standards like mango, jackfruit, coconut etc. The commercial crop is usually established by training the vines of specially planted support trees (standard) such as *Erythrina indica, Gravellia robusta* etc. Standard plants preferably may be planted one year in advance at a distance of 3–4 metres. However, standard trees should have certain special characteristics like (i) They should be quick growing. (ii) Withstand heavy pruning and (iii) Have a deep penetrating root system so as not to complete with pepper feeding roots. It is always advisable to have leguminous species as standard. Rooted cutting of pepper are then planted in June–July at the rate of 2–3 cuttings per standard about 30 cm away from the base of the support tree preferably on the northern side to avoid the scorching sun.

Nutritional Requirements and Their Management

For laterite soil, which are low to medium in major nutrients, the fertilizer recommendations at present for a pure black pepper crop is 100 g nitrogen, 40 g phosphorous and 140 g potash per vine per year. Only one-third of this quantity is applied during the first year. It is increased to 2/3rd in the second year. The full quantity is given from the 3rd year onwards. It is better to apply the fertilizer in two splits, one in May-June and the other in August-September.The fertilizers are applied at a distance of about 30 cm all around the vine and covered with a thick layer of soil. Care is taken to avoid direct contact of fertilizers with the roots of the pepper vines. Besides, organic manure in the form of cattle manure or compost is applied @ of 10 kg per vine during May. Application of lime at the rate of 500 g per vine during April-May in alternate years is also recommended.

Intercultural Operations

The pepper vines need proper care to achieve their vigorous growth. During the dry months, leafy twigs are tied to the basal portion of the standards to serve as mulch round the vines and also as a protection against heat. In the second years during the monsoon, replanting with rooted cuttings is done when there is a failure of establishment. On hill slopes, cover or catch crops should be grown in the rainy season to protect soil loss by erosion. Pepper vines generally prefer weed free conditions. Therefore, regular weedings should be done. Being a shallow rooted crop, earthing is also required, especially on slopes. Since, pepper vines are shallow rooted, they respond well to mulching with banana trash and dried grasses. The pepper vine grow vigorously and after one year attains a height of 1.5-2 m. During the initial stage, the vines are trained by tying with standard at an interval of 30 cm. The operation has to be carried out at regular intervals. The tying is done firmly around the node so that the nodal region is firmly attached and pressed against the standard so as to allow the roots to cling with the standards. The pepper vine is allowed to grow on the main stem with the lower portion kept clean and unbranched at least one metre from ground levels. Since pepper vines grow rapidly and it attains a height of 5-6 m within 3-4 years, the growth should be regulated by pruning. Regular pruning is done to produce lateral branches and planting at the same time while training the plant. The vines are trimmed at the top and prevented from growing too tall for convenience of pickings. If hard wood or dead supports are used. The vines are pruned back 7-8 times to encourage productive lateral shoots and also for easy harvestings. Partial removal of leaves had increased yield while total removal of leaves significantly reduced the yield. Pruning of standards is also required for proper development of pepper vines. All the branches of the standards at the lower half are removed to retain an upright single stem in the third year in March-April. Standard pruning is repeated every year in March-April as it reaches a height of 8 m.

Harvesting, Yield and Storage

The maturity of the crop depends on many factors like location, soil type, varieties etc. Pepper vine may commence bearing berries after one year of planting but it is not advisable to allow the flower-spikes so early. The first harvest is allowed during third year after planting, by the time vines should have reached the top of their support. Commercial bearing starts from the sixth year onwards. Duration of cropping life of varieties/hybrids the proper vine varies from 20-25 years. The black pepper dry yield ranges from 1.0 to 2.5 t/ha and the average is 1.8-2.0 t/ha. This is mainly depends on variety/hybrid used, agro-ecological situation, type of standard used and management practices followed. The dry recovery (per cent) varies from 31 to 35 per cent. Pepper berries of different maturity (green, yellowish-green and red), peeled or unpeeled, packed and sealed in clear polythene bags and stored at 4 ^{0}C and 42 per cent RH remained viable for 40 days. Red berries gave the highest mean germination (65 per cent) followed by yellowish green (52 per cent) and green berries (17 per cent). Peeling did not lead to higher germination percentage but hastened the initial rate of germination. Green berries are low in viability and vigour and unsuitable for planting. Those varieties, which start bearing late, have a longer life span. The productivity period of different varieties and suggested that the variety. Travanean requires earlier replanting than the Malabar. The variety Cherriyakaniykkadan requires the earliest replanting (9-12 years). On the other hand, Kalluvally could yield upto around 50 years. Main flowering starts in May-June. The light showers during this period are considered beneficial for the fruit set due to production of bisexual flowers. However, the flowering season is spread nearly 6 – 8 months from flowering to harvesting. The season for havesting of mature berries is from November to March. Plucking the spikes generally harvested when one or two berries become bright orange or red. As the spikes are tall, ripened berries are harvested with the help of ladders.

Curing of Black Pepper: For the preparation of black pepper, the berries are harvested slightly early while for white pepper, it is harvested at a slightly advance stage of ripeness, that is when the berries turned red. In black pepper, the spikes are heaped for 1-2 days then the berries are separated by rubbing or trampling and dried in the sun. The spikes are also directly dried in the sun for 5-7 days on mats or clean concrete floors, until the outer skins become dark brown to black and shrivel. This is the black pepper for commercial use. Generally, 100 kg of fresh berries yield about 26-30 kg of black pepper is due to commerce. Blackening of pepper is due to enzymatic oxidation of phenols, which is present in the epicarp and mesocarp. The white pepper is prepared by removing the outer pericarp (skin) of the harvested berries, either before or after drying by any one of the following technique .These are as follows:

(A) Water Steeping Technique

(i) Using ripe fresh berries: The harvested ripe spikes or berries are packed in gunny bags or steeped in water tanks or under running water for 7-10 days. The pinhead (undeveloped berries) and light berries floated are separated, dried and sold as 'pin heads' and 'light pepper'. The remaining sound berries are stirred 2-3 times daily while drying. After steeping on the eleventh day, they are heaped on a tarpaulin and rubbed by hand or trampled to remove the outer softened skin. The deskinned berries are then washed, drained and put into a galvanized iron vessel containing a solution of bleaching powder for two days. Then they are drained, dried in the sun and cleaned.

(ii) Using dried berries: The dried black berries are steeped in water for 10-15 days after which they are removed, rubbed, washed thoroughly, steeped again in bleaching solution for 2-3 days, drained, dried in the sun and sold as white pepper. However, the white pepper is more easily prepared from fresh ripen berries than from dried black pepper.

(B.) Steaming or Boiling Technique: This is an improved and more hygienic technique developed at the Central Food Technological Research Institute, Mysore. This process consists of the steaming or boiling fresh ripened berries for about 15 minutes. The boiled or softened berries are then passed through a motorized fruit-pulping machine for removing their outer skin. The deskinned berries are then washed and bleached with powder solution or any other bleaching chemical. The bleached white berries are drained and dried in the sun to get white pepper. The skins of the berries are collected at the other end of the machine and are immediately utilized for steam distillation for the recovery of valuable pepper oil. The recovery of white pepper is about 25 per cent of ripe berries.

14.10.2. Small Cardamom

Title	Description
Climate Requirements	Elevation, moisture and shade are the fundamental factors for the successful cultivation of cardamom. Hence, the cardamom areas are lie in the higher elevation of the western ghats in the southwest of India. The limits of elevation for successful cardamom cultivation in south India appear to be 600 and 1,500 m, but their most productive range seems to be from 900 to 1,350 m. The upper limits are probably largely determined by temperature and also depend on the maximum elevation in the locality. Cardamom is extremely susceptible to wind and therefore areas exposed to high winds are not suitable. At these elevations in the cardamom growing areas, the maximum temperature (from March to May) is rarely likely to rise above 35 °C and the minimum (December to January) may fall to 10°C. In the Western Ghats, cardamom is grown under rainfall conditions ranging from about 150 cm to over 580 cm.

Proceeding from south to north, generally, the rainfall in the southern parts of the Western Ghats where cardamom is grown, is much less i.e., 255 to 380 cm than in the heavier rainfall districts in the north. The rainfall however, is much better distributed in the southern hills than in the northern hills, where it is more seasonal and broken by long spells of dry weather. In the south, especially south of Shencottah, the north-east monsoon extends up to February while in the northern regions, it is usually over by November. Consequently, the rainfall is much better distributed in the south. In the extreme north eastern regions such as the hills of West Bengal, Assam and North-West Frontier Agency, the much greater distance from the equator may make up for higher elevations and cardamom could perhaps be grown in these regions at much lower elevations than those at which, it is grown in south India, provided other conditions are satisfied.

Soil Conditions

The cardamom requires a soil rich in humus. Water logging or excessive moisture accumulation is injurious to plantations therefore, sloppy land with good drainage should be preferred. The cardamom is raised chiefly on well-drained, rich forest loam and red, deep, good textured latrite soils with plenty of humus or leaf mould. A pH range between 6.0 and 7.0 is most favourable for the availability and effectiveness of most of the nutrients. Cardamom requires are usually acidic with a pH of 5.0 to 5.5 and therefore, application of lime at 5000 to 7500 kg per hectare is recommended particularly in Kerala and Karnataka so as to increase the pH to 6.0.

Sowing Time

In Mysore, sowing is usually done in September when good seeds are available. Germination in this region is generally satisfactory and takes about a month. In the southern areas of Nelliampathies, Annamalais, the cardamom hills of Kerala, Rajapalayam and Singampatti, there is rarely any likelihood of getting good seed early enough for sowing in September. In those areas, sowing is usually done in November and germination is irregular and takes a considerably longer time, even up to two months. The differential behaviour of the seeds sown at these two different times may be attributed to the temperature prevailing at the different times. In November and December, a sudden drop in both air and soil temperatures occur in the cardamom growing regions, and this may accounts for some of the difficulties experienced with cardamom seeds sown late in the year in the southern areas. Suckers planted in August survived best, with a mean mortality rate of 25 per cent and those planted on the surface has the lowest mortality rate of 17.5 per cent. However, in low rainfall areas, it may be planted in June – July.

Seed Rate, Methods of Sowing and Planting Distance

The cultural methods employed in the production of cardamom show considerable variations. They may be classified into four types: (i) Coorg "male" system (ii) North Kanara system (ii) Southern system (iv) Mysore system

The first two are quite distinct and seem to represent the opposites poles of agricultural development while the last two approximate to one another and no sharp line of demonstration is really possible between these two systems. Originally, as with all crops, the collection of cardamoms from the jungles sufficed to meet the requirements of local consumption and trade. Even at the present time, a certain amount of this spice is obtained in this way.

The next step involved the encouragement of the growth of cardamom in the jungles in which they were known to occur. This is done by felling a few large trees in suitable sites and waiting for cardamom seedlings to sprout. These are thinned out and bare patches supplied with the seedlings. The "male system" in Coorg practically amounts to this type of cardamom production. In a suitable area of jungle, plots of a size varying from 16 and 25 cents are cleared and planted with cardamom, either with self-sown or nursery raised seedlings. After this only weeding and harvesting of the crop takes place. These cardamom plots are always surrounded by tall untouched jungle and after some years, they are allowed too regenerate natural vegetation and new plots are opened.

In "North Kanara System" of cardamom production, there is a development of spice garden. These gardens are suited almost invariably at the lower ends of hill valleys and consist of small areas, which are planted primarilly with arecanut and grow pepper and cardamom as secondary crops. In this system, the cardamom is taken quite away from its natural environment and grown as a garden crop.

Under the "Southern System", practiced in Kerala, Madras and Mysore states, cardamom is planted in larger or smaller areas of jungle which have been cleared of all undergrowth and the overhead shade slightly thinned out. Planting is done either with seedlings obtained by jungle collection or by raising a nursery or with rhizomes from some earlier established plantation. The individual areas vary from a few hectares to more than 400 hectares. The standards of management vary very greatly from that of a highly organised plantation with a permanent labour force, staff and buildings to small areas with watchman and occassional visits from the owner and casual labour for weeding and harvesting.

The "Mysore system' is very similar to the southern system but consists essentially of the utilization of moist ravines for the crop in estates, which mainly grow coffee. The greater part of the area under cardamom is under southern sytstem and the description of the methods given later concern this system.

Seedlings are transplanted in pits with a size of (50 cubic cm) filled with compost and top soil at a spacing of 1.5-2.0 m either way. While planting, healthy seedlings are uprooted from the nursery, clumps separated and over grown roots are trimmed. The rhizome or suckers are planted 5-8 cm deep and soil is pressed well. They are planted in the pits in such a way that the taller tillers stand in the centre with the smaller ones on the sides. It is also ensured that the tillers are made to lean towards the soil to prevent wind damage. The seedlings are tied with wooden stakes to prevent it from being dislodged by the strong winds and monsoon rains. After planting, leaf mould is spread to serve as thick mulch.

Nutritional Requirements and Their Management

Application of well rotten farm yard manure or compost, poultry manure or jungle leaf mould @ 2-5 kg/plant or neem cake @ 1-2 kg/plant may be given once in a year during May-June along with super phosphate (180 g/plant) and muriate of potash (90 g/plant) are necessary for better growth of plants. The manure and fertilizer are thoroughly mixed with surface soil after application. For the subsequent application to be done in September, organic manure need not be applied. In valley areas and in high fertile soils, soil application of chemical fertilizers may be avoided and instead one application of organic manure may be added during May-June and NPK fertilizers given as foliar sprays @ 2 per cent twice in a year. The use of micronutrients especially zinc in deficient soils improves the cardamom crop by the application of 500 ppm of zinc on the foliage and 1.5 kg of zinc sulphate will be sufficient for one hectare.

Intercultural Operations

Immediately after planting, the plant base should be mulched well with available dry leaves to protect from erosion and conservation of moisture. It also helps in controlling weeds, better rooting and protection from direct exposure of sun and rain. Crop remains/leaves etc. makes better mulch and 4-5 tonnes/ha mulch are sufficient.

In established plantations, the annual operation under interculture consists of weeding, digging, removing of old and dried stems, lopping of shade trees, manuring and plant protection. First weeding is carried out in May-June after the last harvest, the second in August – September at the commencement of harvest and third in December – January in the beginning of the dry period. Weeds are spread round the clumps to serve as mulch. In the later part of monsoon, the light digging is done around the plant to a radius of about 60-75 cm to conserve the moisture.

In cardamom, for good yield, intercultural operations like forking, trashing and earthing up are essential. In forking, the plant base to a distance up to 90 cm and to a depth of 9-12 cm is found to enhance root proliferation and better growth of plants. Trashing consists of removing of tillers and dry leaves and leaf sheaths. This operation may be carried out once in a year at any time one-month after the final harvest. These materials can also be used as mulch. Earthing up operation is not required in normal plantation. However, due to erosion of soil or mismanagement, at that times, it is noticed that the top soil covering the plant base is washed away and the rhizomes and roots are exposed and in such situation, earthing up or the plant base with top soil is recommended during December-January. While carrying out this operation, care should be exercised to ensure that only the top soil is used, it is spread evently at the base covering only half the bulb portion of the rhizome. This operation helps to keep the top 10-15 cm soil loose and friable enabling root penetration and water percolation.

Use of Plant Growth Regulators

Sucker production (for propagation) is increased with treatment of 225 ppm ethrel (ethephon).

Water Management

Number of irrigations required depends on the rainfall received during its growth period. Judicious irrigations during summer months ensure increase in yield by at least 50 per cent. Irrigation is required generally from February to April. March to August is the critical period when development of young tillers and panicles takes place. If plants suffer at this stage, yield will be reduced. Irrigation can be done through pot irrigation, sprinkler irrigation and drip irrigation depending on the facilities available in the plantation.

Harvesting, Yield and Storage

Cardamom plants start bearing from the third year of planting, though an economic yield is usually obtained only from the fourth year onwards. The bearing span varies from 15-20 years. The fruiting period is about

	3-4 months from the opening of the flower to the ripening of the fruit. In most area, the peak-harvesting season is October-November. In Kerala and Tamil Nadu harvesting starts from August-September and continues till February-March, whereas in Karnataka, it starts in July-August and continues upto December-January. Harvesting is continued at intervals of 30-40 days and completed in 5-6 months. Capsules along with peduncles are picked in the correct stage of ripeness with specific objectives viz; • For making pickles, it is harvested at tender stage. • For curing, capsules are picked at dark green stage. • For seed purposes, picked at fully ripened stage.

14.10.3. Large Cardamom

Title	Description
Climatic Requirements	Large cardamom is a shade loving plant. Its natural habitat has been the humid subtropical semi-evergreen forests of mountaneous Sub-Himalayan region. The tracts receive a well-distributed annual rainfall, spread around 200 days to a total of about 2000-3500 mm. The weather remains mostly cloudy and foggy during monsoon months. The crop is grown at varying altitudes from 600-2000 meters above mean sea level. However, it is seen that the lower altitudes of cooler areas (near to the snow line) and higher altitudes of warmer areas are found well suited for its cultivation. The tract receives a monthly temperature ranging between 6 °C in December-January and 30 °C in June-July accompanied by constant high relative humidity. Frosts and hail storms are injurious, where as the heavy and continous rains during flowering are deterimental.
Soil Conditions	The crop requires moist but well drained loose soils having sandy loam to loam textures. The depth of the soil varies from few centimeters to several meters depending upon the topography and soil formation. Due to high rainfall conditions, the soils are mostly acidic with pH values ranging between 5.0 and 6.0. These soils are rich in organic matter and nitrogen due to constant leaf-fall from the shade trees and are generally found medium in phosphorus and medium to high in potassium contents of available forms.
Sowing Time	Suckers planted in August survived best, with a mean mortality rate of 25 per cent and those planted on the surface has the lowest mortality rate of 17.5 per cent in high rain fall area. However, in low rainfall areas, it may be planted in June – July.
Seed Rate, Methods of Sowing and Transplanting Distance	Large cardamom can be multiplied by seed as well as by vegetative methods of propagation. Plantation by raised seedlings commences bearing fruits after five years of plantation. Whereas, plants raised from separated rhizomes start fruiting after three years of planting. Therefore, vegetative method is generally preferred for commercial plantation of large cardamom. On large scale plantation, beds are made along side mountain streams, when water is taken along the narrow channels. This arrangement secures constant moisture supply and also to avoid water logging. During land preparation unwanted vegetation

and seeds are removed. Soil is dug properly and farm yard manure or compost is mixed into the soil sufficiently. However, large trees are left to provide the shade, as large cardamom prefers shady conditions. Individual pits can also be prepared with a size of 25 x 25 x 25 cm at spacing of 1 – 1.5 m and are filled with compost or farm yard manure (8-10 kg) alongwith top soil on the onset of monsoon. While planting, healthy rhizomes or suckers are separated from mother plants and transplanted in the pits at a depth of 8-10 cm and soil is pressed well. Planting is generally undertaken during May-June after receipt of sufficient rainfall.

Nutritional Requirements and Their Management

A ratio of nitrogen, phosphorous and potash @ 60:50:60 kg per hectare, respectively along with 18-20 tonnes per hectare of farm yard manure /compost/forest soils are recommended for robust varieties. These are applied during onset of monsoons (May-June) and durng harvesting (October-November). The fertilizers are applied either in bands or spreading and mixing with soil around each clump. For quick response, fertilizers may be dissolved in water as a 2-4 per cent solution and drenched around each plant.

Intercultural Operations

In early stage of plantation, weeding is more important for normal growth of plant. This can be achieved by three to four weedings in first years, two to three weedings in second year and two weedings annually. Thereafter, once or twice hoeings are helpful for growth and development of plants. In second and third years, gap filling should be undertaken. Lopping or prunings of shade trees are also essential operation as very dense shade causes hinderence in production. During dry period, irrigation are essential for constant growth and better production. In Sikkim, the tree of Utis (*Ulnus nepalensis*) has been adopted as shade trees for large cardamom.

Water Management

Cardamom plants do not thrive any drought or severe moisture streess conditions. A continuous dry spell of about two months may result in huge mortality of young plants and may also cause a year long delay for recovery of partially dried plants. Constant keep up of good soil mositure ensures better crop growth. Irrigation once in every 10 days in dry period commencing from December to April through ground channels, drip or sprinkler may be provided. Irrigation through ground channels require heavy water source and difficult to manage under steep slopes. In such cases either drip or sprinkler sets have been proven efficient specialized and advance system.

Harvesting, Yield and Storage

Vegetative propagated plants start fruiting after three years of planting. Flowerings start from March and continue upto August. After fertilization, fruit ripe within 4-6 months. The fruits of 'Sawaney' are ready for harvest in August-September and of Ramshai and Golshai in October-November. Harvesting is done by cutting the mature panicles with the help of a long narrow knife, which is specially made for this purpose. The harvesting is done only once a year. After harvesting, the individual capsules are separated from branches by hand. At the time of harvesting, old sterile dried shoots which do not bear fruits are also removed, by the same knife locally known as 'Elaichi Chhuri". Generally, large cardamom is harvested from August to November. Bearing span of large cardamom varies between 12-15 years, however, some well managed plantation profitable yield is can be taken upto 20 years. During the third year, when first flowering in new plantation, the yield of dry fruits is negligible (25 kg or so per hectare). In subsequent years, every year the yield increases till it maximum in the sixth and seventh years. Yield at this stage varies greatly. Three to ten tonnes of dry cardamom per hectare can be harvested according to the management and growing conditions of the plantation. Large cardamom is usually stored in bulk (on bamboo matting spread on the ground) or in gunny bags. The farmer practice is adopted usually by growers for storing cardamom in their homes and the later by traders in assembling and distributing markets. The retailers use glass or tin containers for storage.

14.10.4. Cinnamon

Title	Description
Climatic Requirements	It can be grown from sea level to 2000 m altitude in Indian conditions. In Sri-Lanka, it is abundant in the regions of 30-220 m above sea level and upto 1200 m. The crop grows best below 500 m altitude. A hot and moist climate is suited for its cultivation with an average temperature of 27 °C. Average annual rainfall ranges from 2000-2500 mm. Prolonged spells of dry weather are not conducive for its normal growth.
Soil Conditions	Cinnamon is a hardy plant, which can grow in any type of soil. Cinnamon prefers relatively elevated land. The quality of the bark is greatly influenced by the soil and ecological factors. A sandy soil mixed with humus is considered better. Waterlogged and marshy land should be avoided, as plants yield an undesirable bitter product, which is much less aromatic. Rocky and stony soils are not suitable for its cultivation.
Sowing Time	The seeds are sown in beds 10 X 20 cm apart and 3 cm deep in the month of June-July in nursery beds. Frequent irrigation is needed to maintain adequate moisture supply. Seeds germinate in about 15-20 days. After four months in the nursery at 15 cm height seedlings are transferred into polythene bags (30 X 15 cm) or baskets containing a mixture of soil, sand farm yard manure in the ratio of 3:3:1. They are transplanted to the main field after 5-6 months.
Seed Rate, Methods of Sowing and Planting Distance	Seedlings may be transplanted in April-May before the monsoon sets in or in the beginning of the monsoon. Before planting, the main field is cleared of weeds and plants however, some of the large trees are left for shade. A spacing of 15 to 20 m is maintained for the shade trees. Pits are dug at a distance of 3-4 metres with 50X50X50 cm size and filled with 20-25 kg of farm yard manure or leaf mould with top soil.
Nutritional Requirements and Their Management	Cinnamon requires large amounts of nitrogenous fertilizer as leaves young shoots and barks are used. Hence, it is necessary to apply nitrogenous fertilizers to encourage vegetative growth. In the first year, two or three months after planting, compost or farm yard manure @ 4-5 kg per plant is applied. During the second year an increased quantity of farm yard manure (8-10 kg) along with 25 g of muriate of potash should be given at the onset of the monsoon. From third year onward when production starts, a fertilizer quantity of 150 g nitrogen, 90 g phosphorus and 100 g of potassium per tree along with 10 kg of organic

manure in two spilt doses may be applied for commercial crop .

Intercultural Operations

Plants are provided with temporary shade by erecting a small pandal with twigs and covering it with leaves after transplanting. The seedlings or the plants are watered periodically specially during the dry months in the early stages of plantation. Weeding is one of the most important intercultural operations. Three to four weedings per year are recommended upto three to four years. After this, weeding may be reduced to one or two. Young trees cut close to the ground produced side shoots. This process is called "coppicing". This is done until the whole tree assumed the shape of a low bush with side shoots springing forth in profusion. Usually, the plants are coppiced after two years, the stem being cut to within 10-15 cm from the ground and covered with earth. This encourages the formation of shoots, of which four to six are allowed to grow for further two years before harvesting. The stem branches, which are kept straight by pruning, these are cut for processing when they are two to three metre height and 1.5-5 cm in diameter. After cutting, unwanted or distorted shoots and stumps are pruned properly and more soil is earthend up round them. The numbers of shoots in the young stools normally increase each year and reach a maximum after about eight years. When the side shoots develop and attain a brown colour and thickness one to two cm, they are ready for peeling of bark.

Use of Plant Growth Regulators,

Hard wood cuttings treated with IBA at 2500 ppm and IAA at 2500 ppm may be used for propogation of cinnamon.

Harvesting and Yield

The first cutting is made after 2nd or 3rd years of transplanting when the plant reaches a height of 150-200 cm. The stems or branches are cut during the rains to facilitate peeling, at the time when the red flush of the young leaves begin to change green and the sap is flowing freely. The cutter usually tests the stems to observe that either the bark lift easily or not. Harvesting season varies from May to November. Although harvesting on limited scale continues through out the year.

Curing: Cutting of the shoots for peeling commences when the rain ceases. The new growth of leaves on bushes should stop and the trees should have mature leaves. This is the indication of the free flow of sap between the bark and the woods. This is the proper stage at which the best quality of the bark can be obtained in the cuttings and this will be ready for cutting in subsequent seasons, within 18 months. Bulk of the bark is obtained from the shoots of 1.5 to 2 years old. Shoots selected for cuttings are usually one-meter long and 1-2 cm thick. So judging the suitability for peeling, the peeler makes an oblique cut and lifts the bark to see whether the bark separates easily with a free flow of sap to facilitate easy peeling. Shoots ready for peeling are removed from the stumps and the terminal ends of shoots are also removed. The cut stems are collected, tied, bundled and carried to the shades.

Peeling: Peeling is done generally with the help of a small knife with a round edge at the end. The cut stems or sticks are given longitudinal slits from one end to the other. The two halves of the entire bark are removed with the help of a knife. The sticks are rubbed in between hard pieces of wood so as to enable easy detachment of the bark if the bark does not peel easily.

Rolling: The barks are packed together and placed one above the other and pressed well. The bark slips are reduced to 20 cm length and are pilled up in small enclosures made by sticks. Then they are covered with dry leaves or mat to preserve the moisture for the next day's operation and also enhance slight fermentation. The retention of moisture is important for subsequent operation piping.

Piping: Rolled slips are taken to the piping yard for piping operation. Three sticks are driven into the ground in such a way that they cross each other at a height of 30 cm from the ground level. This serves as a support to keep the fourth stick, resting on the knot. The operator sits down and places the slips one by one on the forth stick to scrap off the outer skin with a small curved knife. The scarped slips are sorted into different grades according to thickness. The graded slips are trimmed, ends are cut and pressed over pipes. Now slips are rolled into pipes and soon after they are followed to dry. During drying smaller quills are inserted into the bigger ones, forming smooth and pale brown compound quills, which are known as pipes. The quills are arranged in parallel lines in the shade for drying as direct exposure to the sun at this stage can result in warpping. The dried quills thus obtained consist of a mixture of coarse and fine types and are yellowish brown in colour. The quills are bleached if necessary by sulphur treatment for about 8 hours and are sorted into grades according to thickness of bark as mentioned below:Fine or continental grade: Ranges from 10-19 mm in diameter.Hamburg grade: Ranges from 23-32 mm in diameter.Mexican grade: Intermediate in quality between fine and hamburg. The lower grades of cinnamon obtained as by products in the preparation of quills are exported in the following forms:

Quillings: Broken length and fragments of quills are sold as quillins.

Feathering: The inner bark of twigs and twisted shoots are sold by the name of feathering. They are also genuine cinnamons.

Chips: This includes terminated cut shoots before they are peeled. They invariably contain more or less woody materials. Chips are marketed after being washed and bleached.

14.10.5. Clove

Title	Description
Climatic Requirements	Clove is strictly a tropical plant and requires a warm humid climate. Although, there has been a general belief that clove requires proximity to sea for the proper growth and yield, experience in India has shown that the trees do well even in the hinterland conditions too. In fact, clove trees growing in sub-mountaineous region have also been found to perform better. Humid atmospheric condition and a well-distributed annual rainfall of 150 to 250 cm are the other ideal requirements of the crop. Clove thrives well in all situations ranging from sea level up to an altitude of 90 m. Elevation between 700 and 900 m is reported favourable for its cultivation.
Soil Conditions	Deep black loam soil with high humus content found in the forest region is best suited for clove cultivation. It grows satisfactorily on laterite soils, clay loams and rich black soils having good moisture and

good drainage. The soil pH should range from 4.0 to 5.6.

Seed Rate, Method of Nursery Raising and Transplanting of Seedling

Seeds are sown at a spacing of 2-3 cm and depth of 2 cm. Raised nursery bed on fertile soil with high percentage of organic matter is prepared in a shady place. The beds are normally 1 meters wide and 2 to 3 meters long. The seed should be placed flat at a depth of about 2.5cm at a spacing of 12 to 15 cm. The seeds completely germinate within 45 days, starting from the 3rd week to the 6th week. The slender and delicate seedling grews very slowly. Judicious watering is necessary throughout the nursery period to maintain optimum moisture in the soil. Six-month-old seedlings are transferred to bamboo baskets or mud pots or polythene bags filled with potting mixture. Seedlings are nurtured properly under shade till they attain an age of one to two years. As the root system of clove plant is delicate, the potting should be done with utmost care, preferably on a cloudy/rainy days.

Planting of seedling in the field is done during June (just at the commencement of monsoon) and August-September. Pits measuring 60-90 cubic centimetres are dug at a spacing of 6 m both ways (at 80 plants per ha) about one month in advance of planting, and are filled with a mixture of compost or cattle manure and loose friable top soil. The seedlings are planted in the centre of the pits and watered regularly in the initial stages on all non-rainy days up to two years to ensure better growth. It is necessary to provide shade to the tender plants. Raising banana in the garden provides ample shade. Provision of shade with coconut leaves (*thatties*) is essential in the first year, and if necessary, in the second year also to protect the plant from 'sun-burn'.

Nutritional Requirements and Their Management

Clove-trees are to be manured regularly and judiciously for their proper growth and flowering. About 15 kg of well-rotted cattle manure or compost may be applied per plant in the initial stage. The quantity should be increased gradually so that a well-grown tree of 15 years and more, should get 40 to 50 kg organic manure. In addition, inorganic fertilizers may be applied start with about 20 g nitrogen (N), 18 g phosphorus (P_2O_5) and 50 g potash (K_2O) per plant in the first year and 40 g nitrogen (N), 36 g phosphorus (P_2O_5) and 100 g potash (K_2O) per plant in the second year, and then gradually increase dose to 300 g nitrogen (N), 250 g phosphorus (P_2O_5) and 750 g potash (K_2O) per plant or tree of 15 years and more.

The organic manure may be applied in May-June with the commencement of the monsoon. The fertilizers are applied in two equal split doses, first in May-June along with the organic manures and the other in September-October. For manuring, shallow trench is dug around the plant about 1-1$^1/_2$ m away from the base.

Intercultural Operations

It is essential throughout the year and usually done for cloves. This not only facilitates growth of clove plant but also prevents pests and diseases. As the branches of full-grown trees have a tendency to over crowd, thining them occassionally may keep growth within manageable proportion. Dead and diseased shoots should also be removed periodically.

Water Management

Irrigation is necessary in the initial stages up to two years. Although, the trees can survive without irrigation, it is advantageous to irrigate grown up trees also on all non-rainy days for proper growth and yield.

	Each plant requires not less than 30 litres of water per day.Since the plants are found naturally in the equatorial atmosphere, they require very good sunlight and copious watering to always keep soil moisture around the plant and have necessary humidity. Therefore, when we raise clove garden below 500m elevation, ensure adequate water supply at the site to irrigate the plants in the summer months.
Harvesting, Yield and Storage	Clove-tree begins to yield cloves from the seventh or eight year after planting. Full bearing stage is attained after 15 to 20 years. It continues for 80 or more years. The flowering season is September to October in plains and December to February at high altitudes. Flower buds are produced on young flushes. It takes about 4 to 6 months for bud to become ready for harvest. The optimum stage for picking clove buds is indicated by the change in colour from green to slightly pinkish tinge or just before opening of bud. If they are allowed to flower, they have no value as a spice clove. The mature clove-buds are carefully picked with hand. Care should be taken to pick buds at the correct time, otherwise the quality of the cured produce will be lost to a considerable extent. When the trees are tall and the clove bunches are beyond reach, platform ladders are used for harvesting. Bending the branches or knocking down the bud-clusters with sticks is not desirable, as these practices affect future bearing of the tree as well as the quality of the product. In most cases, there are two crops in a year-one in late summer or early fall and the second in late fall of the first of the year. It is the nature of the clove tree to vary its yield from 'bumper crops' to light ones in cycles, which range from 2 to 6 years. In volume of production, a mature healthy tree may produce from 3 to 18 kg in one harvest. It is no wonder that a 350-years old tree in Ternate Island of Moluccas of Indonesia still gives a yield of 75 kg to 200 kg of dry cloves per year. Whole or grind (powdered) cloves shall be packed in clean and sound containers made of a material which does not affect the product and protects it from moisture in gress and from the volatile matter during storage/transhipment. The containers of cloves should be stored in covered premises, well protected from sun, rain and excessive heat. The store room should be dry, free from objectionable odours and proofed against entry of insects and vermin. The ventilation should be controlled so as to give good ventilation under dry conditions and to be fully closed under damp conditions. In a storage warehouse, suitable facilities should be available for fumigation as well. For safe storage free from mould, the optimum conditions are (a) moisture: 6.5 per cent; (b) storage temperature: 25-28^{0} C and (c) relative humidity: 30-40per cent (dry condition).

14.10.6. Coriander

Title	Description
Climatic Requirements	Coriander is grown as *rabi* or winter season crop for commercial seed production in India. The cultivated areas should be free from severe frost during the months of February-March when the crop is in flowering and seed setting stage. Cloudy weather and high atmospheric humidity

	during flowering and fruiting stage encourages pests (aphids) and disease incidence. The plants require relatively cool weather during the early stage for better vegetative growth while a dry and relatively high temperature favours higher seed production.
Soil Conditions	Coriander can be cultivated on almost all types of soils provided sufficient organic manure applied under irrigated conditions. Unirrigated crop may be cultivated only on heavy soil, which has better water retention capacity. Black soil with high retention of moisture is best suited under rainfed conditions of Andhra Pradesh, Rajasthan, Tamil Nadu etc. It can be grown successfully in soil with a pH 6-7.
Sowing Time	Sowing of coriander is undertaken from September to November for *rabi* crop. The best time for sowing of coriander is from 15 October to 15 November in most of the commercial growing areas for seed crops. The early sown crop may come to flowering stage earlier and become more vulnerable to frost damage in north Indian conditions. Late sowing affects the crop growth and its yield adversely, but it is safe in areas vulnerable to frost incidence. In Malwa region of Madhya Pradesh, *kharif* crop is sown during August-September and in June-July under Coimbatore conditions of Tamil Nadu, but the *rabi* crop gives better seed yield than the *kharif* crop.
Seed Rate, Methods of Sowing and Planting Distance	Seed rate varying from 20-30 kg per hectare in Punjab and 12-19 kg per hectare in south India. The seeds are split into halves before sowing. Split seeds germinate little earlier than whole seeds. Soaking the seeds in water for 12 to 24 hours and drying them in the shade for 12 hours which causes quicker germination. Soaking coriander in warm water, 10 ppm IAA, 20 ppm NAA or 50 ppm GA increased germination percentage and leaf yield. Before sowing, seed treatment is given with thiram at the rate of 2.5 g/kg seed. Sowing is done with gorru (seed drill) adopting a spacing of 20 x 15 cm in between and along the lines in Andhra Pradesh.
Nutritional Requirements and Their Management	Generally, farmer do not apply manures in coriander crops. Apply 10.0 to 12.0 t/ha well rotten farm yard manure at the time of field preparation. For getting high yield, apply 20-30 kg of nitrogen, 40 kg phosphorus and 20 kg potassium per hectare as basal doses in last ploughing have been recommended under irrigated conditions of Andhra Pradesh. Full quantity of phosphorus and potassium and half quantity of nitrogen may be applied at the time of sowing and remaining quantity of nitrogen is applied four to five weeks after sowing.
Intercultural Operations	In coriander, germination is completed in about 12-15 days after seed sowing. The first hoeing and weeding is done in 30-35 days after sowing. Thinning of plants are also done simultaneously to plant distance in line-sown crops, leaving two plants per hill and at this time the remaining half quantity of nitrogen may also be given. Second and third weedings are generally done at an interval of 30 days depending upon the weed growth. Weeding and hoeings are done to remove the weeds, which provides better soil aeration to the crop and to preserve the soil moisture. Pre-emergence application of 0.9 kg/ha fluchloralin or 0.75 kg/ha oxadiazon pre-emergence can be used as weedicides for control weeds in coriander.
Use of Plant Growth	Sex-expression in coriander as affected by growth regulators. Coriander

Regulators	plants at the five leaf stage sprayed with GA, ethrel (ethephon) or CCC (chlormequat) each at 100 ppm. Male flower numbers/umbels are increased by GA but reduced by other growth substances.
Water Management	No irrigation is necessary for coriander grown in black cotton soils, whereas, in light soils two to three irrigations are required in south Indian conditions. For irrigated crop in addition to pre tillage irrigation, three to four irrigations are required under north Indian conditions. First irrigation is given after 30 to 35 days from date of sowing, second after 60-70 days and third after during seed development stage. If sowing is done by broadcasting, first irrigation may be given immediately after sowing for better germination. Subsequent irrigations are given according to requirement of crop. At the time of flower initiation and seed development stage, sufficient soil moisture should be available to the crop.
Harvesting, Yield and Storage	The crops come to maturity in about 90-150 days depending upon variety, soil and growing season. The *kharif* season crop matures earlier than *rabi* season. Harvesting is done when the grain changes its colour to straw or light brown colour. The plants are cut or pulled and filled into small stocks in the field to wither for two or three days. Threshing is done by beating with sticks or by rubbing with hands. The produce is winnowed, cleaned and dried in partial shade. For storage, seeds should not contain more than six per cent moisture. After drying, produce is stored in gunny bags lined with paper or in polythene bags to avoid entrance of moisture.

14.10.7. Cumin

Title	Description
Climatic Requirements	Cumin is a tropical crop, but it prefers mild climatic conditions. It is cultivated mainly in the semi-arid or arid tracts of Rajasthan and Gujarat. It can be cultivated as a winter crop in areas where prevails a dry period during February and March when flowering and seed setting processes take place. High humidity during flowering and fruiting period induces the development of diseases like blight and powdery mildew causing damage to the crop. It is grown as irrigated crop during winter in Indian conditions.
Soil Conditions	It can be successfully cultivated on well-drained, medium to heavy textured soils of average to high fertility. The crop thrives well on deep, friable, medium and well-drained soil in mild climates. However, continuous cropping of cumin in the same field is not desirable because of the problems of soil borne diseases particularly wilt.
Sowing Time	The proper time for sowing is from mid November to first week of December. However, high yield can be obtained by sowing around 15 November.
Seed Rate, Methods of Sowing and Planting Distance	The optimum seed rate is 12 to 15 kg per hectare. Seeds may be sown either by the broadcasting method or in lines. After broadcasting, the seeds should be covered lightly by soil with help of iron teeth rakes. Line sowing at 30 cm row to row spacing is better than broadcasting for intercultural operations. The seeds may be drilled at a spacing of 15 cm along the line. Care should be taken to see that the seeds do not go deep

	inside the soil while being covered with soil.
Nutritional Requirements and Their Management	For getting good yield, farm yard manure at the rate of 15.0 to 20.0 tonnes per hectare is applied as basal dressing during land preparation. Fertilizer quantity of 50 kg nitrogen and 20 kg phosphorus per hectare are applied.
Intercultural Operations	The first hoeing and weeding should be done when the plants are 5-6 cm in height. During this operation remove all the weeds, unwanted, off type plants and those showing poor growth to maintain optimum spacing of 15-20 cm for getting better yields. The subsequent inter-cultural operations are done on appearance of weeds. The weed seeds like zeeri (*Plantago pumilla* W.) and pariian in cumin seed reduces quality and brings less prices. Zeeri plant is serious weed in cumin and can not be distinguished from the cumin field up to the stage of flowering. Zeeri plant should be removed by hand weeding at flowering for getting higher yields of better quality cumin .
Water Management	Light irrigation is given immediately after sowing followed by another irrigation after 8-10 days. Germination will start only after second irrigation. The first irrigation should not be heavy otherwise it results in the uneven distribution of plants. However, if the day temperature is high with dry spell, a third irrigation may be given after another four to five days to allow completion of germination and for better survival of plants already germinated. Thereafter, the crop should be irrigated at intervals of 20-30 days depending on the weather conditions and soils type. The last irrigation at the time of grain formation should be slightly heavy which will supplement moisture requirement during the crop maturity stage should be avoided, as it is likely to affect the seed quality adversely.
Harvesting Yield and Storage	The crop matures in 80-120 days depending upon variety and agroclimatic conditions. It should be harvested with sharp sickle in the morning hours to avoid shattering, as it is prone to it. After harvesting the crop, it should be collected and spread on the threshing flour or tarpaulin in the open sun for drying in thin layer. The seeds are separated by heating with wooden sticks or nowdays the modern thresher are/can be used for threshing of commercial scale. The cumin produce is again dried in the sun till it is left minimum moisture content. If the cumin seed is not dried to the minimum moisture level will be infested with fungus during storage. The produce should be properly cleaned, graded packed in the optimum sized standard packed containers and well levelled. The average yield of cumin seed is 0.8-1.0 t/ha.

14.10.8. Fennel

Title	Description
Climatic Requirements	Fennel is cultivated mostly as garden or home yard. It can be grown throughout India at altitudes up to 6000 fit. Being is a cold weather crop but grows well in fairly mild climate, hence it is grown as winter season crop in parts of north India and does not thrive in south India except at higher elevations. It can be grown as a summer season crop in temperate regions. Dry and cold weather favours higher seed production.

High temperature leads bolting. Autumn cultivation results high yield and less bolting while summer cultivation leads to more bolting and less yield. Prolonged cloudy weather at the time of flowering is conducive to diseases like blight and powdery mildew and pests like aphids.

Soil Conditions

Though fennel is grown in a variety of soils yet it thrives best in rich, well drained loamy or black sandy soil containing sufficient lime. However poorly drained and too much alkaline soils are not fit for fennel crop. In Gujarat, which is the major grower of fennel, the crop is grown in deep black to medium black clay loam soil by utilizing the residual moisture. In sandy loam to clay loam soils, the crop is grown as a transplanted crop under irrigation during *rabi.* In Rajasthan, fennel crop is raised in sandy loam to clay loam soils by utilizing the residual soil moisture during *rabi* as cold weather crop and also in friable alluvial and sandy loam soils.

Sowing Time

October-November is the best sowing time under north Indian conditions. It can be sown in the hills during March-April. For Punjab, last week of October is better than November, while, late sowing leads to lower yield and lower recovery of oil). Whereas, for Rajasthan, first week of October is the best time for sowing. Late flowering i.e. after 30 October resulted low and uneconomic yield.

Seed Rate, Methods of Sowing and Planting Distance

The seed rate varies with method of sowing. In direct seeding, 10-12 kg/ha and for transplanted crop, 3-4 kg/ha. For minimizing seed requirement, fennel can also be grown by raising nursery and transplanting in main field. For this, seeds are sown in nursery beds during May-June and seedling of one and half or two months age are transplanted in the main field in August-September at a spacing of 60-80 cm or even up to 1 meter in rows and keeping 40-80 cm spacing between plants within the row . Nursery beds of 3.0 X 5.0 m size are prepared. Seeds are broadcast by 15th June for *kharif* fennel, while by 15th August for *rabi* fennel. Fennel is also sown by broadcast method particularly where it is cultivated as a crop mixed with chillies or cole crops.

Nutritional Requirements and Their Management

States	FYM (t/ha)	N (kg/ha)	P_2O_5 (kg/ha)	K_2O (kg/ha)	Time of application
Bihar	60	40	20	-	-
Gujarat	25	60	80	-	Basal in nursery
	20	40	60	-	Basal at transplanting
		30	-	-	30 days after transplanting
		30	-	-	60 days after transplanting
North Gujarat	25	15	30-	-	As basal dose
		15			Top dressing with 0.6 per cent Zn, 0.2 per cent B as foliar application at 30 days
		15			Top dressing with

					0.6 per cent Zn, 0.2 per cent B as foliar application at 60 days
		25			Basal 30 days after sowing
	Rajasthan	90	-	-	N in 3 equal splits
	Punjab	100	40	-	
	Uttar Pradesh	90	60	90	
Intercultural Operations	Three to four weedings and hoeing before flowering are desirable to maintain proper growth of plants and to obtain a good crop. In later part of plant growth, earthing the plants is desirable to prevent the lodging. In chemical weed control, application of pre and post emergence premetryne and aresin (monolinuron) at 3.0 kg/ha and aflon (linuron) at 2.0 kg/ha have been recommended for controlling weeds in fennel.				
Water Management	Fennel requires frequent watering and the frequency depends on the soil type and prevailing water conditions. However, the crop should be irrigated at 20-25 days interval in the early stage and at 10-15 days interval in March-April at the time of seed formation. Seven to eight irrigations are required in fennel crop.				
Harvesting and Yield	Since all the fruits do not mature together, harvesting of the umbels is done four to five times at 10 to 15 days interval. Umbels should be plucked before the fruits fully ripen when they are just changing from deep green to slightly yellow. Picking of umbels at half-length fruit size of green colour is economical. The umbels should be dried under shade. Heaping of the umbels may be avoided as it deteriorates the quality. The dried umbels are threshed and the seeds are separated and cleaned by winnowing. On an average yield at 500 to 900 kg per hectare can be obtained but improved varieties can yield 2500 kg per hectare.				

14.10.9. Fenugreek

Title	Description
Climatic Requirements	It is cool season crop. It can tolerate frost and freezing weather for short period. Due to wide adaptability and acclimatization, fenugreek can be grown successfully even under hot climatic conditions. The plants need relatively cool and low temperature during the early stages for better vegetative growth, while a dry and relatively high temperature favours better ripening and high seed production. It is mainly cultivated as an irrigated crop during the winter for seed production, but it can also be grown as a rainfed crop during summer on hills for leafy vegetables.
Soil Conditions	It can be grown successfully in different types of soil from loamy to sandy loam. But light soil is most suitable for fenugreek cultivation. The optimum soil pH should be between 6.0 to 7.0 for better growth and production.
Sowing Time	Sowing of seeds may be done from third week of October to second week of November for seed production while for leafy vegetable the

common fenugreek is sown from the middle of September to middle of March. First fortnight of November is the best time for sowing of fenugreek .

Seed Rate, Methods of Sowing and Planting Distance

In order to sow one hectare crop about 20-25 kg healthy seeds are required for seed crop. For leafy vegetables, 30 to 35 kg seed per hectare is required. The seed is generally broadcast in beds and the surface is raked to cover it. Improved seeds should be sown after inaculation with *Rhizobium* culture in rows 30 cm apart at 2 to 3cm depths on well-prepared friable soil. Line sowing in rows 20-25 cm apart facilities wedding and interculture operations during the initial stages of crop growth.

Nutritional Requirements and Their Management

For getting good yield of fenugreek, fifteen tonnes of farm yard manure are required per hectare land and it should be incorporated during last ploughing. It will give very high foliage yield if nitrogen applied at the rate of 20 to 30 kg per hectare as side dressing just after first cutting, which should be followed by a light irrigation. Fenugreek is a legume crop as it fixes nitrogen from the atmosphere. Field inoculation with *Rhizibium melilotii* and obtained taller plants with a higher seed yield but the maturity was delayed.

Intercultural Operations

Fenugreek may take 5 to 8 days for germination. The crop should be thinned when three to four leaves start sprouting to retain the plant distance of about 10 cm within the rows. Two weeding and hoeings are necessary during the early stages of the crop. The crop is slow growing at the initial stage. The growth becomes faster after four to five weeks and the crop does not allow seeds to compete with it. To keep the crop free from weeds first weeding and hoeing is done at the time of thinning and the second within 45-50 days after sowing. Avoid chemical weedicides for controlling the weeds in fenugreek.

Use of Plant Growth Regulators

GA_3 (10 to 100 ppm) greatly enhanced internodal length and more number of leaves. Sodium 2, 3 – Isobutyrate at 0.05 per cent applied before intitiation of floral buds produced higher yield with less pollen sterility.

Water Management

Frequent watering is necessary to obtain quick and constant growth of crop. Pre-sowing irrigation gives better seed germination and subsequent irrigation should be done at the time of thinning. Four to six irrigations are required at fortnightly intervals.

Harvesting, Yield and Storage

The crop takes 50 to 60 days for flowering after sowing. The crop should be harvested at maturity. Over ripening will result in shattering of seeds while early harvesting results in shrinking of seeds. At the time of maturity, all except the upper leaves becomes yellow and fall. After harvesting, plants are allowed to dry under the sun. Seeds are separated by threshing and cleaned by winnowing. The yield of common methi is 7.0-8.0 t/ha green leaves while 8.0-10.0 t/ha green leaves of kasuri methi. Leaves are very perishable in nature, therefore, they are marketed soon after harvesting. However, well-dried leaves can be stored for about 10 to 12 months.

14.10.10. Ginger

Title	Description
Climatic Requirements	Ginger is mainly a crop of tropics, however, it can be cultivated from sea level to 1500 mean above sea level. As such, it is grown in hilly states like Himachal Pradesh, Sikkim, North Eastern States, hilly parts of West Bengal (Kalimpong) and Uttaranchal (Gharwal) where the climatic conditions are different from plains especially in terms of rainfall and temperature. It does not grow well in those areas where, the temperature exceed 32 ^{0}C with poor relative humidity whereas the low temperature results in dormancy. The foliage and rhizome are also destroyed by frost resulting in poor storability.
Soil Conditions	Ginger can be grown in all types of soils having 6-7 pH. It is mostly grown as rainfed, however, irrigation is useful for high yield. However, it is very sensitive to water logging. In Himachal Pradesh, maximum area under ginger is in Sirmour, which is situated at an altitude of 600-1200 mean above sea level having clay to sandy loam soil. The soil should be rich in humus, lights, friable and fairly dry. Water logged soil should be avoided for higher cultivation.
Sowing Time	The yield of ginger is greatly influenced by the time of sowing. In all the ginger growing states of the country, it is planted during the month of April. In low hills, it is sown during May-June while in mid high hills during April-May. Number of experiments have shown the beneficial effects of early sowing probably because the crop make sufficient growth and withstand rains and grows rapidly when are heavy rains during July-August. In West Coast of India, the best times for planting ginger is during the first fortnight of May with the receipt of pre monsoons. Under irrigated conditions, it can be planted well in advance during mid February or early March. Burning the surface soil and early planting with the receipt of good summer shower consistently gives higher yield and reduces the disease incidence.
Seed Rate, Methods of Sowing and Planting Distance	Twenty to twenty five quintals / ha rhizomes are required and planted at spacing of 30X 20cm. Ginger is universally propagated from the cuttings of the rhizome i.e. known as bits. Bits are separated from the mother rhizome with a length of 3-5 cm, weighing 20-30 g and having at least one sound bud. In small plots, bits are placed at prescribed distances at a depth of 4-5 cm and covered on large scale plantations. It is sown in furrows made by country ploughs at depth 5-7 cm, then the bits are covered with soil and levelled. In the hills of the North Eastern region, ginger is usually cultivated in raised beds or in the jhum field. Traditionally, the field is brought under fire as an integral part of jhumming, which helps in reducing the weed growth, soft rot disease and increases the avaibility of certain plant nutrients, particulary potassium.
Nutritional Requirements and Their Management	Ginger is long duration and nutrients exhaustive crop and requiring heavy manuring. For good yield farm yard manure 25-30 tonnes/ha, nitrogen 100 kg/ha, phosphorous 100kg/ha and potash 80 kg/ ha are required. Farm yard manure is applied 15-20 days before planting, however, 1/3 nitrogen, full phosphorous and full or half potash at the

time of planting. Remaining 1/3 nitrogen, one month or 40-60 days after planting (1/2 K_2O can also be given at this time) and1/3 nitrogen, 2-3 months after planting.

Intercultural Operations

Mulching: The ginger beds/crop with green leaves is essential to enhance germination and to prevent washing-off soil due to heavy rain. It also helps in maintaining optimum soil temperature, conserves moisture and adds organic matter during the cropping season. The first mulching is done at the time of planting with green leaves @ 10-12 tonnes/ha or dry leaves @ 5-6 tonnes/ha. It is also repeated at 40th and 90th days after planting immediately after weeding and application of fertilizer @ 5 and 2.5 tonnes/ha green and dry leaves, respectively. In hilly areas, where farm yard manures with litter is available, used for mulching. However, different types of mulches are used keeping in view the easy and economic availability in ginger growing areas. Since, the requirement of mulch is heavy, the crop is not finding a proper place in these areas where mulch material is in scarcity. Therefore, locally available mulch material like vomica leaves, green leaves, tree leaves (pine, oak, mango and shisham, etc.), banana leaves, dry grass, paddy straw and cane trash etc. may be used.

Earthing-up: Earthing-up helps in pulverizing the soil leading to proper aeration, suppresses the weed growth and covers the growing rhizomes, besides provide support to the growing stem. At least two earthing-up should be done, first after 50 days at the time of second mulching and second after about 75 days of planting.

Generally, 2-3 weeding and hoeings are done in ginger and the same practice is thoroughly followed by the ginger growers of the state. While doing hoeings, the care should be taken that the rhizome should not be disturbed, injured or exposed. Pre-emergence application of 2,4-D @ 1 kg/ha or attrazine is as effecitve weedicide followed by four hand weedings.

Use of Plant Growth Regulators

Several workers tried have been plant growth regulators in ginger for growth and yield. Pre planting treatment with ethaphon at 750 ppm in combination with a 51^{0}C water soaking for 10 minutes is found beneficial for increasing yield.

Water Management

Ginger is generally grown as a rainfed crop in coastal belts as well as in hills. However, in low rainfall areas, crops are watered immediately after sowing if there is no rainfall for better germination. In the dry season from October to January, the ginger beds require irrigation at interval of 15-20 days for proper growth of plants and rhizomes, otherwise their growth stops and the aerial portion starts drying early. Light irrigation is done 5-6 days before harvesting for easy harvesting and to avoid breakage of rhizome.

Harvesting, Yield and Storage

Maturiy Indices: The stage of maturity of rhizome has a significant influence on its quality and suitablity for consumption and processing for preserved, seed ginger and dried ginger. The appropriate stage and maturity indication will depend upon the purpose for which it needs to be harvested. **(i) Preserved Ginger:** In this case, the main indications are when there is a minimum of crude fibre, maximum of volatile oil, oleoresin and starch. The rhizomes are harvested for the direct sale or manufacture of preserved ginger at immature stage i.e. green immature

	and green mature **(a) Green Mature:** The rhizomes are tender, succulent, fibreless and on breaking the rhizomes break easily after 5-6 months of planting. It should not be watery but attained solidity and mild in pungency and **(b) Green Mature:** The rhizomes are fully developed, mature, skin hard, leaves start turning yellow and stem lodges. The rhizomes become more fibrous and pungent. **(ii) Dry Ginger:** Yellowing of leaves and withering of stem indicates the crop maturity. The rhizomes are fully mature after 7-8 months and become more fibrous, skin hard and more pungent and **(iii) Seed Ginger:** The rhizomes are allowed to remain in the field for 3-4 weeks more and the skin of rhizome ripe, thickened and leaves. Pseudo stem completely dries and falls down. Ginger becomes ready for harvesting 7-8 months after sowing. Early harvesting can also be done keeping in view the price and demand. It is generally harvested when the aerial parts start turning yellow or wilting. Early harvesting is also done when the produce is to be used for processing because of less fibre and pungency while for drying purpose (fibrous and pungency), the harvesting is delayed. The yield of ginger varies with variety and locality where it is grown. Maximum yield to the tune of 30.0-40.0 t/ha have been reported, however 12.0-15.0 t/ha is generally obtained. The yield of dry ginger is 15-25 per cent of fresh ginger depending on the variety and locality. In order to get good germination, the seed rhizomes are to be stored properly in pits under shade. For seed materials, big and healthy rhizomes from disease free plants are selected immediately after the harvest. For this purpose, healthy and disease free clumps are marked in the field when the crop is 6-8 months lid and still green. The seed rhizomes are treated with a solution containing 0.1 per cent quinalphos and 0.3 per cent dithane M-45 for 30 minutes, it has been observed that ginger rhizomes harvested after 8-12 months can be stored at 10-15 °C and 45-55 per cent RH or 25-30 °C and 75 per cent RH for 4 to 8 weeks. Oil and oleoresin yield increased with storage. The refrigerated storage upto 4 weeks did not affect quality but storage at room temperature had adverse effect.

41.10.11. Turmeric

Title	Description
Climatic Requirements	Turmeric prefers a warm and humid climate. It needs a well-distributed annual rainfall of 2500-4000 mm for successful production as a rainfed crop. It can also be grown in areas where the rainfall ranges from 120 to 150 cm during the growing period. However, some irrigation is required during later part of the growing season. It is grown as a rainfed crop in the north eastern hill region and the West Coast because of the heavy rainfall. The cultivated types are found to grow from sea level up to an altitude of about 1000 meters in the North Eastern region of India. Fairly medium rain at weekly intervals in September and October increase the size of the rhizomes. If no rain is received with in about three weeks of harvesting, the rhizomes cure better, resulting in a better

keeping quality. Temperature ranges of 30-35°C during germination, 25-30°C during tillering, 20-25°C during rhizome initiation and 18-20°C during bulbing stage have been identified as optimum for turmeric. Higher temperature and low humidity cause slow emergence of the pseudostem and leaves.

Soil Conditions

Turmeric can be grown in all types of soils but well drained loam to heavy loam, sandy loam soil, rich in organic matter is preferred for its cultivatrion. The pH of the soil should be in the range of 5.0-7.5. Light red, brown or ashy coloured sandy loam is also suitable for turmeric cultivation. Alkaline soils are not suited for its cultivation.

Sowing Time

Generally, the turmeric is sown/planted from April to May but in the west costal areas, it can be planted immediately with the receipt of the pre-monsoon showers. Healthy and disease free rhizomes from the fresh crop, harvested in November or December, should be selected for seed and stored in under ground pits. By the beginning of April when the seeds start sprouting, it should be taken out from the pits for planting. Care should be taken to protect the sprouting buds from mechanical injury.

Seed Rate, Methods of Sowing and Planting Distance

About 2.0-2.5 tonnes of healthy disease free rhizomes is sufficient to plant in a hectare. Turmeric rhizomes are planted in the furrows by dibbling. After dibbling, the rhizomes are covered with the loose soil from the ridge. Before sowing/planting, the rhizomes should be treated with the 0.25 per cent diathane M-45 solution for 30 minutes and then dry them in the shade before planting. Precautions should be taken not to plant the turmeric rhizomes in field of solanaceous crops as to avoid nematodes. Whole rhizomes are planted by the ridge and furrow method (36 cm between rows and 22.5 cm between rhizomes) has highest yields. To maintain the plant density in an area spacing of 30 cm between rows and 20 cm between the plants may be adopted.

Nutritional Requirements and Their Managements

Turmeric needs very heavy manuring under mid-hill dry conditions specially of Mizoram, the highest yield and maximum profit was obtained from the application of 50.0 q/ha of farm yard manure alone followed by the application of 90 kg/ha nitrogen, 60kg/ha phosphorous and 90 potash kg/ha in the form of Urea, DAP and MOP. Under Himachal Pradesh conditions, turmeric performs well if 20.0 tonnes of farm yard manure/ha is applied with 30kg/ha nitrogen, 30kg/ha phpsphorous and 60kg/ha potash. Whole quantity of the phosphorous and 1/2 of potash should be applied at the time of planting. Apply 20kg nitrogen/ha 40 days after planting and the balance 10kg/ha and 30kg/ha potash three months after planting. The beds are earthed up after each top dressing with fertilizers.

Intercultural Operations

Interculture operation, mulching, earthing, hoeing and weeding are important operations for getting good yield of tuemeric. Turmeric requires 2-3 mulching, first immediately after planting while second 40-50 days after sowing to preserve moisture and ensure better germination. Third mulching is beneficial when rain ceases to conserve moisture during rhizome development. After weeding and fertilization, earthing is essential in turmeric to save the rhizomes from exposure to sun and also for better expansion of rhizomes. It is very imortant to keep the weeds under control and to maintain desirable soil conditions

	for the normal growth of crop. The first weeding may be done in June, followed by subsequent hoeing and earthing from July to September at fortnightly intervals. One hoeing may be in October, depending upon the intensity of the weeds in the crop. Pre-emergence application of any one of the weedicides like fluchloralin (1.0 and 1.5 kg/ha) oxadiazone (1.0 and 1.5 kg/ha), oxyfluorfen (0.2 kg/ha) and pendimethalin (1 and 1.5 kg/ha), may be used for chemical weed control.
Use of Plant Growth Regulators	Spraying of planofix (NAA) at 10 ppm once at six months after sowing increased yield.
Water Management	Turmeric is grown as rainfed crop in heavy rainfall tracts of the country. The irrigation/water requirement depends on the type of soil and temperature. Generally, 15-20 irrigations are given during the cropping season. During the summer days, the irrigation should be given after 7 days but during the rainy season when its over or in between the irrigation should be given after 10 days interval. It is desirable to give a light irrigation, 3-4 days before harvesting, as it facilities harvesting.
Harvesting, Yield and Storage	The crop is ready for harvesting when the leaves turn yellow and start drying up. The harvesting begins from the middle of November and continues till middle of December.The crop is ready for harvesting in about 8 to 9 months after sowing in the North Eastern region depending upon variety, fertility status of soil and moisture availability. At the time of maturity dry leaves are cut close to the ground. The rhizomes are dug and mother rhizome and fingers are separated before curing. Rhizomes free from fibrous roots and tops should be kept in shade for seed 2 to 3 days for making the skin hard to mechanical injury. Rhizomes for seed purpose are generally heaped in compact shade of trees or in well-ventilated shade and it should be covered with turmeric leaves. The yield of turmeric can be obtained from 15.0 to 20.0 t/ha. In good management 4.0 to 5.0 tonnes of cured turmeric can be obtained from one hectare. The fresh harvested rhizomes are well developed and free from mechanical injury and diseases are selected for seed and stored till the end of April. The rhizomes should be dried in shade for 4 to 6 days after removing the dirt and leaves. They are put in underground pits, locally known as *kattir*. The rhizome should be spread at the bottom of each pit before the rhizomes are stored. The upper layer of the produce should be covered with dry grass and the mouth of the pits may be sealed by plastering them with mud to protect the rhizomes against the heat of the sun and to prevent water from entering the pits and damaging the rhizomes. It is very important to open the pits in January or February for sorting out the diseased and rotten rhizomes. There after, the pits are sealed again.

14.11. Plant Protection Measures

14.11.1. Tomato

Common Name	Strength and formulation	Target Pests	Dose/Ha			Waiting period (days)
			a.i. (g)	Formulation (g/ml)	Dilution in water (Litre)	
Insecticides						
Azadiractin	1%	Fruit borer	-	1000-1500	500	3
Azadiractin	5%	Aphids, Whitefly, Fruit borer	-	200	400	5
Carbofuran	3% G	Whitefly	1200	40000	-	-
Chlorantranilprole	18.5% SC	Fruit borer	30	150	500	3
Dimethoate	30% EC	Whitefly	300	990	500-1000	-
Imidacloprid	17.8% SL	Whitefly	30-35	150-175	500	3
Indoxacarb	14.5% SC	Fruit borer	60-75	400-500	300-600	5
Lambda Cyhalothrin	5% EC	Fruit borer	15	300	400-600	4
Malathion	50% EC	Whitefly	750	1500	50-1000	-
Methomyl	40% SP	Pod borer	300-450	750-1125	500-1000	5-6
Novaluron	10% EC	Fruit borer	75	750	500-1000	1-3
NPV of *H armigera*	0.43% A S2.0% AS	*Helicoverpa armigera*		250-1500	400-6000	-
Oxydemeton methyl	25% EC	Whitefly	250	1000	500-1000	-
Phorate	10% G	Whitefly	1500	15000	-	-
Phosalone	35% EC	Fruit borer	450	1285	500-1000	-
Quinolphos	20% AS	Fruit borer	300-350	1500-1750	750-1000	7
Thiamethoxam	25% WG	Whitefly	50	200	500	5
Trichloforon	5% GR	Fruit borer	500-750	-	-	-
	5% Dust	Fruit borer	500-750	-	-	-
	50% EC	Fruit borer	500-750	-	-	-

Contd.

Common Name	Strength and formulation	Target Pests	Dose/Ha			Waiting period (days)
			a.i. (g)	Formulation (g/ml)	Dilution in water (Litre)	
Fungicides						
Azoxystrobin	23% SC	Early/late powdery mildew	125g	500g	500	3
Copper Sulphate	2.62% SC	Early/late blight		1.0 L	500	3
	75% WP	Damping off (Nursery)	0.25%	2500g	1000 Soil drenching the nursery	NA
		Early and late blight	1250g	1667g	1000	6
	75% WS	Damping off (Soil drench)	15-25g/kg seed	20-30g per kg seed	1	-
	50% WP	Early and late blight	1250g	2.5 kg	750-1000	-
Iprodione	50% WP	Early blight	0.75 kg	1.5 kg	500	15
Kresoxim-methyl	44.3% SC	Early blight	30-37.5 ml	1000-1250g	500-600	03
Kitazin	48% EC	Early blight	0.10% or 100g in 100 L of water	0.20% or 200ml in 200 L of water	As required depending upon crop stage and plant protection equipment used	5
Mancozeb	75% WG	Early blight	750 gm	1000 gm	500 L	5-6
	35% SC	Early and late blight	0.175% or 175g/100 L water	0.5% or 500 gm/ 100 L water	500 L water or as required depending upon crop stage	10
	75% WP	Late blight, buck eye rot, leaf spot	1.125-1.5 kg	1.5-2 kg	750 l	-

Contd.

Common Name	Strength and formulation	Target Pests	Dose/Ha			Waiting period (days)
			a.i. (g)	Formulation (g/ml)	Dilution in water (Litre)	
Mrtarim	70% WG	Alternaria blight	1750g	2500g	500-750 L	6
Propineb	70% WP	Buck eye rot	0.21% or 210g/ 100 L water	0.30% or 300g/100 L water	As required depending upon crop stage and plant protection equipment used	10
Pyraclostrobin	20% WG	Early blight	75-100g	375-500g	500	3
Streptomycin Sulphate + Tetracycline Hydrochloride	9% + 1% SP	Bacterial leaf spot	-	Spray seedlings with streptocycline with 40 to 100 ppm solution in seed beds after appearance of first true leaves. Two sprays of streptocycline one before and one after transplanting.		
Thiophenate Methyl	70% WP	Ring rot	500g	715g	750-1000	7
Ziram	80% WP	Early blight	1.2-1.6 kg	1.5-2.0 kg	750-1000	3
Zineb	75% WP	Early and late blight, grey leaf mould	-	-	-	-
Cymoxanil 8% + Mancozeb 64%	WP	Late blight	1080 g	1500 g	500-750 L	10 days
Famoxadone 16.6% + Cymoxanil 22.1%	SC	Early and late blight	210	500	500	3

14.11.2. Brinjal

Common Name	Strength and formulation	Target Pests	Dose/Ha			Waiting period (days)
			a.i. (g)	Formulation (g/ml)	Dilution in water (Litre)	
Insecticides						
Azadiractin	1%	FSB**	-	1000-1500	500	3
Azadiractin	0.03%	FSB, beetles	-	2500-5000	500	7
Carbofuran	3% G	Nematodes	2000	66600	-	-
Chlorantranilprole	18.5% SC	FSB	40	200	500-750	22
Chloropyrifos	20% EC	FSB	200	1000	500-1000	-
Cypermethrin	0.25% DP	FSB	50-60	2000-2400	500-750	3
	10% EC	FSB	50-70	550-760	150-400	3
	25% EC	FSB, Epilachna beetle	37-50	150-200	500	1
Dicofol	18.5% EC	Mite	250-500	1350-2700	500-1000	15-20
Difenthiuron	50% WP	Whitefly	300	600	500-750	3
Dimethoate	30% EC	Jassids	600	1980	-	-
		FSB	200	660	500-1000	-
Emamectin benzoate	5% SG	FSB	10	200	500	3
Fenzaquin	10% EC	Mites	125	1250	500	7
Fenpropathrin	30% EC	Whitefly, FSB, mites	75-100	250-340	750-1000	10
Fenvalerate	20% EC	FSB	75-100	375-500	500-750	5
Flumite/Flufenzine	20% SC	Mites	80-100	400-500	500-1000	5
Lambda-Cyhalothrin	5% EC	FSB	15	300	500	4
	4.9% CS	FSB	15	300	500	5
Malathion	50% EC	Mites	750	1500	500-1000	-
Phorate	10% G	Jassids	1500	15000	-	-
Phosalone	35% EC	FSB	500	1428	500-1000	-
Phosphomidon	40% SL	Jassids, aphid, Whitefly	250-300	625-750	500	10

Contd.

Common Name	Strength and formulation	Target Pests	Dose/Ha			Waiting period (days)
			a.i. (g)	Formulation (g/ml)	Dilution in water (Litre)	
Quinolphos	20% AF	FSB, Jassids, epilachnna beetle	300-350	1500-1750	750-1000	7
	25% EC	FSB, leaf hopper	375	1000		
Spiromesifen	22.9% SC	Red spider mite	96	400	500	5
Thiodicarb	75% WP	FSB	470-750	625-1000	500	6
Thiamethoxam	25% WG	Whiteflies	50	200	500	3
Thiameton	25% EC	Aphids, jassids, FSB	250	1000	750-1000	
Trichloforon	5% G, 5% dust, 50% EC	FSB	250	1000	750-1000	-
Triazophos	40% EC	FSB, epilachana beetle	500	1250	500	5
Deltamethrin + Triazophos	1% +35% EC	FSB, epilachana beetle	-	1000-1250	-	21
Fungicides						
Benomyl	50% WP	Powdery mildew	100g	200g	600	-
Carbendazim	50% WP	Leaf spot, fruit rot	150g	300g	600	-
Captan	75% WP	Damping off in nursery	0.25%	2500g	1000 soil drench in nursery	-
Zineb	75% WP	Blight	1.12-1.5kg	1.5-2 kg	750-1000	-

FSB= Fruit and shoot borer.

14.11.3. Chilli

Common Name	Strength and formulation	Target Pests	Dose/Ha			Waiting period (days)
			a.i. (g)	Formulation (g/ml)	Dilution in water (Litre)	
Insecticides						
Acetamiprid	20% SC	Thrips	10-20	50-100	500-600	3
Buprofezin	25% SC	Yellow mite	75-150	300-600	500-750	5
Carbofuran	3% G	Thrips	1000	33300	-	-
Carbosulfan	25% EC	Whitefly, aphids	200-250	800-1000	500-1000	8
Chlorfenpyre	10% SC	Yellow mite	75-100	750-1000	500	5
Deltamethrin	2.8% EC	Fruit borer	10-12.5	400-600	400-600	5
Difenthiuron	50% WP	Mites	300	600	500-750	3
Dimethoate	30% EC	Mites, thrips	200-300	660-960	500-1000	-
Emamectin benzoate	5% SG	Fruit borer, Thrips, mites	10	200	500	3
Endosulfan	35% EC	aphids	140	400	500-1000	21
Ethion	50% EC	Mite, thrips	750-1000	1500-2000	500-1000	05
Fenazaquin	10% EC	Yellow mite	125	1250	400-600	10
Fenpropathrin	30% EC	Thrips, Whitefly, mites	75-100	250-340	750-1000	7
Fenpyroximate	5% EC	Yellow mite	15-30	300-600	300-500	7
Fipronil	5% SC	Fruit borer, Thrips, Aphids	40-50	100-800	500	7
Flubendamide	39.35% SC	Fruit borer	48-60	100-125	500	7
Hexythiazox	5.45% EC	Yellow mite	15-25	300-500	625	3
Imidacloprid	70% WS	Jassids, aphids, thrips	700-1050	500-1000 (per 100 kg seed)	-	-
Indoxacarb	14.5% SC	Fruit borer	50-60	333-400	300-600	5
Lambda cyhalothrin	5% EC	Thrips, mite, pod borer	15	300	400-600	5
Methomyl	40% SP	Pod borer, tobacco caterpillar	300-450	750-1125	500-1000	5-6
Milebemectin	1% EC	Mites	3.25	325	500	7

Contd.

Common Name	Strength and formulation	Target Pests	Dose/Ha			Waiting period (days)
			a.i. (g)	Formulation (g/ml)	Dilution in water (Litre)	
Novaluron	10% EC	Fruit borer, tobaco caterpillar	33.5	375	500	3
Oxydemeton methyl	25% EC	Aphids, mites, thrips	250-400	1000-2000	500-1000	-
Phorate	10% GR	Aphids, mites, thrips	1000	10000	-	-
Phosalone	35% EC	Aphids, mites, thrips	450-700	2000	500-1000	-
Propargite	57% EC	Mite	850	1500	500-625	7
Quinalphos	25% Gel	Aphids	250	100	500-1000	-
Spinosad	45% SC	Fruit borer	73	160	500	3
Spiromesifen	22.9% SC	Yellow mite	96	400	500-750	7
Thiacloprid	21.7% SC	Thrips	54-72	225-300	500	5
Indoxacarb + Acetamiprid	14.5% + 7.7% SC	Thrips, fruit borer	88.8-111	400-500	500	5
Fungicides						
Azoxystrobin	23% SC	Fruit rot, powdery mildew	125g	500g	500-750	5
Benomyl	50% WP	Powdery mildew, fruit rot, leaf spot	100g	200g	600	-
Copper sulphate	2.62% SC	Fruit rot, anthracnose		1.0 L	500	3
Captan	50% WG	Fruit rot, anthracnose	750g	1500g	500	5
	75% WP	Damping off in nursery	0.25%	2500g	1000	-
	75% WS	Damping off (Soil drench)	15-25g	20-30g	1	-
Copper hydroxide	77% WP	Anthracnose, cercospora leaf spot	625g	1250g	500	-
Chlorothalonil	75% WP	Fruit rot	600g	800g	750	10
Difenoconazole	25% EC	Die-back fruit rot	0.0125% or 12.5g/100 L water	0.05% or 50 ml/100 L water		
Dinocap	48% EC	Powdery mildew	108g	225g	750	-
Fenarimol	12% EC	Powdery mildew	0.005%	0.04ml	As required	15
Flusilazole	40% EC	Powdery mildew	108g	225g	750	

Contd.

Common Name	Strength and formulation	Target Pests	Dose/Ha			Waiting period (days)
			a.i. (g)	Formulation (g/ml)	Dilution in water (Litre)	
Hexaconazole	2% SC	Powdery mildew & fruit rot	60g	3.0 L	500	7
Kitazin	48% EC	Fruit rot dieback	0.10%	0.20%	As required	3
Mancozeb	75% WP	Damping off, fruit rot, leaf spot	2.125-2.25g	1.5-3 kg	1	-
Myclobutanil	10% WP	Leaf spot & dieback	0.004%	0.04%	500	03
Propineb	70% WP	Die back	0.35%	0.5%	As required	10
Sulphur	80% WP	Powdery mildew	2.5 kg	3.13 kg	750-1000	-
Streptomycin Sulphate + Tetracycline Hydrochloride	9% + 1% SP	Bacterial leaf spot	-	Spray seedlings with streptocycline with 40 to 100 ppm solution in seed beds after appearance of first true leaves. Two sprays of streptocycline one before and one after transplanting.		
Triadimefon	25% WP	Powdery mildew	38g	0.150 kg	750	15
Tebuconazole	25.9% m/m EC	Fruit rot, powdery mildew	0.1875	0.50-0.75 Kg	500	5
Zineb	75% WP	Fruit rot & leaf spot	1.125-1.5 kg	1.5-2 kg	750-1000	-
Captan + Hexaconazole	70% + 5% WP	Fruit rot anthracnose	375-750 g	500-1000g	500	5

14.11.4. Okra

Common Name	Strength and formulation	Target Pests	Dose/Ha			Waiting period (days)
			a.i. (g)	Formulation (g/ml)	Dilution in water (Litre)	
Insecticides						
Azadirachtin	0.03%	FSB**, whiteflies, jassids	-	2500-5000	500-1000	7
Azadirachtin	5%	FSB**, whiteflies, Jassids	-	200	400	5
Carbaryl	5% DP	Jassid	1000	20000	-	-
Carbofuran	3% G	Aphiids	1000	33300	-	-
Chlorantranilprole	18.5% SC	FSB	25	125	500	5
Cypermethrin	10% EC	FSB	50-70	550-760	150-400	3
	25% EC	FSB, jassids	37-50	150-200	500	3
Deltamethrin	2.8% EC	FSB, jassids	10-15	400-600	400-600	1
Dicofol	18.5% EC	Red spider mite	250-500	1350-2700	100-500	15-20
Dimethoate	30% EC	Aphid, jassids	700-600	2310-1980	500-1000	-
Emamectin benzoate	5% SG	FSB	6.75-8.5	135-170	500	5
Endosulfan	35% EC	Aphids	140	400	500-1000	21
Fenpropathrin	30% EC	Whitefly, FSB, mites	75-100	250-340	750-1000	7
Fenvalerate	30% EC	Whitefly, FSB, Mites	75-100	250-340	750-1000	7
Imidacloprid	70% WG	Jassids, aphids, thrips	21-24.5	30-35	375-500	3
	48% FS	Jassids, Aphids	300-540	500-900	-	-
	70% WS	Jassids, aphids	350-700	500-1000	-	-
Lambda-Cyhalothrin	5% EC	Jassids, FSB	15	300	3000-400	4
Malathion	50% EC	FSB, aphid, jassids	750	1500	500-1000	-
Oxydemeton-methyl	25% EC	Whitefly, jassids	250-400	1000-1600	500-1000	-
Permethrin	25% EC	FSB, aphids, jassids	100-125	400-500	750-1000	-
Phosalone	35% EC	FSB	525	1500	500-1000	-
Pyridalyl	10% EC	FSB	50-75	500-750	500-750	3

Contd.

Common Name	Strength and formulation	Target Pests	Dose/Ha			Waiting period/ PHI* (days)
			a.i. (g)	Formulation (g/ml)	Dilution in water (Litre)	
Quinolphos	20% AF	FSB	250-300	1250-1500	750-1000	7
	25% EC	FSB, jassid, mites	250	1000	500-1000	-
Spiromesifen	22.9% SC	Red spider mite	96-120	400-500	500	3
Thiamethoxam	25% WG	Jassid, aphid, whitefly	25	100	500-1000	5
	70% WDG	Aphids	200	286	-	-
Fungicides						
Dinocap	48% EC	Powdery mildew	108g	225g	750	-
Sulphur	80% WP	Powdery mildew	2.5kg	3.13 kg	750-1000 L	-

14.11.5. Cucurbits

Common Name	Strength and formulation	Target Pests	Dose/Ha			Waiting period (days)
			a.i. (g)	Formulation (g/ml)	Dilution in water (Litre)	
Insecticides						
Chlorantranilprole	18.5% SC	Fruit borers, caterpillars	20-25	100-125	500	7
Dichlorvos	76% EC	Red pumpkin beetle	500	627	500-100	-
Dicofol	18.5% EC	Red spider mite	250-500	1350-2700	100-500	15-20
Imidacloprid	70% WG	Jassids, aphids	24.5	35	500	5
Trichloforon	5% Gr	Red pumpkin beetle	500-750	-	-	-
	5% Dust	Red pumpkin beetle	500-750	-	-	-
	50% EC	Red pumpkin beetle	500-750	-	-	-
Fungicides						
Benomyl	50% WP	Powdery mildew, anthracnose	100g	200g	600	-
Carbendazim	50% WP	Powdery mildew	150g	300g	600	-
Thiphanate Methyl	70% WP	Powdery mildew, anthracnose	1000g	1430g	750-1000	1
Zineb	75% WP	Downy mildew, anthracnose, leaf spot	1.125-1.5 kg	1.5-2 kg	750-1000	-
Cymoxanil *% + Mancozeb 64%	WP	Downy mildew	1080g	1500g	500-600	10

14.11.6. Cruciferous Vegetables (Cabbage & Cauliflower)

Common Name	Strength and formulation	Target Pests	Dose/Ha			Waiting period (days)
			a.i. (g)	Formulation (g/ml)	Dilution in water (Litre)	
Insecticides						
Acetamiprid	20% SC	Aphids	15	75	500-600	7
Azadirachtin	0.03%	Aphids, DBM**	-	2500-5000	500-100	7
Azadirachtin	5%	DBM, spodoptera, Aphids	-	200	400	5
Bacillus thuringiensis var. kurstaki	5% WP	DBM	25-50	500-1000	500-1000	-
Carbaryl	5% DP	Borers	600	12000	-	8
Carbofuran	3% G	Nematodes	1000	50000	-	-
Chlorantranilprole	18.5% SC	DBM	10	50	500	3
Chlorfenpyre	10% SC	DBM	75-100	750-1000	500	7
Chlorophyrifos	20% EC	DBM	400	2000	500-1000	
Cypermethrin	10% EC	DBM	60-70	650-760	100-400	7
Difenthiuron	50% WP	DBM	300	600	500-750	7
Dimethoate	30% EC	Aphids, Bugs	200	660	500-1000	
Emamectin benzoate	5% SG	DBM	7.5-10.0	150-200	500	3
Fenvalerate	20% EC	DBM, borer	60-75	300-375	600-750	7
Fipronil	5% SC	DBM	40-50	800-100	500	7
Flufenoxuron	10% DC	DBM	40	400	500-1000	7
Indoxacarb	14.5% SC	DBM	30-40	200-266	400-750	7
	15.8% SC	DBM	40	266	500-1000	5
Lufenuron	5.4% EC	DBM	30	600	500	14
		DBM	30	600	500	5
Malathion	50% EC	Aphids	750	1500	500-1000	-
		Head borer	750	1500	500-1000	-
Metaflumizone	22% SC	DBM	165-220	150-1000	500	3
Novaluron	10% EC	DBM	75	750	500-1000	5

Contd.

Common Name	Strength and formulation	Target Pests	Dose/Ha			Waiting period (days)
			a.i. (g)	Formulation (g/ml)	Dilution in water (Litre)	
Permethrin	25% EC	DBM	50-125	200-500	750-1000	
Phorate	10% G	Aphids	2000	20000		
Phosalone	35% EC	Aphids	500	1428	500-1000	-
Pyridalyl	10% EC	DBM	50-75	500-750	500-750	
Quinolphos	25% EC	Aphid	250	1000	500-1000	
		Head borer	500	2000		
Spinosad	2.5% SC	DBM	15-17.5	600-700	500	3
Trichloforon	5% G	DBM	500-750	-	-	-
	5% Dust	DBM	500-750	-	-	-
	50% EC	DBM	500-750	-	-	-
Fungicides						
Captan	75% WP	Damping off (Nursery)	0.25%	2500	1000 soil drench in nursery	-
	75% WS	Damping off (Soil drench)	15-25 g	20-30 g		
Mancozeb	75% WP	Collar rot	2.25 g	3g	-	-
		Leaf spot	1.125 kg	1.5-2 kg	750	-
Zineb	75% WP	Leaf spot	1.125 kg	1.5-2 kg	750-1000	

14.11.7. Legume Vegetables

Common Name	Strength and formulation	Target Pests	Dose/Ha			Waiting period (days)
			a.i. (g)	Formulation (g/ml)	Dilution in water (Litre)	
Benomyl	50% WP	Powdery mildew	100g	200g	600	2
Carbendazim	50% WP	Powdery mildew	125g	250g	600	-
Fenarimol	12% EC	Powdery mildew	0.005% (5g/100L)	0.04% (40 ml/100L)	As required	15
Sulphur	80% WP	Rust	2.5 kg	3.13 kg	750-1000	
	80% WG	Powdery mildew	1.50-2.00 kg	1.875-250 kg	750-1000	
	40% WP	Powdery mildew	2.25-3.00 kg	5.65 kg	750-1000	
	52% SC	Powdery mildew	1.04 kg	2.00 L	400	
	85% DP	Rust, powdery mildew	12.7-17 kg	15-20 kg		
Triadimefon	25% WP	Rust, powdery mildew	0.025%	0.100%	750	25
Dinocap	48% EC	Powdery mildew	108g	225g	750	
Captan	75% WP	Damping off (Nursery)	0.25%	2500	1000 soil drench in nursery	-
Streptomycin Sulphate + Tetracycline Hydrochloride	9% + 1% SP	Halo blight		Spray seedlings with streptocycline with 100 to 150 ppm solution thrice at interval of 7 days. For prevention apply first spray 10 days after emergence of leaf.		

14.12. Physiological Disorders

14.12.1. Garlic

Crop	Disorders	Symptoms/reasons	Control measures
Garlic	Rubbering of garlic bulbs	Dent formation with the pressure applied through tip of the thumb. The dent returns to original form on release of the pressure.The rubberized bulbs become spongy when dried.	Application of 75 kg/ha nitrogen, 75 kg/ha potassium, 75 kg/ha phosphorous, 50 kg/ ha magnesium sulphate and 500 q/ha of well-rotten farm yard manure has been found best.
	Premature Sprouting of Bulbs	Cloves, after initiation, continue to sprout in the field by producing leaves instead of bulbing. The sprouts from the cloves will burst out through leaf sheath.	It is always better to apply optimum dose of straight fertilizers based on soil test. Recommended dose of nitrogen should be applied in the form of ammonium sulphate. Application of 50 per cent of nitrogen and potassium fertilizers as basal dose and 50 per cent in two splits at 45 and 60 days after planting.In soils with high nitrogen level, when potassium level increases, particularly beyond 75 kg up to 150 kg potassium /ha, premature sprouting and rubbering decreases. There is significant interaction between nitrogen and potassium, indicating that ill effects of excessive nitrogen could be alleviated by increased dose of potassium application. Application of burnt ash 50 kg/ha, 30 days after planting. By closer planting of cloves at 15 cm x 7 cm, healthy and optimum sized bulbs can be harvested. By spraying micronutrient mixture containing boron at 0.1 per cent and sodium molybdate at 0.05 per cent. Spraying of growth regulators either cycocel or maleic hydrazide at 1,500 ppm (1.5 gm in 1 litre of water) .

14.12.2. Onion

Crop	Disorders	Symptoms/reasons	Control measures
Onion	Bolting in onion	(i) It may be due to heredity. (ii) Differences in variety (iii) Extreme changes in temperature (iv) Check in the growth of plants in seed bed. (v) Poor seed quality. (vi) Poor soil. (vii) Cultural practices affecting growth. (viii) Relative length of days and night and (ix) Spacing and size of seedlings *etc.*	(i) Application of more nitrogen reduced bolting. (ii) Application of potash, in combination of zinc, reduced bolting (iii) Transplanting from first week of December to the end of December (iv) Bolting can also be minimized by planting on ridges instead of flat bed planting
	Splitting and Doubling of Bulbs	(i) Water deficiency at the initial growth stages and irrigation after a long spell of drought (ii) Higher quantities of nitrogen (iii) In kharif onion, doubles increased with increase in the size of sets	(i) Follow proper irrigation scheduled. (ii) Apply balanced quantities of nitrogen, phosphorous and potassium.
	Thick necking	A failure to develop mature bulbs. Onions with thick necks are difficult to dry after harvest, and are predisposed to sprouting and decay during storage. Incomplete bulbing may be the result due to delayed sowing, a cool growing period, or the over use of fertilizer.	(i) Sow only healthy seeds. (ii) Avoid over aged seedlings for transplanting. (iii) Select particular seasons. (iv) Avoid excess soil moisture by withholding irrigations as soon as bulbs reach maturity. (v) Apply optimum quantity of nitrogen to the crop. (vi) Application of MH-2000 ppm at 75 days after transplanting (vii) Avoid bulb injury during harvesting, curing, transportation & storage..
	Water staining	Skin is a dark imprint of the mesh known as 'bag-print'. Staining is sometimes traced to wet condition in the field during and after harvest.	Water staining can be minimized by harvesting the crop directly and curing it in store instead of in the field. Good ventilation is necessary to dissipate respiratory moisture during storage and transport

14.12.3. Cauliflower

Disorders	Symptoms/reasons	Control measure
Riceyness	Elongation on peduncle wearing flower buds, rendering curds, granular, loose and somewhat velvety. A premature initiation of floral bud and is considered to be of poor quality for marketing Riceyness mainly develops during the warm weather when the crop is closed to maturity and harvesting has been delayed. If late variety planted early, riceyness develops due to the prevalent of high temperature, however, it can also appear at lower temperature. Hereditary factors have also been reported for riceyness. Heavy dose of nitrogen and high relative humidity also contributes to riceyness.	Cultivation of genetically pure seed and appropriate varieties with recommended cultural practices
Fuzziness	Flower pedicels of velvety curds elongate. The anomaly is both hereditary and non-hereditary. Cultivation of cauliflower out of their normal season encourages fuzziness.	Sowing good quality seed in right season under proper cultural practices
Leafiness	Extremely small green leaves appear in between the curd segment due to inheritable or non-heritable factors. Prevalence of high temperatures during curding phase aggravates leafiness. Certain varieties are more sensitive to leafiness or bracketing than other.	Selection of varieties according to their adaptability.

Disorders	Symptoms/reasons	Control measures
Browning (Brown rot or red Rot)	It is caused by boron deficiency, which is influenced by soil pH. It is characterized by sign on the young leaves that become dark green and brittle. The old leaves puckered, chlorotic and often drops off. Sometimes the downward curling of older leaves followed by development of blisters when boron deficiency is sever. The leaves remain small and the growing point may die. However, in later stage water soaked, light brown to dark brown spots formed on the stem and branches may, ultimately lead to the formation of cavities and a hollow stem. Curds may also show irregular water soaked spots, Which later change to a rusty brown colour. The affected curds remain small and acquire a bitter taste.	Application of borax or sodium borate or sodium tetraborate at the rate of 20 kg/ha as soil application. In case of acute deficiency spray of 0.25 to 0.50 per cent solution of borax at the rate of 1 to 2 kg/ha depending upon growth, soil reaction and extent of deficiency.
Whiptail	Deficiency of molybdenum causes “whiptail” syndrome especially in highly acidic soils. Because high manganese concentrations in such soils hinder the uptake of molybdenum which seldom occurs when the soil pH is 5.5 or higher. The young cauliflower plants become chlorotic and may turn white, particularly along the leaf margins. They also become cupped and wither. The leaves blades fail to develop properly, and the leaves are ruffled and distorted. In older plant, the lamina of the newly formed leaves are irregular in shape, frequently consisting of only a large bare midribs and hence the common name	Application of lime or dolomite limestone to raise the soil pH up to 6.5 or higher. soil pH up to 6.5 or higher. Sodium or Ammonium molybdate at the rate of 1-2 kg/ha as soil application.

Disorders	Symptoms/reasons	Control measures
	"Whiptail".	
Buttoning	Development of small curds with inadequate foliage in cauliflower is known as buttoning. It is also referred to as premature heading. The leaves are so small that can not cover the formed head. Causes of buttoning are (i) Transplanting of more than 6-week-old seedling. Generally, over aged seedlings when transplanted in the field take more time in establishment due to less developed root system. A poor development of root system is possible due to insufficient availability of nutrients and inadequate space for the development of root system due to crowding of seedlings allowed for longer duration in the nursery beds. The growth rate of such over aged seedlings are usually slow. Not only this they could not put on optimum vegetative growth, and start forming curds, which further could not grow into normal size and causes buttoning. Temperature below the optimum during growing period delays maturity. (ii) Planting as early variety in late *vice versa* leads buttoning. (iii) Hot and dry weather is unfavorable for vegetative growth of plants but favorable for inducing curd formation and inhibits further enlargement. Curds remains very small in size like buttons. (iv) When soil moisture becomes limiting factor it checks the growth of the plants, which in	(i) Nursery should be properly look after to avoid any check in the plant growth. (ii) An adequate amount of nitrogen and water should be applied. (iii) Do not delay transplanting and (iv) Cultural practices should be carried out well in time and water logging and overcrowding should be avoided.

Disorders	Symptoms/reasons	Control measures
	turn, causes early formation of curds without maintaining their further enlargement. (v) Transplanting of seedlings obtained from poorly managed nursery bed. Such seedlings may not have high potential for their vegetative growth, which is almost important for the formation and enlargement of normal curds. (vi) Slow plant growth in the nursery, over crowding, insufficient water, lack of weeding, bad condition of the soil, excessive salt concentrations, low lying area or field with shallow and poor top salt may also causebuttoning. (vii) Vigorously grown nursery plants with thickened stems and sessile foliage being already generative have a tendency of button formation in the field. The check in growth may be caused by root injury by insects or by some diseases (especially *Rhizoctonia spp.*).	
Blindness	Plant without terminal buds or when the growing point collapse at an early stage and the terminal buds fails to develop and plant becomes blind. It occurs in overwintered plants and any practice interfering in growth of the terminal bud may lead to blindness. Plant grows without terminal bud and fail to form any curd. It is characterized by the leaves that develop are large, dark green, thick and leathery owing to the accumulation of CHO. Sometimes the axillary bud develops, but the plant fails to produce a marketable curd. The main cause of blindness are low temperature when	Avoiding young plant from low temperature exposure, care seedlings while planting and handling and avoid damage from insect-pests.

Disorders	Symptoms/reasons	Control measures
	plants are small and when damage occurs to the terminal bud during handling of the plants or injury by insect-pests.	
Chlorosis	Magnesium deficiency causes chlorosis when grown on highly acidic soils. Chlorosis shows on interveinal and yellow mottling of lower leaves. The affected leavesturn bronze in colour and become stiff. In severely deficient plants, abscission of the lower leaves occurs and results into small curd formation.	Applying magnesium oxide @ 300 kg/ha, liming the soil with dolomite limestone to bring the soil pH to 6.5. Use of a fertilizer containing soluble Mg also keeps it under control.
Hollow Stem	It may be due to boron deficiency and higher supply of nitrogen nutrition. Hollowness caused by boron may be identified, by water soaked and discoloured tissue, whereas, hollowness caused by nitrogen, the stem is perfectively clear while with no sign ofdisintegration.	Spraying of borax at 0.1 to 0.3 or soil application of borax @ 15-20 kg/ha. For normal type of hollowness spacing the plants closer together or by reducing the fertilizer doses.
Frost Injury	Leaves of young seedling turn yellowish-white on both the surfaces. Petioles become flaccid and , white midrib along with adjacent parenchyma and stem may also be injured. Fully grown curds of cauliflower are more sensitive to frost damage, than the smaller ones. However, in cabbage the younger leaves are particularly sensitive to frost, as that the centre of the head turns brown, while outwardly the head appears healthy, similar symptoms also occurs in Brussels sprout.	Irrigating the field on anticipating the danger of frostand by raising the field temperature by creating smoke.
Pinking	Sometimes curds show pink tinge, this appears due to the exposureof curds to high light intensities. Under this condition anthocyanin form and gives rise pink colour curds.	(i) Grow self-blanched varieties/ hybrids (ii) Avoid curd to the exposure o high light intensities

14.12.4. Tomato

Disorders	Symptoms/reasons	Control measures
Blossom – end rot (BER)	In the beginning brown discolouration starts on the blossom end portion of the fruit. Gradually a black spot develops to encompass on-e–half to two–third portion of the fruit. In the advanced stage, the tissues shrink and the skin becomes dark grey to black. A secondary infection by soft rot or other fungal diseases may occur. The affected fruits are totally unfit for human consumption. The cause of this disorder may be (i) Use of ammonium sulphate for nitrogen supply (ii) An imbalance of magnesium and potassium under saline conditions magnesium is distinctly higher than calcium and thus may cause the disorder. (iii) Depletion of calcium in the blossom-end portion and (iv) GA has caused a high with CCC, SADH and IAA	(i) Cultural practice that conserves soil moisture and maintains a fairly uniform moisture supply aids (ii) Transplanting in early April instead of an early June (iii) Single foliar spray of 0.5 per cent calcium chloride solution at the time of fruit development (iv) Apply nitrogenous fertilizers in the form of urea.
Blotchy ripening (BR)	Greenish yellow and whitish patches on the ripened fruits particularly on the stem end portion. Sometimes white and in certain cases brown, tissues are present in the blotched area. The disorder arises (i) When there is an imbalance of nitrogen and potasic nutrient in the soil and (ii) Water deficiency at the time of excessive transpiration may also cause BR.	(i) There is a need for a balance between nitrogen and potassium fertilizer in the soil. When the level of potassium is very high, the application of magnesium (ii) Use resistant variety, which have the capacity to utilise potassium more efficiently.
Cracking	These conditions occur from mid-May onwards and could be counteracted by verntilating at night, or heavy to increase the green house temperature. Reduced transpiration has increased cell turgidity	(i) Use of resistant cultivars likes Sioux, Manalucie Crack Proof Punjab Chhuhara, Koshi Aman etc. (ii) Picking of the fruits before the full ripe stage reduces the incidence of radial cracking.

	and contributed to tomato fruit cracking. Cracking is also common during the rainy season when the rains follow a long dry spell. The presence of water on the surface of the fruit is more conducive to cracking than high soil moisture. Fruit water potential increase of two bars has been found to be associated with fruit cracking. Boron deficiency in the soil also causes fruit cracking in tomato. There are four types of cracking: radal, concentric, burst and cuticular. Of these, radial cracking is mostly at the ripe stage while concentric cracking is more at the mature green stages	(iii) Soil application of borax at the rate of 10-15 kg/ha or its spray at 0.25 per cent at the fruiting stage. (iv) Proper control of moisture in the soil particularly at the ripening stage.
Puffiness	Fruit reaches about two-third normal size, the outer wall continues to develop normally but remaining internal tissue growth is retarded. As a result, tomato fruits are light in weight, they lack firmness and partially filled. This is due to non-fertilization and necrosis of vascular and placental tissue after the fruit is well developed. Casual factors are high or low temperature and low soil moisture.	(i) Maintain soil Moisture in field (ii) Avoid tomato crop with very low or very high temperature (iii) Grow tomato varieties leaving high pericarp thickness
Catfacing	Distortion or opening of large scar of the blossom - end portion of the fruit. Such fruits have ridges, furrows and blotches. At the blossom – end portion, there is malformation. It looks like a modified blossom end rot. There are several reasons which causes catfacing are (i) Low temperature is the main causes of catfacing. (ii) Faulty pollination and fertilization due to low temperature cause catfacing and (iii) The time of nitrogen application may be another probable cause by altering the transition of	Delayed pruning, balancing the internal nutrient,.regulating temperature, the assimilation rate, and the endogenous growth regulators can control catfacing.

Disorders	Symptoms/reasons	Control measures/reasons
	vegetable growth into reproductive phase.	
Sunscald	When the fruits and the leaves are exposed to the sun, the suscald symptoms appear. First, there is the appearance of yellow or white patches on green and ripened fruits. Further, these patches may have a secondary infection of fungus, which show black dark spots. Sometimes such spots start rotting and the fruits are absolutely unfit for use. When the varieties have sparse foliage, sunscald is more severe. In India, this is a serious problem in the month of May and June. A high temperture treatment along with a high light intensity may result in 100 per cent sunscald.	Use of varieties with ample foliage and following good cultural practices may reduce the incidence.

14.12.5. Beet Root

Disorders	Symptoms/rcasons	Control measures/reasons
Internal black spot or Brown heart	Boron deficient plants usually remain dwarf or stunted. The leaves are smaller than normal. The young unfolding leaves fail to develop normally and eventually turn brown or black and die. The leaves may assume a variegated appearance due to development of mixture of yellow and purplish red blotches over parts or whole, the stalk of such leaves shows longitudinal splitting. Frequently the affected plant has twisted leaves and exhibits a light shortening and distorting of its leaf stalk in the centre of its crown. The growing point may die and decay. The roots do not grow to full size and under condition of severe boron deficiency they remain very small and distorted and have a rough, unhealthy, greyish appearance instead of being clean and smooth. Their surface often are wrinkled and cracked. Within the fleshy roots hard or corky spots are found scattered throughout the roots, but more numbers on the light coloured zones or cambium layers.	Application of borax to the soil.
Magnesium deficiency	Magnesium is one of the constituents of chlorophyll. Deficiency of Mg causes pale areas between the leaf veins. Eventually these discoloured areas turn brown and die. Very acid or limey soils cause unavailability of Mg.	(i) Spray magnesium sulphate (zypsum salts) at 0.1 per cent concentration once or twice at a fortnight interval, (ii) Apply well rotten farmyard manure or compost and (iii) Apply lime in very acidic soils.

	Disorders	Symptoms/reasons	Control measures
	Manganese deficiency	Affected plants have leaves with yellow blotches between the veins, and the leaves and to curl up, usually in mid-summer, Generally Mn deficiency occurs in very sandy soil and very alkaline soils.	(i) Apply manganese sulphate at 0.02 per cent as a foliar feed. (ii) Avoid too sandy soil for cultivation of beetroot crop. (iii) Avoid growing beet root on alkaline soils and (iv) Add adequate amount of well rotten farmyard manure or compost during land preparation.
Carrot	Carrot splitting	Splitting or cracking of carrot root is a major problem. Splitting tended to reduce by low nitrogen and to increase by chlorides. It may also be caused by a fluctuating water supply. When there is a heavy rainfall after a period of drought, the inner flesh of the carrot expands faster than the toughened skin, causing the skin to fissure. Sometimes, roots splits, often exposing core.	(i) Apply balance quantity of nitrogen and (ii) Do not allow to grow carrot for long period of time without water.
	Cavity spot	This physiological disorder is associated with an increased accumulation of potassium and a ecreased accumulation of calcium. It is observed that cavity spot disorder root is a manifestation of calcium deficiency, which may be induced by excess potassium uptake during the ontogeny of carrot plants.	Increase in calcium level in the growing medium results in increased calcium accumulation in the plant and a significant reduction in the incidence of cavity spot.

Glossary

A

Abiotic stress: Adverse conditions for crop growth and production caused by environment factor such as deficiency or excess of nutrition, moisture, temperature and light, the presence of harmful gases or toxicants, and abnormal soil condition such as salinity, alkanety and acidity.

Abnormal seedling: Seedling which are unable to develop in to normal plants.

Acclimatization: The process of introduced plants to adapt or adjust to the new or changed environment.

Acentric chromosomes: A chromosomes without centromere.

A-chromosomes: Normal member of chromosomes complements of a species which are essential for normal growth and development.

Acicular: Long, narrow and cylindrical; i.e., needle-shaped as the leaves of onion, etc.

Acid foods: Foods having pH 4.5 to 3.7 which are usually spoiled by non-spore forming aciduric, butyric anaerobes, etc. e.g., products of tomato, etc.

Acrocentric chromosomes: A chromosomes in which centromere is located very near to one end or has sub terminal position.

Active collection: Germplasm which is meant for medium term storage (10 to 15years). Such collection is subjected to regeneration, multiplication, evaluation, distribution and documentation after every 10 to15 years.

Adaptation: The process by which individuals (or part of individuals), population or species change in form of function in such a way to better survive under given environmental conditions.

Additive gene effect: Gene action in which the effect on a genetic trait are enhanced by each additional gene, either an allele at the same locus or gene at different loci.

Additive variance: That portion of genetics variance which is produced by the average effects of genes at all segregating loci.

Additive X additive epistasis: Interaction between two loci each exhibition lack of dominance individually.

Additive X dominance epistasis: Interaction between two loci, one exhibiting lack of dominance individually.

Adjacent 1-segregation: Segregation of one normal chromosomes with one translocated (t_1+n_2 and t_2+n_1)

Adjacent 2- segregation: Segregation of t_1n_1 to one pole and t_2n_2 to another pole.

Adult resistance: Resistance exhibited by young seedling.

Adventive embryony: Development of embryo from the diploid cells of ovule lying outside the embryo sac belonging to either nucellus or integument.

Alien addition: Addition of one chromosome of yield species to the normal compliments of a cultivated species.

Aline substitution: Replacement of one pair of chromosomes of cultivated species with those of wild donor species.

A-line: The male sterile line.

Alkylating agents: Chemical mutagens which cause mutation by adding alkyl group at various positions in DNA.

Allele: An allele is an alternative form of a gene.

Allelochemical: Chemical substances which are liberated in allelopathy and inhibit the growth of another species growing together.

Allelopathy: Suppression of plant growth on the same piece of land in a year multiplied by hundred.

Alliin: A colorless, odorless, water soluble amino acid present in the uninjured bulb of garlic which, on crushing, breaks down in presence of the enzyme alliinase to allicin, the principal ingredient of the odoriferous diallyl disulfide.

Allogamy: When pollen grains from flowers of one plant pollinate the flower of other plants.

Allohaploids: Polyhaploid which develop from a autopolyploid species.

Allosomal linkage: Linkage of genes which are located in allosomes or sex chromosomes.

Allosomes: Those chromosomes which differ in number and morphology in male and female sex, also known as sex chromosomes.

Alternate segregation: At anaphase movement of two normal chromosomes ($n_1$and n_2) towards one pole and that of two translocated chromosomes ($t_1$and t_2) to another pole.

Amino acid: Organic: compound which contains carboxyl (COOH) or acidic group and an amino (NH_2) or basic group. Amino acids are of two types, essential and non-essential.

Amphidiploid: An allopolyploid combining genomes of two diploid species.

Analysis of covariance: The statistical procedure which splits simultaneously the variation of two variables in various components.

Aneuhaploids: Haploid which develops from a aneuploid species. Aneuploids are four types, viz. disomic haploid, nullisomic haploids, substitution haploid and miss division haploid.

Aneuploidy: The change in chromosomes number which involves one or few chromosomes of the genome. Aneuploids are of three type, viz., .monosomic, nullisomic, and polysomic.

Anther culture: The culturing of anthers *in vitro* for the purpose of generating haploid plantlets.

Anthesis: Full flower expansion including anther extrusion.

Antibiosis: Adeverse effects of the host on feeding, development and reproduction of insect - pests.

Antibody: Substances in a tissue or fluid of the body that acts in antagonism to a foreign substance (antigen).

Antigen: A substance, usually a protein, introduced into a living organism that elicits antibody formation.

Antimutator gene: Gene which decreases the frequency of spontaneous mutation of other genes in the same genome. Such gene has been reported in bacteria and bacterio-phases.

Apical dominance: In plants, the inhibition of lateral buds by high level of auxins, produced in the lead shoot or apical meristem.

Apogamy: Development of embryo either from synergids or antipodal cells of embryo sac.

Apomixis: Development of seed without sexual fusion (fertilization). Apomixis are 4 types, parthenogenesis, apogamy, apospory, and adventive embryony.

Apospory: Development of another embryo sac without reduction from the cell of ovule outside the embryo sac may develop either from archesporium (generative apospory) or from nucellus or integument (somatic apospory).

Arithmetic mean: Sum of all observation in a sample divided by their number.

Aroids: A group of vegetable crops under the family Araceae where edible plant parts are corm and cormels e.g., *Colocasia* spp., *Amorphophallus* sp., etc.

Artificial selection: The practice of choosing individuals from a population for reproduction, usually because these individuals possess one or more desirable traits.

Aseptic conditions: Pathogen free environment.

Asexual reproduction: Any processes of reproduction that does not involve that formation and union of gamets from the different sexes or mating types.

Asiatic carrot: Carrot cultivars which do not require any low temperature treatment for flowering and produce seed freely in the plains of India. e.g., Pusa Kesar.

Asnapsis: The failure or partial failure in the pairing of homologous chromosomes during the meiotic prophase.

Assortive mating: Mating in which the partners are chosen because they are phenotypically similar.

Autogamy; Transfer of pollen grains from the anther to the stigma of the same flower, also called self-pollination various machanism which promote autogamy include, bisexuality, homogamy, cleistogamy etc.

Autohaploids: Polyploids which develop from an autohaploid species.

Autopolyploid: A polyploid that has multiple and identical or nearly identical sets of chromosomes (genomes). A polyploidy species with genomes derived from the same original species.

Autoradiograph: A record or photograph prepared by labelling a substance such as DNA with a radioactive material such as tritiated thymidine and allowing the image produced by decay radiations to develop on a film over a period of time.

Autosomal linkage: Linkage of autosomal genes.

Autosomes: Those chromosomes which do not differ in number and morphology in male and female sex.

Autozygote: A diploid individual in which the two genes of a locus are identical by descent from an ancestral gene.

Auxotroph: A mutant microorganism (e.g., bacterium or yeast) that will not grow on a minimal medium but that requires the addition of some compound such as an amino acid or a vitamin.

Avoidence: Escape of a variety from insect attack either due to earliness or its cultivation in the season when insect population is very low.

B

B- line: The fertile counterpart of a line. This line does not have fertility restorer genes and used as the male parents to maintain the A- line.

Back cross method of breeding: It is method of breeding in which the desirable character (s) of a non-recurrent (donor) parent is added to the genetic back ground of recurrent (recipient) parent through subsequent generations of back crossing and selection.

Back cross: Crossing the F_1 hybrids with either of the parents. This may be done to test the genotypic ratio of F_1 or to transfer specific gene complex from one species to another.

Balanced heterosis: It is a type of true heterosis, which occurs from the balanced combinations of genes in a hybrid.

Balanced polymorphism: Regular occurrence of several phenotypes in a genetic population due to superiority of heterozygote over homozygotes.

Base collection: Plant materials which are meant for long term storage (up to hundred years).Seed of such material is stored at -18° to -20°c.

Base station: The RTK-GPS receiver and radio that are placed in a stationary position, functioning as the corrections source for roving tractor units in an area. These stations can be either portable or permanently installed systems and their coverage can range from 5 to 10 miles depending on topographic conditions, antenna height, and radio-transmit power.

Base temperature: The threshold temperature level below which plant do not develop. Each plant has its own base temperature. e.g., pea (4.4°C), French bean (10°C), asparagus (5.5°C), spinach (2°C), pumpkin (13°C), tomato (15°C), etc.

Basic number: The number of chromosomes in ancestral diploid ancestors of polyploids, represented by x.

B-chromosomes: Chromosomes which are found in addition to normal chromosomes compliments of a species and are not essential for normal growth and development. Also known as accessory, supernumerary or extra chromosomes.

Beaded root: Root possessing swellings at frequent intervals, seen in *Basella*, *Momordica*, etc.

Bhasinda: The underground stem of *Nelumbium*, a popular vegetable in North India.

Bi-directional replication: Replication of DNA in both directions from the point of origin.

Biennial: Plant having a two-year life cycle, vegetative in the first season and reproductive in the second season, and this transition from vegetative to reproductive stage often requires environmental trigger such as vernalization or photoperiod. e.g., cabbage, onion, carrot, etc.

Biological yield: Total dry matter production per plant.

Biochemical mutation: A mutation that alters biochemical function of an individual.

Biometrical genetics: A branch of genetics which utilizes various statistical concepts and procedures in the study of genetics. It includes quantitative genetics and population genetics.

Biometrical pathway: A definite sequential path of biochemical reaction.

Biometrics: The science dealing with the application of statistical methods to biological problems.

Biotechnology: The application of recombinant DNA, cell and tissue culture, and other methods used to develop new and improved plants and plant products.

Biotic stress: Adverse condition for crop growth and production caused by biological factors such as diseases, insects, and parasitic weeds.

Biotype: Distinct physiological race or strain within morphological species. A population of individuals with identical genetic constitution. A biotype may be made up of homozygotes, of which only the former would be expected to breed true.

Biparental cross: Crossing of randomly selected plants in F_2 or sub-sequent generation of a cross between two pure lines in a definite fashion. Concept of biparental mating was originally developed by Comstock and Robinson (1948, 1952). There are three mating designs of biparental cross, viz North Carolina Design 1and 2 North Carolina Design 3, also called NCD1, NCD2, and NCD3.

Bisexuality: A system of producing both stamen and carpel in the same flower on a plant.

Bit: A binary digit, 0 and 1.

Black leaf speck of cabbage: Small, sharply sunken brown or black specks on leaves which occur under refrigeration in transit and storage and under sharp temperature drops in the fields, also found in Chinese cabbage and cauliflower.

Blanching (cultural): Exclusion of light from the edible parts of salad crops like asparagus, leek, cauliflower, etc., which makes the crop crisp, reduces acrid flavor, improves flavor and tenderness.

B-line: The fertile counterpart of a line. This line does not have fertility restorer genes and used as the male parents to maintain the A-line.

Bolter: Sporadic occurrence of abnormally big sized tuber in potato.

Bolting: Significant stem elongation that proceeds flowering; also includes the case of premature emergence of flower stalk.

Bract: A more or less modified subtending a flower or belonging to an inflorescence.

Breeder seed: Seed increased by the originating, or sponsoring, plant breeder or institution, used as the source for production of foundation seed.

Breeder's rights: Legislation giving the equivalent of patent right for plant cultivars. The effect is to give the developer of a cultivar sole legal possession of that cultivars and a legal basis for compensation for its use by others. Breeder's rights may be referred to as "Plant cultivar protection".

Breeding methods: Various procedures (selection, hybridization, mutation etc.) which are used for genetic improvement of crop plants, also called breeding procedures. Breeding methods which are commonly used in autogamous species include, introduction, pure line selection, mass selection, pedigree method, back cross method, bulk method, single seed descent method, multiline breeding, mutation breeding etc.

Broad sense heritability: Ratio of total genetic variance phenotypic variance.

Bud pollination: Pollination of flowers before they attain maturity (open and shed pollen grain) with the pollen grains collected from the same plant/ genotype.

Bulb crops: Vegetable crops under the genus *Allium* which include onion, garlic, leek, shallot and chive, whose bulbs are eaten raw or cooked or they and their leaves are used to flavor other vegetables, meat, fish and sauces.

Bulb scale: Fleshy 'leaves' that together form the bulb.

Bulb tunic: The dead, papery, leathery or fibrous covering that surrounds most bulbs.

Bulb: A specialized underground organ consisting of a short, fleshy, usually vertical stem axis bearing at its apex a growing point or a flower primordium enclosed by thick, fleshy scales, e.g., onion, etc.

Bulbil: Vegetative part that is actually the modification of flower(s). It develops into plant directly without formation of seeds; seen in onion, garlic, etc.

Bulblets: Miniature bulbs produced around the base of the mother bulb due to development of meristem in the axil of scale leaves.

Bulb-to-seed method: A method of seed production of bulb crops where the bulbs harvested during warm weather are selected, stored and again replanted in winter for seed production.

Bulk breeding: A selection procedure is segregating population of self-pollinated species in which material is grown in bulk plots from F_2 to F_5 with or without selection; next generation is grown from bulk seed and individual plant selection is practiced in F_6 or later generations.

Bus: A group of lines used to transfer bits between micro procedure and the components of computer system.

Byte: A group of 8 bits.

C

Callus: A mass of unorganized callus in culture medium (plural calli).

Capsanthin: A carotenoid pigment responsible for the characteristic orange-red coloration of ripe chilli.

Caruncle: An outgrowth near the hilum of the seeds as seen in dolichos bean

Celery lettuce: Stem type cultivar of lettuce, grown for its thick stem which is eaten after peeling.

Cell culture: Regeneration of a whole plant from a single cell in nutrient medium. It may include somatic cell or germinal cell (pollen).

Cell cycle: The period in which one cycle of cell division is completed. It consists of interphase and mitotic phase.

Cell division: The process of reproduction of new cells from the pre- existing cell.

Cell: A basic unit of structure and function in all living organisms.

Centers of diversity: A placed, region or area where maximum variability of crop plants is observed, also called centers of origin. Center of origin include, China, India, Indo-malaya, Central Asia, Near East, Mediterranean, Abyssinia, South Mexico and Central America, Chile and Brazil.

Certified seed: The progeny of a foundation or registered seed, which maintains the satisfactory genetic identity and purity and has been certified approved by the certifying agency.

Chasmogamy: Opening of flower after the completion of pollination.

Chemical dormancy: Type of seed coat dormancy in which germination inhibiting chemicals *viz.,* various phenols, coumarin and abscisic acid accumulated in the fruit as well as in the seed coverings strongly inhibit germination; found in cucurbits, tomato, etc.

Chiasma terminalization: The movement chiasma away from the centromere towards the end of tetrad.

Chiasma: The point of exchange of segment between non- sister chromatids of homologous chromosomes during pachytene.

Chlorophyll: Containing plastids, sites or photosynthesis in green plants.

Chloroplasts: Plastid of green color that is associated with photosynthesis.

Chromatine: A partially clumped and tangled mass of nuclear chromosomes.

Chromoplast: Plastid with other than green color.

Chromosomal DNA: This is found in the chromosome.

Chromosome models: The pattern of organization of chromatin fibers in a chromosome.

Chromosomes maps: Line diagrams which depict position of various genes on chromosomes and recombination frequency between them also known as genetic maps or linkage maps.

Chromosomes: Darkly staining nucleoprotein bodies that are observed in cells during division. Each chromosome carries a linear array of genes.

Circular Chromosomes: A chromosomes with circular shape and structures, found in bacteria and viruses.

Circular DNA: DNA which has a ring or circular shape such DNA is usually found in prokaryotes, chloroplast and, mitochondria.

Cis position: Presence of two yield allele in one homologous chromosomes (++/ab) also called coupling phase of alleles.

Cistron: The largest elements within a gene which is the unit of function.

Cleistogamy: A built-in breeding mechanism where flowers remain closed at the time of pollination which favour self-pollination, as seen in lettuce.

Clonal selection: A procedure of selecting superior clones from the mixed population of asexually propagated crop such as sugarcane, potato etc.

Clone: A group of individuals derived by a single original plant propagated by vegetative means.

Closed anther mutant: A mutated anther type which through produces viable pollen grains but does not shed them due to non- rupturing and causes bareness in plants particularly where self-pollination is the rule. Closed anther mutants can be maintained by hand pollination with the pollens collected from such flowers by force opening at full maturity.

Co-repressor: A combination of repressor and metabolite which parent's protein synthesis. Such process is termed as co repressor.

Codominance: Expression of both the alleles in the heterozygote or F_1.

Codominant genes: Alleles, each of which produce an independent effect in F_1.

Codon: Triplet sequence of RNA bases which codes for a particular amino acid.

Co-heritability: Ratio of genotypic covariance to the phenotypic covariance. It measures simultaneous inheritance of two characters.

Colchicine: Alkaloids extracted from seeds or corms of *Colchicum autumnale,* which induces pollyploid by arresting, spindle formation during mitosis.

Colchiploidy: Polyploid which is induced by colchicine treatment.

Cole crops: A group of vegetable crops which originated from wild cabbage of Mediterranean region and belonging to genus Brassica (Brassicaceae) which include cabbage, cauliflower, Broccoli, Brussels sprouts, knol-khol, Chinese cabbage, etc., whose leaves, unopened flower buds, inflorescences or swollen stems are used as cooked or raw vegetables.

Combinational heterosis: The heterosis in quantitative characters resulting from the overall combination of the favorable cumulative effects of a number componential character.

Compatible: Capable of fertilization.

Complementary genes: Those genes which have more or less similar phenotypic expression individually but when they come together they interact to produce a new character expression. If two such genes are complementary for a dominant effect, a 9:7 ratio results in F_2; if two are complementary for a recessive effect, a 15:1 ratio results in F_2.

Complete diallel: All possible single crosses among n parents that are n (n-1) /2.

Complete linkage: Linkage in which crossing over does not occur.

Complete penetrance: Expression of a gene in all the individuals which carry it.

Completely randomized design: Experimental design which is used when the experimental plot is small and homogenous such as pot culture.

Composite variety: In cross-pollinated species, a variety developed by mixing the seed of various genotypes which are similar in maturity, height, seed size, seed colour, etc.

Composites: The advanced generations seed mixture of an interval or interracial cross.

Computer: An electronic device that can transmit, store and process information or data. Computer are of four types; micro, mini, main frame and super computer.

Conical roots: When the root is broad at the base and gradually tappers towards the apex like a cone as in carrot.

Conservation: The protection of genetic diversity from genetic erosion either under natural condition or by storing in gene banks.

Conservative replication: DNA replication in which one new DNA molecule has parental strands and other contains both newly synthesized strands there is no experimental proof for this method also.

Constitutive enzyme: An enzyme whose production is constant irrespective of metabolic state of cell.

Consumptive use of water (CUW): Water used to meet the evapotranspiration (ET) need and metabolic activities of plant is collectively known as consumptive use of water.

Contrasting character: Feature of an individual with marked (observable) phenotypic differences, such as red and white, tall and dwarf.

Contributing alleles: Those alleles which contribute to continuous variations also referred to as effective alleles.

Convergent improvement: A system of double back crossing for the purpose of improving each of two inbred lines without greatly modifying the yield of their F_1 cross.

Coordinate projection: Refers to a coordinate system using a specific model of the Earth. UTM coordinates would be considered to be a coordinate projection as it uses a model of the Earth that is cylindrical. UTM's are projected onto a map based on latitude and longitude.

Coreless carrot: Good quality cultivars of carrot in which the core or xylem is small and deeply pigmented so that the cortex or phloem and the core is evenly colored.

Corm: Bulky, short and vertical underground modified stem in which foods are stored as in Elephant's foot (*Amorphophallus* sp.), etc.

Correction factor: The square of grand total divided by number of observation in the analysis of variance.

Correlation: A statistical measure which is used to find out the degree and direction of relationship two or more variable. It is of three types viz. simple, partial, and multiple.

Coupling: Linkage between dominant (AB) or recessive (ab) genes.

Cover crops: Crops that are grown both for the protection of the soil from erosion and for soil improvement. e.g., cowpea.

Cris –cross inheritance: Inheritance of sex linked gene from grandfather to grandson through daughter.

Critical differences: Least significance differences greater than which all the difference is significant.

Critical moisture periods: Critical periods of irrigation needs can best be defined as that time when soil moisture stress can reduce yield most in an otherwise healthy crop. This is not to say that it is the only time in the life of the crop that moisture stress reduces yield. It is, however, the time when stress has the greatest effect.

Crop ideotype: A plant model which is expected to yield greater quantity of grains, fibers, oil or other useful product when developed as a cultivar.

Cropping index: Number of crops grown on the same piece of land in a year multiplied by hundred.

Cross incompatibility: In ability of a functional pollen of one species or genus to effect fertilization of the female gametes of another species or genus of the same family.

Cross pollinated crops: An assembly of genetically heterozygous individuals under commercial cultivation which share a common gene pool and in which each individual takes new genotype generation after generation.

Cross- pollination: Transfer of pollen from the anther of one plant to the stigma of another plant. It affects the union of genetically dissimilar gametes.

Cross: The products of the mating between two or more parents are dissimilar genetic constitution. The various type of crosses utilized in heterosis breeding programs are single, three-way, double crosses, top crosses, multiple crosses etc.

Crossing over: Inter change of parts between no sister chromatids of homologous chromosomes during pachytene.

Crossing: Artificial mating of two or more parents of unlike genetical constitutions.

Cucurbits: A large and diverse group of vegetable crops under cucurbitaceae, used as vegetables (pumpkin, different gourds, etc.) pickles (cucumber) and as desert fruits (muskmelon, watermelon).

Cultigroup: An intraspecific category below subspecies which includes cultivated types such as *Vigna unguiculata* cultigroup sesquipedalis (vegetable cowpea).

Cultivar: An assemblage of cultivated plants which is clearly distinguished by any character and which, when reproduced, sexually or asexually, retain the distinguishing characters.

Culture medium: A nutrient medium which contains all essential micro and macronutrients, carbohydrate vitamins and hormones.

Curd size index: A curd character of cauliflower which is the equatorial × polar diameter of the curd.

Curd: Edible part of cauliflower which is actually the repeatedly branched prefloral fleshy apical meristem.

Cyclic selection: Selection in one direction for one generation or season and in opposite direction in next generation or season.

Cytogenetic/cytonuclear male sterility: Male sterility is determined by interaction of gene and cytoplasm but none of them singly can control sterility.

Cytokinesis: The process of division of cytoplasm.

Cytoplasmic and genic male sterility: Sterility of pollen grains which is governed by the interaction between sterile cytoplasm and recessive gene, seen in onion, beet, carrot, etc.

Cytoplasmic DNA: The DNA which is found in cytoplasm either in chloroplast or in mitochondria.

Cytoplasmic genic male sterility (CGMS): Pollen sterility which is controlled by both cytoplasmic and nuclear genes.

Cytoplasmic inheritance: Inheritance which is governed by cytoplasmic gene or plasma gene, by chloroplast or mitochondrial DNA. also known as extra chromosomal inheritance or extra nuclear inheritance or organeller inheritance or non- mendelian inheritance.

Cytoplasmic male sterility (CMS): Pollen sterility which is caused by cytoplasmic genes.
Cytoplasmic mutation: A mutation in cytoplasmic gene.
Cytoplasmic sterility: Transmission of male sterility by the cytoplasm.
Cytoplasmic: Concerned with the cytoplasm in the cell.

D

D2-statistics: Statistical procedures which measures forces of differention at intra and inter cluster levels and determines the relative contribution of each component trait to the total divergence. This technique was developed by P.C.Mahalanobils (1928) and first used for assessment of variability in plant breeding by C.R.Rao (1952).

Data layer (in GIS): A layer of information on a GIS map. A map can have many layers to present different types of information. For example, the first layer of a map may be a satellite image of an area. The next layer may have only lines that represent roads or highways. The next layer may contain topographic information and so forth.

Day-neutral plant: Plant in which flowering is not influenced by day length. e.g., tomato, cucumber, okra, asparagus, capsicum, snap bean, etc.

Decompound leaf: When the leaf is more than thrice pinnate as in carrot, etc.

Defective seed: Seed which are broken, disease, infested, insect damaged, undeveloped and unfit for germination.

Degreening: The process of decomposing the green pigment in fruits by applying ethylene (1000-2000 ppm) or similar metabolic inducers to give a fruit its characteristic color as preferred by consumers, generally followed in citrus fruits but also practiced in banana, mango, tomato, etc.

Dehaulming: Removal of the top portion (haulm) of potato in the seed crop to avoid the infestation of virus carrying insect vectors.

Dehiscence: Splitting open of a fruiting structure or anther.

Dehiscent fruit: Fruit whose peri carp bursts to liberate the seeds at maturity as seen in okra, etc.

Deletion: Loss of a segment from a chromosome, also called deficiency.It is of two types, viz. terminal and interstitial.

Denaturation: The process of separation of DNA strands on heating of DNA molecule at high temperature.

Diakinesis: A sub stage of meotic prophase 1st in which bivalents are distributed throughout the cell.

Diallele cross: A diallele cross can be defined as all possible combinations i.e.; n (n-1)/2of single crosses among one parents.

Dichogamy: The maturing of male and female gametes at different time when the male gametes matures earlier than the female, it is called protandry, but when female matures first, it is called protogyny, this situation is called dichogamy.

Dicliny: A situation, where plants produce unisexual flowers.

Differential Global Positioning System (DGPS): This system operates using the same GPS satellites, with the addition of a differential corrections source (WAAS satellite or Coast Guard Beacon) to increase the accuracy of the system. In both cases, multiple ground stations provide the information about satellite error. Accuracy is typically better than 10 feet (3 meters) and can be better than 40 inches (1 meter).

Dihaploid: A haploid which develops from a tetraploid species.

Dioecious: Plant species in which unisexual flower, staminate or pistillate, is borne on separate plants, as in pointed gourd, etc.

Dioecy: Where male and female flower or borne singly and different plants.

Dipeptide: A product of union of two different amino acids.

Diploid number: The somatic chromosome number of a true diploid species.

Diploids: Individual with 2x somatic chromosome number.

Directional selection: Selection in favor of extreme types, viz; earliness and lateness or tallness and dwarfness.

Disomic haploid: A haploid which develops from a tetrasomic species (n+1).

Dispersion: The degree to which numerical data tend to spread about the mean value. It is a measure of variation in a sample.

Dispersive replication: DNA replication in which the new DNA molecules have old and new DNA in patch. This method is not accepted as it could not be proved experimentally.

Displaced: Presence of duplication away from the original segment but on the same arm of chromosomes.

DNA probes: The small segments of DNA with known base sequences, origin and function.

DNA replication: The process by which a DNA molecule makes it identical copies.

DNA: Deoxyribonuclic acid; the information –carrying genetic material that comprises the genes.

Dominance hypothesis: Heterosis due to superiority of dominant alleles over recessive alleles. Heterosis is directly proportional to the number of dominant genes contributed by each parent.

Dominance variance: That portion of genetic variance which arises due to deviation from the additive scheme of gene action resulting from intra –allelic interaction. It is due to the deviation of heterozygote (Aa) from the average of two homozygotes (AA and aa).

Dominance: The phenomenon in which the dominant gene has an overriding effect on its allele in such a way that heterozygote (Aa) is phenotypically indistinguishable from the dominant homozygote (AA).

Dominant (inhibitory) epistasis: Gene interaction in which a dominant allele at one locus can mask the expression of both (dominant and recessive) alleles at second locus resulting in 13:3 ratios, also known as inhibitory.

Dominant gene: When two parents contrasting characters are crossed, the character of one parent appears in F_1 generation to the inclusion of the character of the other parent even through both the genes are present in the hybrid.The gene, which expresses itself ,is said to be dominant over the other recessive.

Dominant: The character which expresses in F_1.

Donar parent: The parent which donates desirable genes also called non- recurrent parent, because it is used once in the crossing programme.

Double cropping: Cultivation of crops one after another on the same field in a year.

Double cross hybrid: A hybrid obtained by crossing two single crosses i.e; (Ax B) x (C x D).

Double crossing over: The formation of two chiasmata between non- sister chromatids of homologous chromosomes.

Double fertilization: A phenomenon in angiosperm where by one male nucleus unites with the egg nucleus to form zygote (2n) which develops into the embryo and the second male nucleus unites with two polar nuclei in the embryo sac to form the endosperm(3n).

Double stranded DNA: DNA which has spirally arranged double strands. It is found in all plants, animals, and bacteria.

Double tetrasomic: Addition of two chromosomes to two different pairs (2n+2+2).

Double top cross: A cross-obtained from crossing single cross with an open pollinated variety.

Drought avoidance: Ability of plants to the maintain a favorable internal water balance under moisture stress.

Drought hardening: Improvement in drought tolerance ability of a genotype through various seeds and seedling treatment.

Drought tolerance: Ability of crop plants to grow, develop and reproduce normally under moisture deficit conditions. In other words, survival of plants under water deficit condition without injury.

Drought: Condition of soil moisture deficiency or water scarcity. There are four mechanism of drought resistance, viz. drought escape, drought avoidance, drought tolerance and drought resistance.

Duplicate dominant epistasis: Gene interaction in which recessive alleles at either of two loci can mask the expression of recessive alleles at the two loci, resulting in 15:1 ratio, also referred to as duplicate gene interaction.

Duplicate recessive epistasis: Gene interaction in which recessive alleles at either of two loci, resulting in 9:7 ratio, also called complimentary epistasis.

Durable resistance: Long lasting resistance. It may be vertical or horizontal.

E

Earthing up: The process of putting the soil just near the base of stems of certain crops like potato, cassava, banana, etc. to provide support and to prevent root exposure.

Effective root zone: It is the depth where the most of the active roots of mature plant are concentrated and are capable of extracting soil moisture.

Effector: The molecule which acts as an inducer or co-repressor in the Operon model of *E.coli.*

Electrophoresis: The migration of suspended particles in an electric field.

Electroporation: A process whereby cell membranes are made permeable to DNA by applying an intense electric current.

Emasculation: In bisexual flowers, the removal of stamens before they burst and shed pollen grains. Its purpose to check self–pollination and is done before effecting cross-pollination.

Embryo culture: The cutting of an immature embryo on a sterile nutrient medium.

Embryo: The portion of seed, which contains the dominant, miniature, rudimentary plant. It arises from the zygote.

Emigration: Outgoing of alleles from a population.

Endoplasmic reticulum: A vast network of membrane enclosed tubules, vesicles and sacs found in cytoplasm.

Endosperm: The nutritive tissue formed inside the embryo sac in the seed. It arises from the triple fusion of sperms nuclei with polar nuclei of embryo sac.

Environmental correlation: The association between two variables which is entirely due to environmental effects. It is estimated from error variances and co-variances.

Enzyme: A protein that accelerates a specific chemical reaction in a living system.

Epidemic: Wide spread uncontrolled incidence of a disease.

Epistasis: The phenomenon in which a non- allelic or gene combination exert a dominant effect over another gene or combination of genes (non- allelic interaction).

Epistatic variance: That portion of genetic variance which arises due to deviation as a consequence of inter-allelic (inter genic) interaction.

Essential amino acids: Amino acids which cannot be synthesized in human body and their requirement has to be met through dietary intake. These are methionine, isoleucine, leucine, lysine, threonine, tryptophan, valine phenylalanine, histidine, and agrinine.

Euchromatin: Lightly staining region of chromosomes during inters phase. Usually found in the middle of chromosomes, genetically active and takes part in transcription.

Eugenics: A branch of genetics which deals with frequencies of genes and genotypes in a population, and also with various forces which tend to alter gene frequencies in a population leading to evolutionary changes.

Euhaploid: Haploid which develop from a euploid species. Euhaploid are of two types, viz, monohaploids, and polyhaploids.

Eukaryotes: Organism whose cells contain well defined nucleus.

Euploidy: The change in the chromosomes number which involves entire set. Euploidy includes monoploids, diploids and polliploids.

European carrot: Carrot cultivars which are biennial in nature and require low temperature (4.8-10°C) treatment for certain periods for flowering, hence do not produce seeds in plains of India, e.g., Nantes, Chanteny, Imperator etc.

Evaporation: It is the loss of water from soil surface of a particular area during a certain period.

Evapotranspiration: It is the total loss of water due to transpiration from a crop plants and evaporation from the soil.

Evolution: The process of the origin of the organisms (varieties, species, genera, families etc.).

Exons: Coding sequence of DNA in split genes.

Exotic collection: The germplasm which is collected or received from other country.

Explant: Plant part which is used for regeneration. It may be a cell, a protoplast, a tissue or an organ.

Ex-situ conservation: The preservation of germplasm in gene banks.

Extinction: Permanent loss of a crop species due to various reasons.

F

F_1: An abbreviation to designate the first hybrid generation. It is composed of progenies raised by showing the seeds obtained from cross between two genetically unlike parents.

F_2: Progeny of F_1 plants obtained by selfing.

Fasciculated roots: Swollen tuberous roots which are developed in a cluster or fascicle at the base of the stem as in asparagas, etc.

Fertility restorer gene: Usually a gene when put into a cytoplasmic male sterile background is able to bring back the production of normal functional pollen grains.

Fertility: The ability of an organism to form viable off spring.

Field application efficiency: The field application efficiency is the fraction of the applied water that is used by the crop. Provided there are no runoff losses, the field application efficiency (%) is the required irrigation depth (mm), divided by the average applied irrigation depth (mm), and multiplied by 100%.

Field capacity (FC): Field capacity is the amount of water that a well-drained soil holds against gravitational forces, or the amount of water remaining when downward drainage has markedly decreased. This situation usually exists one to three days after the field has thoroughly been wetted by rain or irrigation. The field capacity is the upper limit of available soil moisture to the plants. The soil moisture tension at field capacity generally varies from 0.1-0.3 atmospheres.

Field resistance: Resistance which gives an effective control of a parasite under field condition.

Five parameter models: A model of generation mean analysis which provides information about five parameters, viz. m, d, h, i and l involves P_1, P_2, F_1, F_2, and F_3 generations of a cross in analysis.

Floating garden: A type of vegetable garden found in the lakes of Kashmir valley where vegetables are grown on a floating base prepared with some grass (*Typha*), compost and other organic matters.

Floppy disk: A thin plastic-coated disk with magnetic oxide which is used for information storage in computers.

Foliaceous stipules: A large paired leafy outgrowth as seen in pea, etc.

Foundation seed: The seed stocks that are so handed as to most nearly maintain the specific genetic identity and purity of the original stock and provide the source for the production of called certified and registered seed.

Founder effect: Establishment of a new population in the main population by single or few individuals.

Frame shift mutations: Mutation which arises due to addition or detection of nucleotides in mRNA.

Fresh under germinated seeds: Viable seeds which can abort water but do not germinate and remain fresh in germination test.

F-test: A test of statistical significance which is used to compare the differences among several means.

Full diallel: All possible both away (direct and reciprocal) crosses among n genotype.

Full slip: A harvesting index of muskmelon or cantaloups for local market when the fruit can easily be removed (slip) with a slight pressure from the stem leaving a clean stem cavity.

Functional male sterility: Where plants produce normal pollen grains but anthers remain closed and caused male sterility.

Fusiform root: When the root is swollen in the middle and gradually tappers towards the apex and the base, being more or less spindle-shaped in appearance as in radish.

F-value: The ratio of treatment variance to error variance.

G

G1: A pre-DNA replication phase it lise between telo phase s- phase.

G2: A post DNA replication phase during which protein and RNA synthesis take place.

Gamete selection: It is a type of selection for detecting and combining of desirable gamete a genetically variable heterozygous population into the back ground of an inbred line of known performance and combining ability.

Gamete: A matured sex cell, capable of fusing with another to form a zygote.

Gametocide: A chemical substance destructive to gametes.

Gametophyte: A phase of life cycle of plants, which has haploid nuclei, during it the sex cells are produced. It arises from a spore produced by meiosis from a sporophyte (diploid).

Garden for vegetable processing: A type of vegetable farming where vegetables are produced with a soe objective of supplying them to the processing factories.

Gene action: The manner in which genes control phenotypic expression of various characters in an organism.

Gene deployment: Planned geographical distribution of major genes for specific resistance to a pest for use in varietal devlopment and production.

Gene expression: The hereditary properties of an organism as represented by the gene and are expressed in generation under a set of environmental factors.

Gene flow: The spread of genes from one breeding population to another by migration, possible leading to allele frequency changes.

Gene for gene hypothesis: This hypothesis states that for each gene controlling pathognecity in the pathogene, also called Flor hypothesis after the name of scientist who developed this concept.

Gene frequency: Proportion of a gene or allele or its series present in a population or a sample thereof. It is usually expressed as number between 0 to 1.

Gene pool: Some total of all genes in a breeding population.

Gene pyramiding: Incorporation of two or more major genes in a variety for specific resistance to a pest.

Gene symbol: Various symbol which are used to represent genes or alleles.

Gene: A heredity determinant of a specific biological function; a unit of inheritance (DNA) located in a fixed place on the chromosome.

General combining ability: The comparative ability of a line or a genetic stock to combine with a tester or a group of testers.

Genetic advance: The expected gain in the mean of the population for a particular quantitative character by one generation of selection of a specified percent of the highest-ranking plant conditions. Genetic resistance is of two types viz. vertical and horizontal.

Genetic architecture: A term used to denote the general genetic structure of a species.

Genetic break down: A term used to indicate the loss of vigour and often the early death of F_2 plants which lack the necessary adaptive complexes of either or both the original parents.

Genetic code: The relationship between the sequences of amino acid in a polypeptide chain.

Genetic engineering: Genetic manipulation that use recombinant DNA methods (gene splicing) to change the genetic makeup of an organism.

Genetic equilibrium: In a random mating population, the stage in which genotype frequencies do not change from one generation to another.

Genetic erosion: Gradual disappearance of various forms of a cultivated species and its wild relatives.

Genetic homeostasis: The ability of a random mating population to equilibrate its genetic composition so as to resist sudden environmental changes.

Genetic male sterility: Sterility of male gametes in a flower governed by genes and is heritable.

Genetic resistance: Ability of some genotypes to give higher yield of good quality than other varieties at the same initial level of disease or insect infestation under similar environmental conditions. Genetic resistance is of two types viz. vertical and horizontal.

Genetic RNA: The RNA which act as DNA or genetic material.

Genetics: The science of heredity and variation.

Genic male sterility: Sterility of pollen grains which is governed by a single recessive gene as found in squash, pumpkin, muskmelon, Brussels sprouts, cabbage, cauliflower, lettuce, sprouting broccoli, etc.

Genome: A basic or monoploid set of chromosomes. In a genome, each type of chromosomes is represented only once.

Genotype X environmental interaction: The interplay in effect of the genetic and non-genetic factors on the development of an organism.

Genotype: The hereditary properties of an organism as represented by the gene constituents. They may be expressed or latent.

Genus (pl.genera): A taxonomic category that includes group of closely related species.

Geographic (spatial) data – Data that contains information about the spatial location (position) and the attribute being monitored such as yield, soil properties, plant variables, seed population, etc.

Geographical diversity: The diversity of the biological population produced by the presence of a geographical barrier such as mountains, rivers, canyons.

Germination: Emergence of normal seed ling from the seeds under ideal condition of light temperature, moisture, oxygen, and nutrients.

Germplasm complexes: The advanced generation of mixed seeds obtained by a purpose ful intermixing of a number of genotypes or hybrids among them.

Germplasm: In plant breeding sense, germplasm is the sum total of genetic stocks of a particular crop species.

GIS – Geographical computer system that records, measures, manages, or analyzes geographically referenced information or data.

Global navigation satellite system (GNSS)- It is the standard generic term for satellite navigation systems that provide geo-spatial positioning with global coverage using time signals transmitted from satellites. The United States GPS and the Russian GLONASS are the only two fully operational GNSS. Top of the line GNSS receivers can communicate with both GPS and GLONASS satellites effectively doubling the available reference satellites at any given time

Global positioning system (GPS)- A system using satellite signals (radio-waves) to locate and track the position of a receiver/antenna on the Earth. GPS is a technology that originated in the U.S. It is currently maintained by the U.S. government and available to users worldwide free of charge. There are 30 satellites in the GPS constellation.

Gourd: Generally, it refers to the fruit of cucurbits. Actually, this epithet refers to the fruit character: hard and tough rind upon complete maturation as in bottle gourd, pumpkin or summer squash, even though the term gourd is applied to other fleshy fruits like bitter gourd or snake gourd whose skin do not become tough when ripe.

Grana: Small cylindrical structures found inside the inner memberane of a chloroplast.

Green pepper: Tender, semi-mature green pepper (*Piper nigrum*) spike which is used commercially in pickles.

Gross irrigation requirement (GIR): GIR is the total quantity of water applied to field including losses due to leakage, seepage and evaporation from open channels.

Growth crack of sweet potato: Longitudinal or transverse splits and fissures due to irregular on interrupted growth.

Guar gum: The mucilaginous seed flour of guar (*Cyamopsis tetragonolobus*) is valued as guar gum (Galactomannan) used in textile, paper, cosmetic and oil industries throughout the world. It is also a useful absorbent for explosives.

Gynandro morphs: Individuals with sex mosaic also called gynanders.

H

Hakuran: An artificial amphidiploid of cabbage, as Chinese cabbage produced through embryo culture technique, which is a good leafy vegetable.

Half diallel: All possible one-way crosses among n genotypes, i.e. (n-1)/2.

Half sib: Progeny having one parent in common.

Half-hardy vegetable: Vegetable crops which can thrive well in cool weather condition but can not tolerate frost. e.g., beet, carrot, cauliflower, lettuce, spinach, etc.

Haploid number: The gametic chromosome number of a species.

Haploids: Individual with gametic (half) chromosomes number. Haploids are of different types.

Hard disk: A disk which is permanently fixed in a computer, also called Winchester disk. Hard disks have more storage capacity and are faster in reading and writing.

Hardware: The physical components of the computer such as key board, processing unit, monitor and printer.

Head shape index: A head character of cabbage, Chinese cabbage, calculated by dividing mean head length (cm) with mean head width (cm).

Head: Edible portion of cabbage, Chinese cabbage and head lettuce which is a structurally distinct, compact leafy portion made up of numerous overlapping leaves covering the terminal bud.

Head-to-seed method: A method of seed production practiced in cabbage where the selected plants with fully matured heads are lifted prior to snowfall, stored and again replanted at the onset of spring for seed production.

Heredity: Resemblance among individuals related by descent; transmission of traits from parent to off spring.

Heritability: Degree to which a given trait is controlled by inheritance.

Herkogamy: Hinderance of self-pollination due to some physical barriers such as presence of a hyline membrane around anther.

Hermaphrodite: An individual with both male and female reproductive organs.

Heterobeltiosis: Heterosis expressed over the better parent of the cross.

Heterochromatin: Chromatin staining darkly even during inter phase, often containing repetitive DNA with few genes.

Heterogametic sex: Sex with dissimilar type of sex chromosomes such as xy, xo, and zw.

Heterogeneous population: A population which is composed of genetically, dissimilar plants such as land races, mass selected populations, composites, synthetics and multilines.

Heterokaryons: Hybrid cell combining protoplast of two different species.

Heteroploidy: Any change in the chromosomes number from the diploid state. It is of two types, viz. Euploidy and aneuploidy.

Heterosis: Hybrid vigour such that an F_1 hybrid fall out side the range of parents with respect to same characters. Usually applied to size, rate of growth or general anthocyanin absent fitness.

Heterostyly: Different lengths of styles and filaments in a flower.

Heterozygosity: The phenomenon in which the homologous chromosomes of an organism possess different genes of the same allelic series.

Heterozygote: An organism with one or more heterozygous pairs of genes or unlike alleles at one or more corresponding loci .As a result of heterozygosity the organism will not breed true.

Heterozygotic potential variability: The variability which is stored in heterozygotes, e.g. AaBb.

Heterozygous: Individual having dissimilar alleles on the corresponding locus of homologous chromosomes.

Holokinetic chromosomes: A chromosomes with diffused centromere.

Homeostasis: The buffering capacity of a genotype to environmental fluctuation. Adaptability is a result of homeostasis.

Homogametic sex: Sex with similar type of sex chromosomes such as xx or zz.

Homogamy: Maturation of anthers and stgma of a flower at the same time.

Homogeneous population: A population of genetically similar plants such as a pure line, F_1 between two pure lines and progeny of a clone.

Homokaryons: Hybrid cell combining protoplasts of the same species.

Homologous chromosomes: Chromosomes that cover in pairs and are generally similar in size and shape, one having come from the male parent and the other from the female parent. Such chromosomes contain the same array of genes.

Homozygosity: The proportion of homozygous individuals in a segregating population. Homozygosity is equal to $[(2m-1)/2m]^n$, where m is the number of selfing generations and n is the number of gene pairs segregating .

Homozygote: An organism with identical genes at corresponding loci on homologous chromosomes.

Homozygotic potential variability: Variability which is stored in homozygotes, viz., AAbb or aaBB.

Homozygous: Individual having similar alleles on the corresponding locus of homologous chromosomes.

Horticultural traits: Character of economic importance in horticultural crops.

Hub crop: Crop which has the greatest comparative advantage over other crops in a sequential cropping system e.g. vegetable crops.

Hybrid inviability: In ability of zygote to grow into a normal embryo under the normal conditions of development.

Hybrid sterility: In ability of a hybrid to produce viable off spring.

Hybrid vigour: Increase in vigor, growth yield or function of a hybrid over the parents that result from the crossing of genetically unlike organisms.

Hybrid. The progeny of a cross between two or more individual plants of unlike genetic constitution.

Hybridization: A method of crop improvement in which two or more plants of unlike genetical constitution differing in one or more characters are crossed together.

Hydroponics: Growing plants in nutrient solution.

Hypersensitivity: A host pathogen reaction which leads to death of infested tissues.

Hypogeous germination: A pattern of germination where the lengthening of the hypocotyl does not raise the cotyledons above the ground and only the epicotyl emerges, as seen in pea, etc.

I

Ideotype breeding: A method of crop improvement which is used to enhance genetic yield potential through genetic manipulation of individual plant character.

Ideotype: A biological model which is expected to perform or behave in a predictable manner within a defined environment.

Immigration: In coming of new alleles in a population.

In situ: From the Latin, meaning in the natural place. Refers to experimental treatments performed on cell or tissues rather than on extracts from them.

In vitro: From the Latin, meaning within glass; biological processes made to occur experimentally outside the organism in a test tube or other container.

Inbred line: A line produced by continued in crop breeding a nearly homozygote line usually originating from continued self-fertilization accompanied by selection.

Inbred: In cross pollinated species, a true breeding line obtained by continuous in breeding.

Inbreeding depression: The loss of vigor as a consequence of inbreeding. It is primarily due to the breakdown of specific gene system governing the expression of vigour, governing a particular trait or traits and is often accompanied by reduction in yield, size, fecundity etc.

Inbreeding: Mating of closely related individuals .example –self-pollinated crops.

Incompability: Failure to obtain fertilization and seed formation after self- pollination, usually due to failure of pollen tube to penetrate stigma, or to reduced growth of the pollen tube in the style tissues.

Incomplete dominance: Partial resemblance of F_1 with one of its parents.

Incomplete linkage: Linkage in which some frequency of crossing over occur.

Incomplete penetrance: Expression of gene in less than 100% of its carries.

Independent assortment: Random or free segregation of chromosomes and gene during gamete formation i. e. during meiosis.

Indigenous collection: The germplasm which is collected within the country.

Induced mutation: Mutation in which are produced by the use of mutagenic agent.

Inducer: The substances which allows initiation of transcription (lactose in lac operon). Such process is known induction.

Inducible enzyme: An enzyme whose production is enhanced by adding the substrate in culture medium. Such system is called inducible system.

Inert matter: Non- living materials such as sand, pebbles, soil particles, straw, etc.

Inflorescence: (1) A flower clusters (2) the arrangement and mode of development of the flowers on a flower axis.

Interference: The tendency of one cross over to reduce the change of another crossover in adjacent region.

Inter-generic hybridization: Crossing between two different genera of the same family. Triticale and raphanobrassica are the outcome of inter generic crosses.

Internal browning of tomato: Gray-brownish discoloration of internal tissues in green fruit which extend to the surface and form lesion that remain greenish or yellow in ripe fruit; caused by water imbalance and high temperature and/or nutrient imbalance.

Inter-specific hybridization: Crossing between two different species of the same genus, also called intra-generic hybridization. Such crosses are called inter specific crosses.

Introgression: Transfer of some genes from one species into the genome of another species.

Introgressively hybridization: A type of hybridization in which a number of genes or gene block of one species are added to the genetic background of another species by crossing and often by back crossing.

Inversion: Structural changes in which a segment is oriented in a reverse order. Inversion are of two types, viz. paracentric and pericentric.

Irradiation: Exposure of plants or plant parts to X-rays or other radiations to increase mutation rate.

Irrigation frequency: It refers to the number of days between irrigation during periods without rainfall.

Irrigation period: It is the number of days that can be allowed for applying one irrigation to a given design area during the peak consumptive use period of the crop being irrigated.

Irrigation requirement: Irrigation requirement for crop production is the amount of water, in addition to rainfall, that must be applied to meet a crop's evapotranspiration needs without significant reduction in yield.

Irrigation: An artificial application of water to the soil or plant for the purpose of crop production is known as irrigation.

Isoallele: An allele which is similar in its phenotypic expression to that of other independently occurring allele.

Isogenic lines: Lines differing from each other genetically at one locus only i.e. lines identical in all traits but one.

Isolation: The condition in which individuals of common ancestry is separated into two or more mating groups that mating between or among groups is prevented.

Isosine: A newly discovered nucleotide which is found in third position in a codon and can pair with A, U, and C. It is of three types, dispersive conservative and semiconservative.

J

J. shape chromosome: A chromosome which assumes J shape at anaphase.

Jumping genes: The genes which keep on changing their position in chromosomes and also between the chromosomes in a genome. Also called transpose or transposable elements. The first case of jumping gene was reported by Mc.Clintock in 1950 in maize.

K

Karyokinesis: The process of the division of nucleus.

Karyotype: The characteristic feature of chromosomes of a species.

L

Lamp brush chromosome: A chromosome having lamp brush appearance.

Landraces: Traditional cultivars with sufficient genetic integrity to be morphologically identifiable and differing in adaptation and to cultural practices, but genetically variable.

Latitude – A global standard coordinate used to identify a position on earth given in degrees, minutes and seconds, indicates the north/south position above/below the equator, positive is in the northern hemisphere and negative is in the southern hemisphere.

Lattice design: Incomplete block design in which the number of varieties or treatments form a square.

Lethal gene: Gene which causes death of its carrier when in homozygous condition.

Leucoplasts: Colorless plastids of green color that is associated with storage of starch, protein and fat.

Line breeding: A system of which a number of genotypes which have been progeny tested in respect to some character or group of characters are composite to form a variety.

Line X tester analysis: A system of lines for combining ability in the genetic background of a number of proven testers.

Line: This term refers to a group of individuals obtained from a common ancestry. In maize programme; it is synonym to inbred line.

Linear DNA: DNA which has a thread like structure with both the ends free. Such DNA is found in eukaryotes.

Linkage: Association of two or more non-allelomorphic genes so that they tend to passed from generation to generation as an inseparable unit and fails to show independent assortment. The potential types appear in greater frequency than expected in F_2. This is due to locating of linked factors on the same chromosome.

Lipase: An enzyme that joins the ends of two strands of nucleic acid.

Locus: A position on chromosomes which is occupied by an allele.

Long-day plant: A plant which requires a day longer than its critical day length for flowering. e.g., lettuce, radish, onion, cabbage, carrot, spinach, beet, etc.

Longitude – A global standard coordinate used to identify a position on earth given in degrees, minutes and seconds, indicates the east/west position around the globe from a reference point which overlays Greenwich, England. Negative values are east of Greenwich and positive values are west.

Luxuriance: It refers to the phenomenon in which the crossing of two parental forms bring an excessive, accidental, un adaptable and often unbalanced expression of a number of an attribute. Or the superiority of F_1 over its parents in vegetative growth, but not in yield and adaptation, also called pseudo- heterosis.

Lycopene: Red pigment found in ripe tomato which is a straight chain derivative of carotene with no vitamin activity. Its chemical composition (C_{40} H_{56}) is same as that of carotene.

Lysimeter: Cemented micro plots of various sizes used for the study of roots and salt tolerance.

Lysosomes: Cellular particles which contain several digestive enzymes.

M

Mainframe computers: Computers which is large storage capacity and very high speed of processing as compared to micro and mini computers.

Maintainer line: A genotype use to maintain the male sterility of cytoplasmic- genic system.

Male gametocides: Chemical which are used for induction of male sterility.

Male sterility: A condition in which either pollen is absent or non- functional in flowering plants.

Marker gene: Common gene differences which assort independently from all other readily testable gene loci are called marker genes e.g. potato leaf in tomato, brown seed in onion, anthocyanin pigment in cotyledons of chilli/ brinjal etc.

Market gardening: Vegetable farming for supply of vegetables to the consumers in the local market; one of the most intensive types of vegetable farming.

Mating system: The system in which individuals are arranged in pairs leading to sexual reproduction.

Matric potential of soil water: It is defined as the amount of work that a unit quantity of water is capable of doing (in equilibrium soil water system) when it moves to another equilibrium system identical in all respects except that there is no matrix present.

Meiosis: Two successive spindle using divisions which reduce the chromosome number from diploid to haploid.

Memory: A medium that stores binary information such as instructions and data and provides that information to the microprocessor whenever necessary. Memory is of two types, viz; read only memory and read and write memory.

Meristem culture: Culture of apical meristems, particularly shoot apical meristem, for production of shoots and plantlets.

Messenger RNA: The RNA which carries information from nuclear DNA to cytoplasm for protein synthesis

Metacentric chromosomes: A chromosome in which centromere is located is in the middle portion. Such chromosomes assume V shape at anaphase.

Microcomputer: A computer that is designed using a microprocessor as its central processing unit (CPU). IT includes four components: microprocessor, memory, input, and output.

Microprocessor: A semiconductor device manufactured by using large scale integration technique. It includes arithmetic logic unit (ALU), register arrays and control circuit on a single chip.

Minicomputer: A medium size computer which is more costly and powerful than microcomputer.

Mitochondria: A rod like cytoplasmic organelle which is the main site of cellular respiration.

Mitosis: The spindle using nuclear division which produces two identical daughter cells from a mother cell.

Modern cultivars: The currently cultivated high yielding varieties.

Moisture content (% by vol.) = Moisture content (% by wt.) x Bulk density of soil

Momeostatic: A genotype giving better performance even in adverse environments because of wide genetic base.

Monoallelic SI: Self- incapability which is controlled by single gene. It is found in some species of the family leguminosae, solanaceae, and cruciferae.

Monoculture: Repetative growing of the same sole crop on the same field.

Monoecious: The condition in which both male and female sex organs are produced separately but on the same plant.

Monoecy: Where male and female flower are unisexual but produced on the same plant.

Monohaploids: Haploids which develop from a normal diploid species.

Monohybrid crosses: A cross involving one gene pair affecting one character.

Monoploids: Individuals with basic chromosomes number.

Multiple cropping: Cultivation of two or more crops on the same field in a year.

Multivitamin green: Chekurmanis (*Sauropus androgymus*), a perennial leafy vegetable crop is called so because of the availability of various vitamins like A, B, C, D, F and K from this vegetable crop.

Mutable gene: A gene which exhibits higher mutation rate than other gene.

Mutagen: Physically or chemical agents which greatly enhance the frequency of mutation.

Mutant: Any plant, which has originated or acquired a heritable variation as a result of mutation.

Mutation: A sudden heritable changes in the phenotype of an individual.

Mutational heterosis: It is a type of true heterosis, which results from the occurrence of the balanced types of mutations plants.

Muton: The smallest element within a gene, which can give rise to a mutant phenotype or mutation.

N

Napiform root: Root which when swollen become spherical at the upper part and sharply tapering at the lower part, as in beet, turnip, etc.

Narrow sense heritability: Ratio of total genetic variance to phenotypic variance.

Negative mass selection: Removal of off type plants from a mixed population allowing rest of the plants to grow further.

Net irrigation requirement (NIR): NIR is the irrigation water which is delivered to the field and available for the crop to use. This is primarily water that is stored in crop's root zone.

Non-contributing alleles: Those alleles which do not contribute to continuous variation, also called non-effective alleles.

Non-essential amino acids: Amino acid which can be synthesized by human body and they need not be supplied through diet.

Non-genetic RNA: RNA which does not acts as genetic materials. It is found in higher organisms where DNA is the genetic material.

Non-recurrent parent: The donor parent in the back crossing programme. The desire character of this parent is added in the genetic background of recurrent parent.

Non-sense mutations: Mutation with codons which do not code any amino acid.

Normal isoallele: An isoallele which acts within the phenotypic range of a wild character.

Nucleic acid: A macro molecule composed of phosphoric acid, pentose, sugar, and organic bases; DNA and RNA.

Nucleic acid: A macromolecule composed of phosphoric acid, pentose, sugar, and organic bases; DNA and RNA.

Nucleoside: A combination of deoxyribose sugar and nitrogen base.

Nucleotide: A unit of DNA and RNA molecule containing a phosphate, a sugar, and an organic base.

Nucleus: The part of a eukaryotic cell that contains the chromosomes, separated from the cytoplasm by a membrane.

Nullisomic haploid: A haploid which develops from a nullisomic (n-1).

Nullisomic: An individual lacking one pair of chromosomes from a diploid set (2n-2).

Nursery bed: A prepared area where seed is sown or into which transplants or cuttings are planted.

O

Obtuse: Blunt pointed.

Okazaki Fragments: Short segment of nucleotide synthesized in lagging strand of DNA as result of discontinuous replication.

Oleoresin: A natural combination of resinous substances and essential oils present in the fruits of certain crop plants like chilli.

Oligogenic traits: Characters which are governed by one or few genes, also called qualitative characters.

Open pollinated: The progeny of individuals where pollination took place automatically in flowers in nature.

Orbicular: Circular, Round.

Organogenesis: The process of differentiation of shoot and root from somatic embryos.

Orthodox seed: Seed which can dried to low moisture content and stored at low temperature without losing their viability.

Osmotic potential of soil water: Osmotic potential can be defined as the amount of work that quantity of water in an equilibrium soil water system is capable of doing when it moves to another equilibrium system identical in all respects except that there is no solution.

Out breeding: Mating of unrelated individuals.

Out cross: A type of natural cross obtained from the crosses of a number of unknown genotypes.

Ovate: Egg shaped; broadest below center (contrast ovate and elliptic).

Over dominance hypothesis: Heterosis due to superiority of heterozygote over both the homozygous.

Over dominance: An effect the heterozygote (Aa) that is greater than the effect of homozygous dominant (AA).

Overlapping Genes: Genes which code for more than one protein. In such gene, the complete nucleotide sequence codes for one protein and part of such nucleotide sequence for another protein. Such genes have been reported in tumor producing viruses such as phi X 174 , Sv40 and G4.

Ovule: The term generally applied to the whole seed forming apparatus inside an ovary i.e; nucellus plus the integument.

P

Parietal placentation: When placentae bearing the ovules develop on the inner wall of the one-chambered ovary corresponding to the confluent margins of carpels as seen in radish, etc.

Parthenocarpy: The development of fruit without fertilization and the formation of normal seeds.

Parthenogenesis: The development of an individual from the female gamete without fertilization.

Pedicels: The flower stalks, which grow from the upper branches of the peduncle.

Pedigree: Record of ancestry of an individual selected plant for its various segregations.

Peduncle: The main flower stalk, often branched once or twice (or more) in its upper part and bearing pedicles near the end of the branches.

Pentagonal: In which the lobes are rather broad than long giving, the corolla a pentagonal or 5-pointed appearance.

Pepo: Fleshy, many seeded fruit which develops from an inferior, one-celled or spuriously three-celled, syncarpous pistil with parietal placentation, e.g., cucumber, melons, squash, gourds, etc.

Perianth: When the calyx and corolla do not differ much in shape and color, they together are said to form the perianth as seen in onion, garlic, etc.

Pericarp : The outer wall of the fruit .

Peripheral embryo: Embryo which encloses endosperm or peri sperm tissue as seen in *Amaranthus*, etc.

Permanent wilting point (PWP): The amount of moisture left in the soil after a plant has permanently wilted is called 'wilting coefficient' or permanent wilting point. At this stage film of water around soil particle are held so tightly that roots in contact cannot take water. The moisture tension at this point varies from 7 to 32 atmospheres, but 15 atmospheres is commonly used tension for this point.

Petiole: The stalk of a leaf .

Petiolate: With petioles.

P^F of Soil: It is a negative pressure of soil moisture expressed in cm (based on the height of water column above free water level in cm). pF= log 10^h, where h = soil moisture tension in cm of water.

Phenotype: The visible manifestation of the genotype produced as a consequence of growth and development.

Phenotypic disassortative mating: Mating of individuals with contrasting phenotypic character. Example –crossing between tall × dwarf plants.

Phenotypic assortative mating: Mating of individuals with similar phenotypes. Example-crossing between tall individual with Aa x AA or Aa or Aa x AA and aa x Aa genotypes.

Phenotypic stability: The stability of a genotype (or genotypes) over a spectrum of environmental condition. It is also known as developmental homeostasis.

Photo dormancy: A type of physiological dormancy of seed where germination of seed is sensitive to light i.e., seeds of some plants require light to germinate whereas others require darkness. e.g., lettuce seed require light and *Allium*, *Amaranthus*, etc. seed require darkness for germination.

Phytoalexin: A phenolic substance having antifungal principle, synthesized by plants in response to parasite invasion or infection by certain fungi, e.g., pisatin, phaseolin, trifolirhizin, orchinol and isocumarin from pea and bean pods, and carrot root, respectively.

Pie plant: Rhubarb (*Rheum raponticum*), one of the oldest cultivated vegetable crops, is commonly known as "pie plant".

Pinnate: A leaf divided into terminal and lateral leaflets.

Pinnatipartite: When the incision of leaf margin is more than half way down towards the mid-rib, as in radish.

Planting ratio: The male and female plants when planted in a certain proportion to ensure proper pollination and fertilization e.g., 10:1 (female: male) ratio in pointed gourd.

Pleiotropy: Phenomenon of a single gene affecting two or more different characters.

Poi: The pressure-cooked taro (*Colocasia esculenta*) corms after being passed through strainer are allowed to ferment which gives an acidic product called 'poi'.

Polyhaploid: Haploid which develop from polyploid species. Polyploids again are of two types, viz. allohaploids and autohaploids.

Polycross: An isolated group of plants or clones arranged in same fashion to facilitate random inter pollination.

Polymerase chain reaction (PCR): A procedure involving multiple cycles of denaturation, and polynucleotide synthesis that amplifies a particular DNA sequence.

Polymerization: Chemical union of two or more molecules of the same kind to form a new compound having the same elements in the same proportions but a higher molecular weight and different physical properties.

Polymorphism: Two or more kinds of individuals maintained in a breeding population.

Polynucleotide: A linear sequence of joined nucleotides in DNA or RNA.

Polypeptide: A linear molecule with two or more amino acids and one or more peptide groups. They are called dipeptides, tripeptides, and so on, according to the number of amino acids present.

Polypetalous: When the petals remain free from each other as seen in cabbage, radish, etc.

Polyploid: An organism with more than two sets of chromosomes (2n diploid) or genomes (e.g., triploid (3n), tetraploid (4n) and so on.

Positional sterility: A type of male sterility, also called functional sterility, where pollens are functional but anthers fail to dehisce, found in some mutants of tomato.

Post-harvest: After harvest.

Pot herbs: A group of vegetable crops whose foliage and sometimes immature stem are used as cooked vegetables; also called leafy vegetables or green e.g., palak, amaranthus, spinach, basella, etc.

Potential evapo-transpiration (PET): PET is defined as the evapotranspiration that occurs when the ground is completely covered by short actively growing vegetation in large area and where there is no limitation in soil moisture.

Pricking: A method of raising secondary nursery for the crops having very small seeds; in the case of high density sowing, it 1elps to develop a thinner stand in the nursery. In Cole crops and lettuce, pricking is done when first pair of true leaves develop.

Progeny testing: The practice of ascertaining the genotype of an individual by mating it to an individual of known genotype and examining the progeny.

Progeny: The off springs of a particular mating.

Program: A set of instructions written in a specific sequence for the computer to accomplish a given task.

Prokaryote: A number of a large group of organisms (including bacteria and blue green algae) that lack true nuclei in their cells and that do not undergo meiosis.

Pseudo – heterosis: See luxuriance.

Pseudo- dominance: The phenomenon of the apparent dominance of a recessive gene in the area opposite a chromosome deficiency.

Pseudo- incompatibility: Incompatibility due to physiological and physical reasons only and is not heritable e.g. physiological factors like temperature, light and physical factors like heterostyly, protandry, closed anther, etc.

Pure line: The descendants obtained from self-fertilization of a single homozygous or an inbred homogenic strain.

Q

Qualitative characters: The characters, which show discrete variation and easily identified by visual observations. Examples, flower color, fruit shape etc.

Quantitative characters: The characters, which show continuous variation such that visual identification of individual genes segregation is not possible. These are usually governed by the cumulative effect of polygenes and are highly influenced by environmental conditions. Examples are yield per plant, fruit per plant etc.

Quarantine: The prophylactic measure which is used to prevent the entry of new diseases, insects and weeds along with plant introduction from other countries.

Quercetin: A pigment which imparts coloration to the outer skin on onion bulb.

Quiescence: Describes the condition in which the seed can germinated immediately upon the absorption of water in the absence of any internal germination barriers. The embryo (or seed) is called to be quiescent.

R

Radiation genetics: A branch of genetics which deals with effects of various types of radiations on chromosomes and genes.

Random mating: Arrangements of pairs is by chance i.e. each individual has equal chances to mate with another. Examples- cross-pollinated crops.

Range: Difference between the lowest and the highest values present in the observation in a sample.

Read only memory (ROM): A memory that stores binary information permanently. The information can be read from this memory but cannot be altered.

Read/Write memory (R/WR): A memory that stores binary information during the operation of computer. This is used as writing pad to write user's program and data. The information stored in this memory can be read and altered easily.

Readily available water (RAW): Soil moisture lying between field capacity and permanent wilting point (15 atmospheres) is referred as readily available moisture. As the water content above field capacity can not be held against the forces of gravity and will drain out, and plant roots can not extract water content below permanent wilting point. The fraction of RAW that a crop can extract from the root zone without suffering water stress is the readily available soil water.

Recalcitrant seeds: The seeds which show drastic loss in viability with decrease in moisture content below 12 or 13 %. Such species include coconut, mango, tea, coffee, rubber, jackfruit, oil palm etc. Such seeds can not be conserved in seed banks.

Recessive epistasis: Gene interaction in which recessive alleles at one locus mask the expression of both the alleles at another locus resulting in 9:3:4 ratio. Also called supplementary epistasis.

Recessive gene: When parents with contrasting characters are crossed, the character of one parent does not appear in F_{1}- even though genes for both the factors are present in the hybrid. The gene, which does not appear, is said to be recessive.

Reciprocal hybrids: Two hybrids produced by crossing the same parents but the male of first is used as female in the another and similarly the female of first is used as male in another such as (A× B) and (B × A).

Reciprocal translocation: Mutual exchange of segments between non –homologous chromosomes.

Recombinant DNA: The DNA which contains genes from different sources and can combine with DNA of any organism.

Recons: The regions (units) within a gene between which recombination's can occur, but the recombination can not occur within a recon.

Recurrent selection: Reselection generation after generation with inter mating of selected plants to provide for genetic recombination.

Registered seed: The progeny of foundation seed that is so handled as to most nearly maintain the satisfactory genetic purity and has been approved by certifying agency.

Relative heterosis: Usually refers to the heterosis expressed over the mid parental value of a cross.

Renaturation: Union of separated (denatured) DNA strands on cooling.

Replication: Repetition of treatments under investigation.

Repulsion: Linkage between dominant and recessive alleles.

Restitution: Union of broken chromosomes segments which restores original gene sequence.

Restriction enzyme: An endonuclease that recognizes a specific short sequence in DNA and cleaves the DNA molecule.

Restriction map: A linear or circular diagram of a DNA molecule showing the sites that are cleaved by different restriction enzyme.

Reverse transcriptase: An enzyme that catalyzes the synthesis of DNA using an RNA template.

Reversion: Restitution of a mutant gene to the wild type condition, or at least to a form that gives the wild phenotype. More generally, the appearance of trait expressed by a remote ancestor; a throwback; atavism.

RFLP (Restriction fragment length polymorphism): A genetic difference among individuals that is decided by comparing DNA fragments released by digestion with one or more restriction enzyme.

Ribosome: Cytoplasmic organelle on which proteins are synthesized.

Ring chromosomes: A physically circular chromosome, usually found in prokaryotes such as bacteria and viruses.

RNA (Ribonucleic acid): The information – carrying material in some viruses. More generally, a molecule derived from DNA by transcription that may carry information (messenger or mRNA), provide subcellular structure (ribosomal or rRNA), transport amino acids (transfer or T RNA), or facilitate the biochemical modification of itself or other RNA molecules.

Rod shaped chromosomes: A chromosomes which assumes rod shaped at anaphase.

Rouging: Process of removal of off types (phenotypically different) plants from the field of an improved variety to avoid contamination.

Root crops: A group of vegetable crops whose swollen tap roots and in some cases hypocotyl along with tap root such as carrot, beet, radish, turnip, rutabaga etc. are cooked or eaten raw.

Root forking: Branching of tap roots in the root crops, particularly in radish and carrot, due to the presence of impediment, undecomposed organic matter or plant refuse in the soil.

Root tuber: The fleshy root of a herbaceous perennial plant with buds or eyes in the upper regions. e.g., sweet potato.

Root-to-seed method: A method of seed production in root crops where the fully matured roots are harvested, selected and after giving proper root and shoot cuts, they are replanted for seed production.

S

Sagittate: Arrow shaped with the basal lobes directed downwards. e.g., leaves of some aroids.

Salad crops: Green leafy vegetables which are usually consumed raw with oil, vinegar and various other condiments, e.g., lettuce, endive, celery, chicory, parsley, etc.

S-allele: A set of alleles controlling sporophyte self-compatibility.

Satellite: A communications vehicle orbiting the Earth. Satellites typically provide a variety of information from weather data to television programming. Satellites send time-stamped signals to GPS receivers to determine the position on the Earth.

Saturation point: When all the pores of soil are filled with water, the soil is said to be saturated or having maximum water holding capacity. At this point soil moisture tension is almost zero.

Scheduling of Irrigation: It is the decision-making process of determining when to irrigate and how much water to apply in each irrigation.

Scooping: Removal of central portion of the curd for easier initiation of flower stalk in cauliflower.

Secondary gene pool: The genetic material that leads to partial fertility on crossing with primary gene pool. It includes genotypes of related species and is designated as GP_2.

Seed parent: The female (pistillate parent of a hybrid).

Seed potato: Potato tubers used for planting.

Seed: The matured ovule having all the essential structures to produce a new plant.

Seedless watermelon: It refers to auto triploid (3x) watermelon which is both male and female sterile due to unequal chromosomal distribution in meiosis resulting in seedless condition in the fruit.

Seed-to-seed method: A method of seed production where the plants are allowed to produce seed in its original place of growing.

Segregating generations: The F_2 and onward generation of a hybrid where separation of parental from material chromosomes at meiosis and consequent separation of genes takes place leading to the possibility of recombination in the off spring.

Selection: The process in which a number of individuals with certain desirable characteristics are favored for further reproduction.

Self– pollinated crops: An assembly of homozygous plants. These crops often have one single genotype and reproduce it as such from generation to generation.

Self- sterile: The organism which fails to fertilize and set seeds after self – pollination.

Self-incompatibility: Failure of fertilization even though both male and female parts of the bisexual flower are fully functional as seen in cabbage, cauliflower, radish, etc.

Selfing: The process of putting the pollen of the same flower on its stigma i.e. enforcing self-pollination. It is extensively practiced in maize and other cross-pollinated crops to obtain inbred lines for utilization in the hybrid programme.

Semi – sterility: A state of only partial fertility in plant zygotes usually associated with chromosomal translocations.

Semigamy: Abnormal fertilization in which the male gamete fertilizes the egg, but does not fuse with the egg nucleus.

Sex determination: The process of sex differentiation which utilizes various genetical concepts to decide whether a particular genotype will develop into male or female sex.

Sex influenced genes: Gene whose expression depends on the sex of an individual such as baldness in humans.

Shoot apex culture: A tissue culture procedure for eliminating virus or other pathogens from plant parts where excision and aseptic culture of the small segment of the terminal growing points done because the terminal growing point of a plant is often free from virus and other pathogens even if the rest of the plant infected; practiced in potato, sweet potato, cassava, etc.

Shuttle vector: A plasmid capable of replicating in two different organisms such as yeast and *E. coli.*

Sib- mating: Sibling or crossing at random the two or more-individual obtained from the same parentage. It is form inbreeding and refers to brother – sister mating.

Sib-pollination: Pollination between closely related biotypes.

Silencer: A DNA sequence that helps to reduce or shut off the expression of a nearby gene.

Simla mirch: Bell-shaped, non-pungent, mild and thick fleshed.

Single cross hybrid: A hybrid involving two cross-compatible lines.

Single cross: A cross between two inbred, A x B.

Single crossing over: Formation of single chiasma between non-sister chromatids of homologous chromosomes.

Software: A group of programmes.

Soil moisture content: The moisture content of a sample of soil is usually defined as the amount of water lost when dried at constant weight. It is usually expressed in per cent.

Soil moisture content (% by wt.) = Wt. of moist sample -– Wt. of oven dry sample X 100 Wt. of oven dry sample

Moisture content (% by vol.) = Moisture content (% by wt.) x Bulk density of soil

Soil moisture stress: It is the sum of the soil moisture tension and osmotic pressure of soil solution. The osmotic pressure developed by the soil solution retards the uptake of water by plants. Plants growing in a soil with a soil moisture tension is say 1 atmosphere, apparently can extract enough moisture for growth. But if the osmotic pressure of the soil solution is, say 10 atmospheres, the total stress are 11 atmospheres. Under such condition, plant cannot extract sufficient water for good growth.

Soil moisture tension: It is a measure of the tenacity with which water is retained in the soil. The tenacity is measured in terms of the potential energy of water in the soil measured usually with respect to free water. Soil moisture tension is expressed in atmospheres or bar or kPa (1 atmospheres=1036 cm of water, and 1 bar = 1023 cm of water column or 100 kPa).

Sole cropping: Raising one crop alone in pure stands, also called solid planting.

Somaclonal variation: The variation which is generated by the use of tissue culture.

Somatic hybridization: Crossing of plants through fusion somatic cells (protoplast).

Somatopalstic sterility: A type of sterility, which results as a consequence of the collapse of fertilized ovules or zygote during the embryonic or early development stages due to disturbance in embryo endosperm relations.

Southern blot: The transfer of DNA fragments from an electrophoretic gel to a cellulose or nylon membrane by capillary action.

Spadix: A spike with a fleshy axis which is enclosed by one or more large, often brightly colored, bracts called spathes, as in aroids, etc.

Spear: The shoot which is the edible part of asparagus.

Special chromosomes: Chromosomes which significantly differ in structure and function from normal chromosomes such as lamp brush chromosomes, polytene chromosomes and *B*-chromosomes.

Species: A unit of taxonomic classification containing group of individuals enough alike so that it may be reasonably assumed that they have arisen from a common ancestor.

Specific combining ability: The deviation in the performance expected on the basis of general combining ability.

Spike: The inflorescence in which the main axis is elongated and the lower flower opens earlier than the upper ones as in raceme, but the flowers are sessile, as seen in amaranth us, etc.

Splicing: The process that covalently joins exon sequence of RNA and eliminates the intervening intron sequences.

Sporophytic incompatibility: Failure of fertilization due to genetic abnormalities.

Stamens. Organ of flower, which produces pollens.

Standard deviation: The square root of the arithmetic mean of the squares of the deviation measured from the mean. It is the square root of variance.

Standard heterosis: Heterosis expressed over the standard or check variety. It is also known as useful heterosis.

Statistics: A branch of applied mathematics which deals with collection, presentation, analysis, and interpretation of numerical data tend to spread about the mean value. It is a measure of variation in a sample.

Steckling: Matured root of carrot, radish, turnip, etc. to be replanted after over-wintering for seed production in root-to-seed method.

Sterility: The phenomenon in which an organism is infertile and is incapable of reproducing.

Stolon: Slender, underground lateral stems arising from buds on the underground portion of the stem which enlarge at its tip to produce the tuber, as in potato.

Strain: The mating group within a variety or species with distinct morphological or physiological features.

Stump method: A method of seed production in cabbage where the head after full maturity is cut off just below the base, keeping the stem with outer whorl of leaves intact.

Substitution haploid: A haploid which develops from a substitution line (n-1+1).

Super computer: A computer with extremely large storage capacity and at least 10 times faster computing speed than other computers. Such computers are used in scientific and engineering disciplines.

Supermarket on a stalk: the winged bean (*Psophocarpus tetragonolobus*) plant is described so, as six different foods are supplied by this plant: leaves like spinach, succulent shoots resembling large thin asparagus, fried flowers for making a sweet garnish, tender pod as vegetable, the seed and the underground tubers are exceptionally rich in proteins.

Sweet pepper: It is the chilli of commercial value (*Capsicum annuum*).

Syneptonemal complex: A protein frame work which is found between paired chromosomes.

Synthetic varieties: These are the open pollinated advanced generation population of a number of hybrids obtained by crossing a number of tested lines grown in isolation.

T

Tabasco pepper: Small fruited, very pungent chilli (*Capsicum frutescens*).

Tandem: Duplication with normal sequence (similar to original segment) of genes.

Tautomerization: The process of sift of hydrogen atoms from one position to another either in a purine or in a pyrimidine base.

Taxa (Sing. Taxon): A general term for taxonomic classification, irrespective of rank.

Template: A macromolecule which provides information for the synthesis of another complimentary macro- molecule.

Tender vegetable: Vegetable crops which cannot withstand frost and some of them even do not thrive in cool weather, e.g., brinjal, okra, chilli, cucurbits, sweet potato, cowpea, tomato, cassava, beans, etc.

Tenderometer: An instrument by which toughness of the seed coat and firmness of pulp is determined and is mostly used to determine the seed quality of pea where high value of tenderometer indicates low quality.

Terminal delation: Loss of either terminal segment of a chromosome.

Tertiary gene pool: The genetic materials which leads to production of sterile hybrids on crossing with primary gene pool. It is designated as GP_3.

Tertiary trisomic: A trisomic in which the additional chromosome is translocated one.

Test cross: The cross of the F_1 with recessive homozygous parent i. e; Aa x aa.

Tetrasomic: Addition of two chromosomes to one pair or two different pairs.

Three-way cross hybrid: Hybrid progeny between a single cross and an inbred, i.e. (A x B) xC.

Three-way cross: The cross between a single cross and an inbred line. With three lines (A, B, C), it could be represented as (Ax B) x C. It has been genetically used in the maize-breeding programme for the production of commercial sweet maize hybrids.

Thrum: In primula, flowers with short style and high anthers.

Tissue culture: The development of an entire organism from plant cells and tissues *in vitro* or artificial media.

Top cross: An out cross of selections clones or inbred, to a common pollen parent. In corn, a commonly an inbred – variety cross.

Total available water (TAW): The total available water in the root zone is the difference between the water content at field capacity and wilting point (TAW= FC–WP). TAW is the amount of water that a crop can extract from its root zone, and its magnitude depends on the type of soil and the rooting depth.

Totipotency: Single cell culture develops in a plant.

Transformation (bacteria): Genetic alteration of bacteria brought about by the incorporation of foreign DNA in the bacterial cells.

Transgenic: A term applied to organisms that have been altered by introducing DNA molecules into them.

Transgressive segregation: The appearance of individuals showing an extreme development of a character than either of the parent in F_2 or later generations. This usually occurs because of cumulative and complementary effect of genes contributed by the parents of the cross

Transition: A mutation caused by the substitution of one purine by another purine or one pyrimidine by another pyrimidine in DNA or RNA.

Translocation: One way or reciprocal exchange of segments between non-homologous chromosomes.

Transpiration ratio: It refers to the quantity of water (in gram) transpired by the plant to accumulate 1 g of dry matter. This ratio varies from 200 to 1000 depending upon crop species, cultivation conditions and crop growth stage.

Transpiration: It is water loss through living plants in the form of water vapour is called transpiration.

Transposition: Existance of one wild and one mutant allele in each homologous chromosome (+a / +b) also called repulsion phase of alleles.

Triple cross: The cross between two three-way crosses. With 6 lines (A, B, C, D, E. F), it could be represented as (Ax B) x C) x (D x E) x F).

Trisomic: Addition of one chromosome to one pair in a diploid set.

Tristyly: Style having two positions, viz., low and high.

Tuber: A special kind of swollen modified stem structure that functions as an underground storage organ as in potato, Jerusalem artichoke, etc.

Tubercle: Small aerial tuber produced in the leaf axils as seen in Yam (*Dioscorea alata*).

Tunic: The papery or fibrous coats covering bulbs and corms.

Tunicated bulbs: Type of bulb where the outer leaves are usually thin, membranous and dry and completely ensheath the inner portion and the central axis of the bulb like a tunic as the bulb of *Allium*.

U

Undeveloped embryo: Partially developed torpedo-shaped embryos that may attain a size up to one half that of the seed cavity at maturity as seen in carrot, etc.

Unidirectional replication: Replication of DNA in one direction only from the point of origin.

Uniform expressivity: Similar on or uniform expression of gene in all the individuals that carry such genes.

Unique DNA: The DNA segments (nucleotides) having only single copy per genome.

Utilization index: Ability of root and tuber crops for better accumulation of photosynthates in the storage organ which can be judged by root: shoot ratio.

V

V- Shaped chromosomes: A chromosomes which assumes V –shaped at anaphase.

Vacuum cooling: A technique of cooling vegetable (leafy vegetables, asparagus, Brussels sprout, etc.) having a high surface to volume ratio, rapidly and uniformly by boiling off some of their water at 1°C and at low pressure (5 mm mercury) into a sealed container. The produce is cooled by evaporation of water from the tissue surface and is more rapid than hydrocooling.

Variable expressivity: Differential or variable expression of a gene in the individuals that carry it.

Variance: The average of the squared deviations from the mean or the square of the standard deviation.

Variation: Differences amongst the individuals arising as a consequence of differences in the genetic makeup; the effect of the environment or interplay of both. It is the chief characteristics of living organisms and is the basis of evolution.

Varietal blend: Mechanical mixtures of seed of two or more varieties.

Varietal deterioration: permanent reduction either in the genetic or agronomic value of a released variety.

Variety: An agricultural variety is a population of similar individuals having common identifiable plant fruit or seed characteristics along with a good agronomic base. This is generally utilized for commercial cultivation.

Vector. An animal or insect, which transmits parasites e.g. white fly, is the vector of viral diseases of tomato okra, chili, etc.

Vegetable forcing: A specialized type of vegetable farming where vegetables are grown out of their normal season. Vegetable forcing requires some special structures like glasshouse, hot bed, cold frame, etc.

Vegetable: An edible plant or plant part eaten cooked or raw as a main part of a meal, side dish, or appetizer.

Vegetative apomixis: A type of apomixis where flowers are replaced in the plants by bulbils or buds which fall to the ground like seeds, found in *Allium cepa* var. *Viviparum*, *Poa bulbosa*, etc.

Vertical resistance: Resistance conferred by few genes, specific to few known races.

Vexiliary: Of the five petals, when the posterior one is the largest and almost covers the two lateral petals as in pea, dolichos bean, etc.

Viability: The capability to live and develop normally.

Virulent: A race of a pathogen capable of attacking a host with specific resistance.

Vital mutation: Mutation in which all mutants survive.

W

Water Management: It is an efficient and planned used of water for crop production.

Water Requirement: It is the quantity of water needed for raising a crop in a given period. It includes; consumptive use, economically unavoidable losses and water needed for some special operation such as land preparation, transplanting, leaching of salt etc.

Water Stress: When the potential energy of the soil water drops below a threshold value, the crop is said to be water stressed.

Water use efficiency (WUE): It is the ratio of crop yield (Y) to the amount of water depleted by the crop in the process of evapotranspiration (ET). WUE (crop) = Y/ ET

Waxing: A short term storage technique of fresh fruits and vegetables under ambient conditions by applying wax emulsion containing paraffin wax, triethanol and aleic acid which provide a thin, discontinuous layer on the fruit surface and thus curtails the respiration and transpiration resulting increase in shelf-life. It also helps to keep away the microbes when fungicides like, Benlate 50 are used in wax emulsion.

Waxy blister of tomato: A disorder where white to cream colored irregular blisters, 3 to 6 mm in diameter and often more than 3 mm high occur which become light to dark brown, depressed and crack as the fruits ripen.

White heart: Whiteness at the central portion of watermelon instead of uniform development of pink color from center to rind, indicating poor quality.

Wide crossing: Mating between different genera of the same family; also called distant hybridization.

Wobble base pairing: The pairing of mRNA codon with tRNA anticodon in which first two bases of a codon have normal pairing and third base has abnormal base pairing.

Word: A group of bits the computer recognizes and processes at a time.

Working collection: The germplasm which is meant for short term storage (3 to 5 year). Seed of such material are stored at 5 to 10°C.

WUE (crop) = Y/ ET

X

X- rays: separately ionizing and highly penetrating radiations generated in x-rays tubes and used for induction of mutations.

X^2-Test: A test of statistical significance which is used to test the significance of differences between observed and expected frequencies. It is used for the analysis of oligogenic characters.

Xenia: The immediate effect of pollen (i.e.; male gamete) on the endosperm. It is frequently observed in open pollinated maize with respect to kernel color.

Y

Yearling: One-year-old bulblets which have been formed on the scale.

Z

Z- DNA: The DNA in which sugar and phosphate linkages follow a zig –zag pattern. Such DNA has left handed double helical model.

Zoning of beet: Under unfavorable conditions, particularly in hot weather, beetroot show alternate white and colored circles when sliced, called zoning.

Z-test: A test of significance which is used to compare two means when the sample size is large (more than 30).

Zygote: The cell formed by the fusion.